BLUE GUIDE **GERMANY**

The interior of Balthasar Neumann's baroque masterpiece, the church of Vierzehnheiligen.

BLUE GUIDE

GERMANY

James Bentley

with route plans by
Andras Bereznay

A. & C. Black
London

W. W. Norton
New York

First edition 1987

Published by A & C Black (Publishers) Limited
35 Bedford Row, London, WC1R 4JH

© Copyright James Bentley 1987

Published in the United States of America by
WW Norton & Company, Incorporated
500 Fifth Avenue, New York, NY 10110

Published simultaneously in Canada by
Penguin Book Canada Limited
2801 John Street, Markham, Ontario LR3 1B4

British Library Cataloguing in Publication Data

Bentley, James, 1937–
  Germany.—(Blue guide)
  1. Germany—Description and travel—1945–
  —Guide-books
  I. Title II. Series
  914.3′04878   DD16

  ISBN 0–7136–2845–6

ISBN 0-393-30470-1 USA

Printed and bound in Great Britain by
William Clowes Limited, Beccles and London

ACKNOWLEDGEMENTS

In many different ways I am deeply grateful for the help of the late and extremely kind Henry Bayley-King; Mrs Kay Bayley-King; Mrs Audrey Bentley; Miss Emma-Jane Bentley; Mr Bernhard Heidemann of the German State Tourist Board, London; Frau Pastorin Gundula Meyer; Dr Eduard Schlieter of the Cologne State Tourist Board; Mr Paul Langridge; Mr Tom Neville; Ms Gemma Davies; Frau Rita Zampesi of Lufthansa; British Airways; and Frau Sabine Wolff-Zerzau.

James Bentley 1987

The Publishers would like to thank Mr A.F. Kersting and the German National Tourist Office for permission to reproduce the illustrations in this book.

EXPLANATIONS

Type. the main routes are described in large type. smaller type is used, in general, for historical, background and practical information, as well as for the description of sub-routes and diversions.

Asterisks (*) indicate places of special interest or excellence. **Double asterisks** (**) denote monuments of extraordinary interest.

Abbreviations. In addition to generally accepted and self-explanatory abbreviations, the following occur in the Guide:

alt. altitude
c *circa* (about, concerning a date)
C century
inhab. inhabitants (concerning population numbers)
km kilometres
m metres
Rte Route

For the most part German words have been translated into English—Cathedral for *Dom*, main railway station for *Hauptbahnhof*, town hall for *Rathaus* and so on. The exceptions involve commonly known words such as *Schloß*.

English visitors will find little difficulty in spotting the equivalent German word as they tour the cities, towns and villages described here: church and *Kirche*, museum and *Museum*, market place and *Marktplatz*, university and *Universität*, high school and *Hochschule*.

CONTENTS

ROUTE PLANS

A. INTRODUCTION TO GERMANY

West Germany and Berlin

The Federal Republic of Germany (FDR), whose capital is Bonn, is divided into ten separate *Länder* (or states) of widely different sizes (and including three cities counting as Länder), namely:

Bavaria (with an area of 70,547km^2, a population of nearly 11 million and Munich as its capital city).

Baden-Württemberg (35,750km^2; population almost 9 million; capital Stuuttgart).

Rhineland-Palatinate (19,838km^2; population 3,650,000; capital Mainz).

Saarland (2570km^2; population 1,090,000; capital Saarbrücken).

Hessen (21,112km^2; population 5,550,000; capital Wiesbaden).

North Rhine-Westphalia (34,057km^2; population 17,075,000; capital Düsseldorf).

Lower Saxony (47,408km^2; population 7,238,000; capital Hanover).

Schleswig-Holstein (15,696km^2; population 2,583,000; capital Kiel).

Bremen (404km^2; population 702,000).

Hamburg (753km^2; population 1,682,000).

West Berlin (480km^2; population 2,020,000).

Berlin was the capital of the German Empire and today is still nominally occupied by the British, American, Soviet and French forces—heirs of those who defeated Hitler in 1945. East Berlin, officially the capital of the German Democratic Republic (DDR), consists of the Soviet zone of the city, all of which lies isolated inside the DDR, though connected to the West by carefully controlled routes.

Each *Land* elects its own parliament, headed by a regional prime minister (or, in the case of Hamburg, Bremen and West Berlin, a Bürgermeister). Head of the whole West German state is the Bundes-president, who sits for five years and appoints the Federal chancellor on the advice of the Federal parliament (the *Bundestag*).

Schleswig-Holstein, Hamburg and Bremen, as well as much of Lower Saxony and North Rhine-Westphalia, comprise the North German Lowland, whose clayey soil was laid down in the Ice Age and which includes the forests and heather of Lüneberg Heath. These are lands of considerable agricultural and pastoral importance, as well as mineral wealth.

The rest of Lower Saxony and North Rhine-Westphalia combine with Hessen, Rhineland-Palatinate and the Saarland to form the mountainous Central Uplands and include the Harz mountains, the Siebengebirge and the Teutoburg, Odenwald and Spessart forests, as well as the mountain resorts of the Taunus. These uplands also take in the Rhine valley and the Mosel, which border on the Eifel mountains (these last penetrating into Belgium, where they are called the Ardennes).

Finally the River Main divides the Central Uplands from the Southern Plateau. Again, here are mountains and rivers, particularly the peaks of the Jura and the River Danube. This is the region of the Black Forest and the Bavarian Alps.

After the Peace of Augsburg in 1555 Germans took as their religious denomination the choice of their temporal ruler, whether Lutheran or

Catholic. Today West Germany consists of roughly half Lutherans, half Catholics, with a few members of other denominations and some non-believers (as well as Huguenots who migrated here to escape persecution in the 17C). East Germany is basically Protestant. In the Middle Ages some 800,000 Jews lived in Germany, most of their descendants to be murdered or escape elsewhere during the Hitler Reich.

West Germany is well served by motorways (nearly 40,000km of major roads, including some 5000km of motorways). The passenger railway system began in 1835 and today comprises some 29,500km. West German industry and freight also deploys 5900km of navigable rivers and canals. Its leading airline is Lufthansa, the successor of the Deutsche Lufthansa AG which was founded in 1926.

In 1950 Germany re-armed, and today the *Bundeswehr* conscripts all males aged between 18 and 25, save conscientious objectors and those who are the only sons of men who were killed in World War II.

B. History

Prehistoric remains discovered in the present region of West Germany include the skeleton of so-called Neanderthal man, found in the Neander valley near Düsseldorf, and the jaw of so-called 'Homo Heidelbergensis', discovered near Heidelberg. Works of Mesolithic art—decorated clay pottery, amber utensils—have been excavated in north and east Germany, dating from palaeolithic times; and late Iron Age graves have been found containing utensils that had been imported from the Mediterranean.

In AD 9 Arminius, one of the rulers of the Cherusci tribe, fought and defeated three Roman legions at a battle in the Teutoburg forest. Traditionally Arminius is perceived as Germany's first national hero. The word 'Deutsch', however, initially used of a Franconian dialect in the 7C or 8C, did not for many centuries come to be used of the whole of present-day Germany. Two tribes of Indo-European origin, the Teutones and the Cimbri, living west of the River Rhine and north of the River Danube at the end of the 2C BC, invaded Gaul and northern Italy, only to be wiped out by the Romans in 102 and 101 BC. Julius Caesar next brought under Roman sway such Teutons as were living west of the Rhine, a process continued in 9 BC when the legions penetrated as far east as the River Elbe. Arminius's victory drove them back.

In AD 98 Tacitus produced his 'Germania', describing in detail (and, most historians agree, with considerable accuracy) the customs and beliefs of the Germanic people. Tacitus suggests that only one tribe—the Tungri—was initially known as Germanic, a term which spread to the rest of the tribes in the area. At this time the Frisii lived in the land between the Ems and the Rhine, the Chatti lived in present-day Hessen, the Suebi inhabited the region that is now Berlin, the Angles lived in Schleswig, the Chauci occupied the estuary of the River Weser, and Arminius's tribe, the Cherusci, lived further south. Both Julius Caesar and Tacitus write of a system of periodic land redistribution by the leaders of the Germanic tribes.

After Domitian had fought the Chatti, the Romans began to construct the *limes*, a series of fortifications 55km long, stretching from the Rhine to the Danube, as a defence against the inroads of the Germanic tribes. Inside Germany the tribes razed the old Roman cities.

The next centuries were marked both by remarkable migrations (including the colonisation of England by Angles and Saxons) and by the conversion of the Germanic peoples to Christianity (initially to the heretical form known as Arianism). Anglo-Irish missionaries founded the diocese of Konstanz in 613, and monasteries at Echternach in 698 and Reichenau in 724. St. Boniface missionised Bavaria and Hessen, his most important foundation being Fulda in 744.

Meanwhile Franks, Alemanni, Bavarians and Thuringians continued to invade and settle different parts of present-day Germany. Only when the Merovingian king Clovis (481–511) unified the Frankish kingdom and defeated the Alemanni did these extensive migrations come to an end (though some German tribes continued to expand eastwards long after the Carolingian Empire had broken up).

Between 772 and 814 Charlemagne's Franconian empire embraced peoples speaking many different languages and dialects, including the Germans. In 825 Charlemagne's successor, Louis the Pious, appointed his son, Louis the German, ruler of Bavaria. His sway gradually spread to the whole of the German part of the empire, and this separation of most of Germany from the rest of the empire was formalised in 843 at the Treaty of Verdun. The Treaty of Mersen in 870 extended this rule from the River Elbe in the east to Alsace and Lorraine in the west.

The first ruler whose claim to be truly Germanic makes political and geographical sense was Conrad I, elected king by the Frankish and Saxon dukes in 911. Conrad was succeeded by the Saxon duke Henry the Fowler (Henry I, 919–36), who consolidated the realm, and took the title of king. For the first time Germany was described as a kingdom ('Regnum Teutonicorum'). Henry's son Otto I (ruled 936–973) was crowned emperor of the Holy Roman Empire in Rome in 962, and vindicated Saxon military prowess by defeating the Hungarians at the Lech in 955. To extend Christianity and his own influence beyond the Elbe he founded the archbishopric of Magdeburg.

The next century saw numerous imperial-papal quarrels. In particular Henry IV (1056–1106), having successfully claimed the right to appoint church leaders in his realms, was excommunicated by Gregory VII (who also absolved the turbulent German princes of their oath of allegiance to Henry). Henry IV humiliatingly submitted to the pope at Canossa in 1077.

The Hohenstaufens began their rule with the accession of Konrad III in 1138. He was followed by Frederick I Barbarossa in 1152. Under the rule of his successors the empire gradually disintegrated, so that by the time the Hohenstaufen dynasty came to an end in 1268, subordinate dynasties were ruling their dukedoms virtually unchecked by any sovereign authority.

The advent of the Habsburgs (the first being Rudolf I, 1273–91) began to check this apparent anarchy. Charles IV issued his 'Golden Bull' of 1356, decreeing that seven electors should henceforth appoint the German sovereign. Soon they were invariably electing Habsburgs. The power of the other princelings declined. At the same time certain cities began to ally themselves in leagues, of which the most important was unquestionably the Hanseatic League, which from the 14C dominated the Baltic.

In the mid 15C Gutenberg invented printing from moveable type at Mainz; and capitalism developed rapidly, under the impetus of such rich dynasties as the Fuggers. Maximilian I (1486–1519) fostered new insititutions, such as the Reichstag (the imperial parliament) and the Reichskammergericht (the imperial high court) which were to survive until the early 19C. Yet these structures contributed to a separation of powers, in which powerful princes could flaunt the imperial power. Such a system enabled Luther's attack on the Catholic church in the early 16C to survive papal censure.

Reformers who did not gain the support of princes were put down as revolutionaries. Such preachers as the Anabaptist Thomas Müntzer and Nikolaus Storch took far further than Luther notions of Christian liberty and the personal inner inspiration of every believer. When in 1524 and 1525 the peasants demanded their ancient rights, appealing to Luther's teachings, Luther himself denounced them, and their revolt was savagely put down.

By the time of the Peace of Augsburg in 1555 Catholicism was seriously weakened throughout Germany, but the Catholic church fought back, founding in 1609 the Catholic League in response to the Protestant Union of 1608. In 1618 the Thirty Years' War began, causing devastation and poverty as well as bloodthirsty massacres, to be ended only by the Peace of Westphalia in 1648. Now the emperor's position was seriously weakened, his country divided into some three hundred virtually independent estates, each with a seat in the Reichstag.

Brandenburg-Prussia now began its rise to power under the Great Elector (1640–88), whose son and successor Frederick managed to win the emperor's consent to crowning himself king in 1701. (The emperor needed his support in the forthcoming War of the Spanish Succession.)

France now began increasingly to influence Germany. German princes modelled themselves on the absolutism of the French court. Prussia in particular (especially under Frederick the Great, 1740–86) became a major power. Frederick the Great obtained Silesia by force from Austria in 1742, and successfully defended it (and his own kingdom) in the Seven Years' War of 1756–63—a war in which he took on Austria, Russia, Saxony, France and Sweden, with Britain and Hanover as his only allies.

Napoleon, as heir to the French Revolution, brought the empire to an end after Prussia and Austria has disastrously attempted to intervene in the affairs of France. By the Peace of Bâle (1795) Prussia was forced to promise neutrality and Germany lost to France the left bank of the Rhine. In 1806 the German states neighbouring on France united under Napoleon's protection in the Confederation of the Rhine, the year in which Franz II ceased to be Holy Roman Emperor. Napoleon's brother Jérôme became king of Westphalia.

Republicanism, or at least new constitutional ideas, spread even to Prussia, where the Jews were emancipated and liberal trade laws introduced. Bavaria, Baden, Württemberg and Hesse-Darmstadt all drew up liberal constitutions, allowing propertied voters to elect new assemblies. After Napoleon's defeat German rulers turned absolutist again. Liberalism was defeated. The Congress of Vienna promoted the German Confederation, an alliance of 35 princely states and four free cities whose assembly at Frankfurt am Main remained dominated by Prussia and Austria.

In 1834, in the first moves towards a unified Germany, the German Customs Union was set up. The railways brought increasing unity. The 1848 revolution affected every German state, and at Frankfurt an Austrian archduke was appointed administrator of the empire and a national assembly attempted to set up a constitutional monarchy.

The revolution failed, and Germany restored most of its older institutions. The Frankfurt parliament was dissolved, the German confederation set up again.

Prussian economic strength continued to increase, translated into political power by Otto von Bismarck who became prime minister of Prussia in 1862. In 1864 he gained Schleswig (adding Holstein in 1866) as a result of the Danish war, and defeated Austria in 1866. The North German Federation, with Bismarck as its chancellor, replaced the old German Confederation.

Bismarck next led Prussia to victory over the French in 1870–71. The southern states were persuaded to join the North German Federation as one Reich, and on 18 January 1871 at Versailles Wilhelm I of Prussia was proclaimed German emperor. For the next 19 years Bismarck was its chancellor—the enemy alike of Liberalism, the political aspirations of the workers and Social Catholicism.

Wilhelm II dismissed Bismarck in 1890, but continued to block the hopes of social democracy in his empire. Between 1898 and 1909 the German navy achieved virtual parity with the British, to the latter's great concern. International tension increased. In 1914 the assassination of the Archduke Franz Ferdinand of Austria brought Austria and Germany into war against Britain, France, Russia and (eventually) the USA. The allies won the war and the rulers of Germany and Austria lost their thrones.

After the war, the German Social Democrats, led by Friedrich Ebert, made common cause with Hindenburg, chief of the general staff, in order to prevent an extreme left-wing take-over (incidentally conniving at the murders of the Spartacist leaders Karl Liebknecht and Rosa Luxembourg). For the next 14 years Germany was a republic, ruled from Weimar with a parliament including Social Democrats and the Catholic Centre Party.

Reparations imposed by the Peace of Versailles after World War I made its economic life precarious. Germany had lost all her colonies, Alsace-Lorraine (ceded to France), North Schleswig (ceded to Denmark) part of Upper Silesia, most of Posen, and other parts including West Prussia, Eupen-Malmedy, Memel. The Saar was under the control of the League of Nations, its coalfields run by the French. The coming years saw repeated financial and political instability, and the Weimar Republic finally collapsed as a result of the major economic crises which began in 1929.

By 1932 Adolf Hitler's racist, anti-Semitic National Socialist Party was the strongest in the Reichstag. Hitler became Chancellor of Germany on 30 January 1933. The following year the death of President Hindenburg enabled Hitler to assume the office of president as well.

The dictatorship of Adolf Hitler saw Germany regain the Saar and the Rhineland as well as march into Austria, the Sudetenland and eventually most of Czechoslovakia. It witnessed the virtual extermination of Germany's Jews and Gypsies, and persecution of other ethnic minorities. On 1 September 1939 Hitler launched an attack on Poland which precipitated World War II. Poland, Denmark, Norway, Holland, Belgium, France, Yugoslavia and Greece were all defeated by Hitler's forces. German troops nearly reached Moscow and almost conquered North Africa. Hitler survived an assassination attempt by German officers, churchmen and politicians on 20 July 1944, and—the war lost—committed suicide on 30 April 1945.

The victorious powers—Britain, the USSR, France and the USA—set up military governors in four German zones. Germany was demilitarised. New political parties were created.

Increasingly the Western powers and the Soviet Union were at odds. In 1948 Russia attempted to prevent all communications between Berlin (in the Russian zone) and the West, an attempt thwarted by a massive Western air lift. In the same year the Western powers unilaterally set up a West German state, of which Konrad Adenauer (former Oberbürgermeister of Cologne) was elected president. Adenauer was elected Chancellor of the Federal German Republic, now known as West Germany, the following year, though the three Western powers ceded full sovereignty to the republic only six years later.

In response the Russians set up the German Democratic Republic (DDR), known as East Germany. On 17 June 1953 a workers' uprising against this state was put down by Soviet troops. In 1961, after three and a half million refugees had fled from the East to the West, the Russian authorities blocked this escape route by building the Berlin wall.

Since that time relationships between the two Germanies have eased, especially through the statesmanship shown by Willy Brandt, former Oberbürgermeister of West Berlin, during his time as Federal Chancellor. A treaty of 21 December 1971 commits the two republics to developing friendly relations.

In 1954 West Germany became a member of the North Atlantic Treaty Organisation. The 'occupation' troops at last became troops of friendly powers, stationed by treaty on the soil of a sovereign republic. Three years later the people of Saarland, still under French control, voted overwhelmingly to become a *Land* of West Germany. Also in 1957, the Federal Republic became a founder member of the European Economic Community.

West Germany was experiencing an 'economic miracle', which included full employment. Adenauer was succeeded by Ludwig Erhard, who resigned when the 'economic miracle' seemed to be failing in the 1960s. In 1969 the social democrat Willy Brandt became Chancellor, and inaugurated the controversial 'Ostpolitik'—a policy of cautious rapprochememnt with the east.

When Brandt resigned in 1974 (because one of his close colleagues was revealed as an East German spy) he was succeeded by Helmut Schmidt of his own party, who lead a coalition with the Free Democratic Party. Schmidt fell from power in 1982, replaced by the leader of the Christian Democrats, Helmut Kohl.

C. Art and Architecture

The medieval emperors and princes of Germany, along with the princes of the church, were the earliest patrons of art. The peripatetic emperors (Carolingians, 768–918; Ottonians, 919–1024; Salians, 1024–1125) needed cities with all their appurtenances—monasteries, palaces, cathedrals—to set up court from which to govern the empire.

Almost invariably these foundations derived initially from a religious colony, usually established according to the rule of St. Benedict and in consequence building along the lines laid down by the Benedictines—a church and cloister, cells, a refectory, a chapterhouse, guest house, infirmary—but also including arrangements for the imperial retinue. In consequence churches were frequently built with two chancels, one at the west end (the *Westwerk*) reserved for the imperial retinue. The finest and most characteristic of these are the palatine chapel of Aachen, consecrated in 805, and the *Westwerk* at Corvey (built 873–85), once the seat of an imperial throne.

At Cologne, Paderborn and Fulda superb abbey churches were built at the beginning of the 9C, to be embellished by wall paintings (many, alas, disappeared) and by the works of goldsmiths and workers in bronze. The cult of relics meant that delicate romanesque shrines (reliquaries) abound from this era.

Throughout the Ottonian period (mid 10C to mid 11C) German art was influenced by Byzantine and Roman originals. Three great churches retain enough of their original form to exemplify this architecture: St. Pantaleon, Cologne; St. Michael, Hildesheim; and St. Cyriakus in Gernrode. Strict geometrical forms predominate. And Bishop Bernward's bronze door (1015) for St. Michael offers the first German sculptured cycle, a series of panels representing scenes from Genesis to the life of Jesus, patterned on models from Carolingian illustrated manuscripts. Comparable are the superb mid 11C wooden doors of St. Maria in Kapitol, Cologne.

Ottonian artists included outstanding gold and silversmiths, as well as ivory carvers. They produced the late 10C Gero cross of Cologne and the Gerresheim crucifix. At Reichenau worked a school of manuscript illuminators, patronised by the emperors, and almost matched in skill by those of Regensburg.

From the mid 11C to the 13C romanesque artists continued to produce masterpieces of the quality of the portable altar of Paderborn (now in the cathedral treasury), created by *Roger of Helmarshausen* c 1100. The prophet panels of Augsburg, c 1140, are the oldest surviving stained glass windows in Germany. Nicholas of Verdun made the shrine of the Magi for Cologne Cathedral c 1200. Also to this period belong fine works of monumental sculpture, in particular the tomb of Henry the Lion (c 1240) in Brunswick Cathedral.

Speyer Cathedral, founded in the first half of the 11C, with vaults c 1180, marks a new era of architectural innovation, with vaulted bays flanking a single central nave—a pattern soon to be followed in the cathedrals of Worms and Mainz. The triple-apsed St. Maria im Kapitol, Cologne, was another much-admired prototype (Cologne itself building two other churches, St. Aposteln and Groß St. Martin, according to this pattern).

At the end of the 12C French sculptors began to influence Germans, the peak of their late romanesque achievement being the decorations of Bamberg Cathedral, the work of masons from Reims, c 1230. Surviving romanesque wall paintings include those in St. Maria in Lyskirchen, Cologne (which miraculously survived WWII) and those in the Cathedral and Marienkirche, Soest.

French gothic was slowly introduced during the 13C. The plan of the Frauenkirche, Trier, was modelled on that of Reims Cathedral; the church of St. Elisabeth, Marburg, is a masterpiece of German high gothic. By the mid 13C French gothic had at last gained acceptance through parts of Germany, exemplified above all in Cologne's new cathedral, which was begun in 1248 and whose choir was consecrated in 1332, as well as in the cathedrals at Regensburg and Freiburg im Breisgau. At the same time the Franciscans and

Dominicans continued to build sparse basilicas that scarcely acknowledged the rich decoration of French gothic.

As the 14C saw the development of a new urban middle class, so these secular patrons began to build impressive town halls, as well as fine hall churches: Münster offers the examples both of its town hall (1355) and its cathedral (1225–65). In South Germany the Parler dynasty contributed their own decisive gothic. In North Germany (particularly Lübeck and Schleswig) brick gothic buildings became increasingly fashionable, after the achievement of the Marienkirche, Lübeck. While Lübeck benefitted from the gothic genius of the sculptor Johannes Junge (fl. 1406–28), Ulm Cathedral (finished 1419) profited from the late gothic naturalism of the sculptor *Hans Multscher* (c 1400– 67). In Bavaria the Frauenkirche at Munich, the church of St. Georg, Dinkelsbühl, and the choir of St. Laurence, Nuremberg, all built in the second half of the 15C, represent a style of late gothic hall church that is, in spite of its affinities with French gothic, uniquely German.

At this time painting was undergoing a renaissance, with *Konrad von Soest* (fl. 1402–04) in Westphalia, *Hans Multscher* (c 1400–67; a painter as well as a sculptor), and above all *Stephan Lochner* (fl. 1442–died 1451) in Cologne. Lochner's work is matched by such painters as *Martin Schongauer* (c 1430–91) of Augsburg (who came from Colmar in Alsace), *Hans Holbein the Elder* (1460/65–1524) and *Matthias Grünewald* (1470/80–c 1530).

Late gothic carving also produced supreme masters: the *Syrlin dynasty*; *Erasmus Grasser*; *Hans Leinberger* (fl. 1516–30) of Landshut; *Veit Stoß* (c 1447–1533); *Adam Kraft* of Nuremberg; the *Vischer dynasty*; *Hans Backoffen* of Mainz; *Hans Brüggemann* at Schleswig; and above all *Tilman Riemenschneider* (c 1460–1531) of Würzburg.

Würzburg is the seat of the Marienburg Schloß, built in the 13C for the prince bishops on the site of a former Celtic hill fort and around Germany's oldest round church (706), enlarged by the Scherenberg family, 1466–95, and again in the early 17C. The German nobility, spiritual and lay, built palaces and Schlößer not simply as dwellings but also to consolidate their power. In 1325 Ludwig the Barbarian built one on an island in the Rhine near Kaub. Many, if not most of these buildings were romantically restored in the 19C. Exceptions are the Schloß at Marburg and Burg Eltz on the Mosel.

The gothic elements were a late flowering. The spirit of the renaissance had already been seen in the Fugger funeral chapel at Augsburg (in the church of St. Anna, 1509–18). In the early 16C Holbein, *Albrecht Dürer* (1471–1528), the sons of Peter Fischer, and Matthias Grünewald brought into Germany the insights and impetus of the renaissance, a tradition developed by Dürer's pupil *Hans Baldung-Grien* (c 1480–1545) and by the *Cranach family*. In Augsburg Town Hall (finished 1620) Elias Holl (1573–1646) created a renaissance masterpiece.

The 17C was marred by the Thirty Years' War and a dearth of German creativity, but it was followed by the extraordinary achievements of baroque and rococo. Inspired by Austrians such as *Johann Bernhard Fischer von Erlach* (1656–1742) and *Johann Lukas von Hildebrandt* (1668–1745), and by Italians such as *Enrico Zuccalli* (c 1642–1724) and *Agostino Barelli* (1627–79), architects of the calibre of the *Dientzenhofer dynasty* (Georg, died 1689; Johann, c 1665–1726; Kilian Ignaz, 1689–1751) and *Josef Effner* (1687–1745) built the Cathedral of Fulda (Josef Dientzenhofer, 1705–12), the church of Ettal

(1710; Zuccalli), the Nymphenburg Palace, Munich (1664 and 1717; Barolli and J. Effner). Two brothers, *Cosmas Damian* and *Egid Quirin Asam* (1686–1739 and 1692–1750 respectively), perfected an unsurpassed blend of architecture, stucco work and painting in their churches (especially St. Johann Nepomuk, Munich). Two other brothers, *Dominikus* and *Johann Baptist Zimmermann* (1685–1766 and 1680–1758 respectively), built the remarkable pilgrimage church of Wies, the masterpiece of Bavarian religious baroque. At the same time *Johann Conrad Schlaun* (1695–1773) introduced the baroque of South Germany and Rome to Westphalia.

By the 18C Germany consisted of over 300 separate principalities, and in consequence this was a period when the princes built palaces consistent with their notions of their proper status: Zuccalli and Barelli, along with the Walloon architect *François de Cuvilliés* (1695–1768), built Schloß Nymphenburg and Schloß Schleißheim (1701–27) near Munich. Schlaun, Cuvilliés and the Frenchman *Robert de Cotte* built Schloß Brühl in 1725 for the archbishop and elector Clemens August. *Johann Balthasar Neumann* (1687–1753) added a monumental staircase. The masterpiece of South German secular baroque is the Residenz built by Neumann for the prince-bishops of Würzburg, 1719–44. The workshops of cabinet makers (such as *Abraham* and *David Roentgen of Neuwied*), and faience and china factories (of which the three most important were those at Meißen, Nymphenburg and Berlin), flourished with the need to embellish these residences. Meanwhile, in Prussia, *Andreas Schlüter* (c 1660–1714) was enriching Berlin architecture, followed by the work done by *Georg Wenceslaus von Knobelsdorff* (1699–1753) for his patron Frederick the Great (the Berlin Opera House and part of Schloß Charlottenburg, as well as Sans-Souci in Potsdam).

The influence of Versailles brought French architects to German courts, especially those of Friedrich II in Berlin and the Rhineland electors. At Karlsruhe between 1751 and 1766 the grand-ducal Schloß, originally erected in 1715, was rebuilt in the baroque style by *Friedrich Kesslau* and the French architect *Philippe de la Guépiérre*.

As the 18C progressed artists of the quality of *Johann Baptist Straub* (1704–84), his pupil *Ignaz Günther* (1725–75), and the Wessobrunn stucco worker *Joseph Anton Feuchtmayr* (1696–1770) developed baroque artistry into the often tormented, always sublime rococo. Neumann matched his baroque masterpiece at Würzburg with the extraordinary rococo pilgrimage church of Vierzehnheiligen in Franconia (1743–72).

The late 18C and 19C reacted against much of this exuberance. Excavations of Roman and Greek sites and the writings of Winckelmann (whose 'History of Ancient Art', published in 1763, exalted the 'noble simplicity and tranquil greatness' of Greek art) brought a different inspiration.

Occasionally virtually new towns were created. Mannheim, whose Schloß is Germany's largest baroque building, was laid out in a strict grid pattern in the 58 years from 1720, when it served as the capital city of the electors of the Palatinate. This was in a sense a mere prelude to the work of the architect *Friedrich Weinbrunner* (1766–1826), who transformed Karlsruhe into a classical city between 1800 and 1826. The neo-classical architecture of *Leo von Klenze* (1784–1864) and *Friedrich von Gärtner* (1792–1847) in Munich and that of *Karl Friedrich Schinkel* (1781–1841) and *Carl Gotthard Langhans* (1732–1808) in Berlin created superb vistas and monumental buildings—all matched by the sculpture of artists of the calibre of *Ludwig von Schwanthaler* (1802–48), *Gottfried Schadow* (1764–1850), *Christian Rauch* (1777–1857), and *Reinhold Begas* (1831–1911).

Neo-classicists and romantics (in painting, among the former *Henry Fuseli*, Swiss, 1741–1825; among the latter *Caspar David Friedrich*, 1774–1840; and *Friedrich Overbeck*, 1789–1869) were soon vying with the Biedermeier School (*Moritz von Schwind*, 1804–71; *Karl Spitzweg*, 1808–85) and landscape painters such as *Arnold Böcklin* (Swiss; 1827–1901), to find new directions in art. In architecture, as in Britain around 1830, neo-classicism was being challenged by neo-gothic, to be followed after 1850 by an ecclecticism that utilised renaissance, classical, baroque, gothic and romanesque elements at will, an eclecticism displayed par excellence in the commissions of mad king Ludwig of Bavaria. During the reign of Wilhelm II (1888–1918) neo-baroque came to be known as the 'Kaiser Wilhelm style' (as, for example, the neo-baroque Bode Museum, by *Ernst von Ihne*, 1898–1904).

After a brief flirtation with art nouveau ('Jugendstil'), represented for instance by *Joseph Maria Olbrich* (1867–1908), the 20C saw an extraordinary flowering of German art. Before World War I two groups of painters and sculptors, *Die Brücke* and *Der Blauer Reiter* developed forms now classified as expressionism. The former group included *Ernst Ludwig Kirchner* (1880–1938), *Karl Schmidt-Rottluff* and *Ernst Heckel*, who founded the movement in 1906, as well as *Emil Nolde*, (1867–1956) *Max Pechstein* (1881–1955) and *Otto Mueller* (1874–1930). The latter, based on Munich, included *Wassily Kandinsky* (1866–1944), *Franz Marc* (1880–1916) and *August Macke* (1887–1914). Other artists—such as *Oskar Kokoschka* (1886–1980), *Paula Modersohn-Becker*, (1876–1907) *Max Beckmann* (1884–1950) and *Ludwig Meidner* (1884-1966)—shared some of the aspirations of both groups without ever formally joining either. Ernst Barlach (1870–1938) produced superb expressionist sculpture.

In 1916 a group of artists met in Zürich to express their anger and disillusion with World War I. Of this group the most important Berlin Dadaists were *Georg Grosz* (1893–1953), *Raoul Hausmann* (1886–1971) and *Hannah Höch*. In Hanover *Kurt Schwitters* (1887–1954) represented the movement. A link between Dadaism and Surrealism was provided by the work of *Max Ernst* (1891–1976). Meanwhile, a group seeking a new objectivity (and therefore known as the 'Neue Sachlichkeit') responded to the war in different ways, their chief exponents being *Otto Dix* (1891–1969), *Christian Schad* and *Rudolf Schlichter* (1890–1955).

These artists flourished during the Weimar Republic, as did the *Bauhaus* school of painting and arts and crafts founded by *Walter Gropius* (1883–1969) in Weimar in 1919. Its members included *Paul Klee* (1870–1940), Kandinsky and *Oskar Schlemmer* (1888–1943); its architectural manifestations included Fritz Höger's Chile Haus, Hamburg; and Gropius's Siemensstadt in Berlin.

The Hitler Reich proscribed Dadaists, expressionists, neo-realists and the members of the Bauhaus alike, the German Führer (who had himself been a painter) patronising a patriotic and heroic style in art.

The devastating consequences of World War II meant that much architectural effort in post-war Germany was dedicated to the heroic and often brilliant restoration of damaged buildings. At the same time some German cities have pioneered new and imaginative projects, such as the Hansa Quarter in Berlin, by such internationally renowned architects as Oscar Niemeyer, Le Corbusier, Walter Gropius and Sten Samelson).

D. Music

Christians brought the Gregorian chant to Germany, and the religious tradition thus established in monastic foundations fostered in the 12C the songs of courtly love (Minne) of which we still possess some 500 examples. The Minnesingers themselves—who include *Walther von der Vogelweide, Heinrich von Morungen,* and *Oswald von Wolkenstein* (died 1445)—owed their education to the monasteries.

Their successors were the Meistersingers. Here again a strong religious bent characterised the finest of them. Many Meistersingers utilised the Lutheran Bible for their lyrics. *Hans Sachs* (1494–1576), the most famous, dubbed the Protestant reformer Martin Luther 'the nightingale of the Reformation'. Meistersingers flourished in Lutheran towns and cities, and Martin Luther himself was a formidable hymnologist.

Other, non-German, influences also came into play. *Heinrich Schütz* (1585–1672), Germany's greatest 17C composer, studied in Venice when Monteverdi dominated Italian music. His contemporary and fellow-Saxon *Jacob Froberger* (c 1617–67) studied the organ under Frescobaldi in Rome. Bach's contemporaries *Georg Philip Telemann* and *J.-A. Hasse* both wrote Italian operas, and Bach's great predecesor *Dietrich Buxtehude* (1637–1707) was born not in Germany but in Sweden.

One month before Bach, *Georg Friederic Händel* (1685–1759) was born. Händel studied first in Italy, before settling permanently in Britain. (He was naturalised in 1726.) Supreme among composers of Biblical oratorios (Saul, Messiah, Judas Maccabeus, Samson, Israel in Egypt), Händel was frequently virtually destitute and yet decisively influenced the course of English music.

His contemporary *Johann Sebastian Bach* (1685–1750) scarcely left Thuringia (for a short time he was an organ scholar at Lübeck), yet he absorbed not only the lessons of his German predecessors, such as Schütz and Buxtehude but also the inspiration of Italian geniuses such as Vivaldi. Prolific at composing sacred and secular music alike, a court official apparently composing to order, Bach succeeded in producing such unequalled masterpieces as the Brandenburg Concertos, the St. Matthew Passion and the Mass in B Minor. His life coincided with those of masterly baroque organ builders (Arp Schnitger and Andreas Silbermann in particular). He fathered a dynasty of distinguished composers, including *Carl Philipp Emmanuel* (1714–88), *Wilhelm Friedmann* (1710–84) and *Johann Christian* (1735–82).

Franz Joseph Haydn (1732–1800) once declared, 'I learned everything I know from Emmanuel Bach'. Basically a Viennese composer, he and the other Austrian genius Mozart managed to rid German music of its dependency on the Italian, as well as extending musical forms further than they had ever previously reached. Their heir was *Ludwig van Beethoven* (1770–1827) who, though born in Bonn, revered Vienna as his spiritual home. Nonetheless Beethoven's father and grandfather had both worked as musicians for the elector of Cologne. Haydn taught Beethoven in Vienna, after Beethoven had also worked for the elector. In 1800 he emerged from Haydn's shadow with his first piano concerto and his first symphony. He wrote eight more symphonies, chamber music, five piano concertos, an opera ('Fidelio') and a violin concerto.

Franz Schubert (1797–1827) spent his whole life in Vienna, though this scarcely distinguishes him from many other German composers of the 18C and 19C: *Giacomo Meyerbeer* (1791–1864), though born in Berlin, lived most of his creative life in Paris. *Felix Mendelssohn* (1809–47) and *Robert Schumann* (1810–56) remained more closely tied to their native land—though Mendelssohn's inspiration included Shakespeare and Scotland ('A Midsummer Night's Dream' and 'Fingal's Cave'). Schumann developed a personal friendship with *Johannes Brahms* (1833–97) which lasted until his death.

The international nature of the German musical scene is perfectly displayed in the career of *Franz Liszt* (1811–86), who was born of a Hungarian father and an Austrian mother but spent most of his active life in Germany as director of music at Weimar. Here he presented the first performance of Wagner's 'Lohengrin', and his daughter Cosima became Wagner's second wife. Wagner's musical debt to Liszt is seen above all in his 'Parsifal' and 'Tristan and Isolde'. *Richard Wagner* (1813–83) was director of music in such diverse places as Würzburg, Magdeburg, Königsberg and Dresden. After some years of exile (because he espoused the revolutionaries of 1848), he became court musician to King Ludwig of Bavaria, whence he fled first to Switzerland and finally to Bayreuth, where the first performance of his complete 'Der Ring des Nibelungen' took place.

Wagner's greatest German successor is undoubtedly *Richard Strauß* (1864–1949), whose collaboration with *Hugo von Hofmannstal* as librettist produced 'Salome', 'Elektra', 'Der Rosenkavalier' and 'Ariadne auf Naxos'. Thenceforth European music took a new turn with the atonal works of *Arnold Schönberg* (1874–1951) and his successors *Anton Webern* (1883–1943), *Paul Hindemith* (1895–1963) and *Alban Berg* (1885–1935). Even more avant-garde has been the work of *Karlheinz Stockhausen*, advocate of the musique concrète developed by the French composers *Olivier Messiaen* and *Pierre Boulez*, who in 1953 took up a newly-created post for composing electronic music established by Cologne radio.

E. Literature

Medieval Germany produced a number of folk songs and sagas, in particular the 12C *Nibelungen*, the love poetry of the troubadour Walter von der Vogelweide (1170–1228), and Wolfram von Eschenbach's 13C *Parsifal*. Meister Eckart and Jacob Böhme created mystical treatises.

Three centuries after *Parsifal* the tales of the Brunswick jester Till Eulenspiegel appeared, at a time when Martin Luther was creating a classically beautiful language in his hymns and his translation of the German Bible (finished 1534).

Paradoxically the savagery of the Thirty Years' War produced a literary masterpiece in Christoph von Grimmelhausen's equally savage and bitingly satirical *Simplizissimus* (1669), almost certainly based on his first hand experience of that war.

The next century saw Germany's greatest period of dramatic literature, under the influence of Gotthold Ephraïm Lessing (1729–81), whose chief works are *Minna von Barnhelm*, *Nathan der Weise* and *Emilia Galotti*. Almost immediately followed a group of writers belonging to the *Storm and Stress* (Sturm und Drang) movement, in particular Johann Wolfgang von Goethe (1749–1832) and Johann Christoph Friedrich von Schiller (1759–1805).

Goethe's epistolary novel *Werther*, and his *Wilhelm Meister* and *Elective Affinities*, as well as his plays (*Goetz von Berlichingen*, *Egmont*, *Tasso*, *Iphigénie*) culminated in his supreme *Faust*. Schiller, inspired by Shakespeare (to whom Germans had already been introduced by Christoph Martin Wieland and whose work Schiller translated) produced at the age of twenty the tumultuous *Die Räuber*, followed by *Kabale und Liebe*, *Don Carlos*, the Wallenstein saga, a play about Joan of Arc and another about Mary Stuart as well as *Wilhelm Tell*.

Their successor Heirich von Kleist committed suicide without seeing a performance of any of his plays. Meanwhile fairy-tales of the brothers Grimm, the *Tales* of E.T.A. Hoffman and the poems in the anthology *The Child with the Enchanted Horn* (edited by Clemens Brentano) ushered in a romanticism that was both mocked and furthered by the poems of Heinrich Heine (1797–1856).

Friedrich Hebbel (1813–63) wrote tragic Schopenhauerean plays (including a Nibelung trilogy), while the revolutionary nihilist Georg Büchner (born in the same year as Hebbel) managed to die in his bed in Zürich 80 years later, having written for the stage *Danton's Death*, *Wozzeck*, *Leonce und Lena* as well as the novella *Lenz*.

The 20C witnessed the careers of the two Mann brothers, Thomas (the more successful, whose *Buddenbrooks* chronicles the decline of bourgeois Lübeck) and Heinrich, whose *Professor Unrat* was the basis of the phenomenally successful (and once considered scandalous) film *The Blue Angel*. At this time Franz Kafka (1883–1924) was writing his nightmarish *Trial* and *The Castle*, while Robert Musil's *Man without Qualities* mocked the pretensions of the Austro-Hungarian Empire.

Like Thomas Mann, the mystical novelist Hermann Hesse and Heinrich Böll both won Nobel prizes. Bertolt Brecht (1898–1955), author of *The Threepenny Opera* which Kurt Weill set to music, by contrast turned his back on the Western alliance and preferred to return from exile after World War II to East Berlin, setting up there his famous Berliner Ensemble (but cautiously keeping bank accounts in the capitalist world) in order to produce his own *Mother Courage*, *Galileo* and *The Good Woman of Sezuan*.

F. Food and Drink

German food varies remarkably from region to region, even from town to town. But a typical menu falls into several parts:

Vorspeisen (first courses) can be smoked salmon or herrings, often salads with mayonnaise; meats and sausages (*Bratwurst* and *Blut-wurst*), canapés with paté.

Suppen (soups) include asparagus soup with cream (*Spargel-cremesuppe*), vegetable soup (*Gemüsesuppe*), consommé (*Kraft-brühe*) and farmer's broth (*Bauernsuppen*).

Fische (fish) invariably included on restaurant menus are trout (*Blaue Forelle*), as well as the ever-accessible herrings and often also eel, pike and carp.

Geflügel (poultry), often includes duck stuffed with apple and ham, originally deriving from the environs of Hamburg (*Vierländer Ente*), chicken broth (*Kukenragout*), turkey (*Pute*) and at Christmas and New Year goose (*Gans*).

Fleich (meat) includes *Schnitzel* and numerous kinds of sausage (*Wurst*), as well as various forms of pork, such as the version that is smoked and known as *Kassler Rippchen*. Throughout Germany can be found the beef dish called *Sauerbraaten*. These dishes are served with inventively-cooked potato, cabbage (often in the form of *Sauerkraut*, i.e. shredded and pickled), asparagus or *Blindes Huhn* (i.e. a mixture of carrots, green beans and bacon).

A meal usually ends with **Süßpeisen** (dessert), often created with whipped cream and rice. In addition meals often include cakes (*Konditorei*), sometimes enhanced with marzipan, often filled with luscious, fattening cream.

German menus also frequently include beautifully cooked game—*Hirsch* (venison); *Reh* (roebuck); *Wildschwein* (wild boar, either served as haunch, *Keule*, or saddle, *Rücken*); and *Hasen* (hare).

Each region has its seasonal specialty: *Berliner Pfannkuchen* (doughnuts) at New Year; Berlin *Kartoffelpuffer* (potato pancakes, known as *Reibekuchen* in the Rhineland); *Himmel und Erde*, which in Cologne means mashed potatoes with black pudding and onions; Rollmops (pickled herrings with onions and gherkins); baked fish with apple wine (*Rippchen mit Kraut*), which you eat in Hessen; *Eisbein*, a huge knuckle of pork with Sauerkraut and pease pudding; skimmed milk cheese (*Handkäse*), served in Mainz with vinegar, chopped onions, salt and pepper; smoked eel, Brunswick style, from the Steinhuder lake; smoked sprats from Kiel; the Bavarian potato-dumpling seasoned with liver or bilberries or diced bacon or ground calf's liver (known generically as *Knödel*); Nuremberg Christmas *Stollen* and *Baumkuchen* (cakes covered in icing or chocolate); Schwabian sweet bread (*Zuckerbrot*); Westphalian sausages baked in puff pastry (*Würste-Brötchen*) and the local wheat loaf baked in egg and milk and loaded with currants (*Korintenstuten*); soused herring (*Matjesfilet*) served with boiled potatoes and green beans on the Baltic; even the Hamburger, known in Hamburg as the *Hamburger Rundstück*.

Apart from its splendid beers (each person on average drinking 130 litres a year), Germany also devotes 98·386 hectares of its land to vineyards, some 62 per cent of its produce classed as Qualitätswein in 1983, 33 per cent classed as Qualitätswein mit Pradikat and 5 per cent classed as table wine.

The British have for many years described German Rheinwein as 'Hock', though officially this term may be used only of wine grown produced from the Sylvaner or Riesling grape. Seven regions produce such wine: Rheinhessen; Rhineland-Palatinate; Rheingau; Nahe; Mosel-Saar-Ruwer; Baden; Franken.

In addition the Germans designate as 'Liebfraumilch' wines from Rheinhessen, Rhineland-Palatinate, Rheingau and Nahe. Sparkling wines (*Sekt*) are made, following the methods of French champagne vineyards, with a light variety known as Perlwein.

The denomination of a wine is strictly cntrolled in Germany (and by the EEC), so that 'Qualitätswein mit Prädikat' always denotes a wine of choice quality that contains no chemical additions, and 'Kabinett' denotes the finest such wines. 'Auslese' refers to the finest grapes, while 'Spätlese' indicates that these grapes have been gathered at the latest possible moment, when every grape is indubitably ripe.

Wine labels are strictly regulated and give: the year of the vintage; the vineyard; the variety of grape; its harvesting (i.e. 'Auslese', 'Spätlese'); the region of production; a quality control number; and details of the wine merchant. The words 'Erzeuger-Abfüllung' mean that the wine has been bottled by the producer.

I BAVARIA

1 Regensburg to Ulm

A. Regensburg

REGENSBURG (also called *Ratisbon*; 134,000 inhab.; alt. 333m), situated at the northernmost point of the Danube, at its confluence with the Regen and the Naab, is the main city of the Upper Palatinate, the fourth largest in Bavaria and (with some 1400 medieval buildings) the largest surviving medieval city in Germany.

Main *railway station*: Bahnhofstraße.

Main *post office*: Bahnhofstraße.

Information office: Altes Rathaus (Old Town Hall), Kohlenmarkt.

Trains to Frankfurt, Munich, Ulm, Vienna.

Boats along the Danube to Passau, taking in Walhalla.

History. The Celts founded *Radasbona* c 500 BC, and were conquered by the Romans in AD 77, when Vespasian had a fortress built here. In AD 179 the legions of Marcus Aurelius constructed a huge camp, *Castra Regina*, large enough for 6000 men and still traceable in the quadrangle of streets at the heart of the city. In the early 6C the Dukes of Bavaria, the Agilolfings, made Regensburg their principal seat. Charlemagne overthrew the Dukes in 788. Regensburg became a free imperial city in the 12C, whence dates its most flourishing era. From Regensburg Konrad II in 1147 and Frederick Barbarossa in 1189 set out on Crusades. In 1541 a conference at Regensburg brought local agreement between Catholics and Protestants. The Swedes besieged the city in 1632. Between 1663 and 1806 Regensburg was the seat of the Imperial Diet. As the emperor's principal representatives at the Diet, the princes of Thurn und Taxis established themselves here in 1748. Karl von Dalberg, formerly Elector of Mainz, took over as prince in 1803; the French seized the city in 1809 (Napoleon was wounded here: plaque where Martin-Luther-Straße meets Hemauerstraße); and a year later it became part of Bavaria. Regensburg was the only gothic city in Germany completely to survive WWII. It has been a university city since 1967. Its sons include Albrecht Altdorfer (c 1480–1538) and the writer George Britting (1891–1964).

Maximilianstraße leads from the railway station N through the park of the *Palace of the Princes of Thurn und Taxis**. Turn left along St. Petersweg to Emmeramsplatz, to reach the *Palace*, a former Benedictine monastery (founded by Theodor II and enriched by Charlemagne; the princes took it as their Residenz in 1809): romanesque doorway, c 1170; free-standing bell tower, 1579. On the left is the baroque church of *St. Rupert*. The monastery church, 8–12C; baroque interior, 1731, by the brothers C.D. and E.Q. Asam; three crypts for the tombs of three saints: St. Emmeram (9C), St. Ramwold (late 10C), St. Wolfgang (1052). Other tombs in main church: Queen Emma (c 1280); Emperor Ludwig 'the Child' and ·Emperor Arnulf of Bavaria, monument to the humanist and historian Ventinus (died 1534).— Stables, now the *Marstallmuseum* (the early history of the postal service, started by the Thurn und Taxis family; coaches, carriages and sleighs); mortuary chapel; gothic cloisters.—The Schloß also houses a museum (Brussels tapestries).

NORTH ALONG WAFFNERG. On the left is the 13C early gothic Dominican church of *St. Blasius*. The philosopher Albertus Magnus lived in the convent here between 1236 and 1240. On the W façade is a statue of St. Dominic (c 1430). Interior: 15C choir stalls; monument to Lukas Lamprechtshauser (c 1500); Virgin and supplicants (c 1500).— Further N, on the corner of Gesandtenstraße stands the Protestant *Dreieinigkeitskirche*, built by the Nuremberg architect Hans Carl (1627–31), with 17C and 18C monuments to famous members of the Diet in the churchyard.

Turn W along Gesandtenstraße to reach the 12C romanesque **St. Jakobskirche**, founded by Irish Benedictines (hence its name 'Schottenkirche', Scots church), with a romanesque *N porch, depicting Christ between SS. James and John, Adam, Eve and the twelve apostles and gothic stone statues on pillars of the choir.

Return to Waffnerg and turn N as far as Ludwigstraße to reach HAIDPLATZ, with its fountain, the Justitiabrunnen (1656). No. 1 Haidplatz is the 'Neue Waage' ('New Weigh House'), a former tavern where the Protestant Melanchthon disputed with the Catholic Eck in 1541, and No. 7 is the Goldene Kreuz, an early gothic house with a tower. (Here in 1546 Emperor Charles V met his future wife Barbara Blomberg.) NW in Kohlenmarkt stands the *Altes Rathaus* (13–18C): W wing the imperial hall, c 1360, with a timber ceiling of 1408, painted

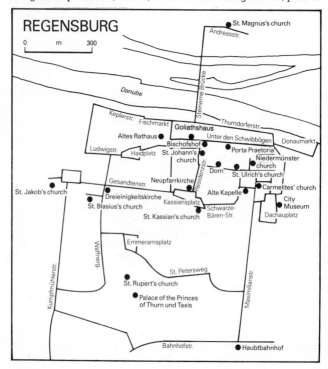

1564; E wing baroque, 1661; eight-storey tower, c 1250; Venus fountain (1661) in the courtyard, with four stone figures (1630) from the Dreieinigkeitskirche. The old town hall now houses the Information Office and Museum of the Imperial Diet: courtroom and torture chamber; tapestries.

This part of Regensburg boasts merchants' houses, built in the Italian style between the 13th and 16Cs and fortified with towers. N is FISCHMARKT, which hosts a fish market each morning (St. George's fountain, c 1600), W of which at No. 5 Keplerstraße (1540) is a museum devoted to the astronomer Johannes Kepler, who died here in 1630. Nos 1 and 3 Keplerstraße retain their 13C towers, and No. 7, the Blaue Hecht, is a former medieval inn.

Goliathstraße, with the 13C *Goliathshaus* (frescoed with a picture of David and the giant by Melchior Bocksberger, c 1573) continues E from the old town hall. S of the Goliathshaus is the WATMARKT, with Regensburg's finest tower-house, the seven-storey mid 13C *Baumburgerturm*, and another mid 13C gothic house, the Bräunelturm, at No. 6. Goliathstraße. Goliathstraße, running into Unter den Schwibbogen, leads past the *Bischofshof* (the bishop's palace from the 11C; now a hotel) and the 2C *Porta Praetoria*, northern gate of the Roman camp. S of the Bischofshof are the 14C *St. Johanniskirche* and the cathedral.

**St. Peter's Cathedral, famous for its boys' choir, the 'cathedral sparrows' (Domspatzen) was begun in the 10C, damaged by severe fires in the 12C and burnt almost to the ground in 1273. The Eselturm on the N side is all that remains of the old building. Bishop Leo the Thurndorfer began a new cathedral in 1250. The main choir was vaulted c 1300, the crossing and the first arch of the nave in 1325. Work started on the S tower in 1341, on the N in 1383. The whole was completed early in the 16C, apart from the 105m-high towers (1859–69, restored since 1950). The cathedral is 85·4m long, 34·8m wide and 31·85m from the ground to the highest point of the central of the three naves; elaborate W façade and doorway, with a rose window behind a crucifix (1480), carvings and statues finished by 1430, including a king riding a curious horned beast and St. Martin of Tours (both mid 14C). The SW porch has a carving of 'St. Peter's release' (1360).—INTERIOR: 13th and 14C glass; stone pulpit (1482); aumbry (1493, to N of high altar) and well (1501, opposite the Eselturm) both by Wolfgang Roritzer; two W pillars of the crossing carrying the Virgin and angel of the Annunciation (c 1280) by the Master of Erminhold; stone statues of the apostles Peter, wearing a conical papal tiara (c 1300), Paul, James and Bartholomew (late 14th and early 15C); tomb of Margaretha Tucher by Peter Vischer of Nuremberg (1521); tomb of Bishop Philipp Wilhelm (1598) in the middle of the nave; high altar 1785 (in silver), by Georg Ignaz Bauer of Augsburg. Silver busts of Mary and Joseph (c 1695), of Peter and Paul (mid 18C), altar cross and seven silver lamps (1777); damaged memorial to first Prince, Karl von Dalberg. Cloisters containing the 12C romanesque Allerheiligenkapelle (All Saints' chapel, built to house the tomb of Bishop Hartwich II) with wall paintings, and St. Stephen's chapel (romanesque; 10C altar). Treasury.

Opposite the W façade of the cathedral is the 14C *Haus an der Heuport*, with a courtyard and open staircase. Residenzstraße leads S from the cathedral to the renaissance *Neupfarrkirche*, built 1519–40 as a pilgrim's church dedicated to Our Lady (picture of 'Schöne Maria', over a side altar, by Hans Leingerger, 1520). It has been a

Protestant church since 1542.—S in Kassiansplatz is the romanesque *St. Kassian's church* (with an 18C baroque interior). From here Schwarze-Bären-Straße leads E to the S side of the picturesque ALTER KORNMARKT and the *Alte Kapelle*, (begun 1002; choir mid 15C; interior Bavarian rococo, with frescoes by the Augsburg painter Christoph Thomas Scheffler; high altar of 1769–75 by Simon Sorg of Regensburg; 13C Italian Madonna in the Lady Chapel). On the NW side of the square stands the 'Roman' (i.e. romanesque) tower; the palace of the Dukes of Bavaria (*Herzogshof*, begun late 10C, the present building c 1200, window arcades of the façade c 1220; behind Herzogshof the romanesque Ducal Hall on the W side, and beyond it the church of *St. Ulrich* (c 1230–50); and on the E side the baroque *Karmelitenkirche* (church of the Carmelites, 1641–60; tower 1681; 18C altarpieces from the cathedral).

In DACHAUPLATZ, E of this church are over 50m of surviving Roman wall and a former 13th and 14C friary now housing the *City Museum* (Bavarian history since the Stone Age; treasures from the city churches; furniture; 16–18C European paintings, including Altdorfer and his school, second floor). The monks handed over this priory to the city in 1544, and here was built the first Protestant press of Regensburg. The priory church (early gothic nave 1260–70; high gothic choir 1330–40; late gothic screen) has gothic and renaissance tombs and a Cruxifixion group by Erhard Heydenreich (1513).—S of this museum is the Neues Rathaus (1936–38).

The Steinerne Brücke at Regensburg, built 1135–46, is Germany's oldest surviving stone bridge. To the left of the bridge gate can be seen the salt warehouse and one of the spires of St. Peter's Cathedral.

N of Alter Kornmarkt are the twin-towered *Niedermünster* church (mid 12C; high altar by the Salzburg stonemason Jakob Mösl, 1763; altarpiece of the Assumption, 1900; excavations inside have uncovered buildings dating as far back as the 2C) and the *Bishops' Palace* (housing the Proske Music Library). N of the palace, Donaumarkt leads left into Thurndorferstraße which runs along the river to Germany's oldest surviving stone bridge: the 310 m-long *Steinerne Brücke* (1135–46), a masterpiece of medieval engineering. (A copy of the Brückenmännchen or Bridge dwarf is on the W parapet.) The Brücktor, sole survivor of three, is 14C. Cross the bridge amd turn right along Andreasstraße to find the baroque church of *St. Magnus*.

B. Regensburg to Ulm along the River Danube

Total distance 233km. **Regensburg**—B16 29km *Kelheim.*—7km *Weltenberg.*—66km **Ingolstadt.**—22km *Neuburg.*—34km **Donauwörth.**—52km *Günzburg.*—B10 23km **Ulm**.

Leave Regensburg by Kumpfmühler Straße along the right bank of the meandering Danube. Turn right before reaching *Bad Abbach*, whose sulphuric baths were known in Roman times (today there are three modern rheumatism clinics here). The Emperor Henry II was born in the town's ruined Schloß in 973. Continue along the B16 into the Danube valley to reach (10km) the pretty market town of *Saal*. From Saal the B299 runs across the Danube to *Kelheim*, with its 13–14C defences (three towers and three gates) and gabled burgers' houses, situated at a strategic point where the Altmühl meets the Danube: late gothic parish church, 15C; remains of mid 12C towers of Wittelsbach's Schloß (the rest of the Schloß buildings are used as a school and government offices). Duke Ludwig I of Kelheim was murdered in the chapel in 1231.

Visible on the Michelsberg, 3km out of the town, is the *Befreiungshalle*, an extraordinary neo-classical building (housing statues of 18 German maidens and 34 goddesses of war, designed by Ludwig Schwanthaler) created by Freidrich Gärtner and Leo von Klenze for Ludwig I of Bavaria in 1842–63 to celebrate the 1813–15 War of Liberation against the French.

The area around Kelheim has several caves with stalagmite and stalactite formations, the best-known being the *Große Schulerloch* and the *Kleine Schulerloch*, close by Oberau (3km on the road W towards Riedenburg).

Cross the river at Kelheim and follow the wooded Jura heights SW and the Danube gorge to the former Benedictine abbey (founded 620) at *Weltenberg*, with its spectacular river gorge (the 'Donaudurch-bruch') and its baroque *church by the brothers Asam (1717–21; high altar depicting St. George and the dragon). The present monastery buildings date from the same period.

From Weltenberg follow the signs to (8km) *Eining* (remains of Roman fort, 1–3C AD).—*Neustadt* is 8km further SW. The countryside is still wooded and hilly, with fields growing hops.—From Neustadt drive 4km E to *Abensberg*, on the River Abens, with parts of its 14–15C fortifications still intact. Its principal sights are the Hofbräuhaus, the birthplace of the historian Johannes Turmair (1477–1534, known as Aventinus); 13C church of St. Barbara (wall paintings); 14C Carmelite church (gothic transepts, later baroque reordering; Aventinus Museum in the former monastery); 16C pilgrims' church at nearby Allersdorf).

The road SW from Neustadt to Ingolstadt leads through *Münchsmünster* (at the junction with the B300 to Augsburg), with a church belonging to its former Benedictine monastery.

From Ingolstadt continue W along the B16 in the direction of Donauwörth. After 5km the road passes through *Oberhausen*. Here a footpath leads left to the 150m-high memorial for the men of the 1st French Grenadiers who fell in the Austro-French war of 1800. Beyond Oberhausen a view of baroque *Schloß Bertholdsheim* appears on the left bank of the Danube. Continue W to Neuburg.

Neuburg (25,000 inhab.; alt. 403m; Information Office in Luitpoldstraße) boasts the oldest Protestant church in Bavaria (the chapel, built 1540, with frescoes by Hans Bocksberger the Elder, 1543, for the renaissance Residenz which is chiefly 1530–45; E wing 1665). Three lines of fortifications and a moat protect the town. In the exquisite KARLSPLATZ stands the court church of Our Lady (1627; renaissance furnishings; Wessobrunn stuccoes; high altar by J.A. Breitenauer, 1752–54; pulpit 1756). Other sights: Chapel of St. Martin (1731; now a library; 18C furnishings); St. Peter's Church (c 1650), opposite the 13C town gate, which is known as the Münz; Holy Cross church (late 12C crypt, the rest reordered in the rococo style in 1755–58; stucco work; high altar by J.M. Fischer, with paintings and frescoes by J.M. Baumgartner); the museum of local history (119 Amalienstraße); and the English Garden.

After 5km driving W from Neuburg a brief deviation S leads to *Rain*, to find in front of the Town Hall (1759–62) a statue (1914) of General Tilly, mortally wounded here in 1632. Rain has a 14C and 15C church of St. John, alongside the chapel of All Souls (1471; now a local history museum).

*Donauwörth, 13km from Rain along the B16, at the confluence of the Wörnitz and the Danube, is where this route reaches the Romantische Straße (see Rte 7B). This Protestant town was mortgaged to the Catholics by Emperor Rudolf II, an act that helped to provoke the Thirty Years' War. The spot was colonised in the 6C; was a free imperial city from the 13C to 1714, and was savagely bombed in 1945. Its treasures include the late gothic Town Hall (1309, restored 1853, at E end of Reichsstraße); the Fuggerhaus (built for Anton Fugger, 1539), at W end of Reichsstraße, near the Town Hall (13–14C) and Information Office; *baroque Heilig-Kreuz-Kirche (1717–22; 17C and 18C monastery building; early 18C pulpit and stalls), with the tombstone of the wife of Duke Ludwig the Stern, beheaded under the accusation of adultery in 1256, and in the crypt a relic of the Holy Cross. The late gothic parish church, 1444–67, has a tabernacle carved by Gregor Erhart, 1503, and medieval frescoes. The late gothic Tanzhaus, on the corner of Reichsstraße and Mangoldstraße, was rebuilt 1974. In Spitalstraße, SW of the Town Hall square, stands the Spitalkirche (1611–12), the Spital (c 1680) and the classical Deutschordenhaus (1774–78). Spitalstraße leads to the Riedertor, one of the two remaining gates of the medieval fortifications of Donauwörth.

21km SW along B16 is **Höchstädt** (alt. 418m) with its Schloß (1589–93), formerly belonging to the Counts of Pfalz-Neuburg, and the church of St. Mary in her Assumption (15C and 16C, fine pulpit and high altar). In 1704 during the War of the Spanish Succession Höchstädt was the scene of a decisive battle between the Franco-Bavarian troops and the English and Imperial forces. The road continues another 6km to reach *Dillingen*, former private country seat of the Bishop of Augsburg and seat of a Catholic university from 1551–1803: 16C Schloß; Catholic church of St. Peter (1619–28); university building, (1688–89; rococo Golden Room, 1761–64); Jesuit College (1736–38, with a baroque library); Jesuit church (1610–17); parish church (1619–28); church of Our Lady, (1734–40); church of Christ the King (1960–62, with a Madonna c 1510).

5km W stands *Lauingen*, which was the birthplace of Albertus Magnus (1193–1280); his memorial is beside the 53m-high Schimmel Gate; 38 Wittelsbachs are buried in the parish church of St. Martin (1518); the former Schloß of the dukes of Pfalz-Neuburg is now a nursing home.

Günzburg, known in Roman times as *Guntia*, lies on the River Günz, 20km SW of Lauingen, along the D16. Domenikus Zimmermann built the rococo *church of Our Lady (1736–39); charming market square; also noteworthy are the 16C renaissance Schloß and the Hofkirche (16–18C); Schloß Autenried (1871).

From here take the B10, driving 23km W to Ulm.

ULM (95,000 inhab.; alt. 478m), situated at the confluence of the Danube and the Blau (which rises 20km W at Blaubeuren), is surrounded by a double set of town walls (14C and 15C) along the Danube, incorporating the leaning Metzger tower and the Eagle bastion (from which the celebrated 'Tailor of Ulm' leapt in 1811 in a vain attempt to fly), this ancient town has become the chief city of Upper Württemberg.

Main *railway station*: F-Ebert-Straße/Bahnhofstraße.

Main *post office*: F-Ebert-Straße.

Information Office: 51 Münsterplatz.

History. Ulm became a Carolingian fief in 854, was under the rule of the Salier (1024–1125) and the Staufen families (1138–1268) and became a free imperial city in 1274. The leading citizens set up a democratic constitution in 1397, celebrated anually in the Swearing-in ceremony (see below). Ulm flourished culturally and commercially in the 14C and 15C, taking the side of the Reformers in the next century. Though culturally and commercially harmed by the Thirty Years' War, Ulm retained its status as a free city until 1802. Nearly three-quarters of the city was detroyed in WWII. The university was rebuilt in 1969. Here was born Albert Einstein (1879–1955). At four-yearly intervals Ulm holds a tradional fish festival and a coopers' festival.

Follow Bahnhofstraße SE to the junction with Wengengasse, which leads N to *Wengenkirche*, a modern bulding housing the remains of a late gothic/baroque church bombed in 1944 (18C altar painting by Franz Martin Kuen). The continuation of Bahnhofstraße E is Hirschstraße, which leads as far as Münsterplatz and the Protestant **Cathedral**, begun 1377(plans by He i nrich Parler the Elder, continued Ulrich von Ensingen and Burckhardt Engelberg) and finished 1890. Among gothic churches only the cathedral at Cologne is larger, and at 161m the tower of Ulm (the lower part largely the work of Matthäus Böblinger, the rest with the spires 1845–90) is the world's highest (768 steps, panorama). Arcaded doorway and renaissance doors, with statue of *Man of Sorrows (1429; by Hans Multscher); other early 16C statues by Jörg Syrlin the Younger. INTERIOR: choir stalls by Jörg Syrlin the Elder (1469–71; note the pagan as well as Biblical motifs);

high altar by M. Schaffner (1521); pulpit by B. Engelberg (1499) with canopy by J. Syrlin the Younger (1510); fan vaulting; fresco of the Last Judgment (1471); 15C glass, (and three modern windows, 1956); *26m-high tabernacle (1464–71, statues by Multscher—upper section—and N. Hagenauer). Major restoration 1965–70.

Along the Lautenberg, SW of the Minster, stands the Neuen Bau (1585–93). In the MARKTPLATZ S of the Minster is the gothic *Town Hall* (1360 and 1420, restored; frescoes of 1540; early 15C sculptures of Electors and Emperors by H. Multscher; astronomical clock, 1520, renovated L. Habrecht, 1580), in front of which is the Fischkasten fountain (1482; by Syrlin the Elder). SW of the town hall is the modern Heiliggeistkkirche, with a bizarre, finger-shaped bell tower. To the E. of the town hall along Neuestraße is the TAUBENPLÄTZLE, with a fountain dated 1585. At 92 Neuestraße is the *Ulm Museum* (open Tuesday–Sunday, 10.00–12.00, 14.00–17.00; no midday break July–September; local masters; international modern masters).

W along Neuestraße turn N along Frauenstraße to reach the old Kornhaus, today a concert hall (1591, by H. Fischer, doorway C. Bauhofer, staircase tower by P. Schmidt, 1591; fountain in courtyard, with statue of St. Hildegard, a copy of C. Bauhofer, 1591).

OTHER SIGHTS: Fishermen's quarter with the Schiefes Haus (i.e. 'Crooked House') over the canal. The Schwörhaus (in Schwörhausgaße, 1613, reordered in the baroque style 1785; restored 1954), where the town officials are annually sworn in, on the festival of Swearing-in-Monday in July. Dreifaltigkeitskirche (Langestraße, 1670, ruined WWII, 14C sacristy). Theatre (73 Olgastraße, 1969) and Theater in der Westentasche (Herrenkellergaße). Bread and Baking Museum, 17 Fürsteneckerstraße (open daily except Saturday, 10.00–12.00, 15.00–17.30). Prehistoric collection, 4 Frauenstraße (open Monday–Friday 9.00–12.00, 14.00–17.00; Saturday and Sunday, 14.00–17.00). Natural History Museum, 3 Korngasse (open weekdays, save Monday, 10.00–12.00, 14.00–17.00; Saturday extension 12.00–13.00).

Cross the Herd bridge to *New Ulm*; modern church of St. John Baptist, in Augburgerstraße, and the Edwin-Scharff-Museum, 40 Silcherstraße (open Tuesday–Saturday, 14.00–17.00, devoted to the 20C sculptor Edwin Scharff). Also the City Heimatmuseum, (12 Hermann-Köhl-Straße; open Wednesday, 14.00–17.00, Saturday, 10.00–12.00; local mineralogy).

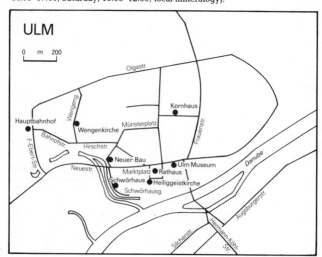

ENVIRONS: *Wiblingen* (7km S across Adenauer bridge): baroque abbey church of St. Martin (18C; frescoes by Janarius Zick; 16C crucifix), with a rococo library (1714–60; open 10.00–12.00 and 14.00 –16.00).

Erbrach (7km SW): church of St. Martin (reordered 1767–79 by I. and A. Finsterwalder; frescoes by M. Kuen, 1768; Madonna c 1490); 16C Schloß (with museum).

2   Regensburg and the Upper Palatinate

A. From Regensburg by way of Amberg to Weiden

Total distance (without diversions) 177km. **Regensburg**—B8 27km *Kallmünz*.—13km *Schmidmühlen*.—27km **Amberg**.—B85 (or B202) 12km **Sulzbach-Rosenberg**.—26km *Auerbach*.—36km *Kemnath*.—A93 36km **Weiden**.

Leave **Regensburg** (Rte 1A) by the B8 towards **Nuremberg**, at *Kneiting* turning N for an excursion (3km) to *Adlersberg*, with its 13C early gothic church (14C wall paintings) as well as the remains of a medieval Dominican monastery. Return to Kneitung and drive S to *Mariaort*, at the confluence of the Danube and the Naab, where you must cross a wooden bridge by foot to visit two tiny baroque churches, the Calvary church (1724) and the Pilgrim's Church of Mariaort (1774–76). 10km further on is *Etterzhausen*, with a 16C Schloß and the 12C romanesque church of St. Wolfgang. The B8 follows the Naab to the hamlet of *Penk* with its 12C church; 6km further on is *Pielenhofen*. Here is a former Cistercian monastery church (1719, by Franz Beer; gable façade; baroque interior, with a shallow cupola by Karl Stauder, 1720; stucco decoration). The 18C monastery is now a school.

Kallmünz is 11km N, a 13C fortress town of the Wittelsbachs. The Swedes demolished its Schloß in 1641, though romantic ruins remain. Kallmünz has narrow streets, exquisite squares and old houses, as well as the stone Naab bridge (1550), a town hall and museum (1603) and the rococo parish church of St. Michael (1758).

From Kallmünz a brief excursion NE leads to *Burlegenfeld*—birthplace of Johann Michael Fischer—with the remains of its 11C Schloß (28m-high keep; walls, 12C towers, gothic armoury), its 16C Altmannsche Schlößchen, town hall (c 1600, and its 18C rococo parish church of St. Veit.

Return to Kallmünz and, leaving the Naab valley, drive to *Dietldorf*, with its Schloß, between 1700 and 1705, built in the style of the late Italian renaissance, containing rococo, Empire and Biedermeier furniture. The road leads (13km from Kallmünz) to *Schmidmühlen* on the confluence of the Vils and the Lauterach. In the Middle Ages this was one of the richest producers of iron ore in the Upper Palatinate, if not in Europe. Forges and smithies were built on the river and the old smith's mill (1311) remains. Schmidmühlen was the birthplace of the sculptor Erasmus Grasser (died 1518). The renaissance Lower Schloß (with its octagonal staircase tower) and the baroque Upper Schloß have been well renovated.

Two routes now lead to Amberg. The westerly route is by way of *Stettkirchen* (tiny baroque pilgrims' church) and the market town of

Hohenburg (ruined Schloß, once a home of the Margraves of Hohenburg; gabled houses; renaissance town hall, c 1560, with early 18C
dormers, now a local museum). Continue NW through *Allersburg*
(gothic church) and then through the picturesque narrow Lauerach
valley by way of Ransbach as far as (14km) *Kastl*, with a Benedictine
abbey founded 1098, whose romanesque abbey church was built in
1129—with a powerful five-storey tower and the oldest barrel-
vaulting in Germany in the choir. The interior contains a frieze with 69
coats of arms of the founder and patrons of the abbey, as well as fine
gravestones in the gothic vestibule.—From Kastl the route turns E
towards (after 20km) *Amberg* (see below).

The easterly route to Amberg from Schmidmühlen leads by way of
Vilshofen and Rieden to **Ensdorf**, with its former Benedictine church
of St. Jakob. A fine doorway, with statues, opens into the interior (by
Wolfgang Dientzenhofer, c 1700; frescoes by C.D. Asam; high altar
painting by Johann Gebhard; wooden statue of the Madonna and
Child, c 1500; stucco decoration). The monastery is now a Salesian
school.

Theuern is 6km N, with a Schloß of 1781, displaying a collection of
minerals, porcelain and glass and an industrial museum. A water-
driven forge has been reconstructed in Theuern, as well as a glass
factory and a grain mill.

Amberg (45,000 inhab.; alt. 373m) lies 8km N of Theuern.

History. Known as *Villa Ammenberg* in the early 12C, Amberg received its city
charter in 1242. The first ironmasters' guild was founded here in 1387, in the late
14C there were 70 or so ironworks here and the 19C Luitpoldhütte remains today
one of the largest ironworks in the region, drawing on the mines to the N.
Emperor Konrad II gave Amberg to the Bishop of Bamberg in 1034; Duke
Ludwig the Severe took control of the town in 1269; and in 1329 it became capital
of the Rhineland Palatinate. The town opted for the Reformation in 1538—the
first town to do so in the Upper Palatinate. Amberg was added to the territories of
Maximilian I of Bavaria in 1628, who restored Catholicism. (The city officially
changed its religious adherence no fewer than five times.) In spite of surviving
attacks and plague during the Thirty Years' War, Amberg was severely reduced.

Amberg's fortifications—gates and towers, the finest being the
renaissance *Wingershof Gate* of 1580 and the *Nabburger Gate*, with
its polygonal upper storey, 1587—remain intact. Other sights include
the 13–14C *Pfalzgrafenschloß* (now a museum of local history); the
gothic church of *St. Martin* (1421–83; tomb of Count Palatine Ruprech
Pipan, 1387; the vault was finished in 1483, the 98m-high W tower in
1584; the gothic interior contains a gothic Annunciation on the N wall,
a bronze font, 1417, and a red marble relief of Martin Merz, died 1591,
on the S wall). The 15C gothic *Town Hall*, with its 16C renaissance
stairway, arcades and balustrade, dominates the old picturesque
market-place; its ogival windows were added in 1880. The imposing
gothic church of *St. George*, founded 1094, rebuilt after a fire in 1359,
has a baroque interior and Wessobrunn stucco, 1718–23, as well as
frescoes depicting the life of St. George, by Josef Adam Müller (1722);
rococo organ case of 1767; high altar with a painting of St. George by
Johann Nepomuk Schöpf (1766).

Other treasures of Amberg are: the 17C Kurfürstliches Schloß; the
*baroque library (stucco by Johann Schmuzer) of the Malt-
esergebäude, formerly the Jesuit college (by Georg Dientzenhofer
and Wolfgang Hirschstetter, 1665–89); and the double-arched sentry
walk across the River Vils (known as the Stadtbrille, or town

spectacles, since its arches mirrored in the water form two perfect circles). NW of the old town is the rococo *Schulkirche (in Schrannenplatz, by Wolfgang Dientzenhofer, 1693–99, enlarged 1738; doorway with statues of SS. Augustine and Francis de Sales; frescoes on nave vault by Gottfried Bernhard Götz, depicting the founding of the Salesian order).

3km NE of Amberg (a 30-minute walk) is the pilgrims' church on the Mariahilfberg, built as the result of a vow when Amsberg was spared the ravages of a plague and the Thirty Years' War in 1634 (stucco interior by Giovanni Battista Carlone; prophets and saints on high altar painted by Carlone's pupil Paul d'Aglio; ceiling and frescoes in choir, side chapels and nave painted by C.D. Asam; 1717).

Travel 12km NE along the main B85 or the quieter B302 to **Sulzbach-Rosenberg** (20,000 inhab.; alt. 450m), dominated by the Ducal Schloß (1582, now an orphanage). From 1353–73 Sulzbach was the Residence of Emperor Karl IV after his marriage with Anna von der Pfalz. The two towns joined in 1934. Minerals have been mined here since the late Middle Ages, and for centuries Sulzbach prospered from the ore. Today it has the largest iron and steel works in Southern Germany. Below the Schloß in the Marktplatz is the 14C gothic Town Hall, with an oriel window in its gable façade. Here too is the 13C Catholic church of *Our Lady in Her Assumption* (nave rebuilt in 1412; 15C font; in the S vestibule a late gothic carving c 1480, in the left side chapel another c 1490; high altar painting by Hans Georg Asam, 1710). From 1652 Catholics and Protestants shared this church until the Protestant Christuskirche (1955–58) was built. Sulzbach-Rosenberg preserves numerous 14C gabled houses with oriel windows. The remains of the 14C town walls can be explored. E of the town the 17th and 18C pilgrims' church of *St. Anna*, at the top of the Annaberg, can be reached by foot.

Return 4km along the B85 towards Amberg and turn right along the Ammer valley to **Oberammerthal** with an early romanesque Frauenkirche (940–1000, with gothic tower, choir and vaulting; 15C stone pulpit and baldacchino) and the 12C romanesque parish church of St. Nikolaus (bottom half of tower romanesque, with gothic enlargement; nave enlarged in 1800, with baroque decoration). Opposite the church is the 16C Hofmarktschloß enriched with an oriel window.

Follow the road W 9km through Götzendorf to *Illschwang* (12C church tower). The road continues towards Weigendorf (short diversions, signposted, revealing pretty **Fürnried**, dubbed 'the most beautiful village in Upper Palatine', and the ruins of Burg Lichtenegg) to *Etzlwang* and *Rupprechstein*. 2km outside these charming spots stands Schloß Neidstein.—20km from Illschwang is *Hirschbach* and the climbing country of the Hirschbach valley. *Königstein*, 11km NE, is the centre for climbing the *Ossinger* (alt. 651m, with its observation tower), the *Steinberg* (alt. 606m) and the *Breitenstein* (alt. 612m, with a ruined Burg and a Burg chapel).

The road continues N by way of *Krottensee*, a centre of potholing (especially the Maximilianshöhle), and *Neuhaus* with the medieval Burg Veldenstein, reaching after 27km *Michelfeld*, where in 1697 the Benedictine monastery was reordered to the baroque plans of Wolfgang Dientzenhofer. 3km E is **Auerbach**, with its gothic town hall (1418). Auerbach owes its past fortune to iron ore and to lying on a main merchant route to Nuremberg. The town hall stands on a long market street. Behind is the church of St. Johann Baptist (1445, baroque reordering by George Dientzenhofer, 1682; late gothic carvings; stone font, 1525; late 18C high altar). The Spitalkirche has rococo altars. 'Auerbach's Keller' appears in Goethe's 'Faust'.

From Auerbach drive 20km NE along the B470 to **Eschenbach**. Kaiser Karl IV gave it city rights in 1358. The 15C gothic church of St. Laurentius in the Marktplatz was enlarged in 1893. Its tower is gothic with a cylindrical renaissance upper part (1541). Inside are baroque choir stalls. Close by is the two-storey 16C town hall. The Maria-Hilf-Kirche (1771–74) has stucco work and three rococo altars.

Much of this region is a legally protected nature reserve. Two routes leads to Weiden. The shorter one (33km) runs by way of the B470 E to *Pressath*. The parish church of St. Georg was burned down in 1759 and rebuilt 1761–65; it retains old gravestones from the former building. The cemetery chapel of St. Stephan dates from 1450 and the Altöttinger chapel from 1754.

3km N of Pressath the 16C *Schlößchen Weihersberg* stands picturesquely on its hill (its chapel has a rococo altar). **Parkstein** lies 12km further towards Weiden, to the N of the B470 (look for the signs), nestling under the basalt peak of the *Parkstein* (596m), on which once stood a castle protecting the town. The Berg retains its pilgrims' chapel (1851). The church of St. Pankratius houses the graves of the major families of Parkstein and a rococo pulpit of 1789. The musician Franz Josef Strauss, the father of Richard Strauss, was born here in 1822.

Follow now the road to Süßenloher Weiher and take the B22 to Weiden.

The longer route from Eschenbach to Weiden leads N to *Speinshart* (5km). Here is a monastery church, dedicated to the Immaculate Conception of Mary, in the Italian baroque style by Wolfgang Dientzenhofer (1696), with paintings by Bartolomeo Lucchese and stucco work by his brother Carlo Domenico. Depiction of Mary's Immaculate Conception on the overpowering high altar. 2km E of Speinshart at *Baraberg* is a 1756 pilgrims' church, restored after WWII.

Continue N to *Neustadt am Kulm* (5km), surrounded by basalt peaks, with its former Carmelite church of 1413 (now a Protestant church and reordered magnificently in the baroque style, with early 18C stucco by Domenico Quadro and fine 17C tombs). The town hall in the Marktplatz dates from 1611. 7km N is **Kemnath**, known as Keminata in the 11C, and boasting ancient houses, the late gothic *Maria Himmelfahrt church (17C side altars; baroque high altar, 1739; tower of 1854). Other noteworthy sights are St. Pirmin's column (1695) and the Sebastian pillar of 1714.

A short diversion E along the B22 leads within 5km to the town of *Waldeck*, again surrounded by high basalt peaks, with a ruined 12C Schloß on the 641m-high Waldecker Schloßberg. The rococo church in the Marktplatz was decorated by the brothers Asam in 1731.

The charming road leads N through Kulmain to *Brand* (birthplace of the composer Max Reger, born 1873) and turns right through *Waldershof* (Schloß, 1471) and SE through the Stein woods by way of Poppenreuth as far as (18km) **Friedenfels**, with its renaissance Schloß. Its Marienkirche (1877) retains on its outside wall the early 18C tombstone of Georg Rudolf von Nothaft and his wife, from an earlier church on this site. Drive now ENE to *Wiesau* (parish church,

1661–63; in front a column to the Virgin Mary; inside medieval tombs). On the nearby *Kreuzberg* 627m high) the Kreuzberg church (1657) has a rococo fresco of 1740 on the ceiling.

3km N of Wiesau lies *Fuchsmühl*, with a pilgrims' church of Mariahilf (1712–25, retaining a chapel of 1688) and the Schloßgut (1510).

Falkenberg is 7km SE of Wiesau in the lovely Waltnaab valley, in the centre of which is *Burg Falkenberg*, founded in 1154. Its 'Hussite tower' is a reminder that the Hussites took the castle in the 14C, as did the Swedes during the Thirty Years' War. Burg Falkenberg was restored in 1934. From here the B299 leads W to *Reuth*, with its renaissance Schloß and on (14km) to *Erbendorf*, once noted for its silver and zinc works, and with a column dedicated to the Virgin Mary (1710) and a late gothic parish church restored after a fire of 1759. (The rococo high altar, 1802, was brought from the Franciscan church at Kemnath after the secularisation of 1802.)

   Windischeschenbach, standing 9km SE of Erbendorf, where the River Fichtelnaab joins the River Waldnaab, is a town devoted to making glass and porcelain. The church of St. Emmeram is neo-gothic (like much of Windischeschenbach, rebuilt after a great fire of 1848).

   Follow now the A93 19km S to *Weiden, the major town of the northern Upper Palatinate (45,000 inhab., mostly living outside the 1000-year-old inner city; alt. 396m). Porcelain, china, glass and textiles are made here, and it is a centre for railway repairs.

History. Weiden became a city in the mid 13C. It flourished as part of the route to Prague in the next century. Fires in 1536 and 1549, plague and destruction during the Thirty Years' War (when the Swedes made the city a centre of their operations) set back its prosperity. In 1777 the city became part of Bavaria. The advent of the railway in 1863 was the beginning of a new prosperity. The composer Max Reger spent much of his youth here and produced his first important works at Weiden.
   The information office is in the town hall. Trains leave for Nuremberg, Regensburg, Munich, Bayreuth, etc.

In Wörthstraße, E of the railway station, stands the *Oberen Tor*, put up in 1911 on the site of the original city gate. From here walk E to the town hall, passing left the Protestant church of *St. Michael* in the Oberen Markt (gothic, reordered in baroque in the 18C; late baroque onion-domed five-storey tower). Interior: remains of late gothic fan vaulting; baroque high altar, 1791; pulpit, 1787; organ case basically 1565). The *Town Hall* in the Unteren Markt (with its 16th and 17C burgers' houses) was built 1539–45 in the renaissance style by Hans Nopl of Weiden. The outdoor staircase and the gable end, with the arms of the seven regional districts of Bavaria, date from 1915. Note the carved hand—symbol of tax collection—and the scales—symbol of justice. Over the gable a mosaic depicts the first historical documentation of Weiden, under Emperor Konrad IV in 1241. The other gable boasts an eight-sided renaissance tower.
   Follow Unteren Markt to the *Unteren Tor*, a late romanesque gateway despoiled by soldiers in 1635 and rebuilt in 1698, surrounded by medieval houses. Narrow streets lead from here to the remains of the city walls. Go through the Unteren Tor to Schlörplatz, with a monument to the last Bavarian trade minister, Gustav von Schlör (1820–83). From here a narrow street leads into Bürgermeister-Prechtl-Straße. Turn right and walk along Sebastianstraße to the church of *St. Sebastian* (15C, restored 1697; memorial to the twin children of Count Palatine Friedrich von Vohenstrauß, 1590).

Return to No. 31, Bürgermeister-Prechtl-Straße, now the *Max-Reger-Haus*, where the composer was taught by Albert Lindner and created celebrated organ works between 1898–1901. Scheibenstraße leads NW from Bürgermeister-Prechtl-Straße to Weiden's only baroque building, the *Waldsassener Getreidekasten* (by the monk Philipp Muttone, 1739–42), where formerly the monks of Waldsassen collected their tithes. From here walk SW along Luitpoldstraße to the neo-romanesque Catholic church of *St. Josef* (1899–1900), with a Jugendstil interior. Kirchenstraße leads S from here into Schulstraße with (right, at No. 4 Pfarrplatz) the seven-storey *Old Schoolhouse* (1566), the two corner houses known respectively as the German school and the Latin school, with the teachers' and clergy quarters in between. The Old School house is now a cultural centre, containing the city archive, library, museum and Max Reger collection; open Monday and Friday, 10.00–11.00, 15.00–16.00).

A gentle walk leads to the Max-Reger-Park on the River Naab, with a memorial of the composer.

B. From Regensburg to Furth im Wald and north along the Czechoslovakian border

Total distance 177km. **Regensburg**—11km *Walhalla*—13km *Wörth an der Donau*—20km *Falkenstein*—15km *Roding*—B85. 15km *Cham*—38km *Lam*—21km **Furth im Wald**—44km *Stamsried*.

At **Regensburg** cross N of the Danube and the Regen by the Nibelungen bridge and drive 9km E along the Landstraße to *Donaustauf*, with a Schloß that was left in ruins in 1634. Turn by the Salvator church for (after 2km) *****Walhalla**, a marble temple, 96m above the river, dedicated by Ludwig I to the memory of eminent Germans and built 1830–41 to designs by Leo von Klenze. Either drive to the well-signposted parking place or climb the 240 steps to the 32m by 67m temple, with its 52 Doric columns and 118 busts of the great. The statues of Ludwig I and six Valkeries were added after WWII (open daily, 10.00–16.00; closed in winter 12.00–14.00).

The road continues along the left bank of the Danube to Sulzbach. NE is the *Thurn und Taxis Zoo*, the largest in southern Germany. Continue 13km SE through *Bach* and *Kruckenberg* (Weinstuben, for tasting and buying local wines) and *Wiesent* (Schloß of 1695 and 18C onion-domed church) to **Wörth an der Donau**, the towers of whose Schloß, once the bishop's palace, appear long before you reach the town. The main gate dates from 1525, the renaissance chapel from 1616; the 'Roundell' and the princely bedroom retain their 18C decorations. The rest of the old town virtually disappeared in a fire of 1841.

Return to Wiesent and turn N for a drive of 18km by way of *Frauenzell* (former Benedictine abbey; the church, with a massive medieval tower, was restored by the brothers Asam in 1747; baroque façade; late 17C pulpit; roof painting by Otto Gebhard, 1752) and *Brennberg*, with its ruined 14C Schloß, as far as *Falkenstein*. The Schloß, high on a granite peak, was founded in the 11C and belonged initially to the bishop of Regensburg. It was given to the town by the Fürst von Thurn und Taxis in 1967. The whole complex, with its chapel and lodgings, has been exceptionally well restored.

The Walhalla, near Regensburg, dedicated by Ludwig I of Bavaria to the great ones of German history and built by Leo von Klenze between 1830 and 1842.

Continue 6km to *Michelsneukirchen* and turn left to reach after 9km **Roding**, a town founded in 844 whose medieval walls and towers partly remain. The renaissance town hall in the Marktplatz carries a baroque bell tower. Note the pillory. The parish church of St. Pankratius is baroque (inside, a romanesque stone font and a Madonna of 1320).

The B85 leads E for 15km to **Cham** (17,500 inhab.; alt. 465m). The 14th and 15C gothic Town Hall bears an oriel window and a tablet commemorating the expulsion of the Jews from Regensburg (1519), and is now a museum of local culture. The 14C Biertor, a defensive gate with two round towers, and the Straubinger Tor (once the city jail) remain from the old fortifications. 15C inn (the 'Krone') in the Marktplatz has 16C battlements. The Spitalkirche of 1519 was reordered in the baroque style in 1750. The late gothic parish church of St. Jakob has an 8C baroque and rococo interior (roof painting by Johann Gebhard). The River Regen washes three sides of Cham, which was the birthplace of Count Nicolas von Luckner, Marshal of France, guillotined in 1794. At *Chammünster*, 4km E of Cham, is a church founded in the 9C, with a 12C charnel house. The present parish church of Maria Himmelfahrt is basically 15C, with a 13C choir and N tower, two 12C romanesque fonts and an interior reordered in the 18C.

Leave the B85 12km SE at *Miltach* (17C Schloß) and travel E for 6km to *Blaibing*, with its Schloß of 1604 and 18C rococo church of St.

Elisabeth. N of the town of *Kötzing*, 4km E, is an 18C rococo pilgrims' church (the Weißenregen), with a 14C picture of the Virgin Mary and a pulpit like a fishing smack. Kötzing itself has a baroque parish church with a rococo high altar, and a baroque town hall. Each Whitsun Kötzing stages a religious horseback procession (the Kötzinger Pfingstritt).—The route continues along the river valley through the mountains as far as *Lam*, a tourist centre (especially for mountaineers and walkers) with an early 18C church (St. Ulrich).

Lam is 21km SE of Furth im Wald. The road runs parallel to the border with Czechoslovakia and through *Neukirchen bei Heilig Blut* with its impressive baroque double church (1720), built in honour of a statue of the Madonna from which blood is reputed to have flowed when a Protestant cut off its head. At **Furth im Wald** is a rail and road pass into Czechoslovakia. The baroque parish church (1727) was redone in the late 19C. The Stadtturm of 1866 now houses a local museum. The statue of St. John Nepomuk was erected in the Stadtplatz in 1767. Furth im Wald is the chief centre for tourism in the forests of Bavaria and the Upper Palatinate. On the second Sunday in August a 500-year-old festival depicts the slaying of the dragon by St. George.

Continue 18km NW to **Waldmünchen**, a town founded in the 10C by monks from Chammünster and now boasting the 15C Pflegamtsschloß. The destruction of the town in 1742 during the War of the Austrian Succession is commemorated by an annual pageant in July and August. The much rebuilt church of St. Stephan was founded in 1660. The statue of St. John Nepomuk and the two fountains were erected in the Marktplatz in the mid 18C. The cemetery chapel dates from 1712, the Spital church from 1767. Water sports at the nearby Perl Lake.

From here the route passes through *Ast* with its 13C early gothic pilgrims' church (with baroque reordering). Note the branch ('Ast') on the old pulpit.—Continue W through *Schöntal* (former Augustinian monastery, founded 1255, closed 1803; baroque parish church, c 1700), to reach after 15km *Rötz*, which became a city in 1495. The ruined Schloß Schwarzenburg towers 706m high on the Schwarzwihrberg (a 30-minute walk from the Marktplatz). The parish church, at Rötz, mostly 1850, has a gothic choir, 1401, and a tower built in 1552.

The Rte ends at *Stamsried*, 10km due S of Rötz, a town razed by the Swedes in the Thirty Years' War but retaining its medieval Schloß. E of the town (signposted) are extensive remains of Burg Kürnburg. A column bearing the statue of the Virgin Mary was erected in the Marktplatz in 1729.

C. North of Schwandorf and along the border of Czechoslovakia

Total distance 234km. **Schwandorf**—18km *Nabburg*—11km *Wernberg-Köblitz*—B14. 10km *Wieselrieth*—20km *Tännesberg*—B22. 11km *Oberviechtach*—12km *Schönsee*—18km *Moosbach*—24km *Neustadt an der Waldnaab*—B15. 35km *Mitterteich*—B299. 7km *Waldsassen*—68km *Pleystein*.

Schwandorf (17,000 inhab.; alt. 365km) has a baroque pilgrims' church (1678, rebuilt 1950–52, after three-quarters of the city was destroyed in 1945), and a 15C tower from its old fortifications. The medieval houses make the Marktplatz particularly attractive. To the N of the city is the renaissance Schloß Fronberg (finished mid 17C). 9km N lies *Schwarzenfeld*, with a pilgrim's church (1720, baroque high altar, rococo pulpit), the mid 18C rococo parish church of St. Dionysius and St. Ägidius, and a 19C Schloß.

Nabburg is 9km further N. Founded in 929, though much was destroyed in the Middle Ages and the Thirty Years' War, the town retains its walls, gates and towers. The basilica of *St. Johann Baptist* dates from the 14C (sculpted reliefs, on S doorway, c 1350; 14C glass in N windows; the 'Nabburg Madonna', c 1470, on left side altar). Renaissance town hall, 1550; 12C romanesque church of St. Nikolaus. The 18C cemetery chapel of St. Georg in the lower town has a romanesque tower.

The way to Pfreimd, 5km N, leads through *Perschen*, with a 12C cemetery chapel and the 13C late romanesque basilica of SS Peter and Paul (gothic vaults and choir, baroque nave, 1752–53). Here is the Upper Palatinate rural museum, in a 12C farmhouse. *Pfreimd*, where the Counts of Leuchtenberg lived 1332–1646, retains part of its medieval Schloß (with two renaissance doorways), and the church of the former Franciscan monastery (1593). Johann Schmuzer built the church of Maria Himmelfahrt (1681–88; retaining by the high altar a marble epitaph of Count Leopold von Leuchtenberg, died 1463). Close by, though a stiff climb, is the *Eixlberg* (517m) with a pilgrims' church and Loretto chapel.

Continue 6km to *Wernberg-Köblitz*, with a 12C Schloß. The B14 leads 10km NE to *Wieselrieth*, where a brief diversion N leads to *Leuchtenberg*, founded in 1124. Burg Leuchtenberg preserves its 14C inner wall, 15C chapel and (newly restored) keep. Return to Wieselrieth and continue S for 10km to *Trausnitz*, with its 13C keep (where Duke Friedrich the Beautiful was imprisoned in 1322 after his defeat by Ludwig the Bavarian at the battle of Mühldorf). Due E, after 10km, is *Tännesberg*, close by which is the baroque pilgrims' church of St. Jodok, 1689 (with a 'plague cross', brought here from Vienna in 1690). Following a vow of 1796, costumed farmers and horsemen process here on the second Sunday in July.

The B22 now leads SE 8km to *Teunz* (baroque church of St. Lambert, with a classical tower and rococo high altar) and another 3km to *Oberviechtach*. The formerly gothic church of St. Johann Baptist now has a splendid rococo interior (1775). From here the route leads NE 12km to *Schönsee*, (once part of Bohemia and known as Kronlehen): a double statue of St. John Nepomuk (1791) looks towards both Bavaria and Bohemia. The present form of the parish church dates from 1868; the chapel of the Fourteen Helpers from 1799. Hunting museum, close by the Hotel St. Hubertus.—An EXCURSION 7km E reaches the pilgrims' church of *Our Lady and St. Michael* at *Stadlern* (late gothic Mary with the Christ Child and the young St. John the Baptist on baroque choir altar; St. Michael fighting the dragon on side altar).

The picturesque road N from Schönsee reaches *Eslarn* after 9km (early baroque church of Our Lady, 1685–87; rococo pulpit). To continue N brings you by way of the nature reserve of *Pfrentsch* after 8km to the border crossing at *Waidhaus* (1754; statue of St. John Nepomuk in the Marktplatz). Turning W at Eslarn, the route leads after 9km to *Moosbach* (pilgrims' church, 1769, with rococo altar, confessionals and pulpit). The route continues through *Burgtreswitz*

(2km; 13C Schloß) as far as (4km) **Vohenstrauß**. The most imposing building in the town is the renaissance *Burg*, with its six round towers, gable and high saddle roof (1586–90). The church of St. Johann Baptist, c 1350, survived a fire of 1839 which destroyed much of the old town. There is a museum of local history in the town hall (1911).

Continue 20km NW to **Neustadt an der Waldnaab**, a town prospering on lead crystal ware, and with many fine gabled houses in the Marktplatz. Church of St. Georg, 1607–66, rendered rococo. Alte Schloß of 1543 and the Italianate baroque Neue Schloß by Antonio Porta and Anton Ritz, 1702. The nearby *Altenstadt an der Waldnaab* preserves the romanesque church of Maria Himmelfahrt, with a late gothic tower and choir and a rococo high altar.

Follow the B15 NW for 24km to *Tirschenreuth* which retains the 1330 Klettnersturm from its old fortifications. Sights include the 12C Fischhof, the stone bridge of 1750 (modelled on that of Regensburg), the town hall (1583; with an oriel festooned with coats of arms), and the memorial in the Marktplatz to the linguist Johann Andreas Schmeller (1785–1852).—The B15 continues to *Mitterteich* (11km): town hall of 1731 in Marktplatz, alongside a statue of St. John Nepomuk and a Virgin Mary column; dance of death inside the Maria Hilf cemetery chapel (1780); 17C tower attached to 1891 church of St. Jakobus.

Follow the B299 for 7km through *Bad Kondrau*, with its medicinal waters, to **Waldsassen**, founded by the monk Gerwig von Wohmundstein in 1133. The superb baroque *church of Maria Himmelfahrt and St. Johann* was built 1681–1704 by Abraham Leuthner of Prague, aided by Georg Dientzenhofer and the brothers Jakob and Bernhard Schießer. The frescoes are by the Prague artist Jakob Steinfels, the stucco work by the Italian G.B. Carlone, the choir stalls by the local woodcarver Martin Hirsch. Karl Stilp created the marble Annunciation and the tabernacle on the high altar. The *Stiftsbibliothek*, a late baroque library, also possesses rich, often humorous carvings by Stilp, with stucco work by Peter Appiani.

A picturesque wooded route now travels S virtually alongside the Czechoslovak border for 68km through a nature conservancy area as far as *Pleystein*, with its cemetery chapel of 1750 and a baroque column of St. John Nepomuk in the Marktplatz. The Kreuzberg dominates the town, with the neo-baroque Kreuzbergkirche.

D. Neumarkt by way of Regensburg to Walderbach

Total distance 157km. **Neumarkt**—24km *Sulzbürg*—B299. 20km *Beilngries*—29km *Parsberg.*—E5. 36km **Regensburg**—B15. 15km *Regenstauf*—33km **Walderbach**.

Neumarkt (30,000 inhab.; alt. 425m) is first documented in 1160; it became a city in 1235. At the very end of WWII the inner city was virtually destroyed and has since been well restored. Two churches and a Schloß (1520) are the major sights of the city. The Catholic parish church of *St. Johannes*, built out of sandstone, begun in 1404 and finished in the mid 15C, has three fine doorways of which the western is famous for its carvings. The early gothic stone font dates

REGENSTAUF **43**

from c 1200, the gravestones and remains of frescoes from the 15th and 16C.

The church of Maria Himmelfahrt was built in 1410, and the nave was redone in the baroque style by Jakob Engel in 1702. The late gothic red marble tomb of Count Palatine Otto II dates from c 1499. The Schloß was burnt down in 1520 and rebuilt in 1539 in the renaissance style. Two other sights are the ruined Burg Wolfstein (with a fine view of the city) and the pilgrims' church of Mariahilfberg (585m high) of 1718, with an altar painting of 1478, depicting the life of the Virgin Mary).

The Heimatmuseum at No. 7 Weiherstraße displays weapons, local art, fossils, and so on (open Thursday, 16.30–18.00; Friday, 17.00–19.30).

Leave Neumarkt SW towards Freystadt, making a brief EXCURSION (right) after 9km to *Seligenporten* where the powerful 15C tower of its gate remains from the old fortifications. The 16C E wing alone remains from the former Cistercian monastery, as well the 13C monastery church (14C choir and stalls). *Freystadt*, with its long market street and burgers' houses and 1550 town hall, possesses an early 18C domed pilgrims' church, by Antonio Viscardi (stucco by Francesco Appiani, 1708). See also the 1750 parish church, with a 13C gothic tower and 16C carvings.

E of Freystadt by way of Rocksdorf and then S is (9km) *Sulzbürg*, notable for its Jewish cemetery (the synagogue was destroyed in 1938 during the Hitler Reich). Continue S along the B299 for 12km to reach *Berching*, which retains its 6m-high walls incorporating 12 towers and the city gates, built 1464–94, and many old burgers' houses. Its important churches are the 11C St. Lorenz (relief c 1220 on N doorway; side altar paintings c 1515; gothic high altar 1500–29) and the early gothic Maria Himmelfahrt, enriched with rococo stucco, c 1750.

Plankstetten lies 4km to the S along the B299, with a Benedictine *church* (1138; tower with a baroque cap; inside, 15C transept with late gothic stellar vaulting and three mid 12C windows; baroque pulpit, 1651; early rococo stucco work, c 1730; *rococo Holy Ghost chapel, c 1760, by Johann Jakob Berg).

The B299 continues S with (right) *Schloß Hirschberg*, once the summer retreat of the Bishops of Eichstätt), built early 14C, much enriched in the 18C. *Beilngreis*, 4km S, at the confluence of the Sulz and the Altmühl, and also on the Ludwigskanal, retains much of its 15C city wall, as well as fine gabled houses with baroque façades and the 15C town hall. The late gothic cemetery chapel dates from the 1470s, the rococo Frauenkirche from the 18C (by Maurizio Pedetti) and the church of St. Walburga from 1913.

The Rte leads E for 4km to *Kottingwörth* (medieval parish church, with early 15C wall paintings, mostly rebuilt in 1760), and 6km further to *Dietfurt* (17C town hall, faced by a 'Chinese' fountain; baroque church of St. Ägidius, 1660, altered in the 19C, with a 65m-high tower). Continue NE for 7km to *Breitenbrunn*, lying in the middle of peaks and woods (16C Gasthof Post; the pilgrims' church of St. Sebastian, with two onion-domed towers, first built 1386 and rebuilt 1702–08; two 18C Schlößchen).—12km further NE is *Parsberg*, with a 16C Upper Schloß and a Lower Schloß of c 1600.

Join the E5 just N of Parsberg and drive SE for 36km to **Regensburg** (see Rte 1A).

Take the B15 N to (13km) *Regenstauf*, where the Schloßberg (436m, with a viewing tower) offers a superb panorama. At *Ramspau*, 4km further N, is a baroque schloß, and at *Hirschling*, 16km further N, a medieval schloß. The Rte continues N along the bank of the River Regen, which bends right (as does the road) at *Marienthal*, where the ruins of 13C *Burg Stockenfels* stand on a high rock. As the Rte continues E towards Nittenau the 10C *Burg Stefling* (restored 1748) and the medieval *Burg Hof* appear. *Nittenau* (22km from Regenstauf) retains parts of its old walls and towers, and a modern parish church, which incorporates a gothic choir and tower with a baroque dome. From Nittenau the road leads ESE for 9km to *Reichenbach* (romanesque monastery church, c 1130, with a gothic choir; tomb of Markgraf Diepold II, 1304; sandstone Madonna, 1420; baroque interior, with frescoes by Andreas Gebhard). The Rte ends 2km E at *Walderbach*, with a 12C romanesque church, formerly part of a Cistercian monastery, whose choir, tower and nave windows date from the 18C. The geometric decoration was added in 1888.

3   From Regensburg to Füssen by way of Augsburg

Total distance 237km. **Regensburg**—B16. 49km *Münchmünster*—B300. 43km *Schrobenhausen*—43km **Augsburg**—B17. 38km *Landsberg*—27km *Schöngau*—15km *Steingaden* and the **Westkirche**—22km **Füssen**.

Leave **Regensburg** by the Kumpfmühlerstraße to take the B16 SW to (49km) *Münchmünster* (with the church of a former Benedictine monastery), for the junction with the B300. This road continues SW through the *Dürrenbucher Forest* for 21km, through *Geisenfeld*, where the valley of the Ilm is crossed before traversing the *Feilen Forest* to reach *Langenbück* and the Nuremberg–Munich motorway. After 5km the B16 reaches *Pörnbach* and the junction with the B13 from Ingolstadt to Munich.

Continue 17km SW to **Schrobenhausen**, a town at least 1100 years old, with remains of its 15C walls. Here the artist Franz Lenbach (1836–1904) was born and is commemorated in a museum, No. 1 Ulrich-Preisse-Gasse (open daily 09.00–11.00 and 13.00–16.00). The late gothic basilica of *St. Jakob* dates from 1425–80 (wall paintings in the choir and nave; Crucifixion group and Calvary c 1500). The church of St. Salvator was built in the 15C. The museum of local history is at 22 Lencbachplatz (open daily, 9.00–11.00 and 13.00–16.00).

An EXCURSION 7km W leads to *Sanizell*, with an 18C rococo parish church by E.Q. Asam and a mid 18C Burg.

14km further is *Unterwittelsbach* (church of 1418, where once stood the family castle of the Wittelsbachs), 2km from *Aichach*, with its 16C late gothic parish church.—After 11km you reach the Stuttgart–Munich motorway, and continue SW along the B300 for 7km to Friedberg.

To the left, shortly before the town is reached, is the pilgrims' church of *Herrgottsruh* (1730–53; stuccoed interior designed by Franz Xaver Feuchtmayr; frescoes in nave by Matthias Günther; ceiling in choir painted by C.D. Asam).

Friedburg on the Lain, once a stronghold of the Wittelsbachs in their opposition to Augsburg, possesses a Schloß (13C walls; tower of 1552, the rest 17C, housing a museum of local history), a town hall of 1680, and, in the neo-romanesque parish church (1872) a memorial stone of Duke Ludwig the Bearded (died 1409).

Augsburg lies 9km SW, reached by joining the B2 from Munich.

AUGSBURG, still moated (245,000 inhab.; alt. 496m), was the chief city of the Bavarian regional district of Schwabia, situated where the River Lech meets the River Wertach. An important trading post with Italy (especially Verona) in Roman times, Augsburg developed a textile industry that still fourishes. By the Middle Ages the city was the seat of important banking families, such as the Welsers and the Fuggers.

Main *railway station*: Bahnhofstraße. Trains to Munich, Nuremberg, Stuttgart, Würzburg.

Information Office: 7 Bahnhofstraße.

Travel Office: main railway station.

Coach trips to the 'Romantische Straße' (see Rte 5B).

History. Drusus, a relative of the Emperor Augustus, established a Roman camp here in 15 BC and in the next century Augsburg (then called *Augusta Vindelicorum*) became the capital of the Roman province of Raetia. St. Afra was martyred here in 304. With the support of St. Ulrich, bishop of the city, who died here in 973, Otto I defeated the Hungarians at Lechfeld near Augsburg in 955. Augsburg received its town charter in the 11C. Fortified in the 12C, in 1276 it became a free imperial city. Luther took refuge in the Carmelite monastery of St. Anne (see below) in 1518. The Augsburg Confession of 1530 set out the fundamentals of European Protestantism. The Peace of Augsburg (1555) granted a limited freedom of worship to Protestants. Prussia and Austria joined with the League of Augsburg in the 17C against Louis XIV's pretensions. After the problems caused by the Thirty Years' War, Augsburg continued as a free imperial city until 1805, being incorporated into the Kingdom of Bavaria the following year. Here in the 1890s was made the first diesel engine. Half the city suffered severe destruction in WWII.

Augsburg was the home of the Habsburg's banker Jakob Fugger (1459–1525), of the finest local architect, Elias Holl (1573–1646) and the birthplace of Bertolt Brecht. Almost equal in wealth to the Fuggers were the Welsers, who discovered and conquered Venezuela ('Welserland') and ran it as their own colony.

From the main railway station follow Prinzregentenstraße into Grottenau to find the *theatre* (1 Kennedyplatz, seating nearly 1000). Turn left from Grottenau along Heilge-Kreuz-Straße to reach Holy Cross Church. Kohler-Gasse leads NE from here into Jesuiten-Gasse as far as Frauentorstraße. Turn N along Frauentorstraße to (No. 30) the *Mozart House*, where the composer's father was born (museum open weekdays save Tuesday, 10.00–12.00, 14.00–17.00; Saturday and Sunday, 10.00–12.00). SE along Frauentorstraße is *St. Mary's Cathedral*, built on 10C foundations, enlarged by Bishop Heinrich II, 1047–63 and gothicised 14C. The romanesque W end contrasts with the gothic choir (built 1326–1431). Exterior: 11C romanesque *S doorway and 32 bronze romanesque panels depicting Old Testament and mythological scenes. *Interior*: five 12C windows depicting the prophets, S side, the oldest important stained glass in Germany; romanesque crypt (1060); bishop's throne, c 1100; tomb of Bishop Wolfhart Rot (1302); wall painting of St. Christopher, S transept (1491); nave altars with paintings by Holbein the Elder (1493); bronze group of crucified Christ with the twelve Apostles, in the E choir, by Josef Henselmann (1962).

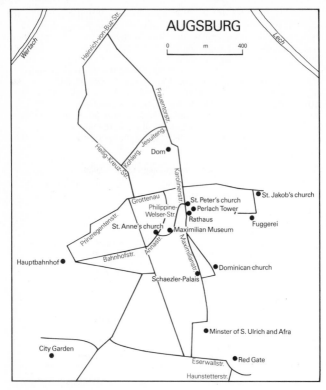

Follow Karolinenstraße S from the cathedral to the renaissance
Rathaus, by Elias Holl (1615–20, seven storeys high, onion domes;
note the town symbol of a pine cone on the gable). Close by are the
Augustus Fountain (by H. Gerhard; 1598–94; the bronze figures
represent the rivers Lech, Wertach, Brunnenbach and Singold), and
the *Perlach Tower* (a romanesque watch-tower, 78m high, restored
17C; panorama). W stands the 12C church of St. Peter.

E of the town hall Jakob Fugger the Rich founded in 1519 a little
town for the poor: the ***Fuggerei**, with four gates, 53 gabled houses
and eight streets. It is still in use. At the N gate stands St. Jakob's
church (1355–1533).

S from the town hall Maximilianstraße, with several renaissance
burgers' houses, leads to the church of *St. Moritz*. In front is the
Mercury Fountain (Adriaen de Vries, 1599, a copy of Giambologna's
Mercury in Florence) and the old *Weavers' House*. At 24 Philippine-
Welser-Straße, NW of the church of St. Moritz, is the **Maximilian
Museum**, in two burgers' houses, late 15–early 16C, transformed
into a museum in the early 20C by Gabriel von Seidl (open daily
save Monday, 10.00–17.00; October–April, 10.00–16.00: goldsmiths'
work of the 16–18C, sculpture including Virgin Mary by Hans
Multscher, c 1440, and Georg Petel's Hercules fighting the Hydra,

1626; firearms, history of Augsburg; architectural models by E. Holl).

W of the museum in Annastraße is the church of **St. Anne**, formerly part of a Carmelite monastery. A gothic church, it was founded 1321, enlarged in the late 15C, rebuilt by E. Holl in 1602–16, decorated with rococo stucco work and frescoes of 1747–49 (gothic Goldsmith's chapel with late 15C wall paintings; *renaissance Fugger funeral chapel, 1509–12, restored 1947, the first renaissance building in Germany—with reliefs on the tombs of Jakob and Ulrich Fugger to drawings by Dürer; portrait of Luther and painting of Jesus as the Children's Friend, both by Cranach the Elder; altar by Hans Daucher; organ wings by Jörg Breu).

S of the church is the Fuggerhaus (built for Jakob Fugger the Rich, 1512–15). To the W is the city *Armory*, built by Elias Holl (bronze of St. Michael, E façade by Hans Reichle, 1603–06). Still further S at 46 Maximilianstraße is the rococo *Schaezler-Palais* (built for the banker von Liebert by K.A. von Lespilliez, 1765–67; baroque banqueting hall). The Palais houses the *City Art Gallery* (open save Monday, 10.00 –17.00, only to 16.00 October–April; baroque masters) and also the *Altdeutsche Galerie* including works by Dürer and Hans Holbein the Elder. In front of the Schaezler-Palais is the *Hercules Fountain* (1602; by Adriaen de Vries).

E of the Fuggerhaus is the former Dominican Church (1513–15; rococo stucco work by F.X. and J.M. Feuchtmayer, 1716–49), now the *Roman Museum* (open daily, except Monday, 10.00–16.00; archaeological finds). Follow Maximilianstraße further S to reach the Catholic **Minster of SS. Ulrich and Afra**, formerly a Benedictine abbey (founded by Maximilian I in the 15C, to replace a church over the tomb of SS. Afra and Ulrich, rebuilt 17C; 93m-high tower with onion dome; baroque grille and three baroque altars by J. Degler the Elder, 1604–07; altar with cross and bronze figures by H. Reichle, c 1605; Crucifixion 1607; chapel to St. Simpert on N side with a Gothic baldacchino and terracotta saints; St. Afra's vault, with the saint's romanesque sarcophagus; St. Ulrich's vault with rococo decoration by P. Verhelst, 1762). Adjacent is the Protestant church of St. Ulrich.

SE of St. Ulrich in Eserwall-Straße stands the brick and golden stone *Red Gate*, or Rotes Tor (16C fortified buildings, tower by Elias Holl, 1622). Next to the Red Gate, is the open-air theatre, which seats 2400 people.

OTHER SIGHTS: City Garden, S of the main railway station (Congress Hall, 1974, with restaurant and the 117m-high Hotel Tower). Canoe slalom stadium (Hochablass, 1972). Renowned marionette theatre—the Augsburger Puppenkiste (15 Spitalgasse) M.A.N.-Werkmuseum, with the first diesel engine and printing presses (28 Heinrich-von-Buz-Straße, open Monday–Friday, 18.00–16.00).

Leave Augsburg by Haunstetter Straße and travel S on the B17. After Haunstetten you pass through countryside bordered by the Rivers Wertach and Lech, in the neighbourhood of which a battle was fought between Emperor Otto I and the Hungarians in 955.—24km *Klosterlechfeld*. Next to the Franciscan monastery (1604; enlarged 1738) Elias Holl built a 17C cylindrical *pilgrims' church* (based on the Pantheon in Rome), later enlarged with a nave and two round chapels. The stuccoed interior is by J.G. Lederer, 1733–41.

14km S, the B17 reaches **Landsberg**, on the banks of the Lech, where Henrich the Lion built a Schloß in the mid 12C to guard the river crossing. The walls and towers derive from the 13C, the Bayer Gate from 1425. The architect Domenikus Zimmermann was Bürgermeister here from 1749–50, and he enriched the early 18C *town hall* with its stupendous façade, in front of which a fountain and statue of the Virgin Mary by J. Streiter, 1783, adorn the lovely Marktplatz. The town hall houses works by the artist Hubert von Herkomer (1849–1914), born in nearby Waal. Zimmermann also created the rococo decor and the horseshoe-shaped chancel of the church of St. Johann (1752). The parish church in Georg-Hellmair-Platz dates from 1458–88, was designed by V. Kindlin of Strasbourg, and contains (in its baroque interior) stained glass of 1450 (by Wolfgang Prielmayr) behind the *high altar (1680; by J. Pfeiffer), as well as a 1437 Madonna in the rosary altar by Hans Multscher. See also the Malteser church adjoining the former Jesuit college (1754; stucco decor of the sacristy by D. Zimmermann; roof painting by C.D. Asam's pupil Christoph Thomas Scheffler and by G.B. Götz; altar painting by J.B. Bader). Landsberg's heated swimming pool has artificial waves.

The B17 now follows roughly the Roman *Via Claudia Augusta* and the medieval trade route from Augsburg to Italy. At *Epfach* was the Roman camp of *Abodiacum* during the era of Augustus. Close by *Hohenfurch* (23km) stands (right) the romanesque basilica of *St. Michael* at **Altenstadt**, built c 1200 and standing with its two towers much the same today (frescoes discovered 1938; restoration of the building, first under Ludwig I in 1826, then in 1936, most recently 1961–63; romanesque sandstone font with carvings of the Baptist, Jesus's baptism, the Virgin Mary and the Archangel Michael; Madonna c 1330 in N aisle; remarkably stern crucifix of 1540). Altenstadt was a seat of the knights templar, who in 1289 brought to the basilica the almost 3·5m-high wooden romanesque crucifix in the main apse (known as the 'Great God of Altenstadt'). The flanking statues of St. John and the Virgin are copies of originals now in the Bavarian National Museum, Munich. Note the 14C frescoes of the Annunciation and the Archangel Michael with saints, and the 15C fresco of Mary and St. John beneath the cross.

Hohenfurch itself boasts a parish church of Maria Himmelfahrt with an interior of c 1750, and a late gothic Madonna (1420). SE of the town on a peak is the chapel of St. Ursula (1520), with a fine contemporary carved altarpiece.

Within 2km the Rte S reaches **Schongau**. The town is ringed by virtually intact walls (15–17C). The parish church of Maria Himmelfahrt was rebuilt in the 18C with an onion-domed tower to replace one that fell down in 1667: chancel stucco by D. Zimmermann (1748), frescoes by M. Günther and F.A. Wassermann, statues by F.X. Schmädl, high altar c 1760. The town hall, though modified in the 19C, dates from 1515. See also the Steingadenes Ritterhaus of 1493, the Holy Ghost Spital church (16th and 17C), the cemetery chapel (16–18C) and the Holy Cross chapel (1689), as well as several burgers' houses. The city museum, at No. 6, Karmeliterstraße, opens at present only on Wednesday, from 10.00–12.00.

Continue S to **Peiting**—a winter sports and convalescent centre, with its parish church of *St. Michael* (romanesque tower and crypt; late gothic choir, rococo pulpit and a high altar of 1758 with carvings by F.X. Schmädl). Peiting also has a pilgrims' church, Maria unter dem Egg (c 1650). A Way of the Cross leads to the *Kalvarienberg*, with a superb panorama of the surrounding mountains.

The road continues for 9km S to *Ilgen* with its late renaissance pilgrims' church of Maria Heimsuchung, by Johann Schmuzer, 1676. After 3km more the route reaches **Steingaden**, where in 1147 Welf VI established a Premonstratensian *abbey*, dedicated to St. John Baptist, whose twin-towered romanesque sandstone basilica of 1176 still remains. The late romanesque transept has a 15C gothic vault. Frescoes of 1580 decorate the vestibule. The Johannes chapel dates from the 12C. The chancel is baroque (1663). The vaulted nave (1729–45) was decorated in the rococo style by Johann Georg Bergmüller with scenes from the life of St. Norbert (founder of the Premonstratensians) and with stucco work by the younger Schmuzer. J.C. Storer created the high altar painting in 1663. The monstery cloister retains 13C romanesque columns. See also at Steingaden the 13C cemetery chapel of St. Johannes, with lions guarding its doorway.

Two hour-long EXCURSIONS may be made from Steingaden. SE is **Wies**, which possesses the richest rococo **church in the whole region. In 1730 a farmer found an apparently weeping statue of the scourged Jesus. When a small church was built to house this statue, the spot became the centre of a remarkable cult, and Dominikus Zimmermann was commissioned with the building of a new, totally rococo church. Zimmermann made sure even that the line of the roof of his remarkable oval building (19m long and 24m wide) matched the nearby mountain ridge. The high altar was painted by B.A. Albrecht; Ägid Verlhest the Elder designed the figures of the evangelists that frame it; Johann Baptist Zimmermann took responsibility for painting the ceilings, his masterpiece being the Last Judgment on the flattened dome; J.G. Bergmüller designed the altars of St. Margaret and St. Mary Magdalen; Anton Sturm created remarkably vivacious statues of the four doctors of the church; Dominikus Zimmermann himself created a trompe l'oeil impression of arches that bend not upwards but downwards! Zimmermann chose to spend the last years of his life in a house next to his masterpiece.

The second excursion goes W from Steingaden to *Urspring*, with its romanesque church, reordered as late gothic and then given a baroque decor in the 18C.

8km S of Steingaden is another holiday resort, *Trauchgau*, at the foot of the Trauchberg (1638m). *Schwangau* lies 19km SW of Steingaden along the B17. Shortly before the town signposts direct towards the royal Schlößer of **Hohenschwangau** and **Neuschwanstein**. The former was constructed in the 12C by the Swan Knights, whose line died out in the 16C. The Schloß was damaged during the Napoleonic wars and restored by King Maximilian II, 1832–36, the architects and artists including Moritz von Schwind and Domenico Quaglio. A park lies to the S. At Hohenschwangau Maximilian's son Ludwig II entertained Richard Wagner. After a visit to the Wartburg Ludwig conceived of the idea of building **Neuschwanstein**. This neo-romanesque and neo-gothic Schloß, though unfinished when Ludwig was declared unfit to rule on 13 June 1886, remains a bizarre masterpiece. The chief artists included August Spieß and Ferdinand von Piloty. Decorations testify to the king's devotion to Wagner before their quarrel. Annual concerts take place here each September. (Both Schlößer are open April–September, 09.00–17.00; in winter, 10.00–16.00.)

Nearby is the Marienbrücke, bridging the Poellat gorge at a height of c 100m, built 1866. A funicular railway runs to a restaurant/hunting lodge on the 1707m-high *Tegelberg*.

E of Schwangau is the resort of **Füssen/Bad Faulenberg** (13,000 inhab.; alt. 800m), with a spa (mud baths, massage); winter sports and sailing on the artificial lake; the Hohes Schloß, the former summer retreat of the Bishops of Augsburg, built between the 13th and 16C (knights' hall, with paintings by Jörg Lederer, c 1500, and a gothic chapel, with a wooden relief of the coronation of the Virgin); and the baroque monastery of St. Mang, by Johann Jakob Herkomer (1701–17), displaying Venetian traits. The statues on the high altar are by Anton Sturm. The abbey buildings include a museum of local history (with a musical collection; open weekdays at 10.30; November–April open only Wednesday). The façade of the *Spital-kirche* on the Lech bridge (1749) is superbly painted in the 18C 'Lüftlmalerei' fashion. The Romans called Füssen *Foetibus*. The town boasts numerous picturesque burgers' houses. S of the spa are the Lech gorge, the St. Mang falls and the 955m-high *Kalvarienberg*.

4   Regensburg to Garmisch-Partenkirchen by way of Landshut and Munich

Total distance 306km. **Regensburg**—B15 48km *Landshut.*—B11 37km *Freisang.*—33km **Munich.**—A95 25km *Starnberg.*—an excursion around the *Starnberg Lake* (50km).—B2 45km *Murnau.*—25km **Garmisch-Partenkirchen.—a round trip back to Murnau** by way of *Ettal, Schloß Linderhof, Oberammergau* and *Bad Kohlgrub* (43km).

Leave **Regensburg** S by the B15 to reach after 14km *Alteglofsheim*, with its fine 18C Schloß of the Thurn und Taxis, built on a former medieval castle, later enriched in the rococo style by J.B. Zimmermann, C.D. Asam and others. *Hagelstadt* lies 3km S, with a baroque church by J.M. Fischer. 14km further S the route turns left at Oberlindhart to reach after 6km *Mallersdorf-Pfaffenberg* where the monastery church has an altar by Ignaz Günther. Return to Oberlindhart and travel S for 17km to Landshut.

**Landshut (52,000 inhab.; alt. 393m) on the Isar is the capital of Lower Bavaria. The Information Office is at No. 79 Altstadt.

History. 'Hut' means 'protection' and the town appears as 'protecting' the surrounding countryside in 1150. In the following century Duke Otto II made it the chief town of his duchy. The history of Landshut was subsequently turbulent, the citizens revolting against their lord in 1409, a plague decimating it in 1444 and another ravaging the region 55 years later. During the struggle for the lordship of the town in 1504–05 Götz von Berlichingen lost his right hand and obtained an iron one from the forges of Landshut. Gustavus Adolphus savaged the town in 1632; plague again scourged the citizens in 1648; Turenne caused much damage in the early 18C; the Austrians occupied the town in 1742.

Yet much survived and was embellished. The 14th and 15Cs were especially happy ones for Landshut. Duke Georg the Rich married a Polish princess here in 1475 (their marriage is still celebrated in regular four-yearly festivals, with some 1200 participants). Duke Ludwig X lived at Landshut from 1514–45 and built the Residenz. Crown Prince Wilhelm V lived in and enhanced the Schloß at Traunitz. Landshut was the seat of a university from 1800–25.

The exquisite street and square known as the ALTSTADT has splendid burgers' houses (especially No. 69, Haus Aldstadt; No. 81, the Papperbergerhaus; No. 300, the Grasbergerhaus) and notable churches at either end. The finest church is the basilica of *St. Martin*. Its 130·6m-high tower (the 'Stethaimer') is the tallest brick-built tower in the world. Hans von Burghausen began it in 1399. His tombstone (1432) lies outside the church on the S side, among many others. His tower was finished only in 1500. St. Martin's basilica has five flamboyant doorways. The interior displays two rows of slender octagonal columns, each 22m high, a stone high altar of 1424 (by Hans Stethaimer, after whom the church tower is named), a stone pulpit of 1429, coloured terracotta figures of the late 15C, choir stalls c 1500, and a famous *Madonna and Child by Hans Leinberger, c 1518.

The Altstadt also houses the triple-gabled *Town Hall*, assembled out of three 14th and 15C houses and with a renaissance oriel window of 1570, a hall with wall paintings of the wedding of 1475 and a neo-gothic façade of 1860 (open weekdays, 14.00–15.00). Almost opposite is the *Residenz*, built for Duke Ludwig X between 1536 and 1543, the earliest Italian palace on German soil (and half of it still emphatically German). The inner courtyard is arcaded. The great hall is frescoed and stuccoed. The living rooms are now an art gallery and regional museum (open daily, 09.00–12.00 and 13.00–17.00 in season, and 13.00–16.00 from October–March).

The second main church in the Altstadt is the *Heiligen-Geist-Spital*, which Hans von Burghausen began in 1407. The Holy Ghost hospice (1722–28) is opposite across the street. Walk NW along Zwei-brückenstraße (so-called because the Isar divides into two at Landshut and must be crossed by two bridges) to the Bismarckplatz and the Cistercian abbey of *Seligenthal*, founded in 1232 by Ludmilla, the widow of Ludwig I. The present monastic buildings date from the 19th and 20C. The monastery church is a rococo building by J.B. Gunetzrhainer of Munich, erected on the walls of the mid 13C church (and incorporating a 1232 chapel of St. Afra). The frescoes and stucco work on the vault and choir are by J.B. Zimmermann, mid 18C. The church is the last resting place of Duke Ludwig X (died 1545; a notable gravestone).

Three fine sights SE of the town are first, the present government building, in a former Dominican monastery, founded in 1271 and rebuilt 1699, with a neo-classical façade of 1802. It contains a 13C church with an 18C rococo interior (much of the detail by J.B. Zimmermann); second, the *Neustadt*, founded to complement the Aldstadt in 1338, with—at its southernmost end—the barrel-vaulted Jesuit church which Johann Holl built, 1613–41; and third, *Burg Traunitz*, only partly restored after a disastrous fire of 1961 and containing the Lower Bavarian state archive: a 13C late romanesque chapel of St. Georg, with a 15C high altar and early 16C statues; and a superb view of the town (visits daily, 09.00–12.00 and 13.00–17.00 in season; 13.00–16.00 October–March).

Landshut also possesses a fine theatre (seating 806, at Nos 2–5, Ländtorplatz), basically a theatre of 1836 which was reordered in 1947.

From Landshut follow the the B11 SW towards Munich, reaching after 10km *Kronwinkl*, with its Schloß (11C, 17C and 18C), and with its fine views back towards Landshut of the tower of St. Martin's basilica and Burg Traunitz. The road reaches *Moosburg* after about 9km. Moosburg, which retains fragments of its old walls, was founded in the mid 8C, and developed around the relics of a Roman martyr, St. Kastulus. Its greatest treasure is the 12C romanesque basilica of *St. Kastulus*, containing a marvellous 15m-high, late gothic main altar by Hans Leinberger (1515), and the medieval shrine of the saint. Other sights are the 13C cemetery church of St. Michael; the 14th and 15C church of St. Johann; its medieval houses; and the 16C Schloß Asch.

18km from Moosburg stands **Freising** (32,000 inhab.; alt. 421m), a city founded as the result of the work of 8C missionaries such as Boniface and Korbinian. Freising flourished in the 14C under Bishop Otto, the uncle of Barbarossa. Its chief treasure is the brick 12C double-towered *cathedral*, with a 13C crypt, late 15C vaulting, gothic choir stalls (1448) and an interior by the brothers Asam (1724). The relics of St. Korbinian are venerated in the crypt, with romanesque animals carved on the crypt columns. Other important buildings include the 13C Benedictine church, which was rebuilt in the mid 14C; the church of St. Johann, which dates from 1359 and is filled with painting and sculpture; and the Spital church dating from 1607. Freising is further enriched by the Bishops' Palace (14–18C) and a monastery church by G.A. Viscardi (1705–15), with decoration by F.X. Feuchtmayr and J.B. Zimmermann and a high altar of 1765 by Ignaz Günther.

The B11 continues for 33km as far as Munich by way of the Isar Valley and Freimann (where the road joins the motorway for Berlin). The route enters **Munich** (see Rte 11) by the Ludwigstraße, Leopoldstraße and Ungererstraße.

Leave Munich on the A95 motorway (the so-called 'Olympia Straße'), taking the spur towards Starnberg. The route passes through the Forstenrieder Park (once a motor racing circuit) and *Forstenried*. Here is a 15C pilgrims' church, dedicated to the Holy Cross and possessing a romanesque wooden crucifix. The church has an octagonal onion-domed tower. Christian Strasser decorated the interior in the rococo style. The 14 life-size wooden statues date from 1670 and the silver tabernacle from 1700. After 15km the route, passing through Wangen, reaches *Percha* at the northern tip of the **Starnberg Lake**.

AN EXCURSION AROUND THE STARNBERG LAKE (Starnberger See; 50km).

This is the second biggest stretch of water in Bavaria, 20km long, between 2 and 5km wide, and reaching a depth of 123m. Popularised among the nobility in the 17C by Kurfürst Ferdinand Maria and his wife Henriette Adelheid of Savoy, today the lake is surrounded by holiday resorts, filled with yachts and traversed by passenger boats.

Just W of Percha is the chief holiday resort, **Starnberg**, with beaches, promenades, swimming pools. The Information Office is at No. 3 Kirchplatz. Trains connect with Munich and Garmisch-Partenkirchen. The Schloß on the Schloßberg dates back to the 13C. An arched bridge joins this Schloß with the rococo church of St. Joseph (1770; high altar by Ignaz Günther, splendid pulpit). In a 16C wooden house nearby is a museum of local history, with an art gallery, including work by I. Günther (No. 9 Possenhofener Straße; open Tuesday–Sunday, 10.00–17.00; closed winter).

Leave by the Possenhofener Straße and follow the W coast to reach in 5km *Possenhofen* with a sailing school and a privately owned Schloß. At *Pöcking* (some 5km along a road W of the lake) is a 17C church with an onion dome. Return to Possenhofen and continue S through *Feldafing* (golf links, 'English Park', the Rose Island with a villa built by Maximilian II and a rose garden given by Ludwig II) as far as *Tutzing* (7km). The peaks of the Johannishügel and the Ilkanhöhe, picturesque ravines and Schloß Garatshausen (1532, now a protestant academy) add charm to this second largest town on the lake. Follow the coast road for 6km through *Unterzeismering* (chapel with a 16C wooden statue of the Coronation of the Virgin), past Schloß Höhenried (now a clinic) to *Bernried*, with its park, the gift of Wilhelmine-Busch-Woods, its former Augustinian monastery (founded 1121), the church of St. Martin (1484 altar, rococo tabernacle), and the parish church of St. Maria (crucifix, and a Virgin with the Rosary, both 16C; altars by Tassilo Zöpf, 1769).

6km further, through Seeseiten, lies *Seeshaupt*, with fine alpine vistas and an onion-domed parish church. Continue round the bottom end of the lake and N along the E coast, through the fishing villages St. Heinrich and Ambach, as far (10km) as *Holzhausen*, with its pilgrims' church (15C monstrance). 3km further is *Münzing*, a centre for mountain walks. To reach Berg (8km N) the route passes through *Allmannshausen* (Schloß and church of St. Valentin by Kaspar Feuchtmayr) and *Assenhausen* (Bismarck gate). At **Berg** is the Schloß of 1640 where in 1876 King Ludwig II of Bavaria built a neo-gothic chapel, where the mentally deranged king was later put under house arrest and close by the spot where on 13 June 1886 he and his doctor were drowned. A plaque marks the place where their bodies were brought ashore, and a neo-romanesque chapel was built here as a memorial for the king in 1900. The late romanesque church of St. Johann Baptist at Berg is worthy of note.

2km SE of Berg lies *Aufkirchen* (15C pilgrims' church of Maria Himmelfahrt, with life-size figures of Jesus, Mary and the Apostles, 1626, and 28 frescoes by Ignaz Biedermann, 1704).
   From Berg the route N reaches Starnberg within 5km, by way of *Kempfenhausen* (rococo church) and Percha.

From Starnberg take the B2 SW for 16km to **Weilheim** (16,000 inhab.; alt. 565m) in the valley of the River Ammer. The town became famous for its woodcarvers and goldsmiths in the 17C. The early baroque parish church of Maria Himmelfahrt contains some of their work: a monstrance of 1698 by Josef Anton Kipfinger and a crucifix of 1699. The church was built by Georg Praun and Bartholomäus Steinle, 1624–28, preserving an early gothic tower. The high altar painting is by Ulrich Loth (1641), the 'Rastaltar' by F.X. Schmädl (1760). See also the Lamentation painted by Martin Knoller for the middle altar on the S side (1790). The gothic cemetery chapel dates from 1449, its tower from 1584 (inside, frescoes by Elias Greither, 1591; shrine and altar, 1470). The church of St. Johann at Töllern dates from 1490 (1⁁C and 17C frescoes). The chapel of the Sorrows of Our Lady (1761) has frescoes by J.B. Bader. In the Marienplatz is a late 18C copy of the fountain of the monastery at Steingaden and a column of the Virgin Mary by Ignaz Degler (1698). The town museum is in the 1788 town hall (No. 1 Marienplatz; *Hans Leinberger's Man of Sorrows; open Saturday–Thursday, 10.00–12.00, 14.00–17.00).
   The B2 now runs 20km S to Murnau; a picturesque journey through such villages as *Etting* (church of 1526 with a rococo decor) and *Obersöchering* (late gothic Madonna in the Frauenkirche). **Murnau** lies at 629m on the warm Lake Staffel (4km long, 3·5km wide, 35m deep, with seven islands), a favourite bathing resort and health centre, at the start of the Bavarian Alps. Many walls of its houses are painted in the traditional fashion of Bavaria. Its treasures include a 15th and 16C Schloß, the church of Mariahilf (1734), the neo-gothic town hall (1842), and especially the church of St. Nikolaus (1734; rococo decor; statues of SS. Anne, Joseph and Joachim by F.X. Schmädl, 1751). On the feast of Corpus Christi is held a procession of boats, and another on 6 November (the 'Leonhardifahrt').

Continue S to *Ohlstadt* (8km) at the foot of the 1790m-high *Heimgarten* (fine 17th and 18C houses; St. Laurentius church, 1759–62, with paintings by Franz Zwinck, the 'Lüftlmaler'). There is a ski lift to Walchensee. *Eschenlohe* (from which the plague came to Oberammergau in 1633) is reached 2km S (parish church of St. Clemens, 1773, designed by J.M. Fischer; rococo tabernacle by J.B. Straub). On its peak remains the chapel of the ruined Burg. The route continues S through *Oberau* (winter sports; churches of St. Ludwig and St. Georg (16C ceiling fresco) and *Farchant* (with its picturesque farmhouses and the church of St. Andreas, 1728 (high altar, 1779), to reach after 15km Garmisch-Partenkirchen.

Lying at the foot of the highest peak in Germany (the 2963m *Zugspitze*) and at the confluence of the Partnach and the Loisach, **Garmisch-Partenkirchen** (28,000 inhab.; alt. 798m) is the country's chief winter sports centre.

Cable cars and mountain railways; theatres; indoor swimming pools (one with artficial waves, next to the ice rink, see below); canoeing; horse- and pony-trekking; concerts; tennis courts; a golf course; health centres, clinics and a health park operate in summer as well as winter. There are more than 300km of mountain paths. Cable cars reach the heights of *Eckbauer* (1239m), *Osterfelderkopf* (2050m), *Wank* (1780m) and from the Hotel Schneefernerhaus (2650m, reached by mountain railway) to the peak of the *Zugspitze*. Railways connect with Munich and Innsbruck.

History. The two separate communities of Garmisch and Partenkirchen (which still retain their village charm) joined together in 1935. Garmisch has existed since the early 9C at least; Partenkirchen derives from the Roman camp *Partanum* and prospered in the Middle Ages from its market (granted in 1361) and its position on the trade route between Augsburg and Venice. Richard Strauss spent most of his long working life here.

For a tour of what was formerly *Partenkirchen*, beginning at the railway station follow Bahnhofstraße E to the Rathausplatz (town hall of 1935, by O. Bieber, decorated with frescoes by J. Wackerle). Cross E over Hauptstraße into Ludwigstraße, where are found (at No. 45) the peasant theatre in the Gasthof 'Zum Rasen' and (at No. 47) the Wackerle House, now a museum of woodcarving and cabinet making (open Tuesday–Friday, 10.00–13.00, 15.00–18.00; Saturday and Sunday only 10.00–13.00). N of Ludwigstraße stands the 1634 'plague chapel' of SS. Sebastian and Roch (both saints having been reputed to be able to protect the faithful against plagues), set in the plague cemetery, which was created in 1776 and made into a war memorial by J. Wackerle in 1924. Return S along Münchener Straße to find on the corner of Sonnenbergstraße the parish church of Maria Himmelfahrt, rebuilt after a fire, 1865–71, but retaining a 16C statue of St. Roch and paintings by Letterini (1731). Due NE of this church, along St.-Anton-Straße stands the pilgrims' church of St. Anton (1704), enlarged by J. Schmuzer 1738, who added an oval dome which J.E. Holzer frescoed in 1739 (stucco decor of high altar by the Venetian B. Letterini). Continue S along Ludwigstraße and then along Mittenwalder Straße and Wildenauer Straße to the Olpympic ski stadium of 1936—which has space for 70,000 spectators, 3000 of them seated.

To visit what was formerly *Garmisch*, start again at the railway station. Bahnhofstraße leads N and then W to Richard-Strauss-Platz, centre of the theatre (in a park) amd health complex. N in Burgstraße is the formerly romanesque church of St. Martin (inside: St. Christopher of 1350; 14th and 15C gothic wall paintings of the Crucifixion and Last Judgment; glass of 1400; late gothic carvings on choir stalls; 15C Passion group; paintings of Christ crucified, St. Erhardt and Popes Urban and Gregory, 1450; 1670, high altar). Continue E along Frühlingstraße and Zoeppritzstraße to find the villa of Richard Strauss (who died here in 1949). Return E along Richard-Strauss-Straße and Maximilanstraße to the so-called 'new' parish church of St. Martin (by J. Schmuzer, 1730–34; ceiling frescoed by Matthias Günther, 1733; statues by Anton Sturm on high altar, 1734; on either side of the organ are paintings by F. Zwinck, 1774). Return along Bahnhofstraße, turning S at Olympiastraße to find the Olympic Ice Rink, the largest in Europe, built 1936, roofed 1964 and seating 12,000 spectators.

The eighteenth century façade of the Benedictine monastery church at Ettal.

A ROUND TRIP TO ETTAL, SCHLOß LINDERHOF, OBERAMMERGAU AND BAD KOHLGRUB (45km).

Drive 9km back along the B2 from Garmisch-Partenkirchen to Oberau and take the B23 W (the 'Alpenstraße') for another 6km to **Ettal**, where a Benedictine monastery was founded by Emperor Ludwig the Bavarian in 1330. The present superbly sited monastery buildings date from the 18C, when to baroque plans by Enrico Zuccalli the gothic church of *St. Maria* was first transformed (1710–26), and then, after a fire of 1744, redone in the rococo style of J. Schmuzer. J.J. Zeiller painted an Apotheosis of the Trinity on the 85m-high dome (1746), the stucco work and organ gallery are by J.B. Zimmermann, the organ case by S. Gantner, the pulpit by J.B. Straub, c 1760. The fresco on the chancel dome is by M. Knoller (1786), the woodcarvings in the choir by R.A. Boos. The marble statue of the Madonna in the tabernacle was brought by Ludwig the Bavarian in 1330.

A 10km excursion due E from Ettal leads to ***Schloß Linderhof** (open daily, 09.00–12.15, 12.45–17.00; October–March closes at 16.00). Here was a farm belonging to the Ettal monastery and (from the 15C) the home of the Linder family. In 1870–78 Georg Dollmann built on the site an Italianate Schloß for Ludwig II, loosely based on the Petit-Trianon at Versailles. The entrance hall has a bronze statue of Ludwig's exemplar, the Sun King Louis XIV. Every detail pays homage to the French 18C court, with portraits of Mme de Pompadour, Louis XV and the rest and a hall of mirrors. Ludwig even called the building 'Meicost Ettal', an anagram of Louis XIV's 'L'état cest moi'. K. Effner laid out 52 hectares of garden, with pools, cascades and fountains, a grotto (based on the Venusberg of Wagner's 'Tannhäuser'), a Moorish pavilion and a temple of Venus, everywhere adorned with sculpture by J. Hautmann and M. Wagmüller. Ludwig II continued to extend and alter this Schloß (using the architect Julius Hofmann) until his death, when Hofmann was engaged on refurbishing the royal bedchamber.

Return to Ettal and drive 5km NW to **Oberammergau**, where the miraculous lifting of a plague in 1633 led to the thanksgiving performance every ten years (with some additions, such as 1934 and 1984) of the now world-famous Passion Play. (The present text, with some anti-Semitisms expunged, is by two parish priests, Othmar Weiss and J.A. Daisenberger, the early 19C music by the local schoolmaster Rochus Dedler.) Oberammergau, dominated by the 1343m-high *Kogfel* with its huge cross, is also a centre for winter sports (an open-air swimming pool, boasting artificial waves, and a cable-car to the 1400m-high *Kolbensattel*), glass painting, and skilled woodcarvers—a carving school was established in 1878 (work displayed in the local museum; No. 8 Dorfstraße, open, 10.00–12.00, 14.00–17.00). In the Middle Ages the town belonged to the Hohenstaufen and after 1269 to the dukes of Bavaria. It prospered, being on the trade route from Italy through Augsburg to the Rhineland. In 1736–42 J. Schmuzer rebuilt its parish church, with stucco work by his son Franz Xavier Schmuzer, and frescoes by M. Günther. The rococo altars are by F.X. Schmädl. The 18C 'Lüftlmalerer' Franz Zwinck painted the outsides of the Pilatushaus and the Geroldhaus, a tradition continued today on other houses (e.g. in the Hansel and Gretel house, painted by Max Strauss in the 1920s). The severely functional passion play theatre is based on one built in 1890 by Lautenschlager, stage manager of the Munich Court Theatre.

4km further NE lies the charming village of **Unterammergau**, with an onion-domed towered parish church of St. Nikolaus (built mainly in the first two decades of the 18C; ceiling fresco by Johann Jakob Würmseer of Oberammergau) and the chapel of the Holy Blood (with a relic of the Holy Blood brought from Italy in 1734, and a baroque organ of 1777). This chapel was plundered in 1704 during the War of the Spanish Succession and later restored, with stucco work and a new painted ceiling by J.J. Schmuzer, 1750–51.

The route leads NE for 6km to Saulgraub and turns E to reach in 3km more *Bad Kohlgrub*, Germany's highest Alpine resort. Its baths are reputed to cure numerous ailments. The nearby *Hörnlegebirge* rises to 1565m. The town preserves numerous painted houses, and its onion-domed towered parish church dates from 1729. From Bad Kohlgrub the road leads 12km directly E to **Murnau**.

5 Würzburg and the 'Romantische Straße'

A. Würzburg

**WÜRZBURG (122,000 inhab.; alt. 182m). Beautifully situated amidst vine-clad hills on the River Main, Würzburg is an old university city, the seat of a Catholic bishopric, and the administrative centre of Lower Franconia. It lies on motorway B8 midway between Nuremberg (102km) and Frankfurt am Main (117km) and at the start of the Romantische Straße. Three bridges cross the river: from N to S the Friedensbrücke, the Alte Mainbrücke, and the Ludwigsbrücke.

Main *railway station*: Bahnhofplatz.

Information Offices: Bahnhofplatz.

Trains to Aschaffenburg, Bamberg, Frankfurt, Ingolstadt, Munich, Nuremberg, Regensburg, Stuttgart. Tramway system.

Boats along the River Main to Veitshöchheim.

History. A Bronze Age settlement c 1000 BC, where later the Celts settled at a spot where the Main could be forded. Irish monks brought Christianity in the 7C. (Three of them, SS. Kilian, Kolonat and Totnan, were martyred in 689.) St. Boniface founded a bishopric in 742. The first bishop was Burkart, and pilgrims increasingly visited the tomb of Kilian. Charlemagne's court was at Würzburg in 788 (when the cathedral was consecrated in his presence) and in 793. The marriage of Frederick Barbarossa and Beatrix of Burgundy was celebrated here in 1156. Twelve years later Barbarossa made the bishops Dukes of Franconia, and they then ruled the city until 1802 (in spite of numerous uprisings against them by the burgers, particularly that of 1397). The citizens supported the peasants during the Peasants' Revolt of 1525. In the late 16C and the 17C the city expanded, especially under the Prince-Bishop Julius Echter von Mespelbrunn (1573–1617), who re-endowed the university in 1582. In spite of its capture by Gustavus Adolphus during the Thirty Years' War, Würzburg continued to prosper in the 17th and 18C, especially under the Prince-Bishops Johann Philipp von Schönborn (1642–73), Johann Philipp Franz von Schörnborn (1719–24) and Friedrich Karl von Schönborn (1729–46). From 1802–05 the city was part of the Electorate of Bavaria, and then was ruled as a Grand Duchy under Ferdinand of Tuscany. Würzburg suffered a devastating air-raid on 16 March 1945. In the 1970s the city began to spread into the new town of Heuchelhof, and the New University was founded in the suburbs.
   Tilman Riemenschneider (died 1531), the greatest limewood sculptor of the renaissance, was mayor of the Würzburg. The painter Matthias Grünewald was born here, c 1465. Distinguished 19C savants at the university (founded 1420) included the philosopher F.W.J. Schelling, the physicist Röntgen, who discovered X-rays, and Gladstone's friend the theologian Ignatius Döllinger ('a remarkable and a very pleasing man').
   Candlelit Mozart concerts in the Residenz each June; autumn wine festival.

From the main railway station follow Bahnhofstraße to the twin-spired *Stift Haug*, the first significant baroque church in Franconia, by the Italian Antonio Petrini (1670–91; impressive dome, interior destroyed 1945; Crucifixion over high altar by Jacopo Tintoretto, 1583). A few yards to the W Juliuspromenade leads W past the baroque Juliuspital, now a Weinstube, founded by Prince-Bishop Julis Echter in 1576; the prince's building (Fürstenbau) has a rococo apothecary's shop, still in use; garden wing by Antonio Petrini, 1699; wing facing street by Geigel, 1789. Behind is a park with a pavilion (used as the university anatomy room in the 19C) by Joseph Greising, 1714, and a baroque fountain by Jakob van der Auvera, 1706. Juliuspromenade continues W to the Old Crane on the riverside, built by Franz Ignaz Neumann (Balthasar's son), c 1770. (Through its alleyway is an impressive view of the Fortress across the river; see below.) N of Juliuspromenade is the church of St. Gertraud (1611, with a modern interior).

S along the river bank and first left leads into Bronnbachergasse, with the *Fichtelhof, the house of Court Chancellor Fichter (1724, superb doorway and staircase). Continue E across Schönbornstraße to reach the former Dominican Augustiner *church* (gothic choir c 1250; central aisle by Balthasar Neumann, 1741; stucco work by Antonio Bossi). Continue as far as Eichhornstraße, turning left here to reach Theaterstraße. NW along Theaterstraße at No. 4 is an ornamental doorway with a statue of the Virgin Mary. Immediately opposite the corner of Eichhornstraße, where Theaterstraße meets Semmelstraße, is the Bürgerspital, today a Weinstube (1319; arcaded courtyard by Müller, 1717; gothic chapel with statues). Return along Eichhornstraße to cross Schönbornstraße into the Marktplatz to find the finest burger's house in Würzburg, the rococo *Falkenhaus* (a former inn; stucco decoration 1752; meticulously restored after WWII). Here the burgers built the late gothic *Marienkapelle*, on the site of a synagogue, having held the Jews responsible for the plague of 1347–52 and driven them away (1377–1481; sculpted doorway—the famous figures of Adam and Eve are now in the city museum.

Interior (renewed after 1945): Madonna c 1430, on S wall of nave, formerly part of W doorway; tombs of knights and townsmen, including *tomb of Konrad von Schaumberg by Riemenschneider; B. Neumann's tombstone).

S of the Marktplatz is visible the romanesque tower of the *Town Hall* (reached by the Marktgasse, the Gressengasse and then the Langgasse). N of the Town Hall, in both Gressengasse and Rücker-mainstraße, is the baroque *Rückermainhof* (1715–23). The Town Hall was formerly the Hof zum Grafen Eckart: romanesque ground floor; 13C Wenceslas Hall on the first floor; upper two storeys 16C; lower half of tower c 1300, upper half 1453. The late renaissance Red Building by Preiss and Villinger (1659) abuts the Town Hall; facing it, to the S, is the baroque Vierröhren Fountain by Lukas van der Auvera and Peter Wagner (1763–66).

Walk E along Domstraße to the Cathedral of **St. Kilian**, the fourth largest romanesque church in Germany, begun 1045, on the site of a 9C building; E towers 1237, destroyed 1945, rebuilt and rededicated 1967. INTERIOR: high baroque, early 18C stucco work by Pietro Magno; ceiling of central aisle painted by F. Nagel; bishops' tombstones, including the earliest, for Gottfried von Spitzenberg (died 1190), and *Riemenschneider's red marble tombstones for Rudolf von Scherenberg (died 1495) and Lorenz von Bibra (died 1519); pulpit by Michael Kern (1609–10, saved in 1945); rococo Schönborn Chapel, burial place for the prince-bishops, by Balthasar Neumann and M. von Welsch, 1721–36, frescoes by Byss, sculpture by Claude Curé; late gothic sepulchre, with modern windows by G. Meistermann; altar, tabernacle and bishop's throne by A. Schilling, 1966–67. Cloisters 1034, with Crucifixion group by Lukas van der Auvera (1761–63).

N of the cathedral stands the *Neumünster* on the spot where St. Kilian was martyred and buried (11C romanesque; 13C choir and tower; dome and baroque façade by V. Pezani and Johann Dientzenhofer, 1710–16. Interior: *Riemenschneider's Madonna (SW niche of the rotunda) and tombstone for the humanist abbot Johannes Trithemius, died 1516); baroque reordering by Joseph Griesing, Nikolaus Stuber, J.-B. Zimmermann, stucco, Dominikus Zimmermann, restored after 1945. In the little garden is the grave of the minnesinger Walter von der Wogelweide (died 1230). Cloisters c 1170, with garden. E is the *Otto-Richter-Hall* (1 Maxstraße; modern art exhibitions). In this area some burgers' houses and courtyards escaped destruction in 1945, including the renaissance Conti in Herrenstraße, now the bishop's palace (1609, with renaissance balcony), and the classical Hof Rannenberg, No. 3 Hofstraße, restored 1965–69. The City Art Gallery is to the S (open Tuesday–Friday, 10.00–17.00; Saturday, Sunday and holidays, 10.00 –13.00; 19th and 20C Franconian painters).

Follow Hofstraße E to reach the Residenzplatz and the baroque ****Residenz** (open daily, 09.00–12.00, 13.00–17.00; varying times for the court church and the gardens): the palace of the prince-bishops, built 1719–44 to the plans of Balthasar Neumann, though these were modified by Johann Lukas von Hildebrandt and Maximilian von Welsch. In the courtyard a fountain (1894) with statues of the minnesinger Walther von der Vogelweide, the painter Matthias Grünewald and the sculptor Tilman Riemenschneider. Neumann's magnificent staircase and cupola, with the ceiling painted by Giambattista Tiepolo, 1750–53 (at 540m^2, the largest fresco in the world, depicting God in his heaven ruling the world: note the portrait of Neumann as an artillery officer, in the representation of Europe); the White Room, with stucco by Antonio Bossi; Emperor's Hall, by Neumann and Hildebrandt, stucco by Bossi, and frescoes by Tiepolo, 1752, depicting the history of Würzburg, chiefly the marriage of Barbarossa and Beatrix of Burgundy; the Garden Hall with ceiling fresco painted by Johannes Zick and stucco by Antonio Bossi; rococo Parade Room, 1740–70, very seriously damaged 1945; court chapel by Neumann (note the light coming from one side only), frescoes by Johann Rudolf Byss, side-altar painting by Tiepolo. Gardens: baroque bastions, cherubs by P. Wagner, rich wrought-iron rococo gates by J.G. Oegg. Martin-von-Wagner-Museum (picture gallery open Tuesday–Saturday, 09.30–13.00; antiquities, Tuesday–Saturday, 14.00–17.00; both galleries open Sunday, 10.00 –13.00; antiques and copperplates). Bavarian national archives in N wing; Garden (and garden front 167m long). The Residenz includes a Weinstube in the Hofkellerei. NE of the Residenz is the neo-gothic Protestant church of St. Johannes (1895, restored after WWII).

From Residenzplatz Balthasar-Neumann-Promenade leads SW to the corner of Neubaustraße. To the S is St. Stephan's Church (J.P. Geigel, 1789; 11C crypt; Crucifixion group above high altar by Helmut Ammann, 1955). E along Neubaustraße are the restored late baroque Jesuit church of St. Michael (1765–98), the Priests' Seminary (by Joseph Greising, 1715–19), the Old University Buildings (renaissance, begun by Georg Robin, 1582) and the renaissance Neubau Church (begun 1586; tower by Petrini, 1696). A little further W is the Franciscan Church (1221, restored after WWII as were its cloisters, with a doorway carved with St. Francis receiving the stigmata, by Michael Kern, first half 17C; *Riemenschneider's Pietà) and then (No. 7) the noble house Zum Rebstock (rococo stucco work).

From Neubaustraße Münzstraße leads S to St. Peter's Church (1717; by Greisang, retaining two towers from the 12C romanesque church that earlier stood here; rococo pulpit by Auvera). To the W you can see across Sanderstraße the Carmelite church built by Antonio Petrini, 1662, the first Italian baroque church in Würzburg. From here a short walk leads to the river bank. Walk N alongside the river to the Alte Mainbrücke, built 1474–1543, adorned with baroque sandstone statues, c 1730, of rulers, including Barbarossa, and saints, including the Irish missionaries of Würzburg; the present statues are copies of originals by Claud Curé, a Frenchman who made his home in Würzburg, and the brothers Volkmar and Johann Sebastian Becker). Across the bridge stands the late gothic *Hospital Church*, neo-classical façade; now an art gallery (open Wednesday–Monday, 10.00–12.00, 13.00–17.00; contemporary works). From here Zellerstraße leads NW to the former church of the order of Teutonic Knights, the Deutschhaus Church (early gothic, 1296, late romanesque tower).

S of the Alte Mainbrücke on the W side of the river stands the romanesque basilica of St. Burkard (consecrated 1140; late gothic transepts and choir, 1493; early gothic capitals; gothic statue of the Virgin; 14C relief of the Crucifixion; bust of the Madonna by Riemenschneider in the S aisle; baroque altars, school of Auvera). NW of St. Burkard's is the church of the former Irish monastery, dedicated to St. John Bosco, a post WWII replacement for the destroyed St. Jakob's church. W of this church is the dominating *Marienberg Fortress*. This fortress, founded 1201, grew around a church consecrated to St. Mary, c 706 (the oldest round church in Germany; interior much altered, baroque altar; tombstones of bishops); Round Tower (the Bergfried, c 1200); Brunnenhaus (1601). The prince-bishops lived here 1253–1719. The main castle dates from 1482, as do the walls; Scherenberg gate c 1600. Julius Echter transformed the fortress into a renaissance palace (Echter bastion and temple above 104m-deep well). The palace became a baroque fortress again, after Gustavus Adolphus's victory over Würzburg in 1631. Princes' Garden; baroque armory (1702–12), now the Mainfränkisches Museum (open daily, 10.00–17.00; November–March closes 16.00; sculpture by Veit Stoß, Ferdinand Dietz, Peter Wagner, and espcially **Riemenschneider; exhibition devoted to regional wines; prehistoric collection).

S of the Marienberg Fortress is the pilgrims' *Käpelle* with its lovely spires and domes, surrounded by vineyards and standing 359m high on the Nikolausberg, by Balthasar Neumann, c 1748. Interior: frescoes by Feichtmayr, stucco by Matthias Günther; rococo organ case, c 1750; classical high altar, 1797–99. Life-size Stations of the Cross on the way to the church by P. Wagner, 1767–75; panorama.

OTHER SIGHTS: Huttenschlößchen, outside the city walls to the S, built by Beyer, c 1720 for the prince-bishop of Hutten. University Mineral Museum (Am Hubland, open Saturday, 14.00–17.00). Civic Theatre (21 Theaterstraße, 1966).

B. Würzburg to Augsburg: the 'Romantische Straße'

Total distance 233km. **Würzburg**—B27 32km
Tauberbischofsheim.—B290 18km **Bad Mergentheim**.—45km
Rothenburg ob der Tauber.—B25 43km **Dinkelsbühl**.—31km
Nördlingen.—B25 28km *Donauwörth*.—B2 36km *Augsburg*.

Leave **Würzburg** by way of the Alte Brücke and make for the B27, which runs SW reaching, after 32km, *Tauberbischofsheim*, crossing the bridge over the River Tauber and continuing along the Hauptstraße to the Marktplatz. The town takes its name from the missionary, Bishop Boniface, to whom it was presented in the year 725. (The name of the River Tauber was added only in 1806.) Around the Marktplatz are numerous well-restored half-timbered houses (especially the baroque Haus Mackert of 1744). S of the pedestrian zone is the SCHLOßPLATZ, with its 14–16C Schloß (with the older Türmers tower). Today it is the local history museum (open Easter until mid-October, Tuesday–Saturday, 14.30–16.30; Sunday and holidays also 10.00–12.00). N of the pedestrian zone is the neo-gothic church of *St. Martin* (1910–14) which still possesses its old gothic furnishings (Marienaltar, part of which is by Tilman Riemenschneider; altar of the cross, 1761). Its chapel of St. Sebastian (formerly the charnel house) displays a Last Judgment over its door.

The Romantische Straße now follows the B290 and the right bank of the river SE under the Heilbronn-Würzburg motorway through *Distelhausen* (baroque parish church, perhaps by Balthasar Neumann, 1731–38), reaching after 6km *Gerlachsheim* (former monastery church of 1725–30, with stucco; high altar painting by Johann Zick; rococo pulpit, 1788). The mid 18C statue of Mary comforting the distressed in the centre of the town was restored in 1878.

From here a short EXCURSION NE would take in *Grünsfeld*, with a town hall c 1580 and a parish church dating from the 14C to the 18C and containing Riemenschneider *tombs (see especially that of Countess Dorothea von Wertheim, died 1503). Continue NE to *Gründfeldhausen* with its 12C eight-sided chapel, to which is attached another smaller eight-sided chapel and a 19C tower. Inside, 12C wall paintings. Further NE lies *Ilmspan*, with a rococo church by Johann Michael Fischer (1766). The excursion now runs SE to *Oberwittinghausen*, with (just outside the town) an eight-sided chapel comparable to that of Gründfeldhausen. Return SW to *Zimmern* (church by J.M. Fischer; 1768) and continue back through Grünfeld and Gerlachsheim.

Lauda, the next place on the Romantische Straße, appears almost immediately, at the other side of the river (crossed by a bridge of 1510–12). A history of the town is laid out in the local history museum (No. 25 Rathausstraße, a restored farmhouse of 1551). The town hall dates from 1591, there are fine 17th and 18C houses and the church of St. Jakob dates from c 1700 (restored 1954). Close by is the sizeable new town of *Lauda-Königshofen*.

Bad Mergentheim, 50km S of Würzburg, is where the Romantische Straße begins to be signposted with green signs (lettered in yellow). Mergentheim derives from the name of a Duchess, Marigund, who ran her son's realm when he was a minor. The Teutonic knights established an important headquarters here in 1525 when they lost their Prussian territories, for they had already invested much in the town; they fortified the town in 1330; their traces are found throughout Bad Mergentheim and above all in their Schloß (1568–1628), on the E side of the town. The grand master had his seat here from 1526–1809. The town now houses a museum of the order (open Tuesday–Saturday, 14.30–17.30; Sunday and holidays and November–February, 10.00–12.00). Its church dates from 1730–36, partly the work of B. Neumann and F. Cuvilliés (inside, tombs of knights and frescoes by N. Stuberm; 1734). In addition its magnesium sulphate springs have made it famous for over a century and a half, since a shepherd discovered its medicinal springs. Medicinal fountains and a pump room were constructed in 1829. The name 'Bad' was added only in 1926. The town has fine houses and a town hall of 1564 in the Marktplatz along with the Michling fountain. S of the Marktplatz stands the 14C Dominican *Marienkirche* (with early 14C wall paintings and a bronze memorial of Grand Master Walther von Cronberg, died 1543, by Hans Vischer). On the N side of the Marktplatz an alley leads to the 13C church of *St. Johannes*, built by the knights of St. John of Jerusalem (with an early 17C gravestone of the Teutonic knight the Marquardt von Eck). Nearby is the frescoed chapel of the Hospice of the Holy Ghost. The poet Eduard Mörike (1804–75) lived here and married a girl of the town.

10km SW of Bad Mergentheim lies *Stuppach*. The church (1607) was extended in 1930 to house the *Stuppach Madonna by Matthias Grünewald, c 1519, which came here in 1812 (from the triptych on the Maria-Schnee altar of the Aschaffenburg hospice church) and was recognised as Grünewald's in 1900.

Another short excursion W from Bad Mergentheim leads to *Boxberg* (with a baroque church by Balthasar Neumann), to *Boxberg Wölchingen* with a 13C late romanesque church), and to *Boxberg-Unterschüpf* (with a church that is part 13C gothic, part early 17C renaissance, with 15C wall paintings and a rococo altar).

From Bad Mergentheim the route runs 11km E to *Weikersheim*, a tiny town with a moated renaissance Schloß built by the princes of

Hohenlohe between the 16C and the 18C and now a museum. The baroque park, orangery and Schloß (knights' hall) are open 08.00–18.00, April–October (otherwise Tuesday–Sunday, 10.00–12.00, 14.00–16.00). In the Marktplatz is the late gothic parish church (1518). The fountain dates from 1768. On the W side are the so-called 'Zirkelhäusern' (compass houses) of 1520. Between these is the way to the Schloß.

The small town of *Weikersheim-Laudenbach*, 4km SE, has a late 15C gothic pilgrims' chapel (altered in the 17C; in the crypt chapel is an alabaster tomb of Fieldmarshal Melchior von Hatzfeld, died 1658). From Weikersheim the Romantische Straße continues E through Röttingen, shortly afterwards turning S to reach after 11km *Biebereh-ren*. Admirers of Tilman Riemenschneider will make a diversion NE to *Aub*, whose parish church has a Crucifixion group partly by him, c 1500. From Aub the route runs S to reach *Creglingen*, where, 2km outside the town, the Herrgottskirche houses Riemenschneider's ****Marienaltar** (c 1505). The wings of the altar depict the life of the Virgin; the centre her Assumption (this piece certainly by the master himself). The church was built to celebrate the discovery of a sacred host by a 14C ploughman. The town of Creglingen has fine houses, and another Riemenschneider in its church.

The Romantische Straße now runs 18km SE to **Rothenburg ob der Tauber**, passing through *Detwang* en route, where the essentially romanesque parish church possesses a Crucifixion altar c 1515, in part by Riemenschneider.

**Rothenburg ob der Tauber (12,500 inhab.; alt. 426m) is a virtually unspoilt medieval town, standing some 100m above the right bank of the River Tauber and preserving its walls intact, situated where the Romantische Straße crosses the Burgenstraße (castle route) between Nuremberg and Heildelberg.

History. By the mid 12C the Hohenstaufen owned castles here, which an earthquake destroyed in 1356. From their chief Burg castle the main street of Rothenburg led to the Marktplatz. The lords of the town fortified it in the 12C (from which epoch remain the Markus tower and the White tower). By the end of the 13C Rothenburg had become a free imperial city. Rothenburg became Protestant at the Reformation, and barely escaped destruction in 1631 for taking the side of Gustavus Adolphus during the Thirty Years' War (see below). The Peace of Westphalia confirmed its free status. Apart from becoming part of Bavaria in 1802, the town slept during the late 17th, 18th and 19C, hence its present unspoilt aspect. Today 1·5 million tourists pass annually through its gates.

Trains connect Rothenburg with Steinach; buses connect with Steinach, Füssen, Creglingen, Würzburg and Schillingfürst. The Information Office is in the town hall.

Annual events include the renactment of the 'Meistertrunk', when the Bürgermeister of the town persuaded the Catholic general Tilly not to raze Rothenburg by accepting and winning a challenge to drink at one gulp a huge draught of wine. Other events are the Schäfertanz ('shepherds' dance') on Whit Sunday and during the summer, and the Hans Sachs festival (Easter and during the summer season).

Begin a tour of Rothenburg in the Marktplatz, with its Town Hall—half gothic (c 1250), half renaissance (1578, with a balcony of 1681). An open-air staircase leads into the renaissance wing and the imperial hall. To the right of the town hall is the Ratstrinkstube of 1446, where daily on the hour from 11.00–15.00 and 21.00–22.00 a window opens for a puppet representation of the 'Meistertrunk'.

Opposite is the fountain of St. Georg (1446; reordered in the renaissance style in 1608).

Obere Schmiedgasse leads from the Marktplatz S. The street comprises fine patrician houses (No. 21, the *Roter Hahn*, the home of Bürgermeiseter Nusch who saved the town from Tilly's wrath in 1631; No. 3, the *Baumeisterhaus*, a renaissance building with a sandstone façade, by L. Weidmann (1596), now a restaurant; next to it stands the *Gasthof zum Greifen*, once the home of Bürgermeister Heinrich Toppler, who led Rothenburg to its greatest prosperity in the 14C, and died in the town gaol). Next to Nusch's house is the 14C church of St. Johannes, with early 17C modifications. Leave here W by Rothenburg's oldest street, the Burggasse, which has at No. 3 a criminals' museum and torture chamber (open daily, April–October, 09.00–18.00; otherwise 14.00–16.00). Follow Burggasse as far as Herrngasse, which includes the 14C gothic Franciscan church (late gothic rood screen; 15C and 16C tombstones) and the 16C Herrn fountain, and leads to the 13C Burgtor (close by which is a puppet theatre). Beyond this gate is the Burggarten (garden), which houses a chapel, c 1200, all that remains of the old Burg. Return to the church of St. Johann and walk S as far as the corner known as Plönlein (from which two streets each lead to a fortified gate). From here continue either right to the Kobolzeller gate (by way of Kobolzellertsteig) or left by way of Untere Schmiedgasse to the Sieber Tower (c 1390), en route for the hospice quarter, which was created in the late 13C (though—apart from the 14C Heiliggeistkirche—the present buildings date from the second half of the 16C, especially the Hegereiterhaus, i.e. horseb.eaker's house, of 1591). Spitalstraße leads from here to the imposing 17C Spital bastion.

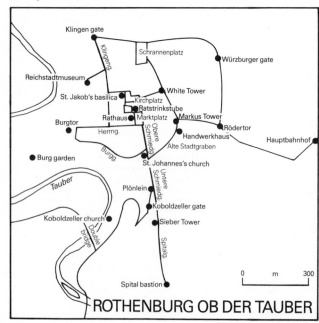

ROTHENBURG OB DER TAUBER

Return from here to the Marktplatz. Pass between the town hall and the Ratstrinkstube to reach the Grüner Markt and then the Kirchplatz, on the W side of which is the 14th and 15C basilica, *St. Jakob-Kirche (inside: a stone Virgin, c 1360; 14C stained glass; early 15C aumbry; mid 15C high altar, with sculpture by H. Waidenlich and painted panels by F. Herlin—note the depiction of Rothenburg itself; and Tilman Riemenschneider's **Holy Blood altar). On the N side of the square is the three-storeyed renaissance former secondary school, by L. Weidmann (1581). Continue N from the church along Klingengasse and then W at Feuerleinserker to reach the town museum (Reichstadtmuseum, at No. 5 Klosterhof), in a 12C former Dominican monastery: containing Bürgermeister Nusch's famous flagon and the 12 paintings of 1494 making up the 'Rothenburg Passion' (open April–October 10.00–17.00; otherwise guided tours 13.00–16.00). Also from the church of St. Georg, Georgengasse leads E to the 12C White Tower. N of here is the former Jewish quarter, with the grain store of 1588 in Schrannenplatz. Two other remains of the 12C fortifications—the Markusturm and the Rödertor—are found by following Pfarrgasse (right from the White Tower), and then the Pfeiffergäßchen and Rödergasse. Follow Hafengasse from here from Röderbogen back to the Marktplatz.

A tour along and outside the walls of Rothenburg ob der Tauber is rewarding. Through the Burg gate (W of the town) and the Burg garden the route crosses the 14C 'Double bridge' (restored after destruction in WW11) by way of the Kobolzeller church (1479), to the W of which stands the Toppler Schloß (1338). Rödergasse leads E of Rothenburg to the Röder gate, from which you walk N to the Würzburger gate (formerly the site of the town gallows) and further to the late 16C Klingen gate, into which is built the fortified church of St. Wolfgang (the 'Shepherds' Church'), c 1490, with a statue of St. Wolfgang, 1489; the high altar by Wilhelm Ziegler, 1514, and the Marienaltar also by Ziegler, 1515.

OTHER MUSEUMS: the *Topplerschlößchen*, No. 100 Taubertalweg, built for Bürgermeister Toppler in the mid 14C, so as to allow him sight of the town mills on the Tauber (open daily, April–October, 10.00–12.00, 14.00–17.00, otherwise 11.00–16.00). The Rothenburg Handwerkhaus and local history museum, No. 26 Alte Stadtgraben (open daily, Easter–October, 09.00–18.00 and 20.00–21.00).

During the tourist season Rothenburg runs a riding school, and the region boasts fine hill-walking country. The nearest motorway is the Würzburg-Randersacker Autobahn, 55km from the town.

Leave Rothenburg ob der Tauber S by the B25, crossing the A7 motorway and reaching *Feuchtwangen* after 31km.

A brief detour E to *Schillingsfürst*, signposted, reveals an early 18C Schloß (open March–October weekdays, 09.30–11.30, 14.00–17.30; Sunday and holidays, 10.00–12.00, 14.00–17.00).

Feuchtwangen developed in the neighbourhood of an 8C Benedictine monastery. On the N side of the Marktplatz is the 13–14C *Sitftskirche* (much renewed in the 20C) with a fine interior (high altar by Michael Wohlgemut, 1484; early 16C choir stalls). S of the church is a calvary, in which plays are held in summer. Nearby are a local history museum and a crafts museum. The church of St. Johann lies to the N of the Stiftskirche, with a fine hall (the 'Kasten', 1565) adjoining.

An EXCURSION from Feuchtwangen follows the B14 for 25km E to **Ansbach**, to see its Italian baroque Residenz (1713–32; 27 rooms, some rococo, some baroque; open summer, 09.00–12.00, 14.00–17.00; winter, 10.00–12.00, 14.00–16.00), its early baroque orangery (1726) and its 200-year-old lime avenue. See also the romanesque church of *St. Gumbertus* (gothic choir, baroque nave, chapel of the knights of the swan; the gothic church of St. Johann (1441); the funeral church of the Holy Cross (1461); the baroque chancellery of 1593 and a town hall of 1623. Some of the wide streets have 18C baroque houses. Ansbach runs an international week of Bach music at the end of each July and a rococo festival every August. Information Office at No. 1 Martin-Luther-Platz.

SW of Ansbach, along the B13 is *Wolframs-Eschenbach*, the birthplace of the medieval author of 'Parzifal', Wolfram von Eschenbach, who is buried in its 13C church. On the way back to Feuchtwangen make a brief excursion S to *Herrieden* to see its 15C Stiftskirche, with a baroque interior.

From Feuchtwangen follow the B25 S to **'Dinkelsbühl** on the River Wörnitz. The medieval town, including its complex fortifications, is completely unchanged, having survived eight sieges in the Thirty Years' War before being taken by Gustavus Adolphus. Because the town's children are said to have saved it in 1632, each summer (mid-July) the 'Kinderzeche' is performed in thanksgiving.

Enter Dinkelsbühl by the 13C Wörnitz gate, to reach the oldest part of the town, with its late 12C 'Burgus Tinkelspuhel', crossing the Altrathausplatz with its old town hall and lion fontains to reach the Marktplatz. To the E stands the 15C parish church of* St. Georg (late gothic interior). Past the present town hall Föhrenberggasse leads to the Schloß of the Teutonic knights (1761–64). Follow the route for the Rothenburger gate, passing the Deutsches Haus (15C; fine 16C renaissance façade) and then the former Corn house (c 1600) and former Hospice (now a local history museum, open daily, 09.00–12.00, 13.30–17.00). At the Rothenburger gate (c 1380) take the Obere Schmiedgasse to the walls and then walk along the walls by way of Kapuzinerweg, to reach the former Capuchin monastery. Close by is a granary (*Kornhaus*) of 1378. Pass the Segringer gate (rebuilt 1655) to reach the mid 16C chapel of the Magi (now a war memorial). From the

A street and one of the four medieval gateways of Dinkelsbühl.

Segringer Gate Oberer Mauerweg follows the town wall to the late
15C Nördlinger Gate, outside which is the late 15C town mill. To walk
outside the walls is rewarding—with parks and a large sports centre to
the W.

The route now travels E through Gerolfingen to *Wassertrüdingen*
(remains of medieval walls; former Benedictine monastery church,
with a renaissance tabernacle by Loy Hering (1512) and an altar
dedicated to the Virgin Mary, by Hans Schüfelin (1513). Continue S to
Oettingen, which retains part of the chapel of its former Schloß and its
'new' 17C Schloß (restored early 19C), as well as the parish church of
St. Jakob with stucco work by Matthias Schmuzer.

Travel SW to **Nördlingen*, with its perfectly preserved town walls
(11 towers, 5 gates; summer plays in the Alte Bastei). Nördlingen
prospered and was built lavishly during the 14th and 15C. The town
became part of Bavaria in 1803 and lost its status as free city. The
Salvatorkirche (1385) preserves 15C frescoes and a high altar of 1497.
Close by is the Winter-Haus (1677). The 13C Town Hall (in the
Marktplatz) has an open-air renaissance flight of steps (1618) and on
the second floor a wall painting by Hans Schäufelin. The bookshop
(1552) E of the town hall was formerly a pawnshop. On the W side of
the Marktplatz is the Brothaus (or Tanzhaus) of 1444 (now the
Information Office), with a statue of Emperor Maximilian I on the
façade. On the S side of the Marktplatz is the 93m-long late gothic
church of *St. Georg* (1427–1519), with an 89m-high tower (finished
1539 when the renaissance copper dome was added), and known as
'Daniel', with 365 steps to the summit, a gothic high altar, a pulpit of
1499 and a sandstone tabernacle of 1525.

Other sights include the nine-storey Hohes Haus of 1442, the
'Klosterle' formerly a Franciscan church (1420; doorway 1686). The
16C Spital, or town hospital, preserves its 13C church (restored in the
19C) and is now a museum (open daily, 19.00–12.00, 14.00–17.00;
Sunday and holidays it opens an hour later and closes an hour earlier).

At Nördlingen the oldest steeplechase in Germany takes place each September.
Each June a fair and festival commemorates the granting of the right to hold a
Whitsun market to the town in 1219. Trains link with Füssen and Donauwörth.

Leave **Nördlingen** by the Reimlinger gate and follow Augsburger
Straße to take the B25 SE to picturesque *Harburg*. The princely
collection in the *Felsenburg*, 12C to 16C (open daily, March–
October, 19.00–11.30, 13.30–17.30), which dominates the town, has
works by Riemenschneider, Gobelin tapestries and a superb library.
Harburg retains a romanesque Schloß church, extended in the 14C,
with a carved Madonna, 1480, and the church of St. Michael, 1510.
After 25km *Donauwörth* (see Rte 1B). The B2 now runs 36km S to
Augsburg (see Rte 3).

6 From Würzburg to Passau by way of Nuremberg and Regensburg

Total distance 326km. **Würzburg**—B8. 19km *Kitzingen*—41km
Neustadt.—40km **Nuremberg.**—37km *Neumarkt.*—65km
Regensburg.—B8 67km *Plattling.*—57km **Passau.**

Leave **Würzburg** (see Rte 5) SE by the B8, crossing the Frankfurt–
Nuremberg motorway, to reach after 12km *Bibelried* (with a crucifix

by Riemenschneider in its parish church) and after 7km further on Kitzingen, on the right bank of the River Main. *****Kitzingen** (18,400 inhab.; alt. 200m) with its noted Falterturm (crooked tower) preserves some of its 13C walls (especially in Kapuzinerstraße) and an ancient stone bridge across the River Main. The Catholic parish church of St. Johannes dates from the 15C, the Italian baroque Protestant parish church (by Petrini, in Gustav-Adolph-Platz) from the 17C. See also the mid 18C *Holy Cross church* by Balthasar Neumann and the renaissance town hall (1561, restored in 1977). Trains run from Kitzingen to Würzburg and Nuremberg.

As this is the centre of the Franconian vineyards, wine tours are available (Tourist Office at No. 34 Markstraße), visiting 13km S (along the Bocksbeutelstraße or 'round bottle road') *Sommerhausen*, with its renaissance Schloß and town hall, medieval walls; *Marktbreit*, with lovely houses, a Black Tower, a town hall of 1579 and a parish church with an early gothic tower; and *Ochsenfurt*, approached across an old bridge, whose 14C parish church has a statue of St. Nicholas by Riemenschneider (and a high altar of 1612) and whose late gothic town hall (1487) has a clock with mechanical figures added in 1560. Next to the parish church is the mid 15C Michaelskapelle, formerly the cemetery chapel. There is a town museum in the Schloß. From **Kitzingen** continue 10km SE along the B8 to *Iphofen*, its 14th and 15C fortifications perfectly preserved with gates and towers. The mid 14C church of St. Veit houses sculpture by Riemenschneider; baroque town hall. Continue through the Steiger woods 14km to Markt Bibart, close by the 17C *Schwarzenberg Schloß* (by Elias Holl) and a further 17km to *Neustadt an der Aisch*. Again the town walls are preserved and a church of 1434, as well as a baroque town hall (1711) on which a model goat bleats the hour of noon.

18km further SE the route reaches *Langenzenn* (early 15C parish church, wall paintings c 1470, renaissance pulpit, Annunciation by Veit Stoß; cloisters of Augustinian monastery; baroque town hall rebuilt after a fire of 1727). 15km further on lies *Fürth*, with a population of 94,000, near where Adolphus Gustavus fought against Wallenstein in 1632 and where the first German railway (to Nuremberg) started in 1835 (gothic church of St. Michael; mid 19C town hall, modelled on the Palazzo Vecchio, Florence). 7km further the route reaches Nuremberg.

NUREMBERG; German NÜRNBERG (490,000 inhab.; alt. 310m). Situated on the River Pegnitz and the Rhine-Main-Danube canal (opened 1972) Nuremberg is the major city of Northern Bavaria and the second largest in Bavaria, was savagely damaged in WWII, though preserving most of its medieval fortifications and some old buildings. Much has been restored, and several fine new buildings (including a new wing of the National Museum, 1958–59) erected since the war. Seat of the Nuremberg-Erlangen University.

Main *railway station*: Bahnhofsplatz.

Main *post office*: Bahnhofsplatz.

Information Office: main railway station; Town Hall, Hauptmarkt; 5 Eilgustraße.

Trains to Bamberg, Bayreuth, Berlin, Frankfurt, Munich, Stuttgart.

Airport: N of the city, 5km from the city centre.

History. An 11C royal Schloß on the River Pegnitz was the basis of the city, which developed in the mid 11C, virtually as two separate settlements on either side of the river. Frederick II granted various charters, early 13C, and Nuremberg became a free imperial city and, in 1256, one of the Rhenish League of commercial cities. Nuremberg was fortified between c 1337 and 1440. The arts flourished in the late Middle Ages—the era of the Mastersingers. Nuremberg opted for the teaching of Luther in 1525 and declared for religious toleration in 1532. Goldsmiths flourished in the 16th and 17C, leading artists being Ludwig Krug, Melchior Bayer and Christoph and Wenzel Jamnitzer. Gustavus Adolphus occupied the city during the Thirty Years' War. In 1806 Nuremberg was incorporated into Bavaria. The first German railway line, 1835, ran between Nuremberg and Fürth, and the city took a lead in the industrialisation of the 19C. At the same time 19C Romanticism flourished (supremely expressed in Wagner's 'Mastersingers of Nuremberg'). The Nazis chose the city for a notoriously successful rally of 1926, and after WWII Nazi war criminals were tried here. Citizens have included the painter Albrecht Dürer (1471–1528), the sculptor Veit Stoß (1445–1533), the humanist Willibald Pirckheimer (1470–1530), Peter Henlein (who invented the pocket watch in 1500) and the mastersinger Hans Sachs (1494–1576). International organ concerts in July; concerts by the Nuremberg Symphony Orchestra, May to September. International Toy Fair.

At Bahnhofsplatz, in front of the main railway station, stands the old city arsenal courtyard, with the craftsmens' alleys (Craftsman's House). From here Königstraße leads past the 14C church of St. Martha (right), home of the mastersingers' school, 1578–1620. Left at the corner of Luitpoldstraße is the church of St. Clare (choir 1273; nave rebuilt early 15C). Further NW along Königstraße stands the imposing former granary or Mauthalle (by Hans Beheim, 1489–1502, later the city customs house, now a restaurant). Continue along Königstraße to reach Lorenzerplatz and the church of *St. Lorenz* (13C nave and 15C gothic choir; N tower finished 1332, S tower 1400; doorway and *rose window in W façade; stained glass in the choir, 1476–83, with tree of Jesse; *Veit Stoß's Annunciation and his crucifix over the high altar, 1517–18; a tabernacle by Adam Kraft, 1493–96; Haller altar, in Haller chapel, built for Ulrich V. Haller died 1456, with a painting of the Crucifixion, c 1450). N of this church is the fountain of virtue (Tugendbrunnen, by Benedikt Wurzelbauer, 1585–89). W of the church is the oldest house in Nuremberg, the Nassau Haus (cellar, ground floor and first floor 13C, upper storey c 1421; now a restaurant). Here in the early 15C Emperor Sigismund pledged his crown to the owner in return for 1500 guilders.

Königstraße (now pedestrianised) leads directly N across the Museums bridge (restored 1954; view to the W of the Fleischbrücke, 1598: a copy of the Rialto Bridge, Venice) over the river to the Hauptmarkt, with the Schöner Brunnen (Beautiful Fountain, nearly 20m high, by Heinrich Parler 1385–96; statues of seven Electors and nine Old Testament heroes). On the way can be seen to the right the Heiligen-Geist-Spital, built on two arches over a branch of the River Pegnitz (1331, enlarged 1487–1527, rebuilt after WWII; now containing an old people's home and a Weinstube; Crucifixion in the courtyard by Adam Kraft). N of this almshouse across Spitalbrücke in Hans-Sachs-Platz, is the Hans Sachs Memorial.

On the E side of the Hauptmarkt stands the 14C church of *Our Lady* (rebuilt after WWII). A clock (1509) over the main door, with mechanical figures representing the seven Electors and Emperor Charles IV, performs daily at 12.00, in commemoration of a bull issued by Charles IV in 1356 undertaking to hold his first Diet in Nuremberg. Interior: Tucher altar and works by Adam Kraft. On the N side stand both the New Town Hall (1954) and the Old Town Hall (by Jakob Wolff, 1616–22, incorporating two earlier buildings of 1332–40 and 1520; dungeons; superb W doorways). Behind the old town hall is the

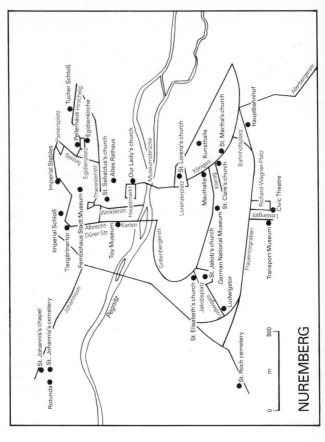

NUREMBERG

Gooseman Fountain (a peasant carrying two water-spouting geese, c 1555). NE, at No. 26 Winklerstraße, stands the **St. Sebaldus-Kirche** (1225–73): 79m-high towers finished late 15C; romanesque doorways in W façade; gothic choir 1379 with—on the outside—the Schreyer-Landauer tomb by Adam Kraft (1492). Interior: Madonna on N aisle pillar (c 1425); *tomb of St. Sebaldus in choir, by Peter Vischer and his sons (1508–09) which incorporates the saint's silver sarcophagus of 1397 (note P. Vischer's self-portrait, chiselling); 6000-pipe organ. N of this church stands the Fembohaus Stadt Museum (built for the merchant Philip Oyrl 1590–1600; open weekdays except Monday in summer, 10.00–17.00, closes in winter 13.00; see history of Nuremberg). W of the Fembohaus in Albrecht-Dürer-Platz is the Dürer Monument (1840, by D. Rauch, cast by D. Burgschmiet).

The bronze and silver shrine of St. Sebaldus, in St. Sebaldus-Kirche, made by Peter Vischer and his five sons between 1508 and 1519.

Go E along Theresienstraße from the Fembohaus. No. 21 is the only remaining baroque house in Nuremberg. Continue along this street and along Theresien-Inn to turn N into Egidienplatz. Here is the baroque *Egidienkirche*, 1711–18, incorporating the romanesque–gothic Eucharius-Kapelle, with the mid 14C Tetzel-kapellem, with the Landau tomb, by Adam Kraft c 1500. At the N side of Egidienplatz is the arcaded courtyard (1605) of the former Pellerhaus, destroyed in WWII and faithfully restored. The Pellerhaus now houses the State archives and library.

Walk E from here to find, in Hirschelgasse, the renaissance Tucher Schloß (1533–44; open weekdays, 14.00–16.00; Sunday, 10.00–11.00, renaissance and baroque furniture, paintings, including glass paintings from the workshop of Augustin Hirschvogel).

Return to Egidienplatz and walk W into Tetzelgasse; turn here NE to the junction with Paniersplatz, where you turn left to reach the Imperial Stables (1595, now a youth hostel; here too is the Graphische Sammlung, open weekdays, 09.00–16.00; prints and original drawings). Adjoining to the W are the five-cornered Tower (Fünfeckigen Turm, c 1040) and the 12C Imperial Schloß (open daily April–September, 09.00–17.00, October–March, 10.00–12.00 and 13.00–16.00; 12C chapel of St. Margaret; courtyard with well; panorama; 12C round Sinwellturm). From the five-cornered Tower Johannisstraße leads some distance W to the cemetery of St. Johannis, where Dürer, Pirckheimer, Stoß and Hans Sachs are buried. Here is the 14C St. Johannis chapel and a 1513 rotunda. Adam Kraft designed the stations of the cross (the present statues are copies) leading from here to the Tiergärtnertor, with its unspoiled medieval square and the 15C Pilatushaus (timbered upper stories—five of them—rising from a red-sandstone ground floor; statue of St. George on the corner).

Directly S is the 15C *Albrecht Dürer's House*, the artist's home from 1509 till his death, now containing an exhibition devoted to him (39 Albrecht-Dürer-Straße; open daily save Monday, 10.00–16.00). The line of the city walls leads SW to the Neu Tor. These walls, built in the 14C and 15C with 80 towers, are the third that have surrounded the city. From Dürer's House follow Albrecht-Dürer-Straße S into Weinmarkt, where No. 2 is a gothic house dating from the 14th and 15Cs. Continue S to the Toy Museum (13 Karsltraße, in a 17C building; open save Monday 10.00 –17.00, Wednesday–21.00). SW of the Toy Museum is the former wine depot, the Weinstadel.

From here Henkersteg leads SW across the river to the Unschlitthaus ('Tallow House', 1491), another former granary. Follow Grillenberger-Straße SW to reach Karl-Kappenstraße, where you turn left to reach the neo-classical church of St. Elisabeth, once the church of the Teutonic knights (part 18C, by the younger Neumann, part 19C). This church is directly N of Jakobsplatz, reached by way of Ludwigstraße, and the 14C gothic church of St. Jakob. Follow Ludwigstraße SW to Ludwigstor, passing through the gate in the city walls to turn right to reach the Planetarium. S of the Planetarium is the St. Roch cemetery.

Frauentorgraben leads E from Ludwigstor to the Civic Theatre (seating 900) in Richard-Wagner-Platz. Here too is the opera house (seating 1100). Lessingstraße leads due S to the Transport Museum

(Verkehrsmuseum, No. 6 Lessingstraße; open weekdays, 10.00–17.00, October–March only to 16.00; archives etc. of the first German railway; model railway, stamp collection).

OTHER MUSEUMS: *German National Museum (1 Kornmarkt, in former Carthusian monastery buildings), based on the mid 19C collection of Hans von Aufseß (open Tuesday–Saturday, 09.00–16.00, Thursday also 20.00–21.00; paintings, sculpture, music, costume). The 'Mensch und Natur' Museum (4 Gewerbenmuseumsplatz; open weekdays save Wednesday, 10.00–17.00, Saturday, 09.00 –12.00; geology, prehistory). Kunsthalle (32 Lorenzerstraße, open daily save Monday, 10.00–17.00, Wednesday also to 21.00; exhibitions of modern art). The Industrial Museum (45 Guntherstraße, to open 1986).

OTHER SIGHTS: Meistersingerhalle (in Luitpoldhain, 1963) and Congress hall. The Sports Stadium. Trödelmarkt (i.e. junk market), on an island where the river divides (14C 'Man's Guilt Tower'). The Zoo (dolphinarium and restaurant), 4400m E of the city along Bahnhofstraße. Harbour of the Rhine-Main-Danube-Canal. 5km SW of Nuremberg.

Leave Nuremberg by the Allersbergerstraße to reach after 9km a brief stretch of motorway as far as Feucht. Continue on the B8 to *Neumarkt in der Oberpfalz* (23km), much destroyed in WW11 and now restored: ruined 16C Schloß Wolfstein; renaissance Schloß; 15C sandstone gothic church of Maria Himmelfahrt, built by Count Johann von Wittelsbach early 15C, with a baroque nave of 1702 and the red marble tomb of Count Otto II (died 1499); parish church of St. Johannes, 1404 to mid 15C; pilgrimage church of Mariahilfberg (1718; 585m high). For the rest of the 64km route to Regensburg see Rte 1A.

Two routes lead from **Regensburg** to **Passau**. The motorway A3 leads 58 km E to Bogen (a town known in the 8C) and another 30km to *Deggendorf* (just N of the motorway). The town hall of 1535 is in the Luitpoldstraße; two fountains (16C and 20C) in the Marktplatz; mid 14C church to the S of the Marktplatz (baroque tower by J.B. Gunetzrhainer and J.M. Fischer, 1727). Further S is the parish church of Maria Himmelfahrt, 17C, with 19C restored façade (high altar by M. Seybold, 1749); nearby the 15C Wasserkapelle. Local history museum in the Oberer Stadtplatz (open Monday–Friday, 19.00–12.00, 14.00–16.00; Sunday, 09.00–12.00). From Deggendorf the motorway continues through Hengersberg for 30km to Passau.

The route by the B8 leads after 35km to *Straubing*. 16km SE of Straubing is *Plattling* (its romanesque church of St. Jakob has a gothic choir). The road now leads SE by way of *Osterhofen* (after 19km), where Benedictine monks founded a monastery in the 8C and J.M. Fischer built part of the present church) to picturesque *Vilshofen* (after 13km; gateway of 1642; baroque church of St. John the Baptist, 1803, with an early 18C high altar and side altars; and an Italian baroque church of Mariahilf) to **Passau** (after 23km).

Passau (32,000 inhab.; alt. 320m) stands at the confluence of the Danube, Ilz and Inn, a city founded by the Celts in the 1C BC. The city was next to a Roman camp and then became the seat of a bishop in the 5C. The treaty of Passau in 1552 was a milestone in the reconciliation of Protestants and Catholics. A tour of Passau, beginning on the banks of the Inn, would encompass (in Innstraße) the 14C church of St. Nikolaus, with stuccoes and frescoes c 1720. NW of this church is the Nibelungenhalle (in Neuburgerstraße), built in 1935 as an exhibition hall and seating 6000 people. Neuburgerstraße joins Nikolastraße, where stands the Heiliggeistkirche (14C, enlarged 1442, much restored in the 19C). To the NW stands the formerly Franciscan Votivskirche.

Follow Ludwigstraße NE to find remains of the old city walls, tracing their origin back to the Romans. Directly E stands the church of St. Paul (rebuilt 1678 after a fire, with 20C stucco decoration). Immediately E is the Domplatz, dominated by a statue of King Maximilian I (1824). The square is bordered by the Lambergpalais rebuilt 1724 (where the 1552 treaty was signed), the 16th and 17C cathedral canonry, the renaissance Herberstainpalais, and the ****Cathedral of St. Stephan**. The cathedral was founded in the 14C, but only its choir (by Hans Krumenauer, 1407–1520) is gothic, for—as a result of a conflagration of 1662—the rest is late 17C baroque, by the Italian Carlo Lurago, (1677; stucco decoration by Giovanni Battista Carlone, 1677–86; domes frescoed by Carpoforo Tencalla of Lugano, 1679–84; pulpit of 1722; high altar by Josef Henselmann, 1953). Its tower (a pastiche of that of Salzburg Cathedral) was finished 1896. The cathedral possesses the largest organ in the world (230 stops, 17,000 pipes; recitals May–October on weekdays, 12.00–12.30; Thursday, 19.30–20.00). In the cloister is the mid 15C *tomb of Heinrich von Ortenburg.

The former bishops' palace is S of the cathedral. In Residenzplatz (E) is the present half baroque, half rococo *Bishops' Palace*, built 1771, with a superb staircase. NE stands the town hall (mostly late 19C, with a late gothic doorway of 1683). From here walk SE to St. Michael-Kirche (1678; by G.B. Carlone), formerly the church of the Jesuit college of 1664, which is now a high school and theological college. Now follow the lanes to the Niedernburg convent (burial place of Gisela, Queen of Hungary, died 1060, memorial of the 15C). Cross the Luitpold bridge to the N to reach the late gothic Salvatorkirche (1478), set into the hillside on the site of a former synagogue, and the Oberhaus fortress, 408m high (a 15-minute walk), housing a gothic chapel (later reordered in the baroque style), the city art gallery, and fireman's museum (open March–October, 09.00–17.00, except Monday). Connected to it by a rampart is the 14C Veste Niederhaus.

7 Würzburg to Hof by way of Bamberg and Coburg

Total distance 205km. Würzburg—B22 45km **Ebrach.**—45km **Bamberg.**—B4 34km **Coburg.**—B303 30km *Kronach.*—B173 51km **Hof**.

Leave **Würzburg** by the Nünrbergerstraße and take the B22 for 18km as far as *Dettelbach* (15C walls, with 36 towers; late gothic town hall; 16th and 17C pilgrims' church), continuing another 27km into the *Steigerwald* to **Ebrach**. Here is one of the best preserved monastic churches in the region, with a romanesque chapel of St. Michael, early gothic features and a classical interior by M. Bossi (alabaster Barnardus altar by V. Dümpel, 1626; sacristy by J.L. Brenno, 1696). Baroque monastic buildings by J.L. Dientzenhofer and J. Greising. After 22km the route reaches Unterneuses, 9km S of which is **Schloß Pommersfelden* (by J.L. Dientzenhofer, M. von Welsch and J.L. von Hildebrandt of Vienna. Inside, trompe l'oeil painting by J.R. Byss (1718) and a painting by J.F. Rottmayr (1717). The picture gallery houses works by Rubens, Titian, Cranach and Breughel (open April–October, 08.00–12.00, 14.00–17.00, except Monday).

After another 8km the route reaches **Bamberg** (see Rte 8). 4km N of Bamberg along the B4 lies *Hallstadt*, a modern industrial town wih a late gothic church, a renaissance town hall and a baroque government building. At *Breitengüßbach* the road meets the B173 (which leads directly NE to Hof by way of Unterleiterbach with its Schloß). From here the B4 runs N for 38km to **Coburg**.

*Coburg (42,000 inhab.; alt. 300m), a former capital of Saxe-Coburg, nestles under its 460m-high Schloß, built 14–16C. Here Luther took refuge in 1530 during the Diet of Augsburg. Today it displays many Luther memorabilia, 16th and 17C sleighs and carriages, arms and armour, Cranach paintings; Luther chapel (open April–October, 09.30–12.00, 14.00–16.00, save Monday; winter, 14.00–15.30; the art gallery stays open until 17.00). In the Marktplatz is a statue of Queen Victoria's consort Albert, who was born here, and the late 16C Stadthaus, with its two corner towers and five rich gables; the late gothic Moritzkirche has a portal with carvings of Adam and Eve and the tomb of Duke Johann Friedrich (1509); the secondary school (1605) has a statue of its founder, Duke Johann Casimir (1586–1633); the Ehrenburg, rebuilt 1816– 38, has a huge library, a giants' gallery, a church and portrait gallery (open except Mondays, 09.00–12.00 and 13.00–16.00). In its park a natural history museum and 8000 species of bird. The Congress Hall was built 1962.

Continue E along the B303 by way of Neustadt bei Coburg and *Mitwitz* (early 16C Schloß with a baroque Oberes Schloß) to *Kronach* (36km), Lucas Cranach the Elder's birthplace. The parish church is 15C; the Rathaus of 1583 has three works by Cranach; the Rosenberg Schloß dominates the town. The B173 now runs 43km NE to **Hof** through the Franconian woods and past the 795m-high *Döbranberg* (reached by foot from Schwarzenbach in 20 minutes). Hof is the most important industrial town (textiles) in Upper Franconia. It has 11–13C church of St. Lorenz (15C Hertnid altar; 16C wooden cross); a 13C twin-towered church of St. Michael (much restored in the 19C); a 13C Spitalkirche, neo-gothic exterior 1836, restored 20C (late gothic altarpiece; late 17C ceiling painting by H.A. Löhe); Martin-Luther-Kirche by R. Reissinger, (1936); a city theatre; the Theresienpark, with its botanical garden; swimming pools; and a symphony orchestra. The Information Office is in the town hall (16C; restored 1823).

8   Bamberg to Lindau by way of Nuremberg and Augsburg

Total distance 366km. **Bamberg**—A73 25km *Forcheim.*—15km **Erlangen.**—19km *Nuremberg.*—A2 16km *Schwabach.*—31km *Weißenburg.*—40km *Donauwürth.*—36km *Augsburg.*—B17 36km *Landsberg.*—B12 9km *Buchloe.*—59km **Ottobeuren.**—9km **Memmingen.**—29km *Leutkirch.*—42km **Lindau.**

BAMBERG (74,000 inhab.; alt. 262m), a city built on seven hills. The River Regnitz on its way to the River Main divides into two at Bamberg, embracing the old burgers' city, which developed from the 12C. The older ecclesiastical city stands on the left bank of the river. A market was founded between the two branches of the Regnitz c 1100.

Today Bamberg also derives trade by way of the Rhine-Main-Danube Canal (the harbour, with its grain elevators, was opened 1962). The musician and writer E.T.A. Hoffmann lived here from 1809–1813. A Bamberg speciality is beer brewed from smoked malt (Rauchbier). Bamberg sponsors a celebrated symphony orchestra.

Main *railway station*, Luitpoldstraße.

Information Office: at main railway station and at No. 16 Hauptwachstraße.

Trains and buses to Coburg, Erlangen, Nuremberg, Würzburg.

History. The Badenbergs established themselves here sometime before the 10C. Their revolt against the Carolingians led to the confiscation of their lands. Duke Henry the Quarrelsome of Bavaria took over their Schloß in 973, and under his son, the Emperor Henry II, the bishopric was set up in 1007. Henry II also founded the cathedral and made the Schloß into a royal palace. In the Middle Ages churchmen and burgers frequently quarrelled, especially over the former's claim to taxes. The city remained predominantly Catholic during the Reformation. Bamberg sided with the Catholic League in the Thirty Years' War and suffered at the hands of the Swedes in 1632. The city was attacked by the Prussians in the Seven Years' War. In the 18C two Prince-Bishops—Lothar Franz and Friedrich Carl von Schönborn—were largely responsible for the baroque richness of the city, deploying the brilliant brothers Georg and J.L. Dientzenhofer. A university, which developed in the mid 18C out of the Jesuit seminary, was closed down in 1803. In 1818 the bishops were elevated to archbishops. Happily, damage during WWII was remarkably slight. Bamberg became a university city again in 1979.

Follow Luitpoldstraße SW from the main railway station, turning left at Königstraße to find (left), in Theuerstraße, the church of St. Gangolf. From here walk SE to the Protestant Erlöserkirche, an octagonal church with a free-standing tower, by Bestelmeyer, 1930. Walk along Kunigundendamm NW along the river bank, crossing the river at Luitpoldbrücke, and then turning right along the river to reach Hauptwachstraße. Hauptwachstraße leads SW into Maximiliansplatz, with the Neus Rathaus (1733–36).

SW from this town hall, along Grüner Markt, is the baroque church of St. Martin (the Jesuit church, 1689–91, partly by Georg Dientzen-

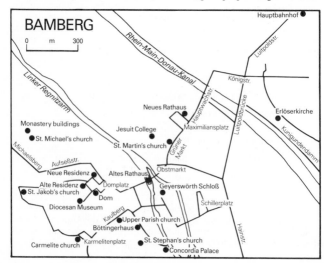

hofer). Behind is the former Jesuit College, now the university faculty of theology. Continue as far as the Obstmarkt. Cross into Karolinenstraße. Where Karolinenstraße crosses the river (by the Obere Brücke, 1453–56) stands the old town hall (by J.J.M. Küchel, 1744–56). The area around the old town hall, with its fishermen's houses, is known as Little Venice. S of the Old Town Hall stands the former palace of the prince-bishops, the Geyerswörth Schloß (1585–86). From the Schloß Geyerswörthstraße leads SE. Turn right to cross the other arm of the River Regnitz at Bischofsmühlbrücke, leading into Judenstraße, along which stands the *Böttingerhaus*, a baroque palace in the Venetian style (1707–13), built for the rich Privy Councillor Böttinger. Judenstraße runs SE into Concordiastraße, at the end of which stands the baroque Concordia Palace (1716–22), Privy Councillor Böttinger's second palace in Bamberg.

Walk back along Concordiastraße to turn almost immediately W and reach Stephansberg and the church of *St. Stephan* (1020; with baroque reordering; late romanesque–early gothic towers), now the chief Protestant church of Bamberg). NW of St. Stephan, on the Kaulberg, stands the 14C upper parish *church*: choir by Parler; gothic ambulatory; baroque reordering of the rest of the interior; representation of the Madonna on high altar, 1320; font with carvings of seven sacraments (1520); 'Marriage doorway' on N side, with the Apotheosis of Mary and wise and foolish Virgins c 1330. Close by is the baroque courtyard by M. Küchel of Ebrach monastery. From here Kaulberg leads S to Karmelitenplatz and the Carmelite church, which belonged to the Benedictines until 1553: a romanesque building, reordered in the baroque style (façade by J.L. Dientzenhofer and others); 14C transept with fine capitals. From here take the street named Sutte NW to reach the 12C St. Jakob's Church, romanesque with a baroque façade. Obere Karolinenstraße leads from this church E to the DOMPLATZ. No. 5 Obere Karolinenstraße is the baroque archbishop's palace (entrance to inner courtyard from 7 Domstraße).

Dominating the Domplatz is the ****Cathedral** (after a fire of 1081 had destroyed the building founded by Henry II, Bishop Otto rebuilt the cathedral, which was again burnt down in 1185; the third cathedral was begun early 13C): romanesque E chancel, 1215–20; on the Prince's doorway (Fürstenportal), N side, with its ten slender receding pillars and arches, is a Last Judgment, apostles and prophets; on Marienporte, on N side of choir, sculpture c 1210, including Apostles' frieze; Adam's doorway, S side of the choir, from which statues of Adam, Eve, St. Peter, St. Stephen, Henry II and his wife Kunigunde, c 1235, have been removed to the Diocesan Museum (see below); cloisters 1457; the stone terrace at the E end (the 'Domkranz') added 1508–11, for the exhibition of the cathedral's relics; spires to towers added by J.M. Küchel, 1766–68. INTERIOR (restored 1828–37 by K. Rupprecht, K.A. von Heideloff and F. Gärtner; second restoration 1969–74): *tomb of Henry II and Kunigunde in front of choir, by Tilman Riemenschneider, begun 1499 (carvings depicting the emperor's death, the weighing of his soul, St. Benedict miraculously removing his gall-stones, Kunigunde dismissing dishonest servants and her ordeal by fire, suspected of adultery); *Bamberg Rider, c 1240; tomb of Frederick I von Hohenlohe, by the Master of Wolfskehl (like Riemenschneider, from Würzburg) c 1352; late romanesque stone sculptures of apostles and prophets on the choir screen, by the Master of the Georgenchor, with statues of the church and the Jewish synagogue (a blindfolded woman) beside the apostles and statues of

Mary and Elizabeth between the prophets; Crucifixion group over
neo-romanesque altar, by the Frankfurt artist Justus Glesker, 1650;
14C choir stalls (restored 1835–38); marble tomb of Pope Clement II
(died 1047, former Bishop of Bamberg) in the W choir, dated c 1450,
with reliefs depicting the pope's death and the four virtues
(Fortitude, Prudence, Justice, Temperance); late gothic Gattendorf
altar in N aisle, third altar from the E; further W in N aisle are
reliquary busts of Henry II and Kunigunde, and statues of St.
Lawrence, by H. Nussbaum c 1500, and St. Sebastian, from
Riemenschneider's workshop; in chapel of the Blessed Sacrament,
S aisle, painting of heaven enclosed in a rosary, attributed to Lucas
Cranach, c 1520; *Christmas Altar by Veit Stoß, 1520–24, against
W wall of S transept. Modern works: Stations of the cross in S aisle
by F. Baumhauer (1921); in apse painting of Christ with SS. Peter
and George, by K. Caspar (1928); modern altar, with bronze scenes
from the life of Christ, by Klaus Backmund (1974); four manual
organs (77 registers), by Rieger and Co. (1976), with sculptures by
Backmund. Crypt (early gothic, extended mid 15C) containing the
sarcophagus   of   Konrad   III,   (died   1153),   bronze   slabs
commemorating the cathedral canons, and three altars: triptych
altar with Apostles, by H. Nussbaum c 1500; altar with crucifix, by
F. Theiler (1675; secondary figures by T. Buscher, 1917); war
memorial altar, by G. Busch (1921).

On the N side of the Domplatz stands the baroque ***Neue
Residenz** with a rose garden in its courtyard; rococo pavilion (by
Johann Leonhard Dientzenhofer, 1695–1704, with 24 apartments,
including the Kaisersaal; now an art gallery; open 09.00–12.00 and
13.30–17.00, closes 16.00 from October–March, paintings by Lucas
Cranach the Elder and Hans Baldung Grien, baroque furniture,
Gobelin tapestries). On the W side of the Domplatz stands the
renaissance ***Alte Residenz** (1571–76; formerly the episcopal
palace; now the Historical Museum). The Domplatz also houses the
canons' residences (Domherrenhöfe), decorated with their coats of
arms, and the chapterhouse by Balthasar Neumann, 1730–33, now
the Diocesan Museum (open weekdays, 10.00–12.00 and 14.20–
18.00; Saturday and Sunday, 10.00–13.00: statues from cathedral,
vestments, stained glass, baroque art). No. 8 Domplatz is the
National Library, with 3400 incunabula (open weekdays, 09.00–
12.00 and 14.00–17.30, Saturday, 09.00–12.00).

A stiff walk from here leads W along Aufseßstraße (to the N of
the cathedral) and then NW along Michaelsberg up to the former
Benedictine abbey (now an old people's home) of Michaelsberg,
founded 1009, with the abbey church of *St. Michael*, with twin
gothic towers and pointed spires (finished 1610): 17C baroque
façade, approached by a magnificent flight of steps (with balustrade, 1723); gothic tomb of St. Otto (Bishop of Bamberg 1102–39);
carving of Man of Sorrows (c 1350); vaulted ceiling and flower
paintings c 1610; renaissance wall memorial to Johann Philipp von
Gebsattel (died 1609), by Michael Kern; statue of grieving Virgin
Mary, c 1720; choir stalls, by F.A.T. Böhm, Servatius Brickhard and
others c 1726; baroque statues of Henry II and Kunigunde, by Peter
Benkert (1726); *rococo pulpit by G.A. Reuß, (1751); sepulchral
chapel on S side, with painted Dance of Death and rococo stucco
work; monastery buildings by J.L. Dientzenhofer (1696–1702), and
by Balthasar Neumann (1742); panorama of the city. Follow St.
Getreu-Straße W from here to the baroque church of St. Getreu

(now a clinic for nervous diseases): Entombment of Christ, c 1500; eight late gothic panels depicting the Passion.

OTHER MUSEUMS: National Archives, 39 Hainstraße (open weekdays, 08.00–18.15, Wednesday until 20.00, Friday until 15.00). Natural History Museum, 2 Fleischstraße (open Friday, 14.00–18.00).

OTHER SIGHTS: Schillerplatz houses both the Municipal Theatre and (at No. 26) the house in which E.T.A. Hoffmann lived (open weekdays, 16.30–17.30, Saturday–Sunday, 09.30–10.30: here the novelist composed his 'Golden Pot'). City Stadium and cycle track in the Volkspark.

Altenburg, 3km SW, 387m-high Schloß; panorama of Bamberg.

The A73 leads SE from Bamberg and travels through the Franconian basin close by the River Regnitz and the Ludwig Canal, which joined the Main to the Danube in 1855. *Forchheim* (29,000 inhab.; alt. 265m) lies 25km SE. Forchheim was a Carolingian palatinate in the 9C and the seat of several imperial diets. Its gothic parish church of *St. Martin* has inside eight 15C altar carvings of the passion and the life of the patron; a dome was added in 1670. Close by stands the moated *Pfalz* (1353–83), built chiefly by Lampert von Brunn and formerly an episcopal palace, with two frescoed rooms, one by the Parler family, c 1370, the other by Jakob Ziegler, 1559. It is now a museum of local history and art (modern works by Georg Mayer-Franken, 1870–1926; open May–October, 10.00–12.30, 14.00–16.30, save Monday). The half-timbered town hall and many burgers' houses, especially in the Marktplatz, date from the 14C to the 16C. From the Pfalz, the nearby Saltertum leads to the renaissance and baroque fortifications. NE of Forchheim beer cellars have been cut into the rocks.

15km S lies *Erlangen** (100,000 inhab.; alt. 280m), a city developed by Huguenot refugees, sheltered by the Margrave Christian Ernst of Kulmbach-Bayreuth, who laid out the new baroque town, to plans by Johann Moritz Richter, after the Revocation of the Edict of Nantes (see the Huguenot fountain, 1706, in the Schloß garden). Erlangen is first mentioned in 1002 and by 1017 belonged to the bishops of Bamberg. Emperor Karl IV granted it city rights in the 14C—the Alstadt dates from this period. In 1440 the city passed into the hands of the Margraves. Erlangen became part of Prussia in 1791 and part of Bavaria in 1810. Johann Gottlieb Fichte (1805–06) and Ludwig Feuerbach (1828) taught at the university. The physicist Georg Ohm (1789–1854) was born here and the city, which is the HQ of Siemens and Co., still prospers on electronics and electrical engineering. Information Office at No. 1 Rathausplatz.

Churches include the 13C SS. Peter and Paul, with its huge tower and baroque interior (ceiling painted by Leinberger); the church of St. Martin, the oldest church in the city; the church of St. Xystus (late gothic, reordered in the baroque style); the 13C Kriegenbrunn church (housing late gothic frescoes); and the former Dominican monastery church of St. Matthew (romanesque porch). Its university, founded 1743, now has its administration in the Schloß (1700–04; G. von Gerdeler). The Schloß garden has an orangery by the same architect (1706–08), and at the NE corner the oldest baroque theatre still in use in West Germany (built for Margrave Friedrich Wilhem, 1517–19, refurbished by the Venetian G.P. Gasperi, 1742). In the Marktplatz is the Palais Sturrerheim (1730), now the city library. The town hall (Martin-Luther-Platz, in the Altstadt) now houses the city museum (open Monday–Friday, 08.00–12.00; Sunday, 10.00–13.00, and some afternoons). The University has noted anthropological, mineralogical and zoological collections, as well as an Art Gallery (self-portraits by Grünewald and Dürer, open Monday–Friday, 09.30–12.00, 14.00–16.00).

19km S of Erlangen is **Nuremberg** (see Rte 6). Leave Nuremberg by the Schweinauer Hauptstraße and travel 16km S along the B2 to *Schwabach*, a town of 35,000 inhab., specialising in tobacco-growing and work with gold leaf, with a late gothic parish church (1469–95), half-timbered houses, a baroque fountain of 1716 and a town hall of 1509. The route after 12km passes through *Roth bei Nürnberg* at the confluence of the Roth, the Rednitz and the Aurach, (16C Schloß Ratibor, with another hunting Schloß on a peak outside the town) as far as Ellingen (rococo town hall; Schloß, once belonging to the Teutonic knights and rebuilt by Franz Keller, 1718–25, its church decorated by C.D. Asam; remnants of fortifications. *Weißenburg*, 3km S, was formerly a free imperial city. It boasts a late gothic town hall, (1476; the tower dates from 1567), a Roman fort and baths, an open-air theatre, the church of St. Andreas (finished 1520 with three altars c 1500), and medieval *fortifications (with 32 inhabited towers, and the especially fine 14C Spital and Ellinger Gates). Nearby, on its 630m peak, stands the 16C Schloß Wülzburg, built for the Margrave von Ansbach by G. and B. Bernwart (inside is the deepest rock well in West Germany). An important *Roman Museum* (No. 3 Martin-Luther-Platz).

The route now leads 40km S to *Donauwürth* (see Rte 1B) and 36km S to **Augsburg** (see Rte 3). Continue S along the B17 for 38km to *Landsberg* (see Rte 3). Continue W for 9km along the B12 to *Buchloe* (parish church built 1400, reordered c 1700, with a rosary picture by Matthias Kager 1626, and the administration centre of the diocese of Augsburg, in a bulding by J.G. Fischer, 1729). From here the B12 runs S for 18km to Kaufbeuren. The older road runs slightly E of this road to **Ketterschwang** (14km), with its mid 18C rococo parish church by Joseph Fischer, wall and roof painting by Johannes Baptist Enderle.

The B18 leads 20km W from Buchloe to *Mindelheim*. En route a brief diversion S leads to *Bad Wörifsheim*, where the parish priest Sebastian Kneipp (1821–97) so developed thermal treatment (hot and cold baths, massages, mud packs, etc.) that today here are 7500 beds for those seeking cures, and spa rooms (1905; modernised 1954). The late gothic church was enriched by Franz Beer (1722), with stucco work by Domenikus Zimmermann. *Mindelheim* is dominated by *Schloß Mindelsburg* (seat of the legendary knight Georg von Fundsberg, 1473–1528, who formed the mercenary Landsknechte in the 16C). The 13C Jesuit church was later reordered in the baroque style (Madonna of 1670 inside). See also the Liebfraukirche of 1510. Gates and towers, c 1400, still surround the town.

Leave the B18 and travel WSW for 10km to reach *Mussenhausen*, with its mid 18C pilgrims' church of Our Lady of Mount Carmel (by Thomas Natterer, ceiling fresco by J.B. Enderle). After 15km the road reaches **Ottobeuren**, another Kneipp health resort. Its Benedictine *abbey, founded 764, was rebuilt 1711–31, most of it the achievement of J.M. Fischer; the monastic buildings are complex and rich (frescoes in the Benedictuskapelle and the Abtkapelle (by the Venetian J. Amigoni). J.M. Fischer built its baroque church (1737–96; with two 86m-high towers; 12C cross over the tabernacle; choir stalls by Martin Hermann, 1760; frescoes Amigoni, J.J. Zeiller and J.B. Zimmermann;

stucco work by J.M. Feuchtmayr; *baroque organ by Carl Riepp, 1756–66). The abbey is open weekdays, 10.00–12.00, 14.00–17.00; Sundays and holidays, 10.00–12.00, 13.00– 17.00; November–March, 14.00–17.00).

The Benedictine monastery church at Ottobeuren, the work of J.M. Fischer (1737–96), with stucco work by J.M. Feuchtmayr and frescoes by J.J. Zeiller.

9km W is **Memmingen** (38,000 inhab.; alt. 601m). Founded in the mid 13C by Duke Welf VI, it became a free town in 1268 and flourished in the 14th and 15C, trading with France, Spain and Flanders, and in the 16C with India and Venezuela. Today the town's industries include foam rubber, textiles, machinery and cosmetics.

Walled with towers, Memmingen has a tax-collection building of 1495; a town hall of 1589 with a façade of 1765; wall paintings, c 1470, in the Liebfrauenkirche; the Kinderlehr church, with its late gothic courtyard; and the gothic church of St. Martin (by M. Böblinger, 1499; choir stalls of 1506 by H. Stark and H. Dapratzhauser). The Sieben-dächerhaus (1601), built by tanners, has seven overlapping roofs. Modern churches are St. Joseph by (Michael Kurz and Thomas Wechs, 1927– 30, and Maria Himmelfahrt by Thomas Wechs, 1956), with sculpture by Josef Henselmann and glass by Franz Nagel. The City Museum (No. 8 Zangmeisterstraße) is housed in a rococo palace by Benedikt von Herman, 1766 (open Tuesday–Friday and Sunday, 10.00–12.00, 14.00–16.00). After 1km follow the signs 9km for the Maria Steinbach pilgrims' church (by D. Zimmermann, enriched by Franz Xavier Feuchtmayr).

20km SE is *Leutkirch* at the heart of the Württemberg Allgäu and a centre of winter sports. Its parish church of St. Martin is gothic (1514), the arcaded town hall is baroque (1739–41; with a stuccoed room by Johann Schütz), the Marktplatz is surrounded by burgers' houses and part of the old fortifications and towers have been preserved. From here the Rte reaches the health resort of *Wangen* after 23km (24,500 inhab.; alt. 402m), at the centre of which is a charming old town, with walls and towers and a baroque town hall of 1721.

Follow the B18 a further 19km to **Lindau** on Lake Constance (26,500 inhab.; alt. 402m). Fishermen established the town in the late 8C and Count Adalbert of Rhaetia established a Benedictine convent here in 810. Fortified as a free imperial town in the 13C, Lindau profited from the trade route into Italy. It became briefly Austrian in 1804 and Bavarian the following year. Today it is a thriving tourist resort. Close by are the springs of *Bad Schachen*, renowned since 1474. Railways connect with Singen and Bregenz, ships with Constance, Bregenz and Rorschach, and buses with Bregenz, Wangen and Friedrichshafen. Tourist Information Offices are opposite and inside the main railway station.

Leave the main railway station and walk NE along Hefenplatz to the Mang tower, part of the old early 13C fortifications. Towards the harbour can be seen the 13C lighthouse and the 6m-high Bavarian lion, (by Johann von Halbig) placed on the Löwenmole in the 19C. In the distance are the Voralberg and Appenzeller Alps. Continue as far as the Reichsplatz, with the Altes Rathaus (1422–46), late gothic, with renaissance elements, seat of an Imperial Diet in 1496. An open-air staircase climbs to its upper storey. The paintings on the façade were made in the 1970s to designs by Josef Widmann. Nearby, at No. 3 Bismarckstraße, is the baroque new town hall (1706–17). In Reichsplatz is the Lindavia fountain of 1884. Follow Ludwigstraße E to find the theatre, which stands on the foundations of a 13C church (and has been, amongst other things, an arsenal and a gaol). Continue NE along Fischergasse to find first the Catholic church of St. Maria (a baroque building by Johann Caspar Bagnato, 1748–51; stucco work mostly renewed 1925) and next the gothic Protestant church of St. Stephan (reordered in the baroque style in the early 1780s). The former monastery buildings connected with St. Maria (1730–36) are now the offices of the town council. N is the Heiden wall, the remains of a Carolingian watch-tower, to the E of which are the town gardens.

Return to the two churches of St. Stephan and St. Maria and continue W across the Marktplatz to find the *Haus zum Cavazzen*, a baroque building of 1729 that now houses the town museum (open Tuesday–Saturday, 09.00–12.00, 14.00–17.00; Sunday, 10.00– 12.00). This area is now a pedestrianised zone with charming alleyways and (at No. 8 Lingg-Straße the home of the poet Hermann von Lingg (1820–1905). Walk W along Maximilianstraße and N along Zeppelinstraße to reach the oldest church in Lindau, *St. Peter*, largely early 11C, which has the only surviving wall painting (the 'Lindau Passion') by Hans Holbein the Elder.

9   Bamberg to Frankfurt am Main along the river Main

Total distance 178km. **Bamberg**—B26 61km **Schweinfurt**.—38km *Karlstadt*.—52km **Aschaffenburg**.—B8 27km **Frankfurt**.

Leave **Bamberg** (see Rte 8) by the Schweinfurter Straße and take the B26 for 19km W to *Eltmann* on the left bank of the Main, a centre of quarrying, overlooked by the 13C Wallburg, with a 19C parish church by Leo von Klenze. 2km further on is *Ebelsbach*, with a Schloß (1564–69), and after 6km the route reaches the walled *Zeil am Main*, with a pilgrims' church on the peak of the Käppelsberg, making a detour en route to Balthasar Neumann's pilgrims' church (1755) of *Maria Limbach*. The route now passes through *Haßfurt* (after 9km), another walled town of half-timbered buildings, the 14C Knights Chapel (with 300 knightly coats of arms inside and outside) and a late gothic parish church containing work by Riemenschneider and his assistants. Continue along the B26, passing the Schlößer at *Untertheres* and *Obertheres* (this Schloß formerly a Benedictine monastery, with a baroque chapel and a rococo parsonage) and through the Steiger woods by way of *Mainberg* (overlooked by a privately owned Schloß) to Schweinfurt (29km).

*Schweinfurt (60,000 inhab.; alt. 218m), which appears in history c 900 as the seat of a Margrave and from 1254–1802 was a free imperial city, today makes ball-bearings and engines and stands on the junctions of the Kassel–Würzburg and Frankfurt–Nuremberg motorways. Much was destroyed in WW11. The town hall of 1572 (by Nicholas Hoffmann) has been well restored. The choir of the gothic St. Johann-Kirche dates from 1554–62, the rest incorporating a romanesque doorway, a transept c 1225 and a nave that is partly late 13C. The former secondary school (No. 12 Martin-Luther-Platz) which dates from the early 1580s, now houses a museum (irregular opening times), partly devoted to the local poet Friedrich Rückert (1788–1866). The theatre (at No. 2 Rossbrunnstraße) was built in 1966. There is a Rückert memorial in the Marktplatz, and the modern Friedrich-Rückert building houses the city library. Post-war buildings include the Catholic church of St. Kilian by Hans Schädel and the Protestant church of the Resurrection by Olav Gulbransson and Wilhelm Wirth.

From here the River Main winds S to Würzburg. Continue W for 9km to *Schloß Werneck*, built by Balthasar Neumann, 1733–45, as a summer retreat for the prince-bishops of Würzburg. 9km further W is the pilgrims' church of Maria Sondheim (containing a baroque ceiling painting depicting the battle of Lepanto). The route continues W to reach after 20km *Karlstadt* (at a junction with the B27, which follows the River Main S for 24km to **Würzburg**, see Rte 5A. Karlstadt is a modern industrial town with a walled inner quarter containing the late gothic church of *St. Andreas* (housing work by Riemenschneider and a romanesque Christ) and a town hall of 1442 (renaissance hall). Continue along the B26 15km W to *Steinbach*, with a Schloß of 1725, much damaged in 1945, and a parish church of the same date, both by B. Neumann. The road crosses the Main again and after 4km reaches

Lohr, a town specialising in glass-making and ironworks, with fine houses in the Altsadt, the gothic church of St. Michael (with 15th and 16C tombs), a town hall of 1601 and a Schloß of 1561–1611, housing an interesting museum of local arts (open Tuesday—Saturday, 10.00–12.00, 14.00–16.00; Sunday and holidays, 10.00–13.00).

After travelling 35km W (through *Laufach*, whose modern parish church houses work from Riemenschneider's studio), the route reaches **Aschaffenburg* (59,000 inhab.; alt. 130m), set among the Spessart hills where the B8 meets the B26 and by the Frankfurt–Nuremberg motorway. For many years Aschaffenburg was ruled by the bishops of Mainz. Between 1803 and 1810 it was capital of one of Napoleon's German principalities. Archbishop Carl Theodor von Dalberg founded a university here in 1808. The town became part of Bavaria in 1814, and 30 years later the opening of the railway to Bamberg and Frankfurt increased its prosperity. Trains connect with Frankfurt, Ulm, Mainz, Wiesbaden, Nuremberg and Darmstadt.

The 12th and 13C church of **SS. Peter and Alexander* (Stiftskirche) possesses fine romanesque cloisters, a 13C portal, and a gable end dating from 1870. Inside: an early 12C crucifix; a stone font of 1487; the Maria-Schnee chapel of 1516; the Resurrection by Lucas Cranach (1520); and the Lamentation by **Matthias Grünewald, c 1525; a renaissance pulpit, 1602, and a Mary Magdalen altar 1620, by Hans Juncker; and a high altar of 1772. The sandstone renaissance *Schloß Johannisburg*, by Georg Ridinger, 1615–24, is now an art gallery (open Tuesday–Sunday, 09.00–12.00, 13.00–17.00; October –March opens 10.00 and closes 16.00). The Schönbusch park (open summer 08.00–13.00, 14.00–18.00, except Monday) has a classical Schloß, lakes, a maze and a temple of joy, 1778–89. The *Pompejanum* is a reproduction of the temple of Castor and Pollux at Pompeii, built for Ludwig I by F. Gärtner (1842–49). The 'English' Park Schöntal (1780) houses a ruined abbey and a pheasant house. The town hall by Diez Brandi dates from 1958. Its bronze doorway decorations are by Ursula Ullrich. The parish church of Our Lady, with its early gothic tower and reordering by Franz Bockorni, 1768–75, was damaged in WW11. A theatre by the Spaniard E.J. d'Herigoyen, 1810, was restored 1960. Aschaffenburg hosts an annual festival in June. Information Office at No. 15 Dalbergstraße.

The B8 leads 16km NW to *Kahl*, on the Bavarian border, and crosses into Hesse to reach after a further 11km **Hanau**, where the brothers Jakob and Wilhelm Grimm were born (1786 and 1787), as was Paul Hindemith (1895). Dutch and Walloon refugees founded the new town in 1597, S of a 12C Schloß and the Altstadt. Hanau became Prussian in 1866. Much of the inner town was destroyed in 1945. In the Marktplatz of the Neustadt is the Grimm memorial (1889–96) and the town hall, 1725–33, as well as the Dutch church of 1608. The former Altstadt contains the Goldsmiths' house (1538), formerly the town hall, the late gothic church of St. Maria (stained glass and gravestones). *Schloß Philippsruhe* (1712), enlarged 1875–80, lies 2km W, and a further 2km W is the 18C spa house *Wilhelmsbad*, in the English Park (with a theatre, fountain and folly).

The route now runs W for 19km to **Frankfurt am Main** (see Rte 34A), passing after 10km, on the opposite bank of the canal, *Schloß Rumpenheim*.

10   Bayreuth to Heidelberg by way of Bamberg and Würzburg

Total distance 298km. **Bayreuth**—B22 61km **Bamberg**.—B22 86km **Würzburg**.—B27 90km *Mosbach*.—61km **Heidelberg**.

The holiday resort of **Bayreuth** (67,000 inhab.; alt. 345m) is first recorded in in the late 12C as *Baierrute* and soon came into the hands of the Hohenzollerns. In 1361 the blossoming town (on the trade routes between Nuremberg, north Bohemia and Saxony) began to mint its own coinage. Hussites ravaged the settlement in 1430. When Margrave Christian von Kulmbach made Bayreuth his principal seat in 1603, the town began an extraordinary period of artistic and architectural expansion. Margrave Christian-Ernst (1661–1712) inaugurated an era of sumptuous baroque architecture. The town was annexed to Prussia in 1791, was under French suzerainty from 1806 and became Bavarian in 1810. Richard Wagner came here in 1872, and in 1876 his 'Ring' began the performances that have made Bayreuth internationally famous through the series of festivals held annually from the end of July to the end of August. The author Jean-Paul Richter lived here, 1804–25 (Museum at No. 84 Königsallee) and is buried in the town cemetery. Wagner's son and grandson, Siegfried and Wieland, and Franz Liszt are also buried here.

Information Office at No. 7 Luitpoldplatz. Air traffic connects Bayreuth with Frankfurt, and railways to Nuremberg and Neuenmarkt-Wirsberg open up the rest of Germany. Coaches also travel as far as Berlin, Munich, Bamberg and Würzburg.

From the main railway station follow Bahnhofstraße S to Luitpoldplatz and the information office. S of the square, in Maximilianstraße, is the *Altes Schloß*, its octagonal tower and spiral ramp by Caspar Vischer, 1566. The medallions are by E. Räntz, 1691, the church by French architect Josef Saint-Pierre, 1753–56. Inside are the tombs of Margrave Friedrich and his wife Wilhelmine, sister of Frederick the Great. W, on the corner of Opernstraße, is the baroque *Opera House*, by Saint-Pierre, 1745–48, with an interior designed by the Bolognese Giuseppe Galli Bibiena. Follow Opernstraße and then Ludwigstraße S to find the mid 18C *Neues Schloß* (rococo rooms, galleries and museum, open daily, 10.00–12.00, 13.30–17.00; winter closes 1½ hours earlier). In front of the new Schloß is a fountain by Elias Räntz, 1700, with an equestrian statue of Margrave Christian-Ernst. To the E of the Schloß garden is the neo-classical *Haus Wahnfried*, built for Richard Wagner by J. Wölfel, 1847, and now a museum (open daily, save religious holidays, 09.00–17.00). Richard and Cosima Wagner lie buried in the garden. The oldest church in Bayreuth is the early gothic *Holy Trinity* in Kanzleistraße, which M. Mebart restored in 1611–14, with massive twin towers, five fine doorways and a high altar by H. Werner, c 1615. Old half-timbered houses, especially in Friedrichstraße and Maxstraße.

Just S of the railway station Tunnelstraße leads E from Bahnhofstraße and then N to Markgrafenalle, on which are the early baroque church of St. George (1705–11) and the little Schloß by Johann David Räntz, c 1730. N of the town lies the Richard-Wagner-

Park with G. Semper's Festspielhaus (1876), seating 9000 spectators. NE stands the *Hermitage*, built 1715–50 according to the French fashion, with a rotunda 'dedicated' as a temple of the Sun, a dragon's cave and a small hermit's chapel.

From Bayreuth the B505 is a fast route of 75km to **Bamberg**. The more picturesque route of 61km is the B22, leaving Bayreuth by the Erlanger Straße and travelling 24km W (through *Donndorf*, with its *Schloß Fantasie*, 1765) to *Hollfeld* (a rococo Schloß and a parish church which was once part of a Dominican monastery, as well as the church of St. Salvator, 1704). Further on is *Würgau*, a centre of walks and rock climbing. 20km from Hollfeld the B22 reaches *Scheßlitz*, with its 15C gothic church of St. Kilian (late baroque interior) and a pilgrims' church on the peak of the Gügel (523m high). The Dillinger Haus of 1692 was built by the brewers' and coopers' guilds. The remaining 9km to **Bamberg** (see Rte 8) pass the towers of *Schloß Seehof*, 1695–1711, the early baroque summer retreat of the prince-bishops.

Follow the B22 86km W to **Würzburg** (see Rte 5A) and the B27 30km SW to *Tauberbischofsheim*. From Tauberbischofsheim the route leads 17km W to *Hardheim*, with its 16C Schloß, and another 9km W to *Walldürn* (Schloß of 1492 and a pilgrims' church of the Holy Blood, 1698–1728). Follow the road 8km S to *Buchen* (late gothic parish church, half-timbered houses and a town hall of 1732). After 26km the B22 reaches *Mosbach*, with more half-timbered houses (the *Palmsches Haus* of 1610) and a 15C parish church. Mosbach is a holiday resort, with outdoor and indoor swimming pools, sauna baths, tennis and riding schools and a narrow guage railway to Mudau. 3km SW lies *Neckarelz*, at the junction with the B37 from Frankfurt to Stuttgart. Neckarelz has a former Teutonic knights' Schloß, and close by is the Schloß of Götz von Berlinchingen, the Hornberg. From Neckarelz, the B27 continues 26km SW to Sinsheim, whence the motorways A6 followed by the A67 lead to **Heidelberg**. A more picturesque route is to take the minor road W from Neckarelz W, to cross the border into Baden-Württemberg thus reaching Heidelberg by means of the B37.

**HEIDELBERG (130,000 inhab.; alt. 245m) situated at the entrance to the Neckar valley, dominated by its Schloß, by the 568m-high *Königstuhl* and by the 440m-high *Heiligenberg*, is the home of one of the oldest German universities and today profits from its electrical, optical, metal and leather industry and above all from tourism.

Main *railway station* (with post office): Lessingstraße.

Main *post office*: Rohrbacher Straße.

Information office: main railway station.

Trains to Dortmund, Basel, Munich, Ludwigshafen, Mannheim and Würzburg.

History. For the Celts this was a holy mountain site. The Romans built a camp on the right bank of the Neckar in the 1C BC, with a temple dedicated to Mithras and Mercury. The Roman settlement was destroyed by the Alemmani in the 3C AD. In the early 11C the bishop of Worms built a castle here, which Konrad von Hohenstaufen (step-brother of Frederick Barbarossa) chose as his chief residence in 1155. He and his successors enriched the town, which remained the capital of the Rhine Palatinate until the Elector Charles Philipp transferred his capital to Mannheim. In 1802 Heidelberg was incorporated in the Grand Duchy of Baden. Ruprecht I von der Pfalz founded the university in 1386, modelled on that of Paris. The Reformation greatly divided Heidelberg. At the head of the

Catholic League, Tilly devastated the town in 1622. Heidelberg was then much damaged in the Thirty Years' War, but recovered, especially when Elizabeth Charlotte, the daughter of Elector Karl Ludwig von der Pfalz, married the Duke of Orleans, brother of Louis XIV of France, in 1671. When the electors' line died out in 1685 the French claimed the town, and the struggles over the succesion again destroyed much of Heidelberg. The old pattern of streets was retained when rebuilding began.

In 1805 Achim von Arnim and Clemens Brentano published here their 'Child with the Magic Horn' (Des Knaben Wunderhorn). Heidelberg escaped injury during WW11, after which it became the US European Military HQ.

In summer parts of the new university and the Schloß are used for open-air performances. Heidelberg hosts a glove fair each June.

To reach the Schloß from the modern main railway station (1955) take the tram to Kornmarkt and then the funicular railway. By foot, which takes 35 minutes, follow Neue-Schloß-Straße from the station, and then take the Friedrich-Ebert-Anlage, crossing Friedrich-Ebert-Platz and leaving right to reach the church of St. Peter. The late gothic *Peterskirche* (15th and 16C, restored 1865, retaining a romanesque tower from a previous church and housing the university chapel of 1489) contains tombs dating from the 16C to the 19C. The new and old university buildings, incorporating the 13C Hexen tower and the 'Domus Wilhelmianna'. of 1712–28 by J.A. Breunig, lie to the W.

Follow the arrows above the church to the.**Schloß**, which towers c 80m above the town. Begun in the 14C, this castle was virtually destroyed by the French in the late 17C. In the 19C a French immigrant, the Count de Graimberg, restored the ruins. A tour takes at least 1½ hours. The oldest surviving parts are 9C granite pillars brought from Charlemagne's palace at Ingelheim and now in the Brunnenhalle. Elector Ruprecht I (1398–1414) added three towers to the E and the Ruprecht building, designed by M. Gertener (note its imperial eagle); all was redone in the renaissance style in the 16C—*chimney on second floor. The Library and Frauenzimmer building (or 'Womens' Wing') date from the 16C, along with the first renaissance palace in Germany, the *Otto Heinrich wing ('Ottheinrichbau'), named after and built by the elector who ruled Heidelberg, 1556–59, a part Italian, part German, part Dutch masterpiece, with a doorway designed by Alexander Colin of Malines (1526–1612). It now houses a pharmaceutical museum (open April–October, 10.00–17.00; Saturday and Sunday opens at 11.00). Opposite is a monument to the Heidelberg physicist Robert Wilhelm Bunsen (1811–99). The Friedrich wing, by Johann Schoch of Strasbourg, was added 1601–07: statues in niches depict rulers from Charlemagne to its builder, Elector Friedrich IV. Its rich chapel was restored in 1959. Friedrich built an 'English Wing' (1612) for his English wife. His English gardener laid out an Italian renaissance garden, the 'Hortus Palatinus'. When the electors claimed a tithe of the annual Palatinate wine harvest, Elector Karl Theodor built the Heidelberg Tun here, capable of holding 220,000 litres of wine. The tun supports a platform for wine-tasting.

The view of Heidelberg from the terrace (laid out, like the gardens, under Friedrich V, 1616–19) is fine. Descend from here to the Kornmarkt, and thence to the Karlstor at the E end of the Hauptstraße. The KARLSTOR is a classical gate, designed 1775–81 by the French architect Nicolas de Pigage. From here follow Hauptstraße NE. No. 235 is the *Palais Weimar* by Johann Adam Breunig, c 1715 (with a Folk Museum, including works from Africa, open Tuesday–Friday, 15.00–17.00; Sunday 11.00–13.00). Opposite (No. 132–4) is the early 18C

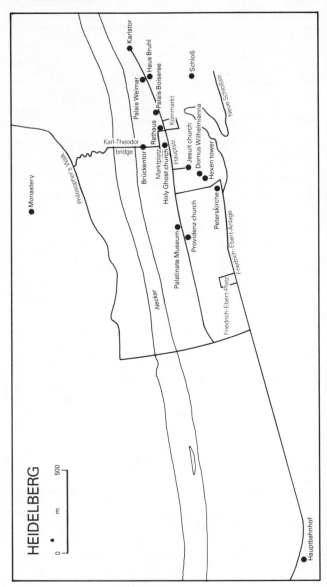

Haus Bruhl, by J.J. Rischer. No. 207–9 is the Palais Boiserée of 1742.

Continue along Hauptstraße to the Marktplatz with its baroque Town Hall (1701; partly burned down 1909 and restored 1924, with more recent restoration 1960–61). The carved façade is by the Hungarian Heinrich Charrasky, who worked in Heidelberg c 1700–20. Here also stands the 15C gothic *Heiliggeistkirche* (housing the tomb of Ruprecht III von der Pfalz, died 1410, and his wife Elisabeth von Hohenzollern). The tower was finished in 1544, save for its 1709 summit; the saddle roof dates from 1698. N of the church is the Fischmarkt (note the Madonna in the corner of the 18C house at No. 4). In Hauptstraße, opposite the church at No. 178, is the Gastof Zum Ritter, built by a French Huguenot immigrant, Charles Bélier, in 1592. (The 'Ritter' on the pediment is St. George.) A little further on is the early 18C Jesuit church, built to the designs of Johann Adam Breunig, finished 1759, apart from the three upper storeys of the tower (1868–70). Part of the church now houses the old university library. The Jesuits also built a seminary here (by Breunig, 1715) and a college of 1750–65 by Franz Wilhelm Rabaliatti. At No. 97 is the *Palatinate Museum* (baroque, by Breunig, 1712, containing early finds of the region and also *Tilman Riemenschneider's 'Windsheimer Altar'; open Tuesday–Sunday, 10.00–13.00, 14.00–17.00). Close by is the Providenz church of 1658–61, with a mid 18C tower). No 52 is the baroque *Haus Zum Riesen* (1707), where in 1859 Bunsen and G.R. Kirchoff (1824–87) succeeded in separating the colours of the spectrum. This is now the University Museum of Geology and Palaeontology (open weekdays, 09.00–12.00), which contains part of the skull of Homo Heidelbergensis.

Return along the Hauptstraße to the Providenz church and thence to the river bank. E stand the 15C stables and 1510 city arsenal. Further E is the BRÜCKENTOR, a classical gateway (1768–88), with statues on the pilars of Elector Karl Theodor and the goddess Pallas Athene (by Franz Konrad Linck). The gateway leads onto the old bridge (also known as the Karl-Theodor-Brücke). Cross the bridge for the Philosophers' Walk (taking about 30 minutes on foot), which passes the Bismarck monument and the Heiligen watch-tower (375m, built 1885), and then climbs to the *Heiligenberg*, with its ruined 11C monastery and 11C basilica of St. Michael. A bus also runs from Bismarckplatz to this 440m-high peak.

11 Munich

**MUNICH (München; 1,350,000 inhab.; alt. 520m) is the capital of
Bavaria and seat of both a Protestant bishop and a Catholic archbishop. Munich has been a university city since 1726 (the Ludwig-
Mamximilans-University today has c 42,000 students, the Technical
University more than 16,000). The philosopher F.-W. von Schelling
was professor here, 1826–40. Other academics were the scientist
Georg Simon Ohm (1787–1854) and the discoverer of X-rays, Wilhelm
Conrad Röntgen (1845–1923). Ibsen lived here, 1877–1891, as did
Thomas Mann, 1893–1933. The Munich 'Blaue Reiter' artists included
Franz Marc, Paul Klee and Wassily Kandinsky. Richard Strauss was
musical director at Munich, 1895–98.

Annual festivals: Fasching (7 January to Ash Wednesday, with the
main events on the Sunday before Lent, between Karlstor and
Marienplatz, and on Shrove Tuesday, in the Viktualienmarkt) and the
feast of Corpus Christi are the occasions of notable celebrations. The
Catholic churches have a joint act of worship followed by processions
in Marienplatz on the second Sunday after Whitsun. Operas, concerts,
ballet and theatre create the 'Festspielzeit' of July and August.
Munich's celebrated Oktoberfest—an October fair on the Theresienwiese, lasting 16 days, during which 4,000,000 litres of beer are
drunk—was initiated in 1810 with the celebrations for the marriage of
Crown-Prince Ludwig and Therese von Sachsen-Hildburghausen.
Other beer festivals, for which particularly strong beer is brewed, are
the Starkbierzeit (March) and the Maibock (May). Beer in Munich is
sold in measures of a 'Quartel' or 'Schoppen' (c ¼ litre), 'eine Halbe' (c
½ litre) and 'die Maß' (c 1 litre). The main markets are the Viktualienmarkt (see below), the Pasingermarkt (Bäckerstraße), the Haid-
hausermarkt   (Wienerplatz)   and   the   Schwabingermarkt
(Elisabethplatz).

Bavarian state radio and TV are based in Munich; and the city has an excellent
underground railway and a tramway system. Taxis take 20 minutes between the
airport and the main railway station (from Arnulfstraße, on the N side):
05.40–20.40). Banks open on weekdays, 10.30–12.30 and 13.45–16.00; Thursday
extension till 17.30. Money can be changed at the main railway station
16.30–23.00 and at the airport 17.00–20.30.

Main *railway station*: Bahnhofsplatz.

Main *post offices*: inside the main railway station; 1 Bahnhofsplatz; 2
Residenzstraße; Airport.

Information Office: 2 Thierschstraße.

Airport Munich-Riem (see above).

History. The capital of Bavaria, Munich makes its first historical appearance in
the early 12C. Its monastic origins have bequeathed the figure of a monk to the
city's arms. Henry the Lion fortified a monastic village here in the mid 12C,
bridged the River Isar and developed a salt market. Count Otto of Wittelsbach
took possession of the village in 1180, and after Ludwig II had granted Munich a
town charter in 1253 the Wittelsbachs settled here permanently. Emperor
Ludwig the Bavarian built another ring of walls and the present city gates in
1310. Munich suffered greatly during the Thirty Years' War and was occupied by
Gustavus Adolphus in 1632. Revival came in the 18C under the patronage of the
court, and especially in the 19C under King Maximilian I (1806–25) and King
Ludwig I (reigned 1825–48, abdicated in the face of scandal caused by his
relationship with Lola Montez and died 1868), who developed and extended the

city, opening out wide streets and squares outside the medieval walls, such as Prinzregentenstraße and Königsplatz. The neo-classical architect Leo von Klenze (1784–1864) built most of Ludwigstraße and the Residenz. Ludwig II patronised Richard Wagner, who lived here, 1864–65. When Ludwig II was drowned in 1886, Prince Luitpold, acting as regent for Ludwig's mad brother, put through an impressive scheme of civic building and design, creating Prinzregentestraße and the City Museum. In 1918 his son was forced to abdicate by Munich revolutionaries.

In 1919 the Nazis established their headquarters in Munich. Hitler attempted and failed to seize power here in 1923. Here in 1938 the Führer met Chamberlain, Mussolini and Daladier, securing their agreement to Germany's annexation of Sudetenland. The city was savagely bombed in WWII, and has since been substantially restored. Munich staged the Summer Olympics of 1972.

Luisenstraße leads NE from the main railway station to the old *Botanical Garden*, created by Ludwig von Sckell, 1808–14, and completely remodelled in the 1930s. Its neo-classical entrance is by E.J. d'Herigoyen, 1812. 33 Luisenstraße is the *Städtliche Galerie im Lembachhaus* (by Franz von Lembach and Gabriel von Seidl in style of a Florentine renaissance villa, 1887–91 (open Tuesday–Sunday, 09.00–16.30); N wing by Hans Grässl, 1927–29; permanent exhibition of the work of 19th and 20C Munich artists, including Spitzweg, Kandinsky, Franz Marc and other members of 'Die Blaue Reiter' group. Continue to Karlstraße and turn right to find the basilica of *St. Bonifaz*, by Georg Friedrich Ziebland, 1835–47, who had been sent to Italy by Ludwig I to study early Christian architecture.

This is an area of great public galleries. The *Staatliche Graphische Sammlung* (10 Meiserstraße; open Monday–Friday, 09.00–13.00, 14.00–16.30; European prints and drawings 14–20C; Rembrandt, Klee, Kirchner). Opposite is the Music High School (venue of the fateful meeting in 1938 between Hitler, Daladier, Chamberlain and Mussolini). Meiserstraße leads NE to Königsplatz, which houses the *Staatliche Antikensammlung* (1 Königsplatz; open Tuesday–Sunday, 10.00–16.30; also Wednesday, 12.00–20.30; building by G.F. Ziebland, 1838–48; frescoes in upper storey by Carl Rottmann; Greek, Etruscan and Roman treasures). At 3 Königsplatz is the *Glyptothek* (by Leo von Klenze, 1816–30, after a design by Carl von Fischer; restored Josef Wiedemann, 1972; open Tuesday–Sunday, 10.00–16.30; Thursday also 12.00–20.30; Greek and Roman sculpture). The *Propylaeen* (1848), modelled on the Acropolis by Leo von Klenze, stands at the W side of Königsplatz. In the gable are sculptures (by Ludwig Schwanthaler) honouring the Greek struggle against Turkey and King Otto of Greece (son of Ludwig I).

Further NE (along Arcisstraße, which is a continuation of Meiserstraße) is the Technical University (left) and the Alte Pinakothek (right), and further on is the Neue Pinakothek.

*Alte Pinakothek (27 Barerstraße; open 09.00–16.30; 19.00–21.00, Tuesday and Thursday). Built by Leo van Klenze, 1826–36 (rebuilt 1952–57) in the Venetian classical style, to house the Wittelsbach Collection, enriched by Herzog Wilhelm IV (1493–1550), Elector Maximilian I (1597–1651; Dürers; Elector Max Emmanuel (1679–1726; 12 works by Rubens, 15 by Van Dyck) and Ludwig I (Raphaels, Murillos, Titians). GROUND FLOOR Rooms I–IIa: Dutch and Flemish primitives (*Rogier van der Weyden*, *Altarpiece of the Magi); IIb–III: *Grünewald*, *Altdorfer*; *Dürer*; IV–V and Rooms 1–5 (*Titian*, Emperor Charles V): Italian masters; VI–VII: Flemish masters, including *Rubens*; Rooms 6 and 11: 16th and 17C German masters; IX: Dutch masters; Rooms 113–22: Dutch landscapes; *Rembrandt*; X and XIIb: Italian painters, including *Tiepolo*; XI, XII and XIIa: French 16th and

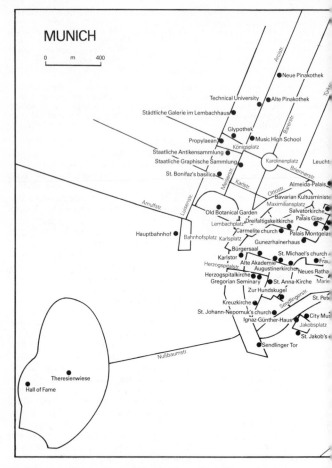

17C landscapes; *Boucher*, Mme de Pompadour and Ruhendes Mäd-
chen; XIII: Spanish masters (*El Greco*, *Christ Despoiled). FIRST
FLOOR: Bavarian paintings; Cologne school; S Tyrol School; Rooms
19–23: *Breughel*.

Neue Pinakothek (29 Barerstraße; open Tuesday–Sunday, 09.00–
16.30; Tuesday also 19.00–21.00), set up in 1846 by Ludwig I to house
contemporary works of art. Rebuilt by Alexander von Branca (1975–
81). Exhibits 18–20C European painting and sculpture, focussing on
Bavarian artists (Caspar David Friedrich and Carl Spitzweg); and the
work of French post-impressionists (Cézanne; Matisse; Gaugin).

Return SW along Barerstraße (E of the Neue Pinokathek) through
Karolinenplatz. SE along Max-Joseph-Straße leads to MAXIMILIANS-
PLATZ (Wittelsbach fountain, 1895, by Adolf von Hildebrandt). This
is the area of fashionable shops (particularly clothes, footwear and art;

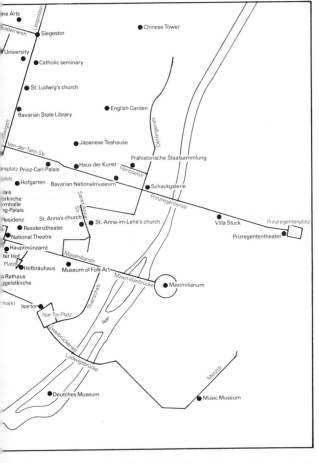

antiques in Ottostraße). NE of Maximiliansplatz, on Briennerstraße, stands the *Almeida-Palais* (by Métivier, 1824, classical façade restored after WWII). Across Breinnerplatz is the Bavarian Kultusministerium. Kardinal-Faulhaberstraße leads S from here to the former *Salvatorkirche* in Salvatorplatz. This late gothic church was built in 1494 by Lukas Rottaler (successor to Jörg von Halspach as city architect) as a cemetery chapel attached to the cathedral. It has a famous six-storey tower. Greek Orthodox Christians have worshipped here since 1829.

Walk E from Salvatorplatz to Theatinerstraße (more elegant clothes shops, shoe shops and art dealers), and turn right to the **Theatinerkirche** (parish church of St. Cajetan). It was built for Theatine monks as a thank offering for the birth in 1662 to the Electress Henrietta Adelaide of Savoy of an heir to the throne, Crown Prince Maximilian Emmanuel. Work began in 1663 under the Italian Agostino Barelli, to be continued in 1674 by E. Zucalli, who built the dome and the towers (the whole inspired by the church of S. Andrea della Valle, Rome). François Cuvilliés built the rococo façade in 1765–68. (The marble figures of SS. Cajetan, Adelheid, Ferdinand and Maximilian are by Roman Anton Boos.) *Interior*: the elaborate stucco work is by Nicolo Petri (1685–86); the three chief altars by Barelli; pulpit by A. Faistenberger (1681); Lady altar with a painting of the Holy Family (1676) by Carlo Cignani; St. Cajetan altar (with painting of the interceding saint by Joachim Sandrart, 1671) in S transept. Here are buried many Electors, King Maximilian I, King Otto of Greece and Crown Prince Ruprecht. Dominican monks now live in the Theatiner monastery, next to the church.

Abutting on the N side of the church is the Moy-Palais, the first classical building on the Ludwigstraße, by Leo von Klenze (1819).

Further S along Theatinerstraße are the Feldernhalle and the Preysing-Palais. The *Feldherrnhalle* is by Andreas Gärtner (1840–44), inspired by the Loggia dei Lanzi, Florence, with statues of General Tilly (Bavarian general in the Thirty Years' War) and Count Wrede (who fought in the campaign of 1814) by von Schwanthaler. Between them a memorial by von Miller to the Bavarian dead in the Franco-Prussian War of 1870–71. Joseph Effner built the rococo Preysing-Palais for Graf Maximiliam von Preysing, 1623–28.

Close by, S along Theatinerstraße and immediately right along Salvatorstraße, Munich boasts another Preysing-Palais, this one built by François Cuvilliés the Elder, with a rococo façade. Opposite this palace, across Prannerstraße, stands the Palais Seinsheim (rococo façade, 1760) and the rococo Palais Gise (1760; by Karl Albert von Lespiliez, a pupil of François Cuvilliés). Close by, No. 12 Kardinal-Faulhaberstraße is the *Palais Porcia*, built in 1684 by Antonia Zuccalli for Graf Fugger. In 1731 it was acquired by Elector Karl Albrecht for his future wife, Countess Porcia. Cuvilliés added for her the rococo façade in 1737. Opposite the Preysing-Palais, across Kardinal-Faulhaberstraße, is the rococo *Archbishops' Palace* (by F. Cuvilliés, assisted by J.B. Zimmermann, 1733–37; inhabited by the archbishops of Munich since 1818). Continue along Briennerstraße to Wittelsbacherplatz. On the same side of the street, further S, stands the classical Palais Montgelas (today part of the Bayerischer Hof), built 1811 by Emmanuel Joseph von Herigoyen for Graf Montgelas.

Kardinal-Faulhaberstraße leads S into Promenadeplatz. To the S of the square stands the Gunetzrhainerhaus, which the court architect J.B. Gunetzrhainer built for himself in 1733. To the W, in Pacellistraße (art shops), are the *Dreifaltigkeitskirche* and the Carmelite church. The city paid for the building of the Dreifaltigkeitskirche (1718; Italian baroque by J.G. Ettenhofer and Enrico Zuccali to plans of G.A. Viscardi; dome fresco by C.D. Asam; stucco by J.G. Bader; tabernacle relief of high altar by J.B. Straub, 1760), prompted by a woman named Anna Lindmayr who predicted great misfortune unless the Holy Trinity were thus honoured. Bronze statue of St. Michael in the gable, by J. Fichtl, 1726. Opposite is the reconstructed tower of the former Herzog-Max castle. The *Carmelite church* (almost directly opposite the Dreifaltigkeitskirche) is the oldest baroque church in Munich. Building began in 1654, to plans by the court architect H.K. Asper. In 1802–22 N. Schedel von Greiffenstein added a classical façade. The Carmelite monastery was destroyed in WWII and the church is now a library. Pacellistraße leads W into Lenbachplatz, SW of which is Karlsplatz, known to the citizens of Munich as the 'Stachus' and an elegant shopping centre. The city courts of justice (late renaissance style, by Friedrich Thiersch, 1891–97) are to the right.

Continue to Neuhauserstraße and turn left to reach Karlspatz and the Karlstor, the former W gate of the city and the start of the pedestrian zone. E along Neuhauserstraße stands the Bürgersaal. The **Bürgersaal** was built for the Marianists by Georg Ettenhofer (1709–10; to plans by Giovanni Antonio Viscardi). The Madonna on a crescent moon over the doorway is by Andreas Faistenberger. Interior: frescoes by Johann Anton Gumpp (18C; restored 1971–80); baroque oratory; angels (under organ) by I. Günther, (1762); 14 oil paintings of Bavarian pilgrimage sites dedicated to the Virgin Mary, by Franz Joachim Bleich (1719); Annunciation (from bombed high altar) by Faistenberger, who also designed the silver bust on the altar; memorial to Jesuit priest and resistance hero Rupert Mayer (1945).

Further E (No. 51) is the *Alte Akademie*, built as a school and seminary by the Jesuits (architect Friedrich Sustris, 1585–97). It became successively the university and the city library. Restored after WWII (renaissance *façade). In front is the Richard Strauss fountain, sculpted in bas-relief depicting his opera 'Salome' (Hans Wimmer, 1962). Immediately E, in Neuhauserstraße, stands the church of **St. Michael**, built for the Jesuits by Herzog Wilhelm V, 1583-90; architects Wendel Dietrich and Wolfgang Müller (façade restored 1972). The sculpture (restored) on the gable represents Christ presiding over Otto's victory at Lech in 955, with portraits of successive emperors and dukes of Bavaria (including the founder, second row of figures, third from right, holding a model of the church). Between the main doors the bronze Archangel Michael, killing the dragon, is by Hubert Gerhardt, cast by Martin Frey (1592; angel on stoop inside also by Gerhardt, same date). Interior: massive renaissance barrel vault; ten altars; high altar by W. Dietrich (1586–89), painting by Christoph Schwarz (1587); Crucifixion, school of Giambologna, right transept; pulpit 1610; memorial to E. Beauharnais (Napoleon's stepson) by B. Thorwaldsen (1830); vault with tombs of 40 Wittelsbachs.

E of St. Michael's church is the former *Augustinerkirche* (Neuhauserstraße 53). The Augustinian monastery church was first built 1291–94 (outside the city walls). It was enlarged during the 14th and 15C, and again between 1618 and 1621. Deconsecrated in 1803, it has housed the Jagd-und-Fischereimuseum since 1966, filled with hunting and fishing memorabilia (open daily, May–October, 9.30–17.00).

Cross Augustinerstraße for Frauenplatz and the cathedral and city parish church of Our Lady, the ****Frauenkirche**, in front of which is a fountain constructed in 1972 from blocks of granite by Bernhard Winkler. Duke Sigismund laid the first stone of the Frauenkirche—a late gothic brick building—in 1468, on the site of a demolished romanesque basilica. The architect was Jörg von Polling (known as Ganghofer), replaced after his death, in 1488, by L. Rottaler. The towers (99m and 100m high, elevator in S tower) were finished 1525. Tombstones from the old cemetery are incorporated in the walls. All five doorways are by Ignaz Günther (1770s). The main, W doorway incorporates statues of Christ and a Madonna from the former basilica; the Arsatius doorway (first on S side) with a 15C statue of St. Rasso; the Bride's doorway (also S side) with statues of Christ and Mary, 1430; the Benno doorway (opposite, N side) with 15C statues of Christ and Mary and (inside) St. Sebastian by Andreas Faistenberger;

the Sixtus doorway (W end of N side) with a 16C statue of St. George.
INTERIOR (restored 1980–81, after war damage): three aisles, 31m
high, separated by two rows of 11 octagonal columns (statues by
Erasmus Grasser on third ones from E end, 1502); stained glass in
choir (middle window by *Peter Hemmel* of Andlau, 1493; Annunciation 1392; Three Kings window 1430); restored choir stalls to designs
of *Erasmus Grasser* (1502); wooden statue of St. Christopher, W end,
1520; bas-relief of Lamentation, *Hans Krumper*, 1618; *memorial
tomb of Emperor Ludwig the Bavarian, S aisle (1619–22, designed *P.
Candid and H. Krumper*; bronze allegorical figures and statues of
Wittelsbachs by *H. Gerhardt and D. Frey*, c 1595); cross in middle
nave· by *Josef Henselmann*, 1954; pulpit, *Blasius Spreng*, 1957.
Statues and memorials in side chapels, beginning E of Arsatius
doorway: tombstone of J.M. Fischer; third chapel E of doorway,
patron saint of bakers, 16C; fourth E, Three Kings, mid 17C; E of
Bride's doorway, baptistery; next but one chapel, Ligsalcz tombstone,
1360; in chapel to right of high altar, mid 15C Crucifixion; high altar,
Mary sheltering Christians under her cloak, c 1510; left of high altar,
Baptism of Christ, c 1510; E of Benno doorway, Assumption, 1620; W
of Benno doorway, painting of Christ with crown of thorns, 1640; next
W, tombstone of first priest of new Frauenkirche, 1520; N chapel at
the W end, Mariahilf altar, c 1475. Crypts (entered behind choir stalls)
with tombs of archbishops of Munich and of Wittelsbachs (from the
son of Ludwig the Bavarian to Albrecht V), as well as the last King of
Bavaria, Ludwig III.

Return to St. Michael's church and take Damenstiftstraße S. No. 1 is
the St. Anna-Kirche, built 1733 by the Gunetzrhainer brothers and
decorated by the Asam brothers.

This part of the city, known as the Altes Hackenviertel, has several
fine buildings: in Herzogspitalstraße (leading E from St. Anna-Kirche)
are the Herzogspitalkirche (inside, wooden statue of Sorrowing
Virgin, T. Pader, 1651), and the former Gregorian seminary (No. 12,
1574, façade 1808); Brunnenstraße (further S along Damenstifststraße
and then E) leads to No. 7 Hackenstraße, home of Heinrich Heine,
1827–28, with a classical façade (1817; by Jean-Baptist Métivier); on
the corner of Hackenstraße and Hotterstraße is Munich's oldest inn,
'Zur Hundskugel' (1440), deriving its name from the six dogs playing
with a ball, over the doorway of the rococo No. 10 Hackenstraße
(1741).

At the corner of Brunnenstraße, Damenstifstraße becomes
Kreuzstraße, on the right of which stands the Kreuzkirche. The gothic
Kreuzkirche, built in brick, has a rococo interior of 1770, a crucifix by
H. Leinberger (early 16C), a tabernacle (late 18C, from the former
Carmelite church), and the 18C so-called Rotenhamm Madonna over
the high altar. The church is now used by Orthodox Christians.
Kreuzstraße meets Herzog-Wilhelmstraße, where you turn right to
reach the Sendlingertor, deriving from the 1318 fortifications of
Ludwig the Bavarian. Nußbaumstraße leads SW from Sendlingertor
to the Protestant church of St. Matthew (Gustav Grassener, 1954–55).
Continue SW (across Kaiser-Ludwig-Platz) to Theresienwiese, scene
of a horse race 17 October 1810 celebrating the marriage of the Crown
Prince and inaugurating the annual Munich Oktoberfest still held on
this site. The W side of the Theresienwiese is flanked by the massive
figure of Bavaria, a lion at her side, by Ludwig Schwanthaler
(1844–50, cast by Ferdinand von Miller; 130 steps inside lead to the
statue's eyes and three other look-outs, for fine views of Munich).

Behind is the huge Hall of Fame (in the Doric style, built by L. von Klenze 1843–53, for Ludwig I). Further on, across Theresienhöhe, is the city exhibition centre (Messe): 330,000m^2 with 20 halls.

Return to Sendlingertor. Running NE from Sendlingertor, Sendlingerstraße houses the church of *St. Johann-Nepomuk*. It was built 1733–46 by the Asam brothers at their own expense on their own land (and known as the Asamkirche). The baroque-rococo façade has portrait medallions of the Pope and the Bishop of Freising. Statue of St. John Nepomuk over the main door, which is carved with scenes from his life. Interior: long and narrow with red stucco marble walls; high altar with a wax model of John Nepomuk in a glass sarcophagus, twisted columns, and medallions of the architects on either side; in a niche left of the high altar is a statue of the Virgin Mary by E.Q. Asam. The two angels of the Bruderschaftsaltar in the gallery are by Ignaz Günther (1767). To the right is the rectory (1771; to the left a house bought by E.Q. Asam, 1733). Turn right where Sendlingerstraße meets Hackenstraße to reach Oberanger and St. Jakob's church, by F. Haindl (1956), replacing a 13C monastery church. N of this is the *Ignaz-Günther-Haus* (1761 rococo; on a gothic base, restored 1977; a small exhibition devoted to the architect Günther) and the City Museum (1 Jakobsplatz), celebrating the history and culture of Munich (*morris dancers, carved by Erasmus Grasser for the town hall, 1480; photographs, musical instruments).

E of the museum is the Viktualienmarkt. In the market square are figures of six Munich theatre artists: Elise Aulinger (1881–1965; by Toni Ruckel); Karl Valentin (1882–1948; by Andreas Rauch); his partner Liesl Karlstadt (1892–1960; by Hans Osel); Weiß Ferdl (1883–1949; by Josef Erber); Ida Schumacher (1895–1956; by Marlene Neubauer-Wörner); and Roider Jackl (1906–1975; by Hans Osel). To the N is the *Heiligegeistkirche* (church of the Holy Spirit), standing where Duke Otto founded a hospital in 1250. This church was rebuilt 1723–30 by Georg Ettenhofer; baroque ordering by the Asam brothers. Almost all of the present church is a restoration, after damage in WWII. High altar by Nikolas Stuber and Antonio Matheo (1728–30); John the Baptist altar (right of high altar) by Matheo; picture of Christ's baptism, Melchior Steidl (1731); paintings by Ulrich Loth (1661); angels by J.G. Greiff (1730); so-called Hammerthal Madonna, middle altar, N side (mid 15C, from a monastery at Tegernsee); war memorial chapel with late gothic crucifix (1501); bronze memorial to Herzog Ferdinand (1588; by Hans Krumper).

To the W stands the parish church of *St. Peter*. The oldest parish church in the city, with a famous tower (1386; views of city from platform: open weekdays, 09.00–17.00; Sunday, 10.00–17.00), St. Peter's was first a romanesque church, rebuilt in the late 12C and again (after a catastrophic fire of 1327) in 1368. Interior: stone Schrenkaltar (1407); red marble tomb of U. Aresinger (1482) and wooden statue of St. Peter (1492), both by Erasmus Grasser); late gothic altar paintings (now in presbytery) by J. Pollack (1517); font by H. Krumper (1620); high altar by Nikolas Stuber (1730); statues of the four doctors of the church, by E.Q. Asam (1732); Corpus Christi altar by Ignaz Günther (1770).

This is the centre of the old city. E along Tal is Isar-Tor-Platz, with the ISARTOR, the E gate of the walls built by Ludwig the Bavarian, restored in 1972. The fresco of Ludwig returning from the battle of Mühldorf in 1322 is by Bernhard Neher (1835). The tower houses a museum devoted to the comedian Karl Valentin (1882–1948; open Monday, Tuesday and Saturday, 11.00–17.30, Sunday opens 10.00). Continue SE along Zweibrückenstraße and across Ludwigsbrücke (1934–35) to find (right) the *Deutsches Museum*, founded by Oskar von Miller (1855–1934). The museum has a library of nearly 700,000 volumes, mostly of a technical, scientific nature, and is one of the greatest scientific/technical museums of the world. Built by Gabriel von Seidl and the brothers Emmanuel, opened 1925, restored after WWII (open daily, 09.00–17.00).

N of Heiligegeistkirche in MARIENPLATZ are both the old and the new town halls: the *Old Town Hall* (Altes Rathaus), built by Jörg von Halspach, 1470–80; barrel-vaulted council chamber, with 99 coats of arms and medallions; tower and much else rebuilt after WWII (1953–58); the *New Town Hall* (Neues Rathaus), by Georg Hauberisser (E building 1867–74; part limestone section 1888–93 and 1889–1908); Glockenspiel—with 43 bells, covering 3½ octaves, the fourth largest in Europe—on the 85m-high tower, playing at 11.00 (and in summer at 17.00): mechanical figures depict the marriage of Herzog Wilhelm V and Renate von Lothringen in 1568 and mechanical dancers celebrate the deliverance from a plague in 1517; lullabies at 21.00.

Burgstraße leads N to the Alter Hof. No. 5 Burgerstaße is the best-preserved late gothic house in Munich (c 1550; courtyard; staircase tower; façade). At No. 6 in 1781 Mozart composed 'Idomeneo'. The court architect François Cuvilliés died at No. 11, 1768; the Bavarian jurist Wigiläus von Kreitmayr (died 1790) lived at No. 12. The *Alter Hof* was the court of the Wittelsbachs from 1253 until they moved to the Residenz (see below), situated in the 13C at the W extremity of Munich. Late gothic W wing built under Herzog Sigismund, c 1460. Half demolished in the 19C, badly bombed in WWII, restored 1946–68; since 1816 the Bavarian Department of Finance. Across Hofgraben is the *Postamt*, built 1747–54 by the Gunetzrhainer brothers for Count von Törring-Jettenbach; transformed into chief post office, 1834–36, by Leo von Klenze, who added the loggia on the N side; restored 1953, after war damage. To the E stands the Bavarian Hauptmünzamt (central mint; 19C façade; former stables; renaissance courtyard; early classical W side, adjoining the Hofgraben, by Andreas Gärtner and Franz Thurm, 1809; façade towards Maximilianstraße by Friedrich Bürklein, 1859–63).

E again along Pfisterstraße lies the celebrated **Hofbräuhaus**, successively a ducal, royal and state brewery. Present building 1896–97, by G. Maxon and Max Littmann; daily music and beer drinking; brass band concerts. An area selling many tourist souvenirs; opposite the Hofbräuhaus, the Platzl stages folk theatre.

Orlandostraße leads NE from the Hofbräuhaus into Maximilianstraße, designed by F. Bürklein in 1852. N of the street is the Hotel 'Vierjahreszeiten' (1856–58; by Rudolf Wilhelm Gottgetreu). A little further E and S of the street stands the art nouveau studio theatre built by Max Littmann and Richard Riemerschmid (1900–01; restored after WWII). Continue E to find, N of Maximilianstraße, the government offices of Bavaria, built by Bürklein under the influence of 19C English gothic, 1856–64. Almost directly opposite (42 Maximilianstraße) is the Museum of Folk Art (19C English gothic style, by Edward Riedel, 1858–65; folk art from outside Europe). The area is dotted with bronze statues: General Deroy (1743–1812); Count Rumford (1753–1814); F.-W. Schlegel (1775–1854); and the astronomer Josef Fraunhofer (1787–1826).

Still further E along Maximilianstraße is the Max-Monument (known to the people of Munich as 'Max-Zwo'; by Kaspar von Zumbusch, 1875; allegorical figures representing the four virtues of a sovereign; cherubs with the coats of arms of Bavaria, Franconia, Schwabia and the Pfalz). En route, Sankt-Anna-straße leads N to the Franciscan church of *St.-Anna-im-Lehe* (1737; rebuilt after WWII) by J.M. Fischer; ceiling painted by C.D. Asam (restored 1971–72); pulpit by J.D. Straub, altars by the brothers Asam. Opposite the church is the neo-romanesque St. Anna (G. von Seidl, 1887–92).—A detour S along Adelgundenstraße, before reaching the Max-Monument leads to the Museum of Folk Art (Volkerkündermuseum). Follow Maximilianstraße across the Maximilian bridge (by F. Thiersch, 1903–05; stone statue of Pallas Athene) as far as the *Maximilianum* (Friedrich Bürklein, 1857, then Gottfried Semper, 1874; now the Bavarian parliament and senate house), flanked by (S) the Maximilian gardens and (N) a Ludwig II memorial (T. Rückel, 1967).

Return along Maximilianstraße to Max-Joseph-Platz (1835 memorial to Ludwig I, designed by C.D. Rauch, cast by J.B. Stigmaier), passing en route the *National Theatre* on the right. The theatre (Leo von Klenze, 1825; restored after war damage at a cost of 63,000,000 DM) houses the Bavarian state opera and ballet. Next to the National Theatre is the Residenztheater (1951; Karl Hocheder), which houses the Bavarian state theatre.

N of Max-Joseph-Platz is the ***Residenz** (enter from Max-Joseph-Platz), which owes its origin to the decision of the Wittelsbachs, in 1385, to leave their Alte Hof (in Burgstraße) and build a new palace. Today it consists of eight courtyards joining together seven buildings: the Old Residenz, the banqueting hall, the superb rococo Cuvilliés Theatre (1731–77, François Cuvilliés; open Monday–Saturday, 14.00–17.00, Sunday, 10.00–17.00), the ruined church of the Holy Spirit (neo-classical, by Leo von Klenze), the Residenz Theatre (built under Max III Joseph) and the National Theatre. The main courtyard, the Königsbauhof, is dominated by a statue of Neptune (1641; G. Petel). The arcaded Grottenhof was built 1581–86 (bronze fountain, 1590; cast by H. Gerhardt). Of the four other courtyards the Brunnenhof boasts a fountain surmounted by statue of Otto von Wittelsbach and depicting the four main Bavarian rivers, as well as gods, goddesses, cherubs and beasts (1611–14; Hubert Gerhardt). The Apothekenhof (1832–42; Leo von Klenze) contains the remains of the earliest building, the Neufeste (begun 1385, burned down 1750). E of this courtyard, the Apotheken Wing houses the Munich Science Academy. The Antiquarium was constructed under Albrecht V (1550–79; the oldest German museum of Greek 'antiques', most of them Roman or renaissance copies). The collection at the Residenz also includes porcelain, weapons, reliquaries, a 'Nibelungensroom' (1827–34; Leo von Klenze), the Court chapel (1601–03), the Golden Room (Cuvilliés, c 1730), the Papal Room (1665–67; Agostino Barelli; named after Pope Pius VI who stayed here 1782) and the *Rich Room (1729; Joseph Effner and J.B. Zimmermann).

The baroque additions to the Residenz are the legacy of Max Emmanuel II (1679–1726). Leo von Klenze built the Königsbau (N of Max-Joseph-Platz, 1826–35) and the 250m-long Festsaal. (N of the Apothekenhof; bronze statues and figures by Ludwig Schwanthaler.) The *Maximilianische Residenz*, adjoining Residenzstraße, was built by Hans Krumper and Heinrich Schön 1611–19 (renaissance façade restored after WWII). The bronze Madonna between the doorways is by Krumper (1616) and the armorial lions by Gerhardt. N lies the Kaiserhof (façade by Hermann Kaspar).

N of the Residenz is the *Hofgarten*, laid out in the French style by Heinrich Schön in 1613–17 for Herzog Maximilian I, with elegant arcades (restored 1950). Temple with (copied) work by Hubert Gerhard and cherubs by H. Krumper. Entrance through Hofgartenertor (1816; L. von Klenze). At the E end is the grave of the unknown soldier (by Bernhard Bleeker, 1924). At the NE corner of the Hofgarten stands Munich's finest early 19C classical building, now the official residence of the Bavarian president, the **Prinz-Carl-Palais** (1803–05; Carl von Fischer; W wing by J.-B. Métivier, 1926). To the W of the Hofgarten lies ODEONPLATZ, laid out Leo von Klenze, who also built the Odeon (1826–28) to the N (originally a music school, now the seat of the Bavarian Ministry of Home Affairs). Opposite is the Retterdenkmal of Ludwig I (Max von Wildenmann, 1862). Further N along LUDWIGSTRAßE (constructed under Ludwig I, 1816–50) is (left) the Leuchtenberg-Palais (1816–21; built for Eugène de Beauharnais, Napoleon's stepson; now the Bavarian Finance Ministry; von Klenze took as his model for this palace the Palazzo Farnese, Rome.) Opposite is the classical Basargebäude (von Klenze, 1824–26). Still further along Ludwigstraße is (right) the former Bavarian war office (1826–30; now the State Archive and the home of the Institute for Bavarian History, the last building in Ludwigstraße by von Klenze). From here most of Ludwigstraße is the work of Friedrich von Gärtner. N stands his Bavarian State Library (1832–39; statues of Homer, Thucydides, Aristotle and Hippocrates), modelled on the Palazzo Strozzi, Florence. Opposite Gärtner built the former Damenstiftsgebäude and the former Blind Institute (both 1840–43). Continuing N along Ludwigstraße you reach the church of St. Ludwig, built at the expense of Ludwig I by Gärtner, 1829–44. Paintings by P. Cornelius (including a monumental Last Judgment). On the left of Ludwigstraße now appears the University (1835–40; F. von Gärtner, in the classical style; fountain also by von Gärtner). Gärtner's Catholic seminary (1834–42) is opposite. To the N is the former Max-Joseph-Foundation for young ladies (1809).

Further N, on the corner of Akademiestraße, rises the *Siegestor*, patterned on the Arch of Constantine, Rome, by von Gärtner (finished Eduard Metzger), 1843–52, to celebrate Bavaria's part in the Wars of Liberation, 1814–15. N of the Siegestor is the residential and artists' quarter called SCHWABING. Schwabing is also noted for antique shops (especially Türkenstraße) and boutiques (Türkenstraße, Hohenzollernstraße, Amalienstraße, Leopoldstraße). To the W of the Siegestor stands the Academy of Fine Arts, Venetian Renaissance style (1874–87; Gottfrield Neurather). From here Ludwigstraße leads NE to Von-der-Tann-Straße, which leads E as far as the *English Garden*, nearly 192m^2 in dimension. Laid out by Ludwig von Sckell, 1789–95, to plans by the American Benjamin Thompson (Count of Rumford), it includes a Chinese Tower (1790; J. Frey, restored 1952) and a Chinese Inn (also 1790); monuments to Benjamin Thompson (1790; J.B. Lechner) and Elector Carl Theodor (a classical temple by L. von Klenze, 1833); the Ökonomiegebaude by Lechner, 1790; and a Japanese Teahouse, given to the city by Mitsuo Nomura after the 1972 Summer Olympics. S of the English Garden, on Prinzregentenstraße is the Haus der Kunst, built by Paul Ludwig Troost in the monumental style of the Third Reich (1933–37) to replace a glass pavilion burnt down in 1931. Further E stands the *Bavarian National-museum*, built by G. von Seidl, 1894–1900 (Prinzregentenstraße 3; open daily save Monday, times vary with the season; arts and crafts from the Middle Ages to 1900; *work by Riemenschneider). Still further E is the *Schackgalerie*, by Max Littmann, 1907–09 (open, except Tuesday, 09.00–14.30; rich private collection made by Adolf Friedrich von Schack, 1815–94, of 19C Bavarian paintings). No. 60 Prinzregentenstraße is the *Villa Stuck*, an art nouveau treasurehouse, (1897–98; to designs by the artist Franz von Stuck; bronze figure over the main doorway of an Amazon throwing a lance, also by Stuck). E (300m), at Prinregentenplatz, stands the Prinzregententheater (1899–1901; Gottfried Semper). From here follow Prinzregentenstraße E over the Luitpoldbrücke (statues of Bavaria, Franconia, Schwabia and the Pfalz) as far as the Friedensengel, a monument supposedly representing the angel of peace, erected 1895 (Joseph Bühlmann, Max Heilmaier, Georg Pezold, Heinrich Düll, restored 1983). The statue is in fact a copy of the Greek goddess of victory, Nike, at Olympia, and the column rests on a structure modelled in part on the Acropolis.

Return along Prinzregentenstraße as far as the Schackgalerie, turning NE here along Oettingenstraße and left along Himbselstraße to reach the *Prähistorische Staatssammlung* (Lerchenfeldstraße 2; open, except Monday, 10.00–16.00, Sunday, 10.00–20.00; prehistorical collection).

Outside the city centre is the Olympic Park ($2 \cdot 8 \text{km}^2$), which was set out for the Summer Olympics of 1972, S of Georg-Brauchle-Ring. The sports hall (1968–72; Behnisch and Partners) seats 40,000 and is used for concerts and the six day races at Fasching. Ice rink by R. Schütze; cycle stadium, H. Schürmann. Olympia lake (part of the Nymphenburg Canal). Television tower (290m high; viewing platform and restaurant). Olympic village (men's quarters by Heinle, Wischer and Partners, women's by Eckert and Wirsing). Nearby is the BMW Museum (open daily, 09.00–17.00; exhibition of automobiles since 1919).

Hellabrunn Zoo (Siebenbrunnerstraße; open summer, 08.00–18.00, winter, 09.00–17.00; animals arranged by geographical origin).

Schlößer

Asam Schloßchen (Benediktbeurerstraße) built by C.D. Asam for himself, 1729–32.
Hunting *Schloß* of *Blutenberg* (Obermenzing), built for Herzog Sigismund, 1439, rebuilt after Thirty Years' War, at present closed for conversion into an international young persons' library. Late gothic *chapel, 1488 (open daily, 14.00–17.00), Holy Trinity altar and limewood statues of Jesus, Mary and the Apostles, by Jan Polack (1491); stained glass.
Former hunting *Schloß Fürstenried* (Forst-Kasten-Allee), by Joseph Effner, 1715–17.
Suresnes-Schlößchen (Werneckstraße, in Schwabing), by Johann Baptist Gunetzrhainer, 1715–18.

Churches

Holy Cross in *Forstenried* (Forstenrieder Allee), late gothic (early 15C), baroque reordering by Gasparo Zuccalli (1672); on high altar, late romanesque wooden crucifix, c 1200.
St. Georg in *Bogenhausen* (Neubergstraße), baroque, by J.M. Fischer (1759), high altar (carving of St. Georg) by J.B. Straub; frescoes by

Philip Helterhof (1770); pulpit and side altar Ignaz Günther.

St. Johann Baptist in Johanneskirchen (Gleißenbachstraße); 13C; 14C frescoes; doorway (1520); stuccoed dome (1688); statues on high altar by Ignaz Günther.

St. Lorenz in *Oberföhrung* (Muspillistraße), Wolfgang Zwerger (1680).

St. Maria in *Ramersdorf* (Aribonenstraße), 15C gothic, baroque reordering (1675); on high altar Virgin Mary and on side altar Crucifixion, both by E. Grasser (c 1510); painting by Jan Polack (1483).

St. Maria in *Thalkirchen* (Frauenbergplatz), 14C, baroque reordering (1692), widened G. von Seidl (1906); high altar Gregor Erhart (1482).

St. Martin in *Untermenzing*, late gothic, by Ulrich Randeck (1499); 17C high altar.

St. Michael in *Berg am Laim*, by J.M. Fischer (1738–51); stucco and frescoes J.B. Zimmermann (1743); pulpit by Benedikt Haßler (1745); side altars (1743–59) and high altar (1767) by J.B. Straub.

St. Stephan in *Berg am Laim* (Baumkirchnerstraße), possibly Munich's oldest church; the present building by Lukas Rottaler (c 1510), baroque reordering (1713).

St. Ulrich in *Laim* (Agnes-Bernauer-Straße), 15C late gothic.

St. Wolfgang in *Pipping* (Pippingerstraße), perfectly preserved late gothic (1478), wall paintings by Jan Polack (1479); carved wooden altar.

Other Museums

Antikensammlung (1 Königsplatz; open, save Monday, 10.00–16.30, and Wednesday, 12.00–20.00): Greek, Etruscan and Roman exhibits.

Architektursammlung (Technical University, 21 Arcistraße; open Monday–Thursday, 09.30–12.30, 14.00–17.00, Friday, 09.00–12.30, 16.00–19.00, Saturday, 14.00–19.00): architectural drawings.

Brewery Museum (in Stadtmuseum, 1 Jakobsplatz, q.v.).

Die Neue Sammlung (3 Prinzregentenstraße; open, except Monday, 10.00–17.00): applied art; historical/cultural collection from 19C to present day.

Egyptian Art Museum (Hofgartenstraße; open, except Monday, 09.30–16.00, Thursday also 19.00–21.00).

Mineralogische Staatssammlung (41 Theresienstraße, entrance Barerstraße; open, except Monday, 13.00–17.00, Saturday and Sunday to 18.00): minerals.

Munich Feuerwehrmuseum (34 Blumenstraße): the Munich fire service through history.

Museum of Railway Technique (Munich-Passing station, 19 Hildachstraße; open Wednesday, 08.00–12.00).

Music Museum (31 Metzstraße; open Friday–Sunday, 16.00–20.00); see also the collection of musical instruments in the Stadmuseum.

Siemens-Museum (10 Prannerstraße; open Monday–Friday, 09.00–16.00, Saturday and Sunday, 10.00–14.00): Siemens electrical developments from 1847.

Sewing-machine Museum (J. Strobel and Son, Ltd, 68–70 Heimeranstraße; open Monday–Friday, 10.00–16.00).

Environs of Munich

**Schloß Nymphenburg, 8km NW from the centre of Munich; open save Monday, 09.00–12.30 and 13.30–17.00 (shorter hours out of season): the former summer residence of the Wittelsbachs. Central pavilion (1664–75; begun by Agostino Barelli, continued by Enrico Zuccalli in 1673), as the Elector's gift to Henriette Adelaide of Savoy after the birth of their son Maximilian Emanuel. Under Elector Maximilian Emmanuel, Antonio Viscardi added the four cube-shaped side pavilions and the connecting buildings (to Zuccalli's plans, 1702). Schloß chapel in second pavilion to N (1715; Viscardi; ceiling painted by Joseph Mölck; statue of Jesus attributed to A. Faistenberger). Semi-circular wings, modelled on Versailles, were added (1715–16) by J. Effner. François Cuvilliés remodelled the ballroom, with stucco and frescoes by J.P. and F. Zimmermann (1756–57; the great Roundel to the N side (home of the Nymphenburg Porcelain Factory since 1740) also by Cuvilliés (1729–58). Hall of Mirrors (1755–57; Cuvilliés and J.B. Zimmermann); gallery of beauties (contemporary ladies, including the dancer Lola Montez, all painted for Ludwig I by Josef Stieler, 1727–50).

In the park stand the octagonal 'Chinese' pagoda (1716–19), the bathing pavilion (1719–21; French style, 18C Chinese wallpaper) and the Magdalen hermitage (a romantic ruin, statue of Mary Magdalen by Giuseppe Volpini; ceiling painted by Nikolaus Gottfried Stuber, 1725–28), all three buildings by J. Effner. Cuvilliés rebuilt the façade and reordered the decor of the pagoda (1767). The *Amalienburg (a hunting lodge and gift of Karl Albrecht to his wife Maria Amalia), by J.B. Zimmermann with carvings by J. Dietrich and paintings by P. Moretti, G. Desmarées and P. Hörmannstorffer: hall of mirrors; blue bedroom; hunting room. Temple of Apollo by L. von Klenze; temple by K. Mühlthaler (1865). The gardens (221 hectares) reached their present 'English' form under F.L. von Skell (1804–23). Sculpture in the Greek style includes works by I. Günther, Roman Anton Boos, J.B. Straub. Waterfall built by Dominique Girard (1731; designed by J. Effner). Marstallmuseum (1719): carriages, sleighs, sedan chairs, sumptuous harness. Orangerie (1723–24). Botanical garden laid out 1909–14 (alpine plants, rhododendrons: open summer, 09.00–19.00, winter, 09.00–17.00 —the greenhouses close half an hour earlier).

18km NW of Munich (S-Bahn service No. 2) lies the old town of *Dachau*, which was granted a market in 1391. The parish church is by Hans Krumper, 1624; remains of a renaisance schloß by Heinrich Schöttl with a staircase by J. Effner. The former concentration camp is now a memorial to the dead, wih a grim museum (No. 95 Alte Römerstraße, open daily, 09.00–17.00).

12 Munich to Fulda by way of Ingolstadt, Würzburg and Brückenau

Total distance 340km. **Munich**—B13. 58km **Ingolstadt**—51km *Weißenburg*—44km **Ansbach**—78km **Würzburg**—B27. 51km **Hammelburg**—25km **Bad Brückenau**—33km **Fulda**.

Leave **Munich** N by the Leopoldstraße and after 16km make a brief diversion 3km W to *Schleißheim*, to see the *Altes Schloß* (Duke Wilhelm V's country house, 1597–1626), the garden Schloß 'Lustheim' of 1689, and the ****Neues Schloß** of 1701–27 (by E. Zuccalli and J. Effner), with its collection of baroque paintings. The staircase vault was frescoed by C.D. Asam; the E entrance is by J. Günther. J.B. Zimmermann provided stucco work and decorated the dining hall. Leo von Klenze reconstructed the façade in 1848.

The B13 continues for 31km through hilly country to *Pfaffenhofen*, with a gothic church of St. Johann (early baroque decor and a high altar of 1672), and then for 3km to *Haimpertshofen* (church with a high altar of the 16C). Continue for 8km to the junction with the B300 at Pörnbach and for another 21km to **Ingolstadt**.

INGOLSTADT (90,000 inhab.; alt. 365m), though deriving its wealth today from oil refineries and assembling motor cars and spinning machinery, retains a fascinating historic centre and much of its 600 year old fortifications.

Main *railway station*: Bahnhofstraße.

Information Office: 1 Schrannenstraße.

History. Ingolstadt began as Frankish court estate in the 8C. It is first documented in 806, when the Holy Roman Empire was partitioned. The Carolingian monarchs ruled it as their personal fief. The settlement was destroyed by the Magyars and rebuilt in the 11C. The Wittelsbachs took possession of the town in 1228. Ludwig II fortified it in the mid 13C. Duke Ludwig the Severe built a Schloß at Ingolstadt in 1260, Duke Ludwig the Bearded founded the Minster in 1425 and in 1472 Duke Ludwig the Rich founded a university. The Jesuit college (founded 1555) was the first in Germany. The Swedish king Gustavus Adolphus besieged the town in 1632 and his general, Tilly, was mortally wounded beneath its walls, dying on 23 April. Only in the 19C, when the university moved to Landshut and the monasteries were secularised, did Ingolstadt begin to decline. King Ludwig I refortfied the town in 1828 and the coming of the railway began to revive its fortunes. After WWII (which destroyed a fifth of the town) Ingolstadt rebuilt and expanded, until today it constitutes the second largest town in Upper Bavaria. An Ingolstadt professor, Adam Weishaupt, founded the secret society of the Illuminati in 1776.

The *Spitalkirche* (1460) in the RATHAUSPLATZ in the centre of the old town, has· 16C frescoes, 17C altarpieces and baroque decoration (1720). In the same square are the *Old Town Hall* (1882; created out of four gothic houses; the inscriptions and escutcheons in the arcades are from the old town gates) and the new town hall (1959). Follow Theresienstraße W to the late gothic, twin-towered ***Liebrauen-münster** (1425). Exterior: SE porch, carved with the Annunciation, the Magi, the Twelve Apostles, the Virgin Mary, the arms of Bavaria and Ingolstadt. Interior: high altar painted by Hans Meulich (1572), showing the Virgin as patroness of Bavaria; bronze memorial to the catholic controversialist Johannes Eck; tomb of Tilly and Fieldmarshal Mercy (died 1645); renaissance stained glass in the E window by Hans Wertingerr (1527); sculptures. N is the rococo *Maria de Victoria* church (1732–35; by the brothers Asam); 'Lep-antomonstrance' by J. Zeckl (1708); altar and allegorical statues of theology, medicine, law and philosophy by J.M. Fischer (1763); ceiling decorated with fresco of the Virgin Mary spreading Christianity, by Cosmas Damian Asam. The SW tower (the 'Pfeif-turm') was initially the town watch-tower. To the W of the church is a seven-towered, fortified gateway, the Kreuztor (1385). A museum of the history of anatomy is in Anatomiestraße close by.

E from Rathausplatz Ludwigstraße (No. 5, the 18C 'Ickstadhaus') leads to the *Ducal Castle*, now a museum of the city and of the Bavarian military. Begun in 1418, its gatehouse dates from 1558, its clock tower from 1771; late gothic interiors. To the S is the Herzog-kasten, built c 1225 by Ludwig I. Other buildings: *Franzikanerkirche*, early gothic (1380), with the 'Schutter Virgin' (1350) on the altar of the first chapel on the S side; woodcarvings in the choir (1613); altarpiece of high altar (1755), and many 16th and 17C tombstones. *St. Moritz* church (founded 9C; rebuilt 13C, 14C, and 15C), which has a romanesque N tower: stone Virgin in N porch (c 1320); font (1608); statues of the Madonna (c 1350) and of Christ the King (1450), placed in the reordered choir after war damage in April 1945. The remains of the Jesuit College (Canisius seminary, 1582) and the Orbansaal (stucco ceiling of 1732). Town theatre (1966).

The medieval walls and fortifications (1368–1434) mostly survive (now laid out as gardens) as do the renaissance fortress and the neo-classical fortifications by Leo van Klenze S of the river.

Neuburg lies 22km W of Ingolstadt along the B16, standing 403m high on the Danube, defended by walls, a moat and outer fortifications. The Residenz (1520) of the Fürst von Pfalz-Neuburg stands on a rock above the S bank of the river. The Schloß chapel is the oldest Protestant church in Bavaria; frescoes (1543) by Boxberger. Hofkirche (1627): stucco decorations. Martinskapelle (1731), now a library of incunabula and humanist works. The medieval Stadtburg is now the town museum.

From Neuburg travel directly N to Eichstatt. For the route along the B13 from Neustadt (or, omitting Neustadt, directly from Ingolstadt) to **Würzburg** see Rte 5A. The motorway A7 is the fast route from Würzburg to Fulda. To take the B27 N leave Würzburg by the Veitshöchheimer Straße and travel 6km to *Veitshöchheim* (superb rococo garden; Schloß 1680–82 and 1750, designed by Balthasar Neumann). After 18km the road reaches **Karlstadt** (see Rte 9) by way of *Thüngerscheim* (walled, with three defensive towers; 16C parish church; half-timbered houses) and *Retzbach* (16C town hall, with a staircase-tower; a church by Balthasar Neumann, 1738; and a pilgrims' church Maria in grünen Tal, in the valley outside the town, founded 1229).

After 27km the Rte reaches **Hammelburg** (12,500 inhab.; alt. 183m), known for its wines in the 7C, still retaining parts of its 13C fortifications (including three towers). Dominating the town is Schloß Saaleck, founded in the 13C (and now devoted to selling wine). The gothic Catholic church has a Madonna by Jakob von Auvera. The renaissance Rathaus dates from 1526, in front of which is a fountain of 1541. The Bavarian Academy of Music, formerly a Franciscan abbey, derives its present buildings from 1649. The modern Protestant church (1962–63) is the last work of the Norwegian Olaf Andreas Gulbransson. On nearby Sodenburg (506m high) is the family seat of the Thüngen family, *Rote Schloß* (1731), a baroque building by Andreas Gallasini, where Götz von Berlichingen spent some of his youth. Continue 25km N to *Bad Brückenau*, whose three mineral springs are therapeutically reputed and which is set among extensive forests.

**FULDA (60,000 inhab.; alt. 261m), 33km N, is the economic centre of eastern Hesse, and the seat of the conference of German Catholic bishops. A speciality is its wax candles.

Main *railway station*: Bahnhofstraße.

Information Office: No. 5 Karlstraße.

Trains connect with Kassel and Frankfurt, *buses* with the Rhön and the spa of Spalzchirt on the Voralberg.

History: In 744 the English missionary St. Boniface founded a monastery here which became pre-eminent in the conversion of Germany to Christianity. In the next century the monastery developed an extraordinary range of learned activity, particularly in copying and illuminating manuscripts. Fulda was chosen for the historic meeting between Pope Benedict VIII and the Emperor Henry II in 1020. The city which grew up around the monastery was given many privileges, receiving its city charter in 1114. Its abbots became prince-abbots in 1220, and Fulda became an independent principality in the 18C, when its architecture received the baroque character that it wears today. In 1734 Abbot Adolf von Dalberg founded a university (which closed in 1805). The abbots became bishops in 1752. Fulda became part of Prussia in 1866 and part of Hesse in 1945.

Walk SW from the main railway station, along Bahnhofstraße, to reach the city museum (fire-fighting equipment from the 14C). Close by stands the Altes Rathaus (principally 16C but founded in the 13C). Friedrichstraße and Pauluspromenade lead NW to Schloßstraße (right) with the former _Abbots' Palace_, a renaissance building transformed into baroque by Johannes Dientzenhofer between 1703 and 1734, now housing the city offices and also part of the Vonderau Museum (sumptuously decorated interior; open Monday–Thursday, 10.00–12.30, 14.30–17.00; Friday, 14.00–17.00; Saturday and Sunday, 10.00–12.30, 14.00–16.30).

Pauluspromenade continues NW to meet Kastanienallee, which runs SW to the baroque _Cathedral_ by Johannes Dientzenhofer (1704–12), partly modelled on St. Peter's, Rome (and replacing an early 9C romanesque basilica). Inside: baroque organ; tomb of Boniface (martyred in 754) in the crypt; high and side altars early 18C; Italianate statues. The cathedral museum, No. 2 Domplatz (opens weekdays, 09.30–12.00, 13.30–16.00; Saturday 09.30–14.00; Sunday, 12.30–16.00). Continue NW along Pauluspromenade, passing on the right the Schloß park (laid out 1714–26) with its baroque *orangery by Maximilian von Welsch, 1724; ceiling painted by Emmanuel Wohlhaubter, stucco by Andreas Schwarzmann and Andrea Pozzi. On the terrace is the baroque 'Flora' vase of 1728. On the left of Pauluspromenade is the Carolingian *church of St. Michael, by the monk Rachulf (820–22), inspired by the Church of the Holy Sepulchre, Jerusalem. The roof is a baroque addition. Continue through the Paulstor (brought here 1771) and turn left along Am Frauenberg for a 15-minute walk up to the Franciscan monastery of 1760, with superb views.

Alternatively (about a 30-minute walk), turn left at Paulstor along Eichsfeld, walk S along Kronstraße to turn right and continue along Langenbrückstraße across the river which meets Bardostraße leads S to the frescoed late Ottonian church of St. Andreas. A bus reaches the church from the bus station S of the Schloß. Another bus runs NE of the city under the railway bridge and along Magdeburgerstraße to the 9C church of St. Lioba, built at the time of Abbot Rabanus Maurus (crypt with wall paintings of 836–47).

OTHER SIGHTS: the Palais Buseck, 1732; the Palais Altenstein, 1752; and the old guard house ('Hauptwache', 1757–59).

6km S of the city (leaving by the junction of Bardostraße and Löherstraße) is Schloß Fasanerie, the abbots' summer retreat (1730–56), largely completed by Andreas Gallasini (Museum; open April–October, 10.00–16.00, except Mondays).

13 The Chiemsee to Ulm

Total distance 237km. **The Chiemsee**—A8. 19km **Rosenheim**—62km **Munich**—B2. 26km *Fürstenfeldbruck*—42km **Augsburg** B10.—54km *Burgau*—34km **Ulm**.

The **Chiemsee** is a lake 503m above sea level, at the foot of the Alps. Covering 80km², and reaching a depth of 73m, the lake is a haven for fishermen and water sports. The Romans settled on its banks (and legend has it that Pontius Pilate came here for a cure and died). One of its islands, *Herreninsel*, was the centre of a bishopric from the Middle Ages until 1805. On the E bank of the lake is *Chieming* (Pfarrhof, c 1530; neo-gothic church of Maria Himmelfahrt, 1882). 4km NE along the lakeside is *Ising* (gothic church of Maria Himmelfahrt, reordered in 1751, with a marble altar; neo-gothic Schloß). At the northern tip is the sports and holiday resort of *Seebruck* (Roman remains). The road now follows the lake SW through Mittendorf to *Gstadt* (late gothic church of SS. Peter and Paul), and then turns W and again S to *Prien an Chiemsee* (8950 inhab.; local history museum, open Tuesday–Friday, 10.00–12.00, 15.00–17.00 and in summer, Saturday, 10.00–12.00; late gothic parish church of Maria Himmelfahrt, enlarged c 1740, with a fresco of the battle of Lepanto by J.B. Zimmermann). Railways connect the town with Munich and Salzburg. Information Office at No. 11 Rathausstraße.

The islands of the Chiemsee are served by steamers from Prien an Chiemsee. A fishermen's colony has been established on one of the islands of the lake, *Fraueninsel*, which houses the former Benedictine monastery of *Frauenwörth* founded in 766, rebuilt 12C. Its church, though altered in the mid 15C, has a 12C choir and romanesque wall paintings. In 1983 Benedictines established on Fraueninsel a school and a seminary for women's work. The neighbouring *Krautinsel*, now uninhabited, was once the site of the monastery garden. The *Herreninsel* is where King Ludwig II commissioned **Schloß Herrenchiemsee**, by Georg Dollmann, 1878–85, modelled on Versailles. The park is also modelled on that of Versailles. *Interior*: the 'ambassadors staircase', based on one demolished at Versailles in 1752, with a fountain of Diana by Philipp Perron; ante-chambers, one with oval-shaped windows (as at Versailles), chandeliers, boulle cabinets, an equestrian statue of Louis XIV, a bedroom for the monarch's lover, a conference hall (with a portrait of Louis XIV and a ceiling painted with the Gods of Olympus); the *hall of mirrors (77m long, with 52 candelabras and 33 crystal lustres); state apartments (especially the rococo one by Julius Hofmann and Franz Paul Stulberger); the blue bedroom (Ludwig slept here for 23 nights); Ludwig's 'cabinet de travail' (where he never worked; portrait of Louis XV; an astronomical clock and the elephant clock by Carl Schweizer of Munich); the rich blue salon; porcelain salon; dining room (after a salon of the Hôtel de Soubise, Paris, with a 'Tischlein-dech-dich' or a table that apparently sets itself); a small gallery; the bathroom; and the unfinished N gallery, with a statue of Ludwig II by Elisabeth Ney, 1870. Open summer, 10.00–17.00; winter, 10.00–16.00. An Augustinian monastery was founded on Herreninsel in 1130. Its church, by Lorenzo Sciasca, 1684, was the cathedral until 1805.

On the lake SW of Prien am Chiemsee is the holiday resort of *Bernau* (ski lift, steamers, sauna, indoor swimming pool). From Bernau the A8 motorway runs directly from Chiemsee to **Munich** and continues to **Ulm**.

After 19km take the exit N for the resort of **Rosenheim** (52,000 inhab.; alt. 450m), which has a college of woodcarvers, parks, a botanic garden, and a concert hall as well as old burgers' houses, especially around Max-Josefs-Platz; the parish church of *St. Nikolaus*, restored in the 19C, though retaining its 15C tower, domed in 1656; the church of the *Holy Ghost*, 1449, with a baroque Loretto chapel, 1635, and the Roßacker chapel of 1737; a 17C baroque church of the Holy Blood; and the 14C *Mittertor*, the sole suviving town gate after a fire of 1641, now housing the local museum (open weekdays, save Monday, 09.00–12.00, 14.00–17.00; weekends 10.00–12.00). Here also is the Max Bram Gallery (open, except Mondays and holidays, 09.00–13.00, 14.00–17.00; Sunday, open at 10.00).

4km N lies *Westerndorf*, with a baroque round church of the Holy Cross, 1691. 12km W is *Bad Aibling*, with its peat baths and lake. The motorway continues 31km W from the Rosenheim junction by way of *Irschenberg* (lying at the foot of the 751m-high Irchenberg peak) to the exit for *Holzkirchen*, close by which is the deep river bed known as the Devil's Ditch. This market town has a late baroque church of St. Laurentius, 1711. Continue along the A8 31km NW to **Munich** (see Rte 11).

Travel W from Munich along the B2 for 26km to *Fürstenfeldbruck* (late gothic church of St. Leonhard, 1440; 17C baroque church of St. Maria Magdalena; 17th and 18C burgers' houses around the Marktplatz; and the *church of the former Cistercian monastery by J.G. Ettenhofer to designs by G.A. Viscardi, 1718–36). 3km further W is *Puch*, with a memorial (1808) to Emperor Ludwig the Bavarian, killed while hunting here in 1347. The road travels for 39km through the industrial town of Mehring as far as **Augsburg** (see pp 45-7).

Leave Augsburg W by the B10, reaching after 54km *Burgau* (with its two Schlößer). Just off the motorway SW is *Wettenhausen*, with an Augustinian monastery founded in 1130. Its church has a late gothic choir, 1523, a Coronation of the Virgin by Martin Schaffner, 1524, the tomb of Provost Ulrich, 1532, a baroque nave by M. Thumb, 1670–83, with stucco work by M. Gigl of Wessobrunn, 1680, and an organ chamber of 1700.

By way of *Günzburg*, the B10 reaches **Ulm** (see Rte 1B) after a further 34km.

14 Wasserburg to Altötting

Total distance 163km. **Wasserburg am Inn**—B304. 21km
Ebersberg—20km Munich by-pass—8km *Aschheim*—B388. 23km
Erding—20km *Dorfen*—B15. 16km *Haag*—B12. 45km
Mühldorf—10km **Altötting**.

Wasserburg (13,000 inhab.; alt. 421m) lies on a strip of land that juts
out into the River Inn, opposite the *Schloß* which Ludwig the Bearded
built in the early 15C and Duke Wilhelm IV enlarged in 1526 (adding
the late gothic Schloß chapel of St. Agidien). Just E and reached by
steps is the parish church of *St. Jakob*, a romanesque 12C building,
rebuilt in the gothic style in the 15C by first Hans Stethainer (who
began work in 1410) and after his death Stephan Krumenauer. After
Krumenauer's own death the work was continued by Wolfgang Wiser
and finished in 1478. The baroque interior dates from 1639–63,
enriched 1879–80, and contains a *pulpit by the brothers Martin and
Michael Zürn, 1639, and baroque side altars. Leave the church square
by Herrengasse, with its picturesque houses, to reach at No. 15 the
late gothic building that houses the local museum (opening times
vary). A little way S is the *Frauenkirche*, 1324–86, tower by Wolfgang
Wiser (late gothic picture of the Madonna, holding grapes, on the high
altar). Further E across the square stands the town hall, two mid 15C
buildings joined together, with a Ratsstube of 1564. Nearby is the
Kernhaus, with a stuccoed façade by J.B. Zimmermann, 1738. Continue S through the gate, by Wiser, 1470, (near which stands the 15C
Heiligen-Geist-Spital) and across the river to Wolfgang Wiser's
church of St. Achatz, 1485. Trains connect with Munich, Mühldorf
and Rosenheim. Information Office in the town hall.

Follow the B304 W for 21km to *Ebersberg* (8800 inhab.; alt. 520m) at
the foot of the 620m-high *Lugwigshöhe*. The town has a rococo
monastery church of *St. Sebastian* by J.G. Ettenhofer, 1734, containing a romanesque reliquary of the saint and tombs from an earlier
building, including the *Gräfin Richardis memorial by Wolfgang Leb,
1501. Nearby is the baroque chapel of St. Sebastian by Heinrich
Mayer, 1689. The B304 continues W through the Ebersberg forest for
20km by way of *Zorneding* (rococo church of St. Martin, 1719),
crossing the ring road E of Munich (see Rte 11) to reach *Haar* (church
of St. Nikolaus with a 13C apse).

Follow the ring road N around Munich for 8km to *Aschheim*, an
ancient town wih a church attested here at the end of the 7C (and the
burial place of St. Emmeram).—Continue along the B388 NE for 23km
through *Niederneuching* with its baroque church of 1649 as far as
Erding (24,000 inhab.; alt. 462m). Of its fortifications remains the 15C
Schöne Turm, with a dome of 1660. The 17C former residence of the
Count von Preysing is now the town hall. Erding also has a late gothic
church, St. Johannes, with a crucifix by Hans Leinberger, 1525; the
church of the Holy Blood, 1675, stuccoed in 1704; and the late gothic
Heiliggeistkirche, reordered in the baroque style in 1688.

Continue 20km directly E to *Dorfen*, with its church of Maria-
Dorfen (1782–86; ceiling painted by Johann Huber, 1786).—Take the
B15 S for 1·5km and make an excursion E to visit the mid 13C
romanesque church of *St. Johann Baptist* at *Rottenbuch*. Return to the
B15 and continue S for 14·5km to *Haag*, with its medieval Schloß, still

retaining the powerful tower of c 1200. From Haag the B12 runs E.—After 6km make a short EXCURSION S for *Gars* (baroque church of St. Maria by Domenico Zuccalli, 1661, with a Pietà c 1425) and *Au am Inn* (another church of St. Maria, designed by Zuccalli, built 1708–17; with the tomb of Gräfin Törring by J.B. Straub).

Continue NE along the B12 for 45km to **Mühldorf** (15,000 inhab.; alt. 383m), whose *STADTPLATZ is surrounded by houses with arcades and the old city tower, and contains four baroque fountains. The late gothic town hall to the N of the Stadtplatz, comprising three buildings in all, has a mid 17C façade. Nearby is the Frauenkirche (1640–43). Leave by the S side of the Stadtplatz to find the church of St. Nikolaus, built to plans of Alois Mair, 1775, with a ceiling painting depicting the life of the saint, by Martin Heigl, 1772. The nearby cemetery chapel of St. Johannes dates from the 14C, with a tower of 1450. Other sights are the late baroque Maria-Eich chapel (1699); the late gothic St. Katharin-Kirche (18C interior, wih 16C monuments); the city library in the 16C Kornkasten; and the museum in the Lodronhaus (No. 7 Tuchmacherstraße, open Tuesday, 14.00–19.00; Wednesday and Thursday, 14.00–16.00; Sunday, 10.00–12.00, 14.00–16.00).

From Mühldorf the B12 leads for 10km directly E to **Altötting** (10,000 inhab.; alt. 402m). Here is the *Heilige Kapelle*, one of Germany's oldest churches, possibly deriving from a 7C pagan temple and containing a miraculous Black Madonna, c 1300, before which kneels an 18C silver figure of ten-year-old Maximilian of Bavaria (by Wilhelm de Groff). The inner octogan of this chapel dates from the 8C, housed in a 14C late gothic church. Inside are many votive pictures and rich gifts, with the hearts of dead Bavarian kings and Field Marshal Tilly. To the S stands the church of SS. Philipp and Jakob, finished 1511 (inside: a chapel of St. Sebastian by Domenico Zuccalli, 1680; altar relief by Andreas Faistenberger, 1690; organ gallery, 1725; treasury). Opposite the Heilige Kapelle is the church of St. Magdalena, 1593, with baroque reordering 1697. Close by is the local history museum (No. 4 Kapellplatz, open daily in summer). Kapuzinerberg leads W from Kapellplatz to the Bruder-Konrad church, 1657, widened 1754, with a modern interior. Trains connect with Munich and Burghausen. Information Office in the town hall.

15 Berchtesgaden and its Region

Total distance 167km. *Traunstein*—B304. 28km *Freilassing*—B20. 17km **Bad Reichenhall**—18km **Berchtesgaden**—9km *Ramsau.*— 39km *Ruhpolding*—37km *Marquartstein*—19km *Prien am Chiemsee.*

Traunstein (17,000 inhab.; alt. 600m) lies on the B304, superbly situated in the Alps c 7km E of the **Chiemsee** (see Rte 13), overlooked by the 900m-high *Hochberg* and where the old Roman road from Salzburg to Augsburg crossed the River Traun. Traunstein is now a winter sports and health resort.

In the Stadtplatz a gothic church, *St. Oswald*, with a high altar of 1731 and a 19C interior, the Liendl-fountain of 1525 and the local history museum (opening times vary). Other churches are the chapel of St. Rupert, c 1630, with contemporary frescoes discovered in 1928, and the church of St. Georg and Katharina, still gothic in spite of being built 1639. The town park houses a culture centre. Each Easter

Monday the St. Georgtritt (St. George's ride), with sword dancing, takes place to the ancient church at Ettendorf. Trains connect Traunstein with Salzburg and Munich.

The B304 crosses the River Traun and leads E through the hilly land of 'Rupertiwinkels' for 18km through Teisendorf to *Freilassing* on the Austrian border (and 7km from Salzburg). Just before Freilassing the B20 leads S along the left bank of the Saalach (with on the left the peaks of the· *Gaisberg* and *Untersberg*) crossing the Munich–Salzburg motorway to reach *Bad Reichenhall* (18,500 inhab.; alt. 470m) after 17km. This celebrated spa and ski resort was famous for its salt mines in Celtic times, and today has remarkable saline springs. The Kurpark contains elegant health centres. A cable car reaches the 1614m-high *Predigstuhl*. Close by is the basilica of *St. Zeno*, 1228, formerly belonging to an Augustinian monastery and rebuilt in the late gothic style c 1520 after a fire of 1412. The inscription FRIDERICUS IMP in a transept chapel refers to Frederick Barbarossa. The romanesque cloisters with a 14C vault survive. Not far from the town hall is the romanesque church of St. Aigidien. The parish church of St. Nikolaus dates from 1181, much altered in the 16C and 19C (frescoed apse; Stations of the Cross by Moritz von Schwind). The railway connects Bad Reichenall with Berchtesgaden and Munich. Information Office at the railway station.

Continue 18km SE by way of the sports resort of Bischofswiesen to *Berchtesgaden*. Berchtesgadener Land was once a separate principality, famous for its Alpine ridges and peaks, its gorges and lakes (especially the Königsee). The town itself (22,000 inhab.; alt. 530–1170m) is situated at the foot of the *Untersberg* (1973m), the *Höher Göll* (2522m), the *Hochalter* (2607m) and the *Watzmann* (2714m). Cable cars reach the *Obersalzburg* (1020m) and the *Jenner* (1874m). Trains connect with Munich and Freilassing; buses with Bad Reichenhall and Salzburg. Information Office at No. 10 Sonnenstraße.

The late gothic church of *SS. Peter and Johannes* (in *SCHLOß-PLATZ) was founded in the second half of the 12C, and retains romanesque features—the W doorway, *transepts, and part of the S tower (though the towers were largely rebuilt 1866). Inside, a baroque high altar by Bartholomäus von Opstal and choir stalls of 1436–43. The buildings attached to the church, once a royal Schloß, now house a Museum (work by Veit Stoß and Riemenschneider; open Sunday–Friday, 10.00–13.00, 14.00–17.00). Close by is the church of St. Andreas, begun 1397, much rebuilt 1699, with a baroque tower. Other sights are the late gothic Frauenkirche am Anger (finished 1519), the 18C Schloß Fürstein, and the salt mines (with an underground railway; daily tours). A museum of salt lore (No. 83 Bergwerksraße) opens daily, 08.00–17.00; in winter, 13.00–16.00. The local history museum (chiefly woodcarving), in the early 17C Schloß Adelsheim, opens daily, 10.00–12.00, 15.00–17.00.

9km W lies *Ramsau* (late baroque pilgrims' church, 1733), from which the Rte leads NW to reach after 39km the health and winter sports resort of *Ruhpolding* (7000 inhab.; alt. 691m), with the parish church of *St. Georg* by Johann Gunetzrhainer, 1738–57 (inside the romanesque Ruhpolding Madonna, c 1230; mid 18C pulpit and choir stalls). The local history museum (No. 2 Schloßstraße), is in a renaissance hunting lodge, 1587 (open weekdays, 10.00–12.30 and Friday also 14.30–17.00). From here the Alpenstraße winds SW as far as Reit im Winkl (with an artificial ski run) and then NW by way of Unterwössen to reach after 37km *Marquartstein* (11C Schloß; theatre) where Richard Strauss conceived his 'Salome and Elektra' between 1897 and 1907 (in the summer retreat 'De Ahna').

The Rte now leads 19km NW by way of *Grassau* (late gothic parish church of *Maria Himmelfahrt*, reordered in the 18C) to **Prien am Chemsee** (see Rte 13).

II BADEN-WÜRTTEMBERG

16 The Black Forest

A. From Basel to Freiburg im Breisgau, thence to Breisach am Rhein

Total distance 108km. **Basel**—22km along the Landstraße to
Badenweiler—56km **Freiburg**—B31. 30km **Breisach am Rhein**

The Landstraße as far as Freiburg is 78km long. Quicker routes: the A5
motorway between Basel and Freiburg is 73km, passing alongside the Rhein and
by Neuenberg. The B3 to Freiburg is 72km, reaching after 40km *Mülheim*
(13,000 inhab.; alt. 350m), the centre of the region's wine trade. 17km further lies
the spa of *Bad Krozingen*, with a Schloß of 1579.

3km out of **Basel** the Landstraße crosses the Swiss-German frontier at
Weil am Rhein (26,500 inhab.; alt. 261m) and 7km later reaches
Binzen by way of the B3. Drive N to *Kandern* (6000 inhab.; alt. 400m):
a summer tourist resort (hiking) in the valley of the River Kandern—
museum of local history. After 12km the road reaches the thermal
resort of *Badeweiler*, known for its curative waters to the Romans:
well-preserved Roman baths of 1C AD, discovered 1784; sub-tropical
park of 16 hectares around the Schloßberg with its old Schloß;
Kurhaus of 1972; 15C, fragmentary wall painting in Protestant
church; renaissance Grand-Ducal palace. This is now the Baden wine
road. 9km further N lies *Sulzburg*, with a 10C (restored) church of St.
Cyriak (crypt; relief of Jesus and two founders on portal; spa),
followed after 5km by *Staufen* (7000 inhab.; alt. 290–715m) at the start
of the valley of the Münster: medieval town centre, the ruined
Staufenberg Schloß, and the Gasthaus 'Löwen' where Dr Faust was
taken by the devil in 1539.
    The Rte continues for 23km to Freiburg through the wine centre of
Ehrenkirchen and then past the former Cluniac monastery church of
St. Ulrich (baroque, by Peter Thumb, 1740; romanesque font in the
presbytery garden).
    **FREIBURG IM BREISGAU (180,000 inhab.; alt. 269m) is situated
on the River Dreisam between the **Kaiserstuhl** (see p 116) and the
Black Forest at the start of the Höllental. The city now dominates an
important crossroads on the borders of France and Switzerland.

Main *railway station*: Bismarck Allee.

Main *post office*: Nos 58–62 Eisenbahnstraße.

Information Office: Rotteckring 14.

Trains to Frankfurt, Basel, Holland.

History. Duke Konrad von Zähringen founded the city, 1118–20, planning it
as an oval town with streets crossing the oval in the fashion favoured by his
dynasty (cf. Villingen-Schwenningen, Freiburg in Switzerland, Bern, Solothurn,
and Offenburg). The city was walled c 1200, when the cathedral was begun. Five
monasteries were set up here in the 13C, when Freiburg was at its richest. In
1368 the Habsburgs became lords of Freiburg (by peaceful agreement with the
citizens), and the university was founded in 1457. The peasants took the city in

1515. In spite of several sieges during the Thirty Years' War (when the Swedes captured Freiburg in 1632 and 1638), the city retained much of its character and buildings intact. Between 1677 and 1697 Freiburg belonged the the French, its defences strengthened by Vauban. In 1806 the city became part of the Grand-Duchy of Baden. Much was destroyed in WWII, but much has been restored. The open medieval sewage streams (the 'Bächle') still flow through the city.

Eisenbahnstraße leads E from the main railway station as far as the Colombipark with its 19C neo-gothic Schloß (now a museum of pre-history and early history). Cross the Rotteckring to reach the church of St. Ursula (18C baroque chapel) and the Rathausgasse with its medieval houses, which leads to RATHAUSPLATZ. Here is a fountain with a monument to the 14C monk Berthold Schwarz who discovered gunpowder. To the left is the *Neues Rathaus*, created by the union of two 16C renaissance houses: oriel windows, richly decorated; a fine courtyard (concerts in summer); carillon in the clock tower. Adjacent is the *Altes Rathaus*, with a renaissance gable and in the courtyard a restored courthouse. Over its clock tower are the coats of arms of the former Habsburg rulers (1368–1806). To the right of Rathausplatz is the gothic church of *St. Martin*, with three naves, dating in part from the 13C, restored 1953 and 1974, with a baroque porch, a crossing of 1246, the tomb of the writer Heinrich Hansjakob (died 1916), and abutting a gothic cloister from the former Franciscan monastery. Follow Franziskanerstraße to the restored *Haus zum Walfisch* ('House of the Whale'), built by the Emperor Maximilian I in 1516 for his retirement and incorporating two flamboyant oriels. Maximilian died in 1519. A plaque records that Erasmus of Rotterdam lived here from 1529–31.

The route reaches the arcaded main street of Freiburg, Kaiser-Joseph-Straße, to find (right) the 15C *Basler Hof*, today the seat of the regional administration, once the cathedral chapter (1500–1510; doorway 1588; staircase tower in courtyard). Turn into Münsterplatz to find the ****Cathedral of Our Lady**, built in four distinct architectural phases between c 1170 and the early 16C. The earliest parts consist of the romanesque crossing (frescoes), and the early 13C clock towers (with later gothic superstructures). The gothic central nave and the

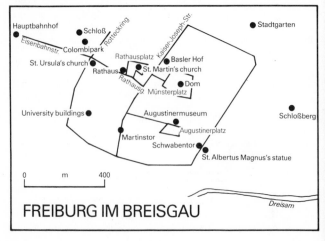

FREIBURG IM BREISGAU

two side aisles date from the mid 13C. The next period of building produced the main tower, begun in 1250 and finished in 1350, standing 115m high, with a delicate stone spire (panorama from the top). It carries one of Germany's oldest bells, the 'Hosanna'. Below is the great door, with statues of SS. Lambert and Alexander flanking the Virgin Mary, along with late 13C sculptures of the wise and foolish virgins, and friezes depicting the life of Jesus, the Last Judgment, and the twelve apostles. The church and synagogue are also represented, the synagogue blindfolded. The late gothic chancel, begun 1354, was designed by J. von Gmünd.

INTERIOR: 125m long, 30m wide, 27m high; in the nave, a gothic pulpit by Jörg Kempf (1561, with the sculptor, perhaps, portrayed by himself underneath the steps), and a fresco by Ludwig Seitz (1877) of the Coronation of the Virgin Mary; on the altar in the transept is an adoration by Hans Wydyz, 1505; the high altar of 1511 carries Hans Baldung Grien's *Coronation of the Virgin; other paintings include Grien's Schnewlin altar; a Man of Sorrows by L. Cranach (1524); the Oberried altar by Hans Holbein the Younger (1521); the rococo font in the Cyriak chapel is by Christoph Wenzinger (1768); the chapel of the tomb dates from 1340; the Locherer chapel contains a Virgin of Mercy, carved in 1524.

N of the cathedral square is the former Corn House, destroyed in 1944 and since restored. To the S is the episcopal palace, built in 1726, and next· to it the half gothic, half renaissance Kaufhaus (c 1520), decorated with statues of Maximilian I, his son Philip I of Spain, his grandsons Karl V and Ferdinand I. From here a little street leads to the 18C Haus 'zum Schönen Eck' by Christian Wenzinger, with a staircase well in the courtyard (and now a music school). Of Freiburg's fortifications remain the much altered Martinstor (originally 13C) and the 12C Schwabentor, restored 1901, with a fresco of the peasant who came with a pot of gold to buy the city. Around the Schwabentor is situated the old Bürgers' quarter of Oberlinden, incorporating Germany's oldest inn, the 'Bären' of 1311. The nearby Schwabentor bridge has on its S side a monument to the battle of Sempach (1336) between the Swiss and the troops of Archduke Leopold III of Austria. Opposite the Tor is a statue of St. Albertus Magnus, 13C provincial of the Freiburg Dominicans. From here rises the 430m-high *Schloßberg*, with its vineyards, a Bismarck monument, and from the top a *panorama. (A chair lift reaches its peak from the Stadtgarten.) Freiburg's other notable peak, the *Schauinsland* (1284m) can also be reached by cable car.

OTHER SIGHTS: municipal theatre of 1910, rebuilt 1963; the university buildings of 1911; the Jesuit church in Bertholdstraße, 1685–1705, destroyed WWII and rebuilt rather spartanly. *Augustinermuseum* in Augustinerplatz (works by Grien and Grünewald, especially the latter's 'Miracle of the Snow'; open, save Monday and Sunday, 10.00–17.00; Wednesday closes 20.00). Also Natural History Museum and Museum of Folk Art, Gerberau 32; Museum of Mechanical Musical Instruments; Museum of Folksong, Silberbachstraße 12.

Each year Freiburg hosts processions on the Monday before Lent and on Corpus Christi, as well as a wine festival at the end of June and a beer festival in early August. Every Christmas a fair is held in the Messeplatz.

Leave Freiburg along the B31 by way of *Umkirch* (Hohenzollern Schloß) and *Ihringen* (Germany's warmest town and a great wine centre) to reach after 30km the fortified town of *Breisach am Rhein* (9500 inhab.; alt. 190–240m), the border town at the crossing of the Rhein for Colmar. The road winds upwards through the 16C walls, past Vauban's Rhein gate (portrait medallions of Louis XIV and his queen) to the minster of *St. Stephan, half romanesque, half gothic, built 10–15C. One tower is romanesque, the other 13C gothic. The gothic *high altar is by Hans Liefrink (1527); fresco (c1490) by Martin Schongauer of the Judgment of the world; late gothic choir screen, c 1500; late 15C choir stalls with grotesques; 15C tabernacle; in N transept an early 16C Deposition; silver reliquary (1496) with the relics of SS. Gervais and Protais. Pre- and early history museum, Münsterbergstraße 21; Galerie Kroner in the Rimsingen Schloß (1773; by F.A. Bagnato).

Approx. 10km NE is the *Kaiserstuhl*, formed from volcanic rocks, where, according to legend, the emperors would meet the people to settle their subjects' grievances.

B. From Ettlingen to Freiburg im Breisgau

Total distance, by way of the B3, 121km. **Ettlingen**—18km**Rastatt**—15km *Steinbach*—3km *Bühl*—10km *Achern*.—9km **Offenburg**.—20km *Lahr*—10km *Ettenheim*—9km *Kenzingen*—11km *Emmendingen*—16km **Freiburg**.
  The motorway from Ettlingen to Offenburg is 74km.

The old town of **Ettlingen** (36,000 inhab.; alt. 340m) lies 8km S of *Karlsruhe* (see Rte 16D) on the River Alb and has a baroque town hall (1737–38) and a renaissance Schloß (16th and 18C, now a regional museum, with the Information Office), in front of which is a well, dated 1549. The Hofkapelle (decorated by Cosmas Damien Asam, 1732) is now a concert hall. Other sights are the 18C parish church and the Lantern tower, remaining from the old town defences.

The Residenz at Rastatt, built on the model of Versailles for Margrave Ludwig Wilhelm of Baden, 1697–1707.

The B3 leads 18km SW to the industrial town of **Rastatt** (40,000 inhab.; alt. 120m). Burnt down by the French in 1689, Rastatt was rebuilt by Margrave Ludwig Wilhelm von Baden (known as 'Louis the Turk'). Here in 1713 and 1715 Prince Eugene of Savoy and the Marshal de Villars met to bring an end to the War of the Spanish Succession. An abortive meeting between the French and their enemies here in 1799 led to a massacre of the French. The town was fortified in 1840. The **Schloß* (1697–1707) is the first in Germany in the baroque style of Versailles, built under the direction of the Viennese architect Rossi with a garden front 230m long. Ludwig Wilhelm's widow, Sibylla Augusta, has a tomb in the baroque Schloß chapel, designed by M.L. Rohrer. The Schloß now houses a regional and military museum. In the gardens is the Pagodenburg (1722; by J. Effner). Rossi designed the MARKTPLATZ, now dominated by the town hall of 1750 and the parish church of 1764.—5km S in the direction of Baden Baden is *Schloß Favorite*, which Rohrer built for Sibylla Augusta in 1711.

The Florentine room of Schloß Favorite, near Rastatt, was created in 1711 by M.L. Rohrer for Sybilla Augusta of Saxony-Lauenburg.

The Rte continues S, passing by the ruins of Ebersteinburg and Hohenbaden on the left, and passing through Baden-Oos to reach _Steinbach_ (3500 inhab.; alt. 142m), with its open-air swimming pool. Here was born Erwin von Steinbach (died 1318), architect of Strasbourg Cathedral (statue in his honour on a hill nearby). 3km S of Steinbach is _Bühl_ (22,000 inhab.; alt. 136m) on the edge of the Black Forest and famous for its fruits: gothic church and Corn Hall. Further S, on the outskirts of _Ottersweier_, is the baroque pilgrimage church of Maria Linden. The town hall is in the former Jesuit's College. The present parish church is 19C neo-gothic. 4km S is the small town of _Sesbach_, where the French Marshal Turenne was killed by a bullet on 27 July 1675. On the spot where he fell is a granite obelisk, 12m high, decorated with a medallion inscribed 'La France à Turenne' and approached by an avenue of pine trees.

After 6km the Rte reaches _Achern_ (22,000 inhab.; alt. 143m) at the beginning of the valley of the Acher. The slightly unsightly St. Nikolaus chapel (14C) has a 16C tower. The monument in the marketplace is to the Grand Duke Leopold who ruled Baden from 1830 to 1852. This is a centre of the brandy industry and of glass-blowing, as well as tourism (golf, tennis, camping). The road continues through _Renchen_ (statue to the poet Jakob Christoph von Girmmelshausen, died 1676) and _Appenweier_ (baroque church of St. Michael with a splendid *interior; railway junction) and reaches Offenburg.

Offenburg (51,000 inhab.; alt. 140–690m) was founded by the Zähringer family in the 12C and in the next century became a free city. Almost entirely destroyed by fire in 1689, it has a baroque parish church, finished 1790, which retains a late gothic choir, a crucifix of 1521 (left side altar); baroque high altar of 1740 by F. Lichtenauer; choir stalls, 1740; pulpit 1790; 18C organ and, outside, a Mount of Olives group of 1524 and 16C tombstones. The former Franciscan monastery at Offenburg dates from 1717. The town hall was created in 1741 by M. Fuchs out of an earlier renaissance building. Nearby (at No. 96, Hauptstraße) is M. Rohrer's baroque Landratsamt, 1717. At No. 10 Ritterstraße is the Ritterhausmuseum of 1775.

The industrial town of **Lahr** (37,000 inhab.; alt. 170m), 20km S of Offenburg and close by the 300m-high _Schutterlindenberg_, lies in the pleasant Schutter valley. At the E end of Kaiserstraße is the old town hall of 1608, restored in the 19C. Markstraße leads from here S to the remains of the 13C Storchen Tower. S too is the 13C Stiftskirche, also restored in the 19C. The new town hall dates from 1808. In the park is a museum of local history. In the suburb of Burgheim is the restored 11C romanesque church of _St. Peter_, with 15C wall paintings.—A brief excursion E reaches _Reichenbach_, with the ruined Schloß Hohengeroldseck, 526m high.

Continue S from Lahr to _Mahlberg_, with its tobacco museum, mid 13C Schloß, restored in the 17C, and an eight-sided chapel of St. Catherine (with 17th and 18C stucco and decoration). After Mahlberg the B3 reaches _Ettenheim_, where in 1804 Napoleon arrested the conspirator d'Enghien. Here lived Cardinal Rohan during the French Revolution, in the present administrative offices (1790–1803). The parish church dates from 1777. _Ettenheimmünster_, 4km E of the town, retains only the walls, a mill and a few other traces of its former Benedictine monastery, as well as a baroque church by Peter Thumb.

The road from Ettenheim passes S through _Herbolzheim_ (a 45-minute climb to the panoramas from the 310m-high Kahlenberg) to reach *Emmendingen* (25,000 inhab.; alt. 201m). Goethe's sister married a town magistrate and is buried here (in the cemetery). Here too died the writer Alfred Döblin. The Markgrafen Schloß (1574) is now a local history museum. The town retains a town hall of 1729 and the Neue Schloß of 1789. The 19C church of St. Boniface contains a gothic altarpiece by Friedrich Herlin (late 15C). To the left, 4km from the town on a 345m hill are the ruins of Schloß Hachberg (11C). The road travels S from here to reach after 16km **Freiburg** (see Rte 16A).

Picturesque alternative route from Offenburg to Freiburg

Total distance 137km. **Offenburg**—39km *Gutach*—10km *Elzach*—15km **Triberg**—15km *Furtwangen*—20km *St. Märgen*—6km *St. Peter*—32km **Freiburg**.

Leave **Offenburg** by the B33, SE in the direction of Donaueschingen, travelling along the valley of the Kinzig through *Gutach im Breisgau* (silk industry). Turn S along the road to *Elzach* (16C church with contemporary glass in the choir). The Rte passes the *Landwassereck* (630m high, with panoramas) and reaches after 48km the tourist resort of *Oberprechtal* (fishing, hunting, miniature golf, spa). Here rejoin the B33 and travel S through the ski country (the *Rohrhardsberg* peak is 1152m high) and the winter sports town of *Schonach* (4200 inhab.; alt. 885m) to reach after 15km Triberg.

Triberg (7500 inhab.; alt. 700–1001m) is situated at the junction of the valleys of the Gutach, Schonach and Prisenach and takes its name from three pine-covered hills (the 847m *Kapellenberg*, the 948m *Kroneck* and the 1006m *Sterenberg*). The spa is open all the year round, and the town specialises both in winter sports and cuckoo clocks. The Black Forest railway passes here, and its constructor, the engineer Robert Gerwig (1820–85) has a granite monument in the Hauptstraße. The pilgrimage church of *Maria in der Tanne* (1705) has a silver antependium before the high altar, given by Louis the Turk in 1706. The spa also has a fine park and a famous waterfall. The administrative offices were built in 1697.

The Rte travels S to the spa of *Shönwald* (covered and open-air, heated swimming pools; sports), reaching after 15km *Furtwangen* (11,000 inhab.; alt. 850–1150m), the main regional centre for clock making (with a clock museum), and on a railway line from Freiburg and Donaueschingen. Travel SW through Neukirch to *St. Märgen* (20km). The former Augustinian church of St. Maria dates from 1725 (interior restored 1907; in the lady chapel a 14C painting of the Virgin Mary). 6km NW lies *St. Peter*, with well-preserved remains of a former Benedictine monastery (*rococo library), today the theological college for the diocese of Freiburg. The twin-domed, baroque monastery church is by Peter Thumb (1724–77), with statues on the high altar by J.A. Feuchtmayr and a painting by S.C. Storer. A short excursion N along a new road leads to the *Kandel*, the highest peak of the central Black Forest region (1240m).

The Rte E from St. Peter passes through the Glottertal wine centre and reaches after 15km Denzlingen before turning S along the B294 and running 17km into **Freiburg** (see Rte 16A).

C. From Freiburg im Breisgau through Freudenstadt to Baden-Baden

Total distance 177km. **Freiburg**—16km *Waldkirch*—39km
Wolfach—10km *Schiltach*—10km *Alpirsbach*—27km
Freudenstadt—13km *Bad Rippolsau-Schapbach*—46km *Kurhaus
Bühlerhöhe*—16km **Baden-Baden**.

Leave **Freiburg** (see Rte 16A), travelling N for 16km by the B294
through Denzlingen as far as Waldkirch at the foot of the 1240m-high
Kandel, which can be attained by a good road (13km). Situated in the
valley of the Elz, *Waldkirch* (18,600 inhab.; alt. 263m) is a health resort
(swimming pools, park, sports, concerts) with a baroque 18C church
of St. Margaret by Peter Thumb. NW of the town stands the ruined
Kastelberg.

Continue along the B294 through *Elzach*, turning NE at Haslach
and continuing by way of *Hausach* (many good walking routes) to
reach after 39km *Wolfach*, at the confluence of the Kinzig and the
Wolf, where the 15–17C Schloß is now a museum with a mineral
collection (renovated Schloß chapel) and some of the medieval
defences remain. Wolfach is also a health centre.

The road continues for 10km to *Schiltach* (4000 inhab.; alt. 325m),
situated where the Schiltach flows into the Kinzig. This health resort is
guarded by the ruined Schloß Schiltach (418m); in its Marktplatz of
mostly 18C houses is a town hall dated 1593.—The Rte passes
Schenkenzel (sports, ruined Schloß Schenkenburg, 390m) and then
traverses the gorge known as the Devil's Kitchen to reach after 10km
Alpirsbach (4000 inhab.; alt. 325m), a health resort with a romanesque *church dating from 1099 and housing several Hohenzollern
tombs. The gothic choir and crossing date from the 15C.

After 27km this Rte (known here as the 'Schwarzwald-Tälerstraße')
reaches the winter sports and congress centre of *Freudenstadt
(20,000 inhab.; alt. 740m), the second most popular health centre of
the region (after Baden-Baden).

Herzog Friedrich I of Württemberg founded Freudenstadt in 1599 as a town for
silver miners. Later Protestant refugees from Austria established themselves
here. The imperial forces sacked and burned it in the Thirty Years' War. Almost
50 per cent of the newly built town was destroyed in WWII. The town has been
brilliantly rebuilt (according to the original plans of H. Schickhardt).

Trains connect Freudenstadt with Stuttgart, Rastatt and Offenburg, buses with
Stuttgart, Baden-Baden and Freiburg.

The arcaded Marktplatz has at its centre the fountain (Wachhaus-
brunnen) of 1763, and houses the Stadthaus (with a local history
museum). The town hall and Protestant church of 1608 (restored 1951)
are found at the NE and SW corners of the square. The church (whose
wings meet at right angles, because of its position in the square) now
houses treasures from other sacred buildings throughout the region,
including a lectern c 1180. The Catholic church was built in 1929, the
Kurhaus inn 1951 and the Kurgarten laid out in 1971. A forest of pine
trees covering 2500 hectares surrounds the town.

From Freudenstadt the 'Schwarzwald-Hochstraße' leads for 85km to Baden-
Baden.

13km W of Freudenstadt lies *Bad Rippoldsau-Schapbach*, known for
its curative waters in the Middle Ages, when the Benedictines

developed and exploited them. The Rte here turns N along the B500 and reaches the village spas of *Kniebis* and *Allerheiligen* (with the ruins of a monastery founded in 1196 and a modern church of 1960), climbing to another spa, Ruhestein, and a further 250m to reach *Hornisgrunde* (alt. 1164m, ski lift), before beginning to descend again and reach after 46km the renowned Kurhaus and sanatorium of *Bühlerhöhe*.

Bühlerhöhe is 16km from ****Baden-Baden**, which is reached by way of Baden-Lichtental. Baden-Baden itself (52,000 inhab.; alt. 150–1002m) has been known for its curative waters since Roman times.

History. The Emperor Caracalla (211–217) constructed baths here that can still be seen in Römerplatz (open April–October, 10.00–12.00 and 14.00–17.30, except Mondays). The name Baden appears for the first time in the late 10C, long after the Romans had left and the town had declined. The Zähringen family acquired the town and built a Schloß in the early 12C. In 1689 Baden-Baden was almost totally destroyed. The first Kurhaus since the Romans was built here in 1765 and is the basis of the present building of 1824. The vogue for visiting the town reached its apogee under Napoleon III and has scarcely declined since. 35,000 visitors a year play blackjack, baccarat and roulette in its Casino.

The thermal quarter of the town consists of a fine park with the arcaded Trinkhalle of 1842 (frescoed by Götzenberger with the 'Four Legends of the Black Forest'), the vast Kurhaus by Friedrich Wéinbrenner (1822–24), which incorporates restaurants and the Casino designed in 1854 by Jacques and Edouard Bénazet. NW of the Trinkhalle on the 210m-high Michaelsberg is the *Stourdza Chapel*, built in 1866 by Leo von Klenze to house the body of a Romanian prince who had died in Paris at the age of 17. In the Kurgarten is also the baroque theatre designed by Edouard Bénazet (1862), from which begins the Lichtentaler Allee, an exotic creation by Bénazet inspired by English parks (housing at No. 8a the art gallery, open save

The nineteenth century Augustus Baths, the setting of Dostoevsky's novel 'The Gambler'.

Monday, 10.00–18.00). It leads to _Kloster Lichtental_ (No. 40, Hauptstraße), a Cistercian abbey founded 1245, whose present buildings
date from the 14th and 15Cs. In the courtyard is a fountain dated 1602.
The church, built in 1330 and restored c 1960, contains numerous
treasures (tomb of the foundress, died 1260, by Wölflin von Ruffach;
pulpit of 1606 by Thomas König). Adjoining the church the Fürsten-
kapelle contains the graves of Margraves.

In Schloßstraße is the 16C _Niederbaden Neues Schloß_, now incorporating the Kavalierbau of 1709 and the Küchenbau of 1572 (and
housing Baden-Baden's history museum, open March–October,
10.00–18.00, except Mondays). The main Schloß contains thermal
baths. In the Marktplatz is the late gothic _Marienkirche_, built over the
ruined Roman baths, with a medieval tabernacle, a late gothic
sandstone crucifix by Nicolaus von Leyden (1467), and the rococo
tombs of 'Louis the Turk' (Margrave Ludwig Wilhelm I, died 1707).
The Kurhaus is celebrated for its concerts as well as its waters.
Amongst composers who have been inspired by Baden-Baden was
Brahms who lived here from 1865 to 1874. The Brahmshaus, at No. 85
Maximilianstraße, is a museum (open Monday, Wednesday and
Friday, 15.00–17.00 and Sunday, 10.00–13.00). In earlier times Baden-
Baden was the home of the noted doctor Paracelsus.

Buses run from Baden-Baden into France and into the Black Forest. Trains
connect with Paris, Vienna, Italy, Frankfurt, Holland and Basel. There is an
airport.

D. From Karlsruhe to Kehl by way of Rastatt and Freudenstadt

Total distance 172km. **Karlsruhe**—29km _Rastatt_—18km
Gernsbach—22km _Forbach_—29km _Klosterreichenbach_—10km
Freudenstadt—20km _Bad Peterstal-Griesbach_—24km
Oberkirch—20km _Kehl_.

*__KARLSRUHE__ (276,000 inhab.; alt. 116m), close to the Rhein and a
major port, is the centre of important industries and refineries and was
thus a key target in WWII, when much of the old city was destroyed.

Main _railway station_: Bahnhofsplatz.

Main _post office_: Kaiserstraße.

Information Office: No. 8 Bahnhofsplatz.

Trains connect with Heidelberg, Ettlingen, Stuttgart, Mannheim, Heilbronn,
buses with Heilbronn and Pforzheim.

History. Established by Margrave Karl Wilhelm of Baden-Durbach in 1715,
Karlsruhe (i.e. 'Karl's rest') was laid out in the shape of a fan, along roads
radiating from the new Schloß. In 1800 Friedrich Weinbrenner (1766–1826; born
and died in the city) was engaged to lay out the rest of the city, which he did with
classical regularity. Karl von Drais (inventor of the bicycle) was born here in
1785, as was Carl Benz (creator of the first vehicle driven by petrol) in 1844. Here
Heinrich Hertz made discoveries in the field of electro-magnetics. Between 1852
and 1870 Edward Devrient dominated German theatre from Karlsruhe. Here
lived the authors J.P. Hebel and J.V. von Schefel. Karlsruhe also possesses
Germany's oldest technical university, and is the centre of the country's atomic

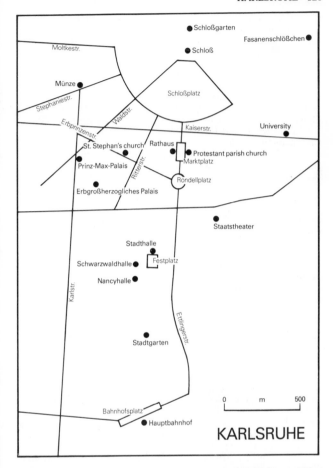

Schloßgarten

Fasanenschlößchen

Moltkestr.

Schloß

Münze

Schloßplatz

Stephaniestr.

Erbprinzenstr.

Waldstr.

Kaiserstr.

University

St. Stephan's church

Rathaus

Protestant parish church

Prinz-Max-Palais

Ritterstr.

Marktplatz

Erbgroßherzogliches Palais

Rondellplatz

Staatstheater

Stadthalle

Schwarzwaldhalle

Festplatz

Nancyhalle

Karlstr.

Ettlingerstr.

Stadtgarten

0   m   500

Bahnhofsplatz

Hauptbahnhof

KARLSRUHE

research as well as the home of EURATOM. The city is also the seat of West Germany's supreme courts and the Federal High Court.

From Bahnhofsplatz take the underground passage to the Stadtgarten (swimming pool, waterfalls, zoo) and cross it to the FESTPLATZ, with the Stadthalle (1915; now a conference centre), the Schwarzwaldhalle (1953), the Gertenhalle (1965) and the Nancyhalle (1967). From here Ettlingerstraße (becoming Karl-Friedrich-Straße) leads by way of the Rondellplatz (column of the constitution, 1826), which contains what remains (the central wing, restored after WWII) of Weinbrenner's 1803 Margrave Palais, to the Marktplatz, in the centre of which is a red sandstone pyramid 6·5m high, enclosing the grave of Friedrich-Wilhelm, founder of the city (died 1738). On the left is the town hall with its square belfry (1815–25), on the right the Protestant parish church (1807–16), resembling a Roman temple, inside which is buried the designer of both buildings, Weinbrenner.

(The interior was not restored to its original style after WWII.) Cross Kaiserstraße to reach the huge triangular SCHLOßPLATZ, whose apex is the octagonal tower of the *Schloß* (1715) and its wings (1749–81; following the original ground pattern of Friedrich von Kesslau and Philippe de la Guêpiérre). Much damaged in the WWII, these buildings have been restored externally (1966) to incorporate the *Badische Landesmuseum* (ranging from prehistory through Egyptian, Greek, Etruscan and Roman sculpture and medieval art to the present; open 10.00–22.00 save Monday, closing Thursday at 17.30). In the centre of the Schloßplatz is a statue of the Grand Duke Karl Friedrich by Schwanthaler (1844). Enter the vast semi-circular *Schloßgarten* by the arcade at the end of the left wing of the Schloß: here are a statue of J.P. Hebel by Steinhüser, 1836; the Wildpark stadium of 1930 (holding 55,000 spectators); tennis and other sports; the botanical gardens, with glasshouses (open weekdays, 09.00–16.00; Saturday and Sunday, 09.00–12.00 and 13.00–17.00); the Margraves' Mausoleum of 1889; and the ornamental Hirsch Gate of 1759 leading to the Fasanenschlösschen of 1765 by Kesslau. To the left of the Schloßgarten, along Moltke-straße, is the youth hostel.

Return to Schloßplatz and by way of Waldstraße reach the **Staatliche Kunsthalle** (No. 2, Hans-Thoma-Straße), with a national collection chiefly built up by the Margraves (Grand Dukes from 1806) of Baden, and including the Crucifixion by Matthias Grünewald and works by Dürer, Grien, Cranach and Holbein, amongst the Germans; and Rembrandt, Rubens and Lucas van Leyden amongst the Dutch, as well as modern works by Max Beckman, Schmidt-Rottluff, Kandinsky, Kokoschka, etc. (open save Monday, 10.00–13.00 and 14.00–17.00). The building is by Heinrich Hübsch (1837–46), with a fresco on the monumental staircase by Moritz von Schwind, depicting the consecration of the Cathedral of Freiburg im Breisgau (1840–42).

Opposite the Orangerie attached to the Gallery, Stephanienstraße leads to the *Münze* by Weinbrenner (1826), which has served as the mint of the Federal Republic since 1948. Karlstraße leads S from the Münze, with on the left at No. 10 the former *Prinz-Max-Palais*, built for the banker August Schmieder (1881–84), and so-named because it was the home of the last Imperial Chancellor, Prinz Max of Baden (1867–1929). It now houses the City Art Gallery and the Museum of the city's history (open save Monday, 10.00–13.00 and 14.00–18.00; Wednesday also 19.00–21.00).

Turn left at the main post office from Karlstraße along Kaiserstraße, which houses the University (1826) and leads to the semi-circular Zirkel, built of identical 19C (well restored) houses for court officials.

Only a short way from the post office along Kaiserstraße is (right) Ritterstraße, which leads to the Catholic church of *St. Stephan* (in Erbprinzenstraße), by Weinbrenner, 1808–14, inspired by the Pantheon, Rome, and housing a Silbermann organ from the abbey of Sankt-Blasien. The post-war restoration has slightly simplfied the building, leaving it with a reinforced concrete dome. Ritterstraße also contains the former Erbgroßherzogliches Palais by J. Durm (1891), now the seat of the supreme court.

OTHER MUSEUMS: Karpatendeutsches Museum of Local History, No. 223 Kaiserstraße (open Monday–Friday, 09.00–15.00); Transport Museum, No. 63

Werderstraße (open Wednesday, 15.00–20.00 and Sunday, 10.00–13.00); Natural History Museum, No. 13 Erbprinzenstraße (open Tuesday 10.00–20.00; Wednesday–Saturday, 10.00–16.00; Sundny, 10.00–17.00).

THEATRES: Staatstheater (1975), No. 11 Baumeisterstraße, with two auditoria of 1002 and 550 seats—opera as well as drama; Kammertheater, No. 79 Waldstraße; Die Insel, Nos 14–16 Wilhelmstraße.

ENVIRONS: at *Karlsruhe-Durlach* (5km E along Durlacher Allee, where the Margraves lived until 1715, is their former Schloß (16–18C), one of whose wings (the Prinzessinenbau) houses a museum with displays of pottery produced at Durlach, 1723–1840, and documents on the Revolution of 1848 (open Saturday, 14.00– 17.00; Sunday, 10.00–12.00, 14.00–17.00). The town possesses richly decorated houses c 1700 and from the fortifications the 16C Basler gate (rebuilt 18C).

From Karlsruhe take the D3 29km SW to **Rastatt** (see Rte 16B). Leave Rastatt SW by way of Niederbühl, passing under the the Basel Karlsruhe motorway to reach after 4km **Schloß Favorite** (see p 117). From here the D462 passes thrugh the village of Gaggenau to reach after 14km the health resort of *Gernsbach* (14,000 inhab.; alt. 185m), situated on both sides of the River Murg (renaissance town hall, 1617; Marienkirche, 14C and 19C; timbered houses and fountains; Jakobskirche with a gothic tabernacle; Storchen tower—the remains of the old Schloß; Kurpark). 2km S is Schloß Eberstein, now housing a restaurant, and after another 20km the village of *Forbach* on the right bank of the Murg (covered wooden bridge of 1778, restored 1955), set amid forests. The Rte continues S through the village of *Raumünzach* (indoor swimming pool) to reach the health resort of Schönmünzach and, after another 27km *Klosterreichenbach*, once the site of a Benedictine monastery (buildings restored in the 19C), now an enterprising health resort. The Rte continues E to *Baiersbronn*, another health resort, and reaches **Freudenstadt** (see Rte 16C) to the S after 10km.

The B28 now winds W to the border crossing of the Rhein into **Alsace**. After 20km it reaches *Bad Peterstal-Griesbach*, whose springs have been reputed since the 16C. The parish church has altars from the former abbey at Allerheiligen. Nearby is *Bad Freyersbach*, noted for its mineral water. The road continues through *Oppenau* (old town gate; cemetery chapel of 1464), travelling along the River Rench to reach *Lautenbach*, with a late gothic pilgrimage church, *Maria Krönung, 1471–83; slightly altered 1900 by the addition of two bays and a tower; inside: choir screen; high altar, with pictures perhaps by Grünewald; glass in the choir from the abbey of Allerheiligen.

After 24km the road reaches *Oberkirch* (17,000 inhab.; alt. 194m), whose September wine festival indicates its importance for that industry. This was the home of J.C. von Grimmelshausen in 1650–67. 20km further W lies *Kehl* (30,000 inhab.; alt. 140m), where the Kinzig and the Schutter flow into the Rhein. Much destroyed during WWII, Kehl has been rebuilt as a modern town, with a town hall of 1969 that also serves as a festival hall. Fine views of the river, which the Europa Bridge crosses on the way to Strasbourg.

E. From Freiburg to Titisee, Donaueschingen, Waldshut, St. Blasien, Lörrach and Bad Säckingen

Total distance 218km. **Freiburg**—B31. 12km *Himmelreich*—18km *Titisee*—30km **Donaueschingen**—B70 and B314. 29km **Waldshut**—B500. 24km **St. Blasien**—23km *Bärental*—B317. 40km *Schopfheim*—12km *Lörrach*—B317 and B518. 30km **Bad Säckingen**.

Leave **Freiburg** (see Rte 16A) E by the Schwardzwalderstraße, passing the sports stadia and through the suburb of Wiehe to join the B31 and the picturesque valley of the Dreisam (known as the 'Valley of Hell' and leading appropriately to Himmelreich, the 'Kingdom of Heaven'), reaching *Ebnet* after 4km (Schloß, 1748–49; in the park sandstone figures of the four seasons by Christian Wenzinger), and after a further 4km *Zarten* (mentioned 1C AD by Ptolemy as *Tardunum*): notable Zartener House. To the S of Zarten is *Kirchzarten* (8000 inhab.; alt. 400m), a health resort; 16C church with romanesque tower. Continue SE from Zarten to Himmelreich (14km S of St. Märgen) and on through *Falkensteig*, with the remains of its old Schloß to the left, as far as *Höllenpaß*, where (at Hirschsprung) a bronze statue of a deer celebrates the legend of a beast which escaped its hunters by springing across the valley in one leap. A little further on is *St. Oswald's chapel* (1148; the oldest still-standing chapel in the Black Forest; restored 1952). Beside the waterfall at the magnificent gorge known as RAVENNASCHLUT is a pathway climbable (up and down) in about 30 minutes.

Further E, 18km from Zarten, the Rte reaches the health and winter sports resort of *Hinterzarten* (camping, tennis, mud bath cures, miniature golf, swimming pools, mountain walks), its old parish church modernised. From here the pass (915m) takes us to the health resort of *Titisee*, situated 858m high between the lake from which it takes its name and the 947m *Hirschbühl* (local history museum; information office in the town hall). 4km further along the B31 lies another health resort, *Neustadt*, founded in the mid 13C (then called Nova Civitas): church of 1797; cuckoo clocks, papermaking and forestry.—The road continues E to Löffingen (game park open to the public) and through Döggingen to reach after 12km **Donaueschingen* (18,000 inhab.; alt. 677m), close by the confluence of the Brigach and the Breg and once the seat of the Princes von Fürstenberg: superb park; Schloß of 1772, altered 1894; baroque, twin-towered church of *St. Johann* (1724–47) housing the relics of St. Valentine and a Madonna c 1525. Here J.V. von Scheffell (1826–86) was court librarian, and the court library (Haldenstraße) houses 140,000 works including 1600 medieval German manuscripts. The source of the Danube is by the Schloß, hence the Donauquelle fountain and statues by Adolf Weinbrenner. Behind the Schloß in the *Karlsbau* (at No. 7 Karlsplatz) is the former princely art collection, which includes paintings by Lucas Cranach, Hans Holbein the Elder and Grünewald (open, except Mondays and November, 09.00–12.00 and 13.30–17.00). Donaueschingen runs a music festival each August and an international music festival in October. Information Office No. 41 Karlstraße. Trains run to Freiburg, Ulm, Stuttgart, Konstanz.

4km E of Donaueschingen, en route to Geisingen, is *Neudingen* where Charlemagne died (888), close by the *Fürstenberg* (795m high), the origin of the name of the noble family.

From Donaueschingen the E70 leads 17km SE to join the B314 which runs 43km SW along the Swiss border to Waldshut, passing through *Stühlingen* (former Capuchin monastery; Schloß Hohenlupfen and Tiengen Schloß). *Waldshut* (23,000 inhab.; alt. 300m), on the right bank of the Rhein, with fine views into Switzerland, is where the peasants' revolt of 1524 broke out. The old town preserves two 13C tower-gates. On the third weekend in August a festival celebrates the emancipation of the Waldshut from the Swiss in 1468.

The B500 now runs 25km N to St. Blasien, passing through the health resort of *Höchenschwand*, at 1015m the highest village in the Black Forest, with superb views in fine weather from nearby peaks as far as Mont Blanc and the Jura mountains.

*St. Blasien** (3200 inhab.; alt. 760m) is the site of a celebrated Benedictine **abbey**, founded in the 9C. After its medieval buildings had been replaced by a huge baroque group (1727–48) a disastrous fire of 1768 meant that almost all had to be rebuilt, by the French architect Pierre Michel d'Ixnard, much of whose work (completed 1772 and in the early classical style under the influence of the Pantheon, Rome) remains. The dome of the church (72m high and 34m in diameter inside) was finished by Nicolas de Pigage in 1781, who respected the plans of d'Ixnard. In the crypt lie the ancestors of the Habsburgs. The monks left St. Blasien in 1806. In consequence many of the treasures of the church have disappeared. The monastery library perished (in Karlsruhe) in WWII. The town today has a noted Jesuit college. Here was born the painter Hans Thoma (1839–1924), whose work is displayed in the town hall.

Titisee, 34km N of St. Blasien, is reached by way of lakes and health and sports restorts: Seebrugg, Schluchsee (whose once tiny lake has become the largest in the Black Forest through damming), Windfällweiher, Altglashütten (where glass has been made since the 17C), and (after 23km) Bärental. At Bärental turn left along the B317 and travel SW through *Todtnau* (5300 inhab.; alt. 600m), situated in healthy winter sports country (cable chair to the 1158m-high *Hesselhorn*; waterfall). 8km SW lies *Schönau* (altar c 1530 in parish church). An excursion 13km NE leads to the *Belchen* (1414m high: orientation table). After another 19km the B317 reaches *Schopfheim* (Höckling chapel, c 1400, with wall paintings; late gothic church of St. Michael, 1482, built on romanesque foundations, with some traces of 14C wall paintings; classical town hall, 1820–30). 12km W is *Lörrach* (43,000 inhab.; alt. 296m) close where the Rhein is crossed into **Basel**, Switzerland. Lörrach produces fine wines, has a Protestant parish church by Weinbrenner (1815–17) and a statue of Hebel, who was professor here. In the suburb of *Haagen* is the ruined Schloß Rötteln and in the suburb of *Tüllingen* a late gothic church with frescoes and a tabernacle of 1474. Trains run into Basel.

Return from Lörrach to Schopfheim and follow the B518 for 18km to *Bad Säckingen**, made famous by Joseph Viktor von Scheffel's 'Trumpeter of Säckingen': Scheffel lived between 1850 and 1852 in the house belonging to the Teutonic knights at the end of the covered wooden bridge (1580). From the old fortifications remain the 14C Gallus and Diebs towers. The gothic minster of *St. Fridolin* (14–17C) is dedicated to the town's patron saint who founded a monastery here. Each March a festival is held in the saint's honour. Bad Säckingen is also a health resort, with swimming pools, mineral springs and clinics. The Hochrhein Museum (in the Schloß, c 1600, much rebuilt 1964–68) contains prehistoric finds, as well as exhibitions connected with Hans Thoma and Scheffel (open Tuesday, Thursday and Sunday, 15.00–17.00). From Bad Säckingen the B34 runs for 28km E to **Waldshut**.

17 From Karlsruhe to Ulm by way of Stuttgart

Total distance 137km. **Karlsruhe**—B10. 27km **Pforzheim**—17km *Vaihingen*—22km **Stuttgart**—29km *Göppingen*—18km *Geislingen an der Steige*—24km *Ulm*.

Leave **Karlsruhe** (see Rte 16D) by the Durlacher Allee and by way of *Durlach* through *Grötzingen* (privately owned Schloß, 16th and 17C) passing under the Munich–Salzburg motorway just before reaching **Pforzheim** (106,000 inhab.; alt. 275m). Once a Roman colony (*Porta Hetcyniae*), Pforzheim was the birthplace of the humanist Johann Reuchlin (1455–1522). Situated at the confluence of the Rivers Enz, Nagold and Würm, it developed jewellery making and goldsmiths' ware in the 18C. Much of the town was destroyed in WWII. Tourist information at No. 1 Marktplatz.

The *Schloß church* (restored and rebuilt, 1949–57), close by the station, was founded in the 11C and retains a romanesque doorway. Its 15C gothic choir has tombs of the Margraves of Baden, who lived at Pforzheim from 1535–65. The church of *St. Martin* in the old town (in Aldstädterstraße) likewise retains a romanesque doorway, finely carved, and in its mid 14C choir late gothic wall paintings, including the Last Judgment.

To the S of the town the *Reuchlinhaus* at No. 42 Jahnstraße houses a museum of 4000 years of jewellery (open weekdays, 09.00–12.00 and 14.00–18.00; Saturday, 09.00–12.00). At No. 243 Karl-Friedrich-Straße is a local history museum. The town theatre is in Osterfeldstraße.

The routes from Pforzheim to **Freudenstadt**, some 90km S, pass through the health and winter sports resorts of the northern part of the Black Forest. From the town the B10 runs NE for 17km to *Vaihingen* (23,000 inhab.; alt. 103m), dominated by the 12th and 16C *Schloß Kaltenstein* (on a 270m peak) and retaining the Haspel and Pulver towers from its old fortifications.

AN ALTERNATIVE ROUTE (45km) FROM KARLSRUHE TO VAIHINGEN BY WAY OR BRETTEN AND MAULBRONN

Leave **Karlsruhe** for *Durlach*. At Durlach drive 20km NE to *Bretten*, birthplace of the humanist and Protestant reformer Philipp Schwarzherd, known as Melanchthon (1497–1560): statue in the Marktplatz; a new *Melanchthon House* (1897–1903 at No. 1 Melanchthonstraße), replacing his birthplace (destroyed 1689) houses the Melanchthon museum with 450 manuscripts in his hand, 800 of his works and 5500 books on the Reformation (open 15 March–30 September daily, 09.00–11.00 and 14.00–16.00). The Protestant parish church dates from the 14C and 18C. Two towers remains from the old town fortifications: the 14C Simmelturm and the 16C Pfeiferturm.

The B35 leads from here E through *Knittlingen*, birthplace in the 16C of Johannes Faust, the inspirer of Goethe's drama (a house near the church, said to be where he was born, is now a museum to him).—6km from Bretten, the B35 reaches **Maulbronn**, where a Cistercian **abbey** was founded in 1146 (romanesque *church conse-crated 1178 with early 15C gothic chapels and a crucifix of 1473; 13C portal—the 'Paradise'— on W side; 13C romanesque–gothic cloister on N side, with a monks' refectory c 1225, and early 12C lay refectory, a late 13C chapterhouse and a fine fountain). In 1556 this abbey became (and still) remains a Protestant seminary, where between 1786 and 1788 Friedrich Hölderlin and between 1891 and 1892 Hermann Hesse were educated.

From here the B35 continues SE for 15km to *Vaihingen*.

Continue SE along the B10 to reach shortly *Markgröningen** (12,500 inhab.; alt. 114m): medieval Marktplatz with fountain (1580), 15C town hall; Protestant parish church of *St. Bartholomew*, c 1300, with 14th and 15C wall and ceiling paintings and choir stalls c 1300; a font of 1426; the huge W towers finished by A. Jörg, 1472. The Catholic parish church (former Spitalskirche), with a choir of c 1300, is next to the 15th and 16C hospital. The Shepherds' Race held here on the weekend after St. Bartholomew's day (24 August) dates from 1443.

After 22km the B10 reaches **STUTTGART** (600,000 inhab.; alt. 207m), lying on the W side of the River Neckar, and the capital of Baden-Württemberg. At the heart of a wine-producing and agricul-tural region, with mineral water springs, and a centre for printing, textiles, cameras and car manufacture, Stuttgart is of economic importance for the whole Federal Republic.

Main *railway station*: Arnulf-Klett-Platz.

Main *post office*: Ehmannstraße.

Information Office: at the main railway station and at No. 5 Lautens-chlagerstraße.

Trains connect with all the other major cities of West Germany and with France and Switzerland. Passenger *boats* ply the Neckar. *Echterdingen airport* is 14km S of the city.

History. Duke Luitolf set up a stud farm (hence 'Stuttgart') here in the mid 10C. The city greatly developed after Ulrich I built here a Schloß (1241–65). In 1321 the city became the seat of the Counts of Württemberg, who were raised to dukes by the emperor in 1495. Duke Karl Eugen (1737–93) founded here a famous school (where Schiller was educated). In 1803 the duke became an elector and two years later Napoleon made him king. Stuttgart expanded greatly under King Wilhelm I (1816–64) who saw the first railway reach the city in 1845. Württem-berg became a free state in 1918, with Stuttgart as its capital. Though savagely bombed in 1944 (losing 60 per cent of its buildings) much of Stuttgart has been restored.

Stuttgart, the birthplace of the philosopher G.W.F. Hegel, boasts a university, and a renowned orchestra. Its 217m-high TV tower (on the wooded Hoher Bopser, itself 482m high) has an observation platform and restaurant at 150m.

The main railway station in Arnulf-Klett-Platz (named after the Oberbürgermeister of Stuttgart from 1945 to 1974), is by Paul Bonatz, 1914–27, and has an observation tower 58m high, with a lift to the top. Cannstatterstraße divides the main railway station from the vast SCHLOßGARTEN, well laid out with fountains and cafés. At the NE end of the park is found Schloß Rosenstein (1823–29), close by the Neckar. Here on the corner of Ehmannstraße is the post office, and to the NW the Wilhelma botanical and zoological gardens (buildings by Zanth, 1851).

Returning to the main railway station (in front of which is the Hindenburg building of 1928), take the Königstraße SW from the station (its shops and other buildings almost entirely rebuilt since WWII). To the left is the modern Schloß garden building fronting this part of the Schloßgarten. Here are to be found the classical *Neues* Schloß (1746–1807; by Retti, de la Guêpiérre and Thouret; restored 1961), once the home of the monarchs, now of the ministry of finance and culture); the art gallery (1913; by Theodor Fischer); the state opera house; the parliament building of Baden-Württemberg (1961; by Viertel, Linde and Heinle); and the state theatre (1962).

Königstraße continues SW past (on the left) the modern church of St. Eberhard (1955) to reach the Schloßplatz, with its chestnut trees, which has two fountains and the 30m-high granite Jubilee Column (with statues by Wagner) erected in 1841 to commemorate the 25th anniversary of the accession of Wilhelm I, as well as a monument to Christoph von Württemberg (died 1568). To the right is the colonnaded Königsbau (by Knapp and Leins, 1856–60; restored and now housing shops and cafés). The Kleiner Schloßplatz, further on, is where the former Palais of the Crown Prince stood until 1944. Left of the Schloßplatz stands the Neues Schloß (see above) and to the SW the irregular *Altes Schloß* with its round towers (1555–78; mostly by A. Tretsch, restored after WWII) with a splendid interior court. The equestrian statue of Eberhard Duke of Württemberg (died 1496) is by Hofer. The Altes Schloß now houses the Land Museum, with treasures depicting the history of Baden-Württemberg from prehistoric times to the 19C.

The Altes Schloß faces onto SCHILLERPLATZ (statue of the poet by Bertel Thorwaldsen, 1839). On the left is the former Chancellery

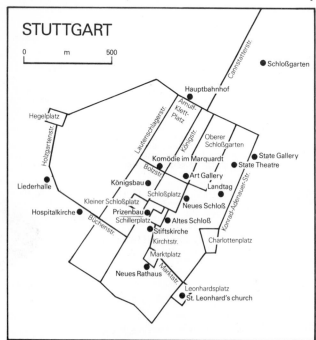

(1543–66, now a restaurant), close by which is a Mercury fountain. Schillerplatz also houses the Prinzenbau (1605–1715; now the ministry of justice); the late gothic tithe house (Stiftsfruchkasten, with a renaissance façade of 1596); and the late gothic *Stiftskirche (1433–56; by Hänslin and Alberlin Jörg; W tower finished 1531; interior restored, with, amongst the tombs, those of the Württemberg counts by S. Schlör, 1576–1608).

Kirchstraße leads from here S to the Marktplatz, with Stuttgart's new town hall (boasting a 30-bell glockenspiel in its 60m-high tower, playing Swabian folk songs at 11.06, 12.06, 14.36 and 21.36 daily). Markstraße runs SE from the Marktplatz to Leonhardsplatz and the flamboyant gothic church of St. Leonhard, by Alberlin Jörg, 1463–1474, tower 1491 (Crucifixion scene a copy of that by Seyffer in the Hospitalkirche, see below). The fountain depicting evening, by the church, is by Fremd (1900).

NW from Königstraße (just SW of Kirchstraße) Büchsenstraße leads past, on the left, the Hospitalkirche by A. Jörg, 1471–93, of which only a tower and the choir remain (in the choir a Crucifixion group by Hans Seyffer, 1501). At the end of Büchsenstraße is found Stuttgart's Liederhalle (by A. Abel, R. Gutbrod and B. Spreng, 1956, with three concert halls, holding respectively 2000, 750 and 350 listeners, and a restaurant). From here Holzgartenstraße runs N to Hegelplatz and the Linden Museum of Natural History.

In 1927 Mies van der Rohe brought together 16 European architects to design houses for an international exhibition. These, by Mies and by such architects as Le Corbusier, are found (many restored after WWII) in the Weissenhofsiedlung.

THEATRES: Staats Theater, No. 6 Oberer Schloßgarten; Komödie im Marquardt, Nos 4–6 Bolzstraße; Altes Schauspielhaus, Kleine Königstraße; Theater der Altstadt, Charlottenplatz.

GALLERIES: State Gallery, No. 32 Konrad-Adenauer-Straße: superb collection of paintings and prints (open save Monday, 10.00–17.00; to 20.00 Tuesday and Thursday); Landesmuseum, in the Altes Schloß, Schillerplatz: scuplture, weapons, musical instruments, textiles, church art, porcelain, etc. (open save Monday, 10.00–17.00); Porsche Motor Museum, No. 42 Porschestraße (open weekdays, 09.00–12.00 and 13.30–16.00); Linden Museum of Natural History, No. 1 Hegelplatz (at present closed); Galerie der Stadt Stuttgart, No. 2 Schloßplatz: 19th and 20C art (open save Monday, 10.00–17.00, closes Wednesdays 19.00). Daimler-Benz Museum, No. 137a Mercedes-Straße (open weekdays, 08.00–12.00 and 13.30–16.30; second Saturday in month, 08.00–12.00).

ENVIRONS: at Rotenburg, W of the city, is the rococo Lustschloß Solitude, built for Herzog Karl Eugen, 1763–67; and the mausoleum (1824) of Wilhelm I's queen, Katharine of Russia (died 1819; Wilhelm also lies there).

For Ludwigsburg see p 138.

Leave Stuttgart by taking Cannstatterstraße NE and turning right before the Neckar bridge. The B10 now runs SE through Wangen (where the Daimler-Benz Motor Museum is found) and through Rotenberg (see above) to reach after 12km *Esslingen (96,000 inhab.; alt. 240m). Situated on the Neckar, surrounded by vineyards, Esslingen was settled in the Bronze Age and apears first in written history in AD 777. Its oldest gate, the Wolfstor (c 1220), carries the Hohenstaufen coat of arms. Esslingen became a free imperial city, and here in 1488 the Swabian League was formed. Esslingen became part of Württemberg in 1802, and the town's industries started to develop. The firm of Kessler began producing Sekt here in 1826 and remains the oldest Sekt producer in Germany. The late 13C Pliens bridge is the oldest stone bridge in Baden-Württemberg.

The old town centre remains intact. Here the Neckar canal is spanned by the Innere Brücke, which incorporates a chapel. 80m above the town stands the *Burg*, a walled Hohenstaufen fortress with defensive towers. The late gothic *old town hall* (c 1430), once the tax house, has a renaissance N façade (by H. Schickhardt, 1586, with a Glockenspiel) and now is the town museum; the baroque new town hall dates from 1746. *St. Dionysius's* church in the Hafenmarkt (13th and 14C) spans the change between romanesque and gothic, its twin towers bizarrely bridged. Inside is a choir screen of 1486 and a tabernacle of 1496 by L. Lechler; stained glass in the choir, 1290–1310. The church houses a museum. Outside, by the choir, is the 13C romanesque Kesslerhouse, close by which (along Archivstraße) is the 13C Totenkapelle. N of the Hafenmarkt stands the gothic church of *St. Paul*, dating from 1233–68, once belonging to a Dominican monastery and the oldest church of a mendicant order in Germany. A bridge leads W over Augustinerstraße to the Marienkirche (1321–1516), close by the old city gate, which boasts a 75m-high tower by Ulrich von Ensingen and fine glass (1320–30) in the choir.

Information Office at No. 16 Marktplatz. Trains connect with Stuttgart, Tübingen and Ulm and buses with Plochingen.

A brief EXCURSION S reaches *Denkendorf*, with a romanesque church (late 12C and early 13C, rebuilt 1377; in the crypt 15C wall paintings of St. Martin, Herod and Salome and the beheading of John the Baptist (also late gothic altar in the choir and early 16C tombstones).

Leave Esslingen by the B10 to reach *Plochingen* (parish church, 1488, with a renaissance pulpit) and then, 39km from Esslingen, Göppingen by way of *Ebersbach* (fortified gothic church), *Uhingen* (17C Schloß) and *Faurndau* (13C church). **Göppingen** (54,000 inhab.; alt. 408m) has a Schloß of 1560, (by A. Tresch and M. Berwart; decorated staircases); a parish church of 1619 designed by H. Schickhardt (tower 1838); and, NE of the town at *Oberhofen*, a 15C church with a late gothic choir, wall paintings of 1499, choir stalls, 1500, and a crucifix, c 1520. The town hall was built in 1783, the Theatre (by Schnitger) in 1890. Göppingen lies at the foot of the 684m-high *Hohenstaufen* with its ruined Imperial Schloß (1079). Most of the old town was destroyed in a fire of 1782. The town *museum* at No. 36 Wühlerstraße is housed in a building of 1536 (open mid-March to mid-November daily, except Sunday, 10.00–12.00 and 14.00–17.00. Information Office at No. 1 Bahnhofstraße.

10km S of the city is *Bad Boll*, with a celebrated Evangelische Akademie (made famous by the Protestant Pastor Johann Christoph Blumhardt, 1805–80, and his son Pastor Christoph Friedrich Blumhardt, 1842–1919).

The B10 continues SE of Göppingen, reaching after 18km *Geislingen an der Steige* (28,000 inhab.; alt. 44m), where five valleys meet: 15C town hall; fortified tower (the Odenturm); ruined Schloß Helfenstein; 15C late gothic church (stalls by Jörg Syrlin the Younger, high altar of 1525, renaissance wooden pulpit by Daniel Hendenberger, 1621); old customs house (15C and 1593) among many fine half-timbered houses. Tourist information at No. 19

Hauptstraße. From here the Rte runs S for 36km to **Ulm** (see Rte 1B).

18 From Ulm to Lindau by way of Friedrichshafen

Total distance 156km. **Ulm.**—B28 20km *Blaubeuren.*—B492 18km *Ehingen.* —llkm *Laupheim.*—B30 18km **Biberach an der Riß** (—B312 11km Ochsenhausen).—23km B30 **Bad Waldsee.**—17km **Weingarten.**—4km **Ravensburg.**—20km **Friedrichshafen.**—B31 25km **Lindau**.

Leave **Ulm** (see Rte 1B), cross the Fahrbrücke and continue along the valley of the Blau. After 8km the road passes through *Klingstein* with a 15C Schlößchen on the left, arriving 12km later at *Blaubeuren* (12,000 inhab.; alt. 520m), to see its Benedictine monastic buildings (now a Protestant seminary), dating from 1466–1510 (interior of church 1499: choir stalls by Syrlin the Younger; *high altar worked on by Gregor Erhart, Bartholomäus Zeitblom and Bernhard Strigel). See also 15C Protestant church and town hall of 1593.

Turn S along the B492 for 18km to *Ehingen* (22,000 inhab.; alt. 511m). In the 13C Ehingen was already an Alamannic settlement and became prosperous in the 15th and 16C. In spite of several damaging fires (especially in 1688 and 1749), Ehringen has retained many architectural treasures: the Ritterhaus of 1692; the late gothic parish church (with 18C transformations and classical and baroque statues); the former Franciscan church of Our Lady (1725; housing a 15C Madonna) and the baroque *Konviktskirche (1719; in the form of a Greek Cross, with stucco decoration). Trains connect Ehringen with Ulm, buses with Tübingen, Lindau and Ulm.

From Ehringen travel 11km SE to *Laupheim* (15,000 inhab.; alt. 515m): Schloß Groß Laupheim (16th and 18C); 17C baroque church of SS Peter and Paul; swimming and camping, parks and walks; processions third Sunday in July. Here are bred Pinsgau horses. Close by at Rottum is Schloß Kleim Laupheim (1789).

Follow the B30 18km S to *Biberach, on the River Riß (29,000 inhab.; alt. 532m). Of the fortifications remain the Gigel tower (1373), the Ulm gate (1410) and the White tower (1480), enfolding numerous half-timbered houses. The Marktplatz houses the 15C town hall, and at No. 17 the Wieland Museum (open Saturday and Sunday, 10.00–12.00 and 14.00–17.00; Wednesday, 10.00–12.00 and 14.00–18.00). The late gothic parish church has a baroque interior (pulpit, 1511; high altar, 1720; nave fresco by J. Zick, 1746; choir screen 1768). Here in 1655 was founded a theatre which Christoph Martin Wieland (1733–1813, born close by at Oberholzeim) took over in 1760, to direct the following year his own translation of Shakespeare. Other noted artists working here were the composer Justin Heinrich Knecht (1752–1817) and the goldsmith Johann Michel Dinglinger (1664–1731). A children's and marksmen's festival takes place in July. The Art Gallery, No. 6 Museumstraße, has a room devoted to the expressionist painter Ernst Ludwig Kirchner (open save Monday, 10.00–12.00 and 14.00–17.00). Trains connect with Ulm and Friedrichshafen, buses with more local spots.

An EXCURSION for 11km E along the B312 leads to *Ochsenhausen* (6500 inhab.; alt. 612m). Its Benedictine *abbey*, founded 1100, became a centre of

learning and culture in the 18C, when the buiuldings, partly destroyed during
the Thirty Years' War, were reconstructed in the baroque style: choir stalls, 1686;
frescoes by Josef Gabler and J.B. Bergmüller, 1728–36 (Gabler also designed the
organ case); stucco by the Italian G. Mola; rococo high altar; pulpit by Ä.
Verhelst, 1741. The monastery buildings still stand intact and are now in part a
school. The classical library was restored 1984.

From Biberach an der Riß the B30 continues S for 23km to *Bad
Waldsee* (15,000 inhab.; alt. 600m), a spa with mud baths, situated
between two lakes, known as the Schloßsee and the Stadtsee (beach
and boating): gothic town hall, 1426, with an impressive gable,
opposite the 15C town granary (Kornhaus), now a local history
museum opening Sundays in summer 10.00–12.00; 15C parish church
with high altar, 1467; 16C and 18C Schloß Waldburg-Wolfegg. The
route now continues S to Ravensberg (21km), passing through *Bad
Waldsee-Gaisburen*, with its tiny romanesque chapel of St. Leonhard,
and *Baindt*, whose romanesque–gothic church was decorated inside
by F.M. Kuen, c 1763, and contains a 14C gothic crucifix and a rococo
high altar of 1764 by Johann Georg Dirr. Next follows **Weingarten*,
celebrated for its **abbey**, which was founded for women in the 10C
and taken over by men in the next. In 1715 Abbot Sebastian Hyller
demolished the 12th and 13C abbey church, replacing it with the
present one, begun by Franz Beer and finished by Christoph Thumb,
A. Schreck and above all by Donato Guiseppe Frisoni (who was
responsible for the dome and the high altar). It is the largest baroque
monastery church in Germany (interior of the nave 102m by 29m, the
vault rising 28m, the dome 66m): frescoes by C.D. Asam, stucco by
Franz Schmuzer, 1718, choir stalls by J.A. Feuchtmayr, 1730, organ
case (4 keyboards and 741 pipes) by Josef Gabler, 1737–50, rococo
pulpit by F. Sporer, 1765. The town also has a restored Kornhaus at
No. 28 Karlstraße (in which is the Alamannenmuseum).

In 1094 Weingarten had been given a supposed drop of Christ's blood, and this
relic contributed to its fame and wealth. Each year on the Friday after Ascension
Day ('Blutfreitag') a procession of over 2000 riders celebrates the 'Blutritt'. The
monks left Weingarten in 1806, to return in 1922.

*Ravensburg (43,200 inhab.; alt. 449m), 4km from Weingarten, in the
valley of the Schussen, is still surrounded by its 14C walls, three gates
and four towers. The *Veitsburg* dominates the town from the SE, once
the site of a Schloß where Henry the Lion was born. Close by here is
an Alamannic burial ground, founded in the 6C and containing more
than 800 graves. The town was called *Ravensburc* in 1088. In 1380 the
Große Ravensburger Handelsgesellschaft was set up to exploit the
profitable linen trade. The town also profited from its close association
with Weingarten.

In the Marktplatz are the Weigh-house, 1498 (once the market hall),
the Blaserturm (trumpeter's tower), 1556, and the 15C gabled town
hall (altered 1876 and 1930) with an oriel window of 1571 (inside, two
fine rooms and wall paintings of 1581). Marktstraße leads to the
Brotlaube, 1625. See also the Leather House of 1574. At No. 36
Charlottenstraße the 15C Vogthaus houses the town museum (open
Wednesday–Saturday, 15.00–17.00; Sunday also 10.00–12.00).

Churches include the 14C Liebfrauenkirche, with 15C glass in the
choir, a 15C high altar and tabernacle, 15C choir stalls. Trains run
from here to Friedrichshafen and Ulm. The Information Office is at
No. 15 Marienplatz.

The B30 now runs 20km SW to **Friedrichshafen** (53,000 inhab.; alt. 400m), on the **Bodensee** (Lake Constance), because of its situation a major tourist centre. Information Office at No. 18 Friedrichstraße. The town dates from 1811, when the Neustadt linked the villages of Buchhorn and Hofen. It profited from passenger traffic on the lake, and from here the first Zeppelin took off in 1900. Much was destroyed in WWII. The Ducal Schloß of 1830 (adapting an older monastery building of 1654–1701) and its twin-towered church (by Christoph Thumb, 1700, stuccoes by the Schmuzers) remain from the old town. The town hall dates from 1956 and houses a Zeppelin museum (open save Monday, 10.00–12.00 and 14.00–17.00). The town has some superb gardens. Trains connect with Ulm and Lindau, boats with Konstanz and Bregenz, buses with Lindau, Ravensburg, etc.

The route to Lindau passes alongside the **Bodensee** (*lacus Brigantinus* to the Romans), Central Europe's third largest (76km by 14km) and bordering on Austria, Switzerland and Germany. Leaving Friedrichshafen by the B31 the lakeside route runs SE for 10km to *Langenargen* (5800 inhab.; alt. 400m), a home of the Montforts from 1290 to 1780. Here Wilhelm I of Württemberg built a Moorish castle in 1861. The baroque church of St. Martin dates from 1722. After 15km the road reaches *Kreßbronn* (camping and tourism), 2km W of *Nonnenborn* (gothic Jakobskapelle; wine press of 1591). After 2km more the road reaches *Wasserburg* (the Fuggers' Schloß of 1592 is now a hotel). The Lieber Augustin Monument is here because the novelist H.W. Gießler who wrote 'Der liebe Augustin' lived at Wasserburg.

Lindau (see p 82) and the Austrian border are reached after 6km.

19 From Konstanz to Heilbronn

Total distance 272km. **Konstanz**—52km *Radolfzell*, through Switzerland. —B34 15km *Stockach*.—B313 21km *Meßkirch*.—17km *Sigmaringen*.—B22 23km *Mengen*.—B311 10km **Riedlingen**.—B312 42km **Reutlingen**.—B27 16km **Stuttgart**.—B27 16km *Ludwigsburg*.—25km *Lauffen am Neckar*.—10km **Heilbronn**.

Konstanz (or Constance) (70,000 inhab.; alt. 400m) on the **Bodensee** (see above) is said to have been founded in the 3C by the father of Constantine the Great, Emperor Constantine Chlorus (283–306). In Alemannic times it became a bishopric (c 590) and enriched itself by the linen trade. The Catholic Council of Constance was held here between 1414 and 1418 and attempted to heal the schism caused by the Avignon papacy. The same Council ordered John Wycliffe's body to be removed from consecrated ground and condemned the Bohemian Reformer Jan Huss to death. (He was executed here in 1415.)

The French essayist Michel de Montaigne lived in the Haus Marktstätte 8 (now the Gasthof zum Adler) in 1580, and in Villa Seeheim (No. 86 Eichhornstraße) lived from 1890 the writer who helped (by his 'Bodensee' and his 'Jew of Konstanz') to make the region famous, Wilhelm von Scholz (1874–1969. In 1848 the revolutionary Friedrich Hecker proclaimed at Konstanz the German Republic.

The major church building is the romanesque cathedral of **Our Lady**, built on the site of a Roman fort. The crypt dates from c 1000 and building ended only when the gothic pyramidical tower was finished in 1856. The W door carvings are from the workshop of Simon Haider,

1470. Interior: *Holy Sepulchre in the Mauritius chapel, c 1280; 15C crucifix; late gothic staircase (known as 'Schnegg') in N transept, with Old and New Testament scenes, 1438; choir stalls, school of Haider, c 1467; altar c 1660, by Franz Morinck; 17C wooden pulpit by Daniel Schenk.

The Kaufhaus on the harbour, 1388, restored 1970, is called the 'Konzil', in the erroneous belief that it was the seat of the Council of 1414–18. Opposite is the Zeppelin memorial (to the Graf von Zeppelin born here 1838). Across the Stadgarten on the 'Half Island' you reach the former Jesuit church of Christ (baroque, now belonging to the Old Catholics) and the *Stadtheater* of 1610 (No. 11 Konzilstraße), the oldest theatre in West Germany. Opposite on the Dominican Island is the former Dominican monastery, now a hotel which incorporates even the church with its gothic transept. The Blessed Henry Suso lived here in the 14C. (He was born at the Haus zur Täsch, No. 39 Hussenstraße.) The cathedral square houses a museum of the linen and silk industries (No. 5, Haus zur Kunkel, open weekdays, 10.00–12.00 and 14.00–17.00) and the city archives in the Haus zu Katze (1424).

Wessenbergstraße leads S from Münsterplatz with (at No. 41) the city art gallery (open save Monday, 14.00–17.00; Sunday, only 11.00–13.00). This street leads to the church of St. Stephan, 1424–86 (interior baroque: Hans Morinck's tomb for his wife; tabernacle c 1600). In Rosgartenstraße is the late 13C church of the *Holy Trinity*, with noted frescoes depicting the history of the Augustinians, 1417. The Rosgarten Museum is close by (Nos 3–5).

Konstanz has an international Casino at No. 21 Seestraße; its Information Office is at No. 9 Bahnhofsplatz. Trains connect with Immendingen and Singen, and boats ply the lake.

To travel around the S side of the Bodensee here means crossing into Switzerland. 3km W of Konstanz is *Gottlieben* (the Druchenberg House of 1617; a Schloß of 1250, redone in the neo-gothic style, 1838,

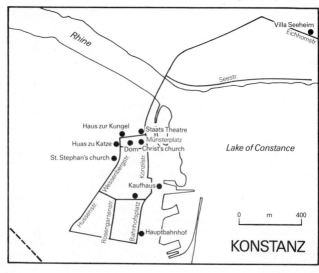

where Huss awaited execution), followed by *Manenbach*, with numerous early 19C Schlößer (the most important of which is a Napoleon Museum) and the medieval town of *Steckborn* (14C and 17C small castles; town hall of 1667), and then *Stein am Rhein*, the most beautiful Swiss medieval town.

Cross back into Germany and drive NE to **Radolfzell** 51km from Konstanz) by way of *Gaienhofen* where Hermann Hesse lived from 1904–1907. (It is possible to drive directly along the B33 from Konstanz to Radolfzell.) On the site of a hermitage built by St. Radolf (9C Bishop of Verona) has grown a town which belonged to Austria until 1805. St. Radolf is buried in the 15C gothic church (Drei-Hausherren-Altar, 1750). Three towers of the medieval fortifications remain. The writer Scheffel made his home here, building the Haus Seehalde, 1873 (No. 14 Scheffelstraße). The town is now a holiday and sports resort, with a bird sanctuary. Trains connect it with Konstanz, Lindau and Munich, boats with Konstanz, Reichenau, Stein am Rhein.

From Radolfzell the B34 runs N for 15km to *Stockach* (12,700 inhab.; alt. 475m) at the foot of the *Nellenburg* with its ruined Schloß, famed for the wildness of its Shrovetide Carnival celebrations whose liberties are said to date back to a 14C court jester Kuony von Stocken (hence the Kuony fountain in the Marktplatz). From Stockach the B313 leads N through wooded hills for 21km to *Meßkirch* (7000 inhab.; alt. 600m). The basilica of *St. Martin* by L. Reder, 1536, is today neo-classical as a result of the work of F.A. Bagnato in the late 18C. It retains from the earlier buiding an Adoration of 1538, a bronze tomb by P. Labenwolf, 1558, and a massive tomb by W. Neidhardt, 1599, as well as the St. Johann Nepomuk chapel decorated by the brothers Asam, 1734. The 14C church of Our Lady was altered in 1576 by Jörg Schwartzenberger, who also designed the ballroom of the Schloß (now the local history museum, open daily, 09.00–12.00 and 14.00–17.00). The town hall dates from the 17C. The philosopher Martin Heidegger (1889–1976) was born here.

Continue along the B313 N for 17km to *Sigmaringen* (15,000 inhab.; alt. 570m), whose *Schloß* was once the home of the Hohenzollern-Sigmaringen family. Rebuilt in the 1893 after a fire, it houses a rich collection (open daily, 08.30–12.00 and 13.00–17.30). The 12C romanesque church of St. Gallus has a 15C choir decorated in the baroque and rococo styles. At Sigmaringen in 1944–45 after their retreat from France the Nazis established a 'French Government', and here was interned Marshal Pétain after his arrest. The road from Sigmaringen winds E, joining the B32 before Mengen, which is reached after 23km. *Mengen* (9400 inhab.; alt. 580m) has fine half-timbered houses of the 16–18C and a gothic church of Our Lady. From here the B311 travels 10km N to *Riedlingen* (8700 inhab.; alt. 540m), still for the most part a picturesque old town, amongst whose fine houses are the mid 15C town hall (with its stork's nest), the former granary of 1686 (called the Alte Kaserne). The 14C church of *St. Georg* has gothic wall paintings and glass of 1898 by the local glassmaker Albert Burkart.

The B312 leads N for 14km to *Zwiefalten*, where the baroque monastery church of **Our Lady* was built to plans of Johann Michel Fischer, 1740–65. Inside: stucco by J.M. Feuchtmayr, painting by A. Meinrad, and F.J. Spiegler, sculpture by J. Christian. The church also shelters a Byzantine reliquary altar of the 12C. Many domestic buildings of the monastery survive, and the large 17C wing is now a psychiatric clinic.

From Zwiefalten take the B312 NE for 42km to **Reutlingen** (96,000 inhab.; alt. 869m), an industrial town (engineering, textiles, tanneries) whose history began in the 11C. Inspite of much damage in WWII, fine buildings remain. Situated on the River Echaz, the town has preserved parts of its medieval fortificatins. In front of the railway station stands a monument to the economist Friederick List (a native of the town, 1789–1846). Wilhelmstraße leads SE from the station past the Nikolaikirche (1358; rebuilt after the war), in front of which is a fountain, 1921. This street leads to the Marktplatz, with a 14C former Spital and a Spitalkirche (now a school) and a fountain, 1570, with a statue of Emperor Maximilian II, as well as the town hall, 1966. Wilhelmstraße continues SE to reach the gothic *Marienkirche* (1273–1343), with its 72m-high tower (inside: 14C paintings, 15C font). Nearby, is a fountain with a statue of Emperor Friedrich II, 1561, and the baroque Landwirtschaftsschule (1728).

Continue along Wilhelmstraße in order to reach the town walls. Otherwise walk SW from the Marienkirche to the local history museum, in a building of 1538 (open at various times Wednesday, Saturday and Sunday). Spendehausstraße leads from here to the 18C Spendehaus (formerly the town granary), from which Lederstraße leads NW to the *Tübingen Gate*, 1240, decorated 16C. At the opposite side of the town stands the Garden Gate of 1392.

Tourist information from No. 1 Lisplatz. Trains connect Reutlingen with Konstanz, Tübingen and Stuttgart, buses with other places.

The road from here leads almost directly N for 41km to **Stuttgart** (see Rte 17).

Leave Stuttgart by the Heilbronner Straße to reach after 16km *Ludwigsburg** (85,000 inhab.; alt. 292m), a town founded in 1709 by Duke Eberhard Ludwig as the chief family seat (which it remained till 1775): MARKTPLATZ, with arcades and a statue of the founder, with a fountain; on the W side Protestant church of 1726; the Catholic church opposite dates from a year later; in Wilhelmsplatz a statue of Schiller, who lived here 1768–73 and 1793–94; at No. 8 Marktplatz was born the poet Justinus Kerner (1786–1862); the poet Eduard Mörike (1804–1875) was born at No. 2 Obere Markstraße; the philosopher and theologian David Friedrich Strauß (1808–1874) was born at No. 1 Marstallstraße.

On the edge of the B27 at Ludwigsburg is the *Schloß* built for Eberhard Ludwig by the French architect L. Ph. de la Guêpiérre, modelled on Versailles and consisting of 452 rooms in all, decorated in the baroque, rococo and empire styles (tours). The vast Schloßgarten is the site of a horticultural show—'Blühendes Barock'—from April till October. Part of the park is a game reserve, and its also incorporates the baroque Lustschlößchen Favorite (1715) as well as the rococo Seeschloß Monrepos (1760–65). Concerts and other festivals take place here from May till October. Tourist Office at No. 24 Wilhelmstraße.

The B27 runs NW across the motorway to reach *Bietigheim* (13,000 inhab.; alt. 220m): town hall 1507; Hornmoldhaus, 1526; walls, gates and towers; followed by *Besigheim* (5500 inhab.; alt. 185m), situated between the Neckar and the Enz: wall paintings c 1380 and carved high altar c 1520 in Protestant church; 15C town hall. This wine road continues through the old villages of Walheim and Kirchheim, reaching, 25km after Ludwigsburg, *Lauffen am Neckar* (9000 inhab.; alt. 172m). Here was born Friedrich Hölderlin (1770–1843), and Lauffen has a monument to him. Parts of the 16C town walls remain. The church of St. Regiswinde (once dedicated to St. Martin) dates from the 13C, with 16C alterations. Close by the early gothic St. Regiwindis chapel contains the saint's bones. A stone bridge crosses the Neckar to join both parts of the town. The town hall is the former Unteres Schloß.

After 10km more the B27 reaches **Heilbronn** (113,000 inhab.; alt. 157m), an important town on the Neckar and the Rhein-Neckar canal. Heinrich von Kleist's 'Kätchen von Heilbronn' (1810) brought it literary fame, and its wines also bring renown. Its name derives from a pre-Christian holy well—'Heiligen Brunnen'. Here was born in 1814 Robert Mayer, who discovered the law of the conservation of energy (monument in Moltkestraße). Much of Heilbronn was destroyed in 1944, though much has been restored and rebuilt. One of the towers of the town fortifications is called the Götzenturm, after the tradition that Götz von Berlichingen was held prisoner there in 1519. The Marktplatz, W of the main railway station, contains the restored gothic town hall, 1579–82, which was partly transformed into a renaissance building at the end of the 16C. It has an astronomical clock, 1580, by J. Habrecht, the maker of that in Strasbourg Cathedral. At the SW of the square is the birthplace of Kätchen von Heilbronn. S is the church of *St. Kilian*, begun 1013, 13C gothic central nave, 15C flamboyant gothic choir, delightful and curious renaissance tower finished c 1530; inside, high altar by Hans Seyffer, 1498. Sülmerstraße leads to the Hafenmarlt, with a tower, 1728, now a war memorial, that is all that remains of the Franciscans' church. Kirchbrunnenstraße leads to the church of the Teutonic knights (SS. Peter and Paul), 13C tower, rest reordered 1721, though basically still gothic. The theatre at No. 64 Gartenstraße dates from 1951.

Information Office in the town hall. Trains connect with Heidelberg, Schwäbisch Hall, Stuttgart, Karlsruhe, and Würzburg, buses with Ludwigsburg, Karlsruhe, Schwäbisch Hall, etc.

20 From Stuttgart to Schwäbisch Hall and on to Nuremberg

Total distance 146km. **Stuttgart**—B14 27km **Schwäbisch Hall.**—32km *Crailsheim.*—20km *Feuchtwangen.*—25km **Ansbach.**—17km **Heilsbronn.**—25km **Nuremberg**.

Leave **Stuttgart** (see Rte 17) by way of Bad Cannstadt and follow the B14 NE for 13km to reach *Waiblingen* (45,000 inhab.; alt. 208m): remains of fortifications; church of St. Michael, 1480–89; 15C Nonnenkirchlein, by Hans von Ulm, a chapel above a charnel house. Continue for 9km to the picturesque town of *Winnenden*, whose former Schloß of the Teutonic knights is now a psychiatric clinic. Its was built in the 13C, reordered in the 18C and contains a 16C chapel. The town also has a gothic church.

After 10km the route reaches *Backnang* (30,000 inhab.; alt. 278m) in the Murr valley: early 17C timber-framed town hall; romanesque parish church, 13C, with gothic modifications; 17C Schloß on the Schloßberg. 6km later it reaches *Openweiler*, with an 18C Schloß serving as town hall and a late gothic church. From here the road continues to Sulzbach, where a brief diversion E reaches *Murrhardt*, with its notable *Walterichskapelle* of 1230 (with early gothic alterations). In the cemetery is the 15C Walterichskirche, with a 17C tower.

The B14 continues NE from **Sulzbach** for 27km to ***Schwäbisch Hall** (32,000 inhab.; alt. 270m), a spa on the River Kocher, crossed here by old footbridges. The town, originally a Celtic settlement, prospered from early times on salt works, was given a charter by Barbarossa in 1156, a royal mint was established, and Schwäbisch Hall became a free imperial city 110 years after receiving its charter. Tourist information at No. 9 Am Markt. Trains connect with Strecken, Heilbronn, Nuremberg and Stuttgart, buses with Heilbronn, Ellwangen, Rothenburg ob der Tauber.

The superb MARKTPLATZ is the scene of annual performances (June to August) of the salt-boilers' dance, etc. on the steps of the late gothic church of *St. Michael* with its huge W tower, romanesque apart from the top two sections added 1527 (nave finished 1456; choir 1527; high altar crucifix by M. Erhart, 1494, with a 15C tabernacle; stalls 1534; 16C Holy Sepulchre). The figure of St. Michael over the doorway is c 1300. Opposite, is the late baroque town hall (1732–1735), alongside patricians' houses, and close by the festival hall, the 'Große Büchsenhaus' (arsenal) of 1505–27, and (at No. 8 Herrengasse) the medieval *Keckenburg*, once the home of a noble town family and now a fine art and historical collection (open save Monday, 09.00–12.00 and 14.00–17.00; opens one hour later in winter). The 13th and 14C church of *St. Katharina* (fine interior, choir 1343) is on the left bank of the Kocher. Of the fortifications remain the Diebs Tower (Salinenstraße) and the Malefix Tower (Saümarkt). The suburb of Unterlimpurg retains ruins of its Burg and the church of St. Urban (13C and 15C).

Unterlimpurger Straße leads 3km SE to *Großcomburg* and the 340m-high peak on which is the defensive former Benedictine **abbey of Comburg**, founded 1079 by Graf Burkhard II of Rotenburg-Comburg. Its romanesque church (now the Catholic parish church) has a baroque interior, 1706–15 (sarcophagus c 1220; antependium of high altar c 1140, altar and baldacchino baroque, 1713–17). The rest of the monastery buildings (in good order and now a teachers' training college) date from the 12C. Hessemtaler Straße leads from here a short distance to another former monastery at *Kleincomburg*, again on a hill, founded 1108 and retaining the romanesque church of St. Gilgen (c 1120, restored 1971).

The B14 continues E from Schwäbisch Hall through *Ilshofen* (remains of fortifications, gate, 1609; 16C church) reaching *Crailsheim* after 32km. Much destroyed in April 1945 at the battle of Crailsheim, this industrial town (25,000 inhab.; alt. 100m) has a history dating back to a 6C Frankish hunting village. Restored are the 15C late gothic church of St. Johannis (high altar and tabernacle c 1490; baroque organ 1709); the cemetery chapel (1580); the gothic town hall (tower 1717). Local history museum at No. 2 Spitalstraße.

The B14 runs E (into Bavaria) to reach after 20km *Feuchtwangen* (10,500 inhab.; alt. 450m), a town deriving from a Benedictine monastery established here 817. Its Marktplatz contains a romanesque church (W façade and cloister), with a high altar by M. Wohlgemut,

1483, and choir stalls c 1510. Feuchtwangen is on the 'Romantische Straße', see Rte 5B.

Continue along the B14 NE (under the motorway) to reach in 25km *Ansbach** (40,000 inhab.; alt. 409m) in the Rezat valley and an important railway junction (Prague, Paris, Stuttgart) as well as the point where the B13 and the B14 meet. Originating as a Benedictine monastery founded 748, it became the chief seat of the Margraves of Brandenburg-Ansbach in 1460. In the 16C Margrave Georg the Pious (1515–43) spread Protestantism here. Today it is the seat of the Mittelfranken administration and the centre of the Lutheran church of this region. Here was born the poet Johann Peter Uz (1720–96).

Karlstraße leads from the railway station NW past (left) the neo-classical Ludwigskirche (1834–40), through Karlsplatz and across the Promenade to Kannenstraße (reached by turning left at Neustadt and right again), which leads to the principal architectural treasures. At the end of Kannenstraße is the *Landhaus*, on the corner of Martin-Luther-Platz, built by Georg the Pious, 1532, now the Stadt-haus and restored 1928. In Martin-Luther-Platz stands the church of *St. Gumbertus*, romanesque (crypt 1039–42), with a baroque nave, 1736, and and early 16C gothic choir. Its N tower was finished 1594, its S tower a century earlier. The choir incorporates the chapel of the Knights of the Swan, with tombs of the members, and a painting attributed to Dürer. The Margraves lie buried in their crypt under the E choir. Adjoining the church is the former Hof Chancellery, by Gideon Bacher, 1591–1600. From here follow Martin-Luther-Platz W to see the 15C late gothic St. Johannis church. To see the Italian baroque **Residenzschloß** follow instead Johann-Sebastian-Bach-Platz E from St. Gumbertus. Now the offices of the Mittel Franken administration, the Schloß is based on plans by Gabriel de Gabrieli, who utilised parts of an earlier renaissance building and designed the long façade of 21 bays. Between 1731 and 1741 work was continued by J.W. and K.F. von Zocha and L. Retti and K.F. von Zocha designed the SE façade, Retti the others. Retti also decorated the *interior in the French rococo style (hall of mirrors; great hall, with ceiling painted by C. Carlone; rooms tiled with 18C Ansbach porcelain, then famous). The Hof garden E of the Schloß, with its double rows of lime trees, was set out in the 16C and remodelled in the 18C. To the N is the Orangery (1726–43). Ansbach, 'the town of Franconian rococo', retains streets with 18C baroque houses, and runs each year a rococo festival as well as an Ansbach Bach week. Information Office at No. 1 Martin-Luther-Platz.

From Ansbach the B14 reaches **Nuremberg** (see Rte 6) after 42km, passing through the resort of *Heilsbronn* where in 1132 Bishop Otto the Holy of Bamberg founded a Cistercian monastery in whose church (restored after WWII) are buried over 20 Hohenzollerns (S aisle, 1412–33; tabernacle, 1515; high altar, 1522).

21 From Stuttgart to the Swiss border by way of Tübingen

Total distance 170km. **Stuttgart**—B27 41km **Tübingen**. —21km *Hechingen.*—40km **Rottweil.**—33km **Donaueschingen**—35km *Schaffhausen* (Switzerland).

Leave **Stuttgart** (see Rte 17) to travel S to Tübingen by the B27, passing through the Schönbuch forest to reach *Waldenbuch* (Schloß, 16C and 18C) and Bebenhausen. At ***Bebenhausen** a Cistercian monsastery was founded in 1185, which became the property of the state in 1806. The buildings are protected by a double ring of walls, in the centre of which is the late gothic cloister (1471–96), The 13C romanesque church N of the cloister was modified in the 15th and 16C. To the E of the cloister is the chapterhouse (c 1200) above which is a 16C dorter. S of the cloister is the gothic refectory of 1335, used only in summer, the monks eating in colder weather in the 15C late gothic refectory on the W of the cloister (daily tours March to October). The kings of Württemberg converted some of the buildings into a hunting lodge in the 19C and early 20C and these now constitute a civic museum.

****TÜBINGEN** (74,000 inhab.; alt. 322m), lying between the Ammer and Neckar valleys, is an 11C city (though the region was inhabited in the 7C BC), dating from the building of Schloß Hohentübingen in 1078. It became the capital of the Dukes of Württemberg. Eberhard the Bearded founded its university in 1477, and a Protestant seminary was established here in 1536. The city was occupied by the Swedes in 1638. In spite of expansions as well as several disastrous fires, the old town, with its picturesque houses, remains the heart of Tübingen. Ludwig Uhland (1787–1862) was born and died here; and Friedrich Hölderlin lived and died (1843) here.

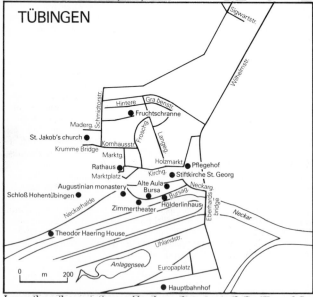

Leave the railway station and by the underpass reach the city park by the Neckar (nymph group by Joseph Heinrich Dannecker, 1758–1841; alley of plane trees). Follow Uhlandstraße E to reach the Eberhards bridge (at the corner of which is the Information Office), and cross the river, turning left into Neckargasse and left again along Bursagasse to reach at No. 6 the house where the poet Hölderlin lived from 1807 till his death (Hölderlinhaus). Further along Bursagasse (on the right) is the classical *Bursa* (1479) once the university faculty of philosophy (Melanchthon was among the students, 'bursares', here, 1514–18). No. 4B is where the humanist Johann Reuchlin lived when he taught at Tübingen, 1481–96 and 1522.

Continue W, taking the Neckargasse, to find the former Augustinian monastery, founded 13C, which became the Protestant theological faculty of the university after the Reformation and was graced by such scholars as Hegel, Kepler, Schelling and D.F. Strauß. Opposite the church steps lead to *Schloß Hohentübingen*, built 1507–40 on the site of the Schloß of 1078 (*Outer Gate by H. Schickhardt, 1606 with sentryposts by Chr. Jelin; *view from terrasses; cellar with huge barrel holding 850 hectolitres of wine, made for Duke Ulrich of Württemberg by Simon von Bönningheim).

Between the Schloß and the old monastery buildings runs Neckarhalde with at No. 24 the birthplace of Uhland and at No. 31 the Theodor Haering House, now the city gallery (open except Monday, 14.30–17.30). Return E along this street to join Münzgasse: No. 20 is the former students' gaol (Alter Karzer) 1515. Continue along Münzgasse to reach the Alte Aula, formerly the site of the university festivals, 1547, altered 1777, and then at No. 32 Münzgasse the superbly vaulted gothic Stiftkirche St. Georg (1470–83). Inside are Württemberg family tombs, especially Countess Mechthild's tomb by H. Multscher, 1450; a rich choir screen with a 16C forged metal grille; stained glass in choir from the workshop of P. d'Andlau; 15C reliefs in N window openings. E of the church, across Holzmarkt, stands the 15C Pflegehof, the former granary and cellar of Bebenhausen monastery (see above), today mostly students' lodgings. Return across the Holzmarkt and turn N along Lange Gasse to reach on the left Konvikt, where once stood a Franciscan monastery that at the Reformation became a school. The present late 16C buildings are now the catholic theological faculty of the university. Lange Gasse leads N to reach on the right Nonnengasse leading to Hintere Grabenstraße, en route to a park with the 15C Nonnenhaus, a former convent.

Return to take Froschgasse and find on the left the church of St. Johannes (1876). Kirchgasse continues from here S to reach (on the right) the Marktplatz with a Neptune fountain of 1617 (restored 1948) and the town hall of 1435 (redone 1698 and 1872; façade 1876, restored 1969; council chamber on first floor; astronomical clock by the astronomer Johannes Söffler, 1511; depiction of 'The Just Judge' by Jakob Züberlin, 1596). From Marktplatz walk N along Marktgasse to Kornhausstraße, with the former town Granary. E along Kornhausstraße appears the Krumme Bridge, leading to the church of St. Jakob, begun 12C, mostly 15C. From here E by way of Madergasse and Schmidtorstraße the route reaches Bachgasse and Tübingen's finest half-timbered house, the 15C *Fruchtschranne*, today the Albert-Schweitzer school.

THEATRES: Landestheater, No. 6 Eberhardstraße; Zimmertheater, No. 16 Bursagasse.

OTHER MUSEUMS: University collections: Archaeology, No. 9 Wilhelmstraße; Dentistry, Nos 2–8 Osianderstraße; Egyptian collection, No. 12 Correnstraße; Geology and Palaeontology, No. 10 Sigwartstraße; History of Medicine, No. 12 Denzenberhalde; Mineralogy, No. 56 Wilhelmstraße; Zoology, No. 3 Sigwartstraße.

Main *post office*, Europaplatz. Trains connect with Stuttgart and Sigmaringen, buses with Riedlingen, Rottenburg, Stuttgart, Donaueschingen.

The B27 continues S to *Hechingen* (17,000 inhab.; alt. 490m), once the chief set of the Hohenzollern-Hechingen family: renaissance church of St. Luzen (pulpit and stalls by H. Amman, 1587–89); classical parish church of St. Jakob, by d'Ixnard, 1783 (in choir bronze monument to Graf Eitelfriedrich von Zollern and wife, by P. Vischer, 1512); Villa Eugenia, 1789, with 19C wings. Hohenzollern collection of sacred art, No. 5 Schloßplatz. 6km left of Hechingen, on a 850m peak, is *Burg Hohenzollern*, founded in the 15C, but largely rebuilt 1850–57 (tours). Remaining from the old castle is St. Michael's chapel (1461), with three romanesque sandstone reliefs from an earlier building (dating from the 13C to the 16C). After WWII the coffins of the Prussian kings Friedrich Wilhelm I (1688–1740) and Friedrich II (1712–1786), as well as that of crown prince Friedrich Wilhelm, were transferred here from Potsdam to the neo-gothic chapel of Christ.

Balingen (30,000 inhab.; alt. 490m) lies 15km S of Hechingen along the B27, in the valley of the Eyach. Founded in 1255, the town has a late gothic church of 1443, with a powerful tower and a 16C stone pulpit; the mid 15C Zollern Schloß, and remains of the town walls (including the water tower). From here the route runs SW for another 25km to reach **Rottweil* (24,000 inhab.; alt. 600m), founded by Konrad von Zähringen in 1140, a free city from 1268 and a member of the Swiss Confederation from 1463. In 1643 the French occupied the town. Before Zähringen's foundation the site had housed a Roman camp (*Arae Flaviae*, c 74 BC) and numerous Roman remains (especially an Orpheus mosaic, c 180, and baths) have been excavated. The old part of Rottweil lies to the right of the Neckar and houses one of the oldest churches in Württemberg, the 11C and 12C *Pelagiuskirche*. Cross the bridge (statue of St. Johann Nepomuk) from Bahnhofstraße and follow picturesque Hochbrücktorstraße to reach, on the right, the *Kapellenhof* with the 14C chapel of Our Lady and its sculpted **Chapel Tower* (Kapellenturm; lower storeys 1330–50, upper storeys sculpted by Aberlin Jörg, 1473). The interior of the chapel was redecorated in the 18C in the baroque style (paintings by Josef Firtmaier, died 1738). Continue along Hochbrücktorstraße to Hauptstraße. At the crossroads is an allegorical fountain, the Marktbrunnen. Hauptstraße leads W past the City Museum (No. 20; Roman collection; open, 09.00–12.00 and 14.00–17.00; closes Fridays and Sundays at noon). At the end of the street is the Schwarzes Gate, from the Hohenstaufen era, once the sole entry by the inner W wall. Further W, along Hochturmgasse, is the Hoch tower, a former city watch-tower.

Rathausstraße (town hall c 1500) leads N from the museum to Kirchplatz and the minster of the *Holy Cross*. Essentially 15th and 16C, the minster houses a 15C tabernacle; gothic altars brought from other churches; an early 16C crucifix, probably by Veit Stoß; a font of 1563; and a 17C pulpit. From here Bruderschaftsgasse leads E to the Protestant *Prediger church*, once the 13C church of a Dominican monastery, reordered as a baroque building in the 18C (roof painting by Josef Wannermacher, 1755). Continue from here E along St. Lorenzgasse to reach the mid 16C St. Lorenz chapel, since 1851 (opening hours as the city museum).

As a holiday resort Rottweil offers swimming, tennis, skiing. Annual events include the Shrovetide Fools' Dance. Information Office in the town hall. Trains connect with Stuttgart and Villingen, as do buses. Schwenningen (just N of the source of the Neckar), with its Schwenninger Moos nature reserve and clockmakers, lies along the B27 18km S of Rottweil, followed after 15km more by **Donaueschingen** (see Rte 16E).

The Rte now continues SE by way of Blumberg on the southernmost tip of the Black Forest, reaching after 35km *Schaffhausen* (33,500 inhab.; alt. 407m), which after **Basel** is the chief point of entry into Switzerland and is the capital of the Swiss canton of that name.

22 The Saar Valley from Saarbrücken to Konz and on to Trier

Total distance 88km. **Saarbrücken**—B51. 10km *Völklingen* (—7km Püttlingen-Löllerbach)—13km *Saarlouis* (—2km Dillingen.—B406. 31km Perl—12km Remich)—17km *Merzig*—8km *Mettlach*—18km *Saarburg*—15km *Konz*—7km **Trier**.

*SAARBRÜCKEN (195,000 inhab.; alt. 182m) is the capital of the Saarland and stands amidst industry and mining where the old Roman bridge crossed the River Saar.

Main *railway station*: St. Johanner Straße.

Main *post office*: by the station.

Information offices: by the station and at the town hall.

Trains connect Saarbrücken with Ludwigshafen, Mainz, and Trier.

History. Over the centuries the city changed hands: the Bishops of Metz (given the Schloß of Saarbrücken by Emperor Otto III in 999), the Counts of the Lower Saar, the Counts of Nassau-Saarbrücken (1381–1793), the French, the Prussians all successively ruling the city until 1919. The Treaty of Versailles ceded the city to the French; a commission nominated by the League of Nations administered the Saarland from 1920 until the plebiscite of 1935 enabled Adolf Hitler to regain the region for Germany. After WWII the Saarland was formally returned in 1957.

N of the main railway station is the suburb of *Malstatt* on Heinrich-Koehl-Straße with a modern church, St. Albert, by Gottfried Böhm, 1954 (a pioneer of churches with central altars). Walk S from the main railway station across the river to Ludwigsplatz, with its 18C baroque

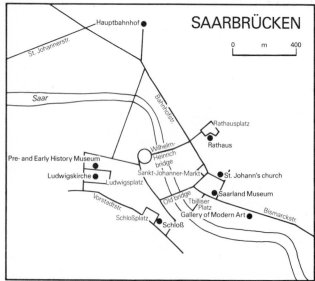

Ludwigskirche by Friedrich Joachim Stengel (restored, with a partly modern interior). W of the platz is the School of Arts and Crafts in one of several baroque buildings designed by Stengel that border this square. No. 15 is the Pre- and Early History Museum (open save Monday, 10.00–16.00; closes Saturday at 13.00 and Sunday at 18.00). From here Vorstadtstraße runs SE as far as Schloßplatz and OLD SAARBRÜCKEN (Alt-Saarbrücken, half destroyed in WWII and well restored). Here stands the baroque *Schloß* built by Stengel, 1739–48 (restored after the revolution of 1793), where the Nassau-Saarbrücken counts lived until the Revolution. Its garden has fine views. The Schloß chapel (15C and 18C, with graves of the Counts), today the Protestant parish church, was restored in 1958 after war damage (modern glass by G. Meistermann). Also restored is Stengel's former town hall of 1760.

Hindenburgstraße contains (just SE of the Schloß) the administrative building of the Saar Landtag.

Return along the riverside (passing the old bridge, by H. Sparer, 1549, modified in the 18C) to cross Wilhelm-Heinrich bridge into the finest part of the city, the district of ST. JOHANN, crossing Bahnhofstraße with its elegant shops to the Rathausplatz, with the monumental town hall, built in 1900 in the 15C gothic style.

Bahnhofstraße leads SE from here to Sankt-Johanner-Markt, with a fountain of 1760 (by Stengel, P. Mihm and the ironworker S. Bockelmann) and at No. 24 the Saarland Museum (in an 18C building). NW of the square is the Catholic church of St. Johann, by J.F. Stengel (1752). S of the square is the city theatre. From here Bismarckstraße leads E (at No. 11 a gallery of modern art, open, except Monday, 10.00–18.00).

SE of Alt-Saarbrücken is the suburb of *St. Arnual*, with an early 14C church of the same name (containing more tombs of the counts and their families, especially Elisabeth von Lothringen, died 1456, and Count Johann III, died 1472). W of Alt-Saarbrücken is the Deutsch-mühlental, with a German-French garden, an amusement park, Gulliver-land', and close by one of the first military cemeteries in Europe (containing c 100 German soldiers who fell in 1870).

The State Theatre is at No. 1 Tbilliser Platz, the Landestheater at No. 10 Scharnhorststraße.

Saarbrücken houses the Saarland University (5km NE, at the foot of the 377m-high *Schwarzenberg*). The zoo is on the B40 in the direction of St. Ingbert, as is the Halberg Schloß, now the HQ of the Saarland Radio.

The B51 leaves Saarbrücken and travels 10km E to *Völklingen* (46,000 inhab.; alt. 200m) in the Köllerback valley, its wealth from iron and steel works, its health from its site, stadium and sports facilities.

From here a brief excursion of 7km reaches *Püttlingen-Köllerbach*, whose church of St. Martin has 15C wall paintings.

From Völklingen travel NW along the valley of the Saar to reach after 13km *Saarlouis*, named after Louis XIV of France at its foundation in 1680, fortified by Vauban, 1681, with walls, gates and a moat (mostly razed in 1890, as was much of the town, since restored, in WWII). Saarlouis remained French until 1815, and many of the citizens' names remain French. A plaque marks the birthplace of Marshal Ney (1769–1815). The town hall contains Gobelin tapestries. An important museum, with Roman finds, is in Alte-Brauerei-Straße (open Tuesday and Thursday, 09.00–12.00 and 15.00–18.00; Sunday, 15.00–18.00).

An EXCURSION for 2km along the B269 reaches *Dillingen*, whose forges were
set up in 1685 by the Marquis de Lenoncourt-Blainville, with a patent from Louis
XIV; 17C church.

The B51 continues NW from Saarlouis, passing through Hilbringen.

From here the B406 runs by way of *Perl* (31km)on the Mosel Wine Road (the
B419), where you can see, except on Mondays, the excavated Roman Villa and
Schloße Berg (early 14C and 16C), to reach *Remich* and the **Luxembourg** border
after a further 12km.

The B51, 15km from Saarlouis, reaches **Merzig** (30,600 inhab.; alt.
174m), a town manufacturing pottery and mosaics: late 12C church of
St. Peter (crucifix c 1300); town hall, 1647–50, formerly a hunting
lodge of Fürst Philipp Christoph von Sötern of Trier; baroque brewery
offices (No. 12 Poststraße); wooded surroundings and walks; train
connections with Saarbrücken and Trier.

From Merzig continue along the B51, reaching after 8km **Mettlach**
(13,000 inhab.; alt. 166m), the 'pearl of the Saarland', site of a
Benedictine *monastery* since the late 9C. The church was rebuilt in
the 14C (restored 19C) retaining the octagonal tower (907) under
which its founder, St. Ludwig, lies buried. The 13C *reliquary of St.
Ludwig is now kept in the modern Catholic Ludwigskirche of
Mettlach. C. Kretschmar rebuilt the abbey, 1727–86, constructing a
façade over 300m long. When the buildings fell into disuse in the early
19C, they were adapted as the famous Villeroy and Boch ceramic
factory. 2km S (an hour's walk) is the ruined *Schloß Montclair* on a
303m-high peak, first built in 1180 by Arnolph von Walecourt to
control the traffic along the River Saar and finally brought low by a
fire of 1778.

3km SW of Mettlach, at *St. Gangolf*, is an octagonal pagoda by
Kretschmar (1745).

Follow the B51 N for 18km from Mettlach through Trassem to
Saarburg (6500 inhab.; alt. 148m), where in the middle of the town the
confluence of the Saar and the Leuk produces a 20m-high waterfall
(the Leukbach): timber-framed house; modern church of St. Laurence
in the gothic style. A tunnel leads through a peak up to the much
pillaged, much rebuilt Schloß of the Electors of Trier. 15km N of
Saarburg the B51 reaches the wine centre of **Konz** (Roman *Con-
tionacum*), where the River Saar joins the Mosel. The Roman remains
here are said to derive from a villa built by Constantine. Cross the
river by a bridge first built by the Romans to reach after 7km **Trier** in
the Rhineland-Palatinate.

23   From Saarbrücken to Homburg

Total distance 31km. **Saarbrücken**—B10 13km *St. Ingbert*—18km
Homburg.

Leave **Saarbrücken** by the Mainzer Straße and travel E along the B10
for 13km to *St. Ingbert* (42,000 inhab.; alt. 229m) on the Rohrbach (a
tributary of the Saar) with its noted brewery tower, its steel works and
glass-making (excursions and walks to the S). St. Ingbert was almost
completely destroyed in 1637. Its industries began to develop in the

next century. It has a modern church, St. Hildegard, by Alfred Boßlet (1929).

18km further E lies **Homburg** (43,000 inhab.; alt. 233m), where the University of Saarbrücken Faculty of Medicine is established: natural park. The site, which had been inhabited in the 3C, derives its modern existence from the now-ruined 12C *Hohenburg*, set on the Schloßberg. In 1755 the town came under the suzerainty of the Graf von Nassau-Saarbrücken. Herzog Karl II August built a Schloß here in 1776. The French destroyed it 17 years later, but the ruins are picturesque.

Information Office at Am Rondell. Trains connect with Ludwigshafen, Saarbrücken, Zweibrücken.

An EXCURSION along the B423 SW in the direction of the French border leads 12km to *Blieskastel*, with part of a baroque Schloß of 1680, and Schloß church, 1778, by P. Reheis, 1778; 18C town hall (formerly an orphanage); a fountain dedicated to Napoleon Bonaparte; N of the town a pilgrims' chapel of the Holy Cross, c 1680, with a 14C Pietà; W towards Alschbach the *Gollenstein*, a 7m-high, 4000-year-old menhir.

24 From Saarbrücken to St. Wendel

Total distance 39km. **Saarbrücken**—B41. 20km **Neunkirchen**—9km *Ottweiler*—10km **St. Wendel**.

Leave **Saarbrücken** NE by the A623 and join the B41 to drive N along the Sulzbach valley, which has the largest concentration of factories and population in the Saarland. The mining town of *Dudweiler* (8km) stands on a prehistoric site. The Inn Zumm Brennenden Berg close by the exit from the town stands at the beginning of a hike through the woods to the Brennender Berg (the coal-bearing 'burning montain', described by Goethe). 4km after Dudweiler is *Sulzbach*, where coal has been mined since the 15C: glass works; chemical products, iron and steel founderies; mineral water.

20km from Saarbrücken is **Neunkirchen** (45,000 inhab.; alt. 257m), the largest town in the Saarland after Saarbrücken. Coal and steel have been the staple products and support of Neunkirchen for 150 years (iron and steel works dating back in fact to the 18C). The Stumm monument commemorates the steel magnate K.F. von Stumm (1836–1901), the fountain at the end of Stummstraße the steel workers. Neunkirchen has a zoo; it also has Europe's steepest street. There is a covered swimming pool and other sports facilities; walks and hikes to the Steinwald, Spiesser Höhe.

Ottweiler (16,000 inhab; alt. 262m), 9km N in the Blies valley, marks the end of the dense industrial area and its Altstadt offers the aspect of a medieval German town, with gabled, timber-framed houses. (Tourist information in Bliesstraße.) The old town is built around the Schloßplatz and its fountain. SW of this square is Rathausplatz (town hall, 1714; 16th and 17C houses). The tower (the Wehrturm) of the Protestant church NW of Rathausplatz was once part of the town's defences. Friedrich Joachim Stengel designed the baroque hunting lodge on the Blies (1759) and the baroque Witwenpalais (1760) in the suburb of Neumünster.

The B41 runs N for 10km to reach **St. Wendel** (27,000 inhab.; alt. 282m).

Information Office at No. 7 Schloßstraße. Train links with Saarbrücken and Strecke, bus links with Saarbrücken and Oberkirchen.

The town is named after a 7C Irish missionary, patron of shepherds and farmers, who is buried in a stone sarcophagus (c 1360) behind the high altar of the 14th and 15C pilgrimage church of *St. Wendelinus* (in the Fruchtmarkt): pulpit of 1462 given by Nicholas of Cusa; 18C sculpture. The church of *Our Lady* has stucco work by K. Zimmermann, 1743; late gothic Kreuz chapel (altered 1869) housing 12C 'Salgau' crucifix; 18C altar. In the Marktplatz is the town hall (1820) and near the church of St. Wendelinus the *Alte Rathaus* with a local history museum (open Saturday, Sunday and Monday, 10.00–12.00 and 15.00–18.00). To the N of the town is the Skulpturenfed, with 14 stone sculptures by modern artists.

The B41 runs N to cross the border of the Saarland into Rhineland-Palatinate. Here, and around St. Wendel, are corn-growing areas: the countryside is less wooded than the rest of the Saarland.

25 From Mettlach to Saarbrücken by way of the 'Eichenlaubstraße', Losheim and Tholey

Total distance 84km. *Mettlach*—16km *Losheim*—15km *Nonnweiler*—B269. 17km **Tholey**—12km *Lebach*—B268. 24km **Saarbrücken**.

The 'Oak Tree route' in the northern Saarland and Rhineland-Palatinate runs for 72km from *Mettlach* to *Friesen-Oberkirchen*, passing through part of the upper Black Forest and incorporating the most beautiful stretch of the Saarland.

Leaving *Mettlach*, travel 16km E by way of Britten to *Losheim* (14,000 inhab.; alt. 300m), whose parish church displays in its crypt Celtic and Roman finds from the neighbourhood. 3km N of the town is the *Losheim Lake* (sailing, windsurfing, swimming, camping, youth hostel). NE of Losheim the Rte takes 15km to reach, by way of *Weiskirchen* (with its clinics and sanatoria) and passing under the A1 motorway, the health resort of *Nonnweiler* (8500 inhab.; alt. 10m). Here are more clinics and the remains of Celtic fortifications—the Hunnenring on the Dollberg—whose walls at times reach a height of 10m.

From Nonnweiler drive 8km SE along the B269 to *Primstal* whose baroque church contains a model of the grotto of Lourdes. Dominating Primstal is the 584m-high *Petersberg*.

The B269 continues SE for 9km to reach **Tholey** (12,000 inhab.; alt. 330m). Buses connect with St. Wendel (10km E) and Saarbrücken. Trains connect with St. Wendel. Louis XIV ceded Tholey to the Palatinate in 1778. It was once the seat of a rich Benedictine abbey (9C foundation) that fell victim to the French Revolution. The abbot's lodgings are now the presbytery and the late 12C romanesque–early gothic monastery church is now the parish church (though the abbey was refounded in 1949 and the monks have returned). Underneath the church have been discovered the remains of the Roman baths, for

Tholey was a Roman settlement, whose name derives from the Latin 'tegula', i.e. tile). On the nearby *Schaumberg* (527m) is an observation tower (38m), with a picturesque hill-top road, the Schaumberghöhenstraße, passing the peak.

From Tholey drive a further 12km SE along the B269 to *Lebach* (5500 inhab.; alt. 275m) in the valley of the Thel: gothic church (12C font; tombs of the van Hagens). Lebach hosts annual races and a fair on the feast of the Nativity of the Virgin Mary (8 September). Tourist information at the Bürgermeisteramt.—The B268 leads S for 24km to **Saarbrücken**.

26 Trier

**TRIER (110,000 inhab.; alt. 130m), situated 10km from the frontier with Luxembourg and 50km from the frontier with France, is Germany's oldest city.

Main *railway station*: Bahnhofstraße.

Main *post office*: am Kornmarkt.

Information Office: Porta Nigra.

Trains connect with Cologne, Koblenz, Saarbrücken, Luxembourg and Paris; *buses* with Mainz, Frankfurt, Kaiserslautern and Luxembourg. *Boats* ply the Mosel to Koblenz and Düsseldorf.

History. Julius Caesar conquered Trier in 56 BC in his attack on the Belgae. Augustus Caesar founded here a Roman town, *Augusta Treverorum*, whose citizens could also become citizens of Rome. Under the Romans trade developed. Constantine the Great lived at Trier from 306–314—indeed emperors frequently preferred living here to living in Rome, and Trier became capital of the part of their lands that stretched from Britain south to Spain and from the Danube west. The Roman walls enclosed some 70,000 people.
 Christianity came in the 4C and the first Bishop of Trier was elected in 328. These bishops (later archbishops) were to become prince-electors in the Middle Ages. The cathedral acquired and still possesses a precious relic, the seamless robe of Christ, displayed rarely (1933, 1959, 1973). In 1473 the university was founded. In 1512 Emperor Maximilian I called a Reichstag here. Then came a century of decline. Several times Trier was captured: by the Spanish in 1545, by the French twice in the 17C, by Marlborough for the English in 1704, by the French again in 1754. For a time Trier was capital of the French *département* of Sarre and began to blossom again. The Treaty of Versailles ceded the city to the Prussians, and the city has continued since then to develop, even though a third of it was destroyed in WWII. Karl Marx was born here in 1818 (died 1883).

Trier still maintains the layout of the old Roman city: Theodor-Heuss-Allee marks the N boundary; the River Mosel the W; Ziegelstraße the S; and Bergstraße, beyond the railway, the E. By the main railway station is a fountain in memory of Prince-Archbishop Balduin von Luxemburg (1308–34). Follow Bahnhofstraße from the main railway station to the right to find on the left, along Bismarckstraße, the church of the former abbey of St. Maximim (see below).
 Return from here by Roonstraße to turn right along Theodor-Heuss-Allee (bordered on the left by the public gardens) to reach the **Porta Nigra**. This gate—the most important ancient monument in Trier—was given the soubriquet 'black' in the Middle Ages, owing to the colour of the stone (in fact sandstone): 36m wide, 22m broad and 30m high, its defensive nature is emphasised by the enormous stones with which (without cement) it is constructed. Over the centuries the gate was modified (with the addition even of a chapel); the Greek monk Simeon lived and taught in the E tower at the beginning of the 11C; but it has been restored to its original form (though part of the romanesque apse of the church remains). Adjoining the gate (right) is the *monastery of St. Simeon*, an early romanesque building of the 11C, today housing the municipal museum (open daily, 10.00–17.00), a restaurant and the tourist information office.
 Follow Simeonstraße SW from Porta Nigra to reach the HAUPT-MARKT, passing St. Nikolaus chapel (1761); at No. 7 a 16C

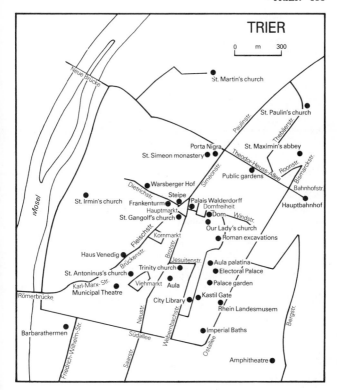

TRIER

0   m   300

St. Martin's church

St. Paulin's church

St. Maximin's abbey

Porta Nigra
St. Simeon monastery

Public gardens

Warsberger Hof
Steipe
St. Irmin's church   Frankenturm   Palais Walderdorff
Hauptmarkt   Domfreiheit
St. Gangolf's church   Dom   Windstr.
Our Lady's church
Kornmarkt   Roman excavations

Haus Venedig
Aula palatina
St. Antoninus's church   Trinity church   Electoral Palace
Viehmarkt   Aula   Palace garden
Karl-Marx-Str.   City Library   Kastil Gate
Municipal Theatre   Rhein Landesmuseum
Römerbrücke

Barbarathermen   Imperial Baths

Amphitheatre

Mosel
Neue Brücke
Paulinstr.
Thebäerstr.
Theodor-Heuss-Allee
Roonstr.
Bismarckstr.
Simeonstr.
Dietrichstr.
Bahnhofstr.
Hauptbahnhof
Fleischstr.
Brotstr.
Jesuitenstr.
Brückenstr.
Neustr.
Weberbachstr.
Ostallee
Bergstr.
Saarstr.
Südallee
Friedrich-Wilhelm-Str.

renaissance house; at No. 8 the house owned by the parents of Karl Marx and where he lived in 1819–35; at No. 19 the 13C house of the Magi, with access only by a ladder to the first floor.

To mark the granting of a market to Trier Archbishop Heinrich erected in 958 the stone cross in the middle of the Hauptmarkt. The renaissance fountain, with statues of the city's patron saint (Peter) and the four virtues is by Hans Rupprecht Hoffmann, 1595. Medieval Trier grew up around the Hauptmarkt. The church of *St. Gangolf* dominates the S side (13–15C; gothic bell tower 1507; baroque doorway 1732). W of the square is the festival hall of the city aldermen, the Steipe (1430–83, totally destroyed 1944, restored 1970), decorated with 15C sculptures of SS. Peter, Helen, James and Paul, with two knights. From here the Rotes Haus of 1684 (also destroyed 1944 and restored) leads into Dietrichstraße and bears the inscription: Ante Roman Treveris stetit annis mille trecentis perstet, et aeterna pace fruator. Amen.

(Trier existed 1300 years before Rome, may she be granted an equally long life and eternal peace. Amen.)

On the left of Dietrichstraße (at No. 5) is the *Frankenturm*, an 11C house in the form of a tower. No. 42 is the 17th and 18C Warsberger Hof. In the Hauptmarkt to the right of the Steipe are at Nos 15–16 a baroque house of 1664; at No. 17 a classical house of 1785; and at the entrance 16C half-timbered houses opening onto the Judengasse and the medieval Jewish quarter. No. 6 Hauptmarkt is Germany's oldest pharmacy, the 13C *Löwenapotheke*. The arcaded Palais Walderdorff to the E side was formed from two canonries, built 1756 and 1768.

Follow Strenstraße alongside this palace to the Domfreiheit, surrounded by more canons' houses, and embracing the oldest *cathedral in Germany, built on the site of a Roman palace (revealed 1946). A Christian basilica has existed here since 336 (the gift of the Empress Helena), destroyed by the Normans, restored in the 10C, extended in 1030 and in the 12C, the victim of a fire in 1717 and restored by 1729. The 12C choir stands over a vast crypt; the nave has 13C ogive vaulting. Furnishings include the tomb of Baldwin von Luxemburg (died 1354) in the W choir; renaissance pulpit by R. Hoffmann, 1520; monuments to 26 archbishop-electors (especially Johann von Metzenhausen, died 1540); baroque high altar by Johann Wolfgang Fröhlicher, 1699; treasury, 1702–16, behind the high altar (funerary altar of St. Andrew; the Holy Coat; open daily, 10.00–12.00 and 14.00–17.00; closed Sunday mornings).

To the right of the cathedral is the church of **Our Lady** (1235–60), influenced by the contemporary gothic of northern France and after St. Elisabeth, Marburg, the oldest early gothic church in Germany: richly decorated W and N doorways; the interior (damaged 1944 and well restored) in the form of a Greek cross, with 12 pillars dedicated to the Apostles (their portraits painted 16C). Next to this church is the episcopal palace of 1786 (on the doorway the arms of Georg von Schönbrünn). In front of the church is the *Palais Kesselstatt* (1745; built for the Count of Kesselstatt).

Return past the cathedral to take the narrow Windstraße (along the N façade) and then right, along the street Hinter den Dom, to find the entrance to the 13C arcaded cathedral cloister, with a statue of the Virgin by Nicolas Gerhaerdt, c 1462. Here can be seen Roman excavations, especially paintings from Constantine's palace (including St. Helena, his mother). Opposite this museum is the huge, rectangular brick *Aula palatina, the early 4C basilican tribunal of the Roman palace, transformed into an electoral palace in the 18C. King Friedrich Wilhelm in the 19C had the original tribunal reconstructed. Partly destroyed 1944, restored 1956, the 67m by 27m basilica now serves as a Protestant church. The *Electoral Palace*, half renaissance, half baroque, with its remarkable inner staircase (by Ferdinand Dietz), now stands facing this basilica (N and E wings 17C; S façade decorated by Balthasar Neumann's pupil Johannes Seitz, 1759–61). In front of this façade is the 18C palace garden, along one side of which are the remains of the medieval wall (incorporating the Kastil gate), separating the garden from the City Library, 1957, (entrance at No. 25 Weberbachstraße), which possesses 4000 medieval manuscripts and 2500 incunabula.

Jesuitenstraße leads from Webernbachstraße and contains the 15C gothic church of the Trinity (once Franciscan, then Jesuit: 13C choir; tomb of the poet Friedrich Spee, died 1635). Close by is a renaissance building, once the Jesuit college, built 1614 with stones from the Imperial Roman thermal baths. Here too is the Aula of 1775, now part of the Catholic theological faculty of the university. The huge 4C imperial baths (*Kaisersthermen*), S of the city library, once measured 260m by 145m. SE (under the railway passage) is the *amphitheatre*, 1C BC, set today amidst vineyards, its axes measuring 75m and 50m, its seating capacity 25,000, with three entrance towers, one to the arena, two for spectators, as well as 14 arched entrance passages.

Return to the imperial baths and continue W along Südallee, which follows the principal street (decumanus maximus) of the old Roman city and now displays a bastion (1543) of the later fortifications of Trier. At the crossing with Friedrich-Wilhelm-Straße was the Roman forum. To the left are the remains of the Barbara thermal baths (Barbarathermen), dating from the 2C (and named today after the medieval suburb of St. Barbara). Partly destroyed in 1673, their stones used for building (see the Jesuit college, above), these baths cover 4 hectares of ground. The cold baths alone consisted of 11 pools and were altogether 54m by 10m. In front is a garden, once a Roman exercise park (the Palaestra). Continue along the Südallee to reach the 190m long, 7·5m wide, eight-arched 11C Römerbrücke, based on Roman pillars, much renewed (save for the second, seventh and furthest from the town). Just upstream are the foundations of an even older Roman bridge, dating from the 1C BC. From here you can walk along the quayside towards Kaiser-Wilhelm-Brücke (new bridge), past old cranes (1474 and 1413) and close by the baroque church of St. Irmin (1771) whose convent now is a hospital. From the Kaiser-Wilhelm-Brücke cross G.-Schmidt-Platz into Lindenstraße, turn left along Peter-Friedhofen-Straße and then right down Maarstraße, to find the 1626 abbey church of St. Martin, with (outside) a Crucifixion group of 1494. Beyond Kaiser-Wilhelm-Brücke is an 18C fisher- and boatmen's quarter whose origins date from the 7C.

Opposite the Roman bridge, Karl-Marx-Straße leads into Brückenstraße (at No. 10, the house where Marx was born, open save Monday, 10.00–13.00 and 15.00–18.00). The 17C Haus Venedig is a little further on. Between Brückenstraße and the Viehmarkt stands the 15C church of St. Antoninus (pulpit, 1762), close by the former Augustinian monastery, 1762 (14C church; bas-relief of Christ 1142), and in front of the Hercules fountain of 1729. Here too is the municipal theatre (1964). Brückenstraße leads into Flieschstraße with, on the right, the Kornmarkt, fountain of St. Georg by Johannes Seitz, 1751; at No. 21 the former Casino, 1825, restored.

Trier is the home of the Rhein Landesmuseum, at No. 44 Ostalle (open Monday–Friday, 09.30–16.00; Saturday closes 14.00, Sunday, 13.00).

S of the city, reached from the Hauptmarkt by Brotstraße, Neustraße, Saarstraße and Matthiasstraße is the basilica of St. Matthias, 1127–1160, transformed at various times between the 15C and the 18C (restored 1967): in the crypt the tombs of the earliest bishops of Trier; 12C choir; W doors 17C; vaulting 1496–1504; tomb of St. Matthias the Apostle (with his alleged relics), as well as those of Trier's first Christian missionaries, SS. Eucharius and Valerius. Of the Benedictine abbey for which this church was built, the 13C cloister has an 18C E wing. Many early sarcophagi.

NE of the city, following from Porta Nigra Paulinstraße and then right along Balthasar-Neumann-Straße, is the church of *St. Paulin, by Balthasar Neumann and Johannes Seitz, 1734–54, on the site of a 6C romanesque church built where the Theban Legion was martyred in 286. (The allegedly exact spot is marked by a cross on the lawn in front of the church.) Inside: stucco and frescoes; high altar by Ferdinand Dietz (fl. 1743–c 1780); tomb of Paulinus (Bishop of Trier, 346–58) in the crypt.

From here take Thebäer Straße back towards the city to find the Carolingian abbey of St. Maximin, whose present buildings (now a school) date from the 17C.

5km SW the 22m-high *Igel column*, a 3C Gallo-Roman funeral monument of the Secundinus family, with moving inscriptions.

27 From Trier to Koblenz (via the Mosel Valley)

Total distance 143km. **Trier**—B49. 10km *Ruwer*—B53. 26km **Neumagen**—21km *Bernkastel-Kues*—23km *Traben-Trarbach*—25km *Alf*—B49. 38km **Koblenz**.

Leave **Trier** (see Rte 26) and take the B49 NE travelling along the right bank of the River Mosel to reach (10km) *Ruwer*, a town which the Latin poet Ausonius praised, surrounded by vineyards, lying at the confluence of the River Ruwer and the Mosel. After 5km the route reaches **Schweich**, the site of a Celtic settlement named *Soiacum*, where the Romans built a bridge across the Mosel. At Schweich in 1924 was discovered a Roman mosaic of Venus and cherubs. The town preserves a baroque Hisgenhaus (1758) which once belonged to the monastery of St. Maximin, Trier, and a basalt fountain commemorating the local poet Stefan Andres, son of a miller.

Cross the modern successor of the Roman bridge and take the B53 for Alf, reaching after 3km the tiny village of *Longen* with a church c 1400.

On the other side of the Mosel stands next *Longuich-Kirsch*, whose baroque church of *St. Laurentius* has a romanesque tower and, inside, a 15C Madonna holding grapes. NE of Longuich-Kirsch is the town of *Riol* (birthplace of Peter Aspelt, died 1300, who lies buried in Mainz cathedral), followed by *Mehring* (a church of 1824, based on a baroque original).

The B53 winds alongside the river, passing through *Plölich* (the Roman *pulchra villa*) and *Schleich* (Schloß of 1700) and through the ancient wine villages of Ensch, *Detzem* (romanesque church; baroque Maximinen Hof) and *Köverich* (where Beethoven's mother was born) to reach *Klüsserath*, 14km from Schweich. From here the Rte continues through *Leiwen* (16C half-timbered houses and narrow streets), after which another curve in the river leads the B53 shortly to *Trittenheim*, another noted wine-producing town that stood here in Roman times, where Roman sarcophagi have been found and where in 1147 Pope Eugenius II founded the chapel of St. Laurence as a gift to the abbey of St. Matthias, Trier. Here was born in 1462 Johannes Trithemius, successively abbot of Sponheim and of the Scottish monastery of Würzburg. The plague cross in the town bears the names of those who died of the plague in 1654; the tower of the parish church dates from 1790.

The B53 continues to follow the bends of the river, crossing again to reach *Neumagen-Dhron* (3000 inhab.; alt. 120m) after 26km. Ausonius also sang about this spot in his poem about the Mosel (calling it *Drahomus*) and is rewarded by a memorial in the church of St. Peter (1718; on an earlier building). Here the Romans built a fort against the Germans (destroyed by the Normans in 822) and Constantine had a villa at Neumagen. Over 1000 Roman finds from this vicinity are displayed in the Landesmuseum, Trier. Amongst the most remarkable finds is the sculpted *Neumagen wineboat, which stands now in front of the church of St. Peter and once marked the grave of a Roman wine-merchant. See also: the *Sayn-Wittgensteiner Hof* (1760; the Counts of Sayn-Wittgenstein were the last lords of Neumagen before the French Revolution); baroque pilgrimage church of *Maria Himmelfahrt* (1793; housing the tombs of Heinrich von Hunolstein, 1485 and Heinrich von Isenburg, 1551); the Martyr chapel, in honour of St. Ricius Varus, allegedly slain under Constantine's orders before the emperor became Christian. Trains connect with Trier and Koblenz, boats with Cologne and Düsseldorf.

3km further along the river the road reaches the hamlet of *Dhron* itself and the beginning of the *Dhronbach*, whose vineyards are noted and the name of whose river (*Drahonus*) means 'full of fish'. The Rte now passes either through or opposite famous wine-producing villages and towns: *Piesport* (parish church of St. Michael, ceiling painting by J.P. Weber, 1778); *Wintrich* (fine timbered houses; stone cross, 1661, in the Weinberg; 13C church); on the left bank *Kesten* (Weinhöfe of 1153) and above it *Monzel*; *Mülheim* (1000 inhab.; alt. 111m), at the entrance of the Veldenz valley (Protestant parish church, 1668, with a 13C romanesque W tower; Catholic chapel, 1772); and finally Bernkastel-Kues, 21km from Neumagen-Dhron. **Bernkastel-Kues** (7500 inhab.; alt. 110m), at the foot of Schloß Landshut (partly ruined) straddles both sides of the Mosel where it is joined by the Tiefenbach. In spite of withstanding numerous sieges and a fire in 1692, Bernkastel, on the right bank, retains many 17C houses and Weinhöfe, especially in the *MARKTPLATZ, with the late renaissance town hall, 1698, its pillory, and St. Michael's fountain, 1606. Two gates survive: the Graacher Tor (rebuilt in the 18C) and St. Michael (the French having torn down the town's 13C defences in 1689). 14C church of St. Michael; 13C romanesque church tower.

A 219m-long bridge of 1905 spans the Mosel to reach *Kues* a settlement in Neolithic times. The birthplace of the philosopher and theologian Cardinal Nicolas Cusanus (1401–64) still stands (the Haus zum Krebs). Cusanus founded here the *hospital of St. Nikolaus* (valuable library; 15C cloister, refectory and Cardinal's room; late gothic chapel, with a triptych, c 1450; a memorial to the cardinal of 1488, containing his heart, the rest of his body being in St. Peter's, Rome). The most famous wine of this town, Bernkasteler Doktor, derives its name from reviving a sick archbishop, Boemund II, in the mid 14C.

Tourist information at No. 5 Gestade. Bus links with Frankfurt, Luxembourg, etc.; boats ply to Düsseldorf, Cologne, Traben-Trarbach.

Here the B53 crosses to the left bank of the Mosel and passes through *Graach* (half-timbered houses; 16C late gothic church), followed by *Wehlen* (with a famous sundial as well as a heated swimming pool), *Ürzig* (whose Celtic name means House of the Bear; railway connections with Trier and Koblenz; boats to Bernkastel and Traben-Trabach), and *Kröv* (2900 inhab.; alt. 105m). The town hall depicts coats of arms relating to Kröv from 755 to 1790, with its own coat of arms (including the double-headed eagle). Kröv produces the noted, delicious, vulgarly named wine, 'Kröver Nacktarsch', a name deriving from the milder 'Nectar'. See the baroque church of St. Remigius (1725), and the mid 17C burial chapel of the Kesselstatts.

The B53 winds alongside the left bank of the river (passing on the right bank the little wine town of *Wolf*: church with early 13C tower and choir) to reach 23km from Bernkastel-Kues the town of *Traben-Trarbach* (7000 inhab.; alt. 113m), two united villages spanning the river, with wine merchants, half-timbered houses, the rococo Haus Kayser, Haus Böcking (once the home of Goethe) and two fine churches: the late gothic Catholic St. Peter and the Protestant hall church.

The Rte now winds through Enkirch, Burg, Pünderich, Briedal, Zell and Merl as far as Bullay. Before Enkirch, *Starkenburg* appears 3km to the right, reached by the footpath known as the Moselhöhenweg and on the site of the ruined 11C Schloß of the same name.

Enkirch has half-timbered houses, a 13C gothic Protestant church and a 15C Catholic church with a romanesque tower, as well as many Weinstuben. Beyond Burg, on the opposite side of the river (which can be crossed here) a road leads from Reil (birthplace of Gerhart von Ryl, architect of Cologne cathedral) to the Marienburg (see below) and into the Alfbach valley to reach after 6km the baroque *Springiersbach abbey* (restored after destruction by fire in 1940; built originally in 1796, with decoration by Franziskus Freund).

Pünderich is on the railway line from Trier to Koblenz and is a 45-minute walk from the ***Marienburg*** which here dominates the Mosel. Here the Archbishop of Trier built a castle on a pagan holy site. On the 205m-high peak Abbot Richard of Springiersbach founded a now-ruined Augustinian monastery in 1127, part of whose church (the gothic choir) is incorporated into the present parish church. The restaurant offers superb views.

At Pünderich the River Mosel turns sharply back on itself and runs SE for 3km to *Briedel*, with charming houses and an early 17C Gemeindehaus. At *Zell* (5500 inhab.; alt. 94m) is produced the wine known as 'Schwarze Katz'. The town has a parish church with an 11C tower and a 13C late romanesque crucifix. In the classical church of St. Peter (1793) is a 15C Madonna.

Merl (united administratively with Zell in 1969) has a parish church first built in 1280 as part of a Franciscan monastery (high altar c 1525). In the cemetery is a 12C romanesque tower (restored 1981). Amongst its wine cellars is the former archbishop's town house (16C).

At *Bullay* (camping, excursions) the B53 crosses a two-tiered bridge to Alf, 25km from Traben-Trarbach. *Alf* (1300 inhab.; alt. 95m), at the mouth of the Alfbach, is a health resort with a history dating back to the Celts. Here the route to Koblenz joins the B49.

After 3km the B49 N reaches *St. Aldegund* (*houses, 12C chapel) and, on the opposite side of the river, a view of *Neef* (13C Burghaus, with late romanesque windows, late gothic oriel, renaissance gable).—*Bremm*, 3km further from St. Aldegund, at the foot of sombre cliffs where the river makes an almost right-angled turn, has a 15C gothic church, St. Laurentius, with a baroque altar; *Ediger-Eller* (1500 inhab.; alt. 92m): late gothic parish church (romanesque font; Entombment of Christ, 1671); the 16C chapel of the Holy Cross on the Ediger Berg houses the late 17C relief *'Christus in der Kelter'—a crucified Jesus being crushed in a wine press. In Eller (where St. Fridolin built a monastery in the 5C) the church of *St. Hilarius* has a five-storey romanesque tower and a sandstone Lady altar, 1621. See also the late gothic chapel of St. Rochus and the 16C wine cellars.

Trains connect Eller with Trier and Koblenz, buses with Cochem and Traben-Trarbach, and boats with Zell and Cochem.

Opposite on the right bank of the river are the ruins of Schloß Beilstein (pulled down 1668). *Beilstein*, often described as a 'miniature Rothenburg ob der Tauber', has a baroque hall church, c 1635 (late gothic Madonna), by the wing of a former monastery; a town hall with a baroque doorway in the Marktplatz (1577; close by the Fachwek-Zehnthaus), and other half-timbered buildings. NW of Beilstein is *Bruttig-Frankel*, birthplace of the humanist Peter Schade (1497–1524), with baroque Schuncksche Haus, 1659, followed (as the river turns S again) by Valwig (chapel of 1643).

5km from Eller along the B49 lies the wine village of *Ernst*, after which the road offers views of Kloster Ebernach (the ancient priory is now a psychiatric hospital) and the cliffs above Sehl, before reaching after 5km more Cochem. *Cochem (7000 inhab.; alt. 86m) is famous for its well-restored (1869–77) medieval *Schloß*, which has been savagely pillaged in 1689; also: baroque town hall, with fine doorway and oriel; Capuchin monastery, 1623 (to which belonged Father Martin of Cochem, 1634–1710); remains of medieval walls (including Ender Gate, 1332); gabled half-timbered houses.

Information Office, No. 1 Moselstraße. Trains and buses between Koblenz and Trier; boats trips.

A 45-minute drive NW from the station along the Ender valley reaches the ruined *Schloß* Winderburg, also pillaged by the French in 1689.

After Cochem the river ceases its abrupt windings and flows more directly NE to Koblenz. 4km from Cochem is *Klotten*, at the confluence of the Mosel and the Dortebach: late gothic church, 1525 (restored 1868); wine cellars; half-timbered houses; nature reserve along the Dortebach valley; ruins of Schloß. The Rte continues through *Pommern* (church with early gothic W tower) to reach *Karden* just above the Muhlbach confluence, once dedicated to the cult of the Roman god Mars, now housing the church of *St. Castor* (three towers, late romanesque apse, early gothic nave, with a terracotta high altar depiction of the Magi, c 1430, and 13C wall paintings); among fine houses the archdeacon's house (Probsteihaus) of 1208, the Zehnthaus (tithe barn) c 1230, the Schulltheissen-Burghaus Broy, 1562, and the Stiftsschule with 1492 wall paintings.

The road crosses to the right bank of the Mosel after Karden to reach *Treis* (7km from Klotten), behind which are two ruined Schlößer, the 15C church of St. Katharina (altar painting, 1552), and the early 17C Zils chapel.

From Karden cross the river for an EXCURSION (3km) to *Burg Elz*, the oldest parts of which date from the 12C, the latest from the 16C, all well restored after a fire in 1920.

The route along the left bank of the Mosel to Koblenz includes *Müden* (whose church tower is based on a Roman look-out tower) and *Moselkern* (half-timbered houses). The route along the right bank passes through *Burgen*, dominated by Burg Bischofstein (built 1270, restored after WWII), continuing to reach (14km from Treis) *Brodenbach* (670 inhab.; alt. 75m), where a good two hours' excursion can be made E along the Ehrbach valley, to see especially **Ehrenburg** (once the home of the politician Baron Karl von Stein, 1757–1831), the finest ruined Schloß in the region, erected mid 12C. Further E at *Buchholz* is the 11C *Burg Schöneck* (now a hotel).

The route along the right bank of the Mosel leads from *Brodenbach Alken*, dominated by the 13C Burg Thurant (only two towers and the 16C buildings remain from a French attack in 1689). In Alken is the gothic church of the Trinity (romanesque choir of 1248).

Kettenes, on the opposite bank, derives its name from the chain with which the Romans blocked the river to demand dues of the traffic. The road runs N along the river by way of Oberfell (romanesque tower of the parish church; 12C pilgrimage chapel on the Bleidenberg; medieval house of Countess Jutta von Pyrmont), through *Niederfell* (baroque altar in the parish church). On the opposite bank at *Gondorf* rise the partly demolished renaissance Schloß of the Leyen family and Schloß Liebig (1280; restored 1830, now a hotel). Gondorf is now linked with *Kobern*, which boasts the oldest half-timbered house in the Rheinland (the *Abteilhof St. Marien*, 1325, alongside other fine houses in the Marktplatz) and the 15C church of the Trinity (in the mountain cemetery). Nearby is the Matthias chapel, a church modelled on that of the Holy Sepulchre, Jerusalem, c 1235, to house the alleged head of St. Matthew the Apostle, now in St. Matthias, Trier.

To drive directly from here to Koblenz (17km) takes you first through *Winningen*, whose romanesque church (altered in subsequent years) was founded c 1200, whose witches' fountain is a reminder of the witch hunts of the Thirty Years' War and whose vineyards cover 220 hectares. The road then passes through *Koblenz-Güls*, with a 13C basilica and a church of 1833 whose three ugly towers have earned it the nickname the 'Toothpick of Güls'.

On the right bank of the Mosel, 3km N from Niederfell along the B49, lies *Dieblich*, a town built on a Celtic foundation, whose modern church houses a late 14C gothic painting of the Madonna; see also the gothic half-timbered Heesenburg. Witches were burnt in the Middle Ages on the nearby Dieblich Berg. From here the road runs for 14km into Koblenz (see Rte 28) through the wine village of *Lay*, opposite which is a camp site superbly set on the edge of the river. From Lay the Rte runs for 8km into **Koblenz** (see Rte 28).

28 From Koblenz to Trier by way of Wittlich

Total distance 123km. **Koblenz**—A48 54km *Ulmen.*—A1 35km *Wittlich.* —B49 23km *Schweich.*—11km **Trier.**

**KOBLENZ (115,000 inhab.; alt. 65m), in English often given its French name Coblence, owes its name to its position at the confluence of the Rhein and the Mosel (Latin 'castrum ad Confluentes', the name Drusus gave to the camp he established here in 9 BC).

Information Office and main *post office* both opposite the main railway station in Bahnhofstraße.

Trains connect with Frankfurt, Trier, and the south; *boats* with Düsseldorf and Cologne.

History. Recognising the strategic importance of this spot, the Franks drove out the Romans. Here in the 5C the Merovingians established a court. An Imperial Diet was held here in 843. Koblenz became a rich medieval city, developing its trade and its vineyards. The Reformation brought upheaval (the elector appealing for help in defence of Catholicism to the Jesuits). During the Thirty

Years' War Koblenz was taken by the French, then the Spanish, then the Swedes and then the imperial forces. For 20 years after the war Koblenz was ravaged by plague. Two thirds of the city was destroyed by Louis XIV's artillery in 1689. The city recovered itself during the next century, to be virtually overwhelmed by refugees from the French Revolution. In retaliation the revolutionary troops took the city in 1794. Koblenz became the chief city of the département de Rhein-et-Moselle. The city again began to flourish and was assigned to Prussia by the Congress of Vienna. Now Koblenz was walled and moated, these fortifications only to be demolished in 1890. Koblenz remained the administrative centre of the Rhineland till 1945. Over 80 per cent of the city was flattened in WWII.

Amongst the natives of Koblenz were Prince Metternich (1773–1849), Josef von Görres (1776–1848) and Clemens Maria von Brentano (1778–1842).

Leave the main railway station and follow (SE), directly opposite, Markenbildchenwege, which leads into Januarius-Zick-Straße, as far as the quayside. Parkland, first planted here in 1609, runs for 4km alongside the Rhine. Walk left towards the Pfaffendorfer Bridge, before which is the Wine Village created in 1925 to represent four typical houses of the region and incorporating restaurants and wine-tasting establishments. Turn left into Julius-Wegeler-Straße and right into Neustadt Straße to find on the right the classical Electoral Palace (Kurfürstliches Schloß) by Pierre Michel d'Ixnard and

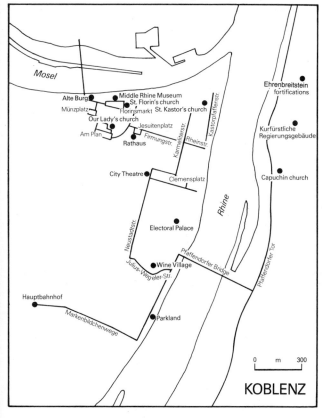

Antoine François Peyre (1778–86; much of the interior was destroyed in 1944). Beyond the Schloß on the right is the city theatre of 1787, in front of which is the Clemensplatz, with its obelisque-fountain, given, according to the inscription, by Prince-Elector Clemens-Wenzeslaus in 1791.

Walk further N along Karmeliterstraße to reach the church of *St. Kastor*, founded in 836 by Archbishop Hetti and today for the most part deriving from the end of the 11C. The vaulting of the nave dates from 1498. In the choir is a monument to Archbishop Kuno von Falkenstein (died 1388) opposite which is the monument to Archbishop Werner von Königstein (died 1418); in the N aisle the sarcophagus of St. Rizza; pulpit by P. Kern, 1625; high altar crucifix by G. Schweiger, 1685. The church abuts onto the 'Deutsches Eck', the corner where the Rhein and the Mosel meet, with the remains of the old city wall. Here the Teutonic knights built a fortress, mostly destroyed in WWII. At the corner stood the monument to Kaiser Wilhelm I (1897) so badly damaged in WWII as to have been later dismantled.

Return to the church of St. Kastor and follow Kastorpfaffenstraße, turning right into Rheinstraße to walk into Firminstraße and reach Jesuitenplatz, site of the former Jesuit college (16th and 17C, now the town hall: courtyard with fountain; renaissance doorway). From here Entenpfühl leads towards the Mosel and reaches Florinsmarkt, where stands the 12C church of St. Florin (a passageway leads to the former monastic cloister and the 13C chapterhouse). On the N side of Florinsmarkt is the Kaufhaus of 1479 (rebuilt 1963, now a museum). Cross the square to see the half-timbered 'Zum Hubertus' and take Burgstraße to reach the *Old Schloß*, or 'Alte Burg', built by Archbishop Heinrich von Vingstingen, 1276–89, to guard the bridge across the Mosel. Here in 1609 the Catholic League was set up in opposition to the Protestant Union. The French destroyed most of the Burg in 1688; reconstructed c 1700, it now houses the city library. The old bridge of 1343 with 14 arches, was built out of Winninger basalt for Archbishop Baldwin of Luxemburg and bears his name. To the right of the Alte Burg the route runs into Münzplatz, in which stands the former electoral mint (the birthplace of Metternich is nearby). To the E stands the church of *Our Lady* (c 1200; choir 1401–31; vaulting of the nave late 15C; towers capped 1693; main doorway 1765). Take the steps S of the square to find the square named Am Plan, on the N side of which is the former town hall (18th and 19C; baroque parts by Sebastiani, 1695–1700; stucco ceiling in staircase hall by Carlo Pozzi) to the W of which are late 17C houses with oriel windows, including the Feuerwache, also once the town hall.

On the opposite side of the Rhein (cross by Pfaffendorfer Brücke and turn left along Pfaffendorfer Tor) you reach the Capuchin church of 1625 (mid 18C baroque altar by Johann Sietz), followed by the Kurfürstliche Regierungsgebäude which Balthasar Neumann built, 1739–49 (stables by Johann Seitz, 1762). The Ehrenbreitstein fortifications, which you can reach by chair lift, constitute a fortress built from the 11C over 700 years (the main part today 1836–42), never taken, and now housing both a youth hostel and the Museum of Prehistory.

A late 18C theatre is at No. 2 Deinhardplatz; little theatre at 13 Florinsmarkt.
    The Landesmuseum, at Hohe Ostfront, Ehrenbreitstein, open in summer daily, 09.00–17.00; Middle Rhein Museum, Florinsmarlt (see above), open save Monday, 10.00–13.00 and 14.30–17.30; Sunday closes 13.00).

Annual events include Shrove tide processions and fireworks on the Rhein in August.

Stolzenfels, 5km S of Koblenz has a *Schloß* by K.F. Schinkel, 1836–42, to replace one destroyed by the French in 1688. 3km further S is *Rhens*, with medieval fortifications, half-timbered houses and a town hall, c 1560.

W of Koblenz join the A48 to drive 55km SW to *Ulmen* and the ruins of a 12C Schloß. The nearby lake (the 'Ulmener Maar') has its origins in a volcanic crater. The A1 now leads S for 35km to *Wittlich* (10,000 inhab.; alt. 165m), known to the Romans as *Vitelliacum*, an old town on the River Lieser, surrounded by vineyards and tobacco fields, SW of which is the last volcano to have been active in the region, the 509m-high *Mosenberg*. Here is also an 18C town hall and church of 1709. The B49 leads S from Wittlich for 26km to *Schweich*, to reach **Trier** (see Rte 26) after another 11km.

29 From Mainz to Worms

Total distance 45km. **Mainz**—B9 18km *Nierstein.*—2km **Oppenheim.**—6km *Guntersblum.*—19km *Worms.*

**MAINZ (188,000 inhab.; alt. 82m), capital of the Rhineland-Palatinate, on the left bank of the Rhein at the confluence wih the Main, is the seat of a university and an archbishopric.

Main *railway station*: Bahnhofsplatz.

Information Office and main *post office*: Bahnhofsplatz.

Trains connect with Basel, Cologne, Dortmund, Frankfurt am Main, Saarbrücken. Rail link with the Rhine-Main airport. *Bus* links with Frankfurt am Main and Luxembourg. *Boats* to Cologne and Düsseldorf.

History. Roman legionaries appeared here in 38 BC and set up castrum Mongontiacum. For a time in ruins after the withdrawal of the Romans, the city began to blossom in the 8C and the Pope sent first Wynfrith as archbishop and then St. Boniface to evangelise the Germans. Mainz became the metropolitan city of Germany. The Archbishop of Mainz became not only patriarch of the German church but from the late 10C chancellor of the Holy Roman Empire. By the mid 13C Mainz was capital of the Rheinish League and known as *Aurea Moguntia*, the golden city. In the mid 15C Gutenberg began printing here. In 1466 the university was founded. After difficulties and decline in the 17C (owing to the Thirty Years' War and Louis XIV depredations), Mainz bloomed again in the 18C. Goethe called it the 'capital of our Fatherland'. In 1792 the city became a republic. French for a time, after the Revolution, the city became part of Hesse in 1815, garrisoned both by the Prussians and the Austrians. After WWII (when 80 per cent of the city was destroyed) a new university was established here, and Mainz became the capital of the region. Johannes Gensfleisch zum Gutenberg, inventor of the printing press and printer of the Gutenberg Bible, 1452, was born at Mainz c 1397.

From the main railway station cross Bahnhofsplatz and follow Bahnhofstraße right, crossing Münsterplatz to reach Schillerstraße. On the left is the baroque Erthaler Hof, by Philipp Christoph von Erthal, 1735–43, with its classical pediment and fine staircase-tower. Opposite is the 19C ministry of supplies (Proviantamt). On the right side of Schillerstraße at Nos 9–11 is the late renaissance Schönborner Hof (by Philipp Erwein von Schönborn. 1647–73, now housing the Institut Français and the University Archaeological Museum), close by which is a modern bronze statue of the Mainz wine drinker. Next,

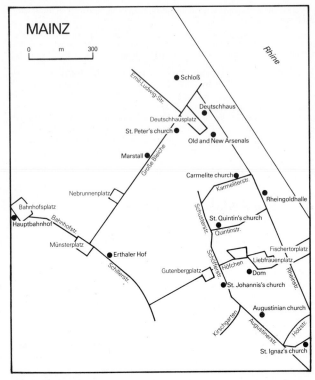

MAINZ

0   m   300

Rhine

Schloß

Emil-Ludwig-Str.

Deutschhaus

Deutschhausplatz

St. Peter's church

Old and New Arsenals

Marstall

Große Bleiche

Carmelite church

Karmeliterstr.

Nebrunnenplatz

Rheingoldhalle

Schusterstr.

Bahnhofsplatz

St. Quintin's church

Hauptbahnhof

Bahnhofstr.

Quintinstr.

Münsterplatz

Fischertorplatz

Erthaler Hof

Liebfrauenplatz

Höfchen

Schöfferstr.

Rheinstr.

Gutenbergplatz

Dom

Schillerstr.

St. Johannis's church

Augustinian church

Kirschgarten

Augustinerstr.

Holzstr.

St. Ignaz's church

at No. 3 Schillerplatz, is the baroque Bassenheimer Hof (by Anselm
Franz von Ritter zu Groenesteyn, 1756).

Turn S along Gaustraße to reach Stefansplatz (Shrovetide fountain,
1967) and the church of *St. Stephan*, a romanesque foundation though
the present building is 14C gothic (late 15C cloister; doorway 1747;
three stained glass windows by Marc Chagall, 1978, representing
reconciliation between Christians and Jews). At the S side of the
square stands the late baroque Osteiner Hof (by Valentin Thomann,
1749, rebuilt 1948–62: rococo façade). Close by this building (NW) is
the Dahlberger Hof (1710; doorway surmounted by a statue of the
Virgin Mary, 1677). Continue across Eisgrubweg and along Zitadel-
lenweg to the Zitadelle, an episcopal palace created 1620–29 by the
archbishop out of the former Benedictine monastery of St. Jakob.

Return to Schillerplatz. From here Ludwigstraße (named after
Ludwig I of Hesse but once called rue Napoleon, after the emperor
who decreed its construction) runs E to Gutenbergplatz (monument to
Gutenberg by Thorwaldsen, 1837), where stands the city theatre,
founded 1833, rebuilt 1950. Behind the theatre, Höfchen (the continuation of Ludwigstraße) contains the former university building,
1615–18 (now housing the European History Faculty of the modern
university). Höfchen continues to the Markt (left, on the corner of
Schusterstraße, an octagonal staircase-tower decorated with a statue

of St. Barbara, 1717). Here in 1526 Archbishop Albrecht of Brandenburg erected the renaissance fountain (commemorating Charles V's victory at Pavia). On the right is the romanesque church of St. Gothard, 1137. The baroque houses with Mansard roofs are by Ignaz Michel Neumann.

Behind them rises the six-towered **cathedral of **SS. Martin and Stephan**: a romanesque basilica (successor to the cathedral built by Archbishop Willigis, 975–1009) with a nave and two aisles, to which in the 13C two more gothic naves were added. The E tower (ruined by Prussian artillery, 1793, rebuilt in a neo-gothic fashion, 1870) is far plainer than the ornate, later W tower, built at various stages between the 13C and 18C, and as it reaches its 82·5m becoming first gothic and then baroque. The cathedral choir was begun at the beginning of the 12C and consecrated in 1239. The W tower was rebuilt by I.M. Neumann in 1767. INTERIOR: 44 of the 84 archbishops of Mainz are buried here, many in superb tombs. In the first chapel left are three early 16C statues (St. Willigis, St. Boniface and the Madonna known as the 'Schöne Mainzerin') and a marble tomb of the Christian socialist Bishop Emmanuel von Ketteler (died 1877); in the next chapel a sandstone Entombment c 1495 and the tombs of Archbishop Konrad III (died 1434), Peter Aspelt (died 1320) and Siegfried III von Epstein (died 1249). The pewter fonts, 1328, are from the former church of Our Lady. In the choir are two renaissance and a baroque altar: rococo stalls by F.A. Hermann, 1767, above which are monuments to Johann Philip von Schönborn (died 1673) and Lothar Franz von Schönborn (died 1729), both by Balthasar Neumann, 1745. Against the N wall of the crossing is a monument to Bernhard von Breitenbach (died 1497). The late gothic door to the 'Memorie' (romanesque chapel in memory of the dead) was sculpted in 1420. In the nave are three funeral monuments by Hans Backoffen: to Berthold von Henneberg (died 1504), Jakob von Liebenstein (died 1508) and *Uriel von Gemmingen (died 1514). The crypt contains the relics of 22 Mainz saints in a modern gold reliquary by R. Wieland, 1960. The high altar dates from 1960 (cross by G.G. Zeuner, 1975). The cathedral cloister (1397–1410) also houses some stone funeral monuments, including one to the Minnesinger Heinrich von Meißen (who was known as 'Frauenlob', died 1318). Next to the cloister is the Diocesan Museum (open weekdays save Thursday, 09.00–13.00 and 15.00–18.00; Saturday, 09.00–13.00).

Return along Höfchen and turn left at Schöfferstraße to come to *St. Johannis* church, the oldest in Mainz, basically the cathedral baptistery and deriving from an early 10C building, to reach, on the right, the picturesque *Kirschgarten* (at the beginning of Augustinerstraße): half-timbered houses, especially the still functioning bakery, and the Mary fountain. Continue along Augustinerstraße (which virtually escaped damage in WWII) to reach on the left the mid 18C Augustinian church, half baroque, half classical, standing close by the former Augustinian *monastery*: sandstone façade; frescoes inside by J.B. Enderle, 1772; wooden statue of the Virgin Mary, 1420.

At the end of Augustinerstraße follow Kapuzinerstraße (E) to reach the Jesuit church of St. Ignaz, by Johann Peter Jäger, 1763–74, at the entrance to which is a 16C Crucifixion by Hans Backoffen. Holzstraße leads from here towards the Rhine. Where it meets Rheinstraße stands the 15C Holzturm. Continue N along Rheinstraße turning right to cross Fischertorplatz (near here the Eisern Tower, from the old fortifications) and find the town hall, by Arne Jacobsen, built posthumously, 1971–74 (reinforced concrete clad in marble).

N of the Rathausplatz stands the Rheingoldhalle, a congress hall holding 3500. Walk from the river back to Markt and turn right along Schusterstraße as far as Quintinsstraße (on the right), where stands the restored 13C gothic church of St. Quintin: rococo pulpit by H. Jung. Further along Schusterstraße you reach (right) Christofsstraße and then Karmeliterstraße, which leads to the Carmelite *church*, an early 14C gothic basilica (restored after WWII): frescoes 1400; gothic retable, 1517, depicting the Virgin, crowned, between SS. Cyril and Jerome; 15C statues, including Mary with a rosary, c 1420. The courtyard of the former convent has an 18C doorway with a statue of St. Joseph and a baroque cartouche of the Coronation of the Virgin.

Turn left at the end of Karmeliterstraße to reach the former old and new Arsenals (Zaughaus, in Zeughausgasse), the first 1604, the second by Maximilan von Welsch, 1740, restored 1958. N of these stands the former headquarters of the Teutonic knights, the Deutsch-haus, by Anselm Franz von Ritter zu Groenesteyn, 1730–38, transformed in the 19C into the grand-ducal palace and now the seat of the parliament of the Rhine-Palatinate. Behind it is a replica of the column of Jupiter erected in AD 66 in honour of Nero. The Deutsch-hausplatz is joined by the Große Bleiche, a main artery of Mainz, across which is the late 16C renaissance *Schloß* of the prince-electors (the Kurfürstliches Schloß: E wing 1627–78, N wing 1687–1752, interior modernised), now the Romano-German Museum (open, except Monday, 10.00–13.00 and 15.00–17.00). Follow Große Bleiche towards the centre of the city. NW along Emil-Ludwig-Straße can be seen the domed church of Christ, 1902. Continue along Große Bleiche, passing on the left the twin onion-domed church of St. Peter (1752–76), then at Nos 49–51 the former stables (Marstall) of the prince-bishops (now housing the Middle-Rhine Museum, open 10.00–13.00 and 15.00–18.00; closed Sunday afternoons). Continue along Große Bleiche to find on the right Nebrunnenplatz, with a fountain of 1726.

MUSEUMS: *Gutenberg Museum (No. 5 Liebfrauenplatz, a museum of world printing, with the Gutenberg Bible, Gutenberg's Last Judgment of c 1455, open Tuesday–Saturday, 10.00–18.00; Sunday, 10.00–13.00); Kupferberg Museum of sparkling wine (at No. 19 Kupferberg Terrasse, open 09.30–11.30 and 14.30–15.30).

THEATRES: City Theatre, No. 7 Gutenbergplatz; University Theatre; Kammerspiele, No. 13 Emerich-Josef-Straße.

Mainz holds a festival at Shrovetide, a wine festival (end of August–beginning of September), a weekend festival (Johannisnacht) in June, and a children's festival (Nikolausfeier) on the first Saturday in December.

Leave Mainz driving S along the B9 (Liebfrauenstraße) through the wine villages of *Bodenheim* (half-timbered town hall, 1608) and *Nackenheim* (birthplace of the playwrite Carl Zuckmayer, 1896–1997, author of 'Des Teufels General', 1946), whose 'Happy Vineyard' ('Der fröhliche Weinberg') celebrates the spot: baroque church of St. Gereon, 1716; 18C town hall. 31km from Mainz lies *Nierstein* (6800 inhab.; alt. 89m), whose wine is famous. In a fortified cemetery (romanesque gate) is the church of St. Martin, 1782–87, bell tower partly 12C, 16C font, renaissance monuments; Schloß with 19C chapel; 18C baroque church of St. Kilian, with a romanesque tower. At the outskirts of the village on the way to Oppenheim were discovered in 1802 Roman thermal baths (the *Stronabad*).

Oppenheim lies 5km S of Nierstein. Known as *Bauconica* in Celtic-Roman times, it was mostly razed by the French in 1688. Oppenheim has retained its gothic church of *St. Katharina, begun 1226; W towers and choir 13C, nave 14C, W end 15C, all restored 1934–37. Behind the church is the gothic chapel and charnel house of St. Michael, many of its skulls and bones said to be those of Swedes and Spaniards fallen in the Thirty Years' War. Oppenheim also has the former Franciscan 14C church of St. Bartholomäus, the Gau Gate of 1566 from the medieval walls, the Luther house where the Reformer stayed on his way to Worms in 1521, a renaissance fountain of 1546, a gothic town hall of 1689, and a Wine Museum. A 15-minute walk leads up to the restaurant in the Imperial Burg Landskrone (13C, destroyed 1689), with fine views of the local vineyards. Train connections with Mainz and Mannheim, buses with Mainz.

The B9 now continues directly S through vineyards by way of *Guntersblum* (6km): romanesque church; two Schlößer, baroque Adelshof, formerly belonging to the Teutonic knights. To the E is a nature reserve on an island created when the Rhine was straightened in 1829. The Rte continues S through the wine village of Alsheim, and (after passing a road to the right which leads for 2km to *Bechtheim* (11th and 12C romanesque church) reaches *Osthofen* (11km): wine festival, last weekend in September; 13C church on the Goldberg; 17th and 18C houses.

Worms (see Rte 30) lies 10km S of Osthofen.

30 From Worms to Speyer

Total distance 37km. **Worms**—B9 11km *Frankenthal.*—5km *Ludwigshafen.*—21km **Speyer.**

****WORMS** (80,000 inhab.; alt. 110m), situated amidst fertile vineyards on the left bank of the River Rhine, profits also from furniture making, sugar refineries, leather goods and light industry.

Main *railway station*: Bahnhofstraße.

Main *post office*: Ludwigsplatz.

Information Office: No. 14 Neumarkt.

Trains connect with Bingen, Kaiserlautern, Mainz and Mannheim, *buses* with Ludwigshafen, etc.

History. Worms was a Roman garrison and before that the Celtic settlement *Borbetomagus* (a name developing into *Vormatia* in the Middle Ages and then Worms). The Nibelungenlied made Worms the seat of Gunther, king of the Burgundians. Emperor Heinrich II gave the city customs rights in 1074. In 1122 the Concordat of Worms brought to an end the investiture controversy between the pope and the emperor. In 1254 Worms allied with Mainz, thus inaugurating the confederation of the Rhine. Several imperial diets took place here, in particular the celebrated Diet of 1521 which condemned Martin Luther. Virtually bankrupted by the Thirty Years' War, Worms was almost destroyed during the war of the Palatinate Succession (1688–97), when its defences were demolished. The city was ceded to the French in 1797 and returned to Hesse-Darmstadt in 1815, when the former great city had been reduced to little more than a small town. Worms began to prosper again, but suffered a further blow when 65 per cent of its buildings were destroyed in WWII. The Biblical and Talmud scholar Salomo ben Isak (1040–1105) lived and worked here.

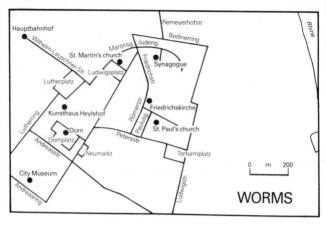

Leaving the main railway station, follow Wilhelm-Leuschner-Straße SE as far as LUTHERPLATZ, with its gigantic monument to the reformer (chiefly the work of Ernst Rietschel, finished by Kietz, Donndorf and Schelling, 1868): the lesser figures are Jan Huss, Wycliffe, Melanchthon, Savonarola, Peter Waldes, Philip of Hesse, Friedrich of Saxony and Johann Reuchlin, as well as statues representing the cities of Magdeburg, Augsburg and Speyer. Take Luthering right to reach, at the crossroads with Andreasring and Andreastraße, the old Jewish cemetery (the oldest and largest in Europe, part of it 11C, used by the Jewish community that lived here from the 10C). Follow Andreasring to reach the City Museum (principally antiquities; open daily, summer, 09.00–12.00 and 14.00–17.00; winter opens at 10.00 and closes at 16.00). NW past Andreastor is the 12th and 13C church of St. Magnus (14C tower), rebuilt 1954. From here en route to the Domplatz you pass some 1·5m of a Roman wall that once was part of the forum.

The **Dom* (cathedral of St. Peter) was first consecrated in 1018, though the earliest parts of the present romanesque masterpiece date from the end of the 12C. The E choir was consecrated in 1110, the W end finished 1181. The ogival vaulted nave is entered from the S by an early 14C sculpted doorway, dominated by a carving of the Church Triumphant, borne on the heads of the four evangelists. INTERIOR: 158m long with the dome rising 40m above the crossing; the W end (once reserved for the emperor and leading civil dignitaries) is architecturally more elaborate than the E, with 18C altar and stalls. The E choir, however, possesses a baroque high altar by Balthasar Neumann (c 1740) and two side altars by Johann Peter Jäger (1750). The chapel of St. Georg is renaissance; the gothic baptistery chapel of St. Nikolaus was finished in 1325; the chapel of St. Anna has two romanesque carvings (Habakkuk and the angel; Daniel in the lions' den). Other 11C reliefs in the cathedral include Christ among saints; 13C frescoes depict SS. Peter, Paul and Christopher; remains of a carved stone cycle of the life of Christ, c 1500; tombs of Eberhard von Heppenheim (c 1430) and Bishop Theodor von Bettendorf (died 1580).

N of the cathedral is the *Kunsthaus Heylshof* (rich art collection, 15C to 19C, of the von Heyl family; open save Monday and Sunday,

09.00–12.00 and 14.00–17.00; in winter opens 10.00 and closes 16.00), and the garden that formerly belonged to the bishops' palace (bordered W by remains of the city walls). Immediately NE of the cathedral is the Lutheran church of the Holy Trinity, 1709–25, rebuilt 1955–59, with modern glass and mosaics representing Luther before the Diet of Worms. Follow Peterstraße to TORTURMPLATZ, which has the Torturm, the Bürgerturm and the Fischerpforte (also called the Lutherpförtchen) from the old city walls. Turn N from Peterstraße along Bauhofgasse to reach the church of *St. Paul* (Pauluskirche), once belonging to a Dominican monastery (11C towers, though the church is basically 13C with an 18C nave and high altar; 13th and 14C cloister). From here take Römerstraße N to reach the baroque Friedrichskirche (1745; paid for by King Friedrich II of Prussia, hence its name), close by the early baroque Red House ('Rotes Haus'), 1624. Friedrichstraße leads N to Judengasse (right), where are more remains of the city walls and which leads to the former Jewish ghetto and the oldest synagogue in Europe, deriving from the romanesque era, almost totally destroyed on the Kristallnacht of 1938, rebuilt 1958–61 (rich Jewish archives); Jewish Mikwe (Frauenbad) behind the synagogue, for women's ritual washing.

Return along Judengasse and continue along Martinsgasse to reach the church of *St. Martin* (13C; partly rebuilt 18C; fine portals, especially the early gothic W door). St. Martin's church borders on Ludwigsplatz (24m- high obelisque, erected in 1895 in honour of Grand Duke Ludwig IV of Hesse). Friedrichstraße leads N to join (on the right) Berlinerring, from which Remeyerhofstraße followed by Liebfruenstift wind N to the three-aisled church of Our Lady (1310–1465: sculptures; 14C painting of the Madonna), surrounded by vines that produce the wine known as Liebfraumilch.

ENVIRONS include the Bergkirche at *Hochheim*, 2km W (11C crypt; 12C romanesque tower); and at *Herrnsheim*, c 4km NW of Worms, the 15C gothic parish church (choir stalls, 1486; late gothic stone pulpit, 1489; tombs of the von Dalberg family), as well as a Schloß in a fine park. At *Pfiffligheim*, 3km W of Worms, is the tree under which Luther and his friends are said to have sat while deciding the reject the findings of the Diet of Worms.

From Worms the B9 runs S passing under the Mannheim–Saarbrücken motorway to reach after 11km the industrial town of *Frankenthal* (47,000 inhab.; alt. 96m), whose porcelain factory was famous between 1755 and 1800 and whose history dates back to the 9C. Of the 18C fortifications remain the Worms Gate (1770–72) and the Speyer Gate (1772–73): classical church of the Twelve Apostles (1820–23; 13C foundations) and the ruined late romanesque monastery church (13th and 14C).

Frankenthal is 3km N of Ludwigshafen, reached by way of the suburb of *Oggersheim*, where in 1729 the crown-prince of Palatinat-Sulzbach built a Loretto chapel (sculpted angels by Paul Egell, 1730), dedicated to the *Assumption of the Blessed Virgin Mary*. The church was rebuilt by Peter Anton Vershaffelt, 1775–77: behind its high altar a marble reproduction of the Holy House of Loretto at Ancona, Italy. At Oggersheim, in 1782 (at No. 6 Schillerstraße), Schiller wrote 'Kabale und Liebe' and worked on 'Fiesko'. The house is now a Schiller Museum (open weekdays save Wednesday, 14.00–17.00; weekends, 10.00–12.00). **Ludwigshafen** (166,000 inhab.; alt. 92m), an important port on the Rhine and the centre of the German chemical industry, developed as a suburb of Mannheim in the 17C and is a totally modern city with a fine park and an enormous sports stadium (holding 85,000 spectators). Named in 1843 after King Ludwig I of Bavaria, it has a Friedenskirche of 1932 (Leuschnerstraße) and the BASF high-rise building of 1937, as well as the most modern main railway station in Europe. The philosopher Ernst Bloch was born here in 1885. The Wilhelm-Hack-Museum, at No. 23 Berlinerstraße, houses medieval to *modern paintings, especially 20C expressionists; open save Monday, 09.30–17.00; Wednesday until 21.00). Ludwigshafen's main theatre is at No. 30 Berlinerplatz. Tourist information in Ludwigsplatz. Train connections with Kaiserslautern, Mainz, Mannheim, Speyer, Worms; buses with Speyer, etc.

SPEYER (44,000 inhab.; alt. 104m) lies 21km S of Ludwigshafen along the B9, on the left bank of the Rhine and dates back to the Celtic-Roman era.

History. Speyer became a bishopric in the 7C and Konrad the Salien made it capital of the empire. A free imperial city from 1294, it was at Speyer in 1529 that the followers of Martin Luther were first called Protestants. Although the Imperial high court sat here in the 16C and 17C, from the Thirty Years' War to the early 19C the city declined rapidly (largely as the result of wars—the French set fire to the city in 1689, sparing only the cathedral, which accidentally caught alight). The French took the city in 1797 and this time deliberately demolished the cathedral. In 1815 Speyer was ceded to Bavaria.

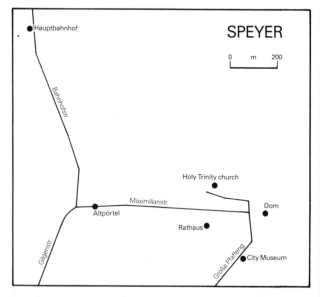

From the main railway station take Bahnhofstraße and Glegenstraße, to pass through the Altpörtel of 1246 (upper storey 1512) and along Maximilianstraße to the cathedral, passing on the left the old Kaufhaus. The *Cathedral*, the largest in Germany (133m by 34m; height 33m), was begun in 1030 and rebuilt by Heinrich IV between 1082 and 1125. The 11C *crypt—the largest in Germany—alone remains from this period and is known as the 'Kaisergruft', since it contains the tombs of eight rulers. After the vandalism of the French Speyer Cathedral was rebuilt in the 19C through the generosity of Kings Maximilian and Ludwig of Bavaria. The bronze doorway is by Toni Schneider-Manzell (1970). The *chapel of St. Afra, c 1110, rebuilt 1850, has carvings brought from elsewhere in the cathedral as well as those originally here (Annunciation, c 1470). In front of the cathedral is the so-called Domnapf, a sandstone basin of 1490 which new bishops were expected to fill with wine after their consecration. In the cathedral garden the 13C Heidentürmchen remains from the old fortifications. Walk left from the cathedral to the church of the Holy Trinity, by J.P. Grabem, 1717: baroque high altar and organ; vault decorated by Guthbier, 1713.

The west façade of the massive eleventh century cathedral at Speyer.

The baroque town hall of Speyer dates from 1712–26. The neo-gothic protestant Gedächtniskirche (1893–1904) is a memorial to the 'Protest' of 1529; the Bernharduskirche dates from 1954 and was built as a symbol of peace with money partly donated by the French. In a building by Gabriel von Seidl (1910, at No. 7 Große Pfaffengasse) is the City Museum, with a Bronze Age golden hat and a wine exhibition (open daily, 09.00–12.00 and 14.00–17.00). In front of the museum are two Roman equestrian statues.

Tourist information at the town hall (No. 12 Maximilianstraße). Train links with Saarbrücken and Frankfurt am Main, buses with Landau and Ludwigshafen.

31 From Mannheim to Zweibrüken by way of Landau

Total distance 111km. **Mannheim**—1km *Ludwigshafen.*—B9 21km **Speyer.**—B9 and B272 20km **Landau.**—B10 14km *Annweiler.*—31km *Pirmasems.*—24km *Zweibrücken.*

MANNHEIM (307,000 inhab.; alt. 95m) is situated in Baden-Württemberg on the opposite bank of the Rhine to Ludwigshafen, at its confluence with the River Neckar.

History. A fishing village existed here in the mid 8C, where in 1606 the Elector Friedrich IV decided to lay out a new town as a bulwark of this strategic position. Although the century saw much destruction of Friedrich's foundations, Mannheim was rebuilt (with the help of Huguenot and Walloon immigrants) in a totally regular fashion whose pattern remains to this day. Although the Vauban personally led a French siege on Mannheim in 1689, the town was not ruined by the French wars. In 1720 the Elector Carl Philipp transferred his seat from Heidelberg to here. The first German national theatre was established at Mannheim in 1779 and three years later produced Schiller's 'Die Räuber'. (Schiller lived in Mannheim 1783–85.) Industrialisation began in the late 19C. In 1886 Carl Benz demonstrated his first motor vehicle here. Mannheim has a massive inland harbour. In the bombardments of WWII the town was seriously damaged.

Leave the main railway station and walk left along Bismarckstraße to reach the baroque grand ducal *Schloß*, 1720–60 (great staircase; knights' hall; Schloß library, 1755–57; church), now the University, behind which is the Schloß garden. Opposite the Schloß stands the *Palais Bretzentheim* (1782–88; only partly restored after WWII) and, further along Bismarckstraße, the Jesuit *church* of 1738–60 by A. Galli-Bibiena of Bologna (finished by F. Rabaliatti and P. A. von Vershaffelt: dome fresco by P.H. Brinckmann; silver Madonna by J.I. Saler, 1747; organ case by P. Egell). Next to the church is the observatory, by F. Rabaliatti, 1772–74.

Turn right here to reach the former Arsenal of Mannheim, 1777–79, the archaeological museum of Mannheim since 1937 (open save Monday, 10.00–13.00 and 14.00–17.00). Turn right again and walk as far as the PARADEPLATZ, laid out in the 18C, with its pyramidical fountain by Gabriel Grupello, 1709–16. Turn left and walk as far as the Marktplatz, with its monument to the four elements (1719) passing the former town hall, joined by a communal tower with the Untere Pfarrkirche (1701–23). From here walk SE to FRIEDRICHSPLATZ, an art nouveau ('Jugendstil') square constructed in 1907, with a 50m-high cylindrical water tower (1886–89), set by a grassy terrace which covers the city reservoir. N of this square of the ROSENGARTEN is

Mannheim's congress centre. The City Art Museum is at No. 9 Moltkestraße: 19C and 20C painting and sculpture (open Tuesday–Thursday, Saturday and Sunday, 10.00–13.00 and 14.00–17.00; Friday, 14.00–20.00); it stands to the S of Friedrichsplatz in a Jugendstil building by H. Billing, 1907, fronted by modern works of sculpture.

Follow Friedrichsring N to reach on the right Goetheplatz, with the new theatre by Gerhard Weber, 1957, opposite the Luisen Park, which covers 41 hectares and has a 205m-high observation tower and restaurant.

Mannheim hosts a fair in May and the Upper Rhine regatta in June.

Tourist information at No. 1 Bahnhofplatz. Mannheim-Neuostheim airport. Boats and buses take passengers to Ludwigshafen.

Cross the Rhine either by the Konrad-Adenauer bridge or the Kurt-Schumacher bridge to reach *Ludwigshafen* (see Rte 30) 1km W. From here take the B9 S to **Speyer** (see Rte 30). After 9km S the B9 meets the B272. Drive SW for 17km to join the B38 1km from Landau.

Landau (40,000 inhab.; alt. 146m), the main wine and tobacco centre of the lower palatinate, grew from a village into a free imperial city in the 13C. Much pillaged during the Thirty Years' War, Landau passed into French hands in 1648. Vauban fortified the city in 1684. The imperial forces vehemently attempted to regain Landau which nonetheless remained French throughout the 18C. Given in the 19C first to Austria and then to Bavaria, Landau grew beyond her fortifications, which were demolished in 1876. Of these remains the German gate, with Louis XIV's motto 'Nec pluribus impar', and the French gate (both baroque, c 1690). In Stiftsplatz is a 13C church, close by the monument to Montclar, governor of Alsace (died 1690). In

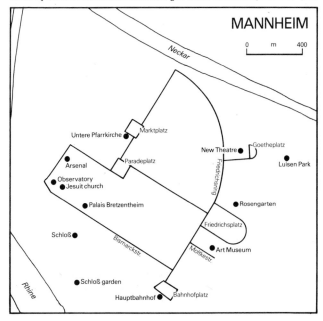

Königstraße is the gothic Augustinian church, 1407 (now the church of the *Holy Cross*: late gothic font, 1506; late 17C Madonna; 15C cloister and 18C monastic buildings). In Max-Josef-Platz is the Luitpold fountain of 1892, close by the 14C chapel of St. Katharina. Museum of local history (No. 8 Marienring, open weekdays except Monday, 09.00–12.00 and 14.00–16.00; Sunday, 10.00–12.30). Flower festival second Sunday in September. Information Office in the town hall; train links with Karlsruhe, Pirmasens, Saarbrücken, Zweibrücken; buses with Heidelberg, Pirmasens, Karlsruhe.

The B10 continues W through Godramstein and Siebeldingen, passing through the country of the Palatinate forest to reach after 14km *Annweiler* (7500 inhab.; alt. 183m), a health resort founded in the 12C by the Hohenstaufen: town hall 1844; Protestant church preserving its older bell tower; Catholic church of 1869; three medieval Schlößer on the Trifels mountain (three peaks c 500m, accessible by foot in an hour).

After 31km the B10 reaches *Pirmasens* (59,000 inhab.; alt. 183m), a town on three hills, once the home of the Landgrave of Hesse and today the centre of Germany's footwear industry, with a biennial footwear fair: Lutheran parish church, 1949. The B10 runs 24km W through Höheischweiler to reach *Zweibrücken* (39,000 inhab.; alt. 266m) at the confluence of the Hornbach and the Schwarzbach. In the centre of the town, reconstructed after WWII, stands the late gothic church of St. Alexander (c 1500: modern stained glass by Erhardt Klonk); the Herzogs' Schloß (1720–25), and the Karlskirche, which King Karl II of Sweden commissioned (1708–11). To the E of the city is the Luitpold park and the famous Zweibrücken rose garden. The 18C town exhibition centre in a late 18C building opens Saturday, 10.00–12.00. Zweibrücken has a famous stud farm and a pheasantry, where the deposed King Stanislas Leczinki of Poland met King Charles XII of Sweden. Information Office at No. 5 Herzogplatz, Zweibrücken. Trains connect with Homburg, Karlsruhe and Saarbrücken, buses with Homburg and Pirmasens.

The ENVIRONS of Zweibrücken include the village of *Hornbach*, 9km S, with the ruins of a Benedictine monastery and the grave of its founder, Pirmin, as well as a Pirmin memorial chapel of 1957.

32   The Eifel

A. From Trier to Cologne

Total distance 176km. **Trier**—B51 23km *Bitburg.*—B257 12km *Kyllburg.* —30km *Schönecken.*—B51 8km *Prüm.*—36km *Blankenheim.*—18km **Bad Münstereifel.**—13km *Euskirchen.*—23km **Brühl.**—13km **Cologne**.

Leave **Trier** (see Rte 26) by the Kaiser-Wilhelm bridge over the Mosel and travel through wooded country 23km NW to *Bitburg* (12,000 inhab.; alt. 338m), once a Roman military station (*Beda Vicus*; the B51 follows the old Roman road from Trier to Cologne) and before that a Celtic settlement. Almost completely destroyed in WWII, Bitburg retains the *Coben tower* from its Roman wall (some 40m of which also remains), the 15C late gothic church of Our Lady (S aisle 16C, N aisle 19C) and the 16C Kobenhof. The beer fountain honours the town's celebrated Pils. Information Office at No. 6 Hubert-Prim-Straße. From Bitburg take the B257 NE for 10km, to turn left at the crossroads for *Kyllburg* (1400 inhab.; alt. 271m), a health resort in the Kyll valley, with the keep of the old Schloß, built for Archbishop Theodor of Trier on the Malberg; a Franciscan *monastery church* (renaissance *stained glass, 1534, in the choir; gothic cloister; 14C chapterhouse); and a 20m-high column of Our Lady.

Drive W and then N for 30km, crossing the Kryll at Erdorf and passing through *Nattenheim* (Roman villa rustica at *Otrang*: mosaic pavement, baths, small museum) to *Schönecken* on the B51: ruins of 13C Burg Schönecken. The B51 continues N to reach after 8km the health and winter sports resort of **Prüm* (5700 inhab.; alt. 425m): Benedictine *abbey*, founded 721, today a school; present buildings by Balthasar Neumann and J.G. Seitz, 1748–65; abbey church (Salvatorbasilika) by Johann Georg Judas: baroque façade, gothic interior, renaissance pulpit, baroque high altar and choir stalls, tomb of the Emperor Lothar I, died 855. From Prüm the B265 leads to the Belgian border.

21km further N along the B51 stands the medieval village and resort of *Stadtkyll*, with the remains of its fortifications. After another 15km the route reaches *Blankenheim* (7500 inhab.; alt. 497m), lying at the foot of its rebuilt 13C Schloß (now a youth hostel) and near the source of the River Ahr, with a gothic parish church, 1495–1501 and half-timbered houses. Follow the B512 18km NW to the walled spa (mud baths) ***Bad Münstereifel** (16,000 inhab.; alt. 280m) on the River Erft: 11C romanesque parish *church*, with 9C crypt, 13C dome, medieval tombs, a font of 1619, a 14C Madonna, and a tabernacle by F. Roir, 1480; Windeckhaus, 1644, on Klosterplatz; 14C and 16C gothic town hall; the former Jesuit *school* (the oldest school in the Rhineland), with a collection of 18,000 schoolbooks; four medieval gates and 17 towers along the 13C walls. The local history museum is in a 12C romanesque house (open May–October, Tuesday–Saturday, 14.00–17.00; in winter Saturday, 14.00–16.00).

At *Iversheim*, 4km N along the B51, is a Roman lime-kiln with six ovens (visits Sunday, in summer, 10.00–17.00). The next village, *Kreuzweingarten*, is the site of a Roman villa with excavated mosaic pavements and baths. An excursion E from *Billig* reveals the 80km-long Roman canal which brought water to the city of Cologne. 9km N of Iversheim the Rte reaches the woollen manufacturing town of *Euskirchen* (44,000 inhab.; alt. 165m): 14C town hall; church of *St. Martin*, 12C romanesque and 14C gothic; remains of the 13C walls.

Continue N through Weilerswist to reach after 23km Brühl, by way of 'Phantasialand' (30,000 square metres of fantasy, including a half-size model of Berlin at the time of the Belle-Époque, a circus, a 'western express', a pirate ship, a marionette theatre, restaurants and bars), and by way of the natural park of Ville. At *Brühl* (44,000 inhab.; alt. 65m) stands the rococo ***Schloß Augustusburg**, by Konrad Schlaun, 1725, interiors by the French architect François Cuvilliés, 1728–40, staircase by Balthasar Neumann, 1740–48. Schloß church with bronze doors by Elmar Hillebrand. In the park (by Le Nôtre's pupil Dominique Girard) is the hunting lodge Falken-lust, by Cuvilliés, 1729–40. The gothic Schloß church of 1493 has a baroque interior (1740–57), with a high altar by Neumann, 1745.

Open daily (save December and January) 09.00–12.00 and 14.00–16.00.

Brühl lies 13km S of Cologne (see Rte 42).

B. From Aachen to Koblenz

Total distance 167km. **Aachen**—B258 9km _Kornelimünster._—25km **Monschau.**—26km _Schleiden._—20km _Blankenheim._—32km _Nürburgring._—26km **Mayen.**—29km **Koblenz.**

**AACHEN (243,000 inhab.; alt. 125m), in French Aix-la-Chapelle, stands on the borders of Holland, France and Germany and was known to the Romans as _Aquis Granum._

Main _railway station_: Bahnhofsplatz.

Main _post office and information office_: Bahnhofsplatz.

Tourist information: Nos 39–41 Markt.

History. The 'Granum' of the Roman name derives from a Celtic god. The Romans relished the town as a spa. Here Pepin the Short (714–68) established his

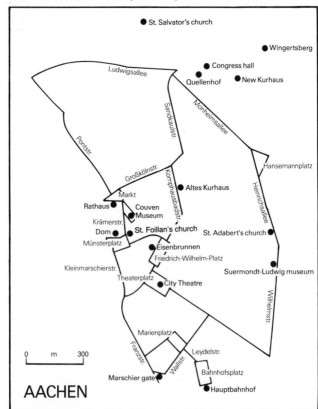

AACHEN

court, and his son Charlemagne made the city capital of his empire, and after his death his collection of saintly relics attracted countless pilgrims. At Aachen 30 Holy Roman Emperors were crowned. After the Reformation the city was frequently at odds with the emperor. A fire destroyed most of the old city in 1656, hence the baroque nature of much of its present-day architecture. Aachen ceased to be a free imperial city in 1794. The city became part of Prussia in 1815. In 1818 the Tsar, the Austrian emperor and the King of Prussia met at Aachen to set up the Holy Alliance. A bishopric was established here, 1802–21 and again in 1930. 80 per cent of the city was seriously damaged in WWII.

From the main railway station walk NW along Leydelstraße to the Marienplatz and the neo-gothic church of Our Lady (Marienkirche). Take Ullstraße, left of the church, to reach the Marschier gate remaining from the 13C walls. Turn right to walk along Franzstraße and Kleinmarschierstraße to reach Münsterplatz and the cathedral. Aachen *Cathedral is built in two distinctly different styles: the octagonal rotunda surrounded by a double-storeyed ambulatory of 16 sides, which Odo of Metz constructed in the Byzantine style between 796 and 805 (the chapel of Charlemagne's palace), and the gothic choir, 1355–1414. Around these are chapels dating from the 14th and 15C (the *Anna chapel of 1449 and the *Hungarian chapel of 1767 on the S side, a gift of the King of Hungary in 1767, redone in the classical style). The rotunda was given its gables in the 13C and the dome was built after the fire of 1656. The base of the bell tower is Carolingian, the upper part 19C. To the cathedral is attached the cloister of 1500 which replaced the previous romanesque building. The main doorway, the bronze Wolfstür, dates from 800, and is set in a baroque porch. INTERIOR: in the entrance hall the she-wolf (a Celtic goddess) dates from c 160 and the bronze pineapple from c 400. The eight pillars came originally from Ravenna, though they were partly renewed in 1854 and all the capitals are reconstructed. Salviati's mosaic on the vault (Christ surrounded by the twenty-four elders of the Apocalypse) was completed by Schaper in 1902. The great *candelabrum was made in 1165 for the Emperor Friedrich Barbarossa as an idealised model of the heavenly Jerusalem. Charlemagne's bones were exhumed after his beatification in 1165 and in 1215 placed in the superb *reliquary on the high altar. The retable (modelled on that in St. Mark's, Venice), was given by Otto III c 1020. The copper-gilt *pulpit was given by Heinrich II c 1101. Charlemagne's former 2C sarcophagus, decorated with the figure of Proserpine, is also here (in the chapel of St. Michael), as is his white marble throne (restored 1889). The altar in the 14C chapel of St. Nikolaus dates from 1962, the font from the 12C. The Treasury (open daily, 09.00–13.00 and 14.00–17.00) contains numerous *reliquaries (including the Lothar cross of c 1000, the Marienschrein of 1238 and Charlemagne's reliquary bust of 1349) along with a remarkable number of dubiously authentic relics.

In Krämerstraße, opposite the cathedral apse, is the church of St. Foillan, 1657–67. S of the cathedral across Ursulinerstraße is Friedrich-Wilhelm-Platz, in which stands the classical Elisenbrunnen by K.F. Schinkel, 1825. N of the cathedral is the Marktplatz, where the Town Hall (almost totally destroyed in 1944 and since reconstructed) was built in 1349 on the base of Charlemagne's palace, of which the Granus tower and the Mark tower remain. On the façade are depicted Pope Leo III and Charlemagne kneeling before Christ; five important historical frescoes in the Reichssaal (out of eight before WWII) by Alfred Rethel (1816–59) have been restored, the rest lost irretrievably. The bronze doors are by the Aachen-born Ewald Mataré, 1965.

Charlemagne's throne, late eighth century, in Aachen Cathedral.

NW of Marktplatz, at No. 13 Pontstraße, is the International Newspaper Museum (open weekdays, 08.00–13.00 and 14.00–17.00), not far from the house (No. 177) where Paul Julius von Reuter established his news agency. Großkölnstraße leads NE from Markt-platz to pass the restored gothic church of St. Nikolaus and turn right into Komphausbadstraße in which stands the Altes Kurhaus of 1782 (restored with the addition of an art gallery, 1969). From here walk N along Komphausbadstraße and Sandkaulstraße to reach Quellenhof. Turning right here leads into Monheimsallee, on which is the New Kurhaus in a park stretching to the foot of the Wingertsberg and housing also the congress hall with its Casino. The route right continues through Hansemannplatz (monument to David Hansemann, 1888) and S along Heinrichsallee (with an equestrian statue of Friedrich III by Lederer, 1911) to reach the church of St. Adalbert, built by Otto III c 1000 and entirely restored 1873–76.

Turning left instead of right at the Quellenhof takes you into Ludwigsallee. N on the Salvatorberg is the restored church of St. Salvator, founded by Louis the Pious and built 814–840. Ludwigsallee leads W to the Marien tower and a gate, both part of the 14C city walls.

MUSEUMS: Couven Museum (architecture, pottery, furniture, at No. 17 Hühnermarkt); New Gallery (modern art, at No. 19 Komphausbadstraße); Suermondt-Ludwig Museum (art and sculpture since the 14C, in a renaissance building at No. 18 Wilhelmstraße); Local History Museum (at No. 68 Rehmannstraße); all are open weekdays save Monday, 10.00–17.00; weekends, 10.00–13.00.

THEATRES: City Theatre by J.P. Cremer and K.F. Schinkel, 1825, rebuilt 1900, in Theaterplatz, close by the Grenzlandtheater (at Nos 5–6 Friedrich-Wilhelm-Platz).

The B258 runs S from Aachen through Brand to Kornelimünster (2700 inhab.; alt. 225m): monastery and church of St. Salvator founded in 814, destroyed by the Normans and by a fire of 1310; replaced by the present baroque buildings, 1728; in the Corneliuskapelle the reliquary of Pope Cornelius from whom the village takes its name.

The Rte passes through Belgium for 6km, passing the 650m-high Hohes Venn and reaching picturesque Monschau (French Montjoie; 11,800 inhab.; alt. 350m, rising to 650m) after 25km. The ruined medieval Burg, partly rebuilt 1899 (keep, knights' hall, 16C asses tower or 'Eselturm' and the Batterie tower) dominates the town: half-timbered houses; old town hall, 1654; the baroque Rote Haus, 1765, of Johann Heinrich Scheibler, founder of the Monschau silk industry, now a museum (rococo interior; open save Monday, 10.00–12.00 and 14.00–17.00); Haus Troistorff, 1783; parish church of Mariä Geburt, 1649; church of St. Maria, from a former monastery, 1726–50. Tourist information at No. 1 Stadtstraße. Trains connect with Aachen.

At Monschau the B258 turns E and runs for 26km to the health resort of Schleiden (12,500 inhab.; alt. 350) in the Ettelscheid valley: Schloß many times rebuilt on a romanesque original; late gothic Schloß church, with the renaissance tomb of Sybille von Hohenzollern and early renaissance stained glass (1525). Close by, the River Ruhr has been dammed for hydro-electricity, creating a large artificial lake.

The Rte now passes through the Schleidener forest, reaching Blankenheim (see p 175) after 20km. 32km further SE the B258 reaches the 29km-long Nürburgring motor racing circuit, set around the health and ski resort of Nürburg with its ruined Schloß. The route passes over and under the actual circuit, continuing through the village of Virneburg (4060 inhab.; alt. 420m), with its 11C Schloß ruined by the French in 1689, its chapel of 1697 and its thatched tithe barn, to reach after 26km **Mayen** (22,000 inhab.; alt. 230m), which the Romans called Megina. Situated in the valley of the Nette at the foot of the 528m Hochsimmer, Mayen is dominated by Schloß Genovevaburg, 1280, partly ruined by fire in 1891 and rebuilt 1893 (Golo tower 32m high). It now houses the Eifel Museum (open save Monday, 09.00–12.00 and 14.00–17.00; Sunday, 10.00–13.00). At either end of the town stand the Brücken gate and the Ober gate (all that remain of the 14C walls). Marktstraße leads from the Brückentor to the 14C gothic church of *St. Clemens*, with a romanesque S tower and a curiously twisted N spire. Continue along Marktstraße to the former town hall, 1717, in the Marktplatz (Information Office). Trains connect Mayen wih Andernach, Daun and Koblenz. 4·5km NW, at the meeting point of the Nette, Nitz, Welchenbach and Fraubach valleys stands *Schloß Bürresheim* 15–17C. The B258 now passes through *Bassenheim* (Schloß of 1614; sandstone relief of the 'Bassenheim rider', c 1240, in the parish church), to reach Koblenz (see Rte 27) by the suburb of Lützel.

C. From Bonn to Bad Tönisstein by way of Kelberg and Maria Laach

Total distance 224km. **Bonn**—B9 21km *Remagen.*—B266 9km *Bad Neuenahr-Ahrweiler.*—18km *Altenahr.*—B257 21km *Adenau.* —8km *Nürburgring.*—17km *Kelberg.*—18km *Ulmen.*—B259 13km *Kaiseresch.*—10km *Monreal.*—30km *Burg Eltz.*—6km *Münstermaifeld.*—B258 and B256 44km **Maria Laach.**—9km *Bad Tönisstein.*

Leave **Bonn** and travel on the B9 for 21km S to *Remagen* (for this stretch of the route see p 212). 3km S of Remagen the B266 leads right into the Ahr valley. 2km W along the B266 lies the spa of Bodendorf, and after another 7km—by way of the ruined *Schloß Landskron* and the mineral springs of Apollinaris—the thermal resort of *Bad Neuenahr-Ahrweiler* (28,000 inhab.; alt. 84m), which boasts Germany's biggest Casino and straddles the River Ahr. In the district of Bad Neuenahr is the church of *St. Willibrord*, founded 990, with today a romanesque W tower c 1200, and the baroque Beethoven house, where Ludwig van Beethoven spent his holidays between 1786 and 1792. The l600m-long 7m-high walls of Ahrweiler were built from the mid 13C to the 15C, and incorporate the Ahr gate, with a 16C relief of the Crucifixion and the Nieder gate, with a relief c 1500 of the Scourging of Christ. Two medieval cannons guard the Kanonen tower. The *Weiß tower* houses a museum (open in Summer Tuesday and Friday, 10.00–12.00 and 14.00–18.00; Sunday, 10.00–12.00). The 13C church of *St. Laurentius* has 14C wall paintings. S of the walls (along Kalvarienbergstraße) is the 15C Ursuline monastery. The region is noted for its red wines and Bad Neuenahr-Ahrweiler has a Wine Museum (at No. 86 Himmelsburgerstraße; open Sunday, 10.00–12.00 and Wednesday, 14.00–19.30). Information Offices at No. 11 Marktplatz and No. 60 Hauptstraße. Train connections with Bonn, buses with Bonn and Remagen.

After 8km the route reaches *Walporzheim*, long noted for its wines and its Kelterhaus (winepress house) of 1717, and then winds through vineyards and the wine villages of Dernau and Mayschoß (ruined Schloß) to reach after 109km *Altenahr* (2350 inhab.; alt. 170m) a centre of walking and hiking (especially to Burg Kreuzberg, 1340, destroyed by the French 1686, rebuilt 1760 with a chapel of 1738, which is also reached by the B257 from Altenahr: half-timbered houses in Kreuzberg itself). Burg Are above Altenahr was destroyed by soldiers in 1714. Altenahr retains three gates of its old walls, and has a romanesque church, c 1170, with an early 14C gothic choir.

Continue S along the B257 to *Adenau* (3300 inhab.; alt. 297m), main town for visitors to the *Nürburgring* (see p 179) and lying 21km from

Altenahr; with 15th and 16C half-timbered houses in the Marktplatz; the parish church an early 13C basilica. From here the Rte continues for 9km S to health and sports resort of *Kelberg* (1500 inhab.; alt. 488m), where four small rivers rise (the Elz, the Lieser, the Trierbach and the Üb): romanesque–gothic church with a 15C crucifix and a 16C Resurrection.

18km S lies *Ulmen* (10,000 inhab.; alt. 436m): its new church, on a peak near the crater of an extinct volcano, incorporates an older tower, the tomb of Philipp Haust (died 1556), a gothic tabernacle and a baroque Lady altar. From Ulmen follow the B259 E for 13km to Kaiseresch, 18km due N of which lies *Monreal* (ruined walled Burg, despoiled both by the Swedes in 1622 and by the French in 1689; remains of a gothic chapel on the Burgberg; gothic cross in the village and a baroque monument to St. Johann Nepomuk; half-timbered houses).

30km SE of Monreal is *Burg Eltz*, 12C to 16C, restored after a fire of 1920. From here the Rte leads 6km NE to *Münstermaifeld* (2700 inhab.; alt. 271m), with the former monastery church of *SS. Martin and Severus*, finished 1332, with a later gothic tower: 12C to 14C wall paintings; 14C sculpted S doorway. From here drive 29km N and left along the B258, to turn right along the B256 in order to reach (15km) the Benedictine abbey of *Maria Laach. Founded in 1093 by the Count Palatine Heinrich II and secularised in 1802, home of the Jesuits from 1863–73, Maria Laach has been restored by the Benedictines and remains a reputed spiritual and liturgical centre. Its Carolingian church was begun in the early 11C to symbolise architecturally the heavenly Jerusalem and consecrated 1156: the choir houses the 13C tomb of the founder; portico 1225; 'paradise' doorway. The nearby lake (Laach) was formed by a volcanic crater, has a circumference of 8km and is in parts 53m deep. 9km NE of Maria Laach is the spa of *Bad Tönisstein*, with a ruined Carmelite monastery. The spa lies just E of *Burgbrohl* (whose name derives from the 11C *Schloß*, rebuilt in the 18C), and 1·5km from *Schweppenburg* (17C Schloß Schweppenburg).

V HESSE

33 The Rhön in Hesse: from Fulda to Gersfeld

Total distance 103km. **Fulda** (and Environs—5km *Petersburg*; 6km *Adolphseck*)—B27 13km *Hünfeld.*—B278 28km *Tann.*—B278 and B284 47km *Wasserkuppe.*—15km *Gersfeld.*

ENVIRONS OF FULDA. Petersbergerstraße leads through the Peters gate and 5km NE to the 508m-high *Petersberg*, on which is built the former Benedictine monastery of St. Peter: in the church are wall paintings and the sarcophagus of Boniface's companion St. Lioba. At *Adolphseck*, 6km S, is Schloß Fasanerie, 1730–50, summer residence of the prince-bishops, now a museum.

SE of Fulda is the Rhön, the vast remains of an extinct volcano, which offers superb opportunities for hang-gliding. Part of the region (around the health resort of Bad Brückenau, 33km S of Fulda along the B27—also easily reached by the Fulda-Würzburg motorway) has been designated the Hesse natural park.

From **Fulda** (see Rte 12), the B27 runs N for 13km to *Hünfeld* (7500 inhab.; alt. 279m), whose previous architectural history disappeared in a fire of 1888, but whose fine surrounding countryside still attracts many visitors. 3km SE of Hünfeld is *Mackenzell*, with a round-towered Schloß.

The B278 continues SE, passing close by the border of the *DDR* and then turns NE to reach after 25km *Tann* (5300 inhab.; alt. 381m), with red, blue and yellow Schlößer (respectively 1558, 1574 and 1714), a town gate of 1557 and half-timbered houses. From Tann drive due S for 42km to *Wüstensachsen*, here turning right along the high Rhön ring (the B284) to reach after 5km the health resort of *Wasserkuppe*, at 950m (*panorama) the highest peak of the Rhön and a major hang-gliding centre (aviation memorial; gliding museum open from May–October, daily, 09.00–18.00). The Rte continues S for 15km by way of *Poppenhausen* (ruins of Schloß Ebersburg) to *Gersfeld* (5400 inhab.; alt. 500m), the most popular tourist centre of this region: thermal springs and mud baths; baroque parish church; 18C baroque Schloß, with a stucco Festsaal, 1765 (now the local history museum, open Wednesday and Saturday, 15.00–16.00).

34 From Frankfurt am Main to Heidelberg

A. Frankfurt am Main

FRANKFURT (640,000 inhab.; alt. 88–212m), on the right bank of the River Main in a large plain bounded by the Taunus Mountains (though its 32 suburbs stretch for 222km² on either side of the river), is the commercial centre of West Germany and—on account of its trade and banking activities—one of the richest cities in the land. Since much of the city centre was razed during WW11, Frankfurt has been rebuilt in a determinedly modern fashion. Apart from housing an enormous trade fair, the city specialises in chemical products, skilled engineering and the electrical industry. It boasts 12 museums, 16 theatres, and more than 40 art galleries. There is a race course at Nierderad and a swimming stadium seating 90,000 spectators. An underground railway system was instituted in 1968. The main railway station information office faces platform 23.

Main *railway station*: Am Hauptbahnhof (also a post office; an information office faces platform 23).

Main *post office*: Große Eschenheimer Straße administrative offices also here).

Bus and rail services connect with all parts of the Federal republic; in summer *boats* ply between St. Goarshausen, Mainz and Cologne. The Rhein-Main *airport* is amongst the busiest in Europe, 10 minutes SW, by the S exit to the motorway). Motorways connect with Hamburg, Würzburg, Cologne and Basel.

History. Frankfurt is first recorded in the late 8C as *Franconofurd* (i.e. Ford of the Franks), on the site of a Bronze Age settlement where the Romans had established a camp. In 794 a conference of imperial leaders was called here by Charlemagne. Louis the Pius built a new palace here in 822 and the city prospered throughout the 9C. Most German sovereigns (from Frederick Barbarossa in 1152) were chosen here. In 1356 the Golden Bull of Charles IV confirmed the city as the permanent seat of such elections. From 1562 the sovereigns were crowned here. Frederick II granted an Autumn Fair in 1240; its Easter Fair was granted in 1330. By the 14C the citizens were emancipating themselves from royal sovereignty, and by the 16C Frankfurt was recognised as a free imperial city. Trading (at home and abroad) increased its wealth. From 1752–63 the French occupied the city. Until the end of the 18C the city was the centre of the German book trade (hence in part its famous 'Buchmesse' today, held in the 90 acre exhibition site near the main railway station). When the empire was dissolved in 1806 Napoleon gave Frankfurt to the primate of the Confederation of the Rhine, Carl von Dahlberg. Its 12C fortifications were razed and replaced with pleasant plantations (the 'Anlagen'). In 1810 the city became capital of the Grand Duchy of Frankfurt and in 1815 one of the four free cities of the German Confederation, as well as the seat of the Diet. The first German parliament met in the Pauluskirche in 1848–49. In 1866 the city was incorporated into Prussia (in spite of a vigorous attempt to stave off the annexation). Here the peace treaty between France and Prussia was signed in 1871. The Johann-Wolfgang-Goethe University was founded in 1914. During the Hitler Reich most of Frankfurt's Jewish community, which had included the Rothchilds and Anne Frank (born here 12 June 1929) was exterminated.

Goethe was born at Frankfurt on 18 August 1749. The philosopher Arthur Schopenhauer moved here from Danzig in 1831. On 26 October 1861 Philipp Reis demonstrated a battery operated telephone before the Frankfurt physics association. Heinrich Hoffmann (creator of Struwwelpeter) and Engelbert Humperdinck were neighbours in apartments at No. 95 Grünebergweg in the late 19C. The composer Paul Hindemith, born at Hanau, died here on 28 December 1968.

Walk SE from the main railway station along Wiesenhüttenstraße to the river and turn left along Untermain Kai, passing the Untermain bridge to reach *Leonhardskirche*. Founded in 1219, its romanesque towers and doorway (now inside, N wall) date from this period, while most of the present building was built in the 13th to 15Cs; the nave, 1500–20. The baptismal chapel, 1425–34 (left of the choir), has a window of 1435 and *hanging vaulting. On the N side is an open-air pulpit. E of the church of St. Leonhard is the Cathedral (so-called, though never the seat of a bishop) of **St. Bartholomew**, where from 1356 the Holy Roman Emperors were elected and from 1562 crowned. 13th and 14C Gothic, restored 1882 and 1950, the 94·75m-high *tower was begun in 1415, its lantern added 1877 in accordance with the original plan (383 steps, open daily, 09.00–17.00, fine panorama from the top). The S doorway dates mostly from the 14C. INTERIOR: in the choir (1315–49) stalls of 1352; on S wall the tomb of Günther von

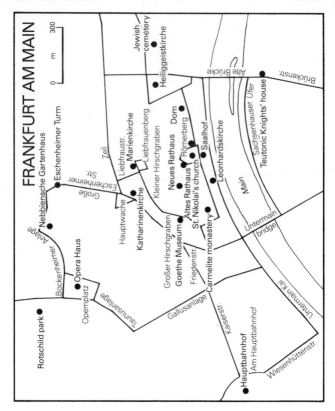

FRANKFURT AM MAIN

Schwarzenburg (died 1352); 15C representations of Charlemagne and of St. Bartholomew on same wall, 1427; high altar, c 1470. In the N transept—Maria-Schlaf altar with sculptures of the twelve apostles and a baldacchino, 1434; above, a rosary window of 1880; 16C altar of St. Anna with the Last Supper; altar of the Sacred Heart, 1505; 15C triptych of the passion; Lamentation by Van Dyck, 1627; memorials of the Thurn und Taxis family. In the entrance hall the Crucifixion by Hans Backoffen. At the crossing is an external relief of St. Bartholomew by Hans Mettel, 1957. When the cathedral was in process of restoration after WW11 the former palace of the Carolingians (840–73) was excavated here. S of the cathedral is the Leinwandhaus, a textile hall, by M. Gertener, 1396 (restored and now an art and photographers' gallery.

NE is the Heiliggeistkirche (13C, restored). Opposite the church, behind the flower market, is the Jewish cemetery (funeral monuments from the 13–19C). Walk W to find the ruined Carmelite monastery (13C to 15C), with 15C frescoes in the cloister and refectory. The refectory is now a museum of decorative arts (open Wednesday–Saturday, 10.00–17.00, 16.00 in winter and Sundays). Continue a little further E to the **Saalhof**, comprising three buildings:

the Renten tower of 1445, the Bernus House of 1717 (with a baroque façade), and the Burnitz House of 1840 which incorporates the palatine chapel of 1125 (the sole vestige of the Hohenstaufen palace that stood here). These three buildings, restored 1952–56, now house the city history museum (open Monday–Friday, 10.00–13.00). Opposite is the Haus Wertheim (c 1600), the sole survivor of some 2000 such fine houses.

The church of *St. Nikolai* (early 13C) stands to the N at the corner of the Saalgasse and the Römerberg. On the outside wall of the apse is a relief of St. Nicholas comforting lepers. Inside, tomb of Siegfried zum Paradies (died 1386) and his wife. The Glockenspiel in the tower plays at 09.05, 12.05 and 17.05. The Altes Rathaus (the 'Römer'), with five gables and a façade of 1610, stands at the N side of the church in the Römerberg square and incorporates three houses: the restored Löwenstein, the Römer of 1405 (balcony, tower and carvings, 1897) and the Alt-Limpurg (1495), with two neighbouring houses, the Frauenstein and the Salzhaus, completing the five gables. Inside: the imperial room where the feasting took place after coronations, with Bürgermeister portraits; gothic Römerhalle; courtyard with *renaissance staircase-tower, 1627 (open weekdays, 09.00–17.00; Sunday and holidays, 10.00–16.00). The rest of the square incorporates N the Haus Goldener Schwann (1731, with a gothic hall), S the Haus Silberberg (1595) and the Hercules fountain of 1904.

S of the Römer are modern municipal administration buildings (1956). W stands the Neues Rathaus of 1900–08, in the renaissance style with a baroque wing and a tower 70m high. The baroque wing overlooks the Paulusplatz, with the church of St. Paul, built 1783–1833, never consecrated and the seat of the parliament of 1848–49; now a festival hall. W of the church, in Großer Hirschgraben, stands the birthplace of Goethe (entirely destroyed 22 March 1944, the furniture saved, the house reconstructed as it was in 1756), joined by an arcade to the Goethe Museum (letters, engravings, manuscripts, open weekdays 09.00–18.00; Sunday, 10.00–16.00). Leave the Goethe House and follow Großer Hirschgraben. which leads by way of Kleiner Hirschgraben and Liebfrauenberg to the gothic church of *Our Lady*, founded 1308, reordered in the 15C, restored 1954, with a S doorway by Madern Gertener, c 1420, and a modern main door by Welker from the 1954 restoration (inside, memorial to the writer Wigel von Wanebach, died 1322). In the square opposite the church is a rococo fountain of 1771.

Liebfraustraße leads shortly NW into the triangular HAUPTWACHE, the centre of Frankfurt, once the site of the old municipal armoury (hence its name). The old guardhouse in the centre (1730, restored) is now a café. On the S side of the Hauptwache is the Katharinenkirche, built for Frankfurt Protestants in 1678 (restored), where Goethe was baptised and confirmed. The Zeil, the central shopping and commercial street of Frankfurt, leads E from Hauptwache. Entirely rebuilt after WW11 with, at No. 110, the post and telecommunications centre of 1951–55, with its 70m-high tower, it incorporates, on the side facinq Große Eschenheimer Straße, a doorway and pavilions that constitute the sole remains of the palace built on this spot by Robert de Cotte, 1732, for the Thurn und Taxis, the imperial postal ministers. The Zeil continues E for some distance to the Frankfurt Zoo.

Schillerstraße leads N from Hauptwache to the Frankfurt stock exchange (1874, restored). Kaiserstraße leads S from the railway station to the Rossmarkt, formerly both a cattle market and a place for

*The sixteenth century fountain of Justice, outside three
gabled houses that make up the Altes Rathaus (the Römer).*

executions (including that of Margaret Brand, the Margaret of Faust).
The Gutenberg monument in Rossmarkt is by Launitz (1858). From
here continue S along Friedenstraße for a tour of Frankfurt's
'Anlagen' or boulevards, beginning at the principal theatre in Unter-
mainanlage (1962, with Marc Chagall's 'Commedia dell'arte' and
Zoltan Kemeny's 'Goldwolken' decorating the foyer). This c 5km
route is best covered by car: Gallusanlage, leading into Taunusanlage, passes right successively the Goethe monument (by Schwanthaler, 1844), the WW1 memorial (by Benno Elkan, 1920), the
Schiller memorial (by Johann Dielmann, 1864) the Heine memorial
(by Georg Kolbe, 1913) and Kolbe's masterpiece the Beethoven
memorial (1951). The Taunusanlage turns right and leads to the
Opernplatz, where you find the Opera House, seating 2500 and
restored in 1981 after war damage. N is the Rothschild park, with a
notable series of statues by Kolbe (1954). From here Bockenheimer
Anlage leads to the Nebbiensche Gartenhaus (c 1810) and to the
*Eschenheimer Turm (1428), sole survivor of the former city gates.

The left bank of the River Main houses important museums. Here
too is the centre of medieval Frankfurt, *Sachsenhausen*. Cross by the
Alte Brücke (present bridge 1926). On the left of Brücken Straße is the
house of the Teutonic knights, incorporating a gothic church and built
1709 (restored 1963). Behind it is the celebrated 'Apfelweinlokale'
with pretty fountains. Return to the Alte Brücke and take the
Sachsenhäser Ufer W to find successively the Post Museum (open
Tuesday–Sunday, 10.00–16.00), the City Art Institute (open Tuesday–
Sunday, 10.00–17.00; Wednesday to 20.00), the Film Museum, the
Museum of Folk Art (open Tuesday–Sunday, 10.00–17.00; Wednesday to 20.00) and the Liebighaus of antique sculpture (open Tuesday–

Sunday, 10.00–17.00; Wednesday to 20.00).

OTHER MUSEUMS: the Albert Schweitzer Archive, No. 15 Saalgasse (open Monday–Friday, 10.00–16.00); the Chaplin archive, No. 5 Klarastraße; the Aircraft Museum at the airport (open May–December, 09.00–19.00); the Heinrich Hoffmann Museum, No. 20 Schubertstraße (open Tuesday–Sunday, 10.00–17.00); the Industrial Hoechst Museum, Schloßplatz; the Schopenhauer archive (in the university library); the Struwwelpeter Museum. No. 47 Hochstraße (open Tuesday–Sunday, 11.00–17.00; Wednesday to 20.00).

B. From Frankfurt am Main to Heidelberg

Total distance 81km. **Frankfurt**—35km **Darmstadt.**—29km *Weinheim.*—17km **Heidelberg**.

Leave **Frankfurt** and drive S by way of the B3, through Neu-Isenburg and Sprendligen, to reach after 35km Darmstadt. **Darmstadt** (134,000 inhab.; alt. 142m), situated amidst extensive forests and at the start of the Bersgtraße-Odenwald natural park, is the former capital of the grand-duchy of Hesse-Darmstadt and prospers on the electronics, pharmaceutical and chemical indusries as well as fine printing. A city by 1330, Darmstadt blossomed from the 15C. In the 18C the Grand-Duchess Karoline patronised writers, and it is fitting that today the city is the HQ of the German PEN club and the German academy of literature. The dramatist Georg Büchner lived here, 1816–31 and again 1834–35.

From the main railway station Rheinstraße leads to Luisenplatz, in the centre of which is a 33m-high bronze monument to Grand-Duke Ludwig I, by Schwanthaler 1844, which has a circular staircase inside. N of the square is the former college of 1780. NE is a monument to the chemist Julius von Liebig (1803–73) a native of the city. Continue across Luisenplatz to reach the huge baroque Schloß, by Louis Remy de la Fosse, whose S façade dates from 1720 and which now houses a museum (containing the 'Darmstadt Madonna' by Hans Holbein the Younger; open save Thursday, 10.00–13.00 and 14.00–17.00). Behind is the Schloß garden, containing the burial mound of Grand-Duchess Henriette-Karoline (1721–74), the technical high school of 1836 and the *Porzellan-Schloß* of 1720, by de la Fosse, with a rich porcelain collection (open save Friday, 10.00–13.00 and 14.00–17.00; closed weekend afternoons). SE of the Schloß stands the 14C White Tower, from the medieval ramparts. In front of the Schloß is Friedensplatz and the neo-gothic Hesse Regional Museum (Jugendstil collection, open save Monday, 10.00–17.00; closes Sunday between 13.00 and 14.00; opens also Wednesday 19.00–21.00). The old town, S of the Schloß, was severely damaged in WWII. It includes the MARKTPLATZ with a fountain of 1780; the Town Hall, 1599, restored (*renaissance façade), and the Protestant *parish church* (choir 1431; nave 1687, redone 1845; bottom half of W tower 1631, top half 1953; tomb of crown prince Philipp Wilhelm, died in his first year, 1579; alabaster renaissance monument to Grand-Duke Georg I and his wife Magdalena, by Peter Osten, 1599. The Catholic parish church of *St. Ludwig* (1820; G. Moller), modelled on the Pantheon in Rome, is in Wilhelminenplatz.

At Matildenhöhe E of the city an artists' colony was set up in 1889, whose architectural memorials are the Jugendstil wedding tower (1908), by the Viennese architect Josef Maria Olbrich, and the Ernst-Ludwig-Haus. Here too is the Russian chapel of 1889, decorated by Berhard Hoetger, 1914.

Tourist information at No. 17 Wilhelminenstraße and at No. 5 Luisenplatz; main post office in Luisenplatz. Trains connect with Basel, Dortmund, Mainz and Munich, buses with local destinations, and boats ply the river to Cologne, Frankfurt and Mainz.

The B3 S of Darmstadt is known as the Bergstraße (and sometimes the 'springtime road'), passing through *Seeheim* (half-timbered houses and town hall of 1599); *Jugenheim* (above which towers *Schloß Heiligenberg*); *Bensheim* (16C wedding house; classical parish church) and *Heppenheim* (renaissance town hall; ruined Schloß Starkenburg). —From Heppenheim a detour W leads to *Lorsch*, with its monastery gate dating from 774–84.

Continue S along the B3 from Heppenheim to reach (29km after Darmstadt) *Weinheim* (30,000 inhab.; alt. 108m): *Schloß Berckheim* (in three parts: 16C, 1725 and mid 19C), whose park includes the oldest cedar tree in Germany; former town hall, 1554; neo-romanesque church of *St. Laurentius*, 1913 (*tower by H. Hubsch, 1850; altars and pulpit 1750; 15C wall paintings); remains of 12C Burg Windeck; Büdinger Hof, 1582; witches' tower from the old walls; Wachenburg, 1913. Local history museum, at No. 2 Amstgasse (open Sunday, 10.00–12.00 and 14.00–16.00; Wednesday, and Saturday, 14.00–16.00).

The Bergstraße continues through Schriesheim at the foot of ruined Strahlenburg, and after 17km reaches **Heidelberg** (see Rte 10).

35 From Frankfurt am Main to Fulda

A. The 'fairy-tale route': Deutsche Märchenstraße

Total distance 94km. **Frankfurt**—19km **Hanau**. —B40 10km
Langenselbold.—12km **Gelnhausen**.—11km *Wächtersbach.*—15km
Steinau an der Straße.—21km Löschenrod—B27 6km **Fulda**.

Leave **Frankfurt** (see Rte 34A) by way of the Hanauer Landstraße
which travels close to the right bank of the Main (after 10km Schloß
Rumpensheim appears on the other bank). Shortly before Hanau
appears the early 18C baroque *Schloß Philippsruhe*, 1km S, now
containing a historical museum (open Sunday and Tuesday, 10.00–
12.00 and 14.00–17.00) and *Wilhelmsbad*, with its spa and health
resort, and its Kurhaus built 1777–82, in an 'English' park containing a
folly, a Hermitage, a ravine with a suspension bridge and a dolls'
museum.

After 19km the route reaches the confluence of the Kinzig with the
Main and the town of **Hanau** (89,000 inhab.; alt. 108m), whose
industries include diamond-cutting, jewellery-making and rubber
manufacture. In the Marktplatz of the Neustadt is a monument to the
brothers Jakob and Wilhelm Grimm (1785–1863 and 1786–1859),
hence the name of this route. The Grimms' younger brother, the
painter and engraver Ludwig (1790–1863) was also born here. Hanau
developed out of the Altstadt, whose former town hall in the Markt
(the *Deutsches Goldschmiedehaus*) was built 1537 (rococo sandstone
porch; goldsmiths' exhibition open, except Monday, 10.00–12.00 and
14.00–17.00). The 14C church of *Our Lady* opposite has contemporary stained glass in the 15C choir. The Neustadt was chiefly a
creation of 17C Dutch and Walloon immigrants who built its 17C
parish church. The town hall of the Neustadt, 1723–33, has a
Glockenspiel. The composer Paul Hindemith (1895–1963) was born at
Hanau. Tourist information at No. 41 Nürnbergerstraße. Trains
connect with Frankfurt and buses with local towns and villages. 4km
S of Hanau along the B45, on a basalt peak on the S bank of the Main,
is *Steinheim* (10,000 inhab.; alt. 115m): gothic Schloß on the Bergfried; gothic church of St. Johann Baptist.

Follow the B40 10km NE to reach *Langenselbold* (10,000 inhab.; alt.
122m), set among wooded hills on the River Kinzig: 18C Schloß of the
Fürsten von Isenberg-Birstein. The B40 continues NE for 12km to
reach **Gelnhausen** (19,000 inhab.; alt. 141m), which Friedrich
Barbarossa made into a free imperial city in 1170. On an island in the
Kinzig he built the Kaiserpfalz—ruined by the Swedes in the Thirty
Years' War—as the first seat of the Reichstag. The many-towered
parish church of Our Lady (the model for the Gedächtniskirche in
Berlin) was begun c 1170, finished 1467: *high altar c 1500, and other
15C altars; 15 tapestries; sandstone rood screen;' 14C stalls. No. 12
Schmidtgasse ('Zum Weißen Ochsen') was the birthplace of the poet
Hans Jakob Christoffel von Grimmelshausen (1622–1676), author of
'Simplicius Simplicissimus'. He is remembered in a museum at No. 2

Kirchgasse, as is another native, Philipp Reis (1834–74), inventor of the telephone (open save Sunday, 10.00–12.00; Tuesday, Thursday and Friday, also 16.00–18.00). A statue to Reis is in the UNTERMARKT, where there is also a romanesque hall of c 1170. In nearby Kuhgasse is the oldest half-timbered house in Hesse, dated 1536. The 13C church of *St. Peter* is in the Obermarkt (it became the Catholic parish church, 1932–38). In Holzgasse is a 14C house belonging to the order of the Knights of St. John. The half-timbered former town hall of 1726 (No. 17 Miroldstraße) is also a museum (open first Sunday in month, 15.00–17.00). Amongst the remaining fortifications are the 15C witches' tower, the brick tower, the Haizer gate and the Holz gate. Tourist information at No. 8 Untermarkt. Trains connect with Frankfurt.

11km along the B40 from Gelnhausen the Rte meets the B276, which leads 1km N to *Wächtersbach* (10,000 inhab.; alt. 148m), situated on the Kinzig, surrounded by forests and with a 15C to 18C Schloß, a brewery, a local history museum in a 1495 half-timbered house (open weekdays 10.00–12.00 and 14.00–16.00; Saturday, 10.00–12.00) and a 14C parish church. Follow the B40 a further 7km NE to reach *Salmünster* (Franciscan monastery founded 1319, with an 18C baroque church by Andreas Gallasine), and then 2km further for *Bad Soden*, a spa overlooked by the ruined 13C *Schloß Stolzenberg*, where Luther stayed: renaissance Hütten-Schloßchen of 1536. 8km from here on the B40 lies *Steinau an der Straße* (10,500 inhab.; alt. 173m), where in the *Amsthaus* (1562), the brothers Grimm spent their childhood—documents and manuscripts of their lives in the renaissance moated *Schloß*, built by Asmus of Steinau 1528–56 (open March–October, 10.00–17.00; otherwise closes 16.00); town hall, 1561, in the Marktplatz; late 13C gothic church dedicated to St. Catherine of Alexandria; Reinhardskirche, 1665–76; baroque cemetery chapel, 1616; marionette theatre. Tourist information at the Amsthaus.

The health resort *Schlüchtern* (14,000 inhab.; alt. 206m) lies on the B40 7km from Steinau and has a former Benedictine *abbey*: gothic church and cloisters; St. Katharina chapel, c 1100; Andreas chapel c 1200; Hutten chapel, 1345; tomb of Petrus Lotichius (1501–67); 8C crypt. The local history museum in the 1440 Lauter Schlößchen has more about the brothers Grimm, as well as mementoes of the poet and humanist Ulrich von Hutten (born 1488 in the Burg Steckelburg (now ruined) in the suburb of Elm). See also the mid 19C church of St. Michael with 14C tower and town hall of 1573. *Schloß Ramholz* in the suburb of Vollmerz was built by the von Hutten family in the 16C. Tourist information at No. 10 Grabenstraße.

The Rte passes through *Neuhof* (Schloß of 1519) to reach after 21km *Löschenrod*, whence the B27 runs for 6km into **Fulda** (see Rte 12).

B. From Frankfurt am Main to Fulda by the Voralberg

Total distance 197km. **Frankfurt**—19km **Hanau**,—B40 23km **Gelnhausen**.—B457 14km **Büdingen**.—B457 9km *Selters*.—B275 18km *Gedern*.—B276 16km *Schotten*.—B276 12km *Laubach*.—B49 34km **Alsfeld**.—B254 16km *Lauterbach*.—B275 14km *Schlitz*.—22km **Fulda**.

Cross the Main at **Frankfurt** (see Rte 34A) to the suburb of Sachsen-hausen and follow Darmstadter Straße (the B3) 3·5km to the Sachsenhüser Berg. From here take the Landstraße left through the Frankfurt woods, crossing the B46 after 3·5km and taking the B45 to **Hanau** and **Gelnhausen** (see above). From here take the B457 N through the Büdingen woods for 14km to the health resort **Büdingen** (17,000 inhab.; alt. 133m): medieval town walls and three gates; town hall, 1458, with a local history museum (open weekdays except Monday, 10.00–12.00; Saturday, 15.00–17.00; Sunday, 10.00–12.00 and 15.00-17.00). Another museum is in the renaissance and baroque *Schloß*, with its late gothic chapel: choir stalls by Peter Schanntz and Michael Silge, 1499; sandstone pulpit by Conrad Büttner, 1610.

The route now passes through the nature reserve of the high Voralberg. Continue along the B457 for 9km to Selters, to join the B275, reaching *Gedern* (16C Schloß) after another 18km. From here the B276 leads for 16km along the SW border of the nature reserve, through the winter sports and summer holiday town of *Hartmanns-hain* and past the *Taufstein* (at 774m the highest peak of the Voralberg) to the winter sports centre of *Schotten* (10,000 inhab.; alt. 282m) on the River Nidda, (lake sports on the Nidda-Stausee): gothic church of *Our Lady* with a winged *altar c 1375, W doorway with Adoration of the Magi and Mary with the founders of the church, late gothic carvings inside, 14C font, organ 1782. Schotten also has a half-timbered town hall, 1530, and a local history museum (at No. 95 Vogelsbergstraße, open Tuesday, Thursday and Sunday, 14.30–16.30; Wednesday, 10.00–12.00; closed winter). This is the site of the motor course known as the Schottenring.

Follow the B276 for 23km to *Laubach* on the River Wetter: 14C *Schloß* of the Grafen zu Solms, with an earlier keep: baroque great hall, 1739; 13C parish church, late gothic wall paintings, nave 1702, organ by J.C. Beck and J.M. Wagner, 1751; near the church a fountain of 1589 and in the Markt another of 1780; numerous half-timbered houses and a 15C watch-tower; 'English' park with a 16C mill.

From Laubach drive 11km N to the B49 and then drive NE for 23km to **Alsfeld* (18,000 inhab.; alt. 264m): *Marktplatz with the Wine House, 1538; the gothic half-timbered *Town Hall* on a stone market hall, 1512–16 (oriels and spires; decorated council chamber, late 16C and mid 17C); and the renaissance Hochzeitshaus, 1564–71. See also Walpurgis *church* in the Kirchplatz: 13C and late 14C gothic, nave 1732 (inside, romanesque font, late gothic wall paintings, 16C altar); the 15C church of the Holy Trinity in Mainzer Straße; in Ritterstraße the Neurath-Haus, 1564–71 and the Minnigerode-Haus (1687; now the regional museum; open week-days, 09.00–12.30 and 14.00–16.30; Saturday closes 16.00; Sunday opens 10.00); and the half-timbered house at Nos 10–12 Hersfelder Straße claiming to be the oldest in Germany.

Take the B254 SE from Alsfeldt for 16km to the health resort of *Lauterbach* (15,000 inhab.; alt, 285m): late baroque parish church, 1791–96, with a partly neo-classical tower, 1820; three-winged rococo *Schloß Hohehais*, 1769–73, stucco by A. Weidemann, now a museum (*'Lauterbach altar' of 1380; open save Monday, 10.00–12.00 and 14.00–16.00; Saturday closed afternoons, Sunday closed mornings). 5km S stands the 14C *Schloß Eisenbach*, with renaiss-ance additions and a chapel of 1675.

Follow the B275 for 14km NE of Lauterbach to reach *Schlitz* (9500 inhab.; alt. 240m), surrounded by a ring of castles: the 13C *Hinterburg*, with its mid 16C Burghaus; the *Vorderburg*, 1565–1600, with two wings joined by a tower (Glockenspiel at 15.00 and 17.00; local history museum open April–October, 14.00–16.00, except Mondays; otherwise only at weekends and holidays); the half-timbered 16th and 17C *Schachterburg*; the late 17C Ottoburg; a youth hostel in the baroque Hallenburg, c 1760. The parish church dates from the 15C and has a font of 1467 and an organ case of 1718. Numerous half-timbered houses. **Fulda** (see Rte 12) lies 22km directly SE of Schlitz.

36 From Frankfurt am Main to Kassel

Total distance 186km (also by motorway). **Frankfurt**—B3 32km *Niederwöllstadt.*—B45 4km *Ilbenstadt.*—B45 and B3 11km **Friedberg.**—5km *Bad Nauheim.*—10km *Butzbach.*—19km **Gießen.**—18km **Marburg.**—51km **Zwesten.**—2km **Fritzlar.**—34km **Kassel**.

Leave **Frankfurt** (see Rte 34A) N by way of the Friedberger Landstraße (B3), reaching after 10km *Bad Vilbel* (25,000 inhab.; alt. 109m), a Roman town set amongst woods and on the River Nidda, today a spa with 22 therapeutic springs; also, remains of the Wasserburg (1414); a half-timbered house, 1747 and a parish church of 1697 wih a 15C W tower. Following the wide river the Rte runs 15km to *Kloppenheim* (Schloß of the Teutonic knights, 1714) and for a further 9km to Niederwöllstadt. Here take the B45 right for 4km to *Ilbenstadt*, where Premonstratensian monks built a romanesque *basilica* in the first half of the 12C (stone carvings by Italian masons; dome c 1500; late gothic wall paintings; apostles and Madonna by C.L. Werr, 1700; organ and gallery c 1735; baroque statues by Burkhard Zamel, 1744); other monastery buildings 1707–15, with the Upper Gate, 1721; Ritterhof of 1742.

Return to the B3 and drive N for 7km more to **Friedberg** (25,000 inhab.; alt. 159m), the furthest point N of the Roman Empire during the time of Diocletian: gothic church of *Our Lady*, 1260–1410 (Ziborien altar, c 1250); late gothic screen with the 'Friedberg Madonna', c 1280; 14th and 15C stained glass; tabernacle, 1482–84); at No. 20 Judengasse a Jewish women's ritual *bathhouse*, 1260, 26m deep; 12C Burg on the site of the Roman fort, 16–18C houses, the Kavaliershaus, c 1605, the house of the Teutonic knights, 1717, and the 50m-high Adolfs tower, 1347 (containing a local history museum open March–October, 10.00–12.00 and 13.00–17.00; closes winter an hour earlier). Trains connect with Frankfurt, Gießen and Kassel, buses wih Bad Homburg, Laubach, Gießen, Schotten.

After 5km the B3 reaches *Bad Nauheim* (27,000 inhab.; alt. 144m) in the fertile Wetterau region, surrounded by woodlands and lying on the W side of the 772m *Vogelsberg*. The town developed as a spa when the Sprudel spring erupted in 1846 after a violent storm: Jugendstil Sprudelhof, by W. Jost, 1905–09, now a youth hostel in the 200 hectare Kurpark reached by a bridge across the Usa, with the Raben tower, 1745; salt museum (Nos 20–22 Ludwigstraße, open

Thursday–Saturday, 15.30–17.30); Roman tower and the ruins of an 8C church on the Johannisberg (268m); National Rose Museum—biennial rose festival in July—in the Altes Rathaus (open Wednesday, 14.00–17.00). Train connections as for Friedberg, buses also connect with Berlin.

The B3 leaves the valley of the Usa, crosses the Frankfurt-Kassel motorway and passes through rose gardens by way of Steinfurth and Oppershofen to *Nieder-Weisel* (early 13C church), reaching after 10km *Butzbach* (22,000 inhab.; alt. 199m) on the NE slopes of the Taunus—once a Roman garrison, now a town making shoes and light machinery: the *MARKTPLATZ contains the town hall of 1560, a fountain of 1575, the two-sided house known as the Goldener Ritter and the Alte Post, 1636, and the Goldener Löwe of 1709 (which inspired Goethe's 'Hermann und Dorothea'); 14th and 15C church of St. Markus, incorporating the Markus chapel of 1433 (organ 1614; memorial tomb of Philipp of Hesse-Butzbach, 1622); 15th and 16C chapel of St. Wendelir (altar c 1500); Solms Schloß, 1481; Hesse Schloß, 1610.

19km N by way of hl-Göns and Klein-Linden is the industrial and university town of   eßen (76,000 inhab.; alt. 150m), situated on the Lahn. The chemist ustus von Liebig (1803–73), lived here between 1834 and 1852; the University, founded 1607, is named after him. His laboratory is preserved at No. 12 Liebigstraße (open save Thursday, 10.00–12.00 and 14.00–16.00; Sunday, 11.00–13.00). Gießen was also the home of the scientist Wilhelm Conrad Röntgen (1845–1923), who was professor at the university (Röntgen memorial, by E.F. Reuter, 1962, in Berliner Platz, near the city theatre of 1907). See also the 14C half-timbered *Leibsche Haus* restored after war damage in 1977; the 1126 former church of the Augustinians, Schiffenberg, with monastery buildings that include a deanery of 1463 and a Kommanderie of 1493; the rebuilt 14C Altes Schloß (now an art gallery, open save Monday, 10.00–16.00); the 16C Neues Schloß, with an arsenal of 1589. The museum of local history is at No. 2 Georg-Schlößer-Sraße (open 10.00–16.00; Sunday, 10.00–13.00; closed Mondays). Tourist information at No. 4 Berliner Platz. Trains connect Gießen with Frankfurt, Marburg and Kassel.

Continue N along the B3, past ruined Schlößer on hilly peaks and through *Staufenberg*, (with its gothic Unterburg and its ruined Oberburg) and Giesselberg (with a neo-gothic Schloß of 1851) to reach after 28km **MARBURG** (75,000 inhab.; alt. 176m), an old university with many half-timbered houses in its Altstadt. The Schloß (where Luther and Zwingli debated in 1429), 400m high, in the centre of Marburg is now part of its university. Here Emil von Behring (professor at the university from 1895–1917) discovered a vaccine for diphtheria and for this achievement won the Nobel prize in 1901.

Leaving the main railway station you cross the two branches of the River Lahn to reach Germany's earliest purely Gothic building, the church of ****St. Elisabeth**, built in honour of St. Elisabeth of Marburg (1207–31), daughter of King Andreas II and also known as St. Elisabeth of Hungary. Four years after her death Pope Gregory IX canonised Elisabeth and building began on the basilica, which stands over her tomb. The church was finished 1285. In the N transept, gothic chapel of St. Elisabeth, with her former tomb, canopied 1280; in the sacristy is the 13C *reliquary containing the saint's bones; S transept, tombs of the Landgraves of Hesse, till the 16C; in the chapel under the

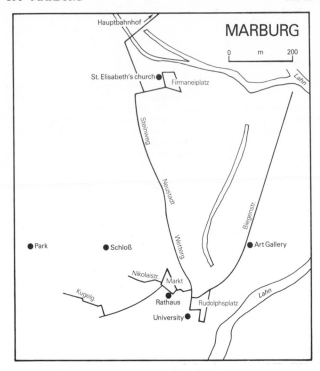

N tower, tomb of Field-Marshal Paul von Hindenburg (1847–1934); in the choir a stone high altar of 1290, 13th and 14C stained glass, a 15C statue of St. Elisabeth and a bronze crucifix by Ernst Barlach, 1931. W of the church is the chapel of St. Michael, 1270, restored 1984.

From the church follow Steinweg, Neustadt, Wettergasse and Reitgasse to reach the University, founded in 1527 by Luther's patron Landgrave Philipp of Hesse (1509–67) as the first German Protestant university: buildings 1874–91, save for the 14C church. It houses the largest library in West Germany (including 1·5 million volumes from the Prussian State Library, Berlin). Biegenstraße leads NE to the University Art Gallery (at No. 11, in the Ernst-von-Hülsen-Haus; 19th and 20C paintings, open save Tuesday, 10.00–13.00 and 15.00–17.00). Continue to climb to the Schloß, at the foot of which is the 13th and 14C Lutheran church (18C tomb of Landgrave Ludwig and his wife). The 13C *Schloß* has a Rittersaal, c 1300, and a chapel consecrated in 1288: *view across the town, the Taunus and Sauerland. It houses a religious history museum (open Monday, Wednesday and Friday, 10.00–13.00). In the park behind the Schloß is an open-air theatre. Marburg's fine houses include the Herrenhaus of 1253, the Brüderhaus of 1254, the 13C Steineres Haus, and the HQ of the Teutonic knights, c 1483, as well as an early 16C bakery (Firmaneiplatz, now a museum of mineralogy, open Monday and Wednesday, 13.00–16.00 and Friday, 10.00–13.00). In the Marktplatz is the Town Hall (1512–27), with a relief of St. Elisabeth by L. Juppe,

1524, a clock with mechanical figures (the Guckelhahn), and a renaissance gable by Eberhardt Böckwein, 1581. The old university building (Am Rudolphsplatz) dates from 1874. The theatre at No. 15 Biegenstraße was built in 1969. Marburg's synagogue was destroyed in the Kristallnacht of 1938 and its site has been dedicated as a memorial garden.

OTHER MUSEUMS: Ethnological Museum (at No. 10 Kugelgasse, open mornings); Cultural History Museum (Schloß, open, except Monday, 10.00–13.00 and 15.00–17.00); Museum of Antiquity (at No. 11 Biegenstraße, open Sunday, 11.00–13.00); Emil von Behring exhibition (at the corner of Kirchplatz in Nikolaistraße, open weekdays 08.00–16.30).

Tourist information at No. 1 Neue Kassler Straße. Trains connect Marburg with Gießen, Frankfurt and Kassel.

After Marburg the B3 crosses the Lahn and travels NE through woods by way of Cölbe and through *Schönstadt*, with timbered houses and a Schloß (4km SE of which is *Rauschenberg*: half-timbered houses, including the town hall, 1558; ruined 13C Burg; romanesque–gothic church).

A DIVERSION 32km N reaches *Haina* (1600 inhab.; alt. 330m), with an early gothic Cistercian monastery, 1216–1328, which in 1533 became a hospital for the mentally ill (and, still a hospital, allows access only to the church and cloister).

Return to the B3 and continue NE. The road skirts the Keller forest and reaches *Zwesten* (3000 inhab.; alt. 240m), 51km from Marburg: a village of old houses, surrounding a church with tower dated 1506. 12km NE of Zwesten lies **Fritzlar** (15,000 inhab.; alt. 230m); in the Marktplatz are half-timbered houses (including the late gothic town hall and the renaissance Hochzeitshaus, the latter a museum of local history opening 10.00–12.00 and 15.00–17.00, closed Saturday afternoons) and the Roland fountain of 1564. Fritzlar retains 12 watch-towers and most of its 14C fortifications, some late gothic stone houses and a romanesque–gothic *cathedral* of the 11–14C, situated where in 724 St. Boniface felled an oak sacred to the pagans. The Cathedral has three crypts (12C statue of St. Peter; reliquary of St. Wigbert, 1340), a gothic Pietà, baroque decoration and 19C spire; it also has a rich museum (12C cross of Kaiser Heinrich IV; open 10.00–12.00 and 14.00–17.00; closed Sunday mornings and in winter at 16.00). See also the church of Our Lady and the 13th and 14C former Minorite monastery church (now used by Protestants), both with wall paintings. Tourist information at the town hall.

11km W of Fritzlar along the B253 is the noted spa *Bad Wildungen*, N of which along the B485 lies the 29km-long *Edersee*.

From Fritzlar the route joins the A49 to reach after 34km **KASSEL** (195,700 inhab.; alt. 163m). Situated on both banks of the River Fulda, Kassel was until 1866 the capital city of Hesse, and until 1945 of Hesse-Nassau.

History. In the 10C the town was known as *Chassala*, owing its origin to an Imperial Schloß built here during the previous century. The town was granted its charter c 1180 and became the seat of the Landgraves of Hesse. The Reformation reached here in 1523. After Louis XIV revoked the Edict of Nantes in 1685 French Huguenot refugees fled here and built Upper-Kassel, which became known as the French new town. During the Seven Years' War the French occupied the city from 1759–62, and in 1807 Napoleon's younger brother Jerome ruled the kingdom of Westphalia from here. The Russians occupied the city in

1813, ceding it back to Hesse in 1814. The city became Prussian in 1866, and after 1945 the chief city of the province of Hesse-Nassau.

Kurfürstenstraße leads from the main railway station SE to Scheidmannplatz where the skyscraper was built by K. Fleischmann and W. Seidel. Ständeplatz, SW of Scheidemannplatz, houses the Ständehaus of 1835. A stairway (Treppenstraße) leads to Friedrichsplatz (monument to Landgrave Friedrich II by Nahl, erected 1783 two years before Friedrich's death). SE of the square is the modern theatre as well as the Ottoneum theatre of 1606, now the Natural History Museum (open weekdays save Monday, 10.00–16.30; weekends, 10.00–13.00), with an inscription recording that Denis Papin used a steam engine at Kassel in 1706. On the NW side are what remains of an electoral palace (now part of a modern shop) and the classical Museum Fridericanum, 1769–76, restored after destruction in WWII.

Due N of Friedrichsplatz is Königsplatz, built in the Parisian circular style in 1766 and approached by six streets, a little way NE of which stands the mid 14C church of St. Martin (badly damaged in 1943, in part restored, though not an accurate reconstruction: with an alabaster tomb of Landgrave Philipp and his wife Christine, by E. Godefroy and A. Liquier Beaumont, 1572; in the vault is the tomb of Landgrave Karl, died 1730). Schöne Aussicht leads E from Friedrichsplatz, overlooking the River Fulda and passing SW by the Schloß Bellevue, by Paul de Ry, 1714, altered by Simon Louis de Ry, (1790; now a museum of the brothers Grimm, open weekdays except Monday, 10.00–17.00; weekends 10.00–13.00, as well as a museum of stringed instruments, open Fridays 10.00–17.00). At No. 1 Schöne Aussicht is the art gallery (open save Monday, 10.00–17.00). From here walk down to the promenade known as An der Karlsaue, where Landgrave Karl created a park, covering 150 hectares, on the left bank of the Fulda (early 18C Orangery, partly rebuilt; open-air statuary), W of which is the Marmorbad, a swimming pool which the French sculptor

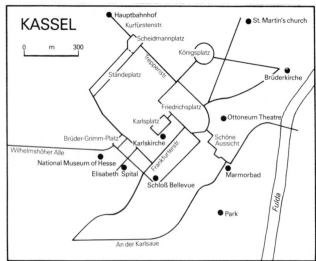

Monnot decorated in the early 18C. NE of An der Karlsaue is the Brüderkirche, 1292–1396, with a *Lamentation c 1500 over the N door. Close by Schloß Bellevue is the Brüder-Grimm-Platz—the brothers Grimm spent much time in Kassel—with (at No. 5) the art collection (*Dutch paintings) and the National Mûseum of Hesse (open, except Monday, 10.00–17.00) and also a Wallpaper Museum (open weekdays save Monday, 10.00–17.00; weekends 10.00–13.00).

From here take Wilhelmshöher Allee, designed in 1781 by Simon Louis du Ry, which runs for 5km to the new part of Kassel and reaches the classical **Schloß Wilhelmshöhe**, by S.L. du Ry and H.C. Jussow, 1786–1803 (housing a gallery displaying seven paintings by Frans Hals, eight by Rubens and 17 by Rembrandt; open, save Monday, 10.00–18.00, in winter closing at 17.00), built at the end of the 18C by Simon Louis du Ry and the palace of King Jerome Napoleon from 1807–13. Ironically, Napoleon III was imprisoned here in 1870/71. This part of Kassel boasts a superb baroque park, designed by G.F. Guerniero—statue of Hercules, waterfall, temple of Mercury, the Octogon (63m high, supported on 192 Tuscan columns), as well as health institutes (Kneipp mud baths). From here visit the Löwenburg, a 'medieval' Schloß built by H.C. Jussow, 1793–1801, for Prince-Elector Wilhelm I (who lies buried in its chapel). The Löwenburg Museum opens March–October, 10.00–17.00, closing 16.00 in winter. From here cross the Teufelsbrücke and reach the aqueduct (250m-long water cascade, with 885 steps, ending in the Neptune basin, with 52m high jets of water).—See also the *Karlskirche* by Paul du Ry, 1698–1710, in Karlsplatz, and the *Elisabeth Spital*, Frankfurter Straße, c 1300, rebuilt after war damage, with cafés and a 15C sandstone statue of St. Elisabeth.

The city arranges summer concerts in Wilhelmshöhe park. *Tourist information* and main *post office* at the railway station. Trains connect Kassel with Dortmund, Frankfurt, Göttingen, Gießen, Marburg, Munich, and Mönchengladbach, buses with more local places.

9km N of Kassel is the rococo *Schlößchen Wilhelmsthal*, built by F. Cuvilliés for Landgrave Wilhelm VIII.

37 From Gießen to Koblenz

Total distance 97km. **Gießen**—B49 15km **Wetzlar**.—22km *Weilburg*.—16km **Limburg an der Lahn**.—20km *Montabaur*.—24km **Koblenz**.

Leave **Gießen** (see Rte 36) SW by way of the B49, passing through Klein-Linden and reaching after 15km **Wetzlar** (52,500 inhab.; alt. 145m), which straddles the River Lahn at its confluence with the Dill. From 1693 to 1806 it was the seat of the highest court of the Holy Roman Empire. Today the town specialises in ironworks and optical goods, cameras, magnifying glasses, telescopes and microscopes. On a peak stands the Altstadt, dominated by the interdenominational cathedral of *St. Maria*, built in the gothic style in 1225 on an earlier romanesque church of 1097, its massive three-storeyed tower finished in the 16C; inside, a Pietà of 1380. The Spitalkirche in Lahnstraße is by J.L. Splittdorf, 1755–64. Burg Hermannstein is a 13C ruin. In Schiller-platz is the Jerusalemhaus of c 1700; the Palais Papius at No. 1 Kornblumengasse (open except Monday and Sunday afternoons,

10.00–12.00 and 15.00–17.00), is a Museum of Furniture. The house of the Teutonic knights (now a Goethe museum, open, save Monday and Friday afternoons, 09.00–12.00 and 14.00–17.00), was the home of Charlotte Buff in 1772, when Goethe came to Wetzlar and was inspired by her to write his 'Die Leiden des jungen Werthers', which in turn inspired Thomas Mann's 'Lotte in Weimar'. Information Office at No. 46 Karl-Kettner-Ring.

The B49 continues for 10km to *Braunfels*, with a thermal spring (the Karlssprudel), half-timbered houses (the Rentkammer, c 1700) and a picturesque Schloß founded in the 13C but now, apart from the 15C tower, the late gothic hall and the early 18C kitchens, mainly 19C (museum open daily, 08.00–17.00). 12km further SW lies *Weilburg* (13,500 inhab.; alt. 128m), a town laid out with military precision, once the home of the dukes of Nassau: *Hochschloß* of 1535–75, enlarged by Graf Johann Ernst, 1703–17, with baroque stables; Orangery stucco by C.M. Pozzi; Schloß *church, wih stucco by A. Gallasini, 1712. At Weilburg J.L. Rothweil designed the baroque Marktplatz (fountain by Wilckens, 1709), as well as a hunting lodge, 1713–26. At No.1 Schloßplatz is a museum of mining (open in summer daily, except Monday, 10.00–12.00 and 14.00–17.00; closed winter weekends). A 300m-long underground canal was built here, 1841–47.

16km SW of Weilburg the B49 reaches **Limburg an der Lahn** (30,000 inhab.; alt. 122m), set between the Taunus range and the mountains of the Westerwald. From the railway station follow Bahnhofstraße to the heart of the city, the Kornmarkt. From here the picturesque Barfüsserstraße leads left to the 14C former Franciscan monastery church and the bishops' palace. High on its peak stands the *Cathedral, founded 909, influenced by the architecture of Laon Cathedral in France and of St. Gereon in Cologne, consecrated 1235, a church that bridges the transition between late romanesque and early gothic, enhanced by the polychrome restoration of 1971. INTERIOR: rood screen c 1235; 13th to 16C frescoes in the nave; 13C tomb of Konrad Kurzbold (died 948); romanesque font, c 1235; tomb of Daniel von Mudersbach and his wife Jutta (died 1477 and 1461 respectively); tabernacle, 1496 (renovated 1628); modern high altar, 1977.

S of the cathedral apse stands the 13th and 14C *Schloß* of the counts of Lahngau, now the Diocesan Museum (a 10C *reliquary of the True Cross, the 'Staurothek', brought by crusaders from Hagia Sophia, Constantinople, and another golden reliquary containing St. Peter's staff, c 980; open in summer, 10.00–18.00). Towards the River Lahn stands the renaissance Walderdorffer Hof, 1665, (at No. 5 Fahrgasse) above the old stone bridge across the Lahn, 1315, with its gate tower. See also the Franciscan church of St. Sebastian (gothic side altars; 15C Pietà; rococo pulpit) and the remains of Limburg's medieval fortifications. Tourist information at No. 2 Hospitalstraße.

From Limburg follow the B49 through Staffel and Görgeshausen to reach afer 20km *Montabaur* (in the Rhineland-Palatinate), with its 14C gothic church of St. Peter in chains (wall paintings, including a Last Judgment over the chancel arch), a fine Marktplatz and a Schloß built at various times between the 13C and the 18C (with four domed towers).

From Montabaur the B49 runs SW for 24km to **Koblenz** (see Rte 28).

38   From Gießen to Siegen

Total distance 78km (64km by motorway). **Gießen**—A429 19km **Wetzlar.**—B272 24km *Herborn.*—7km *Dillenburg.*—28km **Siegen**.

Drive W from **Gießen** (see Rte 36) along the A429 to reach the B277 at Wetzlar (see Rte 37) after 19km.

The Rte now leaves the Lahn valley and enters the valley of the Dill, following the B272 NW by way of *Hermannstein* (dominated by a ruined Schloß) and *Greifenstein* (ruins of Burg Greifenstein, 418m high) for 24km to **Herborn** (108,000 inhab.; alt. 205m): picturesque alleyways and half-timbered, slate-roofed houses, especially the 16C local history museum (open Tuesday, Thursday and Saturday, 15.00–18.00), once the town hall, two storeys high with a courtyard and fine staircase tower. Here Protestant theologians set up a university (1584–1817). The theologians now work in the 14C Schloß (three towers), once the home of the Dukes of Nassau. 2km later, at Burg, the route meets the B255 from Marburg (see Rte 36). Continue NW along the B272 for 5km to *Dillenburg* (25,000 inhab.; alt. 220m), at the foot of a Schloß whose 40m-high Wilhelmsturm is so named because here in 1533 was born William the Silent, who later was to drive the Spaniards out of the Netherlands. The mid 13C Schloß (with 16th and 17C bastions) was partly destroyed by the French in 1760. A museum in the Wilhelmsturm commemorates William the Silent (open, save Monday, 09.00–12.00, 14.00–18.00; closed November–Easter). Part of the town suffered in a fire of 1723, but the parish church, 1489–1524, survived (15 tombs of members of the Nassau-Oranien dynasty), as did numerous half-timbered houses. The town hall was rebuilt after the fire.

The Rte now passes into Northrhine-Westphalia, before reaching, after 28km, **Siegen** (120,000 inhab.; alt. 236m), the geographical mid-point of the German Federal Republic. Situated on the River Sieg, Siegen is surrounded by forests and good hiking country. Here was born (to refugee parents) the painter Peter Paul Rubens (1577–1640). In 1623 the Nassau–Siegen family divided into a Catholic and a Protestant wing. The Catholics lived in the 13–16C Upper Schloß, the Protestants occupying the Lower Schloß (rebuilt 1698–1714 after a fire) in which the family mausoleum (1669–70). The Upper Schloß, modified in the 17th and 18C, houses the Siegerland Regional Museum with eight paintings by Rubens (open, save Monday, 10.00–12.30 and 14.00–17.00). In spite of much damage in WWII Siegen has a late romanesque (13C) rotunda church of St. Nikolaus, with a mid 15C four-storey tower (modern bronze doors by G. Marcks) and the gothic church of St. Martin, 1511–17, which incorporates from an earlier church on this site a mosaic pavement c 1100 and a romanesque W door. The town hall of Siegen is late 18C and early 20C. Here are two theatres: the Sigener Theater, 1957, and the Kleine Theater Lohkasten, 1974. Information Offices at the main railway station and at No. 73 Koblenzer Straße.

39 The Rheingau

Total distance 30km. **Wiesbaden**—B263 and B42 9km *Eltville.*—4km
Kloster Eberbach.—7km *Winkel.*—B42 6km *Geisenheim.* —4km
Rüdesheim.

WIESBADEN (270,000 inhab.; alt. 117m), former capital of the duchy
of Nassau, chief city of the Prussian province of Hesse-Nassau from
1866 and since 1946 capital of Hesse, is sheltered by the wooded
slopes of the Taunus. A city of parks and gardens, it welcomes visitors
to its Kurhaus each May for an international festival, for the Rheingau
wine festival in September, and all the year round for its 26 thermal
springs.

History. The site was occupied at the time of Drusus, in the 12C BC, and the
Romans, who knew its spa as *Fontes Mattiaci*, built a town here with a temple to
Jupiter. In 330 the name *Wisibada* appears. The town was the site of a Frankish
court. The dukes of Nassau ruled Wiesbaden from the 13C (from 1744 it was the
residenz of the Nassau-Usingen line), and it passed in 1866 into Prussian hands
along with the duchy. Between 1919–39 when French and Belgian troops
occupied the Rhinelnd, Wiesbaden was chosen as their administrative seat. The
city was much bombed in February 1945. In 1970 an important research hospital
was established here.
     Goethe frequently visited the city (an obelisk at Frauenstein commemorates
this). Dostoevsky and Turgenev gambled at Wiesbaden. Richard Wagner
composed his 'Mastersingers of Nuremberg' here. At Wiesbaden Brahms
composed his second symphony. Richard and Clara Schumann lived here. Pastor
Martin Niemöller died here in 1984.

The main railway station, built by Klingholtz, 1906 is situated S of the
city on its inner ring road (the Ring, which runs in a semicircle
SE–NW). W of the station is the Martin Luther church. E in Main-
zerstraße are the Hesse state archives (including Nassau documents
from the 10C onwards) in a building of 1878, E of which in
Wittelsbacher Straße is the 13-storey Bundesamt building of 1955.
Cross the gardens in front of Bahnhofsplatz and follow Friedrich-
Ebert-Allee to the Rhine-Main congress hall (1956, holding 4000
participants). Opposite is the City Museum (natural history, antiquities, paintings, including Cranach and Max Beckmann and the
Wiesbaden-born member of the 'Blaue Reiter' school, Alkexej von
Jawlensky, 1861–1941; open, except Monday, 10.00–16.00, Tuesday
also 17.00–21.00).
     Rheinstraße (in which is the main post office, opposite the congress
hall) runs W from the museum to reach on the right, half way to
Ring-kirche, Luisenplatz: Catholic parish church of St. Bonifatius
(neo-gothic, 1845–49); monument to those who fell at Waterloo (an
obelisque, set up in 1865). On Rheinstraße is the State Library (early
16C engravings, 300 ancient manuscripts). At the far end of
Rheinstraße is the Protestant Ring-kirche, by Otzen, 1892. From the
City Museum Wilhelmstraße (filled with shops, hotels and banks, and
named after the duke of Nassau who laid it out in 1812) runs N, past
the Warm-Damm-Anlage gardens on the right (monuments to
Schiller by Uphues, 1905, and to Kaiser Wilhelm I by Schilling, 1894),
reaching on the right the civic theatre and on the left Kaiser-
Friedrich-Platz, with its fountain. On the right of Kaiser-Friedrich-
Platz is the Kurhaus (built by Friedrich von Thiersch, 1905–07: concert

hall, casino which inspired Dostoevsky's 'The Gambler', indoor and outdoor restaurants; summer concerts and tennis courts in the Kurpark). N of the Kurhaus is the Brunnenkolonnade, 1825 and the Theaterkolonnade, 1839.

Taunusstraße leads NW from Wilhelmstraße. Immediately left is the Kochbrunnen hall, which embraces 15 thermal springs capable of delivering 23,000 litres of mineral water every hour. Along Taunusstraße is an 1870/71 war memorial and the Nerotal thermal clinic, at the foot of the Neroberg (funicular railway to the park, gardens, restaurant and the swimming pool given to the city by the motor car manufacturer W. von Opel, in 1933). On the Neroberg is the Greek chapel (with five golden domes, by Philipp Hoffmann, 1848–55; open 08.00–20.00; closed Sunday mornings), built as a mausoleum for the Russian born Herzogin Elizabeth, who died in 1845 one year after her marriage. Her tomb is by E. Hopfgarten. Immediately left after the

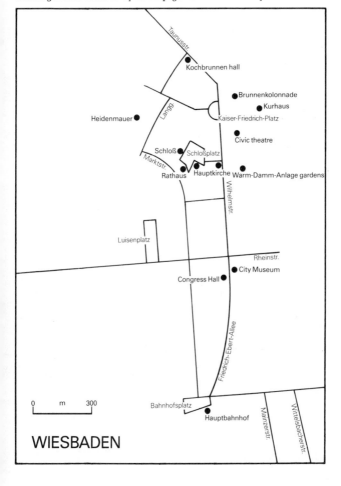

WIESBADEN

Kochbrunnen, Langgasse leads to the Kaiser-Friedrich-Bad of 1913, and then to the Marktstraße. Follow Marktstraße left to reach Schloßplatz. The Town Hall, built in the German renaissance style by Hauberrisser, 1884–87, was severely damaged in 1944 and has been perfectly restored (including a Ratskeller). The square also houses the former Schloß of the dukes of Nassau (built by Georg Moller, 1837–71, used by both Kaisers Wilhelm I and Wilhelm II as a royal residence, and now the parliament building) and the Protestant Hauptkirche (neo-gothic, by Boos, 1853–62). The Schloß borders onto Schloßplatz, with the Lion fountain of 1525 and the oldest building in Wiesbaden, the Alte Rathaus (1609; its formerly half-timbered upper storey rebuilt in stone 1828). NW of Schloßplatz is the Heidenmauer, the remains of the late 4C Roman defences. The so-called Roman gate was built 1902.

National theatre by the Kolonnade; Little Theatre, Am Kochbrunnen. Information office the Brunnenkolonnade. The Rhein-Main airport is 30 minutes away. Trains connect with Basel, Darmstadt, Dortmund, Limburg and Munich. Boats ply the river to Mainz, Cologne and Frankfurt.

ENVIRONS: NE of Wiesbaden (a 30-minute walk, or drive, by the Sonnenberger Straße) are the valleys of the Rambach and and Sonnenberg, with a **Schloß** of 1200 ruined in 1689. 4km NE of the town is the hunting lodge *Kranichstein*, built in the renaissance style, 1571–79 (with a hunting museum). 10km S of the city is the ruined 13C *Schloß Frankenstein* (on a 397m peak).

An avenue of chestnut trees leads SW along Rheingaustraße to reach after 3km *Wiesbaden-Biebrich*, where beside the Rhine stands the baroque **Schloß Biebrich*, built 1699–1706 and embellished and enlarged 1711–45. It now houses the German Film Institute. L. von Sckell laid out the 'English' garden in 1811. On the park is the Wiesbaden racecourse. At No. 142 Biebricher Allee the firm of Henkell makes and sells sparkling wines.

The B42 continues W through *Wiesbaden-Schierstein* (vineyards; sparkling wines). 2km NW is the ruined Schloß Frauenstein. The route continues from Wiesbaden-Schierstein reaching (7km from Wiesbaden) Niederwalluf, where the River Walluf flows into the Rhine (nurseries, fruit growing, sailing). Pass through Walluf to reach 2km later the oldest town in the Rheingau, *Eltville* (8500 inhab.; alt. 89m), founded in 1332: the keep, with the addition of an E wing dated 1681, survives from the Schloß, 1345, of the archbishops of Mainz; 14C late gothic church of SS. Peter and Paul; old houses; annual festival the first weekend of July. 1km further is *Erbach*: Schloß Reinhardshausen, 1745; 15C church of St. Markus; the 'Markobrunnen' wine. 4km N is **Kloster Eberbach*, a former Cistercian abbey, founded in 1116, whose monks are wrongly said to have brought the vines to the Rheingau. The Romans grew grapes here; the monks greatly developed the skill, and their monastery became the greatest wine-producing centre of Germany. Secularised in 1803 and becoming the property of the state, it remains celebrated for its wines. The restored monastery church was consecrated in 1186: chapter-house (1345), wine cellars with old presses, cloister, refectory; new gateway 1774.

Return S to *Hattenheim* (1500 inhab.; alt. 81m): partly ruined Schloß, 1411; church 1740 with a mid 13C bell tower; Crucifixion group, 1510, in front of the church; upstream the 18C Schloß Reichardtshausen is built on the spot from which in the 12C and succeeding centuries boats sailed laden with wine from Kloster Eberbach. 3km W lies *Oestrich*, with the half-timbered Gasthaus

Schwan of 1628 and a wooden crane of 1652: 3km N is Hallgarten ('Hallgarten Madonna' in the parish church).

The road from Oestrich along the right bank of the Rhine runs through *Mittelheim* (romanesque church of St. Ägidius, 1140), reaching after 2km *Winkel*, which has Germany's oldest dwelling, the Graues Haus, c 800, and the Brentanohaus, so-named because the author Clemens Brentano and his sister Bettina lived here in the 18C. Drive N from here to reach after 3km *Schloß Johannisberg*, built on the site of an abandoned Benedictine abbey by Johannes Dientzenhofer, 1718–25, partly rebuilt in the classical style, 1826–33, restored after war damage, 1946; reputed wines. The former monastery church was also restored after war damage.

Return to the river bank and *Geisenheim* (12,200 inhab.; alt. 96m), seat of the Hesse institute for wine culture: gothic church, 1510, enlarged by Philipp Hoffmann, 1838–41 (baroque high altar, 1700; 16C to 18C tombs and memorials), known as the Cathedral of the Rheingau; 600-year-old lime tree; old houses; Schloß Schörnborn, 1550, where an end to the Thirty Years' War was negotiated in 1547 (a year before the peace of Westphalia). 3km N in the middle of the forest is *Marienthal* (medieval monastery church, 1330, restored 1897, outside which is a Crucifixion group c 1520); 4km NW *Eibingen*, with a Benedictine monastery founded 1148.

Geisenheim is 4km E of **Rüdesheim* (10,000 inhab.; alt. 90m) known to the Romans and famous for its wine: Drosselgasse (thrush street), with 17th and 18C houses; early 15C church of St. Jakob in the Marktplatz, with a romanesque chapel; town walls; the 16C Adelshöfe; the Mäuser tower on an island in the the river, built in 1208 by Philipp von Boden on the site of a wooden one set up by the Romans in the 8C BC. The romanesque Oberburg tower dates from 1609. The Adler tower at the E end of the town is 15C. The Rheingau Wine Museum (at No. 2 Rheinstraße, in the early 13C Brömserburg, restored 19C) displays 2000 years of viticulture and opens, except Monday and December–January, 09.00–12.00 and 14.00–17.00. At No. 29 Oberstraße is a mechanical musical instrument museum (open April–October daily, 10.00–22.00). A cable car runs to the Niederwald national monument, with a 10·5m high figure of Germania weighing 32 tons, commemorating the Prussian Empire (by J. Schilling, 1883), N of which is the Niederwald hunting lodge of 1764 (now a hotel). Tourist information at No. 16 Rheinstraße.

VI THE RHINE VALLEY

40 The Right Bank: from Bonn to Rüdesheim

Total distance 130km. **Bonn**—B42 10km *Königswinter.* —17km *Linz.*—22km *Neuwied.*—17km **Koblenz.**—6km **Lahnstein.**—28km *St. Goarshausen.* —10km *Kaub.*—20km **Rüdesheim**.

The small university city of **BONN** (289,000 inhab.; alt. 56m) was chosen in 1949 to be the capital of the Federal Republic of Germany. Since 1969 the city has embraced the neighbouring communities of Bad Godesberg and Beuel (on the left bank of the Rhine), more than doubling its original population of c 130,000.

Here were born Ludwig van Beethoven (1770–1827) and the poet Ernst Moritz Arndt (1769–1860). The grave of Robert Schumann and his wife Clara Wieck (1880) can be found alongside the central alley of the old cemetery (near the main railway station). Here too is buried Schiller's wife Charlotte and their son Ernst; also Beethoven's mother, Ernst Moritz Arndt, A.W. von Schlegel and Otto Wesendonck. The cemetery also houses a chapel of the Teutonic knights, built c 1250 and brought here in 1846

History. The city stands on a Celtic site, known by the Romans as *Castra Bonnensia*, to which the Roman Emperor Claudius sent a Legion in c AD 44. Present day Adenauer-Allee follows the route of the Roman road which led to Koblenz from the Roman camp N of the present Rosenthalstraße. This camp was bisected by the Via Principalis, whose exact route is followed by Römer-Straße. Bonn was settled by the Franks in the 5C, came into the possession of the Kurfürsten of Cologne and joined the Rheinish League in 1677. After becoming part of Prussia with the rest of the Rhineland in 1815, a university was founded here. The historic centre of the city was virtually destroyed in WWII.

W of the main railway station at No. 16 Colmantstraße stands the Museum of the Rhineland, founded 1820, rebuilt 1969 (prehistory, history, art, sculpture, furniture; open save Monday, 10.00–17.00, closing Wednesday, 21.00). From the main railway station follow Poststraße to Münsterplatz: Beethoven monument by Jähnel, 1845, and the former Schloß Fürstenberg. Here stands the romanesque **Münster**: 11C W choir (finished outside 12C), mid 12C apse, late 12C vault, early 13C aisles, 13C and 14C wall paintings, seated Virgin, 12C, tombs of Archbishop Engelbert II of Cologne (died 1275) and Archbishop Ruprecht of Cologne (died 1480), 16C Virgin and Child, 17C marble retables. To the S are the cloisters, 1126–69.

From Münsterplatz follow Am Hof NE alongside the university, in the former Schloß of the prince-electors of Cologne, built by Robert de Cotte and Enrico Zuccalli 1697–1725 (rebuilt 1926–30), to reach the triangular Marktplatz: Town Hall by M. Leveilly, 1737–38, with an annex of 1954 housing the City Art Collection (entrance at No. 7 Rathausgasse: works by the 'Blauer Reiter' and 'Brücke' artists, especially August Macke; post 1945 works, including pop art; open save Monday, 10.00–17.00). N of the town hall is the 15C church of St. Remigius.

Leave the Marktplatz by Bonngasse to see on the right the gothic church of the *Holy Name*, 1688–1717, baroque decoration, *façade 1692. Beethoven was born at No. 20 Bonngasse, and his house is now

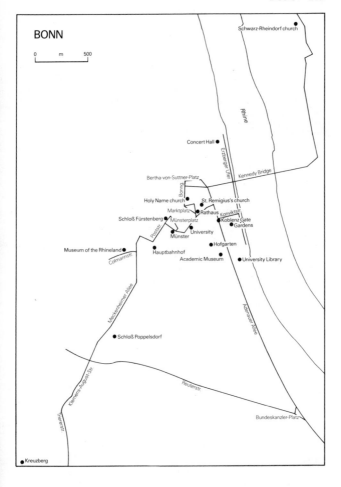

BONN

0   m   500

Schwarz-Rheindorf church

Rhine

Erzberger Ufer

Concert Hall

Kennedy Bridge

Bertha-von-Suttner-Platz

Bonng

Holy Name church   St. Remigius's church

Marktplatz   Rathaus

Konviktstr.

Schloß Fürstenberg   Münsterplatz   Koblenz Gate

Gardens

University

Poststr.

Münster

Museum of the Rhineland

Hofgarten

Colmannstr.

Hauptbahnhof

Academic Museum   University Library

Adenauer Allee

Meckenheimer Allee

Schloß Poppelsdorf

Klemens-August-Str.

Reuterstr.

Thierstr.

Bundeskanzler-Platz

Kreuzberg

a museum (open weekdays, 09.00–13.00 and 15.00–17.00, weekends, 09.00–13.00; including various instruments with which the composer tried to combat his increasing deafness). Follow Bonngasse to Bertha-von-Suttner-Platz, across which you take Berliner Freiheit to reach the 432m-long Kennedy-Brücke that crosses the Rhine to Bonn-Beuel. Erzberger Ufer leads left to the huge congress and concert hall, the Beethovenhalle, by Siegfried Wolske, 1959. Brassert Ufer leads right past the city theatre, by Beck-Erlang and Gessler, 1965, to reach the Alter Zoll, where the bastion that controlled river traffic and took tolls once was. Here is a statue of Ernst Moritz Arndt, with the city gardens close by.

Walk E from Alter Zoll along Konvikt Straße as far as the Koblenz gate, from where you follow Adenauer-Allee S. On the right are the Hofgarten, with the university library (in front of which is a statue by Hans Arp) and the academic museum, by Karl Friedrich Schinkel, 1824 (open save Saturday, 10.00–13.00; Thursday also 16.00–18.00). At No. 79 was born Ernst Moritz Arndt (museum; open save Monday, 10.00–17.00). At No. 50 is the Zoological Museum König (open weekdays, 09.00–17.00; weekends, 09.00–12.30).

Continue S and SE along Adenauer-Allee. The president of the Federal Republic has his official residence opposite the museum in Villa Hammerschmidt (1863–65), close by the federal administrative office in Palais Schaumburg (1858–60). Just beyond the Palais Schaumburg is Bundeskanzler-Platz, with the Bonn-Centre and (to the left) the parliament buildings. From here Reuter Straße leads some distance NW to the botanical gardens in which stands *Schloß Poppelsdorf*, built for the prince-electors of Cologne by Robert de Cotte, 1715–45, and now housing the Mineralogical Museum (open Thursday, 15.00–17.00 and Sunday, 10.00–12.00). Zeppelin Straße leads S from Schloß Poppelsdorf to the forest-clad Venusberg, with the university medical school, an elegant modern residential quarter and game reserve. The route (20 minutes) to the 125m-high Kreuzberg, with its Franciscan monastery and pilgrims' church of 1628 (baroque chapel of the Scala Sancta by Balthasar Neumann, 1746–57), runs from Schloß Poppelsdorf by way of Meckenheimer Allee, Klemens-August-Straße and Trierer Straße.

For Bad Godesberg see Rte 41.

Bonn hosts a triennial Beethoven festival. Tourist information at Cassius-Bastei opposite the main railway station. Trains connect with Cologne and Frankfurt.

Cross the Kennedy-Brücke to Bonn-Beuel, to see (upstream) the romanesque *church of Schwarz-Rheindorf* (1151–73, with an upper nave and a lower nave: frescoes depicting Ezekiel's vision). The route along the banks of the river (Rheinuferstraße) leads SE to the B42, passing through *Oberkassel* (11C romanesque church tower; here was found prehistoric 'Oberkassel man') and reaching after 8km Niederdollendorf. From here a road runs 3km left to the ruins of the 13C Cistercian abbey of *Heisterbach*, whose basilica, 1202–37, was, apart from the choir, demolished in 1808. Close by is an 18C convent. 2km SE lies *Königswinter* (37,000 inhab.; alt. 50m), at the foot of the Drachenfels: parish church of St. Remigius, 1799 (14C reliquary of St. Margaret); Siebengebirge local history museum (at No. 11 Klotzstraße). For the Sibengebirge (including Schloß Drachenfels) see p 240.

After 5km the Rte reaches *Bad-Honnef-Rhöndorf* (45,000 inhab.; alt. 78m), two united towns. In the cemetery of Rhöndorf is buried the

Schloß Poppelsdorf by Robert de Cotte, 1715–40, which stands in the Botanical Gardens·

former federal Chancellor Konrad Adenauer (1876–1967). The house in which he lived, No. 8c Konrad-Adenauer-Straße, is now a museum (open except Monday, 10.00–16.30). Bad-Honnef, situated between the Drachenfels and the Rolandsbogen, dubs itself 'the Nice of the Rhine': gothic church with 12C tower; chapel of St. Servatius, 17C and 18C with a late romanesque choir; Kurhaus (with the Drachen spring providing the waters) in a fine park. A bridge leads to the island of *Grafenwerth* in the middle of the river (open-air swimming pool; mineral waters).

Drive a further 6km to Unkel by way of *Rheinbreitbach* (gateway to the Rhein-Westerwald natural park: ruined Schloß and the home of the writer Rudolf Herzog, 1869–1943). *Unkel* (4000 inhab.; alt. 52m) is an important wine centre with half-timbered houses and a parish church dating in parts as far back as the 13C. Unkel lies 2km NW of *Erpel*, itself lying at the foot of the basalt peak known as the Erpe Ley (96m high). After another 4km the Rte reaches the still partly fortified town of *Linz* (6500 inhab.; alt. 60m)—celebrated by Turgenev in his novel 'Asja'—with a superb view, painted half-timbered houses, late gothic town hall, late romanesque church of St. Martin (13C), a gothic pilgrims' church on the 178m-high Kaiserburg and a Schloß of 1365. Tourist information at No. 13 Burgplatz.

Bad Hönningen (6000 inhab.; alt. 65m) lies 6km SE of Linz, and is another point of access to the Rhein-Westerwald natural park: thermal establishments, swimming pools, camping, Schloß Arenfels and several fine inns, view across the river of Schloß Rheineck. Bad Hönningen runs a wine festival at the beginning of June and a summer festival at the end of July. 3km SE lies *Rheinbrohl* (Roman remains), whose springs are dedicated to the Magi.

The B42 now runs through *Oberhammerstein*, at the foot of a 198m-high peak on which is a ruined 10C Schloß where in 1105 Kaiser Heinrich IV took refuge from his son. After 6km it reaches the wine town of *Leutesdorf* (3000 inhab.; alt. 65m): half-timbered houses, 14C parish church, pilgrims' church of the Holy Cross with a baroque altar. 7km further SE by a new Rhine bridge is *Neuwied* (64,000 inhab.; alt. 62m), whose industries include chemical and iron works and paper-making: 18C Schloß and park; municipal museum (Raffeisenplatz; open weekdays 10.00–13.00 and 14.00–17.00; Saturday, 10.30–13.00). Schloß, 1706–56 (stucco by A. Gallasini). At Neuwied lived and worked the cabinet-maker David Roentgen (1743–1807). Information Office at No. 50 Kirchstraße. Theatre at No. 1 Schloßstraß. Train connections with Frankfurt and Cologne, buses with Mainz and Koblenz. Boat trips. Further E is *Neuwied-Engers*: partly walled, half-timbered houses, plague chapel of 1662, Schloß of 1759 (with hall of mirrors). Here the Romans first bridged the Rhine. Continue along the B42 to reach (9km from Neuwied) *Bendorf* (17,000 inhab.; alt. 67m).—2km further is *Sayn*, with an early 13C former Premonstratensian monastery, a ruined Schloß of the Sayn-Wittgenstein-Sayn family: catholic parish church of St. Madardus, 1204, with a modern glockenspeil. Trains connect Bendorf with Cologne, Frankfurt and Limburg, buses with Koblenz and Neuwied.

The B42 continues through *Vallendar* (10,700 inhab.; alt. 68m): Catholic church of 1839 with a 15C tower; half-timbered gabled houses; Kloster Marienburg, 1240. On an island in the Rhine (the Niederwerth) is a 15C former monastery, and from Vallendar you can see across the river to **Koblenz** (Rte 28). The route along the right bank continues S through Urbar to reach (8km from Bendorf) Koblenz-Ehrenbreitstein: fortress built 16C to 18C, now a youth hostel and museum (open March–October); massive fortress church. The former town hall is by Balthasar Neumann, 1749. Beethoven's mother was born at Ehrenbreitstein, as was Clemens von Brentano.

Lahnstein (20,000 inhab.; alt. 7m) lies 6km S along the B42, at the mouth of the River Lahn. The town is divided into Nieder-Lahnsten at the foot of the Allerheiligenberg (on the peak of the Lahn: Schloß Lahneck, 13C, pillaged 1689, restored 19C; late 13C Schloß Martinsberg; gothic town hall, with a fountain in the Marktplatz; romanesque church of St. Johannes (10C and 11C); church of St. Martin (romanesque tower, baroque interior); romanesque Heimbach house; the Salhof, c1150. By the riverside is the Wenzel chapel of 1400. In 1774 Goethe stayed at the Wirtshaus an der Lahn, built 1697 (at No. 8 Lahnstraße). Tourist information in Ober-Lahnstein, in the Marktplatz.

The B42 now runs for 4km to *Braubach* (3800 inhab.; alt. 71m), from which a road runs for 2km up to the powerfully defended **Schloß Marksburg* (square 13C keep in a triangular courtyard created by three 12C to 14C wings; gothic living quarters; 13th and 14C battlements, open daily, 09.00–19.00), passing en route the 13C chapel of St. Martin (rich collection of 16C statues and memorials). Braubach is 6km from Osterspai, dominated by *Schloß Liebeneck*, after which the route reaches *Filsen* on a picturesque bend in the river (former town hall, 17C; half-timbered houses). *Kamp-Bornhofen*, which lies next on the route (12km) is dominated by two ruined Schlößer known as the enemy brothers, since they are said to have been built by two brothers at odds with each other: gothic church in Kamp; church of 1435 and Franciscan abbey of 1680 in Bornhofen.

From here the road and river run SE for 12km through wine village of *Wellmich* (with its little gothic church and the dominating Deurenburg, known as Burg Maus) to *St. Goarshausen* (2500 inhab.; alt. 74m), over which towers the ruined Schloß known as Burg Katz, built 1371 by Graf Johann III von Katzenellenbogen. St. Goarshausen has a neo-gothic Protestant church, by Eduard Zais, 1860–63, and a neo-baroque Catholic church by Hans and Christoph Rummell, 1923. Tourist information at No. 126 Bahnhofstraße. Trains connect with Cologne and Frankfurt, buses with Koblenz. River trips. 2km from St. Goarshausen, along the B274, is the 14C Burg Reichenberg. 4km SE of St. Goarshausen is the *Lorelei rock*—sung by Heinrich Heine in 1824 in a poem set to music by Friedrich Silchers, 1838, which recounts the legend that here mermaids are said to lure sailors to their deaths—followed after 6km by *Kaub* (1600 inhab.; alt. 79m): N of the village is Burg Gutenfels, a Schloß (rebuilt 19C) from which tolls were levied on river traffic from the 12C to the 19C; here Gustavus Adolphus had his HQ during the Thirty Years' War. Here on 1 January 1814 Blücher crossed the Rhine in the course of his campaign against Napoleon, and at No. 6 Metzgergasse is a Blücher museum (open April–November, except Tuesdays, 10.00–12.00 and 14.00–16.00; in winter only mornings): fine patrician houses, especially in the Marktplatz and Metzergasse; 12C church. In the middle of the river is the pentagonal island fortress of Pfalzgrafenstein (known as the stone ship or 'Steinernes Schiff'), a toll station built 1327 with a bastion added 1607. Kaub hosts a wine festival in September. Tourist information at the town hall; train connections with Frankfurt and Koblenz; boat trips.

The B42 continues SE along the river banks to *Lorch am Rhein* (5000 inhab.; alt. 85m), dominated by the 11C Burg Nollich: late gothic tithe barn; half-timbered houses; renaissance Hilchenhaus, 1573; gothic church of *St. Martin, largely 13C (13C crucifix; late 13C choir stalls; a superb high altar, 1483; and the tomb of Johann Hilchen von Lorch, died 1550). Fine wines. 9km SE of Lorch is *Aßmanshausen* with remains of the town walls, and red wines; a Kurhaus, and thermal springs. After another 5km the B42 reaches **Rüdesheim** (see Rte 39).

41 The Left Bank: from Bingen to Bonn

Total distance 123km. **Bingen**—B9 17km *Bacharach.*—12km *St. Goar.*— 15km *Boppard.*—20km **Koblenz.**—18km *Andernach.*—16km *Sinzig.*—4km *Remagen.*—14km **Bonn-Bad Godesberg.**—7km **Bonn.**

Bingen (22,500 inhab.; alt. 77m) is a long-established wine-trading town, a Celtic settlement fortified by the Romans and lying on the Roman Rhine road. On the Drusus bridge over the Nahe is one of the oldest bridge chapels in Germany, it was built on Roman foundations. Burg Klopp is a Schloß of 1879 built on the site if the 13C one destroyed in 1711. It now houses the local history and astronomical museum (open May–October, daily except Monday, 09.00–12.00 and 14.00–17.00). The town has 17th and 18C houses, some of its medieval fortifications, and a parish church in Zehnthofstraße built in 1410 over

an 11C crypt (13C statues of SS. Katharina and Barbara). Near the
festival hall is a monument to Grand-Duke Ludwig IV (1913). St.
Hildegard von Bingen (1098–1179), the 'Sybil of the Rhine', was
abbess of the nearby Benedictine monastery at Rupertsberg and
founded a daughter house at Eibingen near Rüdesheim. Tourist
information at No. 21 Rheinkai; train connections with Cologne,
Luxembourg, Koblenz, Mainz and Kaiserslautern; bus connections
with the same cities; boat trips.

Cross the River Nahe, which flows into the Rhine here, by the
bridge to take the B9 NW, noting on cliffs in the middle of the Rhine
the 11C Museturm (mouse tower), where the rapacious Bishop Hatto
of Mainz is said to have been eaten by mice. (The name almost
certainly derives from Mautturm or 'toll tower'.) The Rte runs by
Schloß Rheinstein (13C and 19C, restored 1976, on a 173m-high peak;
museum of arms and early gothic art, open 09.00–18.00) and (1km
towards the river) the 12C romanesque chapel of St. Klemens, before
reaching *Trechtinghausen* (1300 inhab.; alt. 74m) and then the tiny
wine village of *Niederheimbach*: 11C church (17C Madonna and
plague altar); medieval walls; Schlößer Sooneck (15C) and Heimburg
(rebuilt 1865).

The B9 continues NW to *Bacharach* (3000 inhab.; alt. 80m), 17km
from Bingen, over which towers Schloß Stahlbeck (12C, razed in
1689). The name of the town derives from the Roman *Bacchi ara* (altar
of Bacchus). Here in 1356 leading nobles elected Ludwig the Bavarian
emperor. At the foot of the Schloß are the remains of the gothic church
of St. Werner, begun 13C, finished 15C, partly destroyed in the Thirty
Years' War and demolished in 1689. The town has numerous old
houses (including the Alter Poshof of 1594), the 13C romanesque–
gothic church of St. Peter (huge tower, the whole restored 1872 and
1970), and the parish church of St. Nikolaus (1688; baroque altars).
Bacharach holds wine festivals on the last weekend in June and the
first weekend in October.

After 6km the B9 reaches *Oberwesel* (5000 inhab.; alt. 71m): known
to the Celts as *Vosolvia* and lying at the foot of the hill on which stands
the 13C Schloß Schönburg (razed 1689). The Swedes and the French
pillaged the town (in 1639 and 1689). The German national anthem
was first sung here, in 1843. In Oberwesel the 'white church', *St.
Martin*, 1303, has 14C sculptures, 15C wall paintings and 16C altars;
the 'red church', the 14C sandstone church of *Our Lady* stands on the
bank of the river, with a rood screen of 1350; Nikolaus altar of 1506;
tomb of Peter Lutern, died 1515, by Hans Backoffen; tomb of the
knights, 1520; baroque organ case; late gothic cloister; and 16 towers
from its medieval fortifications (which incorporate the Werner
chapel). On the opposite bank of the river can be seen St. Goarshausen, as well as the Lorelei rock (see p 209). The B9 continues NW
for 6km to reach *St. Goar* (3800 inhab.; alt. 71m), dominated by Burg
Rheinfels, built by Graf Dieter III von Katzenellenbogen, 1254, which
the French largely demolished in 1797 and which now houses a
museum (open daily, 09.30–12.30 and 13.00–17.30). The 13–15C
Protestant romanesque–gothic parish church of *St. Goar* (*pulpit
1470) was built on an 11C romanesque crypt, matched in size and
splendour only by those of Speyer Cathedral and St. Maria im Kapitol,
Cologne. The neo-gothic Catholic parish church, 1889–91, made use
of a baroque tower from the town walls and has an altarpiece of c
1510. On the opposite side of the river is the twin town of *St.
Goarshausen*, dominated by Burg Katz (see Rte 40).

15km NW of St. Goar the road reaches *Boppard* (by way of *Hirzenach*, with a romanesque church and the spa *Bad Salzig*—mud baths and mineral waters—which lies at the foot of the 530m-high Fleckertshöhe). Still partly protected by Roman walls, Boppard (17,000 inhab.; alt. 70m), whose name is derived from the Roman *Bodobriga*, became renowned in the 10C when it obtained the relics of St. Severus, still preserved in the twin-towered 12C romanesque church of *St. Severus*, with its polygonal choir (colourfully restored 1967; see also the Madonna of 1300 and the early gothic crucifix over the high altar). A Carmelite monastery was founded here in 1265, with a gothic church begun in 1319 whose nave and N aisle were finished 1444 (wall painting of 1407; mid 15C choir stalls; baroque high altar, 1699). Its 14C Burg is now a museum (open weekdays, save Monday, 10.00–12.00 and 14.00–16.00; Saturday mornings and Sunday afternoons). Information office in Karmeliterstraße; train connections with Cologne and Mainz, buses to Mainz and Koblenz, boat trips.

The Rte now passes through partly walled *Rhens* (14C gates and towers, half-timbered houses), near to the 14C *Königstuhl* where the electors of Germany would choose their king. 3km NW of Rhens (and 15km NW of Boppard) is *Kapellen-Solzenfels*. On the 95m-high Bergnase was a mid 13C Schloß which the French destroyed in 1689. In 1842 Karl Friedrich Schinkel built the present 'English gothic' Schloß on the same site. Ernst Deger designed the chapel in 1853. A romantic footpath (waterfall and aqueduct) leads up to the Schloß (now a museum) and gives views of Schloß Lahneck on the other bank of the Rhine.

In 5km the B9 reaches **Koblenz** (see Rte 28). From here cross the River Mosel and pass through the suburb of Lützel to reach after 13km *Weißenthurn*, with a castle keep dating from 1370. Its white tower, after which the town is named, served from the late 13C as a boundary mark, setting the limits of the territory of Trier. After leading French troops across the Rhine in 1797, General Hoche died here. His corpse, taken for burial to St. Petersburg, was brought back by Marshal Foch in 1919, hence the Hoche memorial (obelisk by Peter Josef Krahé, bronzes by Louis Simon Boizot). After 5km more the route arrives at **Andernach** (29,000 inhab.; alt. 64m). Of its medieval fortifications survives the Round tower, 1148–1532 (now a youth hostel) as well as the 14C debtors' tower (Schuldturm) and the Rhine gate. This Roman station (formerly *Antunnacum*) has a town hall, 1572 (with an older Jewish ritual bath in its courtyard), and the catholic church of *Maria Himmelfahrt*, begun 1198, restored 1877–99: gothic tabernacle (in the sacristy), 14C 'plague' crucifix, 18C pulpit. The ruined Schloß dates from the 15C. The tiny romanesque cemetery chapel of St. Michael was attached to a monastery where St. Thomas Becket served. See also the 14C church of the Minorites (now the Protestant parish church) and the church of St. Albert by Rudolf Schwarz, 1952. The restored 14C to 17C Burg was once a seat of the Archbishops of Cologne. Town Museum at No. 14 Schaitbergerstraße (open April–October weekdays 10.00–12.30 and 14.00–17.00; closed Friday afernoons). Tourist information at No. 46 Bahnhofstraße; train connections with Cologne, Mainz, Wiesbaden; buses with local towns (including Maria Laach); boat trips.

The route continues past the old crane of 1554 (in use till 1911), with a view of the island of *Namedywerth* (mineral water spring; 14C church of St. Bartholomäus; 13C Burg Namedy, restored 19th and

20C) and across the river the ruined Burg Hammerstein, reaching after 7km *Brohle*. From Brohle the B412 leads SW for 13·5km, by way of Bad Tönisstein to *Maria Laach*, see p 181.

The B9 continues to follow the Rhine, passing after 4km through the health resort and spa of *Bad Breisig* (6600 inhab.; alt. 61m): thermal swimming pools, park (with concerts); October onion fair; 13C church of St. Viktor (13C and 14C frescoes). In Oberbreisig are the 18C baroque church of Our Lady, restored Burg Rheineck (begun 12C), and along the riverside half-timbered customs houses. 5km NW lies *Sinzig-Bad Bodendorf* (14,000 inhab.; alt. 71m), still partly walled, with numerous thermal baths and springs, close by the confluence of the Rhine with the Ahr. The Romans knew Sinzig as *Sentiacum*. Secular buildings of interest include the medieval Königshof the Zeltenhof (1697–1740), and the 19C neo-gothic Schloß (local history museum, open Sundays, 10.00–12.00). Late romanesque church of *St. Peter* (c 1230, well restored 1964): late 13C frescoes; 15C altar.

After 4km the route reaches *Remagen* (15,000 inhab.; alt. 64m), the Celtic-Roman *Rigomagus*. The parish church of SS. Peter and Paul, enlarged 1902 by Caspar Clemens Pickel (romanesque nave, gothic choir, 16C Pietà, 17C tower) occupies the site of the Roman fort. In the former monastery chapel, 15C, is now a local history museum (with Roman remains). Opposite was erected the Roman Pfarrhof gate in 1902. See also on its hill the pilgrims' church of St. Apollinaris, based on a 6C chapel, restored 1839–57 by Ernst Friedrich Zwirner. At Remagen in 1916–18 on the orders of General Ludendorff was built the superb bridge which the 9th American armoured division took on 7 March 1945. In 1980 a Museum of Peace was established on this bridge (open weekdays, 15.00–17.00; Saturday, 10.00–12.00 and 14.00–17.00; Sunday, 10.00–17.00). Burg Schloß is a classical building by Ernst Friedrich Zwirner, 1839–43. At *Remagen-Oberwinter*, 4km further N, is the neo-gothic Schloß Marienfels and the Haus Ernich, by Ernst von Ihne, 1906–08. The church of St. Laurentius, Oberwinter, is neo-gothic (1866; by Vincenz Statz) incorporating a late gothic choir. *Rolandseck* (1km further N) offers superb views of the Sieben-gebirge across the river and of the river island of *Nonnenwerth* with its nunnery founded 1122 (now a girls' school) and thermal baths. A good road leads for 3·5km up the peak on which rests the *Rolandsbogen* (*views), a Schloß supposedly built by Roland, partly destroyed 1475, renewed by Ernst Friedrich Zirner, 1839.

Rolandseck lies 6km SE of **Bonn-Bad Godesberg** (75,000 inhab.; alt. 65m), whose spa was known to the Romans. From the central railway station Rheinallee leads to a riverside park (with boats moored for trips on the Rhine; car ferry to *Königswinter* (see Rte 40). Poststraße leads E from the railway station to the Stadtpark and the Redou-tenpark, divided by the Kurfürstenstraße. In the Stadtpark stand the modern Trinkhalle, the congress hall and the city theatre. Redou-tenpark takes its name from the rococo Redoute, the former Kurhaus, built for Archbishop Max Franz in 1792 by Martin Leydel, finished c 1820 by his son Adam Franz Friedrich Leydel (now used for concerts and receptions). Here is the new Kurfürstenbad, the thermal estab-lishment called the Draitschbrunnen and the Hof theatre, 1792, which in the 19C became the town hall. In 1863 Vincenz Statz built for Bad-Godesberg a neo-gothic Catholic church of St. Marien (enlarged 1894). The neo-romanesque Protestant Rigalsche chapel dates from 1858.

From here Kurfürstenstraße and the Deutschherrenstraße lead S to Muffendorf (10C church of St. Martin; house of the Teutonic knights, 1254). To reach *Schloß Godesburg* follow from the the Stadtpark Kirchstraße and Winterstraße. The Schloß was built for Archbishop Dietrich of Cologne in 1219; it was ruined on 17 December 1583 by besieging Bavarians except for a few walls and the 48m-high round keep. The romanesque chapel of St. Michael, also damaged in the siege, was restored by Archbishop Josef Clemens, 1697–99 and given a baroque nave. At the foot of the Godesberg is 'Zum Lindenwirtin', an inn rebuilt 1976.

Since 1969 Bad Godesburg has been an integral part of **Bonn** 7km away (see Rte 40), which is reached by way of Bonnerstraße and Kölnerstraße (en route the gothic Hochkreuz, set up by the Archbishop of Cologne in 1350: 11m high, with a sculpted Christ among angels and the four evangelists; restored E.F. Zirner, 1859).

Trains connect with Cologne and Koblenz, buses with Bonn, boats with Königswinter and Niederdollendorf.

42 Cologne

COLOGNE (987,000 inhab.; alt. 50m), in German *Köln*, was capital of the Rhine in Roman times. Almost totally destroyed in WWII (losing 90 per cent of its inner city—save for its cathedral, in spite of 14 direct hits by bombs—and 70 per cent of the outer suburbs) the city has rapidly rebuilt itself, and trade has also been redeveloped. 9,000,000 tonnes of goods are annually loaded and unloaded in the port; Ford-Cologne employs 28,000 workers, Klöckner-Humbolt-Deutz another 17,000 (making diesel engines). The Cologne trade fair (see below) has an annual turn-over of 700,000,000 Marks. Weekly the city creates up to 10,000,000,000 litres of its celebrated perfume eau de Cologne ('4711'). Cologne houses the HQ of West German radio and television.

Main *railway station*: Bahnhofstraße.

Main *post office*: Am Dominikanern.

Information Office: No. 19 Unter Fettenheim (near the Cathedral).

Boats connect with Düsseldorf, Basel and Rotterdam.

Köln-Bonn airport.

History. The city in Roman times was called first *Ara Ubiorum* and then *Colonia Agrippinensis* (in 38 BC, when Agrippa was commanding the legions in Gaul). The colony prospered, making pottery and tiles for the empire. Here Trajan was proclaimed emperor in AD 98. The Romans walled the city, which was the centre of a network of fine roads. Constantine built a bridge across the Rhine. Cologne became the seat of archbishops (some of whom frequently preferred to live in Bonn). In 795 Charlemagne made his court chaplain Hildebold Archbishop of Cologne. Cologne's 12 superb romanesque churches, built on tombs and in former cemeteries, indicate the remarkable power of relics over the medieval Christian mind. In 1180 a ring of walls far wider than the Roman fortifications was built to house the population. In the Middle Ages Cologne was an imperial city and became yet richer as a member of the Hanseatic League (a mercantile alliance of seafaring citizens, set up by Cologne and Lübeck c 1250). At Cologne in 1367 the Hanseatic League declared war on Denmark. From time to time trouble flared between the patricians and the guilds of artisans. The Reformation brought further strife. Luther's works were publicly burnt in front of the cathedral by the university faculty of theology in 1520. In 1794 the city was taken by French Revolutionary troops. Protestants and Jews were at last allowed to settle here. The Congress of Vienna (1814–15) ceded Cologne to Prussia.

In 1881 the medieval walls were demolished to construct wide boulevards around the city. Between then and 1930 the Rhine was twice bridged, and great industrial companies set up here. Nine railway lines today meet at Cologne. After the destruction of WWII an international competition to re-plan the city was won by Fritz Schaller. All 12 of Cologne's *romanesque churches were restored by 1985.

The musician J. Cochläus (1479–1552) taught at the university. The composer Carl Rosier (1640–75) was a native of Cologne, as were Friedrich Schlegel (1772–1829; he taught philosophy here 1804–09), the socialist politician August Bebel (1840–1913) and the socialist journalist Emil Rosenow (1871–1904). Jacques Offenbach (1819–80) ran the city opera. At Cologne a sudio for electronic music was founded under the leadership of Karl-Heinz Stockhausen. The novelist Heinrich Böll was born here in 1917. Konrad Adenauer, Federal Germany's first post-war chancellor, was Oberbürgermeister from 1917–33.

The main railway station is close by the cathedral square and looks out on it through the glass façade of the great shed, rebuilt (1957). In front of the station stands Deichmannhaus (1911). W of the station

Marzellenstraße leads to the church of St. Mariä Himmelfahrt, designed for the Jesuits by Christoph Wamser of Alsace, 1618 (finished 1678, restored 1964: five altars and a pulpit, all early 16C, by Valentin Boltz, a lay-brother who carved himself smoking a pipe on the pulpit). Next door is the former Jesuit college (also by Wamser, 1618–89).

Walk N to Ursulaplatz and the church of **St. Ursula**, built in a Roman cemetery at the the beginning of the 12C on the site of a 4C building. On the interior of the S wall an inscription preserved from the earlier church records that a Roman named Clematius built it over the saint's tomb. Legends soon developed about Ursula, an allegedly English queen, and her 11,000 martyred companions, and inside the church are a sarcophagus of the saint, by Johann Lenz, 1659; *13th and 14C reliquary busts and the 17C baroque *Golden Chamber decorated with bones (reliquary of St. Etherius, c 1170; 120 bust reliquaries). The church's W tower was extended early 13C; late 13C choir extensions; baroque crest on romanesque tower, with a crown (supposedly representing that of England).

Follow the passage underneath the railway line right of the church to reach the church of **St. Kunibert**, the last of the city's romanesque churches (later ogive vaulting), consecrated 1247 on the site of a 9C church built over Bishop Kunibert's 7C grave: glass of 1230 (tree of Jesse; legends of SS Kunibert and Clemens); *Annunciation group by Konrad Kuyn, 1439. From here follow Konrad-Adenauer-Ufer NE alongside the river to reach (at No. 80) the restaurant Bastei. On one of the bastions built by the Prussians when they razed the city's medieval walls Wilhelm Riphahn built this expressionist steel, concrete and glass restaurant in 1924 (destroyed 1943, restored by Riphahn himself). Konrad-Adenauer-Ufer leads further NE to the Cologne Zoo (at No. 173 Riehlerstraße) and botanical gardens (swimming pool, miniature railway, open 08.00 till dusk).

Return SW along Konrad-Adenauer-Ufer to pass under Hohenzollernbrücke and turn right to the cathedral, set on a spacious terrace aproached by flights of steps. NW of this terrace has been re-erected a Roman gate discovered here in 1826. Fritz Schaller built the bank directly W of the cathedral (1953), in front of which is the pigeon fountain of the same year.

Cologne **Cathedral** stands on the site of a romanesque church and was begun under the direction of Master Gerard in 1248 when Archbishop Konrad von Hochstaden laid the first stone, and was completed only in 1880, when the two W towers stood, at over 153m, taller than any other buiding in Western Europe. In the square is the reproduction of a tower finial 9·25m high, 4·58m wide. Stone was quarried for the building from the Drachenfels (see p 240). The choir was finished 1322; work started on the transepts in the 14C. Work stopped in 1559. A campaign to finish the cathedral was started in 1824 and the work was completed at a further cost of 21,000,000 Marks. Bomb damage was repaired 1956. The S doorway has decorations designed by Schwanthaler; the N door has four bronze doors by Ewald Mataré, 1948–53. 509 steps lead 95m up the S tower (*view), which houses the heaviest bell in the world.

INTERIOR (144m long, 44·8m wide, 43·5m high): the glass in the N aisle windows dates from the early 16C; that in the S aisle from 1848, made in Munich. Of the nave sculptures all are 19C save an Entombment of the 15C and the 1914–18 war memorial, by *Grasegger*. In the S transept are a stone Madonna, 1420; a statue of St. Christopher by *Tilman van der Burch*, c 1470; the retable of

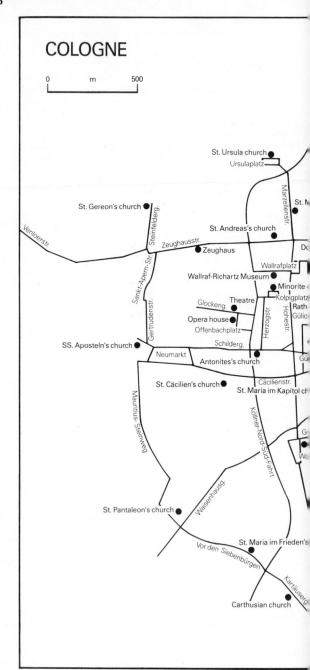

COLOGNE

0 m 500

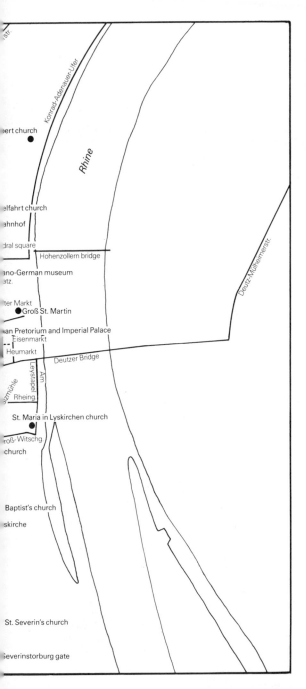

…str.

Konrad-Adenauer-Ufer

…bert church

Rhine

…elfahrt church

…ahnhof

…dral square

Hohenzollern bridge

…ano-German museum

…atz.

…ter Markt

Groß St. Martin

…an Pretorium and Imperial Palace

Eisenmarkt

Heumarkt

Deutzer Bridge

Deutz-Mülheimerstr.

Leystapel

Am

…zmühle

Rheing.

St. Maria in Lyskirchen church

…roß-Witschg.

…church

…Baptist's church

…skirche

St. Severin's church

…everinstorburg gate

St. Agilolph, 1520. In the N transept are St. Ursula protecting her maidens, early 16C; St. Peter and the Virgin Mary, both 18C; an altar and octagonal marble tabernacle by *Elmar Hillebrand*, 1960 and 1964; organ case by *Peter Hacker* 1948; a statue of the master builder Konrad Kuyn, died 1469. The *choir has the series of *stained glass windows depicting the Adoration of the Magi, 1315–29; the three kings (amid 45 others); canons' stalls of 1311; frescoes c 1322. The *high altar c 1320 was the gift of Archbishop Wilhelm von Gennep (1349–62). Behind it is displayed the **shrine containing the relics of the Magi (stolen from Milan in 1164), *Nicholas of Verdun*, late 12C: sculpted with prophets and apostles, Jesus's Baptism and Second Coming, and The Adoration of the Three Kings. The surrounding chapels include (beginning from left to right) that of the Holy Cross, housing a romanesque crucifix from the earlier church (the figure c 970, the cross mid 17C). The chapel also houses the tombs of Archbishops St. Engelbert (1216–25), Wilhelm von Gennep (1349–62) and Engelbert von der Marck (1364–68). This chapel gives entry to the chapel of the Holy Sacrament in which are the Madonna of Milan (14C), a tabernacle c 1460, and 16C glass. The chapel of St. Engelbert, to the right, houses the early 16C retable of St. Georg, the renaissance tomb of Archbishop Anton von Schauenberg (died 1558), by *Cornelis Floris*, and modern glass by *W. Rupprecht* (1956). The next chapel, of St. Maternus, houses the tomb (1336) of Archbishop Philipp von Heinsberg (died 1191) who, as the design indicates, gave Cologne its medieval walls. Next, in the chapel of St. Johannes, is the bronze tomb of the cathedral's founder (died 1261; tomb c 1320) and the sarcophagus of Queen Richeza of Poland (died 1059); 13C glass, (*All Saints' window); 14C wall paintings. Next is the chapel of the Magi where formerly their relics lay: glass c 1320, including an Adoration of the Magi and the *Bible window. A marble plaque at the entrance covers the heart of Marie de Medici, who died at Cologne (1642). Nearby is the tomb (1460) of Archbishop Dietrich von Moers (1414–63). The chapel of St. Agnes has 1340 frescoes and the gothic tomb of St. Irmgard; glass 1320 and 19C. In the chapel of St. Michael are an altar triptych of the Crucifixion by *Barthel Bruyn* (1548), and the tomb of Archbishop Walram von Jülich (died 1349), 16C glass and the tomb of General Philipp Bertram von Hochkirchen (killed at Landau, 1703), by *Fortini*. The chapel of St. Stephan houses the 10C tomb of Archbishop Gereon (969–76), preserved from the former church; the tomb of Archbishop Adolf von Schauenberg, by Cornelis Floris, c 1560; and another *Bible window, c 1290. Next is the chapel of the Virgin: modern altar by *Willy Weyres*, 1956; modern tabernacle by *Carl von Ackeren*, 1956; *Stephan Lochner's **triptych depicting the Magi, SS. Gereon and Ursula (closed, the wings depict the Annunciation), c 1440; tomb of Archbishop Friedrich von Saarwerden, c 1415; modern glass by *W. Gayer*, 1956; and—at the entrance—the tombs of Archbishop Rainald von Dassel and Count Gottfried von Arnsberg.

The Cathedral Treasury houses a 12C Byzantine reliquary of the Holy Cross; the Hillinus codex, c 1000; St. Peter's staff, variously dated; and a chasuble (16C) of St. Charles Borromeo (open 09.00–18.00; Sunday, 13.00–17.30).

S of the cathedral stands the Romano-German Museum, built on the site of a 72m² mosaic (open, except Monday, 10.00–17.00; Wednesday and Thursday to 20.00). Behind the Domhotel is the fountain of the dwarfs (1900), commemorating the story of the little men who used to entertain the citizens. Unter Fettenheim reaches Wallrafplatz, with the Cologne broadcasting house, by P.F. Schneider (1948–52), from which An der Rechtschule leads to the Wallraf-Richartz Museum Ludwig (by Rudolf Schwarz and Josef Bernard, 1957: 14–16C Cologne artists, especially *Stephan Lochner; *contemporary works given by Dr Peter Ludwig, soon to be moved to a new museum (open daily, 10.00–17.00; Tuesday and Thursday to 20.00).

Continue left to reach Kolpingplatz: part of the Roman aqueduct; statue of Adolf Kolping (1813–65); Minorite church, 1250–1410, with the modern tomb of Duns Scotus (1266–1308), by Josef Höntgesberg, 1957. S of the church stands the chapel of St. Kolumba, by Gottfried Böhm, 1950, incorporating the remains of a romanesque church bombed 1945 (statue of Our Lady of the Ruins, 1460; Pietà, c 1440; St. Anne, Virgin and Child, c 1500; statue of St. Antony of Padua by Ewald Mataré, 1937; glass by Georg Meistermann, 1950, and Ludwig

Gies, 1954). W of Herzogstraße, beyond Tunisstraße, is Offenbach-platz, which contains the 1957 expressionist Opera House and the 1953 Theatre (both by W. Riphahn). Between these two buildings runs Glockengasse, so-named because of the Glockenspiel on the façade of the house where 'eau de Cologne' was first created. Continue along Herzogstraße turning right at Schildergasse to reach the *church* of the Antonites, built 1350–84, transferred to the Protestants in 1802 (the first Protestant church in Cologne): choir window 1520, aisle windows 1966, by Alois Plum; 12C font (cover by Wyland, 1934); bronze statue of the Commissioning of the Apostles, (Ulrich Henn, 1964); organ 1968; cast of the *Angel of death, by Ernst Barlach, 1927 (the original destroyed as 'degenerate art' by the Nazis, 1937: the face is that of Käthe Kollwitz).

Return W long Schildergasse to cross Hohe Straße and walk into Gürzenichstraße, to reach the Gürzenich, built as a concert and exhibition hall by R. Schwarz and K. Band (1955), where the 15C Gürzenich stood, until its destruction in 1943. The building abuts onto the ruined church Alt-St. Alban, which (as a war memorial) has a reproduction of 'suffering parents', a statue by Käthe Kollwitz.

Gülichplatz (Carnival fountain by G. Grasegger, 1913) lies between the Gürzenich and the old and new town halls (restored early 15C belfry, with a Glockenspiel; gothic, richly decorated Hansa-Saal, c 1360; mannerist Vorhalle by Wilhelm Vernukken (1569); new build-ing by Theodor Teichen and Franz Löwenstein (1955), with a stained glass window by Georg Meistermann depicting the city's history, and the Europe mosaic of Hans-Jürgen Grummer). Close by are the remains of the Roman Pretorium and Imperial palace (open 10.00–17.00; Wednesday also 19.00–22.00).

Follow from here Große Sandkaul S to reach the romanesque church of **St. Maria im Kapitol** (consecrated 1065), so-named from its site on the old Roman Capitol where in the 8C the stepmother of Charles Martel founded a nunnery. Severely damaged in WWII (the apse partly collapsed in 1948), the church has been entirely restored: *carved wooden doors of the mid 12C, illustrating the life of Jesus; 12C and 13C tombs (including that of the foundress, Plectrudis, 1180); renaissance rood screen, 1525). Outside is a weeping angel, by Gerhard Marcks, 1949. N of the church is the late 15C tower of Klein St. Martin, whose church was demolished 1803. Walk towards the river, taking first An der Malzmühle and then Rheingasse (at No. 8 the 13C Overstolzenhaus, restored 1956 now the Kunstgewerbemuseum and housing 13 secular frescoes). The quayside reaches the church of **St. Maria in Lyskirchen**, built 1220 on the site of a 10C church: 12C font; 13C *frescoes of the Old and New Testament (remarkably unscathed in spite of war damage); 15C 'sailors' Madonna; 16C glass. The gothic windows are 17C.

Continue N along the quay to the Deutzerbrücke (1948; where the Romans bridged the Rhine, to find on the left the Cornmarket (Heumarkt, with picturesque 16C to 18C houses, dated on the ouside walls, several restored after WWII) and the iron market (Eisenmarkt, with Cologne's marionette theatre). The Alter Markt is situated N of Heumarkt, with a fountain (statue of Jan van Werth, died 1651, general in the Thirty Years' War). Towards the river stands **Groß St. Martin**, built 1150–1230 on the site of a Carolingian monastery (ravaged by fire in 1150): the great tower, totally destroyed in WWII, was restored 1963. Groß St. Martin copies and modifies the clover-leaf choir of St. Maria im Kapitol. The old patterns of the streets have been

retained here. To the E of Groß St. Martin are the renaissance houses
Zum Dorn and Zum Bretzel (1580, restored) and the house Am Hanen,
decorated by Edward Mataré, 1962–65. Unter Seidmacher contains
the renaissance Gasthaus zum St. Peter (built by Terlaen van Lennep
1563, destroyed 1945, rebuilt 1946). Follow Am Leystapel S along the
river bank past St. Maria in Lyskirchen, turning right at Groß-
Witschgasse and continuing by way of Georgstraße to the Waidmarkt,
where stands the **church of **St. Georg**, founded 1059, consecrated
1067, to replace a Frankish chapel which stood on the ruins of a
Roman temple: vaulting mid 12C; W end rebuilt c 1190 (the sole part
that needed no restoration after WWII); the romanesque crucifix is a
replica of the original, now in the Schnütgen Museum (see below);
14C crucifix; 16C altarpiece by Barthel Bruyn; glass by Jan Thornprykker (1930).

From here Severinstraße leads S (along the route of the Roman
road) for a 650m walk to the **church of St. Severin, passing on the
right first the church of St. Johann Baptist (12C basilica, enlarged
14–16C, redone by Karl Band, 1962) and then (a little distance from
Severinstraße) the Elendskirche, 1765–71. The church of **St. Severin**
(13th and 14C) stands on the site of a 4C chapel which stood in the old
Roman cemetery. It owes its present form initially to the crypt built for
the bones of St. Severin in the 10C (and extended in the next). The
romanesque choir was rebuilt in the 13C: mosaic floor, 13C canons'
stalls, 14C wall paintings; two towers at the E end finished in the
gothic style, 14C; huge W tower and spire finished 1411; vaulting of
the interior and the high windows 15C, when the cloister was also
redone; Madonna, c 1290; Severin's present reliquary (behind the
high altar), 1819; in the sacristy, Christ crucified, surrounded by
angels and saints, c 1420. Difficult of access (permission from parish
priest) is the Romano-Christian **cemetery excavated under the nave
of the church. Severinstraße continues S to the 13C Severinstorburg
gate, to the E of which is the Bayen tower, again from the medieval
walls. Around St. Severin's church are a number of 16C houses. NW
from the church follow Kartäusergasse to the Carthusian church
(Kartäuserkirche, 1393: modern glass by Carl Cordel and modern
fittings by Gerhard Marcks, save for a 15C retable on the N wall and a
15C triptych).

Kartäuserstraße leads into Vor der Siebenburgen (with on the right
the baroque church of St. Maria im Frieden, 1643–1716, restored
1965) which leads to the church of **St. Pantaleon** (7C, rebuilt c 950,
consecrated 980). The W façade is 10C, the aisles were added in the
12C, the choir and gothic windows in the nave redone in the early 17C
by Christoph Wamser (choir glass 1622). The 12·80m-high nave
houses a late gothic *rood screen, 1502–14; head of Christ; baroque
organ. The ceiling was not restored in its original form after WWII.
Sarcophagus of Empress Theophanu, died 991, by Sepp Hürten, 1965.

From here follow Waisenhausgasse NE, turning left at Köllner-
Nord-Süd-Fahrt to reach in Cäcilienstraße the church of *St. Cäcilien*,
which adjoins and houses part of the Schnütgen museum of religious
art (and in consequence was not restored inside with complete
faithfulness after WWII, open 10.00–17.00 and also Wednesday,
19.00–21.00). Here in 881 was founded a ladies' collegiate church,
rebuilt in the 10C, with further reconstruction in the 12C: St. Cecilia
with her companions sculpted over the N door, c 1160; the skeleton
sprayed on W end of the former convent is by the Zürich 'spray-artist'
Harald Nägeli. W from the church cross the NEUMARKT (Germany's

largest medieval square, invaded by handloom weavers in December and always a fine market) to reach the church of **SS. Aposteln**, restored and serving as a concert hall: built 1020 on a 9C chapel; partly rebuilt 1192 after a fire, vaulted 1219, the date also of the present choir; 12C square tower; steeple to W, with a diamond-shaped spire, mid 12C; painting of the archangel Michael by Friedrich Overbeck, 1850; 13C statues of Christ and the twelve intercessors; 15C statue of St. Michael; woodcarvings of the twelve apostles, c 1330; *Christ suffering by Tilman von der Burch, c 1450; modern chapel to the right of the nave, glass by Ludwig Gies, 1955; other modern glass by Willy Weyres. To the S along Mauritius-Steinweg is the neo-gothic church of St. Mauritius (1864, restored 1957).

Walk due N from St. Aposteln along Gertrudenstraße and then follow Sankt-Apern-Straße to the Roman tower (50 BC). To the right along Zeughausstraße is the brick-built former arsenal (Zeughaus, 1594–1606; baroque doorway 1594 by Peter Cronenborch, now the City Museum, open daily, 10.00–17.00 and Thursday also 19.00–21.00), whose S façade is built on the former Roman wall. The building abutting on the Zeughaus is the former city guard house (Alte Wache, 1840, restored 1958). To the S by way of Landgasse is the church of St. Maria in der Kupfergasse (1705–15, restored 1955). Zeughausstraße leads further E to the church of **St. Andreas**, in the centre of Cologne's banking area: its choir, once 10C, was rebuilt in the late gothic style of the 15C (late gothic *shrine of Albertus Magnus; early 16C altar by Barthel Bruyn; 19C glass); the nave and crossing tower were begun in 1200; the side aisles are essentially 13th and 14C extensions; N transept modified and S transept (shrine of the Maccabees c 1527) rebuilt 15C. Modern additions include bronze doors by Karl Winter (1962), and the present Dominican convent, by Karl Band, 1955.

Return along Zeughausstraße to Sankt-Apern-Straße and turn N along Steinfeldergasse to reach the church of **St. Gereon**, built in a Roman cemetery, the well-restored 4C decagon wrongly alleged to have been built by Constantine's mother St. Helena: alterations (1056–75) under Archbishop Anno include the mosaic floor, a long E choir, lengthened in the next century and embellished with two flanking towers. At this time early gothic windows were added to the decagon, closed with ten ribs and a hanging keystone 34m high (completed 1227). The baptistery was added shortly afterwards (wall paintings). The vault of the choir and its gothic windows date from the 15C, as does the sacristy. Modern glass by Georg Meistermann.

OTHER MUSEUMS: Diocesan Museum at No. 2 Roncalliplatz (open, save Monday, 10.00–17.00, closes Sunday, 13.00); Motor Museum at No. 111 Deutz-Mülheimer-Straße (open weekdays 09.00–16.00); Police Museum at No. 16 Verloerstraße (open on request); Folk Museum at No. 45 Ubierring (open save Mondays 10.00–17.00 and Wednesday till 20.00); Theatre Museum in the rococo Schloß Wahn (open weekdays 09.00–17.00).

Rhine regatta in early June; Corpus Christi procession along the Rhine.

43 From Cologne to the Dutch border: the Left Bank of the Rhine

Total distance 149km. **Cologne**—B9 23km **Dormagen**.—13km
Neuß.—23km **Krefeld**.—B57 19km **Moers**.—29km **Xanten**.—14km
Kalkar.—13km *Kleve*.—B9 11km *Kranenburg*.—4km the Dutch
border.

An EXCURSION along the B9 from Krefeld to Kleve by way of
Geldern and *Kevelaer* 65km. Taking the B57 between **Krefeld** and
Mönchengladbach 20km.

Leave **Cologne** (see Rte 42) N (which offers a view of the highest flats
in Europe, the 137·3m high Colonia-Hochhaus) by way of
Neußerstraße, and take the B9 for 16km to *Worringen* (known to the
Romans as *Buruncum*, where in 1288 the citizens of Cologne fought
and won against their archbishop and his allies of Brabant). Continue
for another 7km to *Dormagen* (56,000 inhab.; alt. 45m). Here (at
Durnomagus) the Romans stationed their 22nd legion.

2km NE of the B9 lies *Zons (10,000 inhab.; alt. 36m), on the river's bank, its 14C
walls the best-preserved medieval fortifications in the Rhineland. Archbishop
Friedrich von Saarwerden built them c 1373 and used Zons (Roman *Sontium*) as
a river toll station: windmill tower, Krötschen tower (once a gaol), the Halb
tower, the Customs tower; fountain 1577. The Museum (at No. 1 Schloßstraße;
Jugendstil collection) opens May–September: weekdays, except Monday,
14.00–19.00; weekends 10.00–12.30 and 14.00–17.00; other months: weekdays
except Monday, 14.00–18.00). Buses to Cologne, Dormagen, and Düsseldorf;
boat trips.

Continuing N on the B9 you reach (13km) the industrial town and
harbour of *Neuß* (150,000 inhab.; alt. 42m), whose town charter was
granted 1190: late romanesque basilica of *St. Quirinus*, with an 11C
crypt and a baroque dome, 1741 (inside, crucifix, c 1350; Madonna of
1420); Ober gate c 1300; former Observaten church (1640), now a
concert hall; church of Christ the King, 1955, preserving pre-WWI
windows by J. Thornprykker; botanical garden; theatre at No. 2
Büttget-Straße. Museum (Am Obertor) open, save Monday, 10.00–
17.00. Tourist information at No. 40 Friedrichstraße; train links with
Holland, buses with Aachen, Cologne, Düsseldorf, Zons, boats with
Düsseldorf; annual festival in late August. From Neuß the B326
crosses the Rhine to Düsseldorf-Süd (6km; see Rte 42).

The B9 continues N, (passing en route the B222 which leads W to
the new town of *Meerbusch*: ruined 17C Schloß (the Haus Meer) and
the Haus Dyckhof (1666)). After 22km it reaches the silk and textile
manufacturing city of **KREFELD** (235,000 inhab.; alt. 38m): classical
town hall, 1893; windmills; patrician houses; church of *St. Klemens*
(12C tower, 14C nave, 17C S aisle, 19C E end); neo-gothic church of
St. Matthias, with a 12C romanesque tower; 12C to 17C restored Burg
Linn (now the Lower Rhine History Museum; open April–October;
daily, except Monday, 10.00–13.00 and 15.00–18.00; otherwise closes
17.00); *Haus Lange*, built Mies van der Rohe, 1929 (at No. 91
Wilhelmshofallee; now an exhibition hall for contemporary art, open
save Monday, 10.00–17.00; Textile Museum in a building of 1880 (at
No. 8 Andreasmarkt; open as the History Museum); Kaiser-Wilhelm
Museum (at No. 35 Karlsplatz; modern art; open save Monday,
10.00–17.00).

Ice rink, racecourse. Tourist information at the main railway station. Train links with Cologne, Düsseldorf, Holland; buses to Duisburg, Düsseldorf and Venlo (on the border with Holland); airport for light aircraft; river trips.

The B9 leaves the river bank here and travels NW, reaching after 27km *Geldern* (19,000 inhab.; alt. 25m), once the capital of the duchy of Geldre: remains of its fortifications, including the Mühlenturm; 15C parish church, formerly belonging to an Augustinian monastery whose refectory still stands. 11km NE is *Kevelaer*, whose mid 17C Madonna and mid 17C shrine developed into a baroque pilgrimage church (1654) as the statue's miraculous powers (mocked in Heine's 'Die Wahlfahrt nach Kevelaer') became famous and whose present neo-gothic basilica of *St. Maria* (1858–64) seats 5000 and attracts 500,000 annually. History of the pilgrimage in the Museum (at No. 18 Hauptstraße; open daily, 10.00–17.00, closed Monday from November–April).

Kevelaer is 12km SE of *Goch* (30,000 inhab.; alt. 16m). Here are a 14C stone gate (twin towers, now the museum, housing 14th and 15C art and a gramophone collection; open save Monday, 10.00–12.00 and 15.00–17.00), the 16C Haus zu den fünf Ringen (at No. 1 Steinstraße), and the 14C to 16C brick-built church of *St. Maria Magdalena* (15C sandstone tanbernacle). From Goch the B9 leads NE for 13km to **Kleve** (see below).

From **Krefeld** the B57 runs for 19km to **Moers** (103,000 inhab.; alt. 29m): remains of the old fortifications; 15C to 17C Grafenschloß, now the local history museum at No. 9 Kastell (open save Monday, 09.00–18.00; weekends opens 10.00); mid 15C parish church with a baroque organ; at No. 1 Altmarkt the birthplace of the hymnologist Gerhard Tersteegen (1697–1769); theatre (at No. 6 Kastell); town museum in the 17C building at No. 1 Meerstraße; open weekdays, 13.00–19.00; Sunday, 11.00–17.00). Tourist information at No. 49 Oberwallstrße.

The B57 continues for a further 12km due N to *Rheinberg* (27,500 inhab.; alt. 25m): parish church 1107 (reredos c 1500); town hall 1449; Zollturm and Pulverturm remaining from the medieval walls.

17km NW along the B57 lies **Xanten* (16,000 inhab.), once an important Roman garrison town and still preserving its Roman amphitheatre and other Roman remains: excavations; archaeological park at No. 3 Trajanstraße (open 09.00–18.00, or dusk if earlier), as well as parts of the medieval walls (the double Klever gate, 1393). The Altstadt retains numerous medieval houses: town hall, 1786; Protestant church 1649; Charterhouse of 1646. Here is also the collegiate church of **St. Viktor* (the Dom), built on the site of a 4C grave of two martyrs (hence Xanten, i.e. 'Ad Sanctos'), with a romanesque–gothic W façade, a gothic five-aisled basilica; the oldest choir stalls in the Rhineland, 1250; 14C glass; high altar with the golden shrine of St. Viktor, 1150, and an altarpiece by Barthel Bruyn the Elder, 1530; Lady altar by Heinrich Douvermann, 1535; gothic cloister and chapterhouse, 1543–46; treasury (open Tuesday–Saturday, 10.00–12.00 and 14.00–18.00; winter: only afternoons). Important regional Museum at Nos 7–9 Kurfürstenstraße (Roman remains, open weekdays save Monday, 10.00–17.00; weekends opens 18.00–18.00).

Tourist information at the town hall. Train links with Duisburg and Kleve, buses with local towns. The 'Nibelungenlied' places Siegfried's home here.

Kalkar (11,000 inhab.; alt. 20m), a member of the Hanseatic League and the centre of north Rhenish woodcarving, 1490–1540, lies 14km NE of Xanten along the B57: turreted town hall 1444–46 and other 15C brick houses in the Marktplatz; 12C romanesque church of St. Clemens; 15C church of *St. Nikolai* with a Crucifixion group c 1500 over the N door and fine furnishings: high altar, with wings by Jan Joest, 1505–08; altar of the Seven Sorrows of Mary by Heinrich Douvermann, 1519; six other carved altars by the Kalkar school (church museum open daily, 10.00–12.00 and 14.00–17.00). Tourist information at the town hall. Train links with Duisberg and Kleve, buses with other local towns.

At *Kleve* (46,000 inhab.; alt. 46m), 13km NE along the B57, the route rejoins the B9. The town includes the former collegiate church of St. Mariä Himmelfahrt, by Master Konrad of Kleve, 1356; nave and W towers finished 1426 (interior much altered after damage in WWII: Lady altar by Heinrich Douvermann and Jakob Dericke, 1510; 14C to 16C tombs, including that of Graf Arnold II and his wife Ida, 1350); Minorite church, 1440, with stalls of 1474; 15C gothic ruins of the Schwanenburg (*view); a *garden-park created by Johann Moritz Fürst von Nassau, 1656 (frequented by Voltaire); a zoo; and at No. 13 Kabarinerstraße the Haus Koekkoek, the home, 1861–62, of the painter Barend Cornelis Koekkoek (1813–62), housing medieval art, works by Heinrich Dovermann (open save Monday 10.00–13.00 and 14.00–17.00). Tourist information at the town hall. Train connections with Amsterdam, Cologne, Düsseldorf, Kranenburg (on the Dutch border) and Klagenfurt; bus connections with Emmerich Geldern, Goch, Kalkar, Kevelaer and Xanten.

11km E of Kleve along the B9 lies *Kranenburg*, 4km from the Dutch border: gothic pilgrimage church; museum on the Katherinenhof (former Augustinian monastery) and the nearby Pulvertum (15C to 20C art, especially drawings and etchings by Daniel Chodowiecki, 1726–1801; open save Monday, 14.00–17.00; Sunday also 11.00–12.00). The distance from Kranenburg to Amsterdam by way of Nijmegen is 120km.

From Krefeld to Mönchengladbach and Rheydt

From **Krefeld** (see above) the B57 runs SW through Neersen and Neersbroich to reach after 20km the industrial town of **Mönchengladbach** (262,000 inhab.; alt. 50m), an important railway junction whose name derives from a former Benedictine abbey. The former abbey church of St. *Vitus* (Münsterkirche) has a 13C gothic choir, finished 1275, built on a romanesque crypt: 12C romanesque font; late 13C *Bible window in the choir; romanesque altar c 1160, now in the treasury (missal c 1001; open Sundays 10.15–12.15). Other churches include that of Neuwerk, originally 12C, rebuilt early 16C, and in the suburb of *Wickrath* the 12C Protestant church (much rebuilt 17th and 18C). In Wickrath is also an 18th and 19C Schloß. The monastery buildings became the town hall in the early 19C. E of the town is Rheindahlen, the HQ of the British Army of the Rhine and also of NATO (Central and N Europe). The theatre is at No. 73 Hindenburgstraße. The town Museum is at No. 27 Abteistraße (contemporary art, including expressionism, constructivism, neo-realism, Rauschenberg and Warhol; open save Monday, 10.00–18.00). Tourist information at the main railway station.

4km SE of Mönchengladbach the B59 reaches **Rheydt** (110,000 inhab.; alt. 67m), another industrial town, with a renaissance Schloß built 1565–85 on medieval foundations and today housing a cultural and weaving museum (open save Monday, 10.00–18.00; November–February only Wednesday and at weekends, 11.00–17.00). Tourist information at No. 60 Stresemannstraße.

44 From Cologne to Emmerich: the Right Bank of the Rhine

Total distance 153km. **Cologne**—B8 12km **Leverkusen**. —31km
Düsseldorf.—10km *Kaiserswerth.*—17km **Duisburg**.—18km
Dinslaken—15km **Wesel**.—41km *Emmerich*.—9km *Emmerich-Elten*
to the Dutch border (en route to Arnhem).

Leave **Cologne** (see Rte 42) by driving NE along Konrad-Adenauer-
Ufer and then Niederlander-Ufer and left along An der Schanze to
turn right and cross the Rhine by the Mülheimer cable-bridge (by F.
Leonhardt and K. Schüssler, 1949–51) to the important suburb of
Mülheim. Once a Frankish settlement, Mülheim now includes a
harbour; the narrow, tall modernistic church of Our Lady by Rudolf
Schwarz, 1955, glass by Anton Wendling, 1958; the baroque church of
St. Klemens, 1692, restored by Joachim Schürmann after WWII,
bronze doors depicting the saint's life, by Werner Schürmann, 1960;
the church of St. Theresia by Gottfried Böhm, 1955. To the S is the
industrial suburb of *Köln-Deutz* (on the site of a Roman fort, *Castel
Divitia*), now the HQ of the Klöckner-Humboldt-Deutz factories. Here
(in 1864) E. Langen and Nikolaus August Otto founded the Deutz
motor car factory. See also the 100m by 14m and 60m-high administrative offices, the Klöckner-Hochhaus by Hentrich and Petschnigg,
1964, and the church of St. Heribert, 1886, restored (St. Heribert's
shrine, c 1170). Motor Museum at No. 111 Deutz-Mülheimerstraße
(open weekdays, 09.00–16.00).

In 1360 Emperor Karl IV granted Cologne the right to hold two fairs
a year, the start of its present highly successful trade fairs. NW of
Mülheim stand the halls of Cologne's trade fair (85m-high Mess-
eturm; cafés and restaurants; the Rhine park). From Mülheim drive N
along the B8 to reach (15km from Cologne) Leverkusen.

Alternatively, leave **Cologne** by driving to the right bank of the river across the
Deutzer bridge and along the B55 to reach after 15km *Bensberg* (44,000 inhab.;
alt. 162m), dominated by the towers of its ruined 12C Schloß, adapted as the
town hall by Gottfried Böhm (1967), and by the baroque Neues Schloß by Matteo
d'Alberti, 1705–10, under the inspiration of Versailles. 4km N of Bensberg is
Bergisch-Gladbach, after which you drive for another 24km to visit the former
Cistercian **monastery at *Altenberg*: 13C monastery buildings; church founded
12C, rebuilt, 1259–1379, after an earthquake, restored 1895. Interior 77·7m by
19·5m and 28m high; 14C glass; 14C Annunciation; late gothic tabernacle 1480;
Madonna c 1530). The A1 motorway leads back to Cologne by way of
Leverkusen.

Leverkusen (170,000 inhab.; alt. 45m), the home of Bayer AG's dye
factories, welcomed also in 1925 the HQ of its chemical industries
(122m-high Bayer-Bürohaus, 1921). The Schloß is now a modern art
museum (open save Monday, 10.00–17.00). In Kaiser-Wilhelm-Allee
is the Agfa-Gevaert Photography Museum (open weekdays, 09.00–
17.00). Trains connect with Cologne and Düsseldorf, buses with
Cologne and Slingen. Boat trips. The B8 continues through the
industrial town of *Opladen* and on to *Düsseldorf-Benrath* (in its
'English' park and late baroque/rococo *Schloß Benrath* by the French
architect Nicolas de Pigage, 1755–73, who also designed the waterfalls; natural history collection and aviary; (at No. 102 Benrather

Schloßallee, open save Monday, 10.00–17.00; Saturday opens 13.00; November–March restricted opening times).

After 31km the route reaches **DÜSSELDORF**, (590,000 inhab.; alt. 38m), situated at the confluence of the 800m-wide Rhine and the Düssel.

Main *railway station*: Konrad-Adenauer-Platz.

Main *post office*: Konrad-Adenauer-Platz. Other post offices at No. 23 Heinrich-Heine-Allee and at No. 15 Graf-Adolf-Platz.

Information Office: No. 12 Konrad-Adenauer-Platz.

Trains connect with major German cities and with Holland; *buses* with Aachen, Belgium and Holland.

Lohausen international *airport* 6km from city centre, with an Aeroplane and Flight Museum (open March–December. 09.00–19.00).

History. The town developed in the early 12C, by the end of which it belonged to the Graf von Berg, whose descendants became the principle family resident in 1288. The Elector-Palatine Johann Wilhelm II lived here 1679–1716. Napoleon made the city capital of the Grand-Duchy of Berg in 1806. The city became Prussian in 1815. In 1838 the first railway of the Federal Republic ran from Düsseldorf, which led to the expansion of the city's trade and industries. After WWI it was for a time under French occupation. Although 50 per cent of the city was destroyed in WWII, the old city escaped destruction. Heinrich Heine (1797–1856) and the artist Peter von Cornelius (1783–1867) were born in Düsseldorf.

Turn left from Konrad-Adenauer-Platz (in front of the main railway station) and continue W along Graf-Adolf-Straße to Graf-Adolf-Platz, which lies at the S end of Düsseldorf's N–S axis, the *Königsallee, known as the Kö (shops, offices and restaurants), created by C.A. Huschberger in 1804 on the site of the old ramparts and straddling the moat (very late Jugendstil building by J. Olbrich, 1909, now the Maufhof). In the garden here are the statues of a girl playing with a ball (W. Schott, 1932) and the Bergisch Lion (Philipp Harth, 1963).

Continue W from here along Haroldstraße to reach the bank of the Rhine and on the right the tall Mannesman-Hochaus by P. Behrens (1912). Take Berger-Allee N and find on the right the City Museum in the Palais Graf Spee, 1755–70 (entrance at Nos 7–9 Bäckerstraße,

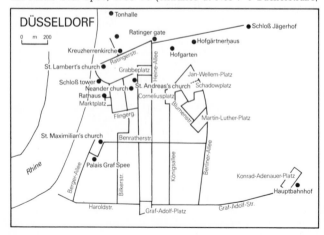

open Wednesday, 12.00–20.00; Tuesday, Thursday and Friday, 10.00–17.00; Saturday 13.00–17.00). From Berger-Allee Citadelle-straße leads N to reach the former Franciscan church of *St. Maximilian* (1734–37; lectern 1450; 18C vestment cabinets and vestments in the sacristy; stuccoed refectory, with frescoes of the life of St. Anthony).

From here Benratherstraße runs E, crossing Königsallee to reach Berliner-Allee. Turn N here and walk to Martin-Luther-Platz, which houses the Ministry of Justice, the Protestant church of St. Johann (1881, restored) and a monument to Bismarck (1889). Blumenstraße leads NW from here to Schadowplatz (bust of the artist Wilhelm von Schadow, director of the art academy at Düsseldorf 1827–46) and the Salinen fountain, by M. Kratz, 1964. N stands Jan-Wellem-Platz (its name derived from the nickname of Kurfürst Johann Wilhelm II, 1658–1716). Königsalle finally ends at Corneliusplatz (basin fountain by L. Müsch, 1882, and a Triton fountain by F. Coubellier, 1902). A subway leads to the Hofgarten, a park of c 26 hectares dating back to Nicolas Pigage, 1767, and enlarged by Maximilian Weyhe, 1813. The garden houses the theatre, the opera, a 26-storey building by H. Hentrich and H. Petschnigg (1959), *Schloß Jägerhof* (1753–63; now an art museum; 20C works, especially Paul Klee; open weekdays, except Monday, 10.00–17.00; Wednesday till 20.00) and the Hofgärtnerhaus (1790; Goethe Museum; open except Monday, 10.00–17.00).

Heine-Allee runs along the W side of the Hofgarten and meets at its N end Ratingerstraße, leading left by way of the classical Ratinger gate (by A. von Vagedes, 1814) to the old city, with its winding narrow (pedestrianised) streets. On the right of Ratingerstraße is the 15C gothic *Kreuzherrenkirche* (now part of the nearby Art Academy Museum, at No. 5 Ehrenhof, in a complex running N along the river bank that includes the domed Tonhalle, by W. Kreis, 1925; open save Monday, 10.00–17.00). On the opposite side of Ratingerstraße, just before the river bank, stands the church of St. Lambert (13th and 14C: Italian baroque interior, 1650–1712; late gothic tabernacle; renaiss-ance tomb by Gerhard Scheben, 1599; stucco; main doors by Ewald Mataré, 1960). S of this church, in Burgplatz, is the 12C Schloß tower (the rest of the Schloß was burned down in 1872); further S in Marktplatz is the town hall (1961; façade, 1573, by Heinrich Tussmann). In front of the town hall is the baroque equestrian statue of Kurfürst Johann Wilhelm II by Gabriel de Grupello (1711). No. 12 Marktplatz carries a Glockenspiel. On the corner with Zollstgraße (gabled houses) is a fountain by W. Hoselmann, 1932; Grupello lived in the 18C house opposite.

From Marktplatz take Flingergasse and Shneider-Wibbel-Gasse back into the Altstadt to reach Bilkerstraße where at No. 53 Heinrich Heine was born in 1797. (The Heinrich Heine Institute, open Wednesday–Sunday, 10.00–17.00 is at No. 14 Bilkerstraße). The Neander church, 1683–87, is named after the Protestant hymnologist Joachim Neander (1650–80). Take on the left Hunrückerstraße to reach the Italian baroque church of St. Andreas, 1620–29: mausoleum of seven members of the Neuburg family, 1667 (Johann Wilhelm II's tomb with a portrait medallion by Grupello); altar by Ewald Mataré, 1959). Opposite the main door is a column with a statue of St. Martin by R. Graner (1965). The former art gallery, destroyed in WWII, has supplied the caryatids by L. Müsch (1880), between the church and the modern art gallery (at No. 4 Grabenplatz, open save Monday, 10.00–18.00; Friday–Sunday closes 20.00).

Other Düsseldorf churches include the romanesque *Alt-St. Martin*, c 1160, to the S of the city in the suburb of *Düsseldorf-Bilk*, with 13C frescoes; side-aisles rebuilt in 1881; and the church of *St. Margareta* in the suburb of *Gerresheim*, finished 1236, with the former convent cloisters and a crucifix c 980.

The Altstadt is packed for festivals on the Monday before Lent and on 10 November.

In the suburb of *Kaiserswerth*, 10km NW along the B8, is the 11C and 12C *Barbarossapfalz*, ruined in 1702 in the War of the Spanish Succession, and the *collegiate church*, founded c 700, rebuilt as a 12C romanesque basilica and housing the golden shrine of St. Suitbertus.

17km further along the B8 is **DUISBERG** (570,000 inhab.; alt. 31m), birthplace of the geographer Gerhard Mercator (1512–94) and the sculptor Wilhelm Lehmbruck (1881–1919), chief port for the Ruhr and the world's largest river port. From the main railway station follow Friedrich-Wilhelm-Straße E, passing on the left the Lower Rhine Museum (at No. 64: Mercator rooms, open save Monday, 10.00–17.00; Wednesday closes 16.00; Sunday opens 11.00) and the Wilhelm-Lehmbruck Museum (entrance at No. 51 Düsseldorferstraße; works by Wilhelm Lehmbruck and 20C sculpture; open Tuesday and Friday, 14.00–22.00; otherwise, except Monday, 10.00–17.00). At the end of Friedrich-Wilhelm-Straße turn N to reach Salvatorkirchplatz and the 13th to early 15C Salvator church (restored 1903–04 and after WWII), housing Mercator's tomb. Return E along Gutenberg-Straße and Kohnenstraße to the Burgplatz: town hall, 1897–1902; theatre; Mercatorhalle concert and congress hall, 1962; Mercator monument.

Zoo on the Kaiserberg (including dolphins and whales). Sports stadia. Tourist information at No. 96 Friedrich-Wilhelm-Straße. Trains connect with Dinslaken, Wesel, and Walsum, buses with Krefeld, and Kevelaer. Boat trips.

The B8 continues N through the suburb of *Duisburg-Hamborn* (romanesque church of a Premonstratensian abbey, 1170), reaching after 18km Dinslaken (62,000 inhab.; alt. 30m): remains of medieval walls; 15C church of St. Vincentius; Protestant parish church 1722; 15C Crucifixion group (Kalvarienberg); Burg theatre, 1722; local history museum (at No. 31 Brückstraße; open save Monday, 09.00–12.00 and 14.00–17.00; closed Sunday).

After another 15km the B8 reaches **Wesel** (61,000 inhab.; alt. 27m) at the confluence of the Lippe and the Rhine. Despite enormous destruction in WWII Wesel preserves of its old defences the Zitadelle gate, 1718, and the Berlin gate, 1722, as well as the church of St. Willibrord, a 15th and 16C gothic church on the base of a romanesque basilica. Wesel has a monument to Peter Minuit, who left for America in 1586, where he founded New York and Wilmington, Delaware. Theatre: Stadtisches Bühnenhaus in Martinistraße. Museum at No. 14 Ritterstraße (gold and silver ware; open weekdays, 10.00–20.15; Saturday, 10.00–13.00).

Finally the B8 reaches Rees and Emmerich. *Rees*, 24km NW of Wesel, preserves from its 13C walls the Mühlenturm and the Toelder gate and a bastion on the riverside. Protestant parish church of 1624 was restored after WWII). 17km NE of Rees is *Emmerich* (30,000 inhab.; alt. 19m), close by the Dutch border (crossing point) and the chief customs point for German shipping, dealing annually with 200,000 vessels. Almost totally destroyed in WWII, Emmerich now boasts the longest suspension bridge in Germany, the restored church of St. Aldigond, 1483 (91m-high tower, ascent and *view) and the restored church of *St. Martin* (11C crypt; crucifix, c 1200; 12C wall paintings; stalls, 1486; in the treasury the chest-reliquary of St. Willibrord, 11C and 15C). Shipping Museum, at No. 2 Martinikirch-gang (open Tuesday and Wednesday 10.00–12.00 and 14.00–16.00; Thursday open till 18.00; Friday and Saturday, 10.00–12.00). Tourist information at the town hall. Train connections with Cologne and Amsterdam. Bus connections with Holland. Boats cross the Rhine.

For the road to Arnhem, *Emmerich-Elten* (9km NE along the B8) is the border crossing: 93m-high Hohenberg; 57m-deep Roman well ('the Drususbrunnen'); and romanesque St. Vitus church, once belonging to a late 10C abbey. Bus connections with Emmerich and Holland.

45 The Ruhr

Total distance 90km. **Duisburg**—B60 9km **Mülheim an der Ruhr**.—B224 6km **Oberhausen**.—A430 18km **Essen**.—B224 20km **Gelsenkirchen**.—B226 19km **Bochum**.—B1 18km **Dortmund**.

To visit the populous industrial Ruhr (German Ruhrgebiet) leave its Rhine port, **Duisburg** (see Rte 44), E by the B60, travelling through the Sobald parkland to reach after 9km **Mülheim an der Ruhr** (980,000 inhab.; alt. 37m), where seven bridges cross the River Ruhr with its wide promenades. Mülheim is dominated by *Schloß Broich* (12C, with 18C alterations) lying on the left of the road from Duisburg as it approaches the Schloßbrücke to cross to the centre of the town. Across the river to the right of Schloßstraße is the old quarter of the town with the church of St. Peter (15C and 19C), and, amongst other 18C houses, No. 1 Tersteegen, the house in which the religious poet Gerhard Tersteegen (1698–1769) died. The town has a number of 13C towers and the gate of a 13C Schloß. At No. 1 Leineweberstraße is the Museum (open save Monday, 10.00–12.30 and 15.00–18.00; closes Thursday at 21.00).

From Mülheim the B224 leads N for 6km to **Oberhausen** (234,000 inhab.; alt. 37m), a town founded around the 1847 railway station in a region of 18C mines, deriving its name from Schloß Overhus (now *Schloß Oberhauses*, which houses the town's collection of contemporary art, open, save Monday, weekdays, 10.00–13.00 and 14.00–17.00; weekends, 10.00–17.00). In the suburb of *Osterfeld*, N of the town centre, is the moated *Schloß Vondern*, part 16C, part 17C. Information Office in Berlinerplatz.

The A430 leads 18km E to **ESSEN** (660,000 inhab.; alt. 108m), the fifth largest city in the German Federal Republic and an important industrial centre. The S part of the city has avoided industrial expansion.

Am Haputbahnhof, in front of the 1964 main railway station, houses the main post office (1935) and the Haus der Technik (1926). From here the 450m-long pedestrianised Kettwiger Straße (boutiques and shops) bisects the city: at No. 22 a Glockenspiel with moving figures. On the left of Kettwiger Straße is Theaterplatz and further along on the right Burgplatz, with the episcopal palace (bronze doors by Ewald Mataré), the gothic church of *St. Johann Baptist* (founded 946, reaching its present form in 1471, with a 17C baroque interior: font c

1600, an altar by Barthel Bruyn 1525, and the altar of St. Georg (1770), and the ***Münster**. A cathedral only since 1958 when Pius XII set up the diocese, the Münster (dedicated to SS. Maria, Cosmas and Damien) was founded c 850 and rebuilt in the 11–13C, the main work being late gothic, 1276–1327, after a fire of 1275. The romanesque W end and the crypt (14C tomb of Bishop Altfried of Hildesheim, died 874) remain from the older building. The treasury has 10th and 11C gold treasures (11C *Theophanu cross; open save Monday, 10.00–15.30). In the atrium, which connects the cathedral with the church of St. Johann Baptist, is a wooden crucifix, c 1400. Interior: late 11C *golden Madonna; seven-branched candelabrum, c 1100; glass by H. Campendonck, 1953.

In front of the church of St. Johann Baptist is Kurienplatz (fountain and garden), leading into Kennedyplatz (statue G. Kolbe, 1914). From the church Kettwiger Straße leads to the Markt, with an 11C church badly damaged in WWII (bronze doors by H. Schardt, 1963) and a statue of Alfred Krupp (1898). E of the Markt is Porscheplatz, laid out in 1954 and containing the town hall (by Theodor Seifert, 1972). The domed former synagogue by Edmund Körner (1911–13), lies on the S side of Porscheplatz (transformed inside in 1961 to house an industrial museum, with documents on Jewish history and the resistance to Hitler, open 10.00–17.00, Sunday closes 18.00).

S of the main railway station lies the city garden, with a lake, the city concert hall and the Städtischer Saalbau (congress centre and concert hall). SW at Nos 64–66 Bismarckstraße is the Museum Folkwang built 1960 (19th and 20C French and German art as well as the regional museum and posters from 1875, open save Monday, 10.00–18.00). Bismarckstraße leads (by car) to the Grugapark, built for the garden exhibition of 1929, enlarged 1965, housing the Grugahalle (exhibition hall of 1958). S lies the Stadwald (ornithological park) and to the E the Schellenberger Wald with the 16th and 17C Schloß Schellenberg and restaurants. Further S by way of Alfredstraße (continuation of Bismarckstraße) stands *Villa Hügel*, above the 8km-long Baldeney lake (water sports), built by Alfred Krupp, 1869–73 and the home of the Krupp Art Gallery (open save Monday, 10.00–18.00). SW of Villa Hügel is the suburb of Essen-Werden, with the Catholic priory of *St. Ludger*, whose church was founded 796 and stands today a romanesque bulding of 1156–75 with baroque furnishings of the early 18C. The treasury houses a 5C pyx and the bronze Helmsted crucifix of 1060. Heckstraße is the church of *St. Lucius*, 995–1003, with 15C alterations (restored 1965).

Tourist information for Essen and district at No. 1 Hollestraße.

The B224 leads for 20km NE to **Gelsenkirchen** by way of Bottrop (parish church of the Holy Cross 1957, and the 'Dreamland' fun park) and Gladbeck (13C moated Schloß Wittringen). Gelsenkirchen (310,000 inhab.; alt. 54m) on the Rhein-Herne canal is an important inland harbour and mining town, with fine parks, a concert hall and theatre of 1960 (in Kennedyplatz), the 16C and 18C Schloß Berge (in its park with the Berger lake). At Gelsenkirchen is the Ruhr zoo, a lion park (in Westerholter Wald, E of the town), the ruined, moated Schloß Horst, 1570, and in the suburb of Buer an art collection (at Nos 5–7 Horster Straße, open except Monday, 10.00–13.00 and 15.00–18.00). Information office in Rathausplatz.

From Gelsenkirchen take the B226 for 19km S to the university city of **Bochum** (430,000 inhab.; alt. 104m). The Schauspielhaus is the home of the city symphony orchestra, founded 1919. The priory church of *SS. Peter and Paulus* in Brückstraße has a 14C tower and 16C nave with a 12C carved romanesque font and a Lamentation of c 1530. At No. 191 Dr-C.-Otto-Straße is a Railway Museum (open March–November, Wednesday and Friday, 10.00–17.00), and at Am Bergbaumuseum a *Mining Museum (open weekdays save Monday, 08.30–17.30, weekends, 10.00–12.00). The University Art Gallery at No. 150 Universitätsstraße, opens Tuesday–Friday, 12.00–15.00 and weekends, 10.00–18.00, the City Art Gallery, at No. 147 Korumstraße, is open weekdays except Monday, 10.00–20.00, weekends, 10.00–18.00). Haus Kemnade is a moated Schloß (renaissance fireplaces; local history museum; open Wednesday–Friday, 13.00–19.00; weekends, 11.00–18.00). The city has a festival on 30 April. Tourist information in the railway station.

From Bochum the B51 leads N for 7km to **Herne** (188,000 inhab.; alt. 59m) situated on the Dortmund-Ems canal and the Rhein-Herne canal: moated 17C renaissance *Schloß Strünkede* (museum open daily except Monday, 10.00–13.00 and 14.00–17.00); thermal baths; festival at the beginning of August. Information at the town hall.
 The B51 continues NW for another 9km to reach **Recklinghausen** (120,000 inhab.; alt. 76m), once a member of the Hanseatic League and in the late 8C an imperial court of Charlemagne, the plans of whose city can still be seen in the central pattern of streets. Here is the 13C and 16C church of St. Petrus (tabernacle c 1520) and the nearby *Icon Museum (at No. 2a Kirchplatz; open save Monday, 10.00–18.00, Sunday, 11.00–13.00 and 15.00–18.00); the 1701 Engelsburg; the Kunsthalle, a former WWII bunker; the city garden with a Henry Moore statue in front of the 1965 Festspielhaus (at Nos 25–27 Große Perdekampstraße. Open as the icon museum). Tourist information office at No. 23 Kuniberstraße.
 Not far from Recklinhausen is the Hohe Mark nature reserve.
From Bochum the B1 leads for 18km E to **Dortmund** (see Rte 55).

46 Münster and Environs

A. Münster

MÜNSTER (270,000 inhab.; alt. 62m) lies on the River Aa and the Münster canal and is the chief city of Westphalia.

Main *railway station*: Bahnhofstraße (also a post office here.

Main *post office*: Domplatz.

Information Office: No. 22 Berliner Platz.

Trains to all major cities. *Buses* connect with Münsterland.

History. Charlemagne set up a bishopric here c 800, after the Friesian missionary Ludger had founded a monastery. Around it developed a settlement that was granted its civic charter in the 12C. The city became a member of the Hanseatic League. At the time of the Reformation it was a noted centre of Anabaptists (led by Jan van Leyden, his step-father Bernard Knipperdolling and Nernhard Krechting), who were put to death in 1535. Here (and in Osnabrück) was signed the peace of Westphalia which brought an end to the Thirty Years' War. The city university was founded in 1780. Münster became French and then Prussian in the early 19C. 90 per cent of its Altstadt was destroyed in WWII (67 per cent of the rest of the city). Clemens August von Galen, Bishop of Münster from 1933 to 1946, was a noted opponent of the Nazis.

To see Münster's oldest church take Bahnhofstraße N from the main railway station and continue along Eisenbahnstraße as far as Mauritztor, E of which (on St. Mauritz-Freihet) is the collegiate church of _St. Mauritz_ (chapel and three towers, c 1070, the W tower capped by baroque dome, 1709). Return to the station, from which Windhorststraße leads NW and crosses Klosterstraße, along which (right) is the Servatorkirche (part mid 13C, part c 1500, restored and altered 18C: late 15C Lady altar). Continue along Klosterstraße, passing on the left the rococo church of St. Klemens (1754; by Johann Conrad Schlaun) and turn left into Salzstraße to find the baroque Erbdrostenhof (1753–57; also by J.C. Schlaun). followed by the former Dominican church (now the university Catholic chapel; baroque, by L.F. von Corfey, 1725, restored). Continue along Salzstraße to find on the right the 14C (restored) *Lambertikirche (main door 15C; Jesse tree on S door; tower, reconstructed 1898, with three cages in which the corpses of the three leading Anabaptists were displayed). Behind the church (in Alter Steinweg) is the former grocers' guild house, the brick-built Kameramtshaus, 1588 (restored 1951).

Turn right from Salzstraße along Prinzipalmarkt into Roggenmarkt. From here walk along Neubrückenstraße NE to find (left) the 13C to 17C church of SS. Aposteln (gothic and early renaissance decoration) and (right) the theatre, by H. Deilmann, P.O. Rave and M. von Hausen, 1956, close by which is the gothic church of St. Martin (romanesque tower—fourth storey 15C with a baroque top of 1760). Near this church (in Hörsterstraße) is J.C. Schlaun's convent chapel of 1772. Return to Salzstraße and find left of the church of St. Lambert the PRINZIPALMARKT, with its arcades and gabled houses, the renaissance 'wine house', by J. von Bocholt 1615, and the 14C gothic *Town Hall (open weekdays, 09.00–17.00, Saturday closes 16.00, Sunday, 10.00–13.00: the Friedensaal, furnished as in 1577; portraits of those present for the signing of the peace of Westphalia in 1648, panelling

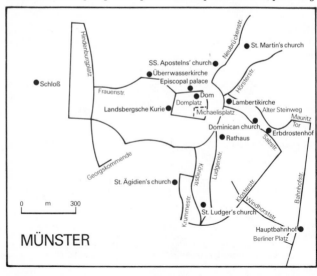

and chandelier, 1577; fireplaces), both restored after WWII.

Leave the town hall and turn into Domplatz where stands the twin-towered **Cathedral**, a romanesque and gothic basilica, built 1172–1265. In the narthex, 13C *statues of the Apostles, with a frieze showing secular events; 1622 reliquary by G. Gröninger; altar c 1520 and a wall painting by Hermann tom Ring, 1590, in the E transept; *astronomical clock, 1420, with performing figures at 12.00 (Sunday 12.30); marble tomb of Bishop C. von Galen, died 1678; modern glass by Max Ingrand. The 14C cloister has a Lady chapel (Marienkapelle), 1390, with an 11C crucifix; in the chapel of the Holy Sacrament, 1667, a tabernacle by M. Gröninger (1540); chapterhouse panelling by Ludger tom Ring the Elder (1590). The cathedral treasury houses *liturgical vestments.

On the W side of Domplatz the early 18C Landsbergsche Kurie houses the University Geological and Palaeontological Museum (open weekdays, 09.00–12.30 and 13.00–17.00). S of Domplatz at No. 10 is the provincial Museum (open save Monday, 10.00–18.00). Here too is situated the episcopal palace of 1732, opposite which is a monument, 1978, to Bishop Clemens August von Galen (1878–1946, see above). Left of the episcopal palace Spiegel-Turm leads to the gothic church of Our Lady, known as the Überwasserkirche, 1340–60, early 15C tower (votive tablet at the entrance by Ludger tom Ring the Elder, 1548; baroque altar painting by M. Kappers, 1763; font by W. Gröninger, c 1720). From here walk along Fruenstraße and cross Hindenburgplatz to reach the baroque Schloß, by J.C. Schlaun, 1767–73, now the main university building. Behind the Schloß is the city botanical garden.

Take from here the Promenade S to the water sports centre on the 40 hectares Aa lake, SW of which is the zoo (1974; dolphinarium). Continue along Promenade, turning left along Ludgeristraße as far as the church of St. Ludger (12C and 13C; high altar 1961; glass 1968). By way of Königstraße (at No. 5 the late 18C Druffelscher Hof and at No. 47 the Heermannscher Hof of 1564) and Krummestraße reach the church of St. Ägidien, by J.C. Schlaun, 1724–29 (font by A. Reining, 1557; *baroque pulpit by J.W. Gröninger, c 1720; mid 19C wall paintings by E. Steinle).

OTHER MUSEUMS: Museum Hans Rüschhaus, at No. 81 Am Rüschhaus, in a building by J.C. Schlaun, 1745–48 (open daily, 09.30–12.00 and 14.30–17.00); Bible Museum at No. 7 Georgskommende (open Wednesday, 11.00–13.00; Thursday, 17.00–19.00; and the first Saturday in the month, 10.00–13.00).

10km W is the 16C moated Haus Hülshoff, the birthplace and home of the poet Annette von Droste-Hülshoff (1797–1848), now the Droste-Museum, open save Monday, 09.00–12.00 and 14.30–17.00). Between 1826 and 1841 she lived at the baroque Schloß Rüschhaus (2km NE in the suburb of Münster-Nienberge), built by Schlaun, 1749–49.

B. West of Münster: to Emmerich and to Gronau

Münster to Emmerich

Total distance 122km. **Münster**—B51 and B67 37km **Coesfeld**.—27km **Borken**.—18km *Bocholt*.—13km *Isselburg*.—10km *Rees*.—17km **Emmerich**.

Leave **Münster** (see Rte above) in the direction of Cologne by the B51 to reach the B67 at Appelhülsen after 17km. From here the B67 runs NW for 6km to *Nottuln* (15C monastery church and monastic buildings). Continue for 14km W to Coesfeld, passing on the right the highest peak of the Baumberge, the *Westerburg* (tower, 189m).

Coesfeld (32,000 inhab.; alt. 81m) was a Hanseatic town and retains vestiges of its medieval fortifications (the Walkenbrücher gate and the Pulver tower, both 14C). In the church of St. *Lambert* (partly romanesque, mostly 1473–1524; W end and tower 1703) is the gothic Coelsfeld cross, early 15C, carried in procession through the town on Whit Monday, and statues of the apostles by J. Düsseldorp, 1506–20. Other churches include the baroque Jesuit church and St. Jakob (destroyed WWII, rebuilt 1949, retaining a 13C *doorway and remnants of the previous furnishings, including a mid 13C font and an altar c 1520). Old houses survived the war, chiefly in Mühlenstraße and Welkenbrückerstraße. Local history museums at No. 10 Bahnhofsallee (visits only by previous arrangement) and in Letterstraße (open Sundays, 11.00–12.30). 5km N is the 18C Schloß Varlar.

25km along the B67 lies *Gemen* (15C and 17C Schloß) followed 2km S by *Borken*, with towers surviving from its medieval walls, and the church of St. *Remigius* (lower part of W tower mid 12C, rest mid 15C: romanesque font, late 12C; 14C crucifix; 15C Entombment). Local history museum in the church of the Holy Spirit, 1404, badly damaged in WWII (Heilig-Geist-Straße; open Sundays, 10.30–12.00). —6km due S of Borken is *Raesfeld*, with a mid 17C renaissance Schloß.

Continue W from Borken along the B67 to reach after 18km *Bocholt* (70,000 inhab.; alt. 26m), an industrial town on the River Aa: gothic church of St. Georg, 1415–86; Dutch renaissance *Town Hall 1618–21, restored 1928–34; both restored after bombing on 22 March 1945 destroyed virtually the whole town. Art gallery in the New Town Hall, at No. 1 Berlinerplatz (open daily, 10.00–13.00 and 15.00–18.00). *Tourist information* at No. 22 Europaplatz. After 13km the route reaches *Isselburg*, situated on the River Issel, with vestiges of its old fortifications. 3km NW is *Anholt* (administratively linked to Isselburg), whose moated Schloß has a 12C keep, other buildings 14th and 15C (staircase tower), the rest redone as Dutch renaissance in the 17C; 18C park. Inside, tapestries by L. van Schoor and paintings (including works by Rembrandt; open April–September, 10.00–18.00).

The road now leads by way of Rees for 17km to **Emmerich** (see Rte 44) and the Dutch border.

Münster to Gronau

Total distance 62km. **Münster**—B57 38km **Burgsteinfurt**.—24km *Gronau*.

The B54 leaves **Münster** (see Rte 46A) and runs NW for 7km to Nienberge, 1·5km SW of which is *Schloß Rüschhaus* (see p 233). After another 23km NW along the B54 the route reaches *Burgsteinfurt* (32,000 inhab.; alt. 50m), with the *Schloß* of the Fürsten zu Bentheim-Steinfurt, the largest moated Schloß in the region, built 16C to 18C on two islands of the River Aa, and incorporating remains of an earlier Schloß, especially the 12C romanesque chapel and the 13C knights' hall and tower-gate; renaissance oriel by Johann Brabender (known as Beldensnyder). SE is the 'Bagno', an 18C park. The Rathaus of

Bursteinfurt dates from 1561. Churches include the 15C Große Kirche and the neo-gothic church of St. Nikomedes (1885, replacing one founded in 968); inside, romanesque altar candlesticks, and the 11C *Heinrich Cross, whose ornaments include the bust of Emperor Heinrich II.

After 12km the B54 runs through *Ochtrup* (monastic buildings and 13C monastery church), which lies 12km from *Gronau* (26,000 inhab.; alt. 42m): textiles, nature reserves; the Dutch border.

From Ochtrup the B403 runs N for 28km by way of *Bad Bentheim* (thermal baths; 15C Schloß Bentheim, with a 12C Crucifixion on its S terrace), and a further 28km to *Nordhorn* (at the confluence of the Ems-Vechte and Süd-Nord canals. The B213 runs from here for 4km to the Dutch border (179km from Amsterdam.

From Bad Bentheim the B65 runs NE for 23km to **Rheine** (72,000 inhab.; alt. 40m): 15C gothic parish church of St. Dionysius; 16C Falkenhof; basilica of St. Antonius, with a 116m-high tower.

C. East of Münster: to Paderborn and from Herford to Dortmund

Münster to Paderborn

Total distance 90km. **Münster**—B51 12km *Telgte.*—B64 15km *Warendorf.*—24km *Rheda.*—3km *Weidenbrück.*—9km *Rietberg.*—12km **Delbrück.**—11km *Neuhaus.*—4km **Paderborn**.

Leave **Münster** (see Rte 46A) by the B51 and drive E for 12km to *Telgte* (16,500 inhab.; alt. 56m) on the River Ems: pilgrimage chapel, 1647, with a 14C Pietà; priory church of 1522 (19C tower; inside the church a 15C Madonna and a carving of Jesus, c 1200); local history museum in the 1600 parsonage (later extended; open save Monday, 09.30–12.30 and 13.30–17.30), with a collection that includes a Lenten veil of 1623 with 33 panels, incorporating scenes of Christ's Passion). The B64 leads SE from Telgte to reach *Warendorf* (34,000 inhab.; alt. 56m), a former Hanseatic town noted for its horses (stud farm; olympic riding committee; army sports school): gothic church of St. Laurentius, 1404 (*high altar painted early 15C). Town Hall, 1404 (one of several 15C and 16C houses, housing the local history museum (open weekdays save Monday, 15.00–17.00; weekends, 10.30–12.30).

—4km S is *Warendorf-Freckenhorst*, with a romanesque *church from a former convent.

The B64 continues SW by way of *Herzebock* (whose abbey was founded in 860) reaching after 24km *Rheda* (moated Schloß of the Fürsten von Bentheim-Tecklenburg-Rheda, 17th and 18C; Kapellen tower early 13C). 3km SW is *Wiedenbrück* (administratively combined with Rheda), which has numerous half-timbered houses, especially in Mönchstraße and Langenstraße. See also the oddly built *Marienkirche* (19m wide, only 13m long, built 1470), and the collegiate church of St. Ägidien, c 1500, 19C choir and tower (late gothic font, tabernacle 1504, early 17C sandstone pulpit).

The road runs NE and then E from Wiedenbrück for 9km to *Rietberg* (half-timbered houses, including the Town Hall; baroque church of St. Johann Nepomuk, by Johann Conrad Schlaun, 1747–48), and then turns SE again reaching *Delbrück* after another 12km (half-timbered houses, 14C pilgrimage church). After another 11km the B64 reaches *Neuhaus*, at the confluence of the Rivers Pader, Alme and Lippe (renaissance Schloß Neuhaus, c 1600, with a monumemt to the discoverer of morphium, Friedrich Sertürner, born here 1783 (died 1841) and now housing part of Paderborn City Art Gallery (open save Monday, 15.00–18.00; Sunday also 10.00–13.00).

4km SW lies **PADERBORN** (115,000 inhab.; alt. 119m), situated on the River Pader between the Eggegebirge and the Teutoburg woods. 200 springs created the river, flowing as five streams through the city and meeting outside.

History. Paderborn was the seat of a bishopric as early as 806 (an archbishopric since 1930). Charlemagne's first Saxon Diet was held here, and he met Pope Leo III at Paderborn in 799 to arrange his coronation in Rome the following year. The city was walled in 1180, was a member of the Hanseatic League in the 13th and 14Cs and founded its university in 1614. Paderborn hosts an eight-day fair beginnning on the Saturday after 23 July.

Tourist information at No. 2 Marienplatz. Train connections with all major towns.

From the main railway station Bahnhofstraße leads by way of Westernstraße to Marienplatz (at No. 2 the early 17C Heisinghaus, gabled, with carved figures). From here Jühengasse leads to Jesuitenmauer and the baroque Jesuit church, 1682–84, restored after WWII. The route continues from Marienplatz to Rathausplatz, housing the theatre and the *Town Hall, 1613–20 (here is also the natural history museum, open save Monday, 10.00–18.00; closes Sunday 13.00). The pedestrianised Schildern leads NE by way of shops to the Domplatz.—Alternatively reach Domplatz by the Markt, with the 12C romanesque church of *St. Ulrich*, known as the Gaukirche: 14C crucifix; Madonna, 1420; Calvary relief, c 1450. In Domplatz stands the 13C gothic **cathedral**, rebuilt after numerous fires (the first in 1058), with a romanesque W tower, late romanesque N door, a paradise doorway on the S side sculpted c 1250 as well as remains of the sculpted Brautportal, gothic cloisters (16C glass depicting three hares, and the Westphalian chapel, with the *tomb of Wilhelm von Westfalen, died 1517). Inside: capitals developing from late romanesque to gothic; 12C crypt with the reliquary of St. Liborius, a romanesque cross and stone tombs; tomb of Bishop Dietrich von Fürstenberg, 1618; late gothic reliquary altar in the choir, c 1440. Close by the N side of the cathedral is the chapel of *St. Bartholomäus*, built by Bishop Meinwerk c 1070 and the oldest hall church in Germany. The Imperial Palace which stood N of the cathedral has been excavated by Professor W. Winkelmann (1964–70): oldest parts 8C, restored parts 11C, with a museum in der Kaiserpfalz (open save Monday, 10.00–17.00). NE of the cathedral in Michaelstraße stands the baroque Michaelkloster.

Other important churches in the city are the Franciscan *St. Josef* in Westernstraße (1668–71; baroque façade by A. Petrini) and in Abdinghof, the *Alexis chapel*, a rotunda of 1673, and the 11C church of *SS. Petrus and Paulus* (crypt). Here are also half-timbered houses and the City Art Gallery (No. 11; open save Monday, 10.00–18.00, closes Sunday 13.00). In Am Busdorf are the collegiate church and cloister founded by Bishop Meinwerk in 1036. The Diocesan Museum is at No. 17 Markt (open save Monday, 10.00–17.00); the City History Museum at Nos 7–9 Hathumarstraße (open save Monday, 10.00–18.00, closes Sunday 13.00).

Herford to Dortmund

Total distance 113km. **Herford**—B61 15km **Bielefeld**.—17km
Gütersloh.—9km *Wiedenbrück*.—14km *Beckum*.—19km
Hamm.—14km *Kamen*.—11km *Lünen* (**Cappenberg-Selm** close
by).—B54 14km **Dortmund**.

Herford (68,000 inhab.; alt. 71m), situated at the confluence of the Aa
and the Werre, a former Hanseatic city whose present prosperity
derives chiefly from furniture and textiles, boasts an Altstadt that
grew up around a convent founded in the 8C and a Neustadt founded
c 1220. The 13C *Münster* of the former convent has a 16C late gothic
font, romanesque capitals and gothic tracery in its windows. Close by
the Münster are the 14C *Jakobikirche* (woodcarvings) and the 13th
and 14C Johanniskirche (stained glass c 1300, with a Crucifixion
window of 1520, as well a fine furnishings). Houses include at No. 4
Höckerstraße the *Bürgermeisterhaus*, built 1583, birthplace in 1662 of
the baroque architect Matthäus Daniel Pöppelmann; at No. 6
Brüderstraße the half-timbered *Riemenschneider Haus* of 1521. W of
the Altstadt in the former village of Berg is 14C the collegiate church
of Our Lady (*Marienkirche*), which houses a Madonna c 1340 and a
gothic reliquary altar. The City Museum is at No. 2 Deichtorwall
(romanesque to baroque sculpture; open Tuesday, Thursday, and
Friday, 10.00–13.00 and 15.00–17.00; Wednesday, 15.00–18.00;
weekends, 10.00–13.00). Tourist information at No. 16 Fürstenstraße;
good train service; bus links with Bielefeld, Bünde and Detmold.

9km W of Herford lies *Enger* (18,000 inhab.; alt. 94m) whose 12C and 14C
collegiate church houses a sculpted wooden altar c 1525 and the 14C sarcophagus of Witikind (11C grave-slab), the Saxon adversary of Charlemagne
who submitted in 785 and was baptised at Attigny-sur-Aisne.

The B61 leads SW for 15km through hilly country with wild boar
hunting, approaching the peaks of the Teutoberg forest, on the N side
of which is the industrial and university town of **BIELEFELD** (315,000
inhab.; alt. 118m). The twin-towered *Neustädter Kirche* stands in
Kreuzstraße on the S side of the Aldstadt; finished in 1330 and
restored after WWII, it has remains of the early 14C choir screen; a
gothic altar painted by the artist of the Crucifixion altar in the
Marienkirche, Dortmund (see Rte 55); 14th and 15C tombs, especially
the 14C tomb of Count Otto III. The 16C *Spiegelfhof* is also in
Kreuzstraße. In the Altstadt, in Postgang, stands the Marienkirche
(the Altstädter Kirche) with a 16C gothic *altar. Close by this church is
the renaissance Town Hall and the fountain of the linen weavers
(1909). At No. 1 Obernstraße is the gothic Crüwelhaus (1530). In
Obernstraße stands also the church of St. Jakobus (1511; with a Black
Madonna c 1220). On the Sparrenburg is a restored 13C Schloß
(37m-high watch-tower). In the Markt are the renaissance Batig Haus
of 1680 and the theatre.
  Bielefeld has a botanical garden and animal reserve. Museums
include one at No. 9 Kantensieck (visits by prior arrangement)
dedicated to the celebrated Protestant Pastors von Bodelschwingh—
Friedrich, 1831–1910; Fritz, 1877–1946 and Friedrich the Younger,
1902–77—founders and fosterers of the German inner mission Bethel
homes, begun by Friedrich the Elder, 1887, and today housing 8000
incurables. There is also the Nauernhaus Museum, at No. 82 Dornber-
ger Straße, focussing on farming from the 16C to 19C (open save
Monday, 10.00–13.00 and 15.00–18.00; November–March, 10.00–

13.00 and 14.00–17.00); the Kulturhistorisches Museum (at No. 61 Welle), housing a collection of porcelain and silver (open save Monday, 09.00–12.00 and 15.00–18.00; Sunday, 10.00–13.00); and the Town Art Gallery, at No. 5 Artur-Ladebeck-Straße (built 1966–68), especially expressionist and cubist art (open save Monday, 11.00–18.00).

Tourist information at No. 6 Am Bahnhof and at No. 47 Bahnhofstraße.

The B61 continues SW, crossing the B68 (Osnabrück-Paderborn) after 3km and reaching Gütersloh 9km later. *Gütersloh* (50,000 inhab.; alt. 94m) is a centre of the German publishing and silk industry; half-timbered houses. 9km SE the route reaches *Wiedenbrück* (see p 235). En route to Beckum, which lies on the B61 24km SW of Wiedenbrück, is *Oelde-Stromberg*, at 156m the highest place in Münsterland and boasting a ruined medieval Schloß and the church of the Holy Cross, 1344. *Beckum* (40,000 inhab.; alt. 110m) has inside its parish church of *St. Stephanus* (14C to 16C) the *shrine of St. Prudentia, 1240, and a 13C octagonal font.

Hamm (179,000 inhab.; alt. 63m), 19km SW of Beckun, is the westernmost part of the Ruhr and an important iron manufacturing community. The suburb Bad Hamm is a health resort (thermal baths, congress hall and a Kurpark). The Gustav-Lübcke Museum, at No. 2 Museumstraße (open except Monday, 10.00–16.00; closes Sunday 13.00), houses works of art from Greek to modern times. Tourist information in Bahnhofsplatz. Trains connect with Dortmund and Soest, buses with local towns.

At *Kamen* (45,000 inhab.; alt. 62), 15km SW along the B61, is the classical *Pauluskirche*, 1844–49, built on romanesque foundations and incorporating a 12C tower capped in the 14C. The B61 continues to *Lünen*, close by which at *Cappenberg-Selm* is the 13C romanesque *church* (late 14C gothic vault) of a former Premonstratensian monastery: 12C Cappenberg crucifix; gothic tomb of the founders (Gottfried and Otto von Cappenberg), c 1330; choir stalls, 1509–20; in the treasury gold-plated **reliquary bust of Friedrich Barbarossa, made in Aachen 1155–71; monastery buildings 1708; *Schloß Capppenberg*, 1708 with mid 19C gatehouses, in a park laid out by the Prussian statesman Karl Freiherr von und zu Stein (died here in 1831) housing a Museum of art and culture (furniture from gothic to Jugendstil, Kachelöfen, porcelain; open April–November, except Friday, 10.00–18.00).

From Lünen the B54 runs for 14km S to **Dortmund** (see Rte 55).

47   The Hill Country of the Weser

Total distance 160km. **Minden**—B65 10km **Bückeburg**. —B83 31km **Hameln**. —55km **Höxter**.—5km *Godelheim.*—9km *Beverungen.*—B80 50km **Hannoversch-Münden**.

Minden (84,000 inhab.; alt. 46m) lies 7km N of the the Minden Gap, known as the *Porta Westfalica* (with a monument of 1896 to Kaiser Wilhelm I, who is blessing the country), and at the northernmost edge of the hill country of the Weser ('Weserbergland')—montainous country on either side of the River Weser, seldom reaching 500m but marked by deep ravines. At Minden Charlemagne established a bishopric at the turn of the 9C. The city received its charter in 1220 and became a member of the Hanseatic league. Its romanesque *cathedral* was restored after destruction in WWII (inside, an 11C bronze crucifix; 13C reliquaries; part of the late 13C choir screen, now set against the S wall of the transept). Minden has houses dating from the 13C to the renaissance; the *Marienkirche* of the 12C and 14C, with a massive tower and a late 16C font; the town hall, principally 13C, though much restored; the 14C church of St. Martin (late 15C choir stalls; bronze font 1583; tomb by A. Stenelt, 1615). N of the city a 400m-long aqueduct carries the Mittelland Canal across the River Weser. Information office at No. 31 Ritterstraße.

10km from Minden along the B65 is **Bückeburg**, with a *Schloß* built c 1300 and rebuilt in the mid 16C in the renaissance style, only to be rendered baroque in the next century (open daily, 09.00–12.00 and 13.00–18.00). In the Schloß park is the mausoleum to Fürst Adolph zu Schaumburg-Lippe, by Paul Baumgarten, 1911–14. Herder was court chaplain and preached from 1771–76 at the parish church, built 1611–15 (bronze font by A. de Vries, 1615; baroque organ restored 1962). Local history museum at No. 22 Lange Straße (open daily, 10.00–17.00).

The B83 leads for 31km SE to **Hameln** (51,000 inhab.; alt. 68m), known to the British as Hamlin because of Robert Browning's poem about the Pied Piper, whose legend is daily performed here from May to September. In spite of Browning's assertions, Hameln is not near Hanover and is in Lower Saxony, not Brunswick. It does stand on the right bank of the Weser, on the site of an early 9C monastery. In Münsterkirchhof stands the 13C minster church of *St. Bonifatius*, with an 11C crypt and a late 12C octagonal tower (inside, a relief of the Coronation of Our Lady, 1415, and a gothic tabernacle). The church of St. Nicolas in the Markt was rebuilt after WWII. In *OSTERSTRAßE* are the Pied Piper's house, 1602 (now a café and wine bar) the Dempter-sche house, the early 17C Hochzeitshaus, the Stiftsherrenhaus (1558), and the Leistsche house (1589), (now the local history museum, open save Monday, 10.00–17.00; weekends, 10.00–13.00).

Due S of Hameln is the health resort of *Bad Pyrmont*, known for its healing springs in the 1C AD, wih a Kurhaus, a Kurtheatre, and the 360m-high Pyrmonter Berg.

The route continues for 55km to reach the walled town of **Höxter**, on the left bank of the Weser, whose deanery in the Markt dates from 1561, whose town hall dates from 1613, and whose Altstadt boasts numerous renaissance houses. The 11C church of St. Kilian (in An der Kiliankirche) has a 15C S aisle, an early 16C Crucifixion group and a pulpit of 1597. To the E of the town is the former monastery of *Corvey*, founded 822, where Widukind wrote the history of the Saxons, the home of the poet Hoffmann von Fallerstein (1798–1874) from 1860–74, who wrote the German national anthem. Although the abbey was rebuilt in the baroque style after the Thirty Years' War, with a gothic *church* of 1671 (Benedictus chapel, 1772; Lady chapel, c 1790; interior baroque, almost all restored after WWII); the W part, 873–885, remains the oldest building in Westphalia. The Schloß at Corvey was built out of part of the monastery buildings, 1699–1721, and now is a local history museum (open daily, April–October, 09.00–18.00). On the other side of the river is the region of Solling, famous for its game (especially wild boar). 10km W of Höxter is the Benedictine abbey of *Marienmünster*, with an organ of 1738. The B83 continues for 14km through Godelheim to reach *Beverungen* (6000 inhab.; alt. 100m), with an early 14C moated Burg, the late 17C church of St. John the Baptist and several half-timbered houses.

From here take the B80 for 50km to **Hannoversch Münden** (also known simply as **Münden**; 20,300 inhab.; alt. 141m), at the confluence of the Weser with the Werra and Fulda, a place still boasting that Alexander von Humboldt regarded it as one of the finest in the world. The Weser is here spanned by a stone bridge first built in 1329. The splendidly restored Altstadt is crammed with half-timbered houses. The *Welfenschloß* of 1560–80 is decorated with renaissance frescoes and is also a local history museum (open Tuesday–Friday, 10.00–12.00 and 16.00–18.00; weekends, 10.00–12.00). In Kirchplatz is the church of *St. Blasius* (13–16C; font, 1392; pulpit, 1493; organ case, 1645; baroque altar, 1700). G. Crossman incorporated into his renaissance new town hall (1603–09) parts of an earlier gothic building.

48 The Siebengebirge

Königswinter (see Rte 40) is the best point of entry to the seven extinct volcanic peaks that make the picturesque Siebengebirge. There are in fact about 30 peaks in the c 50km^2 range, but the name arose because only seven can be seen from Bonn, namely the **Ölberg* (461m), the *Löwenburg* (455m), the *Lohrberg* (435m), the **Petersberg*, the *Nonnenstromburg* (336m), the *Wolkenburg* (325m) and the **Drachenfels* (321m). The top of the 321m-high Drachenfels can be reached by foot, motor car or rack railway (modern Schloß Drachenburg; early 13C Schloß Drachenfels, built by an Archbishop of Cologne). Half-way up is the cave of the dragon, celebrated in the legend of the Nibelungen. Buses run to the 331m-high *Petersberg*. The highest of the seven peaks is the 461m *Großer Ölberg*, reached by car and then on foot (20 minutes) through woods (ruined Schloß Löwenburg).

49 The Bergisches Land: from Wuppertal to Düsseldorf

Total distance 55km. **Wuppertal**—B51 and B229 llkm **Remscheid-Lennep** (—Altenberg 20km). —B229 10km **Solingen**.—B229 14km *Langenfeld.*—B8 9km *Düsseldorf-Benrath.*—B8 llkm **Düsseldorf**.

Wuppertal (418,000 inhab.; alt. 157m), straddling the River Wupper was formed in 1929 from the union of Barmen, Elberfeld, Beyenburg, Vohwinkel Cronenberg and Ronsdorf. The textile industry was well established here by the 16C. Between 1898 and 1901 an overhead railway 13·3km long was built to join Elberfeld, Barmen and Vohwinkel. Here were born Friedrich Engels (1820–95), Marx's collaborator and patron (Engel's House, at No. 10 Engelsstraße; open save Monday, 10.00–13.00 and 15.00–17.00), and Johan Carl Fuhlrott (1803–77), the discoverer of Neanderthal man (Fuhlrott natural history museum at No. 20 Auer Schulstraße, open as the Engel's house, with some extensions). A university was founded here in 1927, reached S of the city by the Kiesbergtunnel, Europe's sole two-storey motor car tunnel. At Barmen in 1934 Protestant opponents of Hitler made a celebrated declaration of the spiritual independence of the church from the state.

Modern buildings include the swimming complex (the Schwimmoper, 1956), the Schauspielhaus (in Bundesallee, by G. Graubner, 1966, in front of which is a statue by Henry Moore), and the opera house (Friedrich-Engels-Allee, 1956). Older buildings include Barmen town hall, 1912–22, and the neo-classical St. Lorenz-Kirche (Friedrich-Ebert-Straße), 1828–32. Elberfeld also has a zoo with 3500 animals, and the Von-der-Heydt museum (at No. 8 Turmhof; *19th and 20C paintings, open save Monday, 10.00–17.00). In Barmen are the botanical gardens.

OTHER MUSEUMS: Clock Museum (at No. 11 Poststraße; open weekdays, 10.00–12.00 and 16.00–18.00; Saturday, 10.00–12.00), and the Missions Museum (at No. 9 Missionsstraße, open weekdays, 08.00–16.00). The Toelle tower in Barmen offers panoramas. Tourist information at Pavillon Döppersberg in Elberfeld.—9km E of Wuppertal is the 5·2km long Klütert cave, reputed to heal asthma.

Take the B51 S from Wuppertal to reach **Remscheid–Lennep** (135,000 inhab.; alt. 370m) on the B229, its prosperity deriving from the manufacture of precision tools. Wilhelm Conrad Röntgen (1845–1923), the discoverer of X-rays, was born at Lennep (Röntgen Museum at No. 41 Schwelmer Straße (open Sunday–Thursday, 14.00–17.00 and Friday, 10.00–14.00). The regional Museum is in a 19C house at Nos 2–6 Cleffstraße (open Wednesday–Saturday, 09.00–13.00 and 14.00–17.00; Sunday, 10.00–13.00).

The Bergisches Land is named after the former dukes of Berg, whose artistic and cultural collection is partly preserved at *Schloß Burg an der Wupper*, 7·5km SE of Remscheid-Lennep (founded 12C, rebuilt 1887; regional history; open March–October daily, 09.00–18.00; except Monday, 13.00–18.00; winter closed Monday, and at 17.00 other days): chapel with wall paintings, *Festsäle. Tourist information at Remscheid town hall.

The B229 leads 10km W of Remscheid-Lennep to reach the industrial town of **Solingen** (177,000 inhab.; alt. 224m). En route the River Wupper is crossed by Europe's highest railway bridge (107m high, 550m long). Solingen makes cutlery and swords (museum at No. 160 Wuppertaler Straße; open except Monday and Thursday, 10.00–13.00 and 15.00–17.00). In the 18C market square is a Protestant church of 1718. The Catholic parish church of Solingen-Gräfrath dates from 1690, the theatre (at No. 71 Konrad-Adenauer-Straße) from 1963. Tourist information at Cronenbergerstraße.

18km S of Remscheid-Lennep by way of Bergisch-Born and Burscheid the B51 reaches the Dhünn valley. Turn right along the valley to reach after 2km *Altenberg* the former Cistercian abbey church now known as *Altenberg Cathedral, built 1255–1379, restored early 19C, and housing the tombs of many of the Berg family. The W window, 18 by 8m, is the largest in Germany; Annunciation group c 1375; 15C tabernacle.

14km from Solingen along the B229 is *Langenfeld* (29,000 inhab.; alt. 44m), where you join the B8 to reach after 9km *Düsseldorf-Benrath* (see see Rte 44) and after another 11km **Düsseldorf** (see Rte 44).

VIII LOWER SAXONY AND HAMBURG

50 Hamburg

HAMBURG (182,000 inhab.; alt. 17m), Germany's second city and one of the premier European ports (serving 200 shipping lines), is situated on the right bank of the River Elbe and around the basin of the Alster.

Main *railway stations*: Steintorplatz.

Main *post office*: Stephansplatz. Every post office facility is also found in Münzerstraße, close by the main railway station.

Information Office: Hachmann Platz (named after Bürgermeister Gerhard Hachmann, 1838–1904).

Trains to all major cities. Fuhlsbüttel *airport*.

History. Late Saxon remains of the 7C and 8C have been discovered in the vicinity of Hamburg and in the Altstadt. Here Charlemagne founded first a church and then a fortress to keep back the heathen, thus creating its name *Burg am Hemmis*. In 831 Emperor Ludwig the Pious founded the bishopric; 14 years later the Vikings plundered and burned the city. Hamburg was again razed in 983, to be rebuilt under the inspiration of Archbishop Unwan, 1013–29. The city now began to prosper again and by the 12C was a rich trading centre, in the next century helping to set up the Hanseatic League and damming the Alster river to create its celebrated lake. In the mid 14C Archbishop Bezelin ordered the construction of the city walls.

In 1529 the city turned Protestant, under the influence of Johann Bugenhagen. The Hamburg stock exchange was instituted in 1558 and the Hamburg bank founded 1619. Recognised as a free city by the emperor in 1618, Hamburg gained a seat on the Imperial Diet in 1770. After the dissolution of the Hanseatic League in the 18C Hamburg kept a special relationship with two other Hanseatic cities, Lübeck and Bremen. Savants of the calibre of Friedrich Gottlieb Klopstock and Gotthold Ephraim Lessing brought the city fame at this time. By the beginning of the 19C Hamburg was amongst the richest cities in Europe. Between 1816 and 1818 Heinrich Heine worked here in his father's bank. French occupation in 1803 (which blocked trade with England and caused swift British reprisals) hampered her trade and in 1810, after three brief years of freedom, Hamburg was incorporated into the French empire. The city regained its free status five years later. Devastated by a fire in 1842, Hamburg was rebuilt. (The British architect Gilbert Scott won the competition to design the Nicolaikirche.) In 1860 Hamburg guaranteed to its citizens freedom of the press, of religion and of assembly. The University was founded in 1919. In 1921 the city set up a new constitution and a democratic assembly. Once more devastated in WWII (in 1943 British bombers demolished all but the tower of Gilbert Scott's Nicolaikirche), Hamburg has since that time both restored some of its old quarters and also built a modern city. Hamburg became a separate Land of West Germany in 1949. A severe flood ravaged the city in February 1962. Hamburg prospers on engineering, ship building, car manufacture, beer and chemicals. In January 1975 the 500m-long Elba tunnel (for pedestrians and vehicles) was officially opened. The city is served by a U-Bahn and and S-Bahn system. Hamburg is today the HQ of the North German radio and TV company (the Norddeutscher Rundfunk) and the publishing house of Axel Springer.

Hamburg was the birthplace of the composers Felix Mendelssohn-Bartholdy (1809–47) and Johannes Brahms (1833–97). C.P.E. Bach died here in 1778. The city boasts an internationally renowned symphony orchestra. The opera company, founded 1678, is the finest in Germany.

Glockengießerwall leads NW from the main railway station (by Moeller, Reinhart and Süssenguth, 1906) by way of the City Art Gallery (built in the Italian renaissance style, 1868, 1886 and 1907, open save Monday, 10.00–17.00, till 19.00 Wednesday) to the Binnen-Alster Lake (separated from the Außen-Alster by the Kennedy bridge and the Lombards bridge (built along the line of the former ramparts). Cross Lombardsbrücke to reach Stephansplatz, with the main post office (and a post office museum, open Tuesday–Friday, 10.00–14.00). To the N is the botanical garden and then the park known as 'Planten un Blomen' (dialect for plants and flowers), which covers 38,000m^2 and incorporates a miniature railway, tropical house, congress centre, trade fair, the Ernst-Marck hall and the 272m-high TV tower (1968, known as the Tele Michel), with a revolving restaurant. To the NE of the park in Edmund-Simers-Allee is the University.

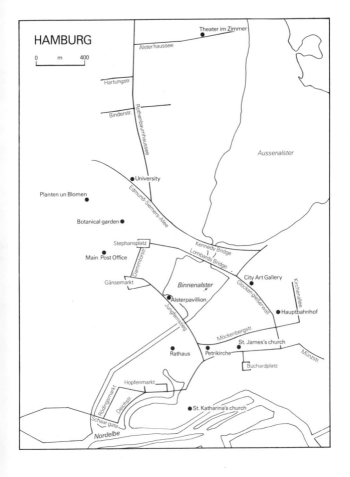

From Stephansplatz Dammtorstraße leads S (left the opera house of 1817, rebuilt 1955) to the Gänsemarkt (the centre of Hamburg's antiquarian quarter), with a statue of Lessing (1881; by Fritz Schaper) and Hamburg's first opera house, founded in 1678 (the present building by Gerhard Weber, 1955). Left of the Dammtorstraße the fashionable shopping street of Jungfernstieg leads to the embarkation point for sailing on the Binnen-Alster and the Außen-Alster. Beside the lake is the Alsterpavillon. Continue to the end of Jungfernsteig and turn right into the Alster arcades along the Kleine Alster, taking the road on the right to cross the Michael bridge and reach in Michaelistraße and the late gothic church of St. Katharina (1380–1425; baroque tower, 115m high, by P. Marquardt, 1659, restored 1957; façade by Johann Nikolaus Kuhn, 1732– 37); inside a statue of St. Catherine c 1400 and a 13C crucifix. The writer Johann Melchior Goeze (1717–86) was once pastor here.

From here take Ost-West-Straße W to reach on the left the baroque church of *St. Michael (by Ernst Georg Sonnin and Leonhard Prey, 1751–77, restored 1907–12 by J. Faulwasser, H. Geißler and E. Meerwein, and after WWII by Gerhard Langemaack), with its 132m-high tower (ascent and *view). The statue of Michael killing the dragon on the doorway under the tower dates from 1912; that of Luther (in bronze N of the tower) is by Otto Lessing, also 1912. In the entrance is the Sonnin memorial by Oscar Ulmer (1906). The Steinmeyer organ dates from 1962. Here after WWII, and until his death in 1986, the anti-Nazi resistance leader Helmut Thielicke brought new renown to this church by his preaching. Behind the church, at No. 10 Krayenkamp, the Mercers' Guild in 1670 set up widows' charitable homes. Continue W along Ost-West-Straße to reach the Zeughausmarkt (34m-high Bismarck monument by Lederer and Schaudt, 1906). The Elba park lies on the W side of the Zeughausmarkt and houses NW of Zeughausmarkt, at No. 24 Holstenwall, the City History Museum (built by Schumacher, 1913–21; open save Monday, 10.00–17.00, closing Saturday, 13.00).

Walk S through the park to reach the river bank and the St. Pauli Hafenstraße. From here the Elba tunnel leads to the pleasure quarters of Sankt Pauli and the Reeperbahn (bars, cabaret, night clubs, the Panoptikon waxworks, etc.). Follow Königstraße W from the Reeperbahn to reach the former Prussian village of Altona, whose church of the Holy Trinity was restored after WWII (see also the 18C Christianskirche in Klopstockstraße and the neo-classical palaces in Palmaille). The Altona fish market opens each Sunday morning. Altona's Jewish cemetery dates from 1611. Continue along Königstraße and then take Museumstraße to find at Nos 21–23 the local history museum (open save Monday, 10.00–17.00; closes Saturday at 13.00).

Return to St. Pauli Hafenstraße and continue E as far as the Schaar gate and then the Deichstraße with (at No. 35) Hamburg's oldest surviving house, 1641, and from here to No. 49 a row of fine 17th and 18C gabled houses (the Nicolaifleet). Just beyond, in Hopfenmarkt, the 147m-high neo-gothic tower from Gilbert Scott's Nicolaikirche (built 1864–74) is all that remains after WWII (see above), now a memorial of victims of the Nazis. Schaar gate adjoins the Rödingsmarkt, which leads to the stock exchange, whose present building is by Forsmann (1841). Close by is the renaissance town hall of 1886–97 (112m-high tower), on whose façade are statues of 18 emperors, of the saints commemorated in Hamburg church dedications, etc. The *Ratsweinkeller* has a statue of Bacchus by the Swiss sculptor Mannstadt, 1770 (open weekdays, 10.00–15.00 and weekends, 10.00–13.00); great Festival Hall, 46m by 18m, 15m high, paintings by Hugo Vogel, 1909). S of the town hall stood a monastery which furnished Hamburg with its first school. From here take Mönckebergstraße (named after Bürgermeister Johann Georg Mönckeberg, 1839–1908, with the Mönckeberg fountain, by Georg Wrba, 1926) to see the 12C *Petrikirche* (rebuilt by Alexis de Châteauneuf and H.P. Fersenfeldt, 1844–49, preserving the lion's head of 1342 on its doorway and a 133m-high tower of 1342—the octagonal crown 1877—climbed by 550 steps: inside, a stone Madonna, c 1470). In Jacobihof stands the *Jacobikirche*, rebuilt in 1959 after destruction in WWII (St. Luke altar in the aisle, by Heinrich Bornemann, 1499; altar in the bapistery chapel, c 1500; 16C Trinity altar; baroque pulpit by Georg Baumann, 1610; *organ by Arp Schnitger, 1689–93; 124m-high tower.

S of the church in Burchardplatz are found two noted 20C buildings: the *Chilehaus*, by Fritz Höger, 1923 and the *Sprinkenhof*, by Höger and his collaborator Gerson, 1930. Hamburg's Ohlsdorfer cemetery contains a Memorial to the Air Raid Victims of Hamburg, by G. Marcks (1951). As well as the Staatsoper at No. 34 Großer Theater Straße, its theatres include the Theater im Zimmer at No. 30 Alster-schaussee, the Schauspielhaus at No. 39 Kirchenallee and the Kammerspiele at No. 11 Hartnungstraße.

MUSEUMS: Museum of Folk Art, at No. 14 Binderstraße (open save Monday, 10.00–17.00); Concentration Camp Museum, at Neuengammer Heerweg (open Tuesday, Wednesday and Sunday, 16.00–18.00); Brahms Museum at No. 39 Peterstraße (open Tuesday and Friday, 12.00–13.00, Thursday, 16.00–18.00); Planetarium, Wasserturm in Stadtpark (open except Saturday, 10.00–15.30); Museum of Tobacco and its history, at No. 51 Parkstraße (visitors by appointment); University Theatre Collection at No. 45 Rothenbaumchaussee (open weekdays, 09.30– 16.00, Tuesday till 18.00).

Hamburg hosts sailing regattas and an annual folk festival, November and December.

ENVIRONS: 17km SE of Hamburg lies the town of *Bergedorf* (13C Schloß, rebuilt 17C and 19C; church of SS.Peter and Paul, founded mid 12C, rebuilt 16C, tower of 1759; observatory of 1915. At No. 2 Sachsentor is the half-timbered inn known as *Gasthof Stadt Hamburg.

N of Hamburg, in the suburb of *Stellingen*, is *Hagenbeck's Zoo, established 1848 and reconstituted 1945–52 (open, 18.00–19.00, closing 16.30 November–March.) In Gerhard-Hauptmann-Platz is the Thalia Theatre, founded 1843, the present building 1912 (restored).

The B431 leads W from Hamburg for 14km to the fishing village of *Blankenese*, by way of *Klein-Flottbek* (with a Museum of the works of Ernst Barlach). Blankenese boasts the 80m-high Süllberg (*view) and the 87m-high Bismarckstein.

51 From Hamburg to Hanover

Total distance 127km. **Hamburg**—B4 15km *Harburg.*—B75 11km *Nenndorf.*—9km to the junction with the B3.—B3 17km *Wintermoor.*—23km *Soltau.*—22km *Bergen.*—23km **Celle.**—7km **Hanover.**

An alternative route via the A7 motorway (148km in total, has stupendous views of Lüneberg Heath.

Leave **Hamburg** (see Rte 50) by the Bilorner Brückenstraße, crossing the river by the New Elba Bridge, built 1883–87, to reach *Veddel* (where the motorway to Hanover begins). Continue over the canal into the industrial suburb of Wilhelmsburg, to cross the river again by a bridge 470m long. Drive along Hanoversche Straße, Moorstraße and Wilhelstorfer Straße to reach after 15km Harburg. *Harburg* was already settled in the 12C and became a chartered city in 1297. It was the seat of a branch of the Lüneberg-Celle family in the 16C and 17C, was taken over by Hanover in 1705 and by Prussia in 1866, before becoming a suburb of Hamburg in 1937. Although most of the old city was destroyed in WWII, Harburg retains a fine park, an open-air theatre, and borders onto Lüneberg Heath.

The B75 continues 20km SW through *Nenndorf* to join the B3, which then runs 17km S across the Heath (much of which is here a nature preserve, with no motor traffic) up to Wintermoor. The route now descends to the Böhme valley and (after 23km) *Soltau* (18,000 inhab.; alt. 68m), known as *Curtis salta* in the 10C. 22km further S lies *Bergen* (18,000 inhab.; alt. 70m) with a local history museum in a 300-year-old farmhouse (at No. 7 Am Friedensplatz, open weekdays, 09.30–12.00 and 15.00–17.00; closed Friday afternoons and weekends), and an African Museum (at No. 9 Buhrstraße, visits by arrangement). E of Bergen is Herrmannsburg with a church dated 972.

The B3 continues for 23km, passing 3km W seven megalithic tombs from the New Stone Age (the 'Sieben Steinhäuser') before reaching *Celle, the former residence of the Dukes of Lüneberg and situated where the River Aller is navigable.

History. *Kellu* or 'riverside settlement' appears first in written history in a charter of 990. It flourished because of the river trade, and in 1292 Otto the Severe refounded the town, with a new Schloß 3km downstream. Celle became capital of the Lüneberg Duchy in 1378. In 1526 under Herzog Ernst the Confessor the town embraced Protestantism. Celle continued to prosper, as is indicated by its many fine buildings (which escaped destruction in WWII). Becoming part of the electorate of Hanover in 1705, Celle was chosen as the seat of a court of appeal in 1711 which later became the supreme court of this province. The royal stud farm founded 1735 by George II of Britain (who was also elector of Hanover), is still flourishing, with some 300 horses.

At Celle in 1666 was born Sophie Dorothea, who married the future King George I of Great Britain and was grandmother of Frederick the Great.

From the main railway station Bahnhofstraße leads by way of Westcelerstraße to the moated *Schloß*, which faces onto Schloßplatz. Traces remain of the 13C foundation, though the present late 17C building is substantially due to Herzog Georg Wilhelm. The renaissance *Schloß chapel, built 1485, was rebuilt in the next century (paintings by the Dutch artist Martin de Voss, see especially the Crucifixion on the altar). The theatre in the Schloß, 1685, is the oldest surviving in Germany (note the stucco and decorations; visits daily, 09.00–12.00 and 14.00–16.00; Saturday closes 12.00).

E of the Schloß across Schloßplatz are the main post office and the Bomann Museum (history of Celle and Lüneberg Heath, with a model of a Lower Saxon farmhouse of 1571; open daily, 10.00–17.00; closes Sunday 13.00). The old town runs further E, with numerous half-timbered houses. Stechbahn was formerly the spot for jousts and leads to the marketplace with the Protestant parish church (14C; altar 1613; baroque alterations 1675–98; renaissance and baroque tombs of the ducal family). Kalandgasse leads N from the Stechbahn to the old Latin School, 1602. Zöllnerstraße leads E from Stechbahn to the old town hall, rebuilt by Jakob Riess in the early renaissance style, 1561–79 (classical façade 18C).

Other houses include at No. 8 Poststraße (a continuation of Zöllnerstraße) the *Hoppener House*, 1532, built for Simon Hoppener, the chamberlain of Ernst the Confessor, and at No. 14 Großer Plan the 17C baroque Stechinelli House. In the southern part of Celle are a French Garden (monument to Queen Caroline Mathilde of Denmark, died 1775, whose lover Struensee was beheaded in 1772) and the Lower Saxon Institute of Bee-Research, and the stud farm.

Tourist information at No. 6a Schloßplatz. Train and bus links with Brunswick, Hamburg and Hanover.

11km SE of Celle along the B214 is the 13th and 14C former Cistercian convent *Kloster Wienhausen*: wall paintings, stained glass, tabernacle of 1445.

The B3 continues S for 7km to **HANOVER** (German 'Hannover'; 557,000 inhab.; alt. 56m), the capital of Lower Saxony.

Main *railway station* and main *post office*: Ernst-August-Platz.

Information office: No. 8 Ernst-August-Platz.

Trains connect with every important German city. Hanover is also served by an underground railway.

Airport: at Langenhagen.

History. An industrial city situated on the Mittelland canal and in the valley of the River Leine, Hanover appears first in recorded history in 1100. Henry the Lion gave Hanover its city charter in 1242. In 1386 Hanover became a member of the Hanseatic League. Under the Elector Ernst August (1679–98) the city continued to prosper and underwent a cultural renaissance. Gottfied Wilhelm Leibniz (born Leipzig 1646, died Hanover 1717) became court librarian. The elector Georg Ludwig united Hanover to Great Britain when he became George

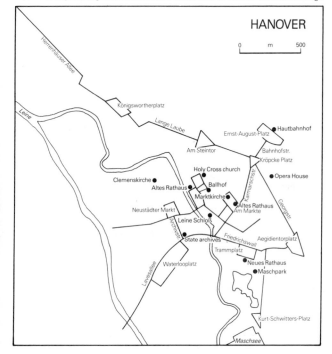

I in 1714, a union which ended only in 1837 when Ernst August became king of Hanover and over the next 14 years gave the city a classical face through the work of his architect Georg Ludwig Friedrich Laves. The city expanded industrially in the 19C, and was taken by the Prussians. Much was destroyed in WWII.

The astronomer Friedrich Wilhelm Herschel was born here in 1738 (dying in England in 1822). Other natives of Hanover were the writers August Wilhelm von Schlegel (1767–1845) and Karl Wilhelm Friedrich von Schlegel (1772–1829).

Opposite the main railway station is the huge Ernst-August-Platz, with a monument to Queen Victoria's uncle, King Ernst August (1837–52). Follow Bahnhofstraße SW (noting the Passerelle: a sunken shopping street 750m long) to another huge square, Kröpcke Platz (with the skyscraper-store known as the Hanover Kröpcke Centre). Bahnhofstraße runs into Karmarschstraße, where stands the former *Town Hall (15C, restored 1875, rebuilt 1953–64). On the right in Am Markt is the brick gothic *Marktkirche* (1340–60, restored after WWII (choir glass c 1400; altar c 1490; font c 1500; bronze doors by Gerhard Marcks, 1958; 95m-high tower.

Continue to the bank of the Leine and take Leinstraße NW to reach Heinrich-Wilhelm-Kopf-Platz and the *Leine Schloß* (begun 1637, restored 1816–26 by G.L.F. Laves, restored again after WW II). The Schloß is now the seat of the Lower Saxon parliament, and George I is buried in its chapel. Opposite the Schloß in Dammstraße is the 1850 extension of the old town hall, popularly known as the Doges' Palace. Continue NW along Leinstraße, then Burgstraße, to reach Ballhopplatz, with the half-timbered *Ballhof* (1649–64), once an indoor tennis court and theatre, now the civic theatre. Kreuzstraße leads N from the Ballhof to the church of the Holy Cross (early 14C, mid 17C tower, all rebuilt after WWII). Today the church is at the centre of an entirely modern quarter of Hanover.

Return to Ballhofplatz by way of Burgstraße (half-timbered houses) and turn right into Rossmühle to reach the river by way of the old stables' gate, incorporated into Remy de la Fosse's Town Hall of 1714 (the city's second town hall). Turn left at the river bank to find the former arsenal (Zeughaus), built 1643–49 and partly demolished in 1886. The Beginen tower, close by in Pferdstraße dates from the 14C. Cross the river by way of Schloß Straße and the Schloß bridge, continuing W along Calenberger Straße (with various ministries) to reach the Neustädter Markt, whose church (by the Venetian H. Sartorio, 1660–70; tower 1700; rebuilt 1872, and again after WW II) contains Leibniz's tomb. The baroque church to the N is the 1718 Clemenskirche, by another Venetian, T. Giusti. Archivstraße leads SE from here, passing on the left the state archives and the national library (by Remy de la Fosse, 1712–25), opposite which is a monument to General Carl Graf von Alten, died 1764. Continue along Archivstraße to Waterlooplatz, with the 47m-high Waterloo column of 1826, on which a goddess of Victory commemorates 800 Hanoverians who fell at the battle of Waterloo.

Return NE along Lavesallee and then SE along Friedrichswall to reach on the right the new town hall of 1900–13, with a domed tower 100m high (lift to the top). Behind the town hall is the March park and artificial lake, created in the 1930s for water sports. The Hanover broadcasting house stands to the W of the lake. NW of the lake is the Lower Saxon stadium, seating 6000 spectators. Friedrichswall contains Laves's 1832 Wangenheim palace, and the house he built for himself in 1922. It continues E as far as Aegidientorplatz (14C

Aegidien church, ruined but retained as a memorial to war dead). From here take Georgstraße NW to reach the Opera House (by Laves, 1845–52). Georgstraße continues through the Kröpcke (turning to the left; fashionable shopping, banks), reaching the square Am Steintor, with another skyscraper to the N (the Anzeiger building by Fritz Höger, 1928). Follow the continuation of Georgstraße (Lange Laube) on the other side of the square to reach Königswortherplatz. From here the pedestrianised Herrenhäuser Allee, laid out with 1400 lime trees in 1734, leads 2km NW to the baroque *Herrenhausen Gardens*, passing en route the technical high school (in the former royal Schloß of 1857–66). Most of the garden Schloß was destroyed in WWII, but the Galeriegebäude of 1698, with its baroque frescoes escaped. The geometrical Großer Garten, with its fountains, garden theatre and orangery, was laid out between 1666 and 1714. The botanical Berggarten to the N contains the royal mausoleum, by Laves, 1842. In the 18C Georgengarten to the left is the Palais Wallmolden, now the Wilhelm Busch Museum, with humorous works of art by Busch (1832–1908) and Heinrich Zille (1858–1929).

OTHER MUSEUMS: Herrenhausen Museum in the Schloß at No. 14 Herrenhäuser Straße, built 1721 for the illegitimate daughter of Georg I; 17C to 20C paintings from the royal household (open April–September, 10.00–18.00; otherwise 10.00–16.00); Kestner Museum, housing the collection of August Kestner (a son of Goethe's friend Charlotte, née Buff), who was the city's representative at the Vatican from 1817–53, at No. 3 Trammplatz (open save Monday, 10.00–16.00, times occasionally extended); City Art Collection, in Kurt-Schwitters-Platz (open save Monday, 10.00–18.00); Lower Saxon provincial gallery, at No. 5 Am Maschpark (open save Monday, 10.00–17.00); Veterinary Museum, at No. 15 Bischofsholer Damm (open Monday, Tuesday and Friday, 14.00–16.30 and by arrangement).

ENVIRONS: E of Hanover is the forest of *Ellenreide*, covering 627 hectares, and containing Hanover zoo and numerous restaurants. SE is the huge fair complex, the 970,000m^2 Messegelände, with the 83m-high Hermes tower and restaurant.
  Further afield are the neo-gothic Schloß Marienberg (1860–68), 20km S near Nordsemmen; and 30km NW the Steedhuder Meer, a large lake with sailing and an island fortress built 1761–65 for Herzog Wilhelm von Schaumburg Lippe.

52 Lüneburg Heath

Total distance 151km. **Hamburg**—B5 17km *Bergedorf.*—10km *Geesthacht.*—11km *Schnakenbek* (—B5 8km to the East German border).—B209 22km **Lüneburg**.—B4 15km *Bienenbüttel.*—20km *Uelzen.*—56km *Gifhorn.*

Adenauerallee and Borgfelderstraße lead SE out of **Hamburg** (see Rte 50) from the main railway station to *Hamm* (Holy Trinity church by Reinhard Riemerschmid, 1957) and on to *Bergedorf* (on the B5), whose moated Schloß dates from the 13C (present buildings 16C, 17C and 19C, now housing the museum of the region, open Sunday, Tuesday and Thursday, 10.00–17.00), and whose half-timbered guesthouse 'Stadt Hamburg' dates from the 17C. See also church of SS. Peter and Paul, rebuilt on a mid 12C foundation in the 16C, tower 1759. The environs of Bergedorf are known as the Vierlände (since they comprise four separate parishes) and are given over to market gardening. One of the parishes, Curslack, has an interesting museum of the countryside (at No. 284 Curslacker Deich, open April–September weekdays, 08.00–17.00; weekends, 10.00–18.00; winter Tuesday–Sunday, 10.00–16.00).

The B5 continues 10km E to reach *Geesthacht*, with its 18C church and fine views from the high bank of the Elbe. 11km further is Schnakenbek. Here the route crosses the River Elbe and takes the B209 to reach after 22km **Lüneburg** (65,000 inhab.; alt. 17m), lying in Lower Saxony on the E side of Lüneburg Heath, which is now a wild-life park and prohibits motor cars and buses.

From Schnakenbeck the B5 continues for 4km E to *Lauenburg* (13,000 inhab.; alt. 45m) marking the SE point of Schleswig-Holstein, a town that grew rich off the salt trade (bridge for railway and road across the Elbe; 16C and 17C half-timbered houses in the lower town; in the upper town the remains of the Schloß of the Herzogs of Sachsen-Lauenburg, partly burnt down in 1618). From Lauenburg the Elbe-Lübeck canal, dug 1896–1900 along the lines of a late 14C canal, runs to Lübeck. The town is only 4km, along the B5, from the East German border.

Lüneburg's thermal institutions treat sufferers from rheumatism and related diseases. In the centre of the street called 'Am Sande' is the 14C brick *Johanniskirche*, with a massive leaning spire, an organ case of 1715, splendid chandeliers and a *high altar dated 1430–1485. 'Am Sande' houses numerous gabled buildings, including at No. 1 the mid 16C Schwarzes Haus. The Town Hall dates from the 12C, though most of it was rebuilt in the 14C and 15C and the baroque façade was added in 1720. Its loggia dates from c 1330, and is flanked by 15th and 16C rooms still preserving their original decor. The main council chamber was built in the renaissance style 1566–84. The The town hall also incorporates a baroque state room built 1706. Other sights include the 15C gothic Nicolaikirche (with a late 19C tower and the Lamberti altar by Hans Snitker the Elder, c 1450) and the medieval crane of 1420. *Lüne monastery*, formerly a Benedictine house, on the outskirts of the city, was built 1379–1412 and possesses fine late 15C tapestries, a renaissance pulpit, 1608, and a baldacchino of 1524. Today it is a Lutheran ladies'institution. The East Prussian Landesmuseum is at No. 25 Salzstraße (open weekdays, 10.00–12.00 and 15.00–17.00; weekends, 10.00–12.30). Information office at the town hall.

From here take the B4 for 15km to the summer resort of *Bienen-büttel*. After another 20km the B4 reaches *Uelzen* (25,000 inhab.; alt. 35m), noted for its two markets (the Griepemarkt and the Kiekemarkt) as well as its *Marienkirche* (built 13C, rebuilt after WWII, containing 13C 'golden ship'; 15C chandelier; memorial tomb of Prior Stillen, died 1702; mid 18C rococo organ). Local history museum at No. 36 Lüneburger Straße (open in summer Tuesday–Friday, 15.00–17.00; Saturday, 10.30–12.30). Information office at No. 43 Veersserstraße.

The B4 now runs for 56km to *Gifhorn* (30,000 inhab.; alt. 65m), situated at the confluence of the Ise and the Aller and boasting half-timbered houses, an 18C church and the Guelph Schloß of 1581 (restored in the 17C and 19C and now a museum).

53 The Harz

A. Seesen to Brunnbachsmühle

Total distance 47km. *Seesen*—B243. 7km *Münchehof*—B242. 8km *Clausthal-Zellerfeld*—26km *Braunlage*—6km *Brunnbachsmühle*—1km border with the German Democratic Republic (Bad Grund; Altenau).

Seesen (23,000 inhab.; alt 250m) lies at the beginning of the so-called Harz high road (Harzhochstraße), in the W parts of the wooded Harz mountains. The town retains the 16C renaissance part of a moated Schloß founded in the 13C. The church of St. Andreas is 17C, and the town possesses a huge park with lakes. Here was born the piano maker William Steinway. Trains connect the town with Brunswick and Hildesheim.

From Seesen the B243 runs for 7km S to *Münchehof*, a summer resort (alt. 210m), meeting here the B242, which leads SE for 7km to where a diversion 2km SW leads to Bad Grund.

Bad Grund (3300 inhab.; alt. 350m), the oldest of the hill towns of the Harz, stands at the foot of the 563m-high *Iberg*, and is noted for its winter sports, thermal and mud baths, and the stalactites and stalagmites of the Iberg cavern.

8km from *Münchehof* the B242 reaches *Clausthal-Zellerfeld* (16,000 inhab.; alt. 560m) situated amidst woods and 66 mountain lakes: *parish church* built of spruce wood (1639–42), with an oak tower, Germany's largest wooden church; swimming pools; open-air theatre; summer and winter sports; technical high school with a *mineral collection (open Mondays, 14.00–17.00; Tuesday–Friday, 09.00–12.00); celebrated mining school and a Museum of Mining in the suburb of *Zellerfeld* (at No. 16 Bornhardtstraße, open save Monday, 09.00–13.00 and 14.00–17.00). See also in Zellerfeld the 17C church of St. Salvator. Numerous buses service the town. Information office at the Kurverwaltung.

The Harz high road continues 26km SE to *Braunlage*, passing the Sperberhaier Damm house from which the B238 leads for 5km to Altenau: summer and winter sports; 18C wooden church, close by the 919m-high *Bruchberg* and its highest point (828m) at *Steiglitzecke*.

The health resort of *Braunlage* (7000 inhab.; alt. 560m), with its ice stadium and monster ski-jump lies close by the 972m-high *Wurmberg* (the highest peak in West Germany) and the 926m-high *Achtermann*. Cableway. Buses connect with neigbouring towns. Information Office at No. 17 Elbingeröderstraße. 6km further the Harz high road reaches *Beunnenbachsmühle*, which is 1km from the border with the German Democratic Republic (DDR).

B. Hildesheim to Hohegeiß

HILDESHEIM (103,000 inhab.; alt. 89m) stands on the NW side of the Harz mountains on the Mittelland canal and has been an episcopal see since 815, founded under Emperor Ludwig the Pious. A market town since the 11C, Hildesheim prospered so that a new town was founded c 1220—not finally united with the old town until until 1803. After the deliberate destruction of the medieval inner city in an air raid of 22 March 1945, the cathedral and the churches of St. Michael and St. Andreas have been splendidly restored.

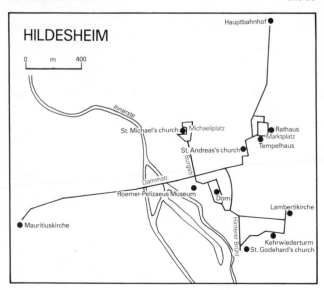

The market square, S of the main railway station and post office via
Bernwardstraße and Almsstraße, houses the rebuilt gothic town hall
(founded 13C) and the Tempelhaus, a building of 1457 which escaped
destruction in WWII (renaissance oriel, 1591). From here Hoher Weg
leads S, to the W of which stands the *St. Andreaskirche*: 78m by 35m;
middle nave 28m high; rebuilt after WWII; choir originally 14C;
romanesque lower tower, raised to its present height of 114m in the
19C.

Continue S past St. Bernward's hospital and along Hinterer Brühl to
reach, on the S side of the moated old city, the romanesque *St.
Godehardkirche*, the only church to escape the bombardment of
March 1945, built 1133–72, with an octagonal, pointed tower. The
sculpture in the tympanum of the N door is of Christ and two saints, c
1205. The interior has romanesque *capitals and mid 15C gothic choir
stalls. In the Treasury is the 12C *Albani Psalter and a 13C chalice.—
The surrounding streets contain most of what remains from the
half-timbered houses of the old city and include the sole remaining
tower of the old fortifications (the Kehrwiederturm, 1465).

From the Kehrwiederturm walk E along Keßlerstraße and then N to
pass the 15C Lambertikirche and reach the the Neustädter Markt.
NW of the Neustädter Markt the route leads to the *Heiligkreuzkirche*,
once a city gate and made into a church in the 11C (baroque façade,
1712; baroque W wall). Walk W along Kreuzstraße to the Domhof and
the romanesque cathedral of *St. Maria*, destroyed 1945 but well
reconstructed in the same style: bronze doors of 1015, with 16 reliefs
from the Old and New Testaments. Bishop St. Bernward (died 1022)
gave the 3·80m-high Christ column (with scenes from the life of Jesus
and John the Baptist); the Hezilo chandelier was made in 1061 and
given by Bishop Hezilo (1054–79); the bronze *font, supported by four
kneeling figures representing the rivers of paradise, dates from c

1230. In the romanesque cloister is a rose tree that has blossomed here since the 13C. The Cathedral Treasury (open Sunday, 12.00–17.00; Wednesday, 10.00–19.00; Saturday, 10.00–16.00) houses the silver cross of St. Bernward, 1007, and the mid 12C Oswald reliquary. Hildesheim Cathedral was given its baroque decorations under Prince-Bishop Joseph Clemens (1724–30).

Continue W to reach the *Roemer-Pelizaeus Museum* (ancient Egyptian collection with statue of Prince Hem On, c 2600 BC; open save Monday, 10.00–16.30). Take Dammstraße by way of the Damm gate further W to reach the romanesque Mauritiuskirche in Moritzberg, built 1058–68 by Bishop Hezilo (12C cloisters; baroque decorations 1744; Hezilo's tomb, carved late 17C; upper part of tower 1765).—Return along Dammstraße and turn N along Burgstraße, which leads to *St. Michaelis-Kirche* (Michaeliplatz), with its six towers and double apse. Bishop Bernward (buried in the crypt) founded the church in 1007, the main church was finished 1033, the choir added late 12C. The square of the crossing repeats itself 16 times in the rest of the church. There are 15C late gothic windows in S aisle and a 13C late romanesque painted ceiling (including Jesse tree).

Trains connect Hildesheim with Brunswick, Hameln, Hanover, Goslar, etc. The nearest airport is at Hanover (50km). Tourist information at No. 5 Markt.

Leave Hildesheim by the Alfelder Straße and drive SE for 11km to *Groß-Düngen*. At Groß-Düngen an excursion 2·5km S leads to the forest health resort of *Bad Salzdetfurth*: mud and salt baths, camping. The B243 continues through the Hildesheim forest for 16km before reaching *Bockenem* (12,000 inhab.; alt. 102m), with its gothic church of St. Pankratius, its motor museum (open April–October weekends and holidays, 10.00–12.00 and 13.00–18.00) and its steeple clock and local history museum (open Friday, 16.30–18.00 and Sunday, 10.00–12.00). Follow the B243 another 16km S to *Seesen* (see Rte 53A).

The B64 leads 24km W from Seesen to the thermal resort of *Bad Gandersheim* (12,500 inhab.; alt. 125m), the home of Germany's first woman poet, the nun Roswitha von Gandersheim (935–1001). Here is the former collegiate church of SS. Anastasius and Innocentius, founded 852. The present building is 11C romanesque with two 15C towers and five 15C chapels (bronze candelabra, c 1425; Bartholomäus altar, c 1490; Lady altar 1521; 15C altar of the Magi; mid 18C tomb in the Andreas chapel). E of the church is the mid 11C chapel of St. Michael. The renaissance abbey buildings are the work of Heinrich Overkate, 1599–1600 (Kaisersaal built 1730). The 15C church of St. Georg is built on a romanesque foundation, with a high altar of 1711. Bad Gandersheim also possesses numerous half-timbered houses, a 16C Schloß, a renaissance *town hall* of c 1580, and (in Clus) the former Benedictine monastery church of SS. Maria and George (Lübeck altar 1487). Local history museum in the town hall (open April–October, Monday and Wednesday, 10.00–12.00; Friday, 16.00–18.00). Train connections with Brunswick.
26km due N of Bad Gandersheim is *Lamspringe*, where a Benedictine monastery was founded in 847. Its church, 1670–91, is now the Catholic *parish church* (*high altar by Johann Mauritz Gröninger, 1695; altar paintings by Hieronymus Ses of Antwerp; choir stalls by Heinrich Lessen the Elder.

From *Seesen* the B243 continues SE through (12km) *Gittelde* (18C half-timbered houses) to reach 10km further another health resort, *Osterode am Harz* (32,000 inhab.; alt. 230m) on the border of the DDR: 16C town hall and church of St. Aegidien, mid 16th to mid 20C (tombs of the Herzöge von Grubenhagen) in the Marktplatz; St. Jakobi in Jakobitorstraße, 1218, restored 18C; granary in Eisensteinstraße, 1719–22; 16C half-timbered houses. Tilman Riemanschneider lived here as a young man. Local history museum at No. 32 Rollberg (open save Monday, weekdays, 10.30–16.00; weekends, 10.00–12.00). Train and bus connections with Hildesheim. Information at the Kurverwaltung. The nearby Söse reservoir is Germany's largest (for drinking water).

Take now the B241 SW for 13km to *Katlenburg*, at the confluence of the Rhume and the Oder (16C ruined Schloß) and then the B247 SE along the Rhume valley, reaching after 25km **Duderstadt*, still walled with the Westertorturm (towered gate); some 400 half-timbered houses: see especially the 13C town hall at No. 6 Marktstraße; the Steinernes Haus, 1752, at No. 91 Marktstraße; and the local history museum, 1767, at No. 3 Oberkirche (open save Monday, 10.00–12.00 and 15.00–18.00; closed Sunday afternoons); priory church of *St. Cyriakus*, begun 1394, finished 16C; mid 19C high altar, 15 baroque figures on the pillars; gothic church of St. Servatius; near by Seeburger lake.

From Duderstadt drive N by way of *Rhumspringe* (with Germany's most prolific spring) to reach after 20km *Herzberg* (18,000 inhab.; alt. 245m), with its 12C Schloß. From here the B243 runs 20km SE to *Bad Sachsa* (passing S of Germany's oldest Kneipp health resort, *Bad Lauterberg im Harz*). The health resort of *Bad Sachsa* (9500 inhab.; alt. 325m), close by the 650m-high Ravensberg, is a noted winter sports centre, lying 5km W of *Walkenried* (2950 inhab.; alt. 275m), which retains the ruins, including the cloisters, 1294, of a Cistercian monastery destroyed by Thomas Müntzer's followers during the peasants' war. Walkenried is 2km from the East German border.—From Walkenried the Rte runs N alongside the border by way of the wooded health resort of *Zorge* (1700 inhab.; alt. 340m), famous for its charcoal, reaching after 10km *Hohegeiß* (1600 inhab.; alt. 642m), on the very edge of the border with the DDR, one of the highest spots in the Harz, and noted for its fir trees.

C. Hameln to Bad Harzburg

Total distance 102km. **Hameln**—B1. 23km *Elze*—8km *Heyersum*—10km **Hildesheim**—B6. 33km *Salzgitter Bad*—15km **Goslar**—5km *Oker*—8km *Bad Harzburg*.

Leave **Hameln** (see Rte 47) and drive 23km E along the B1 by way of *Coppenbrügge*, with its ruined Schloß, to the industrial town of *Elze*, and another 18km through *Heyersum* (N of which is Schloß Marienburg, neo-gothic, 1860–68) to *Hildesheim* (see Rte 53B).

33km E of Hildesheim along the B6 is the health resort of **Bad Salzgitter** (116,000 inhab.; alt. 138m), with a former Benedictine *monastery church*, 1504–1694; tower 1695; extended c 1790; rococo interior, with a wooden crucifix c 1000. The Protestant parish church of St. Jakobi dates from the mid 18C. The city museum is in the 17C Schloß, built mostly by Paul Francke in the early part of the century (Hinter dem Knick, open save Monday, 10.00–17.00). Train connections with Bad Harzburg, Brunswick and Hanover. Tourist information at the railway station. In the region are mined Germany's richest veins of iron ore.

15km further SE, lying on the northern rim of the Harz, is **Goslar** (53,000 inhab.; alt. 320m), a winter sports resort exploiting the 726m-high *Bocksberg*.

Goslar was already prosperous in the 10C, since the nearby Rammelsberg was rich in silver, copper, lead and zinc. Emperor Heinrich II made it his capital in the early 11C, and here in 1056 Pope Victor II and Henrich III staged a historic meeting. Goslar joined the Hanseatic League in the 13C, when it also became a free imperial city. Although the city fathers quarrelled over religion with the powerful Dukes of Brunswick in the mid 16C, only in the 17th and 18C did the city fall into relative decline. Happily Goslar completely escaped destruction in WWII.

Leave the main railway station, crossing the square and reaching Rosentorstraße. To the left is the powerful Achermann tower (1501), close by remains of the old fortifications, behind which is the richly decorated *Neuwerk church*, a romanesque former Benedictine abbey church (1186; Byzantine style wall paintings, 1230, including a Madonna enthroned; stone rood screen of 1230, with statues) and the hospice of 1719. Follow Rosentorstraße past on the left, in Mauerstraße, remains of the medieval fortifications (Weber tower; Devil's tower) to Jakobikirchhof and the church of *St. Jakobi* (12C romanesque, gothicised in the 15C: inside 13C frescoes; Pietà in painted wood by Hans Witten of Brunswick c 1520; font, 1592). To the S side of the church is Jakobistraße leading to the 1528 *Mönchehaus* (at No. 1 Mönchestraße, now a Museum of Modern Art, open except Monday, 10.00–13.00 and 15.00–17.00; closed Sunday afternoon) and at No. 15 a house of 1612.

Rosentorstraße leads by way of Fischemäkerstraße to the MARKT-PLATZ, with its 13C bronze fountain surmounted by the imperial eagle; the former drapers' guild house (the Kaiserworth, 1494, decorated with statues of eight German emperors and mythical subjects—for example Hercules and a renaissance naked man called the 'Dukatenmännchen'); a Glockenspeil, set up in 1968 to commemorate a thousand years of silver mining; the twin towered romanesque-gothic church of *SS. Cosmas and Damien* (13C stained

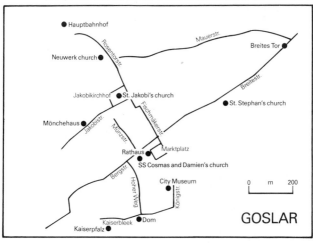

glass; bronze font by M. Karsten, 1573; pulpit 1581; altar painting 1659; towers rebuilt mid 19C); and Goslar *town hall* (11–17C, mostly late gothic, with an open-air staircase, 1537; visits in summer, 09.00–18.00; winter, 10.00–16.30), in front of which is a romanesque fountain, 13C, on top of which is the imperial eagle.

Opposite the twin towers of the church, at the corner of Hoher Weg and Bergstraße, is the house known as the *Brustuch*, with satirical carvings. In a house built 1510 at No. 5 Hoher Weg is a musical instrument and puppet museum (open April–October, 10.00–18.00, otherwise closing at 14.00).—To the N of the church of SS. Cosmas and Damien, Schuhhof contains fine old houses, as does nearby Münzstraße (at No. 10 the former 15th and 16C mint, and at No. 11 the 17C 'Zum Weißen Schwan'). Hoher Weg leads to all that remains of the cathedral (pulled down 1820)—the mid 12C narthex, with the 11C Imperial throne on which Kaiser Wilhelm I sat to announce the Reichstag of 1871.

To the W of the cathedral remains, in the vast square known as Kaiserbleek, the Imperial palace—the *Kaiserpfalz*—built under Heinrich II (1039–56), with the great hall and the early 12C chapel of St. Ulrich, the lower part a Greek cross, the upper part an octagon (restored 19C; open May–September, 09.00–18.00; otherwise 10.00–16.30), the home of 11 German emperors from 1050 to 1253.

OTHER SIGHTS: the Siemens family house, built by an ancestor of the inventor Werner von Siemens in 1693 (museum open weekdays, 09.00–12.00); the ramparts (views; 16C wide gate or 'Breites Tor'; powerful tower known as Zwinger, 1517); the birthplace of Marshal Hermann Maurice of Saxony (1696–1750) at No. 95 Breite Straße; ruined 11C hospice of St. Peter; 15C hospice of St. Ann; church of St. Stephan (rebuilt in 1730, after a fire; 18C altar); the romanesque Frankenberger church of SS. Peter and Paul (13C ogive ceiling; 13C frescoes; baroque carvings, including an altar by H. Lessing the Elder); the hospice of St. Cross (Kleines Heiliges Kreuz, 1686 with a doorway of 1510).

OTHER MUSEUMS: the City Museum, at No. 1 Königstraße (open weekdays, 09.00–13.00 and 14.30–17.00;· Sunday, 10.00–13.00); Domvorhalle in Kaiserbleek (open June–September weekends, 10.00–13.00 and 14.00–17.00; winter weekends, 10.00–12.00).

Tourist information at No. 7 Markt. Trains connect Goslar with Bad Harzburg, Brunswick and Hanover. Buses to other localities.

Continue SW along the B6 to reach *Oker*, 5km from Goslar (ironworks and chemical factories; the Romkerhalle waterfall, 6km S). After another 8km the route ends at the health resort of *Bad Harzburg* (27,000 inhab.; alt. 300m) at the beginning of the Radau valley, surrounded by the peaks of the *Rabenklippe* (555m), the *Kästeklippe* (602m) and the *Burgberg* (483m), with the ruined Schloß, built by Heinrich IV in 1065, from which the town derives its name. Bad Harzburg is 5km from the border with the German Democratic Republic. Train and bus connections with Hanover, Goslar and Brunswick. Information at the Kurverwaltung.

54 From Hanover to Helmstedt

Total distance 101km (to Berlin 293km); total distance via the motorway 82km (to Berlin 275km). **Hanover**—B5. 42km **Peine**—11km *Vechelde*—B1. 12km **Brunswick**—21km *Königslutter am Elm*—8km *Süpplingen*—7km **Helmstedt** (—B244. 11km *Schöningen*; 192km Helmstedt to Berlin).

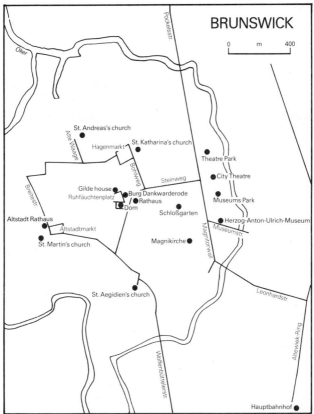

BRUNSWICK

By the Hans-Böckler-Allee leave **Hanover** (see Rte 51) E to join the B65, which runs for 42km to the industrial town of **Peine** (28,000 inhab.; alt. 80m), with its many oil rigs. 11km E of Peine is *Vechelde*, where the B1 leads right for 12km to **BRUNSWICK** (German 'Braunschweig'). Brunswick (262,000 inhab.; alt. 72m), the second largest city in Lower Saxony, lies between two streams of the River Oker, close by the Mittelland Canal.

History. Brunswick was founded in 860 by Bruno and Dankward, the two sons of Ludolf of Saxony. Henry the Lion (Heinrich der Löwe, 1129–95), who made the city his permanent home in 1166, gave Brunswick its city charter, and in 1247 the city joined the Hanseatic League. At the time of the Reformation Brunswick supported the Protestants. The Dukes of Brunswick ruled here from 1753 to 1918. In WWII destruction was colossal.

The jester Till Eulenspiegel was born c 1300 9km SE of Brunswick at Schöppenstedt. The first performance of Goethe's 'Faust' was given here in 1828.

Walk N from the main railway station along Altwiek-Ring to find, on the right, the city hall, to the W of which is the main cemetery, where are buried Gottfried Ephraim Lessing (born 1729, died in Brunswick 1781) and Friedrich Gerstäcker (died in Brunswick 1872). Continue along Altwiek-Ring and turn left into Leonhardstraße, where is the museum to the poet Wilhelm Raabe (born here 1831, lived here 1870–1910; open Wednesday, Friday and Sunday, 11.00–13.00). Turn right along Magnitorwall to find the city theatre, built in Florentine renaissance style in 1861.

From here Steinweg runs W to the Ruhfäuchtenplatz, which houses *Burg Dankwarderode, at the centre of the old city. The Schloß, said to have been built by Dankward in the 9C, was rebuilt by Henry the Lion in 1170 (restored in 1873 after a fire, and again after WWII; visits, except Monday, 10.00–16.00). To the W of the Schloß the bronze lion set up in 1160 by Henry the Lion stands on its pillar (Germany's first free-standing sculpture). N of the square is the sculpted Gilde house of 1526.

S is the romanesque cathedral of *St. Blasius (1176–1250) which Henry the Lion founded in 1173 on his return from the Holy Land. Inside is his tomb and that of his wife Mathilde (died 1189), daughter of Eléanor of Aquitaine (sculpted c 1250); also a seven-branched candelabrum made for Henry the Lion; wooden Immerwald crucifix, c 1160; romanesque wall paintings; tombs of the Dukes of Brunswick in the crypt with notable wall paintings of 1220–40; remarkable twisted pillars and nave vaulting.

To the E stands the neo-gothic town hall, built by Winter in 1899 with a 61m-high tower. From here continue E into the huge SCHLOß-PLATZ with the 13th and 14C Magnikirche (modernised after WWII), by which is a fountain (1931) in memory of Wilhelm Raabe. From here walk along Am Magnitor and into Steintorwall to reach at No. 14 the city museum (open save Monday, 10.00–17.00). Continue N by way of the Steintorwall into Museumstraße (the *Herzog-Anton-Ulrich-Museum* with paintings by Rubens, Rembrandt and Vermeer; open save Monday, 10.00–17.00), to the N of which is the Museum's park and the Theatre park, between which stands the Brunswick city theatre (1861, restored 1948).

Take Steinweg W from the theatre and then turn right along Bohlweg to reach the very large HAGENMARKT, where you find the 13th and 14C *Katharinenkirche*, restored after WWII, with a baroque organ of 1620, and a fountain and a statue of Henry the Lion (1874). W of the square is the romanesque church of *St. Andreas* (12C, gothicised in the 13th and 14C, 92m-high tower 1518–32). From this church Alte Waage leads S to the ruined 15C church of the Brothers, from which the street called Hintern Brüdern passes the ruined 13C church of St. Peter to reach the Bäckerklint square with a statue of Till Eulenspiegel (1906), whose drolleries tormented a baker in Bäcker-klint.

Follow Breite Straße S to reach the Altstadtmarkt, with the 15C fountain of Our Lady and the superb Altstadt *Rathaus (13th and 14C; statues c 1460; restored after WWII). S of the square are the Gewand house (cloth house) of 1250, with a renaissance *gable of 1590–91 by Hans Lampe, and the former customs house (Zollhaus). W of the square stands the late 12C church of *St. Martin* (modelled on the cathedral, altered during the 13th and 14C; font held up by four figures symbolising the rivers of paradise, by Bartond Sprangken, 1441; late gothic chapel of St. Anna by Sprangken, 1441).

Walk SE from the square to find the former Benedictine church of *St. Aegidien* (12C, rebuilt 13C; baroque pulpit with reliefs by Hans Witten; some 12C buildings remaining from the former convent, now housing the Ethnographical and Regional History Museum).

The late baroque Schloß Richmond in Wolfenbüttlerstraße was built by Duke Karl Wilhelm Ferdinand for his wife Augusta of England (1768). The house of Wilhelm Raabe is at No. 29 Leonhardstraße (open by arrangement). The Natural History Museum is at No. 10a Pockelstraße (open save Monday, 09.00–17.00; Wednesday also 17.00–19.00).

Trains connect Brunswick with Hanover, Helmstedt and Hildesheim. The main post office and tourist information office are in the main railway station.

Continue E from Brunswick along the B1 for 21km to *Königslutter am Elm* (17,000 inhab.; alt. 123m): view of the Elm hills and forest, and the former cathedral, founded by Emperor Lothar in 1135 as the church of a Benedictine monastery (14C vaulting; 15C gothic W end and gothic spires; 17C vaulting in the nave; wall paintings 1894, based on earlier work; *N cloister). Mineral and fossil collection of the textile magnate Otto Klages, at No. 1 Sack (open weekday mornings).

The Rte continues 8km E through Süpplingen (2·5km N of which is Süpplingenburg, the birthplace of Emperor Lothar).

Follow the B1 7km E to reach **Helmstedt** (28,000 inhab.; alt. 140m), at present the chief border crossing into the German Democratic Republic, and 192km from Berlin. As the neolithic tombs (the Lübbensteine) on the St. Annenberg to the W of the town indicate, Helmstedt has been inhabited for millenia. An important Christian settlement in the 9th and 10C, Helmstedt flourished between the 16C and the early 19C, when it was the seat of a Protestant university (the 'Juleum') whose late 16C renaissance buildings still grace Juliusplatz. From the medieval defences survives the *Hausmann Tower* (c 1500) in Neumärker Straße. The so-called double-chapel of *SS. Peter and John the Baptist* in the Passhof dates from the 12th and 13C (wall paintings; dome 1666), and belonged to a Benedictine monastery founded in the 9C. The monastery church of St. Ludger was restored after WWII (Felicitas crypt). In Klosterstraße is the former convent church of *St. Marienberg* (romanesque nave; gothic choir, 1488; romanesque stained glass in the N transept; wall paintings 1250; *antependium c 1250, displayed in the convent buildings).

The Brunnen theatre, founded 1815, present building 1924–27, at No. 7 Brunnenweg. Local history museum at No. 2 Bötticherstraße (open weekdays, 09.00–11.00, and on Monday and Saturday, 15.00–17.00; Sunday, 11.00–12.30).

Train links with Hanover and Berlin. Information Office at No. 2 Lindenplatz.

11km S of Helmstedt along the B244 is *Schöningen*: 11C church of St. Lorenz (nave vaulting late 15C); church of St. Vincenz, 1429–60; renaissance Schloß, 1569; 16th and 17C half-timbered houses.

55 From Hanover to Dortmund

Total distance 207km. **Hanover**—B217. 10km *Weetzen*—15km *Springe*—20km **Hameln**—B1. 15km *Grießen*—15km *Blomberg*—10km *Horn-Bad Meinberg*—B239. 13km **Detmold** and the Hermann monument)—5km the 'Externsteine'—13km *Bad Lippspringe*—8km **Paderborn**—12km *Salzkotten*—7km *Geseke* (—13km *Büren-Wewelsburg*)—13km *Erwitte*—17km **Soest**—8km *Ostönnen*—6km **Werl**—16km **Unna**—17km **Dortmund**.

Leave **Hanover** (see Rte 51) by Deisterstraße, taking the B217 SW for 10km to *Weetzen*, a point of entry into the hill country of the Weser, W of which is the hilly range of the Deister. Drive for 15km more to reach *Springe* (15,000 inhab.; alt. 113m), a summer resort, with half-timbered houses and views of the 345m-high *Sauerpark* and the 419m-high *Osterwald*. A further 20km SW the B217 reaches **Hameln** (see Rte 47), having passed the *Süntel* peak (437m).

The B1 leaves Hameln SW, crossing the Weser and reaching *Grießem* after 15km (close by the 258m *Klüt* peak—with a view tower and restaurant), a health resort boasting a superb Kurpark. After 15km the route reaches *Blomberg* (15,000 inhab.; alt. 235m), noted for its medieval half-timbered houses, and another health resort, (18km from Hameln) *Horn-Bad Meinberg* (18,000 inhab.; alt. 210m). S of the suburb of Horn is the *'Externsteine'*, a striking group of five sandstone rocks (one 3·75m high), carved with pagan motifs which were later transformed into a carving of Christ being lifted down from the cross (c 1120; chapel in the rock). This is the region of the Teutoburg woods.

13km NW of Horn-Bad Meinberg lies **Detmold** (315,000 inhab.; alt.134m), a furniture-manufacturing city in the Werre valley and on the N slopes of the woods. Written history records Detmold as *Theotmalli* in 783. Here Charlemagne defeated the Saxons. Receiving its municipal charter in the 13C, Detmold was from 1613 to 1918 the principal seat of the Grafen (later Fürsten) zur Lippe. Today it is the home of the North German Music Academy. Here were born the the the poet Ferdinand Freiligrath (1810–76) and the dramatist Christian Dietrich Grabbe (1810–36). The princely *Schloß* was rebuilt by J. Unkair and C. Tönnis, 1551–57, though the medieval keep remains (visits April–October daily, 09.00–12.00 and 14.00–17.00; otherwise daily at 10.00, 11.00, 15.00 and 16.00: eight tapestries by Jan Frans van den Hecke of Brussels, 1670); the Neue Palais, 1706–18, now houses the Music Academy. The Lippe provincial and local history museum is at No. 4 Ameide (open save Monday, 09.00–12.00 and 14.00–17.00). The Marktplatz houses a 16C church and the 19C town hall.

Trains and bus connections with Herford and Osnabrück. Tourist information at the town hall.

S of Detmold a group of peasant and farm houses have been reconstructed, in 80 hectares (at the *Krummes Haus*, open April–October, 09.00–18.00).

6km SW of the city is the 386m-high *Grotenburg*, where Ernst von Bandel erected the Hermann monument, 1838–75, commemorating the legendary defeat of the Romans by the chieftain Hermann in AD 9.

The B1 continues SW from Horn-Bad Meinberg, reaching after 13km the thermal resort of *Bad Lippspringe* (10,000 inhab.; alt. 150m), situated at the Senne (heath land on the S side of the Teutoburg woods): open-air swimming pool; ruined Schloß; two sources of the River Lippe (hence the name of the spa). Tourist information at the Kurverwaltung. 8km SW is **Paderborn** (see Rte 46B).

Leave Paderborn SW by the B1, reaching after 12km *Salzkotten*, with its 13C ruined Schloß and half-timbered houses. After 7km in the same direction the B1 reaches *Geseke* (12th and 13C convent church).

A DIVERSION 13km S leads to *Büren-Wewelsburg*, with its Schloß, built in the Weser renaissance style 1604–07; and a local history museum, with memorials of the Niedarhagen concentration camp, run by the SS 1933–45 (open save Monday, 10.00–12.00 and 13.00–18.00). See also the 12C church and the 18C church.

The B1 continues from Gesecke SW, arriving after 13km at *Erwitte* (12C church of St. Laurentius; moated Schloß) and reaching after another 17km **Soest**. **Werl** (30,000 inhab.; alt. 90m) lies 14km SW (by way of *Ostönnen*, with its 12C romanesque church). Werl has a gothic priory church of *St. Walburga* with a romanesque tower (Calvary group, c 1520; 15C and 16C altars; 17C Pietà); 18C pilgrimage church of the Capuchins; 13C Madonna and Child in the Franciscan church, 1903–05; local history museum at No. 1 Am Rykenberg (open at various times, save Mondays). The Franciscans run a Missionary Museum at No. 15 Meisterstraße (open weekdays, 09.00–12.00 and 13.00–17.00; Sunday, 11.00–12.00 and 15.00–17.00).—After 16km the B1 reaches **Unna** (55,000 inhab.; alt. 103m), an important coalmining and industrial centre of the Ruhr, with salt and thermal baths in the suburb of Unna-Königsborn. The 14C parish church has a tabernacle of 1451 and a baroque pulpit, 1667; there is a late 17C Schloß, renovated 19th and 20C; a local history museum, the Hellweg-Museum at No. 8 Burgstraße, open weekdays save Monday, 10.00–12.30 and 15.00–17.00; Saturday, 11.00–13.00; Sunday, 11.00–13.00 and 15.00–17.00).

Unna is 17km from the former Hanseatic city of **DORTMUND** (618,000 inhab.; alt. 87m), the largest and one of the oldest cities in Westphalia, with a harbour on the Dortmund-Ems canal covering 192 hectares and including nine docks. Dortmund's role as a centre of sporting events has been increasingly developed and its beers are renowned.

History. First known in the 9C as *Throtmanni*, when the Carolingian kings established here a settlement to guard the rich Hellweg, Dortmund developed into a free imperial city (in 1220) and a member of the Hanseatic League, defended by mid 13C fortifications (marked today by the circle of streets named Königswall, Burgwall, Ostwall, Südwall and Hoher Wall). The Thirty Years' War ruined its trade and Dortmund began to prosper again only in the mid 19C, when its iron and steel works were massively developed, as well as its breweries (the most productive in Germany). After WWII 90 per cent of the city had to be rebuilt. Dortmund University, 3km SW, was founded in 1968.

In front of the main railway station climb the steps to Westenhellweg (fine shops, as also in Ostenhellweg) to find the *Petrikirche* (14C, restored 1963; huge high altar—the largest in Westphalia—1521, by Master Gilles of Antwerp, with 633 gilded statues). Continue S to the *Propsteikirche* on Schwarze-Bruder-Straße (14C, restored 1965: winged altar by Derick Baegert, 1480, with a view of Dortmund in one panel; 15C tabernacle). Next comes the *Marienkirche* on Ostentorwall (12C and 14C, restored 1957: altar c 1390 and another by Conrad von Soest c 1420; late gothic choir stalls, 1523). Adjoining the Marienkirche is the *****Reinoldikirche**, founded 11C, rebuilt 13C, restored 1956, with a tower 105m high, finished 1701 and carrying the heaviest set of bells in the province: 15C statues of Charlemagne and St. Reinold; font by J. Winnenbrock, 1469; late gothic high altar; modern windows in the choir by Gottfried von Stockhausen. Walk along the W side of Marienkirche to reach the Markt, with the Westphalian Civic Library (Haus der Bibliothek, 1957). The civic theatre (1958–66) is on Hiltropwall.

MUSEUMS: Museum am Ostwall (20C art; open save Monday, 09.30–18.00; Sunday, 10.00–14.00); Natural History Museum, at No. 34 Ritterhausstraße (open save Monday and Saturday, 10.00–17.00).
    Tourist information at No. 8 Königswall.

Other sights are the *Volkspark* (SW), whose Westfalenhalle (1925; rebuilt by Walter Hötje in 1952) seats 24,000 and whose stadium seats

54,000 (show-jumping in March; races October): ice rink, rose garden (3000 species) and running track. S is the 70-hectare *Westfalenpark*, whose TV tower, the Florianturm (220m high), has a revolving restaurant (137m high). The park leads SW to the botanical gardens and the zoo in *Rombergpark* (Schloß Romberg, 1682). Further S is the Bittermark forest.

Dortmund's southernmost suburb is *Syburg*: Hengstee lake, with water sports; two panoramas, from the Kaiser Wilhelm memorial and the Saxon **Schloß Hoheynsburg* (which Witikind ceded to Charlemagne in the 8C and whose church dates from the 12C).

56 From Hanover to the Dutch Border by way of Osnabrück

Total distance 202km. **Hanover**—B65. 28km *Bad Nenndorf*—13km **Stadthagen**—14km **Bückeburg**—10km **Minden**—23km *Lübbecke*—21km *Harpenfeld*—B51. 24km **Osnabrück** (—B51. 15km *Bad Iburg*)—B65. 40km *Rheine*—16km *Schüttorf*—5km *Bentheim*—8km Dutch border (—175km **Amsterdam**).

The B65 leads W from **Hanover** (see Rte 51) reaching *Bad Nenndorf* after 25km. This spa (4200 inhab.; alt. 71m) lies on the slopes of the Süntel (part of the hill country of the Weser) and has sulphurous springs and mud baths. Panorama from the 146m-high *Rodenberg*.

Continue W along the B65 for 13km to reach the old town of **Stadthagen** (17,000 inhab.; alt. 68m): 16C gabled Rathaus in the Marktplatz, set amid other 16C houses; the 16C half-timbered Amtspforte; 16C *Schloß* in Obernstraße, built in the style of the Italian renaissance, with a late 16C summerhouse in the Schloß garden; 16C Kavaliershaus in front of the Schloß; some early 15C fortifications; church of *St. Martin* (at No. 3 Am Kirchhof), begun 1318, 15C and 16C extensions (inside: altar, 1585; 16C pulpit; late 16C panelling and tombs); and the baroque **Mausoleum* (adjoining the church), built for Fürst Ernst von Schaumburg and his family by J.M. Nosseni, 1609–25, with sculptures by A. de Vries, including a marble ***Resurrection*. Local history museum in Obernstraße (opens Wednesday and Saturday, 15.00–17.00, and Sunday, 11.00–12.30).

The B65 now runs SW through (14km) **Bückeburg** (see Rte 47) and (10km) **Minden** (see Rte 47).—23km W of Minden is *Lübbecke* (11,000 inhab.; alt. 100m) at the foot of the 319m-high *Wurzelbrink* (topped by a tower): renaissance town hall; ruined 13C Schloß; local history museum in the 16C Burgmannshof, in the market square (open save Sunday and Monday, 10.30–12.00 and 15.00–16.30; Saturday only 10.00–12.00).

21km W of Lübbecke along the B65 is *Harpenfeld*. 1km S on the wooded Wiehengebirge (the western extension of the hill country of the Weser) lies *Bad Essen* (3000 inhab.; alt. 190m): salt springs; 13C church. At Harpenfeld the B65 joins the B51, which runs 24km SW into **OSNABRÜCK** (160,000 inhab.; alt. 64m) on the River Hase.

History. After Charlemagne had overcome the Saxons in this area, in the year 783, he built a church on the site of the present cathedral of Osnabrück, around which the city developed and prospered. By the end of the next century Osnabrück was minting its own money and was an important trade centre. Its fortifications were built under Frederick Barbarossa in the mid 12C. A new town had developed, centred on the Johanniskirche, and this was merged with old Osnabrück in 1306. Osnabrück became an important member of the Hanseatic League. Here (and in Münster) the preliminary negotiations took place which in 1648 led to the end of the Thirty Years' War. After the peace the Bishops of Osnabrück were alternately Protestant and Catholic. The prince-bishops who ran the city developed strong diplomatic and dynastic relationships with France in the 18C, relationships that have left artistic traces on Osnabrück. Numerous émigrés escaped here from the French Revolution. In the last quarter of the 19C Osnabrück again began to expand, and most of its fortifications were demolished. Much was destroyed in WWII, and has since been carefully restored or rebuilt. The university was founded in 1970. Here was born the novelist Erich Maria Remarque (1898–1970), author of 'All Quiet on the Western Front'.

From the main railway station Möser Straße (named after the historian and statesman Justus Möser, 1720–94) leads NW past the main post office, and reaches Schillerstraße. The Herrenteichswall, which abutts onto Schillerstraße, contains the remains of the old fortifications (the Helling wall, the Pernickel tower, now in a garden, and the two Helling towers).

Left of the Herrenteichswall and across the Hase can be seen the three towers of the **Cathedral** (badly damaged 1944, restored 1952). Dedicated to St. Peter, this cathedral was begun in the 11C, with an octagonal tower added in the early 12C. The nave and choir were rebuilt 1218–27, after a fire; 28 altars were built in the 14C. The NW tower was added in the 13C, the ambulatory in the 15C and the SW tower in the 16C. In the nave are eight sandstone statues of the Apostles (1525). Other treasures include a cross c 1250; the 13C *font; a tomb statue of Bishop Konrad von Diepholtz (died 1482); a 15C Pietà; the tomb of Ferdinand von Kerssenbrock by J.C. Schlaun. The cathedral treasury houses a cross of c 1050 (open weekdays, save Monday, 10.00–13.00 and 15.00–17.00; weekends, 10.00–13.00).—In front of the cathedral is the episcopal chancellery, by F. Schädler, 1783, and a bronze statue of Justus Möser, by Drake, 1836.

Across the Domhof square is the three-sided MARKT, with the late gothic *Rathaus* (1487–1512), from whose open-air staircase the Peace of Westphalia was proclaimed. The town hall is enriched with sculptures of German emperors. Inside is the Peace Hall, where the treaty was drawn up, with council chamber furnishings of 1554 and 16C wrought-iron candelabrum. The treasury houses a 14C imperial goblet (the 'Kaiserpokal'), with renaissance ornamentation. Opposite the town hall is the 14C gothic *Marienkirche* (bombed 1944 and well restored): gabled W end, with sandstone statues; Bride's doorway; inside, tomb of Justus Möser; Antwerp retable of 1530, above which hangs a cross c 1320; font by Johann Beldensnyder, 1560; numerous tombs.

Return to the cathedral and walk N along Hasestraße to the Vitischanze of 1636 and the Barenturm, 1471, a tower from the former fortifications. From here follow the site of the fortifications SW by way of Hasemauer to reach the Bürgerhorsam tower, opposite which is the former Dominican abbey church (14C).

From the Dominican church cross Rissmüllerplatz.—Bierstraße, which leads from here back to the Markt, includes old houses, especially at No. 24 the Wallhalla of 1690. Continue S to find the Buckstum, a tower now housing a museum of torture, with instruments that have tortured among others Anabaptists and witches. Outside is a WWI memorial by Hosaeus, 1922. Further S is the Heger Gate, a monument to the dead of Waterloo (erected in 1817). At No. 27

Heger-Tor-Wall are Osnabrück's City Museum and Natural History Museum (both open weekdays save Monday, 09.00–17.00; Saturday, 10.00–13.00; Sunday, 10.00–17.00).

Continue S along Heger-Tor-Wall and turn left along Katharinenstraße to find the 14C Katharinenkirche, with its tower 103m high. S of this church in Neuer Graben is the 18C *Schloß* of the *prince-bishops*, built by P. Carato, rebuilt after a fire in 1945, and now a school. Follow Neuer Graben E to reach the Neumarkt, from which Große Straße (with baroque houses) leads N, and Johannisstraße leads S to the gothic church of *St. Johann* (1256–91): mid 15C sandstone sculptures of Christ, his mother and the apostles; tabernacle, c 1440; carved altar of 1511.

See also the romanesque church of *St. Gertrud*, in Gertrudenberg, N of the city, begun 13C as the church of a Benedictine nunnery; the abbess's house, 1757–65, also survives. Osnabrück hosts a summer music festival and a picturesque children's peace parade on 25 October. Tourist information at No. 22 Markt.

ENVIRONS: 4·5km N of Osnabrück are two prehistoric tombs: the great and the small Karlsteine. 4km E are two more: the Teufelsteine and the Hermannsteine. 14km E is the moated Schloß Schelenburg, by J. Unkair, 1528–32 (romanesque keep).

15km S of Osnabrück the B51 reaches the spa of *Bad Iburg*, with a hill-top Benedictine abbey, founded 1070 (church rebuilt 13th and 15C with a stucco ceiling by J. Geitner, the 11C tomb of Bishop Benno, and a chapel of 1665; abbey by J.C. Schlaun, 1751–53), and the 17C prince-bishops' Schloß (decorated by the Italian A. Aloisi; knights' hall 1656, designed by J. Crafft; as well as the 331m-high Dörenberg.

From Osnabrück to the Dutch border the B65 runs for 40km to **Rheine** (see Rte 46B). After 17km you pass through the industrial town of *Schüttorf*, reachng after another 5km *Bentheim* (14,500 inhab.; alt. 50m). Here has been a Schloß since the 10C, rebuilt for the Princes of Bentheim in the 15th and 17C, but retaining its 13C chapel and towers. On the terrace stands a sandstone *crucifix dating certainly from the 12C and perhaps from the 11C. (Bentheim quarries were for centuries an important source of sandstone, and supplied the builders of Bremen town hall.) To the N of the town is a popular spa and casino. Tourist information at No. 2 Schloßstraße. Trains connect Bentheim with Hamburg and the Hook of Holland. The town museum is at No. 28 Schloßstraße (open daily, 09.00–17.00).

Bentheim is 8km from the Dutch border.

57 From Hamburg to Emden by way of Bremen, Oldenburg and Wilhelmshaven

Total distance 336km. **Hamburg**—B4. 15km *Harburg*—B73. 9km *Neugraben-Fischbek*—12km **Buxtehude**—10km *Horneburg*—13km **Stade**—B74. 28km *Bremervörde*—29km **Osterholz-Scharmbeck**—9km *Burgdamm*—B6. 13km **Bremen**—B75. 13km **Delmenhorst**—19km *Varel*—25km **Oldenburg**—B69. 13km *Rastede*—19km *Varel*—37km **Wilhelmshaven**—B210. 12km *Jever*—8km *Wittmund*—25km *Aurich*—B72. 11km *Georgsheil* (—B70. 16km *Norden*)—16km **Emdem**.

Jever—Carolinensiel-Harle, the islands of *Wangerooge* and *Spieckeroog*, and the other East Frisian islands, 20km, excluding the trips to the islands.

Leave **Hamburg** (see Rte 50) S by the B4, reaching after 15km **Harburg** (see Rte 51).

From Harburg drive W along the B73 through wooded hills. At *Neugraben-Fischbek* the Rte borders on the Altes Land to the N (a vegetable, cherry and apple region whose fertility and old farmhouses were created by Dutch settlers in the 12th and 13C and whose main towns include Jork, c 4km N, with a 17C church).—12km W of Neugraben-Fischbek is the former Hanseatic town of **Buxtehude** (32,000 inhab.; alt. 5m), chief town of the Altes Land: 12C church of *St. Peter*, reordered as a brick N German gothic church in the 14C (pulpit 1674; high altar 1710); excavated foundations of a former Benedictine cloister; restored medieval houses; the 'Marschtorzwinger' from the old fortifications; local history museum at No. 9 Petriplatz.

The Rte now enters the strawberry, plum and cherry country known as the *Lühe*, reaching after 10km *Horneburg* and then running NW for 13km to reach **Stade** (45,000 inhab.; alt. 7m), another former Hanseatic town.

Stade once lay on the Elbe, since when the river changed course, so that the present harbour is on a tributary 5km from the main waters. From 1648–1712 Stade belonged to Sweden; from 1712–15 to Denmark. Its chief glories are the 13C church of *SS. Cosmas and Damian* (baroque spire on crossing, 1682; furnishings late 17C, except one 15C altar; pulpit 1663; font 1665; high altar by C. Precht, 1674; *organ the first work of A. Schnitger, completed 1688); the late gothic *Wilhadikirche* (dating back in parts to the 12C; baroque organ by E. Bielfeldt, 1735); half-timbered houses in the Altstadt; the *Burgermeister-Hintze-Haus*, with a baroque *façade added by Mayor Heino Hintze, 1621; the House of the Brauerknechte, 1604; town hall, 1668; Arsenal, 1698.

Museums include the *Schwedenspeicher Museum* at the picturesque harbour, built 1705 (Am Wasser West, prehistory and medieval history; open save Monday, 10.00–17.00) and the Alte-Stade in Baumhaus, in a farmhouse of 1773 on the site of an earlier one of 994 (Am Wasser Ost; opening times vary). A local history museum is at No. 12 Inselstraße (open May–September, except Monday, 10.00–12.00 and 14.00–17.00).—Trains connect with Bremen and Hamburg. Tourist information at the town hall.

From Stade the B74 leads SW through peat and cattle country for 18km to reach *Bremervörde* (18,600 inhab.; alt. 4m) on the River Oste. Museum at No. 8 Amstallee (pre-and early history of the district, open weekdays, 08.00–12.30; Sunday, 14.00–16.30). Remains (stables) of former Burg Vörde. Modern swimming pools and 78 marked walks and hikes through the moors and woods.

The Rte continues to the end of the Teufelmoor to (29km) *Osterholz-Scharmbeck* (see p 274) and then for 9km to *Burgdamm*, joining there the B6 which runs 13km S to **Bremen** (see Rte 59).

From Bremen the B75 leads 13km W to the industrial town of **Delmenhorst** (78,000 inhab.; alt. 18m): modern swimming pools and sports complex; ascent to tower of the modern town hall; 17th and 18C parish church. Tourist information at the railway station.

25km W of Delmenhorst is **Oldenburg** (137,000 inhab.; alt. 7m), the administrative seat of Weser-Ems, set on the River Hunte.

History. Oldenburg first appears in written history in 1108 as Aldenburg. The Counts of Ammerland chose it as their family seat in 1150, and Oldenburg received its municipal charter in 1345. After the death of Count Anton Günther (1603–67) Oldenburg passed into the hands of the Danes. The plague devastated Oldenburg in the following year, and in 1676 almost every old building was burned down in a disastrous fire. The grand-dukes of Holstein-Gottorf lived here in 1773–1918. Oldenburg was a free state in 1918–45. The university was founded in 1970.

From the railway station follow Bahnhofstraße SW and then Gottorpstraße S to reach the *Grand-Ducal Schloß* (medieval, rebuilt late 16C, partly rebuilt in the 18th and 19C, Holmerscher wing 1778, theatre 1899; now the regional art gallery, open save Monday, 10.00–13.00 and 15.00–17.00; closes Sunday 13.00). In the 18-hectare Schloß park (set out 1806) is the 19C neo-renaissance Elisabeth-Anna-Palais.

Follow Dammstraße SE to reach the Museum of Natural and Pre-history (open weekdays save Monday, 09.00–13.00 and 14.00–18.00; weekends, 09.00–13.00). Return to Schloßplatz and find NW the gothic church of St. Lambert, restored 18th and 19C. W of the church, Theaterwall leads to the city theatre (1893).

Other sights include, in the Markt, the *Haus Degode* (1618, restored 19C), opposite which is the Town Hall of 1887. In Lange Straße at No. 76 is the 17C frescoed house of Count Anton Günther and at No. 3 Oldenburg's oldest building, the *Lappan* (1468; part of the former Heiligen-Geist-Spital, with its tower and a golden clock). The exhibition hall (Weser-Ems-Halle) was built in 1954. The botanic garden is NW of Oldenburg. In the Gertruden cemetery is a chapel—the grand-dukes' mausoleum—with 15C wall paintings.

Trains connect with Bremen, Emden, Hamburg and Wilhelmshaven; buses with Bremen, Aurich and Wilhelmshaven. Tourist information at No. 3 Lange Straße.

12km NW of Oldenburg is the 3km by 2·5km *Zwischenahner Lake* (the spa Bad Zwischenahner has thermal establishments and mud baths).

From Oldenburg the B60 leads N, reaching after 13km *Rastede*, a health resort with an 11C church of St. Ulrich and a *Schloß park laid out in the 19C. After 16km the Rte reaches a road that leads right 3km to **Varel-Dangast** (25,000 inhab.; alt. 13m) in the Jade bay: 13C *Schloß church* (15C frescoes; early 17C *altar, font and pulpit by Ludwig Münstermann). Local history museum at No. 3 Neumarkt (open save Monday, 15.00–18.00).—6km to the N is *Dangast*, a bathing resort founded in 1797.

Return to the B69 and drive 24km N to **Wilhelmshaven** (105,000 inhab.; alt. 12m), lying at the western end of the Jade bay.

Wilhelmshaven was founded in 1853 by Wilhelm I of Prussia as the chief base for the Prussian navy (and in 1869 it took his name). In 1937 Wilhelmshaven merged with Rüstringen. In spite of much damage in WWII and industrial reconstruction, this remains a popular seaside resort. The construction of the 1958 pipeline with Köln-Wesseling has made Wilhelmshaven Germany's largest oil port.

The town hall, orginally that of Rüstringen, was built by Fritz Höger, 1927–29 (50m-high belfry); in Heppenser Straße is the 16C Heppenser Wurt church (pulpit by L. Münstermann, 1633). See also the garrison church, 1872; salt water aquarium (open 10.00–18.00); two museum ships moored at Kaiser-Wilhelm bridge; and the Ornithological Museum at No. 21 An der Vogelwarte (open Tuesday, 09.00–13.00; Thursday, 13.00–17.00). N of the town is Schloß Knyphausen.

Train connections with Bremen, Hamburg, Hanover, Oldenburg, Osnabrück; buses with Aurich, Emden and Oldenburg; boats with Heligoland (see Rte 57). Tourist information at No. 29 Virchowstraße.

Follow the B210 W across E Friesland through *Jever* (12,400 inhab.; alt. 5m): 14–18C hunting Schloß, with an *audience chamber of 1560 (now the local history museum, open save Monday, 10.00–13.00 and 15.00–17.00); town hall by A. von Bentheim, 1616; 18C church with Friesian *funeral chapel (1511; marble renaissance monument to Edo Wiemken, died 1511, by Cornelis Floris 1560). Tourist information at the town hall.

11km S of Jever is the moated *Schloß Gödens* (1669).
   Just W of Jever a road leads 20km N to *Carolinensiel-Harle*, whence boats serve the East Frisian islands of *Wangerooge* (9km by 1·5km) and *Spiekeroog* (8km by 2km), whose church contains frangments of a wrecked galleon of the Spanish Armada.

The other six East Frisian islands are, from W to E:
Borkum (the largest at 36km², with 7800 inhab), with a 6km promenade and a sandy beach, a Kurhaus; a 63m-high 16C lighthouse. Boats reach Borkum in 2 hours from Emden, aeroplanes in 20 minutes.
Memmert, 11·5km², Germany's largest bird sanctuary, attainable by foot from the island of Juist at low tide.
Juist, 17km by 1·5km, with a population of 1500, nature reserve, sandy beach and a lake with an island. Juist has its own airfield and is also reached by boat from Norddeich.
Nordeney, with a seaside resort—Germany's oldest—founded 1797, 15km by 2km, with a population of 7800, a 5km-long promenade, forests and sand flats. Connections with Norddeich.
Baltrum, the smallest island (6·5km²) with a population of only 850, has 8km of sandy beach.
Langeoog, at 19km² the island with the highest dunes, is a North Sea health resort, boasts a gull colony, 14km of sandy beach, a population of 300, beds for nearly 7500 visitors and boat connections with Bensersiel.

The B210 leads 8km W to *Wittmund* (Schloß, ruined 1674; woodland excursions) and for another 25km to **Aurich** (34,000 inhab.; alt. 8km), administrative centre of East Friesland. Here in the 13C the Counts of Oldenburg built a church. The following century was founded the Schloß. The present Schloß (housing the administrative offices) dates from 1852, with 18C stables. The East Frisian Landschaft is housed in a neo-renaissance building of 1897–1900. The church of St. Lambert (1835) has an early 16C carved altar from Antwerp. In a five-storey windmill is a museum devoted to the history of mills (open April–September, save Monday, 10.00–12.00 and 15.00–17.00; closed Sunday afternoons). A major cattle and horse market. Tourist information at the Pferdemarkt.
   The B72 runs 11km W from here to *Georgsheil*, whence the B70 runs for 16km NW to **Norden** (25,000 inhab.; alt. 8m). Norden has a church of *St. Ludger* (1445), with a free-standing bell tower, set in the exquisite tree-lined MARKTPLATZ. Inside the church: eight mid 13C sandstone statues, the 16C tomb of Unico Manninga, and Arp Schnitger's finest **organ, 1685–88. The 1000-year-old Theelacht (peasant landowners' association) still meets in the town hall (1542), which also houses the local history museum (open Wednesday, Friday

and Saturday, 15.00–17.00).

In the Markt is also a house of 1662 now used as a Mennonite church. The gabled Schöningh house in Oberstraße dates from 1576.

From Norden the B70 continues to the North Sea health resort of *Norddeich*, with boat excursions to the islands of Nordeney, Juist and Baltrum.

Close by Norden is *Schloß Lütetsberg*, rebuilt in 16C renaissance style after a fire of 1959.

From *Georgsheil* the B72 runs SW for 16km to **Emden** (52,600 inhab.; alt. 4m), at the mouth of the Ems and possessing on the Dortmund-Ems canal Lower Saxony's largest harbour.

The town was trading as early as the 9C and by the 16C was one of Germany's major ports. When the Ems changed course the prosperity of Emden disastrously declined, to revive again in the 20C with the digging of the canal and the building of a new harbour. Today it constitutes the third biggest port on the North Sea.

Worth seeing are the medieval church of SS. Cosmas and Damian, ruined as a result of WWII; the Calvinist new church (in Brückstraße), 1643–48; the town hall, a copy of that of Antwerp, by L. van Steenwinkel, 1576, rebuilt after WWII (now the City Museum, open weekdays, save Monday, 10.00–13.00 and 15.00–17.00; weekends, 11.00–13.00); the new town hall of 1962.

Train connections with Bremen, Hamburg, Münster and Norddeich. Tourist information at No. 2 Gräfin-Anna-Straße.

58   From Hanover to Göttingen

Total distance 102km. **Hanover**—B3. 14km *Pattensen*—16km *Elze*—7km *Banteln*—12km **Alfeld an der Leine**—15km **Einbeck**—18km *Northeim*—9km *Nörten-Hardenberg*—11km **Göttingen** (—6km *Nikolausberg*).

Drive S from **Hanover** (see Rte 51) along the B3, reaching after 14km *Pattensen* (with fine views of the Diester and Osterwald hills and the Weserbergland). After 16km the Rte reaches *Elze*.

Continue through *Banteln* (with a Schloß in a park) to reach, 19km from Elze, **Alfeld an der Leine** (15,500 inhab.; alt. 93m): Rathaus, 1584–86; old grammar school, half-timbered and brick, 16C, with coloured carvings of classical a well as Old and New Testament characters; steel-framed shoe factory by Walter Gropius and A. Meyer, 1911–14; romanesque and gothic church of St. Nikolaus; local history museum and exotic zoo at No. 5 Am Kirchplatz (open weekdays, 10.00–12.00 and 15.00–17.00; weekends, 10.00–12.00). A private zoo supplies imported animals world-wide.

15km SE of Alfeld an der Leine lies the partly fortified former Hanseatic town of **Einbeck** (23,000 inhab.; alt. 114m), in the valley of the Ilse. Einbeck has over a hundred sculpted renaissance houses, including the public weigh-house, 1565; the bakers' house, 1552; the pharmacy, 1562; and the town hall, 1593. Einbeck also has the oldest brewery in Germany (1378; from 'Einbeck' possibly derives the term 'Bockbier'); the church of *St. Jakob*, founded 13C, chiefly 17C baroque (W façade, pulpit and furnishings); the *Münsterkirche*, 13th and 14C, with remains of the 12C church (choir stalls, 1288; font, 1427); bicycle museum at No. 1 Papenstraße, and town museum at

No. 11 Steinweg. In the 16C chapel of St. Bartholomäus is buried Friedrich Setürner (1783–1841), who discovered morphia and worked here as a pharmacist, 1806–20.

The B3 travels 18km SE along the Leine valley to reach **Northeim** (25,000 inhab.; alt. 121m), another former Hanseatic town and like Einbeck still partly fortified with many half-timbered renaissance buildings. See also the surviving Benedictine monastery buildings, 1474 and late 16C, including the Münsterkirche; the Heiligen-Geist-Spital; the late gothic hall *St. Sixtus-Kirche* (late 15C stained glass; high altar 1430; two early 16C altars; font 1509; organ case c 1740). Local history museum Am Münster (open save Monday, 10.00–12.00 and 15.00–18.00). Train connections with Basel and Hamburg. Tourist information at No. 12 Markt.

From here the B3 runs due S through *Nörten-Hardenberg* (half-timbered houses; 18C and modern church; nearby ruined 11C Schloß) to reach after 20km **GÖTTINGEN** (115,000 inhab.; alt. 150m).

History. Göttingen is first documented in 953 as *Guitingi*. The town's municipal charter was granted in 1210. In 1351 the city became a member of the Hanseatic League. A new period of importance was inaugurated when Georg I of Hanover founded the university in 1734. Amongst its teachers have been Freidrich Wöhler, who discovered aluminium in 1827 and, Karl Friedrich Gauss (1777–1855), who discovered the magnetic field in 1833. Otto von Bismarck was a student here from 1832–33. In 1772 in a grove (*Hain*) at Göttingen a league of Romantic poets (the 'Hainbund') came together the reform German poetry. In Göttingen is buried Max Planck, who conceived Quantum Theory. Göttingen became the HQ of the Max Planck Society after WWII.

Cross into Berlinerstraße from the main railway station and walk S (following Goethe Straße) to turn left into Groner Straße, reaching on the left the 14C church of *Our Lady* (bell tower 15C; painted 16C altar panels). Next to the church is a gatehouse adjoining the 14C house of the Teutonic knights (who endowed the church). Papendiek leads NE from Groner Straße, from a corner of which Johannisstraße runs E to the oldest church in Göttingen, *St. Johann*, begun in the 13C (romanesque N doorway; two unequal 15C towers; ascent of and view from N tower). This church lies on the S side of the Markt, whose 1396–1443 *Rathaus* is itself in two unequal parts (Ratskeller; guard house). In front of the town hall is Göttingen's goose girl fountain (1901). A half-timbered house of 1553, NE of the Markt, contains the old pharmacy, which was founded in 1332.

From the pharmacy follow Barfürstraße to reach at No. 5 the decorated Junkenschänke of 1549 and at No. 12 the Bornemann Haus, 1536. Barfürstraße continues as far as the 'Aula' or great hall of the university (1837; with pediment sculpture by Ernst von Bendel).

Continue E to reach the 15C church of *St. Albanus* in Geismarstraße (inside, altar depicting the beheading of the saint and scenes from the life of the Blessed Virgin Mary, by H. von Geisman, 1499).

From the church of St. Albanus proceed N to Theaterplatz (at No. 11 the Deutsches Theater, by Schnittger, 1890). From here follow Wall (the site of the former fortifications) to the botanical gardens, laid out in the 18C.

The chief shopping street of Göttingen, Weender Straße, leads S from Wall back to the Markt. Museums in the city include the University Art Gallery, at No. 10 Hospitalstraße (renaissance and baroque art; visits by arrangement); the City Museum, at Nos 7 and 8 Ritterplan (medieval to baroque religious art; open save Monday, 10.00–13.00 and 15.00–17.00; Sunday, closes afternoons); the University Zoological Collection, at No. 28 Berlinerstraße (open Sunday, 10.00–13.00).

Göttingen hosts an annual Handel festival. Tourist information at the railway station and the town hall.

6km NE of Göttingen on the *Nikolausberg* stands the 12C former abbey church of Augustinian nuns (high altar c 1490; N altar c 1400); *view of Göttingen.

59 From Hanover to Heligoland by way of Bremen

Total distance (excluding ferry to Heligoland) 203km. **Hanover**—B6.
24km *Neustadt am Rübenberge*—24km **Nienburg** (—5km
Marklohe)—B215. 19km *Hassel* (—5km *Hoya*—3km *Bücken*)—14km
Verden—A27. 20km **Bremen**—B6. 13km *Burgdamm* (—B74. 9km
Osterholz-Scharmbeck)—18km *Worpswede*)—45km **Bremerhaven**—
44km **Cuxhaven** (—B73. 8km *Altenbruch*—9km *Otterndorf*—9km
Neuhaus). Ferry to **Heligoland** 45km.

Leave **Hanover** (see Rte 51) by way of the Herrenhäuser Gardens taking the B6 for 24km NW to *Neustadt am Rübenberge* (13,000 inhab.; alt. 37m), once the seat of the Dukes of Calenberg: Schloß Landestrost, 1570; 13C collegiate church of St. Peter.

The Rte continues through woodland a further 24km NW to reach **Nienburg** (30,000 inhab.; alt. 25m) on the River Weser: several half-timbered houses including the arcaded renaissance *Rathaus in Lange Straße, c 1590; late gothic church of St. Martin, 15C; the Stocktower, from a former 15C Schloß; local history museum at Nos 4 and 7 Leinstraße, a classical building of 1821 (open save Sunday and Monday, 10.00–12.00; open Wednesday and Thursday, 14.00–17.00). Train connections with Bremen and Hanover. Tourist information at No. 39 Lange Straße.

At *Marklohe*, 5km NW, is a 13C romanesque church with an altar of 1420, late 15C wall paintings and an early 16C tabernacle.

From Nienburg take the B215 N for 19km to *Hassel*.

5km W of Hassel, across the River Weser, is the town of *Hoya*, with a 14C Schloß. 3km S of Hoya lies *Bücken*, with a 12th and 13C romanesque *church, housing a triumphal cross of 1270 and 13C stained glass in the choir.

The B215 continues N from Hassel to reach after 14km **Verden** (24,000 inhab.; alt. 23m), on the River Aller (boat trips; canoes) close to its confluence with the Weser. Once an imperial and Hanseatic city, Verdun was the see of a bishop from 786 and today hosts an important horse fair (horse museum at No. 7 Andreasstraße; open save Monday, 09.00–16.00). The 11C *cathedral*, extended 15C, has three naves and a copper roof, a romanesque font, a early 14C gothic sedilia, and numerous tombs. In the church of *St. Andreas*, Grüne Straße, is the oldest surviving monumental brass, to Bishop Yso, died 1231, and a curious baroque altar. The *Johanniskirche* in Ritterstraße is North Germany's oldest brick church (12C, enlarged and gothicised 15C, with a 15C triumphal cross and tabernacle; medieval wall paintings; stuccoed Last Judgment). Vestiges of the old fortifications. Verden also has a 'Märchenland' (fairy-tale land) with electrically operated models.—Local history museum in a house dated 1708, at No. 10 Große Fischerstraße (open save Monday and Thursday, 10.00–13.00 and 15.00–17.00; Sunday only 14.00–17.00).

Train connections with Bremen, Hanover and Rotenburg. Tourist information at No. 7 Ostertorstraße.

On the Halse 2km N of Verden are 4500 stones (the *Sachsenhain*) commemorating 4500 Saxons massacred by Charlemagne's troops in 782.

From Verden take the A27 for 20km NW to **BREMEN** (558,000 inhab.; alt. 5m), Germany's oldest seaport and lying on either side of the Weser.

Main *railway station*: Bahnhofstraße.
Main *post office*: Domsheide.

Information Office: No. 29 Bahnhofsplatz.

Bremen has an international airport and is served by inter-city trains.

History. Charlemagne established a bishopric at Bremen in 787; and its importance was enhanced in the following century when an archbishopric was created. Bremen gained market rights in 888, and under Otto the Great in 965 the right to mint its own coins and dispense justice. Archbishop Adalbert

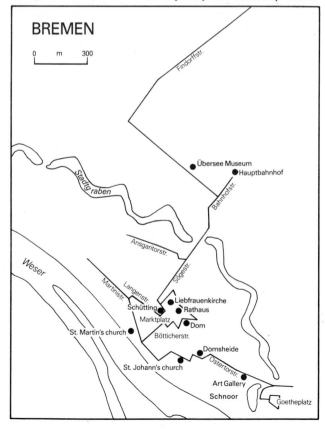

The late gothic north aisle of Bremen Cathedral, facing west.

(1043–72) enlarged its influence and prestige. The city joined the Hanseatic League in 1358. In 1525 the citizens opted for the Reformation. Bremen became a free imperial city in 1646. At the Peace of Westphalia the archbishopric was united with that of Hamburg and the see transferred there. The Swedes attacked Bremen in both 1654 and 1666. Napoleon took the city in 1810. It regained its independent republican status from the Treaty of Vienna (1814–15) and joined the German League. When silting of the Weser jeopardised its trade in the 19C, the merchants of Bremen first founded Bremerhaven and then, between 1886 and 1895, vigorously deepened and regulated the river so as to open up the port once more. Much of the harbour was destroyed in WWII. Reconstructed, it now serves 140 shipping lines (with a large container harbour, constructed 1973). Today Bremen is the capital city of the Land of Bremen. Its university was founded 1970.

The main railway station is flanked by the *Übersee Museum* (founded 1896; ethnology, palaeontology; open save Monday, 10.00–18.00) and the city library.—From the main railway station Bahnhofstraße leads by way of the Herdentor across the gardens with which Altmann replaced the moat in 1805 (along the site of the old fortifications) as far as Sögestraße.

To the left of Herdentor can be seen Bremen's sole surviving windmill. Left of Sögestraße stands the 13C *Liebfrauenkirche*: romanesque S tower; W tower 1229; three aisles. Left of the church is the MARKTPLATZ, where stands the 5m-high Roland statue and pillar, now the city's emblem (1404; on the shield is inscribed: 'Freedom do I give you liberally'—'Vryheit do ik ju openbar'). The statue, symbol of civic freedom, faces the cathedral, whose archbishops had threatened the citizens privileges.

The **Cathedral of St. Peter** stands on the spot where Bishop Willehad built a church in 787. The present building was begun in 1043: romanesque double crypt, with a romanesque bronze font, c 1220; an enthroned Christ, c 1050; and the 'Bleikeller', or Lead Cellar, with mummified bodies (visits weekdays. 09.00–12.00 and 14.00–17.00; Sunday, 09.00–12.00). The W façade was completed in the 13C, follwed by the S aisle chapels (14th and 15C) and the late gothic N aisle. The *organ gallery is by H. Brabender, 1518. The twin towers c 100m high were restored in the romanesque and early gothic styles in the late 19C. Next to the cathedral stands the gothic *__Rathaus__ (1405–09; renaissance façade by Lüder von Bentheim, 1609–12; Ratskeller of 1408, with 18C barrels and reputedly 400 local wines on sale; statues of Charlemagne and seven electors, 1409–10; superb gothic chamber; upper chamber partly renaissance; *Güldenkammer, with early 16C renaissance frescoes; hourly guided tours). The bronze statue by the town hall represent the Bremen 'musicians' (a donkey, dog, cat and cock, by Gerhard Marcks, 1961) from a story by the Brothers Grimm. The modern part of the town hall dates from 1909–12.

Opposite the town hall is the *Schütting* (dialect for 'money making'), i.e. the Guild House of the Bremen merchants, with a façade by Johann den Buscheneer of Antwerp, 1538, a late gothic W gable and a renaissance E gable (doorway and balustrade 19C), today housing the chamber of commerce. The Marktplatz also contains several patrician houses and the modern parliament building (Haus der Bürgerschaft, 1966).

In Langen Straße, which runs between an 18C house and the Schütting, is the office of weights and measures, *Staatwage* (originally 1587–88, destroyed in WWII, rebuilt 1961).

To the S of the Markt is the narrow *BÖTTICHERSTRAßE, an old street of craftsmen's shops, which Ludwig Roselius, the founder of Kaffee Hag (producers of the first caffeine-free coffee in 1907), had redesig-

The gothic Rathaus of 1405–09 stands next to the north tower of the Cathedral.

ned 1926–31; much of the work by the sculptor Bernhard Hoetger (1874–1949). It comprises the Roselius-Haus, 1588; Paula-Modersohn-Becker-Haus, by Hoetger 1927, with his sculptures on this and other façades (see below, museums); the Robinson-Crusoe-Haus; a porcelain carillon on the Haus des Glockenspiel plays at noon, 15.00 and 18.00; the Kammerspiel theatre.

Bötticherstraße leads to Martinistraße and the 13C _Martinskirche_ on the bank of the Weser, rebuilt after WWII (modern windows; Bockelmann organ, 1619; carillon in tower plays noon, 15.00 and 18.00). Close by here is the landing stage for boat trips along the Weser.

Martinistraße leads E to the 14C gothic hall-church of St. Johann, at the centre of the district known as *_Schnoor_ (15C, 16C and 18C houses; art galleries, restaurants). N of the church the street called Am Landherrenamt leads past Domsheide (main post office) to Ostertorstraße, to find at No. 207 Am Wall the ****Kunsthalle** (art gallery; rich collection, 15C to 20C paintings and drawings, open save Mondays 10.00–16.00; Tuesday and Friday also 19.00–21.00). Next door, at No. 208, is the _Gerhard-Marcks-Haus_ (expressionism; open save Monday, 10.00–18.00).

Continue E to find in Goetheplatz the city theatre and at No. 24 _Villa Ichon_, a cultural centre built 1852 and 1871, restored 1982.

OTHER MUSEUMS: Roselius-Haus, with Ludwig Roselius's own collection (open Monday–Thursday, 10.00–16.00; weekends, 11.00–16.00); Paula-Modersohn-Becker-Haus, with paintings by Paula-Modersohn-Becker and modern art exhibitions (open weekdays 10.30–12.30 and 15.00–19.00; weekends, 10.00–14.00). In the suburb of _Schwachhaus_, at No. 240 Schwachhauser Heerstraße, is the Focke-Museum, partly housed in a building of 1768 (daily life in Bremen and north German history; open save Mondays 10.00–18.00). The local history museum is in the moated Schloß Schönebeck, 1660, at Nos 3–5 Im Dorfe (open save Monday and Friday, 15.00–17.00; Sunday, also 10.00–12.30). The Bremen Broadcasting Museum is at No. 85 Findorffstraße (open weekends, 10.00–12.30). See also the 17C renaissance House of the Guild of Artisans (Gewerbehaus) in Ansgaritor Straße.

Annual events include ice sports on 6 January; a traditional banquet in the town hall in February and a market held since 1035 in the last two weeks of October.

The B6 leaves Bremen NW, crossing the Weser and passing through _Burgdamm_ after 13km.

The B74 leads NE from Burgdamm to reach after 13km _Osterholz-Scharmbech_ (24,000 inhab.; alt. 8m), with its 12C romanesque monastery church; farmstead; stone graves; windmills and watermills; local history museum at No. 32 Rollberg (open save Mondays, weekdays, 10.30–16.00; weekends 10.00–12.00).

Follow the B74 for a further 3km and then drive 15km E across the Teufelmoor to the artists' village of _Worpswede_ (800 inhab.; alt. 51m) on the slopes of the 57m-high Weyerberg, made famous in the early years of this century by Rainer Maria Rilke, Paula Modersohn-Becker, Bernhard Hoetger and Heinrich Vogeler.

45km N of Burgdamm, by way of the Garlstedter heath, marshland and sandy ridges, the B6 reaches **Bremerhaven** (142,000 inhab.; alt. 3m), bought from Hanover in 1827 as an alternative port by Burgermeister Johann Smidt of Bremen when the silting of the Weser threatened his city's economy. Its eleven docks and over 12km of quays (including the 1250m-long Columbus Quay) help to make it the busiest passenger and fishing port of the FDR. Bremerhaven incorporates the suburbs of Geestemünde (which is reached first from Bremen), Wesermünde and Lehe.

The fishing harbour, with its vast fish markets (auctions begin at

07.00), lies SW of the main railway station. To the right, at No. 6 Kaistraße, is the Morgenstern museum (prehistory and local history; open weekdays save Monday 10.00–16.00; Saturday, 10.00–13.00; Sunday, 10.30–12.30). Close by, at No. 12 Handelshafen, is the North Sea and Fishing Museum (open weekdays, 08.00–18.00; weekends, 10.00–18.00). Enter Geeste Straße, passing the radar tower (116m; panoramic view), to reach the new Museum of Navigation (Schiffahrtsmuseum, entrance in Von-Ronzelen-Straße; open save Monday and Sunday, 10.00–18.00).

Other museums in Bremerhaven include the Museum of 20C Art, at No. 4 Karlsburg (open save Monday, 15.00–18.00; Sunday only, 11.00–13.00) and the Travel Museum (in a building dated 1912 at No. 17 Hansastraße, open weekdays, 08.00–12.00). Bremerhaven also has a zoo and an aquarium (both open daily, 08.00–16.30).—N of the town at *Speckenbüttel* is an open-air museum with reconstructions of Lower Saxon houses of the 16C and afterwards.

Train connections with Bremen, Hanover, Cuxhaven, Bremervörde and Stade. Buses connect with Cuxhaven. Boat trips to Heligoland and Bremen. Tourist information at No. 58 Friedrich-Ebert-Straße.

43km further N from Bremerhaven along the B6 is **Cuxhaven**, the road to which runs not far from the coast—resorts include *Wremen*, 7km W, with mini-golf, etc.; connected to Bremerhaven and Cuxhaven by train and to Bremerhaven and Dorum by boat; and the health resort of *Sahlenburg*, 4km W, with a 3km-long beach at the foot of the wooded Wolfsberg. 1km N of the road to Sahlenburg the B6 reaches **Cuxhaven** (62,000 inhab.; alt. 3m), on the 15km-wide mouth of the Elbe. Cuxhaven, now part of Lower Saxony, belonged to Hamburg from 1394 to 1937, and with its two fine beaches has been renowned as a thermal sea spa since 1816. In Schloß Ritzebüttel is the town's historical museum. After Bremerhaven and Altona this is Germany's largest fishing port (auctions begin at 07.00). Its emblem is the Kugelbake beacon. The suburb of *Döse* has a church dated 1528. Trains connect Cuxhaven with Hamburg and Bremerhaven; boats with Hamburg and Heligoland. Tourist information at the Kurverwaltung.

Boats for the 1700m by 600m red limestone island of *Heligoland*, (German 'Helgoland'), 45km away, leave from the pier known as Alte Liebe (derived from the name of a ship, the 'Olivia', which sank here in 1732): bathing, cliff walks, duty-free goods. Other excursions to the islands of *Neuwerk* (600-year-old lighthouse, attainable by horse carriage along the mud flats) and *Scharnhörn* (bird sanctuary). Neuwerk is best reached from the seaside resort of *Duhnen*, 5km from Cuxhaven along the B73.

8km W of Cuxhaven on the B73 lies *Altenbruch* (4500 inhab.; alt. 3m), a seaside resort with a twin-towered romanesque church of *St. Nikolaus*, gothicised and then rendered partly baroque (high altar 1480; baroque organ).—Just beyond Altenbruch a road leads 1km right to *Lüdingworth* (romanesque stone church).

Continue W along the B73 for 9km more to the walled town of *Otterndorf* (6200 inhab.; alt. 5m): Rathaus, 1583; half-timbered houses including the Kranichhaus of 1696 with the local history museum; ruined Schloß of the dukes of Lauenburg; church of St. Severin, 1261; house of Homer's translator, the poet Johann Heinrich Voss, who taught in the grammar school (1614) from 1778 to 1782. 9km further W is *Neuhaus*, close where the River Oste flows into the Elbe.

IX SCHLESWIG-HOLSTEIN

60 From Hamburg to Lübeck

A. By way of Ahrensburg and Bad Oldesloe

Total distance 58km. **Hamburg**—B75. 23km *Ahrensburg*—6km *Bargteheide*—14km *Bad Oldesloe*—15km **Lübeck**.

Leave **Hamburg** (see Rte 50) NE by the suburb of *Wandsbeck*, given glory by the poet Matthias Claudius (1740–1815) who lived and is buried here close by the market place in the cemetery of the *Christuskirche* (which houses the classical mausoleum, 1782–91, of Count H.C. von Schimmelmann). After 16km the Rte (the B75) passes the open-air village museum of *Volksdorf* (open save Tuesday and Thursday, 09.00–12.00 and 14.00–18.00).

7km further the B75 reaches *Ahrensburg* (25,000 inhab.; alt. 40m): on the N edge of the city the moated renaissance Schloß and Schloß church (both built by Count Peter Rantzau, c 1595, with baroque alterations, 1759–82; 19C ballroom; open save Monday, 10.00–dusk). Tourist information at No. 39 Rathausplatz.

4km N lies *Bargteheide*, with its Schloß, hotel Tremsbüttel and a 13C church. The B75 continues for 14km to reach **Bad Oldesloe** (20,000 inhab.; alt. 17m) at the confluence of the Rivers Trave and Beste. A church has existed here since the mid 12C. Bad Oldesloe, though no longer a spa (the Kurpark remains, with fine sports facilities), was treasured for its springs by Henry the Lion. The town was the birthplace of the composer Dietrich Buxtehude (1637–1707). The present church building (on the site of the first) dates from 1757–64 (tower 1886). The neo-classical town hall dates from 1806. Close by here (1·5km N, on the road to Bad Segeberg) is *Menno-Mate*, refuge of Menno Simons, founder of the Mennonites (died 1561).

The B75 continues NE for 15km to reach **LÜBECK** (220,000 inhab.; alt. 11m), entering by the Moislinger Allee, which runs as far as the central railway station.

Main *railway station*: Am Bahnhof.

Main *post office*: Marktplatz.

Information Office: No. 14 Rathaushof and at main railway station.

Trains and buses connect Lübeck with major towns and cities; *ships* with Denmark, Finland, Sweden and Trellenborg. Lübeck has an *airport*.

History. Count Adulf II of Holstein founded Lübeck in 1143, on a spot once settled by the Wends where the River Trave meets the Schwartau. Henry the Lion took possession of the town in 1159, setting up a mint here. In 1160 the bishopric of Oldenburg was transferred to Lübeck, a sign of the city's growing importance. Frederick Barbarossa ratified the city's privileges in a charter of 1188. Lübeck escaped the domination of Denmark and in the early 13C began building its city walls and gates as a symbol of that freedom. Declared a free imperial city in 1226 by decree of Emperor Friedrich II, Lübeck's favourable position on the Trave (only 20km from the Baltic Sea) enabled it to prosper and become one of the three dominant members of the Hanseatic League (in effect the leader, and for a time the largest German city after Cologne). Between 1300 and 1350 Lübeck rebuilt all five of its main churches in the gothic style. The last meeting of the League in 1630 consisted only of Lübeck, Bremen and Hamburg. Lübeck's fortifications spared her some of the atrocities of the Thirty Years' War. After a period of decline (mitigated in part by the wine trade), during which Lübeck was the theatre of struggles between the two sides of the French Revolution and became in 1810 capital of the French département of Bouches-de-l'Elbe, the city began in part to prosper again. Lübeck joined the German Confederation in 1815 and the North German Confederation in 1867. After Napoleon's defeat, Lübeck, Bremen and Hamburg had united as three free Hanseatic towns, a status lost only in 1937 when the city voted to become part of Schleswig-Holstein (whereas Bremen and Hamburg have remained free cities within the German Federal Republic). Further prosperity has come from the establishment of new industries at Schlutup on the border with the DDR and the construction of the Elbe-Trave canal, opened 1900. The city was severely damaged in WWII in an air raid of 29 March 1942, and has been splendidly restored. Today its port has 12 docks.

Here were born the novelists Heinrich Mann (1871–1950) and Thomas Mann (1875–1955), whose first major work, 'Buddenbrooks' (1901) depicts the decline of a Lübeck bourgeois family throughout the 19C.

Lübeck's marzipan is famous.

From the main railway station follow Konrad-Adenauer-Straße E across the PUPPENBRÜCKE (decorated with statues by Dietrich Jürgen Boy, 1778, one of which, Mercury, inspired a noted poem by Emmanuel Giebel, 1815–84) to reach the city's symbol, the *Holstentor, a medieval fortified gate, built 1469–78 by Heinrich Helstede,

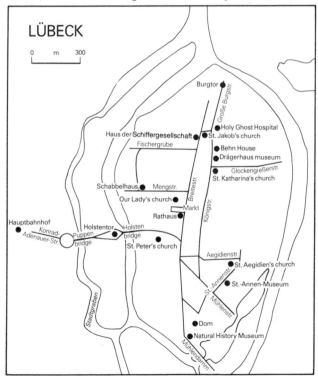

which now houses a historical museum (open April–September, 10.00–17.00; closes winter 16.00). The motto 'CONCORDIA DOMI FORIS PAX' was added in the 19C. To the right of the Holstentor are former salt barns dating from the 16th and 17C.

Cross the Holstenbrücke (right the Upper Trave, left the Holsten harbour) to reach the Markt, passing en route on the right the 12th and 13C romanesque church of *St. Peter*, built with a nave and two aisles in the 14C, two more aisles added 16C, burned down 1942, restored; a lift ascends the 50m-high tower (crowned with its spire c 1430, restored after 1942), which offers a splendid view of Lübeck. The street known as Große Petersgrube contains numerous half-timbered houses.

In the Markt is situated the ***Rathaus**: brick gothic façade, 1230, ornamented further 1434; renaissance loggia, 1570, with a 13C Ratskeller; S wing built 1298–1398, with long gothic arcades, a wing embellished in 1442 (inside this wing, the War Hall, whose furnishings were destroyed in the 1942 air raid); yet further enriched by a renaissance staircase and bay window of 1594 (in Breite Straße). In Breite Straße (N) is also the main entrance to the town hall, with two brass side panels, cast 1452, depicting the enthroned emperor and a wild man whose shield bears the Lübeck eagle; bronze mountings on the double doors depict the emperor amidst the seven electors. Tours of the interior (on the hour from 10.00–16.00 weekdays and at 11.00 and 12.00 weekends) include the late baroque audience chamber (1754–61), with a renaissance doorway (by Tönnis Evers the Elder, 1573) and paintings by the Italian Stephan Torelli, 1754–60; the cellars, with romanesque pillars (1220–26), as well as various halls (the Hansa Hall, the Rose Room, the Admiral's Room and the Bridal Chamber (whose fireplace of 1575 is inscribed in low German: 'Many a man sings loudly when he brings home his bride; if he saw into the future, he would weep'); and the Bürgerschaftshalle with 17th and 18C portraits of the city fathers.

A passage leads from the corner tower of the town hall (1425) to the part gothic, part renaissance *Chancery* (1480–85, extended in 1588 and 1614), with wall panelling by Tönnies Evers the Younger. The modern wing of the town hall, by way of the *N façade (1887), is flanked by a garden and leads to the gothic, three-aisled, brick-built *Marienkirche*, destroyed in WWII and since restored (architect B. Fendrich). The choir was finished 1291, the W end 1337. The two towers (each 125m high) were built 1304–10. The nave measures 70m by 40m. *Inside*: 13C roof paintings, discovered after the conflagration of 1942; font by Hans Apengeter, 1337; bronze gilt **aumbry, by Nikolais Grude (the brazier) and Nikolaus Rughese (the goldsmith) 1476–79 (its Madonna was added by C.J. Milde 1855); late 15C altar of the Annunciation (behind the high altar); bronze tomb of Godhard Wigerich (died 1518) and his four wives, by Peter Vischer of Nuremberg; high altar bronze crucifix by Gerhard Marcks, 1959. In the S tower lies a bell as it lay smashed after the air raid of 1942.

From here Mengstraße leads to the *Buddenbrook house* (No. 4), a building that belonged to Thomas Mann's family (1841–91), and where the Mann brothers were born (originally built 1239, rebuilt 1758, from which century dates the façade).

Return along Mengstraße towards the harbour, passing several old houses and at No. 49 the merchant's 'Schabbelhaus' (13th and 14C, baroque interior, now a restaurant).

From here walk N and then E along Fischergrube to reach (at No. 2 Breite Straße) the *Haus der Schiffergesellschaft*, set up as a house for sailors, 1535, and now a restaurant (inside, intricate models of sailing vessels; painting of Lübeck's largest flagship, the Adler, built 1566; wall paintings of Biblical stories). No. 6 Breite Straße is the merchants' company house (*Haus der Kaufmannschaft*), neo-gothic 1819, on the site of a building constructed in the 15C. Inside are 16th and 17C furnishings, especially the superb pannelling by Hans Dreger, 1572–83, with 1035 mythological and Biblical figures, brought here in the 19C from another renaissance house (the Fredenhagen Haus), and known as the Fredenhagen room).

Opposite the Schiffergesellschaft is the 13th and 14C *Jacobikirche. Inside:* pillar paintings, mid 12C; font by Klaus Grude, 1466, supported by three kneeling angels and depicting the twelve apostles; small organ 1515; larger organ, 1504; spiral staircase to the W gallery, 1619; carved altar by Jakob Budde, 1698; renaissance choir stalls; baroque high altar by Johann Hieronymus Hassenberg, 1717; and the *Brömbse altar, 1498–50, whose sculptor also made the four stone reliefs of the Passion on the trellis work of the choir. The flèche dates from 1623. The top storey of the tower was added in 1636, and the city architect Kaspar Walter added the slender baroque spire in 1658. In the N chapel under the tower is the wrecked vessel, the 'Pamir'.

Walk E to find across the road the **Heiligen-Geist-Hospital**, an old people's home, founded c 1230, the present buildings 1276–86, with three gables, an octagonal tower and (inside) a chapel with early 14C wall paintings, gothic altars, star vaulting of 1495, a five-arched screen with an early 15C frieze depicting 23 scenes from the story of Elizabeth, and a 16-branched chandelier, 1673; and the Long House, 88m long, whose roof trusses date from the 13C with 170 small rooms (or cabins) for the pensioners, built 1820. The hospital archive has 15C gothic wall cabinets, and the warden's room has a fireplace of 1672.

From here follow Große Burgstraße N to reach Lübeck's other gate, the five-storeyed *Burgtor*, the lower four storeys from the old fortifications of 1230, the fifth built by Nikolaus Peck in 1444. The cap-like roof replaced a slender spire in 1685. To the right is the former customs house (1571; terracotta frieze by Statius van Düren).

Return past the Heiligen-Geist-Hospital to find on the left the classical *Behn House*, built in 1779–83 for the city father Peter Testorf (art gallery with works by Franz Overbeck, Caspar David Friedrich, Emil Nolde, Schmidt-Rottluff, etc.; open April–October, except Monday, 10.00–17.00; winter closes 16.00). Close by (at No. 9 Königstraße, the continuation of Große Burgstraße) is the *Museum Drägerhaus*, in a late 18C building (memorials of the Mann brothers, open as the Behn House gallery), beyond which, on the corner of Glockengießerstraße, is the 14C former Franciscan *Katharinenkirche* (13C; asymmetrical façade begun 1335; late 15C triumphal cross; gothic choir stalls; in the niches of the W façade three terracotta figures by Ernst Barlach, 1947 (Woman in the Wind, Beggar and Singer), and six figures by Gerhard Marcks, 1949. On the inside S wall is a Raising of Lazarus by Tintoretto.

Continue S to find (right) Aegidienstraße which leads to Lübeck's brick gothic church of *St. Aegidien*, whose earliest building (1227) possessed a single nave, extended in the 14C to become a hall church with three aisles. St. Aegidien's *organ has an early baroque case (1624–26) by Michael Sommer, following the specifications of Hans Scherer of Hamburg, with reliefs and mosaics by Baltzer Winne, 1626, and foliage and trumpeting angels of 1715. The font was cast by

Heinrich Gerwiges in 1453 (font cover and trellis-work 1710). The pulpit dates from 1706 (figures by H. Freese). The rood screen was made by Tönnies Evers the Younger, 1586–87. The gothic wall paintings were discovered in 1907.

St.-Annen-Straße leads SW from here and contains at No. 15 the *St.-Annen-Museum*, devoted to the history and treasures of Lübeck (*Crucifixion altarpiece by Hans Memling, from the cathedral; open as the Behn House gallery). Built into the museum is a baroque hall of 1736 from Glockengießerstraße.

Take Mühlenstraße to reach Fegefeuer Straße (purgatory street, leading in theory from the Hell of the city to the Paradise N entrance of the cathedral, 1250, but at present a one-way street running the other way), along which you reach the *Cathedral*, begun when Henry the Lion laid the foundation stone in 1173 and finished 1247, with two 120m-high towers, partly romanesque, partly gothic. From the bombings of 1942 escaped a triumphal cross by Bernt Notke, 1477, the bronze font by Lorenz Grove, 1455, a Schöne Madonna of 1509, a mid 15C Virgin Mary crowned with stars and the renaissance pulpit of 1568 (railings 1572).—The cathedral museum is open at the same times as the Behn House gallery. The natural history museum is at Nos 1–3 Mühlendamm. At Nos 4–6 Kleine Petergrube is a puppet museum (both open, except Monday, 09.30–18.00).

B. By way of Ratzeburg

Total distance 90km. **Hamburg**—B5. 18km *Bergedorf*—B207. 20km *Schwarzenbek*—21km *Mölln*—B207 and B208. 8km **Ratzeburg**—B208 and B207. 11km *Groß-Sarau*—4km *Klein-Grönau*—8km **Lübeck**.

Leave **Hamburg** (see Rte 50) E to reach *Bergedorf* by way of the B5. Continue E along the B207 to reach (20km) *Schwarzenbek*.

Take the B404 from Schwarzenbek through the Saxon woods in the direction of Trittau, reaching after 6km the signposted *Schloß Friedrichsruhe* (destroyed 1946, rebuilt) in the heart of the forest, the Bismarck family retreat (Bismarck mausoleum, completed 1889, with the mortal remains of Otto von Bismarck and his wife; visits except Monday, 09.00–17.00).
The health resort of *Trittau* (5500 inhab.; alt. 17m) lies along the B404 16km from Schwarzenbek.

From Schwarzenbek drive N along the B207 (the route of the medieval salt road between Lübeck and Hanover) for 21km, crossing the Elbe-Lübeck canal, to reach **Mölln** (15,500 inhab.; alt. 18m), a town surrounded by lakes, with picturesque houses (including a gothic town hall in brick, staircase gable 1373) and, near the Markt, the 13th and 15C church of *St. Nikolaus*, romanesque with a gothic tower (inside, seven-branched candelabrum, 1436; font by P. Wulf, 1509; triumphal cross, 1504; baroque organ by Peter Scherer, 1558; pulpit, 1743). On the church wall is the 16C memorial stone of the merry jester Till Eulenspiegel (depicting an owl and a mirror: 'Eule' and 'Spiegel'), said to have died of the plague here in 1350. (He is remembered in the local history museum, at No. 2 Am Markt, open April–October, weekdays save Monday, 09.00–12.00 and 15.00–17.00; weekends, 09.00–12.00). Mud baths and Kneipp health centre. Trains and buses connect with Lübeck, Lüneburg and Ratzeburg, buses also with Hamburg. Tourist information at the Kurverwaltung.

Continue along the B207 for 6km, turning E along the B208 for 2km
to reach **Ratzeburg** (13,000 inhab; alt. 16m) on a promontory of the
Ratzeburg lake. In 1154 Henry the Lion founded its bishopric and
Cathedral, one of the oldest in Germany (completed 13C), with a
powerful W tower. The exterior is patterned in yellow and red brick.
Inside are the gravestones of 23 bishops, a romanesque triumphal
cross, flanked with statues of Mary and John, romanesque choir stalls,
a gothic ducal pew, pulpit 1567, baroque altar in the S transept 1629.
The cathedral cloister has medieval wall paintings. Outside is a copy
of the bronze lion set up by Henry the Lion in Brunswick.

In the Domplatz are the *Andreas Paul Weber Museum* (a collection
of his satirical lithographs and drawings) and the regional museum (in
a rococo house built 1764–66 for Duke Adolf Friedrich von
Mecklenburg-Strelitz), both open, save Monday, 10.00–13.00 and
14.00–17.00.

Because the old town was razed by King Christian V of Denmark in
1693, its oldest secular buildings are the Kreis house and the
Weigh-house in the market square (c 1700). Close by is the classical
parish church, 1787–91, whose neighbouring (c 1840) presbytery was
the home of the sculptor and poet Ernst Barlach (1870–1938) from
1878–84. (It is now a Barlach Museum, open save Monday, 09.30–
12.00 and 15.00–18.00.) Barlach is buried in the cemetery on the E
bank of the Ratzeburg Lake (over the Königsdamm), his grave
marked by a copy of his statue of a singing choirboy.

Trains connect Ratzeburg with Kiel, Lübeck and Lüneburg; buses with local
places. Tourist information at No. 9 Am Markt.

Return to the B207 and travel N along the Ratzeburg Lake (which
comes close to the border with the DDR), passing *Einhaus*, with a
2·8m-high stone cross commemorating the martyrdom of Abbot
Answerus, stoned to death by the Wends in 1066.

Continue through the villages of *Groß-Sarau* and *Klein-Sarau* to
reach after 23km **Lübeck** (see Rte 60A).

61 From Hamburg to Kiel

Total distance 95km (by motorways A7 and A215 90km).
Hamburg—B4. 46km *Bad Bramstedt*—19km **Neumünster**—12km
Bordelsholm lake—18km **Kiel**.

Leave Hamburg (see Rte 50) NW by the Kieler Straße, passing
through the suburbs of *Eimsbüttel* (19C church) and *Sellingen* (0·5km
E of Hagenbeck's zoo), to reach by the B4 (46km) **Bad Bramstedt**
(10,000 inhab.; alt. 14m), a spa with peat and saline baths: modern
health centre 2km S of the town; gothic church of St. Mary Magdalen,
with a 14C altar; statue of Roland (dressed as a Roman legionary)
1693, in front of the baroque Kavalier house given by the Danish king
Christian IV (1588–1648) to his third wife, who was born here.

Trains connect the spa with Hamburg and Neumünster. Tourist information at
the town hall.

Neumünster (81,000 inhab.; alt. 22m) lies on the B4 19km N of Bad
Branstedt. The name derives from the new monastery which Bishop

Vicelin founded here in 1127 (in a small settlement called Wip-
pendorf), all of its buildings destroyed in air raids in WWII, along
with most of the old town. Today Neumünster is a modern textile-
and metalworking town. Sights include the neo-classical church of
St. Vicelin, with a green domed tower, by F. Hansen, 1829–34; the
baroque Caspar-von-Saldern house built by the statesman Caspar
von Saldern in 1746; and the zoo (in the city forest, NW of the town,
with over 400 animals and an aquarium, open 09.00 to dusk). The
textile museum opens weekdays, 07.30–16.00; Sundays, 10.00–
13.00). Train connections with Bad Oldesloe, Flensburg, Hamburg
and Kiel. Tourist information at the Stadthaus.

12km N along the B4 is the *Bordesholm lake*, beside which lies the
village of *Bordesholm*: Augustinian monastery, founded 1332, later a
college which was the basis of Kiel University. The only building
remaining from the monastery is the late medieval gothic church
(tomb inscribed J.H. Voß; choir stalls of 1509; bronze tomb of
Herzogin Anna von Holstein-Gottorf, died 1514). The Bordesholm
altar by Hans Brüggemann, 1666, is now in Schleswig Cathedral.

Continue N through the Obereider valey to reach in 18km **KIEL**
(250,000 inhab.; alt. 5m), on the Kiel fjord which gives shipping
access to the Baltic.

History. The name Kiel derives from 'the city by the spring' (*Kyle*) and was
founded by Count Adolf IV von Schauenburg in 1242. The settlement prospered, became a member of the Hanseatic League in 1283 and established a
thriving market and stock exchange. The city voluntarily chose Christian I of
Denmark as its ruler in 1460, one of whose descendants, Herzog Christian
Albrecht of Gottorf, founded the university in 1665. Kiel was where the
provisional government of Schleswig-Holstein sat in 1848 to declare its
opposition to Denmark. The city became Prussian and a major naval base, a
role continued under the German empire. In 1895 its naval resources were
enhanced by the opening of the Kiel canal. In 1917 the city was made capital of
the Prussian province of Schleswig-Holstein. Here in 1918 a naval mutiny
began the November Revolution. The damage suffered by Kiel in WWI, though
severe, was far outweighed by that of WWII, when 80 per cent of the city was
destroyed. Kiel has recovered, redeveloped its shipbuilding industry, built a
new city and since 1945 has been capital of the federal province of Schleswig-
Holstein.

Of the former *Franciscan monastery* in Falckstraße have survived
the mid 13C refectory (now students' lodgings) and the cloister (with
the tombstone of Adolf IV von Schauenburg, died 1261). In the old
MARKT is the 14th and 15C church of *St. Nikolaus*, partly modernised during restoration after WWII, but still retaining its bronze font
cast by Johann Apengeter in 1344, the patriarch's altar of 1460, a
triumphal cross of 1490 and a baroque pulpit of 1705. Outside the
church is Ernst Barlach's bronze 'Spiritual fighter'. The former
Schloß (in Schloßstraße), much damaged in the war, has been rebuilt
in the 16C renaissance style and is now a cultural centre and local
history museum (open weekdays save Mondays and Wednesday
afternoons, 10.00–13.00 and 15.00–19.00; Sunday, 11.00–13.00),
with a splendid garden.

In 'Kleiner Kiel', W of the Markt, are: the Opera House, by
Christian Heinrich Seeling, 1905–07, restored; Heinrich Billing's
Jugendstil Rathaus of 1911, with its 106m-high copper-covered
tower, standing on a tributary of the fjord at No. 9 Fleethörn (visits
daily 10.30 and 11.30, May–September); and the art and
archaeological collection, at No. 1 Düsternbrooker Weg (open save

Monday, 10.00–13.00 and 15.00–18.00; closed Sunday afternoons).

OTHER MUSEUMS: the Geological and Palaeological Collection and the Theatre (both at Nos 40–60 Olsenhausenstraße, open Wednesday, 14.00–18.00); University Zoological Museum, at No. 3 Hegewischstraße, (open except Monday, 10.00–17.00, closes Sunday at 13.00). In the suburb of *Rammsee* 6km S of the city is the Schleswig-Holstein open-air museum (reconstructed farmhouses and workshops; open except Monday, 1 April–15 November, 09.00–17.00).

The Olympic centre and Olympic harbour (used for the Olympic games of 1933 and 1972) is on the outer fjord in the suburb of *Schilksee*. The environs of Kiel include 19km N, by the sea, the naval monument of Laboe, by G.A. Munzer, 1927–36.

Boats ply to Bagenkop, Göteborg and Oslo; trains connect with Flensburg, Hamburg and Lübeck. Tourist information at No. 18 Auguste- Viktoria-Straße.

62   From Lübeck to Kiel

A. By way of Bad Segeberg and Neumünster

Total distance 85km. **Lübeck**—B206. 28km *Bad Segeberg*—B205. 27km **Neumünster**—B4. 12km *Bordesholm lake*—18km **Kiel**.

Leave **Lübeck** (see Rte 60A) by the Fackenburgen Allee, taking the B206 W through woodlands to reach after 28km **Bad Segeberg** (15,000 inhab.; alt. 52m), a town built by Emperor Lothar in the 12C as a bulwark against the Slavs. The town's development as a spa dates from 1884. The 91m-high *Kalkberg*, E of the town, is today a protected national monument, and includes a limestone cave with nine chambers sheltering uniquely developed species both of animal and plant. Bad Segeberg has an open-air theatre (1934–37) seating 10,000, and hosts an annual Karl May theatre festival. See also the brick-built romanesque church of *Our Lady*, begun 1160 (font 1447; late gothic altar 1515; triumphal cross 1515; renaissance pulpit 1612. Lübecker Straße has numerous 15th and 16C half-timbered houses, including, at No. 15, the 16C local history museum (open daily, 10.00–12.00 and 15.00–18.00).

The B205 continues a further 27km NW to *Neumünster* from where the Rte runs N along the B4 for 30km by way of the Bordesolm lake to **Kiel** (see Rte 61).

B. By way of Bad Schwartau, Eutin and Plön

Total distance 73km. **Lübeck**—B206. 7km *Bad Schwartau*—14km junction with B76—8km *Eutin*—15km *Plön*—13km *Preetz*—16km **Kiel**.

Leave **Lübeck** (see Rte 60A) N by the B206, passing after 7km through the spa of *Bad Schartau* (20,000 inhab.; alt. 16m), close where Blücher surrendered to the French in 1806, and after a further 14km reaching the junction with the B76. This road runs W through the hilly

*'Holstein Switzerland' for 8km to the lakeside town of *Eutin* (17,000 inhab.; alt. 43m), for many years the home of the Bishops of Lübeck. Here was born the composer Carl Maria von Weber (1786–1826)—birthplace at No. 48 Lübecker Straße. Herzog Peter Friedrich Ludwig, who ruled 1785–1829, generously patronised artists such as Homer's translator Johann Heinrich Voß, the poet Friedrich Leopold Graf zu Stolberg and the painter Wilhelm Tischbein. Voß's house with a façade of 1784–1802 is now a hotel. See also the late romanesque *Michaelskirche* in the Marktplatz, with a gothic choir (inside: candelabrum, 1444; bronze font, 1511). The Marktplatz also houses several half-timbered houses, the Stadtpalais of 1786 and the classical Rathaus of 1788–91. The *Schloß*, begun 13C, enlarged by the bishops in the 17th and 18C (with princely portraits and work by Tischbein: tours daily except Monday, 11.00, 15.00 and 16.00, May–September). The *Schloß park*, set out in the 'English' style, has hosted an annual Carl Maria von Weber festival since 1951.

Trains connect Eutin with Hamburg, Lübeck and Keil, as do buses; boats ply the lake. Tourist information at the house of the Kur guests, at No. 9 Am Markt.

The *Bungsberg*, 16km N, at 164m is the highest peak of Schleswig-Holstein.

Continue NW for 15km through forests and lakeland to *Plön* (11,500 inhab.; alt. 25m), which lies between the Great Plön Lake and several smaller ones (water sports) and long ago was a Slavish settlement. The *Schloß*, now a boarding school, was built for Duke Joachim Ernst von Schleswig-Holstein, 1633–36, and retains Italianate stuccoed rooms and a rococo panelled library. In the Schloß park is the rococo *pavilion called the Prinzenhaus, 1747–50 (with wings dated 1896). To the E of Plön is the Max Planck hydro-biological institute. Regional museum at No. 1 Johannisstraße (open May–September, 10.00–12.00 and 15.00–18.00; Sunday, 15.00–18.00; winter Tuesday–Saturday, 10.00–12.00).

1·5km N of the town rises the 64m-high Parnaß (hotel and view-tower). Trains and buses connect Plön with Kiel and Lübeck. Tourist information at No. 12 Bahnhofstraße.

The Rte continues NW between the small Plön Lake and the Trammer Lake to reach (13km) *Preetz* (16,000 inhab.; alt. 34m): 13C abbey, present buildings dating partly from the 17C, with a 14C abbey church; 17th and 18C parish church.

From Preetz the B76 runs 16km NW to **Kiel** (see Rte 61).

63 From Lübeck to Puttgarden

Total distance 112km. **Lübeck**—B75. 16km *Travemünde*—the Bäderstraße, 5km *Niendorf*—3km *Timmendorfer Strand*—7km *Haffkrug*—5km *Süsel*—B207. 8km *Neustadt in Holstein*—2km *Merkendorf*—13km *Lensahn*—8km *Oldenburg in Holstein*—11km *Heiligenhafen*—12km *Großenbrode*—22km *Puttgarden*.

Leave **Lübeck** (see Rte 60A) NE by way of the Burgtorbrücke and then along Travemünder Allee past a large military cemetery. After 5km the B75 reaches the B105 (which leads E 4km to Schlutup and the border crossing with the DDR). 16km from Lübeck the B75 reaches *Travemünde* (13,000 inhab.; alt. 3km), a port founded in 1178 by Count Adolf von Schauenburg, and bought by the citizens of Lübeck in 1329. Today an elegant bathing and health resort, on the Baltic where the River Trave empties itself into Lübeck bay, Travemünde also has a casino, golfing, campsites, the four-masted sailing ship 'Passat' (visits May–September, 09.30–12.30 and 14.30–17.30), and in the oldest part of the town several half-timbered houses and the church of St. Lawrence (1557). Train connections with Hamburg and Lübeck, buses with Lübeck and the Bäderstraße (see below). Boat trips in the bay and to Scandinavia (Gedser, Trelleborg, Bornholm, Helsinki), with a car ferry to the promontory of Privall on the right bank of the Trave. Since 1899 Travemünde has hosted an annual summer regatta with more than 1000 yachts participating. Tourist information at No. 1b Strandpromenade.

The Bäderstraße now follows the coastline W and N from Travemünde, reaching after 5km the small seaside and fishing resort of *Niendorf*, with a 4000m-long sandy beach, and after 3km more, *Timmendorfer Strand*, with an even longer beach and pine woods (Tourist information at No. 73a Strandallee). The family-orientated resorts of *Scharbeutz* and *Haffkrug* are reached, respectively, 4km and 3km further on (tourist information at No. 134 Strandallee). All these resorts have good train and bus connections.—After 5km W the Bäderstraße reaches *Süsel*. From here take the B207 for 8km N to *Neustadt in Holstein* (16,000 inhab.; alt. 4m), a port and bathing station on Lübeck bay founded c 1200. Its gothic *parish church* dates from 1238–44 (W tower 1334; gothic wall paintings; *altar 1643, designed for Schleswig Cathedral). The Holy Ghost hospital dates from 1408, the corn house from 1830. the Kempertor, sole survivor of the medieval fortifications, now houses the local history museum, including works by the local painter Adam Hölbing, (1855–1929) and a steamship of 1850 (open May–September, weekends, 14.00–17.00), with the same times weekdays July and August). Train connections with Hamburg, Cologne and Lübeck; local bus services; boats to the other resorts on Lübeck bay. Tourist information at the Kurverwaltung.—4km N on the road to Schönwalde is the village of *Altenkrempe*, with a 13C romanesque basilica.

The B207 continues for another 2km to *Merkendorf*.

From Merkendorf NE along the coast are more bathing resorts: after 9km *Grömitz*; after 6km more *Cismar*; and after a further 3km *Dahme*, with a bathing pool using heated sea water.

The B207 continues NW from Merkendorf by way of (13km) *Lehnsahn*—gothic parish church, with a 15C carved altar; nearby, Schloß Gildenstein—to reach after another 8km *Oldenburg in Holstein* (16,000 inhab.; alt. 4m), a bishopric in 940; flanked by two lakes; and with numerous megalithic tombs in the vicinity. Continue NE for 11km to *Heiligenhafen* (10,000 inhab.; alt. 3m), a bathing resort on the Baltic, founded in the Middle Ages as a fishing port and now a nature reserve for seagulls and other coastal birds.—12km NE of Heiligenhafen is *Großenbrode* (2000 inhab.; alt. 3km), a resort noted for its seagulls' egg dishes: beach; boats to Gedser; trains to Lübeck and Puttgarden; local buses.

The B207 now runs NE fro 22km to the port of *Puttgarden* on the island of *Fehmarn*, crossing en route the 963-long bridge across the Fehmarn Sound. The island (185km²) is farmed by some of its 14,000 population, it has good beaches, the towns of *Burg* (Peter Wiepert local history museum near the 13th and 15C church of St. Nikolaus; open June–September, Monday, Wednesday and Saturday, 14.00–18.00); *Landkirchen* (15C church of St. Peter); and *Lamkenhafen* (windmill of 1737).—4km N is the Niobe memorial, in memory of 69 marines lost with the sailing ship 'Niobe' in 1932. From Puttgarden, trains run to Hamburg and Lübeck, buses to Kiel and Neustadt in Holstein, and ships sail to Denmark.

64 From Kiel to Flensburg

Total distance 80km. **Kiel**—B76. 14km *Gettorf*—13km
Eckernförde—10km *Fleckeby*—8km *Haddebey*—2km
Schleswig—25km *Oeversee*—8km **Flensburg** (—6km Glücksburg).

Leave **Kiel** (see Rte 61) by the Eckernförder Allee, driving NW along the B76 through the Danish woods and crossing the Nord-Ostsee canal by the Levensauerbrücke, reaching after 14km *Gettorf*: 13–15C early gothic **church*, with a bronze font, 1424; carved altar c 1510; renaissance pulpit by H. Gudewedt the Elder, 1598.

The B76 continues in the same direction for 13km, running alongside the Eckernförde bay, to reach *Eckernförde* (25,000 inhab.; alt. 5m), a town known in the late 13C and lying at the W end of the bay. Eckernförde was virtually destroyed in a fire of 1416 and began to flourish again only in the 16C. It became noted for its pottery in the 18C and was developed as a seaside health resort in the 19C. Sights include the brick hall church of *St. Nikolaus* with superb interior decor (**baroque altar by H. Gudewerdt the Younger, 1640; bronze font supported by four lions by Michael Dibler, 1588); 14C town hall, with staircase of 1588 in the fine Markt; the bathing suburb of *Borby*, with an early 13C romanesque stone church (contemporary font; altar perhaps by Gudewerdt the Younger, 1686). Local history museum at No. 59 Kieler Straße, open Wednesday, 16.00– 18.00 and weekends, 10.00–12.00. Boats to Denmark; trains to Kiel and Lübeck. Tourist information at the Kurverwaltung.

From here drive W along the B76. The road runs at first along the fishing lake called the Windeby Noor and passes the 97m-high Hüttener Berg. You pass through the villages of *Fleckeby* (Schloß Luisenlund, now an international school) and *Haddeby* (close to which was the Viking setlement of *Haithabu*, whose 10C walls follow the banks of the fishing lake, the Haddeby Noor). Nearby stands a romanesque church, c 1200, with a superb gothic altar.

20km from Eckernförde is **Schleswig** (29,500 inhab.; alt. 14m), at the end of a long narrow bay stretching 30km NE into the Baltic and known as the Schlei.

History. Schleswig developed out of *Haithabu*, and is recorded in 808 as *Sliesthorp*. Its bishopric was established in 947. The bishops of Schleswig and

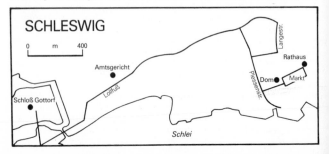

the dukes of Schleswig-Holstein helped to enrich the city from the Middle Ages until 1720. In 1866 Schleswig became the chief town of Schleswig-Holstein, retaining that status until 1945. Schleswig remains the seat of the supreme court of this region. Its welcome to tourists has included building a holiday centre— Port Viking—with a block of flats 85m high.

From the main railway station walk N to Friedrichstraße, at Nos 7–11 the *Von Günderoth'sche Hof*, built for Herzog Friedrich III as the the ducal guest house, 1633–35, and today serving as the city museum (open save Tuesday, 09.00–17.00, closing Sunday 13.00). N of this guest house stands *Schloß Gottorf*, the largest ducal Schloß of Schleswig-Holstein, the residence of the Schleswig-Holstein- Gottorf family from 1544–1713: chapel c 1500; Königsaal c 1520; some fine furnishings first half of the 17C; baroque conversion, c 1700; 18C façade and central tower. Schloß Gottorf now houses the regional museum, and the pre- and early history museum of Schleswig-Holstein, with a celebrated 'bog man' (both museums open April– October, 09.00–17.00; winter 09.30–16.00).

From here walk NE along Lollfuß to find the Amstgericht, built by C. Friedrich Heespen, 1754. The continuation of Lollfuß, Stadtweg, leads N of the ****Cathedral**, in Süderdomstraße at the centre of the Altstadt. Founded in the 11C, St. Peter's Cathedral was rebuilt in 1440 as a three-aisled gothic hall church (tower 19C). It houses the 12·6m *high altar by Hans Brüggemann, 1514–21, which in 1666 was transferred to here from Bordesholm on the orders of Duke Christian Albert and boasts 392 sculpted statues in wood, depicting the life of Jesus. The cathedral wall paintings date from the 14C (restored 1938). Other treasures are the altar of the Magi, c 1300; the choir stalls, 1512; the Kielmannsack altar of 1644 (paintings by J. Ovens); the restored 15C rood screen and the 16C choir screen; the 17C and 18C chapels containing the ducal tombs, with a baroque entrance to the Schacht vault. In the N choir is the memorial tomb to King Frederick I of Denmark (died 1533; he was also Duke of Schleswig-Holstein), by Cornelis Floris, 1551–55. The cathedral cloister has 13C wall paintings.

The town hall in the Markt just E of the cathedral is a classical building of 1794. On the Schleistraß, SE of the town hall, is the former Benedictine *convent of St. Johann (begun late 12C; 15C tabernacle; pulpit 1717; 18C choir; vaulted cloister and refectory); now a Protestant ladies' convent. See also the 17th and 18C houses in Lange Straße.

Schleswig hosts a July regatta on the Schlei. Trains run between Hamburg, Flensburg and Neumünster. Sailing trips in summer. Tourist information at No. 7 Plessenstraße.

25km NW of Schleswig along the B76 lies the village of *Oeversee*, with a 12C romanesque stone church. Near here the Austrians fought the Danes on 6 February 1864 (war memorial). Potholing and walks.

The B76 runs N for 8km to reach **Flensburg** (88,000 inhab.; alt. 3m) on the 36m-long Flensburg Fjord, a busy port that first appears in written history in the 12C. The town was Prussian in 1864, became the home of a naval academy, by a popular vote in 1920 opted to remain German, and at the end of WWII served as the seat of Admiral Doenitz's three-week-long government after Hitler's suicide.

From the main railway station take Bahnhofstraße to the Süder-markt, passing the library in the Deutsches Haus of 1923. Südermarkt contains, as well as half-timbered houses, the *Nikolaikirche*, in a building from 1390, W tower begun 1516 and given a neo-gothic aspect in 1877 (pulpit, 1570; organ case by H. Ringerrinck, 1604; altar, 1749).

Take Angelburger Straße E of the Südermarkt (and over the railway bridge) to reach the 12C church of *St. Johann* (dome c 1500; W tower 1741; pulpit by Hans von Bremen, 1587).

Return to the Südermarkt and walk N along the Holm (shops; at No. 13 and 18C pharmacy) to find the town hall. Große Straße continues N to the *Heiliggeistkirche* of 1385 (baroque gable; services here in Danish) as far as the Nordermarkt, with its arcaded Schrangen house of 1595 and its Neptune fountain of 1785. On the N side of the market square stands the *Marienkirche*, built in brick in the 13C and given a neo-gothic tower in 1880 (inside, pulpit of 1579; bronze font by Michael Dibler, 1591; high altar by H. Ringeringk, 1598).

Continue N along Norderstraße (shops) to find at No. 8 the *Alt-Flensburger house* of 1780, birthplace of Hugo Eckener (1869–1954), who flew the first Zeppelin across the Atlantic. The symbol of Flensburg, the brick Northern gate of 1595, is at the end of Norderstraße.

The natural history museum is at No. 40 Süderhofenden, and the city museum is at No. 1 Lutherplatz (both open except Monday, 10.00–13.00 and 15.00–17.00, closing Sunday afternoons).

The B76 reaches the Danish border after 7km. Trains to major cities of Schleswig-Holstein. Boats to Denmark. Tourist information at No. 6 Norderstraße.

6km NE of Flensburg by way of Mürwik with its naval officers' academy, lies *Glücksberg* (Schloß Glücksberg, built for Duke Johann the Younger, 1582–87), with a sandy beach at the nearby health resort of Sandwig.

65 From Flensburg to Itzehoe

Total distance 108km. **Flensburg**—B76. 8km *Oeversee*—25km **Schleswig**—B77. 7km *Jagel*—21km **Rendsburg**—8km *Jevenstedt*—39km **Itzehoe**.

Follow the B76 for 33km from **Flensburg** to **Schleswig** (see Rte 64). Take the B77 S for 7km to reach *Jagel*, to the E of which have been excavated the foundations of the wall built by the Danes as a defence against Charlemagne in 808.

Continue along the B77 to cross the River Eider and reach after 21km **Rendsburg** (34,000 inhab.; alt. 7m), first documented, in 1199, as *Reynoldsburg*, and whose iron and steel works are served by the Kiel canal. A tunnel (1961) carries traffic under the canal to the W; to the SE is the huge high-level Rendsburg bridge (42m high, built 1911–13) carrying rail and other traffic over the canal. Here are based the main theatre companies of Schleswig-Holstein. The old city, based on an island in the River Eider, houses in the MARKT the half-timbered former town hall of 1566, and the church of *Our Lady* (1287; 14C paintings on the vault; pulpit by Hans Peper, 1621; baroque altar by H. Claussen, 1649), as well as the half-timbered 'Zum Landsknecht' at No. 3 Schleifmühlen Straße (1541).

The suburb of *Neuwerk* was built S of the Alstadt, 1690–95, and houses in Paradeplatz, the Christuskirche (1685–1700), with a baroque interior.

The regional theatre is at No. 7 Jungfernstieg; the local history museum in the former town hall (open save Monday, 10.00–12.00; also Friday–Sunday, 15.00–17.00). Train and bus connections with Flensburg, Hamburg, Husum and Kiel. Tourist information at No. 25 Herrenstraße.

The B77 continues S by way of *Jevenstedt*, 8km away (fine view of the high level railway bridge) and for another 39km to **Itzehoe** (see Rte 66).

66 From Itzehoe to the island of Sylt

Total distance 133km. **Itzehoe**—B204. 38km *Albersdorf*—14km
Heide—B5. 17km *Lunden*—9km *Friedrichstadt*—15km
Husum—5km *Hattstedt*—12km *Bredstedt*—23km *Niebüll*—motorail
by way of *Klaxbüll* for the island of Sylt.

Itzehoe (38,000 inhab.; alt. 7m) lies on the River Stor where Charlemagne established a bulwark against the Danes c 818. The town was Wallenstein's HQ during the Thirty Years' War. Its chief treasures are the Rathaus of 1685 (extended 1893); the baroque church of St. Lawrence (1716, with numerous fine tombs); the small church of St. Jürgen (1657); a Bronze Age grave (at Am Lorsenplatz), c 1200 BC; the remains of a mid 13C Cistercian monastery; and—5km E of the town—Schloß Brietenbur, rebuilt 1750 and 1898. The local history museum is in a 17C building (the Prinzesshof) at No. 20 Viktoria Straße, (open Wednesday and Saturday, 14.00–16.00 and Sunday, 10.00–12.00). Train connections with Hamburg and Husum. Tourist information at No. 8 Bahnhofstraße.

The B204 runs 27km N from here to *Hademarschen* (where the novelist Theodor Storm died in 1888), and then W for 11km to *Albertsdorf* (7000 inhab.; alt. 6m): church with a 15C font.—To the S the 'Brutkamp', a New Stone Age megalithic tomb; to the N the 'Schalen stone', another megalithic tomb, with curious carvings.

Heide, 14km NW (22,000 inhab.; alt. 14m), has the largest marketplace in the Federal Republic, with the gothic church of St. Jürgen (pulpit, 1570; font, 1640; Carl-Diem Hall, with the space for 500 persons; sports stadia). The Klaus Groth Museum is at No. 48 Lüttenheid, devoted to the poet (1819–99; open Monday–Saturday, 09.30–12.00; afternoons except Wednesday and Saturday, 14.00–16.30); local history museum at No. 8 Brahmstraße (open April–September except Monday and Saturday, 09.00–12.00 and 14.00–17.00; winter closed mornings). Tourist information at No. 1 Postelweg.

From Heide the B203 leads SW for 20km to the North Sea health resort of *Büsum* (crab fishing; institute of maritime research; long walks along the tidal flats; boats to Heligoland), 10km N of which is *Wesselburen*, the birthplace of Friedrich Hebbel (1813–63): Hebbel Museum at No. 6 Osterstraße (open daily, May–October, 10.00–12.00 and 14.00–18.00; Sunday closed 17.00), and a monument outside his home (at No. 49 Süderstraße). See also the baroque church of St. Bartholomäus, by J.G. Schott, 1738.

From Heide the B5 continues 17km N to *Lunden* (church 12–15C).—The seaside resort of *Garding*, W of Lunden on the Eiderstadt peninsula, is reached by the B202 through Tönning. Follow the B5 for another 9km to reach *Friedrichstadt* (2700 inhab.; alt. 4m), where the

River Treene meets the Elder, a town built by Dutch Protestant refugees welcomed here by Herzog Friedrich III von Gottorf in 1621, and now a health resort with many sporting facilities: Dutch renaissance façade to the former mint, 1626; shared Catholic and Protestant church, 1643–49. Trains run to Hamburg and Westerland. Boats ply to *Heligoland* and the *Halligen*—a group of nine islands once attached to the coast (separated by a storm and floods in 1634) and including Hooge, Langeness, Grode, Süderoog, Nordstrand, Pellworm (whose romanesque church has 12C wall paintings and an 18C organ by Arp Schnitger) and Südfall, most of them connected again to the mainland by causeways. Their inhabitants breed cattle, fish commercially, and welcome tourists.

After 5km the B5 reaches *Hattstedt* (from which a 2.5km causeway runs to the island of Nordstrand). Continue 12km along the B5 to *Bredstedt* (5600 inhab.; alt. 5m): agricultural market; North Friesland nature centre. The route continues across the Bordelum Heath (10km E of which is the Kalkerheide narure reserve), reaching after 23km *Niebüll* (7000 inhab.; alt. 5m), from which trains serve both Hamburg and (including motorail) the island of **Sylt** (by way of Klaxbüll and the 11km-long Hindenburg Damm, built 1923–27). A branch line leads to *Dagebüll*, the port for the islands of Amrum and Föhr (whose chief town is Wyk, a seaside resort since 1819; Hoeberlin Frisian Museum (open March–May and September–October, except Mondays, 10.00–12.00 and 14.00–18.00; November–January, except Mondays, 10.00–17.00).

Sylt, at 102km^2 the largest of the islands, has a beach almost 40km long on the W coast. Its villages include *Hönum* (dunes and fishing; boats to Hamburg and Cuxhaven); *Kampen* with sandflats and the Abessina naturist beach; *List*, at the N tip of Sylt (boats to Denmark); the health resort of *Wenningstedt* (whence Angles, Saxons and Jutes set sail for England in 449); and the main town, *Westerland*, with sophisticated holiday and health baths; a sanatorium; a 'graveyard of the homeless', for those drowned at sea and washed up here; and a church dated 1635 (part romanesque, part gothic); casino; aquarium; more naturism. Tourist information at the railway station and the Kurverwaltung.

X BERLIN

History. The city of Berlin (1,200,000 inhab.; alt. 30m) developed from two 13C settlements on the River Spree, both set up by the Margraves of Brandenburg.

Kölln, which is first documented in 1237, stood on a island in the middle of the river. Berlin was set up on the right bank and first appears in written history in 1244. The name 'Kölln' derives from the city of Cologne (Köln); the origin of 'Berlin' remains obscure.

On a major trade route, Kölln and Berlin prospered, and their achievement of independence was aided by the disappearance of the Brandenburg line in 1320. In 1359 they joined the Hanseatic League. In 1411 they fell under the suzerainty of the Hohenzollerns (who became electors of Brandenburg). Friedrich II of Hohenzollern built a Schloß here, and in the late 15C Elector Johann Cicero made Berlin his permanent home.

After the ravages of the Thirty Years' War the towns began to prosper again. Friedrich Wilhelm, the 'Great Elector' (1640–88), fortified his capital, welcoming Dutch artists and architects. The population grew to over 20,000, and Berlin's boundaries extended especially with the need to house French Huguenot refugees after the revocation of the Edict of Nantes in 1685. In 1674 the Great Elector established a third town, Dorotheenstadt, named after his second wife. In 1709 the first king of Prussia, Friedrich I, united the three towns in one city, Berlin, adding the township of Friederichstadt and decisively influenced its architecture by patronising the baroque genius, Andreas Schlüter. Friedrich Wilhelm I (1713–40) found it necessary to replace the old fortifications by a far more extensive ring of walls and gates. By the end of the reign of Frederick the Great (1740–86) another 100,000 persons lived in Berlin. The Berlin porcelain factory was established in 1763. Frederick the Great also brought to Berlin the rococo architect Georg Wenceslaus von Knobelsdorff, as well as French and Dutch artists and savants of the calibre of Voltaire.

After the battle of Jena in 1806 Berlin was occupied by the French till 1808. Two years later Wilhelm von Humboldt founded the university. Its professors included Alexander von Humboldt and G.W.F. Hegel. Berlin also began to develop as an industrial city, especially with the coming of the railways in 1838. Classical architects, particularly Karl Friedrich Schinkel, stamped their mark on the city. The monarchy survived the upheavals of the 1848 Revolution, and with the coming of the German Empire in 1871 Berlin became the capital city of the whole of Germany, reaching a population of over 1·5 million by the end of the century. The Congress of Berlin in 1878 settled the quarrels of the East, just as the conference of 1880 decided the Turkish-Greek frontier and another conference of 1885 divided up Africa amongst the great powers.

All three Kaisers lived here. The city attracted avant-garde artists, especially expressionists and neo-realists of the stamp of Max Beckmann, E.L. Kirchner, Georg Grosz and Karl Schmidt-Rottluff, many of whom continued to flourish until driven out by Hitler. Bertolt Brecht stayed until the Nazis forced him to flee to the USA, only to return to East Berlin after WWII.

The collapse of the empire after WWI did not impede the growth of Berlin, which took seven satellite towns and 59 communes into Groß Berlin. The Hitler regime increased its prestige, especially by staging the 1936 Olympic Games in a city whose population was rapidly approaching 4·3 million. The Olympic stadium (by Werner March) represents the new feeling in architecture at this time. After 1943 the city was subject to repeated air attacks and suffered deeply. It was taken by the Russians on 2 May 1945 and two months later divided into four sectors, occupied by Russians, French, Americans and British. The Russians blockaded Berlin in 1948, a blockade overcome by a massive air-lift organised by the three Western powers and lasting until May 1949.

On 13 August 1961 the Russians separated their sector, now known as East Berlin, from West Berlin by constructing a concrete and barbed wire wall, guarded at all times. Ten years later the four occupying powers signed an accord agreeing that West Berlin should be closely linked with the Federal Republic, though not one of its constituent parts, an accord which considerably eased the access to East Berlin of West Berliners.

67 West Berlin

West Berlin is served by three airlines: Pan-American, British Airways and Air France. Trains runs from West Germany to the main station, Bahnhof Zoological Garten. Buses also run from West Germany, either by way of the Helmstedt/Marienborn frontier (on the Hanover–Brunswick motorway) or the Töpen/Juchöh frontier (on the Munich–Nuremberg motorway). Car routes run by way of those two frontiers and also via the Herleshausen-Wartha frontier (on the Frankfurt am Main–Bad Hersfeld motorway). The East Germans charge motorway tolls, payable in West German currency.

Transport in West Berlin is by bus, by the underground railway (the U-Bahn), or by the electrified trains known as the S-Bahn, and run by the Eastern zone of the city.

Pleasure *boats* ply the River Havel and the River Spree.

Principal *post offices* are at the main railway station, at Nos 93–95 Kurfürstendamm and at No. 50 Derburgstraße.

Tourist information at the main railway station; at Nos 7–8 Fasanenstraße and at Tempehlhof airport.

The city is still divided into a Russian sector ('East Berlin'), a British, an American and a French sector, since the four-power victory over Germany in 1945.

West Berlin is also divided into 12 districts ('Bezirke'):
1. Tiergarten (British sector)
2. Charlottenburg (British sector)
3. Wilmersdorf (British sector)
4. Spandau (British sector)
5. Schöneberg (American sector)
6. Steglitz (American sector)
7. Zehlendorf (American sector)
8. Kreuzberg (American sector)
9. Tempelhof (American sector)
10. Neukölln (American sector)
11. Wedding (French sector)
12. Reinickendorf (French sector).

The following description of West Berlin's districts begins with Tiergarten, which houses the main railway station, and then continues in a roughly anti-clockwise direction, thus:
Charlottenburg, Wedding, Reinickendorf, Spandau, Wilmersdorf, Zehlendorf, Steglitz, Schöneberg, Kreuzberg, Tempelhof and Neukölln.

A. Tiergarten

Trains from the Federal Republic arrive in West Berlin at the Bahnhof Zoo, in the borough of **TIERGARTEN**, which has the oldest park in the city.

S of the station stands the memorial church to Kaiser Wilhelm (*Kaiser-Wilhelm-Gedächtniskirche*), by Franz Schwechten, 1891–95, tower 53m high, all virtually destroyed in 1943, and reconstructed by Egon Eiermann, 1959–61, (aluminium doors by Gerhard Marcks; glass of the E end by Georg Meistermann; blue Chartres glass; W Crucifixion glass by Willy Fries; Eternity mosaic behind the high altar by Carl Crodel; organ 1962; risen Christ, by Karl Hemmeter; Glockenspiel music by Prinz Louis Ferdinand of Prussia).—E of the church is

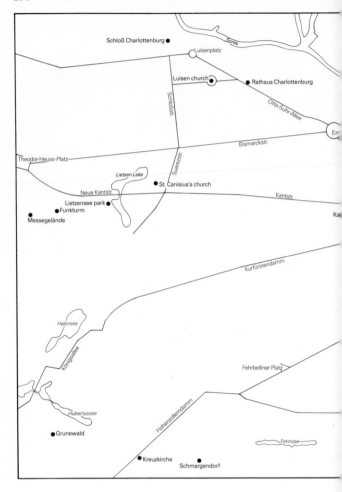

Schloß Charlottenburg ●

Spree

○ Luisenplatz

● Luisen church

● Rathaus Charlottenburg

Otto-Suhr-Allee

Schloßstr.

○ Err

Bismarckstr.

Theodor-Heuss-Platz

Suarezstr.

Lietsen Lake

● St. Canisius's church

Neue Kantstr.

Kantstr.

Lietzensee park ●

● Funkturm

Kai

● Messegelände

Kurfürstendamm

Haiensee

Königsallee

Fehrbelliner Platz

Hubertussee

Hohenzollendamm

Fennsee

● Grunewald

● Kreuzkirche

Schmargendorf

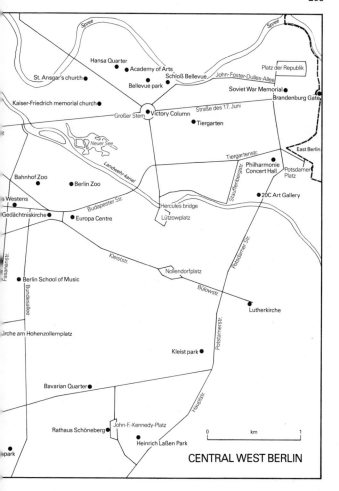

CENTRAL WEST BERLIN

the *Europa Centre*, a 22-storey shopping and business centre, designed by H. Petschnigg, W. Düttmann, E. Eiermann and H. Hentrich, 1963–65, with an Irish pub, a swimming pool, two cinemas, a gambling casino, restaurants and bars, cabaret, and a water clock.

The ruined Kaiser-Wilhelm-Gedächtniskirche alongside E. Eiermann's new blue glass church, in the Kurfürstendamm.

From the Kaiser-Wilhelm-Gedächtniskirche follow Budapester Straße E, N of which is the **Berlin Zoo**, set up in 1841–44 by the explorer Heinrich Lichtenstein, the geographer Alexander von Humboldt and the gardener Peter J. Lenné. An aquarium was built in 1913. Only 91 animals survived WWII, since when it hs been restored virtually to its former splendour.

To the S is Lützowplatz, with the *Haus am Lützowplatz* (Berlin's cultural institute) and on the N side the Hercules bridge across the Landwehr canal. To the N side of the canal is the Federal office of insurance, once the Admiralty (1911–14). Walk E along the canal bank (Reichpietsufer) to Stauffenbergstraße, at the corner of which is the multi-storey Shell building by Emil Fahrenkamp, 1931.

Follow Stauffenbergstraße N to the *Tiergarten*, noting the memorial to those German officers who attempted to assassinate Hitler on 20 July 1944 (in the courtyard of Nos 11–13). Close by the Tiergarten is the city porcelain factory, first set up by Frederick the Great in 1763.

To the right of Stauffenbergstraße is the new national gallery and the church of St. Mathäus (by A. Stüler, 1846). At the end of Stauffenbergstraße turn right along Tiergartenstraße to reach Kemperplatz, housing the *Philharmonie concert hall* of 1960–63, by Hans Scharoun (bust of Wilhelm Furtwängler by A. Archipenko), the home of the Berlin Philharmonic Orchestra, founded 1882 and directed by such conductors as Hans von Bülow (1882–94), Artur Nikisch (1895–1922), Wilhelm Furtwängler (1922–54) and today by Herbert von Karajan. S of the Philharmonie is the new city library (1965–70), opposite the 20C Gallery, by Ludwig Mies van der Rohe, 1968: entrance at No. 50 Potsdamer Straße).

Immediately to the E of the Philharmonie is POTSDAMER PLATZ, formerly the hub of Berlin life, now a desolate square because of the wall and the division of the city. N is the **Tiergarten, 2·8km by 1·2km, converted into a park under Elector Friedrich III, landscaped by Peter Joseph Lenné (1789–1866) and filled with different species of trees and shrubs until the destruction of WWII necessitated a completely new start. The statues mostly escaped destruction: Lessing, by Otto Lessing, 1890; Goethe, by F. Schaper, 1880; Queen Louise, by Encke, 1880; Friedrich Wilhelm III, by Drake, 1849; an Amazon, by Tuaillon, 1895; Wagner, by Eberlein, 1903; Kaiser Wilhelm I, by Brütt, 1904; Fontane, by Klein, 1910. C. Rauch designed the Lions bridge to the W of the park in 1838.

The road through the park (now called the Straße des 17. Juni) is famous as the last runway for aeroplanes in forlorn Berlin in 1945. To the W, where the Straße runs into the Große Stern (meeting place of five roads) is the *Victory Column* designed by Heinrich Strack (1865–73), commemorating German victories against Denmark in 1864, Austria in 1866 and France in 1871. The goddess of Victory surmounting the tower is by Friedrich Drake, and the Salviati factory contibuted the frieze of Venetian mosaics depicting the battles of the Franco-Prussian war; 285 steps lead to the panoramic view from the column's platform.

Straße des 17. Juni leads E to the the Brandenburg Gate (see below) and the Soviet war memorial of 1946. Walk N from here to the PLATZ DER REPUBLIK (statues 1961–63), with the former **Reichstag building** by Paul Wallot (1884–94), inscribed 'Dem Deutschen Volk, 1916'; set alight 1933; scarred 1945; restored 1968.—To the left once stood the Congress Hall, given to Berlin by the USA as part of the International Building Exhibition of 1957. Built in 15 months, its roof fell in in 1980. Walk W along John-Foster-Dulles-Allee to reach *Schloß Bellevue* (the Berlin residence of the Bundes president), by Daniel Philipp Boumann (1785), behind which is the 20-hectare *Bellevue park* (including the English garden, recreated in 1952 with the help of the Shropshire Horticultural Society and other British philanthropists: thatched cottage, now a restaurant).

W of the park is the HANSA QUARTER, a residential district designed by Gerhard Jobst and Willi Kreuer (including five multi-storey blocks in Bartningallee) the scene of the International Building Exibition of 1957 when no fewer than 48 architects took part (including Walter Gropius, Arne Jacobsen, Luciano Baldesari, Oscar Niemeyer, Pierre Vago, Sten Samuelson, Fritz Jaeneck, Klaus Müller-Rehm and Gerhard Siegmann, the two last designing the then socially revolutionary flats for the unmarried). Each architect's name is attached to the buildings he designed. Here is the *Kaiser-Friedrich memorial church* by Ludwig Lemmer (1892–95; restored after WWII). The Hansa church of *St. Ansgar* is by Willy Kreuer, 1957 (copper doors by Ludwig Gabriel Schreiber; stations of the cross by Ludwig P. Kowalski). E of the Hansa quarter is the *Academy of Arts* by Werner Düttmann, 1960, fronted by a reclining woman sculpted by Henry Moore.

MOABIT, N of the Hansa quarter, includes the *Schauspielhaus Hansa* theatre and the little park known as the Kleiner Tiergarten, at the E end of which is the church of *St. Johann* by Schinkel (1835; doorway and tower by A. Stüler, 1856). In Moabit was once a prison where the martyr Dietrich Bonhoeffer and the patriot Martin Niemöller were imprisoned for opposition to the Nazis. The harbour here is twinned with Greenwich and boasts a traditional British post box, telephone booth and fire alarm, all unusable.

B. Charlottenburg

The KURFÜRSTENDAMM (or Ku-damm), which leads SW from the Kaiser-Wilhelm-Gedächtniskirche for almost 4km, was laid out to reach the hunting lodge of Kurfürst Joachim II in the 16C. In 1881 it was widened and at the end of the century lined with Jugendstil buildings, of which only Nos 29, 50, 60, 78, 172 and 188 surivived WWII (mosaics above No. 172). Most of the other buildings are post 1945. Today the street is Berlin's most fashionable, with cinemas, bars, cafés, restaurants, two theatres, hotels and shops. (The Café Kranzler takes its name from one founded in Unter den Linden in 1825 by the noted Austrian confectioner Johann Georg Kranzler.) At No. 25 is the Hotel am Zoo, 1895. At No. 217 (over what is now a film theatre) Robert Musil wrote part of his 'Man without Qualities' in 1932–33.

N of the Kurfürstendamm is Kantstraße, which runs E from the Kaiser-Wilhelm-Gedächtniskirche and is prolonged by Neue Kantstraße as far as the Lietsen Lake. It houses the *Theatre des Westens* (1896), with the Vaganten-Bühne (a miniature theatre specialising in avant-garde productions) in the basement. Just beyond the theatre Kantstraße is crossed by Fasanenstraße, in which stands the Jewish community house (restaurant, library, synagogue) built in 1959 to replace the one burnt down on the 'Kristallnacht' of 1938.

Kantstraße continues as far as Uhlandstraße, close by which (at No. 152) is a plaque to the Nobel prize winner Carl von Ossietsky (1889–1938) who edited 'Die Weltbühne' from here between 1927 and 1933. Continue along Kantstraße (finding Suarezstraße to the left, with the Roman Catholic church of *St. Canisius*, Berlin's first post-war church, by R. Hofbauer, 1955) and into Neue Kantstraße, to cross the Lietzen Lake, by which is the Protestant church am Lietzensee by Paul Baumgarten, 1959.

The *Lietzensee park* contains the Schiller monument by Reinhold Begas (1868). W of the lake are Berlin's trade fairgrounds (the *Messegelände*). First set up during WWI, the most celebrated of the fairground buildings date from the 1930s and are by Richard Ermisch; they are augmented by numerous post-WWII buildings, as well as the radio tower (Funkturm), built by Heinrich Straumee (1924–26; lift to the restaurant and panorama). Next to the Messegelände is the Germany Hall ('Deutschland Halle', rebuilt 1957), housing 14,000 spectators, and the Avus motor-racing track of 1921.

Continue W from the Funkturm, along the extension of Bismarckstraße, Theodor-Heuss-Straße, to reach (to the N of the street, in Sensburger Allee) the *Georg Kolbe museum*, home of the sculptor (1877–1947) from 1929 until his death. The nearby park called Georg Kolbe Hain contains four of his statues. To the NW is the

Olympic Stadium, 300m by 230m, built by Werner March (1894–1976) for the 1936 Olympic Games, a vast oval seating 85,000, with another 15,000 spectators standing. The bell tower (76m high) was rebuilt in 1962 (its Olympic bell weighs 6500kg).

Close by are the Maifeld parade ground: tennis courts, the horse stadium, the House of German Sport (1931) and the open-air theatre built by W. March in 1934–36. N of the theatre is the Fließwieße nature reserve. To the S lies the Grunewald forest.

Continue from Theodor-Heuss-Straße W along Heerstraße. At No. 2 Richard Strauss lived from 1913–17. N of the street can be seen a block of 527 flats which Le Corbusier designed in 1957. The **British War Cemetery** lies further N, with the graves of 3500 dead and a monument with the words 'Their name liveth for evermore'. Continue along the Heerstraße to reach the River Havel (boat trips).

Return along Heerstraße, Theodor-Heuss-Straße and Bismarck-straße, passing on the left the **Berlin Opera House**, a rebuilt version of the famous pre-WWII theatre of 1912–35 (by Franz Bornemann, 1961, incorporating such as remained from the air raids of 1943), in front of which is an abstract statue by Hans Uhlmann. Bismarck-straße continues E to reach the huge ERNST-REUTER-PLATZ, designed by W. Düttmann and B. Hermkes after WWII, with lawns and fountains (41 jets), 1960s housing blocks and the Telefunkenhaus. The monument to Ernst Reuter (Burgermeister of Berlin, 1948–52), in the form of a bronze flame, is by Bernhard Heiliger, 1963. Around the square stand the buildings of the *Technical University*, the oldest 1878–84, the newest all post-WWII. To the S of the building are preserved fragments of Berlin in former days (a column of the old cathedral, terracottas from the 1858 Borsig factory), as well as a memorial to Werner Siemens.

From Ernst-Reuter-Platz take Otto-Suhr-Allee NW. At No. 18 is the Tribüne Theatre, to the right of which Loschmidtstraße leads to the Lietzow church (by Ludwig von Walthausen, 1961). Continue along Otto-Suhr-Allee by way of *Charlottenburg town hall* (Jugendstil, 1899–1903 and 1913; restored), behind which is a power station of 1900 with a huge chimney.—In nearby Gierkeplatz is the *Luisen church* of 1716, rebuilt by K.F. Schinkel (1823), restored externally after WWII (modern stained glass by P.L. Kowalski). In the church square (Luisenplatz) is a statue of Prince Albert of Prussia (died 1872). Schloßstraße (with a former imperial barracks, by August Stüler, 1850) leads from here to ****Schloß Charlottenburg**. Built first as a Prussian royal country house for Queen Sophie Charlotte by Arnold Nering in 1695–99, the Schloß was transformed into a three-winged castle by Eosander von Göthe in 1701–12, and then enlarged with a new wing by G.W. von Knobelsdorff in 1740–43, commissioned by Frederick the Great. The theatre was finished in 1788. The Schloß was finely restored after WWII (see Museums, below). K.F. Schinkel built the summer house in 1825 in the Neapolitan style.

The park—once a French garden by Siméon Godeau (1697), trans-formed into an 'English' garden in the 19C—reaches as far as the River Spree, and contains the *Belvedere* by Langhans, 1788. An avenue of firs leads to the *royal mausoleum*, by Henrich Gentz, 1810, enlarged by Friedrich Hesse, 1841. It contains, among others, the bodies of Queen Louise (died 1810), and King Friedrich Wilhelm III (died 1840), with statues by C.D. Rauch; and Kaiser Wilhelm I (died 1888) and his empress (died 1890), their tombs by Erdmann Encke, 1894.

Andreas Schlüter's equestrian statue of the Great Elector guards Schloß Charlottenburg.

C. Wedding

WEDDING lies N of Tiergarten and Mitte. At the heart of the district is WEDDINGPLATZ, a triangular 'square' close by the Berlin Wall and housing a sandstone statue to the reunion of East and West Germany, by Hilde Leest, 1962. Müllerstraße, in which are the administrative offices of Schering and Co., leads NW from Weddingplatz. From Weddingplatz Schulzendorferstraße and Grenzstraße lead to the *Humboldt-Hain*, a park laid out in the 1870s in memory of the naturalist Alexander von Humboldt (1769–1859). It has an artificial hill, 86m high (panorama and restaurant), a rose garden with 75,000 bushes and an open-air swimming pool.

E of the park is Brunnenstraße, which runs S along the Wall to join Bernauer Straße, again running alongside the Wall, this time SW. The houses on the East Berlin side of the street have been abandoned and walled up, as has the Church of the Atonement.

Following Brunnenstraße N leads one by way of Badstraße to the Panke, a small tributary of the River Spree. Both names ('Brunnen' and 'Bad') refer to a healing spring, discovered in 1757 and lost again in 1882 through injudicious building.

Uferstraße leads SW along the Panke. From Uferstraße take Wiesenstraße, crossing Reinickendorfer Straße and taking Plantagenstraße to reach the *City Cemetery*, laid out by W. Müller in 1912 (where lies the physician August von Wassermann, 1866–1925). From the NW corner of the cemetery follow Ruheplatzstraße to LEOPOLDPLATZ, with two churches: the *Nazarethkirche*, designed by Schinkel (1832–35), and the *Neue Nazarethkirche* by Spitta (1893). At the corner of Limburger Straße is the town hall (1928–30; tower 1964).

Take Müllerstraße NW, to meet Seestraße, on the corner of which is the cemetery in which are buried those killed in the uprising of 17 June 1953. To the right along Seestraße is the *Schiller Park*, 25 hectares laid out by F.-R. Bauer (1906–13), with a copy of Schiller's statue by Begas and a Schiller oak.

From the junction with Müllerstraße, Seestraße leads left to the *Westhafen*, West Berlin's largest harbour, and the Berlin–Spandau canal, which joins the Rivers Spree and Havel. W of the canal is the notorious *Plötzen gaol*, built 1876–78, where were executed the leaders of the plot to assassinate Hitler on 20 July 1944. (There is a memorial to Nazi victims in the courtyard.) Heckerdamm leads from the gaol to the church of *Maria Regina Martyrum*, built by the Würzburg architects Hans Schädel and Friedrich Ebert (1961–62) as another memorial to National Socialist victims (a 48m tower was planned but kept to 25m for air traffic reasons; altar and stations of the cross by Otto Herbert Hajek; in the crypt memorial stone to Provost Lichtenberg of Berlin and the ashes of Dr Erich Klausener).

N of the canal is the 800m-long *Plötzen Lake* (harbour with over 20 cranes), N of which again is the *Rehberge people's park*, laid out in 1929 on 86 hectares of sand-dunes by Barth and Germer (open-air theatre, animal reserve, sports grounds).

Müllerstraße runs along the E side of this park to the Quartier Napoleon, the quarters of the French occupying forces and their families (church of St. Louis de France on the Kurt-Schumacher-Damm, by Raymond Joly, 1953).

D. Reinickendorf

The second largest of the Berlin districts, **REINICKENDORF** was formed in 1920 out of six villages, hence the six golden ears (as well as a fox) on its coat of arms. Of the six villages *Reinickendorf* has a late 15C church (in Alt-Reinickendorf), with a tower of 1713 and a painted altarpiece of 1515. From this village Humboldtstraße runs SW to *West Reinickendorf*, famed for its dahlia nurseries.

N of the former village of Reinickendorf is *Wittenau*, with a 15C *church* (baroque altar; tower of 1799 with two bells, one 16C, the other 17C), set amidst old and famous trees. On the S side of the square is the town hall, 1911, enlarged 1957 with the addition of the Ernst-Reuter hall. NW is the Steinberg Park and the Tegel brook (the Tegeler Fließ). The *Tegel airport* (built in 1948 to aid the Berlin air lift and now one of two chief entry-points into Berlin for planes) lies on the S side of Reinickendorf and NW of the Quartier Napoleon (see above). Scharnweberstraße, NE of the airport, leads NW into Siedelstraße, on the left of which is the prison of 1898, where were held enemies of the Nazi regime (including the martyrs Dietrich Bonhoeffer and Graf von Moltke). Take Holzhauserstraße (right) from here to reach the *Russian cemetery*: Russian chapel of 1894; memorial to the composer Michail Glinka 1804–57, who died in Berlin.

Berliner Straße leads N from the prison, containing the *Borsig engineering factories* (85m-high 12-storey tower building by E. Schmohl, 1924), and then fine shops, before reaching Alt-Tegel, with its neo-romanesque church of 1912. To the W is the 4km-long ****TEGEL LAKE**, which covers more than 400 hectares: boats to Spandau and Tegelort; bathing; promenade; open-air restaurants; campsites; five islands, including the island of *Scharfenberg* (park and farming school).

Continue along Berliner Straße, and then Schloßstraße and Karolinenstraße to reach ****Schloß Tegel**. Here Schinkel rebuilt the family villa for Wilhelm von Humboldt in 1821–23. Inside is Von Humboldt's collection of antiques (some plaster-cast reproductions of objects looted at the end of WWII). The Schloß garden houses copies of antique sculptures. An avenue of limes leads to the family cemetery, laid out by Schinkel in 1829. Here lie Caroline von Humboldt (died 1829), her husband Wilhelm (died 1835), his brother Alexander and his daughter Gabriele von Bülow. The copy of 'Hope' by Thorwaldsen was placed here in 1831. By the lakeside is a noted oak tree, 7m in circumference, known as 'Dicke Marie' ('fat Mary').

Take Heiligenseestraße left through the firs and beeches of the Tegel woods to the village of **Heiligensee** on the River Havel: 15–16C *church*, altered in the 17th and 18Cs, with a baroque tower of 1761, set in a square of old houses.

From here Hermsdorfer Damm leads to the 13C village of *Hermsdorf*, now enhanced by fine late 19C villas. To the NE of Hermsdorf is the garden suburb of *Frohnau*, founded 1910 by Prince Henckel von Donnersmarck: railway station with a 30m-high restaurant tower; church of St. Johann, 1936; the Buddhist House built for Dr Paul Dahlke, 1922–24.—From here walk E along the Fließ to the village of *Lübars*: old cottages and an inn; church (1793); open-air swimming pool.

E. Spandau

The district of **SPANDAU**, situated almost entirely W of the Havel, incorporates the remarkable settlement known as SIEMENSTADT, reached from Charlottenburg by the Siemensdamm and built by the electrical engineering firm of Siemens between 1928 and 1930 to house its employees. The *Werner factory* (the 'Wernerwerk', named after Werner Siemens), was designed by Hans Hertlein, with a 74m-high clock tower.

N of the city is the *Jungfernheide people's park* (1920–26): open-air theatre, bathing pool, animal reserve, monument to police chief Hinckeldey, killed in a duel in 1856. Close by is the housing estate called GROß-SIEDLUNG SIEMENSTADT, built by the famous group of architects known as the Ring, led by Hans Scharoun, Walter Gropius, Otto Bartning and Hugo Häring.

To reach Alt-Spandau from Siemenstadt, follow Am Juliusturm and Nonendamallee, which pass the massively fortified moated *citadel ('Citadelle'), whose present Italianate style derives from the work of the Venetian De Gandino (1560-94). (Open weekdays except Monday, 09.00–16.00; Saturday, 14.00–17.00; Sunday, 10.00–13.00 and 14.00–17.00.) Included in this work are earlier buildings; see especially the 12C Julius tower and the former castle. In the Julius tower in 1402 was incarcerated the baron-bandit Dietrich von Quitzow; the Kavalier house served as a prison for such as the Great Elector's admiral Benjamin Raule and Joachim II's mistress Anna Sydow. The gatehouse has a plaque celebrating the recovery of the citadel from the French by General von Thümen in 1813.

Old Spandau was once the home of an important convent; it was a fortified village in the 14C. (Parts of its fortifications survive at Hoher Steinweg and at the Altstädter Ring.) Its citadel was founded in the 12C. In the Altstadt is the 14C brick church of *St. Nikolai*: font, 1398; Crucifixion group of 1540; renaissance high altar, 1582; pulpit, brought from Potsdam in 1903, the gift of Frederick Wilhelm I; gothic Lady chapel, with a candelabrum of 1651 and stained glass by Sigmund Hahn, 1959. The church square (Reformationsplatz) contains a memorial to the fallen in the Napoleonic wars by Schinkel (1816), and a monument to Elector Joachim II by E. Enckel (1889). To the S of the church Carl-Schurz-Straße leads to the town hall of 1910–13.

Cross the River Havel by the Charlottenbrücke to reach the shipbuilding area on the S bank of the River Spree in the suburb of **Stresow**. On the N side of the Altstadt (on the W bank of the River Havel) is the *Neustadt*, at a point where the river includes an island, the Eiswerder, with bridges connecting to each bank.—Further N is the **Berlin municipal forest**, covering 1500 hectares, with nature reserves and marked tracks for hikers.

Environs of Spandau include *Kladow* (with a 14C church, rebuilt in 1818 after a fire, and a tuberculosis clinic); the boating village of *Pichelsdorf* and the agricultural and holiday village of *Gatow* (restored church, 1953, with a Pietà of c 1495). Gatow has a small airport.

F. Wilmersdorf

The residential district of **WILMERSDORF**, S of Charlottenburg, is crossed by the Bundesallee which runs N–S. In the Bundesallee is the former grammar school of 1875–80, now the *Berlin School of Music*, with a renowned collection of musical instruments. At No. 216 are the offices of the Federal Republic of Germany's representatives. (the 'Bundeshaus Berlin'). Bundesallee crosses Berliner Straße to reach the *Volkspark*, left: sports stadia, lakes, a bronze spear thrower by Karl Mobius, 1921. To the N is the *Schoelerschlößchen* of 1753 and a neo-gothic church of 1897.

Continue S to Bundesplatz, from which Detmolderstraße leads W to the octagonal church of *Our Father* (concrete dome; 32m-high tower), by Werner March, 1961. Detmolderstraße leads W into Heidelberger Platz, S of which, by way of Assmannshauser Straße, is the **Rheingau** suburb, which houses the Free University of Berlin. To the W is the suburb of **Schmargendorf**: 14C church in Breite Straße (with the tombs of Johann and Eva von Wilmersdorff (died 1635 and 1644 respectively); town hall of 1902 in Berkaer Platz.

Cunostraße leads N from Breite Straße to join the Hohen-zollerndamm, which runs SW from Bundesalle and contains at No. 130 the octagonal *Kreuzkirche* and its tower, designed by Ernst and Günther Paulus (1929), and at the Hohenzollernplatz the *Kirche am Hohenzollernplatz*, by Fritz Höger (1931–33). Hohenzollerndamm passes through FEHBERLINER PLATZ, with the Wilmersdorf town hall whose courtyard has 25 coats of arms from East and West Germany, done in mosaic by L.P. Kowalski. The square houses numerous government offices, including the 18-storey building of the housing office (exhibitions open weekdays, 08.00–16.00). N of the square is the *Preussenpark* (statue to Prussia, 'Borussia', by Reinhold Begas, 1885).

The northern boundary of Wilmersdorf is the Kurfürstendamm, reached from Bundesallee by the Lietzenburger Straße (post office, with a permanent exhibition of post office history, at Nos 93–95). The Kurfürstendamm leads SW to the Königsallee, which runs to the *Grunewald* suburb, set up as a residential quarter on the orders of Bismarck in 1889 and well rebuilt after WWII.

N of the Königsallee is the *Halensee*, a lake with summer sports and bathing. SE of Königsallee stands the Bismarck memorial. Where Königsallee meets Wallotstraße is a plaque recording that the German foreign secretary, Walther Rathenau, was assassinated here on 24 June 1922. (His home was No. 65, Königsallee.) Grunewald contains numerous other lakes: the Herthasee, the Dianasee, the Grunewaldsee, the Schlachtensee, the Krumme Lanke and the forest lake of Hundekehlesee, most of them interconnected by narrow canals.

The **Grunewald** itself is a forest covering 13km², bounded on the W by the River Havel and containing 18 million pine trees (half of them planted after the destruction of WWII) and 6 million trees of other varieties. Parts of the forest are designated as nature reserves, protecting deer, wild boar, foxes and birds. A mound of rubble, created from bombed buildings after the war, is known as the *Trümmerberg* (or 'Teufelsberg') and incorporates ski jumps and a toboggan run. From Königsallee a road leads left to the hunting *Schloß Grunewald*, built by Caspar Theyss in 1542, and extended by Arnold Nehring (1693–95). It is now a concert hall and museum containing German paintings from the 15th to the 19C (open 10.00–18.00; closed Sunday).

Königsallee is continued by Onkel-Tom-Straße, on the right of which are the Krumme Lanke, the little lodges in the quarter known as Onkel Toms Hütte, and the church of Ernst-Moritz-Arndt (1934).

The W boundary of the Grunewald is marked by the Havel-chaussee, which runs alongside the river and leads by the Schildhorn peninsula, where in 1845 Friedrich Wilhelm IV set up a monument in memory of the last Wend chief to convert to Christianity.

The Havelchaussee runs towards the KARLSBERG, on which is the red brick *Grunewald tower* (also known as the Kaiser Wilhelm tower: restaurant and panorama on the 105m-high platform, reached by 204 steps), by Franz Schwechten, 1897. From the tower can be seen the villages of Gatow, Kladow and Potsdam. Follow the Havelchaussee further S to reach the *Lieper bay*, with ferries to the island of Lindwerder, and the Große Steinlanke bay.

G. Zehlendorf

The district of **ZEHLENDORF**, the most southerly of those of West Berlin, is traversed by the old road to Potsdam. It comprises the parishes of Zehlendorf, Nikolassee and Wannsee, as well as the old enclaves of Dahlem, Kleingelienicke and the Pfaueninsel.

Onkel-Tom-Straße leads S from the Grunewald by way of the suburb of *Fischtalgrund*, which dates from 1929 (Fischtal park), to **Zehlendorf**, from which the whole district takes its name, a suburb settled according to archaeological finds as early as the Bronze Age. The octagonal *church* of Zehlendorf was built by Frederick the Great in 1768 (rebuilt in 1953, with a late 15C altarpiece and 11 17C panels from other churches).

Teltower Damm runs S from the church by way of the church of St. Paul to the Town Hall, by H. Stier (1905). To the E (along Mühlenstraße) is the pyramid church of *St. Stephen* (1961). Follow Teltower Damm to reach the *Schweizerhof park*, once the site of the Schweizerhof mental hospital, founded by Heinrich Laehr in 1854. The Heinrich Laehr park lies further S. To the W is the Kirchliche Hochschule, a Protestant theological faculty. Yet further S, by way of the suburb of Schönow, is the Teltow canal.

Potsdamer Chausee leads W from the centre of Zehlendorf village, running for 7km to reach the Wannsee. En route it runs S of the Schlachten lake (which covers c 31 hectares), the Paul Ernst park, and the Nikola lake, which (as a result of silting) covers no more than 5·6 hectares.

Continue along Potsdamer Chausee to reach first the *Protestant community centre* (1960–62), the *Free University students' lodgings* (founded 1948, main buildings by H. Fehling, P. Pfankuch and D. Gogel, 1960), and the church of the *Twelve Apostles* (carvings of the Apostles by Hanns Schrott-Fiechtl, 1955). Between the Potsdamer Chaussee and the Königsweg is the *Zehlendorf forest cemetery*, laid out in 1946, where are buried Burgermeister Ernst Reuter and 2000 Italians killed in WWII. Continue along Potsdamer Chausee which passes close by the frontier with East Berlin, houses a bronze statue of the Berlin bear by Renée Sinntenis (1956), and eventually reaches the ***Wannsee**.

The Wannsee comprises two lakes—the Großer and Kleiner Wannsee—and scattered homes, set up here since the mid 19C. The **Großer Wannsee** covers 260 hectares and has a superb bathing resort, the *Strandbad Wansee*, created in 1907. Boats, bathers, windsurfers, the island of Schwanenwerder with a Corinthian column brought from the Tuileries gardens, Paris, in 1883, (at No. 3 Bismarckstraße the grave of the suicidal poet Henrich von Kleist and his fellow-suicide Henriette Vogel, died 21 November 1811), the panoramic view from the Großes Fenster, the Flensburg Lion (a copy of the victory memorial by H. Bissen, 1853), convalescent homes and open-air restaurants make this Europe's largest inland bathing resort.

At No. 42 Am Großen Wannsee (now incorporated into a hospital) lived the painter Max Liebermann (1847–1935). The southern part of the suburb is bounded by the Friedrich-Leopold canal, connecting the Wannsee with the River Havel by way of a series of lakes. W of the district is the village of *Stolpe*: church by August Stüler (1958), with a Glockenspiel playing 'Praise to the Lord, the Almighty, the King of creation' on the hour. W of the church is the *Hahn-Meitner Institute of Nuclear Research* (named afer Otto Hahn, who managed to split the uranium atom in 1938, and his colleague Lise Meitner).

Königstraße continues W from Wannsee through the Düffel forest, passing the Berlin-Wannsee golf course to the S and the Post Office tower of 1962 to the N and finally reaching the River Havel. Here is the westernmost point of West Berlin and the village of *Kleinglienicke*. The *Glienicker bridge* here, half of which is in East Germany, is dubbed the bridge of unity. In a park N of Königstraße stands *Schloß Kleinglienicke*, built by K.F. Schinkel in 1826, restored as a centre for the disabled in 1951: antique and renaissance sculptures; stables; tower.

At Kleinglienicke P.J. Lenné laid out what is now the PEOPLE'S PARK in the early 19C (acquired by the city of Berlin in 1934): Schinkel built the Casino in 1824; he modelled the lion fountain (1828) on one in the Villa Medici, Rome; he built the Jägerhof (with a deerpark) in the same year; the semicircular pavilion known as the *Stibadium* contains a female statue by C. Rauch, 1850; the Kleine Neugierde contains 3rd and 4C tomb reliefs; in 1850 parts of a Venetian Carthusian monastery were brought here and reconstructed as the Klosterhof (with a wall tomb of the philosopher Pietro d'Abano, died 1316).

To the S of the Schloß park in Mövenstraße stands the *Jagdschloß Glienicke*, built in the renaissance style in 1862 on the site of a hunting lodge built for the Great Elector in 1682, and now a youth hostel.

From the E side of the People's Park take Nikolskoer Weg N to pass the restaurant of *Nikolskoe* (panorama), situated where in 1819 Friedrich Wilhelm III built a hut for his daughter Charlotte (who married Tsar Nicholas). The church of *SS. Peter and Paul* by Stüler and Albert Dietrich Schadow (1834–37), has an onion dome, a Glockenspiel, a mosaic of SS. Peter and Paul presented by Pope Clement XIII and a royal burial vault.

To reach the *Pfaueninsel* ('Peacock island') continue along the Nikolskoer Weg to the ferry. The island itself incorporates a summer home built for Friedrich Wilhelm II in the 18C with a park laid out by Lenné. Bendel built a Schloß at the SW corner of the Pfaueninsel in 1794–97, including a folly and twin towers (façade 1909–11; furnishings 1790–1830). The island also embraces the Castellan's house of 1795; the dairy, a picturesque 'ruin' of 1795; an aviary (1824); Schinkel's Swiss Cottage (1825); and his Kavalierhaus (1826), which incorporates an older gothic house.

The district of Zehlendorf also includes the suburb of **Dahlem**, the home of the state archive and numerous scientific and practical institutes, as well as the *Free University of Berlin* (founded 1948, with the historian Friederich Meinicke as its first chancellor, built 1952–54 by F.H. Sbotka and G. Müller, and paid for by the Henry Ford Foundation). Clayallee, which separates Dahlem from Grunewald, is named after General Lucius D. Clay, who was military governor, 1947–79. The *United States HQ* is in the former Luftwaffe building of 1936–37 (by E. Sagebiel). The orthopaedic clinic, Oskar-Helene-Heim, was founded in 1908. The *Dahlem Museum* (by Brun Paul, 1912–16) totally escaped damage in WWII (see **Museums**, below).

Also in Dahlem are the 14C church of *St. Anne*, with a 15C chancel and a tower of 1781 (14C wall paintings; 18C Wilmersdorff monuments), whose pastor during the Hitler Reich was Martin

Niemöller; the Thiel park, and the Jesus-Christus-Kirche of 1931.

H. Steglitz

STEGLITZ, first noted in written history as a village in 1242, gave is name in 1920 to a district formed out of the village itself, three other villages dating from the Middle Ages (Lankwitz, Lichterfelde and Giesendorf) and the Südende suburb created in 1872. Its main shopping street is the elegant Schloß Straße, part of the old Berlin–Potsdam road. Its N end houses the *Titania-Palast* of 1927, once a cinema, now a theatre.

Steglitz town hall in Schloß Straße was built in brick in 1896–98. Kieler Straße leads S from close by the town hall, passing the neo-romanesque church of the Holy Rosary, 1900, and under the railway to reach the post office of 1909 and Heesestraße, where is situated the grammar school at which in 1901 Karl Fischer founded the German youth movement known as the 'Wandervogel'. The road continues over the Teltow canal, constructed 1901–06, and joins Siemensstraße (Werner Siemens started the world's first electric tramway in Lichterfelde in 1881). The W side of the canal here is occupied by a housing estate set up in 1956 for refugees from East Prussia (the 'Ostpreußensiedlung').

Follow Siemensstraße NE back over the canal to reach Steglitzer Damm, a continuation of Albrechtstraße which runs SE from the town hall and is flanked by parks and gardens. Return NW to Schloß Straße and the town hall. Grunewaldstraße continues NW (for Dahlem), with a plaque to Franz Kafka who lived at No. 13 from 1922–23. Follow Schloß Straße SW to see the bronze memorial to the victims of the Hitler regime, the church of St. Matthew (1876–80; through a passage to the right) and the Schloßhotel, by Heinrich Gentz (1803). At No. 48 is the *Schloßpark theatre*, with a porcelain bust of the actress Tilla Durieux by Ernst Barlach in its foyer.

Schloß Straße now takes the name Unter den Eichen. To the right (entry at Nos 6–8 Königin-Luise-Straße) are the ***botanical gardens**, lying at the foot of the Fichtenberg, covering 42 hectares and containing 18,000 species, glasshouses, a palm house, and a geographical garden setting out the plants of the north temperate zone. The gardens were laid out here after outgrowing their former home in 1896–1903. Botanic museum. (Gardens open daily from 08.00 till dusk; opening 09.00 Sunday.)—From here Unter den Eichen leads to the American hospital, the Stubenrauch-Krankenhaus.

To reach the suburb of **Lichterfelde** take the Hindenburgdamm S from the Schloßhotel. In Lichterfelde village square stands the church of *St. Paul* (1900), and the 14C village *church* (restored 1939: baroque burial chapels). Beside the canal is the *Lichterfelde Schloßpark*, with a classical Schlößchen dated 1860. Close by is the *Klinikum*, the medical centre of the Free University (by the American architects Davis and Curtis, 1966). Across the canal stands the Lichterfelde stadium of 1929. The surrounding gardens contain a monument to the pioneer airman Otto Lilienthal (1848–96), by Peter Breuer, 1914.

Hindenburg Damm becomes Goerzallee, S of which is the *park cemetery* (where lies the writer Moeller van den Bruck, died 1925). Take Wismarerstraße S across the Eugen-Kleine bridge (rebuilt 1956) to reach the Ostpreußendamm and further S the *Lilienthalberg* (on

Schütte-Lanz-Straße), an artificial mound created by the airman in 1894 from which he experimented with gliders; a Lilienthal memorial was built on it in 1932.

From Lichterfelde take Lankwitzer Straße E to join Kaiser-Wilhelm-Straße and reach, en route for the suburb of **Lankwitz**, the church of the Holy Trinity, 1906. From here Leonorastraße runs left to the neo-renaissance town hall of Lankwitz (1911). Take Schulstraße NE to the centre of _Alt-Lankwitz_ with its lime trees, a church built in 1943 (restored 1956, and housing an altarpiece of 1540 borrowed from the Marienkirche in East Berlin).

I. Schöneberg

Because its Town Hall is the seat of the senate and the governing Burgermeister of West Berlin, the district of **SCHÖNEBERG** is the focus of the city's political life. The town hall square, named John-F.-Kennedy-Platz, is the scene of numerous political rallies. Each day a replica of the Philadelphia liberty bell (which rang to celebrate the beginning of the Amercan War of Independence) is rung at noon from the town hall tower.

Tauentzienstraße, filled with shops and office blocks, runs SE from Breitschied Platz reaching Wittenbergplatz, which houses the largest department store in Berlin, the 'KaDeWe' ('Kaufhaus des Westens'), founded 1907 and rebuilt 1950. Kleiststraße continues SE by way of numerous multi-storey buildings and at Nos 13–14 Berlin's _Urania_, a cultural centre first established in 1888 (present building 1962). Close by (at the corner of Martin-Luther-Straße and Lietzenburgerstraße) is an 18-storey block of flats, erected in 1963.

Kleiststraße runs into Nollendorfplatz (theatre and cinema; *flea market, with antiques, etc., in 16 former U-Bahn carriages; open 11.00–21.30, closed Tuesday). NE (in Kurfürstenstraße) is the church of the _Twelve Apostles_, by Hermann Blankenstein. To the SE (along Bülowstraße) is the neo-gothic _Lutherkirche_, by Otzen (1894).

To reach the Lutherkirche, Bülowstraße passes through Potsdamerstraße, which runs N–S through Schöneberg. Turn S along the street to find the _Sports palace_ of 1910 (reconstructed 1951: ice rink; winter beer festivals) and further S past Pallas Straße, the _Kleist park_ (right), once a vegetable and herb garden of the Great Elector and the former site of the Steglitz botanical gardens (see above). It houses the Königskolonnaden (1777–80) by Karl von Gontard, designed for the former Königs bridge and brought here in 1910.—W of the park stands the former high court of appeal, the _Kammersgericht_ (neo-baroque, 1913), in front of which are copies of the horsebreakers of Leningrad (the originals by Baron de Clodt, 1844), a gift of Tsar Nicholas I to Friedrich Wilhelm IV.

Potsdamerstraße runs into Kaiser-Wilhelm-Platz and continues SE as Hauptstraße, flanked by the _Heinrich Lassen park_, with the former village church of 1764 (rebuilt after WWII), whose churchyard contains a mausoleum to peasant farmers grown rich when their land was bought for the expansion of Berlin. Hauptstraße continues as far as the suburb of **Friedenau** by way of Friedenau town hall (1913–17), reaching Friedrich-Wilhelm-Platz (neo-gothic church of the Good Shepherd, 1893). Take Knaus Straße SE from here to reach the mound created from WWII rubble and known as _Der Insulaner_, on which are the Wilhelm Foerster Observatory of 1962, the Planetarium of 1965, and the Insulaner open-air swimming pool.

Return along Hauptstraße, to where it is crossed by Dominikus Straße, which leads SE to the Sachsendamm and the Schöneberg sports stadium. It leads NW from Hauptstraße to reach the JOHN-F.-KENNEDY-PLATZ: Tuesday and Friday markets; *town hall* by Peter Jürgensen and Jürgen Bachmann, 1911–14. The tower was rebuilt in 1950 by Kürt Dubbers, and can be ascended by 374 steps. The W wall of the town hall has a relief of the Freiherr von Stein, by Hugo Lederer, 1914. The memorial plaque to President John F. Kennedy is by R. Scheibe (1964). The liberty bell replica, weighng 10 tonnes, was presented by the Americans in 1950 (and cast at Croydon in the UK).

Martin-Luther-Straße leads from here N into the BAVARIAN QUARTER of Berlin. (In Bayerischer Platz is a statue of the Bavarian Lion by Anton Rückel, 1958.) Albert Einstein lived in this quarter at No. 8 Nördlingerstraße.

J. Kreuzberg

KREUZBERG at present owes its principal importance for visitors to Berlin to the location here of 'Checkpoint Charlie', the motorists' crossing point between East and West Berlin for non-Germans. The suburb derives its name from the 66m-high hill on which K.F. Schinkel built a memorial to the Wars of Liberation (1813–15), against Napoleon.

The centre of the district, MEHRINGSPLATZ, was laid out N of the Landwehr canal in 1734 and today is enhanced by the Column of Peace, set up to commemorate the peace of 1815: bronze statue of Victory by C.D. Rauch; marble figures representing Peace by A. Wolff and Clio (writing the history of the wars against Napoleon) by F. Hartzer.

To reach **Checkpoint Charlie** from Mehringsplatz follow Friedrichstraße N. To the right the 20-storey publishing house of Axel Springer gazes across the Wall. Kochstraße leads right as far as Oranienstraße, named after French Protestant refugees from the principality of Orange, at the W end of which is the Federal printing house (1879–82).

Running S from Mehringsplatz, Mehring bridge leads across the Landwehr canal to Blücherplatz, which houses the *American Memorial Library* (by the consortium G. Jobst, W. Kreuer, F. Bornemann and H. Wille, 1954). Running from Blücherstraße is Stresemannstraße, with, at No. 29, the *Hebbel theatre*, by Oskar Kaufmann (1908). Mehring Damm curves SW from Blücherplatz. It meets Yorckstraße (right), which houses both the *Kreuzberg town hall*, by W. Kreuer (1957) and the twin-towered brick church of *St. Boniface*, 1903–07.

Continue S along Mehring Damm to reach Kreuzbergstraße (right), S of which rises the KREUZBERG, with Schinkel's monument in the form of an cast-iron Eleanor cross, with 12 symbolised battles won by the Germans and their allies in the Napoleonic wars.

Bergmannstraße leads E from Kreuzstraße as far as the Südstern: Missions church, 1897, and a *cemetery* in which lie the painter Adolph von Menzel (died 1905, tomb and bust by Reinhold Begas), the theologian F.D. Schleiermacher (died 1834, tomb by C.D. Rauch) and the poet Ludwig Tieck (died 1853).

K. Tempelhof

TEMPELHOF, the West Berlin district lying to the S of Kreuzberg, was formed out of four 13C villages: Tempelhof, Mariendorf, Marienfelde and Lichtenrade. Until 1318 Tempelhof belonged to the Knights Templar. From 1722 the Berlin garrison had its parade ground here, which was converted into Tempelhof airport in 1934–39 by Ernst Sagebiel. Here, before the airport was built, the brothers Orville and Wilbur Wright in 1908 displayed their motor-powered aeroplane. Civilian air transport began from the field shortly after WWI. From here the Soviet blockade of West Berlin was broken by the Allied airlift from 28 June 1948 to 11 May 1949, an event commemorated by the air lift memorial by Eduard Ludwig (1951), set in the Platz der Luftbrücke in front of the airport building and symbolising the three air corridors from the W to Berlin.

From the memorial Tempelhofer Damm (nicknamed the 'Te-Damm') runs S, by way of the NEUTEMPELHOF housing estate (by F. Bräuning, 1928, with many streets named after WWI fighter pilots and Bräuning's Protestant church of 1928). The Tempelhofer Damm continues S by way of the town hall of 1936, the 13C *Templars' church* (rebuilt after WWII: altarpiece of 1596 by Daniel Fritsch) and the Francke park.

Tempelhofer Damm continues S, becoming the Marien Damm and crossing the Teltow canal by the Stubenrauch bridge to pass the Tempelhof docks and the Ullstein printing house (Eugen Schmohl, 1926). Marien Damm continues S into the suburb of **Mariendorf**, its 13C church with 16C pillars dividing the nave and a tower topped in 1737; people's park; race course; windmill of 1888.

The two other suburbs of Tempelhof are **Marienfelde**, with the oldest church in Berlin (early 13C, weather vane of 1595; barrel vault 1921) and **Lichtenrade** (14C church with a tower of 1902, all rebuilt 1949; Salvator church, 1938).

L. Neukölln

Curiously, WWII enhanced the economic status of the district of **NEUKÖLLN**, since scarcely more than 15 per cent of its property was destroyed and businesses flocked here once the war was over.

Hermannplatz in the centre of the district houses the department store of *Karstadt*, built 1929, with a roof garden and restaurant. To the W runs Hasen Heide, with a dance hall and other entertainment centres, leading to the Lilienthalstraße (church of St. Johannes, built 1897). To the S of the street is the *Hasen Heide public park* (bronze statue of the gymnast Friedrich Ludwig Jahn, 1778–1852, by Encke, 1872; open-air theatre; mound created out of war rubble, known as the *Rixdorfer Höhe*, with a statue by Katharina Singer, 1955, in honour of Berlin women).—S of the park is the Columbia Damm, skirting Tempelhof airport.

Return to Hermannplatz and take Karl-Marx-Straße SW to reach *Neukölln town hall* (1905–08; tower restored 1950, with the goddess of fortune on the top). Karl-Marx-Platz houses a 15C church (run by the Moravians, with Bohemian graves in its cemetery) and several 15C cottages.

Jonas Straße leads W from Karl-Marx-Straße to the *Körner Park*, where Ice Age remains have been discovered. Jonas Straße joins Hermannstraße, which runs S and becomes the Britzer Damm, reaching the former village of *Britz*, with a 13C church (charnel house, 1766; much restored 1888; restored again in the 1950s). The park contains a house of 1706 in which lived Count Hertzberg, who in 1763 gave his name to the treaty (which he negotiated) ending the Austro-Prussian Seven Years' War.

Flanking Fritz-Reuter-Allee in Britz is the horseshoe housing estate built by Bruno Tait and Martin Wagner (1925–31). In the Allee are a Protestant church by Karl Streckebach, and a Catholic church by Johann Jackel, both built in 1955.

Buckower Damm leads S from Britzer Damm by way of *Buckow* (church c 1250, with a tower of the same date and vaults of c 1500). Take Johannis Chaussee left to reach the housing estate known as GROPIUSSTADT (1962–70): 15,000 flats housing 45,000, the highest building 90m, all named after its creator Walter Gropius.

From here Rudower Straße leads SE to the industrial suburb of **Ruckow**: 13C church with a modern interior since the restoration of 1954 (including a modern Pietà by Schreiter); hunting lodge of Elector Friedrich III, c 1680.

M. Museums and Theatres

Museums

Air Flight Museum, at Tegel airport, open March–December 09.00–19.00.

Antiquities Museum, at No. 1 Schloßstraße, open 09.00–17.00, closed Friday.

Arts and Crafts Museum ('Kunstgewerbmuseum'), at Schloß Charlottenberg (see below), open 09.00–17.00, closed Friday.

City Art Gallery, at Nos 23–27 Arnimallee, open 09.00–17.00, closed Monday.

Bauhaus Museum, at No. 14 Klingelhöferstraße, open 11.00–17.00, closed Sunday.

Berlin Museum (cultural history), at No. 14 Lindenstraße, open 11.00–18.00, closed Monday.

Charlottenburg Local History Museum, in the town hall of Charlottenburg, opens at complex times, as do the local history museums of Kreuzberg, Neukölln, Reinickendorf, Schöneberg, Spandau, Steglitz, Tempelhof and Zehlendorf.

Cinema Museum, at No. 57 Großbeerenstraße, open Wednesday and Saturday 18.00–23.00.

*Brücke Museum, at No. 9 Bussardsteig, open 11.00–17.00, closed Sunday.

Egyptian Museum, at No. 70 Schloßstraße, open 09.00–17.00, closed Friday.

National Gallery (founded 1861: German 19C masters, French impressionists), at No. 51 Potsdamer Straße, open 09.00–17.00, closed Monday.

Peace Museum, at No. 27 Stresemannstraße, open daily 06.00–20.00.

World War II Resistance Museum, at No. 14 Stauffenbergstraße, open weekdays 09.00–18.00 and weekends 09.00–13.00.

Schloß Charlottenburg (including the pre- and early history museum), open 09.00–17.00, closed Monday.

In front of Schloß Charlottenburg is a baroque equestrian *statue of the Great Elector, designed by Andreas Schlüter in 1698 and cast by Johann Jacobi in 1700. The *rococo state apartments are by G. von Knobelsdorff and J.A. Nahl, 1740–44.

Theatres

Deutsche Opera, at Nos 34–37 Bismarckstraße.
Schiller Theatre, at No. 110 Bismarckstraße, connected with a theatre workshop.
Hansa Theatre, at No. 47 Alt-Moabit.
Youth Theatre, at No. 99 Alt-Moabit.
Scholßpark Theatre, at No. 48 Schloßstraße, Steglitz.
Free Volksbühne Berlin, at No. 24 Schaperstraße.
Theater am Kurfürstendamm.
Vaganter-Bühne, at No. 12 Kantstraße.
Theater des Westens, at No. 12 Kantstraße.
Tribüne, at Nos 18–20 Otto-Suhr-Allee.
Schaubühne am Lehniner Platz, at No. 153 Kurfürstendamm.
Children's Theatre, at No. 22 Altonaer Straße.

68   East Berlin

Non-German visitors crossing to the capital city of the German Democratic Republic ('East Berlin') enter either by the Friedrich-Ecke Zimmerstraße crossing known as 'Checkpoint Charlie' or by rail to Friedrichstraße. The East Germans make no restriction on photography, apart from forbidding pictures of military posts and personnel (with the exception of those guarding the Neue Wache, see below).

Theatre tickets can be bought in West Berlin (from the travel agency Berolina, at No. 25 Kurfürstendamm) and at the chief information office in East Berlin, at No. 5 Alexanderplatz. At Friedrichstraße S and U-Bahn railway station, and in various East Berlin hotels, FDR currency can be used to purchase goods. The authorities specify the minimum amount to be spent for each day's stay in the capital, and visitors are required to change a specified amount of West German money for East German, at a rate of 1:1.

Visitors by train should follow Friedrichstraße to Unter den Linden to start their tour at the Brandenburg Gate. Tourists arriving by car by way of 'Checkpoint Charlie' can park by Marx-Engels-Platz or near the Staatsoper and then make their way on foot to the Gate.

East Berlin's *airport* is Berlin-Schönefeld, to the SE of the city. Berlin is also served by the *S-Bahn* (aerial railway) and the *U-Bahn* (underground railway).

The main *post offices* are at the main railway stations (including Friedrich-straße), at Nos 8–10 Fruchtstraße, in the Berolina Building at No. 1 Alexander-platz, and at Nos 9–12 Französische Straße.—*Tourist information* at the Berolina Building, at No. 67 Unter den Linden, at No. 100 Friedrichstraße.

A. East Berlin

The ****Brandenburg Gate**, one of 18 formerly guarding the city walls, was set up in 1734 where Frederick the Great and his successor Friedrich Wilhelm II planned the long wide street Unter den Linden. In 1788–91 Carl Gotthard Langhans created the present superb gate, 26m high, 65·5m long, 11m wide, modelled on the Propylaea (the entrance to the Acropolis, Athens). The statues and the Quadriga with the goddess of Victory were finished three years later by Gottfried Schadow. The sculptures underneath represent the triumph of the goddess; 32 other sculptures represent scenes from Greek mythology, by Bernhard Rode; 20 reliefs depict the life of Hercules; and on the N and S sides are statues of Athena and Ares. The French removed the Quadriga to Paris in 1806. It came back in 1814. Throughout the 19C the square was the scene of military parades. In 1848 and 1918 it was the rallying point of the revolutionaries. The gate, much shattered by bombs in WWII, has been completely restored.

To the E is Pariser Platz, laid out 1734, at the SE corner of which is Otto-Grotewohl-Straße, E of which stand various ministries and embassies, including the *Soviet Embassy*, designed by the Russian architect A.P. Strijewski (1950–52). Inside is a stained glass representation of the Kremlin, illuminated at night and visible outside.

E from the Pariser Platz runs *UNTER DEN LINDEN ('Under the Lime Trees'), 1·4km long, 60m wide, set out by the Great Elector and Frederick the Great. Unter den Linden is crossed by the busy Friedrichstraße (to the N the railway station: on the corner with Unter den Linden the Interhotel, 1966, and the cafés and restaurants of the Lindencorse, 1966).

Continue along Unter den Linden past the *State Library* (in the neo-baroque former building of the Prussian State Library, 1903–14) to find (left) the **Humboldt University**, built as a neo-baroque palace for Prince Heinrich by Johann Boumann in 1748–68; N wing by Ludwig Hoffmann added 1913–19.

It became the Friedrich-Wlilhelm University in 1810 and was renamed in 1949. In front are the memorials to Wilhelm and Alexander von Humboldt, respectively by Paul Otto and by Reinhold Begas, both 1883. The latter's statue has an inscription in Spanish: 'To the second Cuban explorer, the University of Havana, 1939'. Alexander planted the gingko tree in the garden. The marble columned entrance hall is inscribed with Marx's dictum, 'Till now philosophers have only explained the world; our task is to change it.'

In the middle of the street is an equestrian statue of Friedrich II by C.D. Rauch (1851), opposite which is the ***Staatsoper**, built for Frederick the Great by G.W. von Knobelsdorff (1741–43), in the style of a Corinthian temple and meticulously restored after WWII. The niches over the doorway are filled with statues of Euripides, Menander, Aristophanes and Sophocles.

Circling the Staatsoper on the same side stand *St. Hedwig's Cathedral*, modelled on the Pantheon, Rome, begun by Jean Legeay in 1747, finished by Johann Boumann in 1773 (restored after WWII); the former *Royal Library* (nicknamed, from its curved front, the 'Kommode'), built by Boumann in 1780 to plans by the Viennese baroque master Fischer von Erlach (restored 1967–69); the *Palais of Wilhelm I*, by Karl Ferdinand Langhans, Carl Gotthard's son (1836; rebuilt); and the *Opera Café*, formerly the Prinzessinnenpalais of 1733–1811, in front of which are statues of Blücher (1826), York (1855), Gneisenau (1855) and Scharnhorst (1822), all by C.D. Rauch (erected here 1962).

On the other side of Unter den Linden from the café stands the *Neue Wache, built by Schinkel as a Roman temple with a Doric portico, 1816–18, a WWI memorial from 1931 and from 1949 a memorial to the victims of fascism and militarism (changing of the guard, 12.00 and 14.30), behind which is the classical *Maxim Gorky Theatre*, built as a music academy in 1827.

Continue along Unter den Linden to find (left) the baroque *Zeughaus (arsenal), begun by Arnold Nering, 1695, continued by Martin Grünberg and by Schlüter and finished by Jean de Bodt, 1695–1706. Today it houses the *Museum of German history* (strong emphasis on revolutionary history; open weekdays, except Friday, 08.00–19.00; weekends, 09.00–16.00). Opposite the Zeughaus stand the *Palace of the Crown Prince* (1663–1857, restored) and the stone *Friedrich-Werdersche church*, by Schinkel (1824–31). Cross the River Spree by the *Marx-Engels bridge* (built as the Schloß bridge by Schinkel, 1822–24) to reach the massive MARX-ENGELS-PLATZ, on the site of the former Berliner Schloß and its garden, both ruined in WWII. The doorway of the Schloß, by Eosander von Göthe, from which on 9 November 1918 Karl Liebknecht proclaimed the Free Socialist Republic of Germany, is set in the façade of the administrative offices of the DDR here. Close by is the *Foreign Ministry* of the DDR, 145m long, 44m high, built 1967.

N, across Karl-Liebknecht Straße, stands the *Protestant Cathedral*, built in the Italian renaissance style by Julius Raschdorff (1894–1905), much damaged in WWII and containing the mausoleum of the Prussian kings and crown princes.

Continue along Karl-Liebknecht Straße into what was formerly the ALTSTADT, a quarter mostly destroyed in WWII. On the right is Berlin's second oldest church, the **Marienkirche**, built in the 15C on a 13C original (tower by Langhans, 1790; main entrance by Achim Kühn, 1970; inside: late 15C Dance of Death fresco, 22m long; baroque pulpit by Andreas Schlüter, 1703). Behind the church is the post office tower and to the S is a Neptune fountain by Begas (1891). S of the post office tower, take Rathaus Straße W to reach the red brick and terracotta *Town Hall* by H.F. Waesemann (1861–70), with a 74m-high tower (access by 287 steps), behind which is the neo-baroque Stadthaus of 1902–11, with a 100m-high tower.

Take Spandauer Straße SE to Molkenmarkt, with the mid 13C restored church of St. Nikolaus. Mühlendamm leads SW across the River Spree by way of the Ministry of Culture (building 1935–39, incorporating a relief of 1798 by Schadow) to reach BREITE STRAßE, with its numerous fine houses: at No. 11 the Ermelerhaus of 1761 was destroyed by bombing and has been re-erected on the Märkisches Ufer (see below); at No. 13 a dwelling house of 1710; at No. 35 the Ribbeckhaus of 1624; the 176m-long Marstall (stables) of 1670, much restored 1896–1901 and now the state library and archives. Breite Straße leads SE by way of Roßstraße to Märkisches Ufer. Turn left here to find on the right the *Märkisches Museum* (1908; Berlin culture and history, especially works by the caricaturist Heinrich Zille; open 09.00-17.00, closed Monday).

Cross the river by way of Brückenstraße and follow Alexanderstraße N to ALEXANDERPLATZ (known as 'Alex')—a military parade ground, named after Tsar Alexander in 1805, with the 365m-high *TV tower* of 1969 (café, observation tower), and numerous post-war buildings including the 39-storey Internhotel (2000 beds), the *HO-Warenhaus* (East Berlin's largest department store) and the 12-storey *Haus des Lehrers*, with a mosaic frieze by Walter Womacka.

From here Karl-Marx-Allee (known as Leninallee till 1961) leads SE, flanked by six- to nine-storey housing blocks and running into the oval Strausbergerplatz, with a fountain by Fritz Kühn, restaurants and cafés in the Haus Berlin, and a children's department store (the Haus des Kindes), which incorporates a puppet theatre, cinema and children's restaurant. From here Lichtenberger Straße runs SW to Leninplatz and the Lenin memorial of 1970.

Other sights in East Berlin

Charlottenstraße leads S from Unter den Linden to the PLATZ DER AKADEMIE, where stand the partially restored 18C German Dom and the almost completely restored French Dom, two churches with columns and domes, both early 18C churches refurbished and aggrandised by Carl von Gontard, 1780–85. For the centre of the square Schinkel restored a fire-damaged theatre, 1819–21. The royal bank of 1901 to the E of the square now houses the DDR Scientific Academy.

The *Soviet war memorial* stands in the 79-hectare *Treptower park* (laid out by Gustav Meyer, 1876–85). It consists of a weeping woman in grey marble and two massive red marble columns with lowered flags. Its 33m-high mausoleum, containing the remains of 4800 Soviet soldiers who died in the battle for Berlin (1945) is topped by a 12·8m-high bronze figure of a Russian soldier, holding a child and crushing with his sword a Nazi swastika.

The 160 hectares of animal park were set out in the Friedrichsfelde in 1955; the park houses c 5000 animals (open summer from 07.00; winter from 08.00 till dusk).

Schloß Köpenick, by Rutger von Langerfeld, 1677–82, now a museum of goldsmiths' work, porcelain, furniture: Schloß chapel by Nering, 1684. *Köpenick town hall* dates from 1903–05 and is memorable for the celebrated exploit of Wilhelm Voigt, the 'Hauptmann von Köpenick'.

The *Müggelsee*, at 746 hectares Berlin's largest lake, reached by the S-Bahn (to Friedrichshagen): swimming; the 115m-high Müggelberge, with a 30m-high tower of 1961, incorporating a restaurant.

Bertolt Brecht's house, at No. 125 Chausseestraße, now a Brecht archive.

Pankow: reached from Alexanderplatz by way of Rosa Luxemburg Straße and Schönhauser Allee (which houses the Jewish cemetery where rest the composer Giacomo Meyerbeer, died 1864, and the painter Max Liebermann, died 1935). From here Berliner Straße leads further N to *Schloß Niederschönhausen*, by Eosander von Göthe (1704), transformed into the rococo· style 1764, with an 'English' park designed by Lenné (entry only to the park). The 15C *church* of Pankow has octagonal bell towers of 1859.

Friedrichshain park, covering c 52 hectares, and set out in 1840 to commemorate the centenary of Frederick the Great's accesssion: fairy- tale fountain by Ludwig Hoffmann, 1913; two rubble mounds; open-air theatre; graves of 183 who died in the rising of 1848; swimming stadium.

B. Museums and Theatres

Museums

East Berlin possesses what is known as the **Museum Island ('Museum-Insel'), the oldest museum centre of the divided city, set up on an island in the Spree on the orders of Friedrich Wilhelm IV.
The complex comprises five museums:
Old Museum (by Schinkel, 1822–30, with a Greek portico of 18 Ionic

columns, adorned with bronzes): antiques, *20C paintings.
New Museum (by F.A. Stüler, 1843–59, left in ruins after WWII).
National Gallery (designed by Stüler, built by Heinrich Strack, 1865–76, in the form of a Corinthian temple, with an equestrian statue of Friedrich Wilhelm IV by Calandrelli, 1866, and numerous garden sculptures): *19C and 20C paintings, drawings, engravings, sculpture.
Bode Museum (neo-baroque building by Ernst von Ihne, 1898–1904, named after its director from 1872–1929, Wilhelm von Bode): Egyptian works and remains; early Christian and Byzantine museum; German sculpture and paintings from the late gothic to the rococo; other European art; coins and engravings.
Pergamon Museum (designed by August Messel, built by Ludwig Hoffmann, 1909–30): antiquities, Greek and Roman architecture, the *Pergamon altar, 180–160 BC, Near Eastern art, Islamic art.

The Old Museum, National Gallery, Bode Museum and Pergamon Museum are open Wednesday – Sunday, 09.00–18.00.

Theatres

Berliner Ensemble at Bertold-Brecht Platz.
Berlin Puppet Theatre at No. 70 Tirolerstraße.
Deutsche Staatsoper at No. 7 Unter den Linden.
Deusches Theater/Kammerspiele at No. 13a Schumannstraße.
Die Distel Cabaret at No. 101 Friedrichstraße.
Komische Opera at Nos 55–57 Behrenstraße.
Maxim Gorky Theatre at No. 2 Am Festungsgraben.

C. Potsdam

The former garrison town of **Potsdam** is where in *Schloß Cecilienhof* (built for the Crown Prince, 1913–13) Roosevelt, Attlee and Stalin met in 1945 to work out Germany's post-war destiny (guided tours and restaurant). Here is also the rococo *Schloß Sans-Souci, built for Frederick the Great (he died here on 17 August 1786) by G.W. Knobelsdorff, 1745–47; new buildings by Büring, 1755; 'Neuen Kammern' by Gontard, 1772–74: 'English' and 'French' park; Italianate orangery, with a Raphael room, by Persius and Stüler, 1850; 'Chinese' tea house, 1754–56; Roman baths by Schinkel, 1834.

INDEX

0713628456

BENTLEY

BLUE GUIDE GERMANY

PUB: BLACK   SUP: BLACK   CAT: TRA

1 COPIES FOR STOCK

DATE: 5/11/87